Compensation

Decision

Making

Frederick S. Hills

Virginia Polytechnic Institute
and State University

THE DRYDEN PRESS
Chicago   New York   Philadelphia   San Francisco   Montreal   Toronto
London   Sydney   Tokyo   Mexico City   Rio de Janeiro   Madrid

Acquisitions Editor: Joan Resler
Project Editor: Jan Doty
Design Director: Alan Wendt
Production Supervisor: Diane Tenzi
Director of Editing, Design, and Production: Jane Perkins

Text and Cover Designer: Margery Dole
Copy Editor: Michele Heinz
Compositor: Donnelley Rocappi
Text Type: Palatino

Library of Congress Cataloging-in-Publication Data

Hills, Frederick S.
　　Compensation decision making.

　　Includes bibliographies and index.
　　1. Compensation management—Decision making.
I. Title.
HF5549.5.C67H55　1987　　　　658.3'2　　　　　86-2668
ISBN 0-03-063339-7

Printed in the United States of America
789-038-98765432

Address orders:
383 Madison Avenue
New York, NY 10017

Address editorial correspondence:
One Salt Creek Lane
Hinsdale, IL 60521

CBS COLLEGE PUBLISHING
The Dryden Press
Holt, Rinehart and Winston
Saunders College Publishing

*To Linda, Karl, Marion
and an Elusive
Muskellunge*

The Dryden Press Series in Management

Arthur G. Bedeian, Consulting Editor

Albanese and Van Fleet
**Organizational Behavior:
A Managerial Viewpoint**

Bedeian
Management

Bedeian
**Organizations: Theory and Analysis,
Text and Cases**
Second Edition

Boone and Kurtz
Contemporary Business
Fifth Edition

Bowman and Branchaw
**Business Communication:
From Process to Product**

Bowman and Branchaw
Business Report Writing

Chen and McGarrah
**Productivity Management:
Text and Cases**

Compaine and Litro
Business: An Introduction

Cullinan
**Business English for Industry
and the Professions**

Gaither
**Production and Operations
Management: A Problem-Solving and
Decision-Making Approach**
Third Edition

Gatewood and Feild
Human Resource Selection

Greenhaus
Career Management

Higgins
**Strategy: Formulation, Implementation,
and Control**

Higgins and Vincze
**Strategic Management and
Organizational Policy: Text and Cases**
Third Edition

Hills
Compensation Decision Making

Hodgetts
Modern Human Relations at Work
Third Edition

Holley and Jennings
**Personnel/Human Resource
Management: Contributions
and Activities**
Second Edition

Holley and Jennings
The Labor Relations Process
Second Edition

Huseman, Lahiff, Penrose, and Hatfield
**Business Communication:
Strategies and Skills**
Second Edition

Huseman, Lahiff, and Penrose
**Readings and Applications in
Business Communication**
Second Edition

Jauch, Coltrin, Bedeian, and Glueck
**The Managerial Experience: Cases,
Exercises, and Readings**
Fourth Edition

Kuehl and Lambing
**Small Business: Planning
and Management**

Lee
Introduction to Management Science

Miner
Theories of Organizational Behavior

Miner
**Theories of Organizational
Structure and Process**

Paine and Anderson
Strategic Management

Paine and Naumes
**Organizational Strategy and Policy:
Text and Cases**
Third Edition

Ray and Eison
Supervision

Robinson
**International Business Management:
A Guide to Decision Making**
Second Edition

Robinson
**The Internationalization of Business:
An Introduction**

Smith
**Management Systems: Analyses
and Applications**

Stone
Understanding Personnel Management

Tombari
**Business and Society: Strategies for the
Environment and Public Policy**

Varner
Contemporary Business Report Writing

Weekly and Aggarwal
**International Business: Operating in
the Global Economy**

Zikmund
Business Research Methods

Compensation decision making is a critical organization activity. Organizations are vitally interested in attracting, retaining, and motivating employees to high levels of performance. Indeed, organizational survival requires that they do so. One only needs to look at the U.S. economy to see organizations that do this well, and those that do not. Some organizations have a difficult time attracting and retaining people, while others do not. As a result, some organizations have achieved unprecedented productivity growth, but others see their productivity slipping to the point where they are no longer competitive, and many fail altogether.

At the same time organizations must compete for the best work force, survival also requires that the firms live within a whole range of other constraints. With the growth in product competition (both domestic and imported) and legal pressures, organizations in the modern world are more constrained than ever in making compensation decisions. Current events show these two constraints at work in the United States. The auto industry has emerged from its most severe recession ever by updating technology and controlling labor costs. The textile industry is in trouble because of the influx of less costly foreign products. The electric razor industry, with one exception, has become entirely a foreign industry because of high labor costs. In the case of legal constraints, organizations are routinely taken to court for violating nondiscrimination and other wage-related laws. As a result, organizations are faced with an incredible tension between needing to compete for the best labor and working within the constraints of their ability to pay as well as legal constraints. This book is about the dynamic tension between these and other competing forces.

The compensation field has been depicted variously as a group of theories, a set of administrative practices, or a set of techniques. These pages are an effort to make sense out of this mishmash by relating theory to practice and presenting techniques to aid in sound compensation practice.

The ultimate goal of the text is to make compensation decision makers out of its readers. No book can provide bromides for all situations. At the same time, all compensation decisions are made under a set of decision-making constraints. This book is also about those constraints. A thorough understanding of them will assist the reader in making compensation decisions, since carefully considering all of the constraints and judiciously weighing them should result in more rational compensation decisions.

Stated another way, the reader will be making compensation decisions for some organization in the future. These decisions will determine whether the company achieves its goals or fails. The decisions have an impact upon the company achieving high productivity or slowly slipping into oblivion. To aid in preparing for compensation decisions, these pages were written to provide readers with the skills to make wise decisions in a complex and ever-changing environment.

Organization of the Text

COMPENSATION DECISION MAKING is divided into six parts. Each part covers a block of material that is critical for compensation decision making. The parts are divided into chapters and are documented with references for further reading. Each chapter also has highlighted key terms, discussion questions, and exercises to use as learning aids.

Parts One and Two set the parameters in which compensation decisions are made. In Part One, Chapter 1 provides an overall introduction to the compensation field. Chapter 2 discusses theoretical frameworks that are useful in understanding human behavior as it applies to compensation, such as why people work and what motivates people. The focus in Chapter 3 is the economics of compensation: that is, why organizations that hire workers face an ability-to-pay constraint. The implications of theories of human behavior and economics are then discussed in each chapter.

The two chapters in Part Two examine institutional constraints that influence compensation decision making. Chapter 4 examines the institutional constraints of internal labor markets and labor unions. Chapter 5 then examines the major federal legislation that affects compensation decision making.

In Part Three, each of the three chapters deals with one or more particular administrative activities that are important in designing a good pay system. Chapter 6 covers job analysis and job descriptions. Studying jobs and documenting the results of these studies are critical for all compensation work. How jobs are studied, uses of the data, and techniques for studying jobs are all discussed in this chapter.

Chapters 7 and 8 discuss four general approaches to job evaluation. Each chapter covers two approaches and develops the methods in some detail. Because Part Three emphasizes skill building, there are cases and exercises to use in mastering job analysis and job evaluation.

Part Four contains three chapters. Chapter 9 completes the design of a basic wage or salary system. It examines the topic of conducting wage and salary surveys. It focuses on the organization's wage payments in light of what other organizations are doing. Chapter 10 discusses how organizations use wage surveys and integrates them with job evaluation data. This chapter also develops the topic of pay ranges and their uses. Chapter 11 is an applications chapter that applies the concepts and tools developed earlier to a particular compensation issue: wage discrimination.

In Part Five, Chapters 12 and 13 discuss individual performance pay. Chapter 12 deals with the important subject of performance assessment in a merit pay context. Chapter 13 focuses on several types of individual and group incentive plans used by organizations.

Part Six completes the discussion of designing a total compensation system. Chapter 14 takes up the subject of employee benefits. The chapter discusses the types of benefits that are provided and trends for future benefits. Chapter 15 focuses on the types of noneconomic rewards which organizations provide and the reasons for providing them.

Finally, Chapter 16 covers the important topic of compensation control and administration. Once a comprehensive compensation program is installed, it must be administered on a day-to-day basis, and control must be maintained in the system.

Instructor's Manual with Test Items

An instructor's manual has been designed to accompany the text. This manual provides a brief overview of each chapter, a battery of multiple-choice questions for each chapter, and possible answers for discussion questions and exercises.

Acknowledgments

Although only one name may appear on the cover of a book, in reality such a project is the collaborative effort of many people. I would like to take this space to thank those who were instrumental in the creation of this book.

My first debt is to those who were instrumental in my own education. While many should be mentioned, I would in particular like to recognize Tom Mahoney, Vanderbilt University. Because of his unswerving commitment to me over many years, this book is a reality. I would hope that Tom would see much of himself in this book, although I also hope that I have enriched and expanded his ideas and in some small way crystallized our thinking about compensation.

As anyone who has attempted a book knows, criticism is easy to get but not always useful. Constructive criticism, therefore, is especially valued. A host of colleagues improved various draft manuscripts with their constructive criticism. I would like to thank Chris Berger, Purdue University; Ruth Curran, California State University–Northridge; Kermit R. Davis, Jr., Auburn University; James W. Hathaway, Appalachian State University; Linda A. Krefting, Texas Tech University; Vida Scarpello, University of Georgia; and Michael N. Wolfe, University of Houston–Clear Lake.

Seven reviewers were particularly astute in their constructive criticisms. They are Thomas J. Bergmann, University of Wisconsin–Eau Claire; Luis R. Gomez-Mejia, University of Florida; Sandra Jennings, Miami University of Ohio; Timothy J. Keaveny, Marquette University; Robert M. Madigan, Virginia Polytechnic Institute and State University; Paul M. Muchinsky, Iowa State University; and Craig J. Russell, Rutgers University. I owe these colleagues a special thanks for the extra effort they put into reviewing the manuscript.

To those of you who may attempt to write a book, allow me to recommend The Dryden Press to you. A competent staff of many, including Joan Resler, Jan Doty, Michele Heinz, Jo Ann Learman, and Teresa Chartos, were just wonderful. They held my hand, cajoled, and always pleasantly nudged the project towards completion. Art Bedeian, thanks for challenging me.

I owe perhaps my greatest admiration and thanks to Linda Hills. She had to put up with me during the evolution of the book. Also, much of the editing and administrative work fell to her. Thank you, Linda.

Finally, I must recognize all of those practitioners and academicians who write, teach, and work in compensation. Whether named or unnamed in these pages, your collage of contributions, I hope, is accurately presented here.

This book is a collection of empirical facts, general compensation beliefs, and my own biases. Errors of fact are my responsibility. My interpretation of general beliefs, I hope, is accurate and my biases tolerable.

Frederick S. Hills
Blacksburg, Virginia
October 1986

CONTENTS

■ PART ONE
Introduction
and
Theoretical
Foundations
3

CHAPTER 1
An Introduction
to Compensation   5

Chapter Outline   5
Learning Objectives   6
The Subject of Compensation   6
Individual Concerns about Compensation   6
Organizational Concerns about Compensation   7
Societal Concerns about Compensation   9
Compensation Defined   10
Wage or Salary   10
Employee Benefits   11
Nonrecurring Financial Rewards   11
Nonpecuniary Rewards   11
Perspective of the Text   11
Goals of the Compensation System   12
Influencing Employment Behavior   12
Constraints of the Compensation System   16
The Roles of Theory and Practice   19

CHAPTER 2
The Theoretical Framework I:
Worker Behaviors   23

Chapter Outline   23
Learning Objectives   24
Introduction   24
Content Theories of Motivation   24
Maslow's Hierarchy of Needs Theory   24
Murray's Theory   26
Alderfer's Theory   26
Herzberg's Two-Factor Theory   27
McClelland's N-Achievement Theory   28
The Employment Exchange Contract   29
A Psychological Contract   29
Both Parties Profit   30
Process Models of Motivation   31
The Equity Model   31
Instrumentality and Expectancy Theory   34

CHAPTER 3
The Theoretical Framework II:
Economic Constraints   43

Chapter Outline   43
Learning Objectives   44
Introduction   44
Wage Differentials — A Technical Meaning   45
Marginal Revenue Productivity Theory   46
Labor Demand as a Derived Demand   46
An Intuitive Example of Labor's Value   46
The Employer's Demand for Labor   49
Labor Supply in the Marketplace   51
Marginal Revenue Productivity Theory and
    Ability to Pay   52
Average and Total Revenue   54
Variable Costs   54
Fixed Costs   55
Profits   55
Labor's Share   55
Labor's Productivity and Ability to Pay   56
A Caution on Labor's Productivity   56
Wage Level versus Wage Structure Concepts   56
Ability to Pay and Industry Characteristics   57
The Importance of Product Market Surveys   58
Elasticity of Demand for the Product   59
Elasticity of Demand for the Brand   61
The Capital/Labor Ratio   61

The Substitutability of Other Factors
  of Production   62
The Supply Curves of Other Factors of
  Production   62
Consequences of Different Wage Levels   63
The Low-Wage Employer   63
The High-Wage Employer   64
The Wage Level Concept   64
Minicase: The Automobile Industry
  Recession   65

■ PART TWO   CHAPTER 4
Institutional   Institutional Constraints: Internal Labor
Constraints in   Markets and Labor Unions   71
Compensation
69
                    Chapter Outline   71
                    Learning Objectives   72
                    Introduction   72
                    The Internal Labor Market Concept   72
                    Organizations and Internal Labor Markets   74
                    Implications of the Internal Labor Market
                      for Compensation   74
                    Pressures to Maintain Internal Labor Markets 75
                    Emergence of Internal Labor Markets   76
                    Labor Unions and Compensation   79
                    The U.S. Labor Movement   79
                    Issues and Process in Collective Bargaining   85
                    General Union Impact on Compensation
                      Decisions   89
                    Specific Union Influence on Compensation
                      Decision Making   91
                    Exercise   102

                    CHAPTER 5
                    The Legal Environment   105

                    Chapter Outline   105
                    Learning Objectives   106
                    Introduction   106
                    The Fair Labor Standards Act of 1938   106
                    Overtime Provisions   108
                    Minimum Wage Provisions   109
                    Child Labor Provisions   109
                    Record Keeping for FLSA   110
                    Enforcement   111
                    The FLSA and Compensation Decision Making   111
                    Wage Legislation for Government
                      Contractors   112

The Davis-Bacon Act   **112**
The Walsh-Healy Act   **113**
The McNamara-O'Hara Act   **113**
The Contract Work Hours Standard Act   **113**
Enforcement   **114**
Contractor Wage Legislation and Compensation
  Decision Making   **114**
Workers' Compensation Laws   **116**
Provisions of the Laws   **116**
Workers' Compensation and Compensation
  Decision Making   **117**
Social Security Act of 1935   **118**
Social Security and Compensation
  Decision Making   **118**
Unemployment Insurance   **118**
Consumer Credit Protection Act of 1968   **119**
Health Maintenance Act of 1973   **120**
Compensation Decision Making and HMOs   **120**
Employee Retirement and Income Security
  Act of 1974   **121**
Fiduciary Standards   **121**
Funding   **121**
Vesting   **122**
Portability   **122**
Reporting and Disclosure under ERISA   **123**
ERISA and Compensation Decision Making   **123**
Civil Rights Legislation   **124**
The Equal Pay Act of 1963   **124**
The Civil Rights Act of 1964   **127**
The Age Discrimination in
  Employment Act of 1967   **129**
Executive Order 11246   **129**
State Legislation   **132**

■ **PART THREE**
**Internal
Equity
Determination**
137

CHAPTER 6
Job Analysis and Job Descriptions   **139**

Chapter Outline   **139**
Learning Objectives   **140**
Introduction   **140**
Tasks, Jobs, and Positions   **140**
Job Analysis   **141**
— *Uses of Job Analysis Data*   **141**
— Steps in Conducting Job Analysis   **143**
— *Determining the Use of the Data*
  and Information   **143**
Selecting a Method of Analysis   **145**

Informing Other Managers of the Study 146
Informing Job Incumbents of the Study 146
Carrying Out the Study 146
Validating the Study 146
Summarizing the Results 147
Job Analysis Techniques and Methods 147
Direct Observation 148
Interviewing Techniques 151
*Standardized Structured Approaches to
  Job Analysis* 153
Custom-Designed Job Analysis 156
Job Analysis Outcomes 158
The Job Description 158
Job Specifications 159
Performance Standards 159

CHAPTER 7
Nonquantitative Job Evaluation 163

Chapter Outline 163
Learning Objectives 164
Introduction 164
Job Evaluation and Relevant Theory 164
An Overview of Job Evaluation 164
The Comparison Standard 165
Quantitative and Nonquantitative Dimensions 166
The Evolution of Job Evaluation 168
Job Assessment and People Assessment 170
Compensable Factors 170
The Ranking Method of Job Evaluation 173
Steps in the Job Ranking Method 174
*Advantages and Disadvantages of the
  Ranking Method* 176
The Whole Job Method of Job Evaluation 178
The Job Classification Method 179
Steps in the Classification Method 179
*Advantages and Disadvantages of the
  Classification Method* 182
Exercises 184

CHAPTER 8
Quantitative Job Evaluation 189

Chapter Outline 189
Learning Objectives 190
Introduction 190
The Theoretical Basis of Job Evaluation 190

Factor Comparison Method of
    Job Evaluation   **191**
Steps in the Factor Comparison Method   **191**
Advantages and Disadvantages of the Factor
    Comparison Method   **198**
The Point Method of Job Evaluation   **200**
Steps in the Point Method   **200**
Advantages and Disadvantages of the
    Point Method   **207**
Other Job Evaluation Techniques   **207**
Single Factor Job Evaluation Methods   **207**
Employee Attribute Techniques   **208**
Maturity Curves   **209**
The Hay Guide Chart Profile Method   **218**
Direct Market Method   **218**
Position Analysis Questionnaire   **218**
Exercises   **219**

■ **PART FOUR**   **CHAPTER 9**
Pay Structure   **Job Pricing: Surveying Labor and Product**
Decisions   **Markets**   **225**
223
                         Chapter Outline   **225**
                         Learning Objectives   **226**
                         Introduction   **226**
                         Labor and Product Market Constraints   **226**
                         Organizations Included in a Labor Market
                             Wage and Benefits Survey   **227**
                         Organizations Included in Product
                             Market Surveys   **231**
                         Wage and Benefit Survey Data and
                             Antitrust Law   **233**
                         Who Conducts Wage and Benefits Surveys?   **234**
                         Third-Party Surveys   **234**
                         Custom-Designed Surveys   **243**
                         Summarizing Survey Data   **254**
                         Benefits Data   **254**
                         Wage Data   **254**
                         Summary Statistics and Wage Data   **255**
                         Reporting Data to Management   **257**
                         Exercises   **261**

                         CHAPTER 10
                         Pay Structure Design: Integrating Job
                         Evaluation and Pay Structure Data   **265**

                         Chapter Outline   **265**
                         Learning Objectives   **266**

Introduction   266
Theoretical Objectives of a Wage Structure   266
Multiple Wage Structures   268
Reasons for Multiple Structures   268
Multiple Wage Structure Relationships   269
Job Evaluation Data and Pay Grades   269
Establishing Pay Grades   269
Administrative Convenience   270
Other Factors   271
Determining the Number of Grades   272
Determining Internal Equity   273
Internal Equity Using a Freehand Line
  of Best Fit   274
Internal Equity with a Regression Line   275
Internal Equity as a Sole Criterion   276
External Equity Determination   278
Wage Rates   279
Slotting in Nonkey Jobs   279
Product Market Constraints   280
Labor Costs and Decision Making   280
Nonlinear Wage Lines   281
Designing Pay Ranges   282
Ranges for Merit   282
Ranges for Seniority   283
Examples of Merit and Seniority Pay Ranges   284
Flat Rate Systems   285
Range Overlap   286
Implementing a Systematic Pay Structure   286
Communication with Employees   286
Initial Adjustment of Rates   287
Pay Structure Maintenance   288
Training of Managers   289
Exercise   290

CHAPTER 11
Wage Discrimination   297

Chapter Outline   297
Learning Objectives   298
Introduction   298
Basic Concepts of Wage Discrimination   298
Fair versus Unfair Discrimination   298
Legal versus Illegal Discrimination   299
Components of Illegal Discrimination   299
Examples of Discrimination   299
Doctrines of Illegal Employment
  Discrimination   300
Disparate Treatment Discrimination   301

Adverse Impact Discrimination   301
Present Effects of Past Discrimination   302
Reasonable Accommodation Discrimination   302
Compensation Audits for Pay
    Discrimination   302
Direct Pay Discrimination   302
Indirect Pay Discrimination   308
Comparable Worth Pay Discrimination   309
Examples of Alleged Comparable Worth
    Discrimination   309
Comparable Worth Court Cases   311
Evolution of the Concept   311

■ PART FIVE   CHAPTER 12
Individual   **Performance Assessment**   317
Equity
315   Chapter Outline   317
                     Learning Objectives   318
                     Introduction   318
                     Performance Assessment and Compensation   318
                     Instrumentality and Expectancy Theory
                         and Performance   318
                     The Performance Appraisal Paradox   319
                     What Is Performance Assessment?   320
                     Work Rules versus Job Outcome Compliance   321
                     Job Outcome versus Behavioral
                         Outcome Dimensions   322
                     People Assessment versus Job
                         Assessment Revisited   322
                     Who Conducts Performance Assessment?   323
                     Immediate Supervisors   323
                     Peer Evaluations   323
                     Subordinate Evaluations   323
                     Other Evaluators   324
                     Multiple Evaluations   324
                     Problems with Performance Standards   325
                     Criterion Contamination and Deficiency   325
                     Measurability of the Criteria   326
                     Combining Performance Dimensions   326
                     Rater Biases and Errors in Performance
                         Assessment   327
                     "Halo or Horns" Bias   328
                     Excessive Strictness or Leniency   328
                     Central Tendency   328
                     Recency Tendency   328
                     Primacy Bias   329
                     Similarity or Difference Bias   329

Order Effect and Contrast Bias 329
Other Factors Influencing Performance
  Assessment 329
Unwillingness to Discriminate 330
Poor Training 330
Superordinate Goals 330
Legal Considerations in Performance
  Assessment 331
Adverse Impact Discrimination under Title VII 331
Equal Pay Act Considerations 332
Age Discrimination in Employment Act of 1967 334
Performance Assessment Techniques 334
Ranking Methods 334
Graphic Rating Scales 335
Behaviorally Anchored Rating Scales 340
Management by Objectives 341
Performance Assessment and Compensation
  Decision Making 343
The Departmental Unit Problem 343
Allocating Percentage Pay Increase Budgets 343
Percentage Increases to a Department 344
Guidecharts 344
Exercises 346

CHAPTER 13
Individual and Group Incentives,
Compensation of Special Groups 349

Chapter Outline 349
Learning Objectives 350
Introduction 350
Incentive Plans and Theory 350
Instrumentality and Expectancy Theory
  Assumptions 350
Work Environment Assumptions 351
Individual versus Group Plans 351
Merit Pay versus Incentive Pay 352
Individual Incentive Plans for
  Production Employees 352
Piece Rate Plans 352
Standard Hour Plans 358
Problems with Individual Incentive Plans 359
Individual Incentive Plans for Salespersons 362
Salary plus Commission 363
Draw plus Commission 363
Sales Commission Plans 364
Special Sales Incentive Plans 364

Problems with Sales Incentive Plans	366
Individual Managerial Incentive Plans	367
Bonus Plans	367
Executive Bonuses	367
Group Incentive Plans	370
Small Group Incentive Plans	370
Plantwide Group Incentive Plans	370
Exercises	375

■ **PART SIX**
Completing the Compensation Package
383

CHAPTER 14
Employee Benefits — 385

Chapter Outline	385
Learning Objectives	386
Introduction	386
Employee Benefits Defined	386
Employee Benefits versus Perquisites	386
Theoretical Foundation for Employee Benefits	386
Growth in Employee Benefits	387
Societal Attitudes	388
Favorable Tax Treatment	390
Employer Self-Interest	390
Group Coverage Effects	390
Employer Paternalism	390
Income and Leisure Preferences	391
Changing Philosophies about People and Work	391
Indirect Returns from Benefits	391
Union Pressures	391
Bandwagon Effect	392
Types of Benefit Programs	392
Pension Plans	392
Issues in Designing Pension Plans	392
Types of Pension Plans	395
Pension Plan Costs	396
Pay for Time Not Worked	397
Vacation Time	397
Holiday Pay	397
Other Paid Time	397
Indirect Costs of Pay for Time Not Worked	399
Insurance	399
Health Insurance	399
Life and Accident Insurance	403
Long-Term Disability Insurance	403
Other Insurance	403
Other Benefits	404
Discounts on Goods and Services	404
Subsidized Meals	405

Moving Expenses 405
Severance Pay 405
Legally Required Benefits 406
Social Security 406
Workers' Compensation 406
Unemployment Compensation 406
Benefits Decision Making 407
Benefit Level and Product Market
  Benefit Surveys 407
Benefit Structure and Labor Market
  Benefit Surveys 407
Benefit Structure and Survey of
  Current Employees 407
Benefit Structure and Goals 408
Contributory versus Noncontributory Benefits 408
Future Trends in Employee Benefits 408
Cafeteria Benefit Plans 409
Retirement Plans 409
Taxation of Benefits 409
Exercise 410

CHAPTER 15
Noneconomic Rewards 413

Chapter Outline 413
Learning Objectives 414
Introduction 414
Noneconomic Rewards 414
Economic versus Noneconomic Rewards 414
Noneconomic Rewards and Human Needs 415
Work Adjustment Theory 416
Job-Related Rewards 418
Intrinsic Job Rewards 418
Extrinsic Job Rewards 419
Non-Job-Based Rewards 420
Organization Status 420
Geographic Location 421
Organizational Responses to
  Noneconomic Rewards 421
Job Design and Redesign 421
Flexitime 423
Professional Development Programs 424
Job Posting and Bidding Systems 424
Supervisory Training 426
Organizational Due Process 426
Quality Circles 426
Management by Objectives 429
Company-Sponsored Events 429

Noneconomic Reward Decision Making   429
Employee Attitude Surveys   429
The Minnesota Satisfaction Questionnaire   430
Impact of Noneconomic Reward Programs
   on Economic Rewards   431
Indirect Impact   431
Direct Impact   432
Exercise   434

CHAPTER 16
Compensation Administration and Control   437

Chapter Outline   437
Learning Objectives   438
Introduction   488
Responsibility for Compensation
   Management   438
Compensation Staff Personnel   438
Organization Line Managers   439
Line Managers and Compensation Staff
   Relationships   439
Top Management Decision Making   442
Maintenance of the Wage Level   442
Wage Surveys   442
Cost of Living Allowances   442
Supply Shortages   443
The Wage Level Adjustment Decision   443
Maintenance of the Wage Structure   445
Job Content Changes   445
Job Reanalysis   446
Pay for Performance Administration
   and Control   447
Size of Merit Increases   448
The Unit Allocation Problem   448
Conducting Performance Appraisals   448
Administration of Pay Change Transactions   450
Wage and Salary and Standard
   Hours Budgets   451
Wage and Salary Budgets   451
Standard Hours Budgets   453
Legal Controls   454
Federal Contract Holders   454
Overtime, Child Labor, and Minimum
   Wage Legislation   455
Equal Opportunity and Affirmative
   Action Regulations   455
Employee Retirement Income Security Act of
   1974   456

Social Security   **456**
Labor Contracts   **457**
Wage and Price Guidelines   **457**
Communication of Compensation
   Information to Employees   **457**
The Importance of Communication   **457**
Communication of Wage Levels and Structures   **458**
Communicating Pay Increase Information   **459**
Communicating Merit, Market, and
   COLA Increases   **459**
Benefits Communication   **460**
Exercises   **462**

Index   **471**

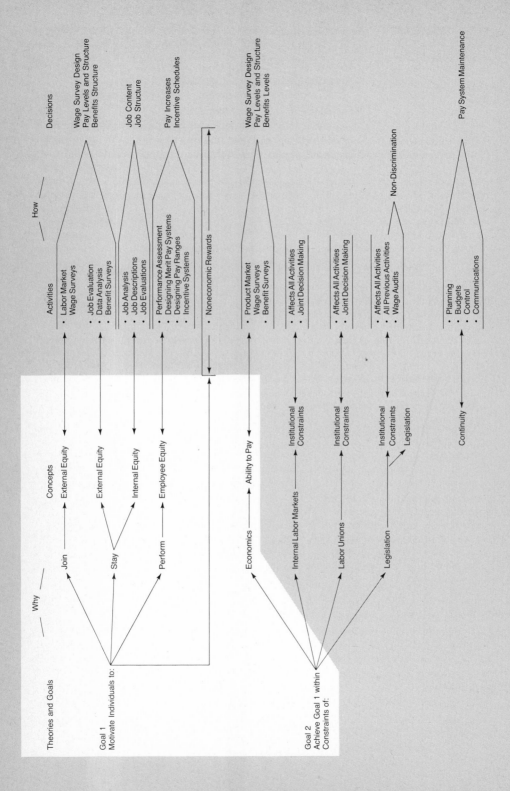

Introduction

and Theoretical

Foundations

Because nothing is likely to be more frustrating to a reader than not knowing where a book is going, Part One sets the stage for this text.

Chapter 1 provides an overview of the text. It also examines in a very general way the importance of the subject of compensation by examining it from the perspectives of the individual, the organization, and society at large. In this chapter the concept of compensation as used in this text is defined. The chapter also focuses upon the goals of a well-designed compensation system and discusses the role of theory in understanding how the world operates.

Chapter 2 focuses upon the individual as a decision maker. Every individual makes a host of decisions about what to do in life. Some of the more important decisions are: should I get a job; what will I expect from my work; am I fairly treated with respect to my job in general and pay in particular; and should I work harder today. Chapter 2 develops several theoretical frameworks that are useful in understanding how and why people make certain decisions for themselves—decisions about joining and staying with an organization, and decisions about performing at high levels.

One of the realities of wage and salary payments is that different employers often pay considerably different wage rates for the same type of worker. This fact is often attributable to union influence over wage setting, to different amounts of labor supplied in different geographic areas, to differences in management philosophy, or to other factors. While all of these reasons may play a role in employer wage differences, this text takes the view that unless the employer is economically capable of paying high wages, no union will be able to demand them, nor will management have a philosophical bent toward paying them. In short, an employer's wage decisions are first and foremost likely to be influenced by its ability to pay. Chapter 3 discusses the concept of ability to pay and identifies key variables that influence it.

The first three chapters lay the groundwork for designing a compensation system. Chapter 1 focuses upon what compensation is, the importance of compensation, and the goals of a well-designed compensation system. Chapter 2 shows the factors that influence individuals to make decisions. Chapter 3 develops the concept of a firm's ability to pay and also discusses the economic constraints faced by organizations that pay wages.

1

An Introduction

to Compensation

- **Chapter Outline**
- **Learning Objectives**
- **The Subject of Compensation**
  Individual Concerns about Compensation
  Organizational Concerns about Compensation
  Societal Concerns about Compensation
- **Compensation Defined**
  Wage or Salary
  Employee Benefits
  Nonrecurring Financial Rewards
  Nonpecuniary Rewards
- **Perspective of the Text**
- **Compensation System Goals**
  Influencing Employment Behavior
  Constraints of the Compensation System
- **The Roles of Theory and Practice**

Learning Objectives

To become aware of the subject of compensation.
To understand how three different elements of society (individuals, organizations, and society at large) are concerned about compensation-related issues.
To define the term *compensation* and to identify the components of compensation.
To introduce the viewpoint (an organizational view) of this textbook.
To identify and discuss the goals of an organization's compensation system.
To recognize that compensation goals are made within a set of constraints (economic, legal, and institutional).
To understand the role of theory as it relates to compensation practice.

The Subject of Compensation

Compensation is of concern to numerous groups. Three of the most interested groups are individual members of society, organizations (public, private, and nonprofit), and society as a whole. To understand why each of these groups is concerned about compensation, it is useful to look at some compensation issues from each of their perspectives.

Individual Concerns about Compensation

Wages as Income   Individuals usually receive income from two sources, earnings and investments. Relatively few people realize most of their income from investments. The largest portion of most people's income comes from what the economist calls **earnings** and what this text calls **wages**.[1] Wages are defined here as income received for labor services.[2] The fact that most people must work to sustain themselves in return for wages influences their lives in numerous ways. For example, Tom, an engineer, may decide to leave firm A in Toledo and move to firm B in Houston because firm B offered him a 30 percent increase in wages.

Wage Comparisons   Why do maintenance workers at the local industrial plant make more than mechanics at the local gas station? Why is a bachelor's degree in engineering worth one-and-one-half to three times in wages what a bachelor's degree in education is worth? Why does one person get a 3 percent raise when another gets a 6 percent raise?

Why does a marketing manager in the electronics industry generally get paid twice what a marketing manager in textiles gets paid for virtually identical work? These and other questions are raised about people's wages.

A more fundamental question is why do people ask these questions? Wages affect people's lives in pervasive and intimate ways. People's wages influence whether they drive a Ford Escort or a Ford Thunderbird, or whether they own a home (and the relative quality of the home) or rent a home or an apartment. Wages help define one's socioeconomic status and influence friendships, neighborhood choice, clothing choice, eating behaviors, and so on. Wages are important to individuals because people are intimately affected by the wages they earn.[3]

Wage Fairness　There are also issues about wages which tap people's sense of fairness. People want to know why one person's raise may be higher. Why does Sally make $12,000 as a first-year teacher in the Montgomery school system when Joe makes $14,500 as a first-year teacher in the Salem school system? Again, the question has an element of concern over the fairness of treatment.

One of the objectives of this book is to answer the questions raised above, as well as others, about why individuals are paid certain wages.

Organizational Concerns about Compensation

The subject of compensation is of concern to organizations because of the variables that influence an organization's ability to pay, the legal implications of the constraints placed on pay systems by society, and the ability of the compensation system to meet the organization's goals.

Labor Costs　Just as individuals have concerns about wages, organizations are also concerned about paying wages to their employees. A principal reason for this concern is that labor costs represent a substantial proportion of total costs to the average company, whether they are in the public, private, or nonprofit sectors of the economy.[4]

Labor costs as a proportion of total costs vary tremendously from industry to industry and even from employer to employer, as depicted in Table 1.1. The fact that labor costs on average represent a substantial cost relative to total costs for employers, however, means that one way to effectively manage business costs is to effectively manage labor costs.

Some organizations are relatively more labor intensive than others. Less labor-intensive employers tend to pay more for the same type of worker than do relatively more labor-intensive employers.

Legal Constraints　Other considerations besides labor costs cause organizations to be concerned about wage payments. Organizations must assure themselves and their employees that they are in compliance with legislative and administrative legal constraints so that they behave in a socially responsible way.[5] For example, the Equal Pay Act of 1963 is a piece of federal legislation that prohibits discrimination on the basis of sex in wage payments. If an organization violates the standards of this law, then it is subject to prosecution (causing more costs). If a violation is found, the organization may be faced with redressing it. This could involve back pay with interest (more costs) plus attorneys' fees for the plaintiff (more costs).[6] Exhibit 1.1 shows the extent of some of these costs.

Table 1.1   *Cost of Labor in Various Industries*

Payroll as a Percentage of Value of Inventory Shipments

	Payroll (in millions)	Value of Shipments (in millions)	Percentage
Food & kindred products	$23,221.5	$255,871.5	9.1%
Tobacco	1,044.8	11,892.8	8.8
Textile mills	9,253.1	44,397.0	20.8
Lumber & wood	8,904.8	47,193.1	18.9
Paper	11,699.3	72,595.4	16.1
Printing & publishing	18,843.1	69,543.9	27.1
Chemicals	18,269.0	161,558.5	11.3
Petroleum & coal	3,615.1	198,673.1	1.8
Rubber & misc. plastics	10,140.5	47,341.8	21.4
Leather	2,199.9	9,739.3	22.6
Primary metal	23,556.4	133,930.1	17.6
Fabricated metal prod.	26,700.6	116,194.3	23.0
Machinery (nonelectric)	44,603.7	180,727.3	24.7
Electric, electronic equipment	32,453.3	128,587.3	25.2
Transportation equipment	38,843.9	186,281.7	20.9

Constructed from information in *Annual Survey of Manufacturers* (1980), (Washington, D.C.: U.S. Department of Commerce, Bureau of the Census, Industry Division, 1981).

Exhibit 1.1   *Legal Costs of Wage Discrimination*

Bias suit costs Allstate $5 million

From wire reports

WASHINGTON—In one of the largest such settlements on record, Allstate Insurance Co. agreed to give $5 million to female sales agents alleged to have been discriminated against, the government announced Monday.

The Equal Employment Opportunity Commission said the back pay settlement agreement, approved by a federal district court in Sacramento, Calif., affects some 3,000 women employees and ends nearly 10 years of litigation.

The settlement came in a class action case in which Lola Hogan challenged the company's policy of basing starting salaries on prior pay. She maintained that she had been frustrated by earning less than men doing the same job.

EEOC Chairman Clarence Thomas called the wage discrimination settlement one of "historic proportions" and said it "should have significant impact on salary-setting practices in all industries nationwide."

A spokeswoman for Allstate, saying she could comment only if her name were not used, said that in signing the settlement the company was not admitting that it had discriminated against women.

Source: "Bias Suit Costs Allstate $5 Million," *Roanoke Times & World News*, October 2, 1984, p. A-4. Copyright 1984 by The New York Times Company. Reprinted by permission.

Influencing Employee Decisions   Finally, employers are fundamentally concerned that their pay systems accomplish the goals they have set. The compensation system should help motivate employees to join the organization, stay with the organization, and perform for the organization. These goals are expanded upon later in the chapter.

Societal Concerns about Compensation

As far back as the Middle Ages, when plagues were sweeping Europe, the Church and State became concerned over the increases in wages for occupations experiencing labor shortages. To assure that relative wages of occupational groups remained constant, the Church and State invoked a Just Wage doctrine. This doctrine held that each occupational group should receive their just wage. "Justness" was defined as the relative wage of the occupation before the plague. Societies have historically been concerned with the wages of their members. This concern is one of the reasons for the myriad of legislation facing compensation decision makers today.[7]

Income Maintenance   Society has expressed its concern over wage payments in various ways throughout U.S. history. Early in this century there was concern over workers becoming injured on the job and not receiving adequate compensation for the injury. An outcome of that concern was workers' compensation laws.[8] In the 1930s there was concern about the financial ability of workers to live in retirement. The Social Security Act of 1935 was passed in part to provide a supplemental retirement income.

Labor Law Reform   In the 1930s society also decided there was a need to permit employees to organize and bargain collectively with management. One of the issues that workers have a right to negotiate under the provisions of the Wagner Act of 1935 is the wage rate. Society also became concerned about whether workers earned enough to keep them out of poverty. In response to this concern, the Fair Labor Standards Act (FLSA) of 1938, among other provisions, established the first minimum wage. The changes in the minimum wage since 1938 are reflected in Table 1.2.

Civil Rights   By the 1960s the United States was involved in the civil rights movement. That movement, supported by interest groups such as the National Association for the Advancement of Colored People (NAACP), the Black Caucus, the National Organization of Women (NOW), and others, fought hard for change. In the case of women, the average woman earned only about 60 percent of what the average man made.[9] In an attempt to eradicate that wage differential Congress passed the Equal Pay Act of 1963.[10] In 1964, Congress acted to prohibit discrimination in the terms and conditions of employment on the basis of race, color, creed, sex, and national origin with the Civil Rights Act of 1964, which prohibits discrimination in pay, among other things.[11]

Table 1.2   *Changes in Minimum Wage*

Month/Year		Minimum Wage
Oct.	1938	.25
Oct.	1939	.30
Oct.	1945	.40
Jan.	1950	.75
Mar.	1956	1.00
Sept.	1961	1.15
Sept.	1963	1.25
Feb.	1967	1.40
Feb.	1968	1.60
May	1974	2.00
Jan.	1975	2.10
Jan.	1976	2.30
Jan.	1978	2.65
Jan.	1979	2.90
Jan.	1980	3.10
Jan.	1981	3.35

Source: U.S. Department of Labor, Employment Standards Administration, *Minimum Wage and Maximum Hours Standards under the Fair Labor Standards Act* (1981), annual, and unpublished data.

Legislation influencing pay decision making is discussed in detail in Chapter 5.

Compensation Defined

Compensation is defined as:

Compensation = Wage or salary + Employee benefits + Nonrecurring financial rewards + Nonpecuniary rewards.

Each component of compensation is discussed in turn.

Wage or Salary

The first component of compensation is wage or salary. Wage or salary can be defined in two ways. First, it can be expressed as the rate of pay per unit of time. Thus, wage can be expressed as dollars per hour while salary is normally thought of as dollars per month or year. (Some legal distinctions between wage and salary are discussed in a later chapter, but for now the two are treated the same.) Wage or salary can also be expressed as the rate of pay per unit of output. For example, under piece rate pay systems an employee is paid so many dollars or cents for each unit produced. Piece rate systems are discussed in more detail in Chapter 14. The concept of wage or salary refers to the gross wage or salary and should not be confused with take-home pay, net pay, or earnings.

Employee Benefits

Employee benefits are defined here as the indirect and recurring monetary rewards that an employee receives from employment. Examples of employee benefits are company contributions to retirement and insurance plans, as well as company-paid vacation days and personal days off. Employee benefits, sometimes called fringe benefits, are an important part of compensation decision making. They are treated separately from wage or salary partly because they tend to influence different worker behaviors than do wage or salary. It is also useful to think in terms of direct economic rewards (wage or salary) as opposed to indirect rewards (employee benefits).

Employee benefits today represent about 40 percent of base pay among large employers.[12]

Nonrecurring Financial Rewards

Nonrecurring financial rewards are defined as those monetary rewards that a person can earn through employment but that do not occur automatically. Examples of these rewards include profit sharing (paid only when the employer has a profitable year), special commissions such as those in sales promotions, and prizes won in special absenteeism or tardiness control programs.

Nonpecuniary Rewards

The three components of compensation just defined (wage or salary, employee benefits, and nonrecurring financial rewards) comprise what many people call the monetary or economic components of a compensation program. Another component to compensation is the nonpecuniary reward. Nonpecuniary rewards are defined in this text as the noneconomic rewards associated with employment. Examples are one's colleagues, a sense of accomplishment in one's job, and a sense of power from one's work. Chapter 15 is devoted to nonpecuniary rewards. The text focuses primarily, however, on the monetary components of pay and on making decisions about wages and salaries, employee benefits, and nonrecurring economic rewards.

Perspective of the Text

The perspective of a text probably will dictate the organization of material, the topics that are included and excluded, and the biases of the author. The perspective of this text is reflected in the title: COMPENSATION DECISION MAKING. The general objective of the text is to answer two questions about making compensation decisions from the organization's perspective: (1) what information shapes compensation decision making; and (2) how do organizations gather this information?

To illustrate this perspective, an example may be in order. A typical fast-food restaurant pays the minimum wage to its employees. If one were to do a wage and salary survey of other types of work that the fast-food restaurant's employees could perform, it would probably be found that these employees could make more money if they worked at other organizations. This finding would mean that this restaurant is a low-wage employer. On top of that, the benefits these employees receive are probably also low. What steps did the fast-food organization go through to arrive at its decision to offer low wages and low benefits (in other words, low compensation) relative to other organizations in the area? Why did the fast-food restaurant decide to be a low-compensation organization—what forces or variables caused or encouraged the organization to be a low-compensation organization?

Goals of the Compensation System

Before an organization can act on compensation decisions it must decide what goals to accomplish. There are in essence two goals of every compensation system. The first is to influence individuals who participate in the labor force to make personal decisions about employment that are congruent with the organization's needs. Exhibit 1.2 shows three parts to this goal. The second goal is for the compensation system to operate effectively within a range of constraints, including the organization's ability to pay, the legal environment, and the institutional constraints of collective bargaining and internal labor markets.

Influencing Employment Behavior

The first goal of all compensation systems is to influence individuals who participate in the labor force to make personal decisions which are congruent with the organization's needs. There are at least three areas of employment covered by this goal: (1) motivate people to join the organization, (2) motivate people to stay with the organization, and (3) motivate people in the organization to perform at above minimum levels.

Motivate Individuals to Join the Organization   Motivating people to join the organization is a critical objective of the compensation system. Every organization utilizes people in the process of producing its unique goods or services. Whether manufacturing tires, fixing teeth, managing a monetary fund, training

---

Exhibit 1.2   *The First Goal of Compensation*

The First Goal of Compensation: To elicit desired behaviors from employees.

1. Motivate people to join the organization.
2. Motivate people to stay with the organization.
3. Motivate people in the organization to perform at high levels.

---

college graduates, or franchising restaurants is the organization's business, labor is an absolutely essential factor in the production process. Organizations must motivate appropriate individuals to join the organization to create this labor force.

Compensation versus Other Motivators It should be apparent that many factors other than economic compensation influence individuals to join a particular organization. For example, an individual may decide to work at organization X because she or he identifies with the product, or a person may decide to join organization Y because it is the only organization within easy commuting distance. Regardless of these forces, compensation is the main area in which the organization can influence individual decisions about joining the organization.

One of the critical compensation decisions that organizations must make is the **wage level**. Wage level is defined as the average wage paid to all workers in the organization. The wage level is important in attracting labor. If one organization pays more than another, the high-wage employer will attract more and possibly better-qualified individuals who wish to work than the low-wage employer will. Wage level is used in a relative sense—that is, workers would value $10 per hour over $8 per hour because of the greater purchasing power of the $10 per hour. The reasons for being concerned about relative wage levels are developed in Chapter 3, where the subject of motivating workers to join from a theoretical perspective is explored. Chapters 10 and 11 cover the administrative aspects of pay structure and wage discrimination.

Motivate Employees to Stay with the Organization Getting people to join the organization does little good if it can't keep them. Just as with motivating people to join the organization, motivating individuals to stay is also influenced by a complex set of variables. The intrinsic rewards from the job itself (nonpecuniary rewards) partly influence the employee's decision to stay. The attitudes and leadership style of one's supervisor can also influence the decision to remain with the organization. Numerous variables beyond the economic compensation system influence this decision.

External Compensation Equity Regardless of these other influences over the individual's decision to stay, organizations can influence staying with the compensation system in at least three ways. First, the organization must continue to provide its employees with a feeling that they are treated equitably in an external sense, referred to as **external equity** here. By external equity we mean that if an employee is hired at a pay rate that is relatively equal to other organizations' pay rates, then this feeling of equity to other organizations must be maintained by continually assuring that the wage level remains at the same relative amount compared to pay in other organizations. External and internal equity are defined in Exhibit 1.3.

Internal Compensation Equity Not all jobs are readily assessed in terms of external equity. Once individuals work for an organization for a while, they

---

Exhibit 1.3   *Definitions of External and Internal Equity*

External Equity: External equity occurs when the organization's pay rates
are at least equal to market rates.

Internal Equity: Internal equity occurs when people feel that performance
or job differences result in corresponding differences in
pay rates.

---

may lose track of their market worth because they move into jobs that are not
readily comparable across organizations, or they simply lose track of pay rates
in the marketplace. This phenomenon is attributed to the operation of the
internal labor market (discussed in Chapter 4), which results in employees
becoming isolated from the external labor market. Once an employee reaches
this point, external equity probably becomes less relevant than **internal equity**
perceptions, defined in Exhibit 1.3. That is, it is more important to insure that
individuals feel they are treated equitably with respect to others within the
organization. This concern over internal equity is explored in more detail theoretically in Chapter 4 and administratively in Chapters 7 and 8, where the
process of establishing the **wage structure** in the firm is explored in detail. For
the time being wage structure within the firm is defined as the system of
relative wage rates among jobs within the firm.

A third way that employers can influence the individual's decision to stay
with the organization is to increase the costs associated with leaving. While
there are probably other reasons for providing employee benefits (these are
explored in Chapter 13) one principal reason is to motivate employees to stay.
For example, many benefits grow as a function of length of service (amount of
vacation time or size of the monthly retirement stipend), so that to change
employers involves costs to the employee that the average person may not be
willing to incur. An example of a progressive vacation schedule (giving more
time off with longer seniority) can be seen in Exhibit 1.4.

Organizations must make compensation decisions that will motivate people to stay with the organization. These decisions focus on internal and external wage levels, internal wage structures, and the types and amounts of benefits to provide.

Motivate Individuals to Perform   Most organizations would like to motivate
employees to perform beyond minimum acceptable levels. Organizations do
many things other than use wage payments to elicit high performance. For
example, there is an extensive body of leadership literature that suggests that
leaders and their behavior can influence the level of performance workers
exhibit.[13] Other literature suggests that the way jobs are designed may influence performance levels.[14] While there may be multiple variables, interacting
in complex ways, that have an impact on individuals' motivation to perform, it

---

Exhibit 1.4   *An Example of a Company's Vacation Policy*

Vacations

Policy
   Newman Co. provides vacation with pay to all eligible employees.

Comment
   Full-time employees will be provided with paid vacation in each calendar year within the following guidelines:
   1. Full-time employees receive 10 days of paid vacation each calendar year. Each employee on the staff on January 1 accrues vacation time as of that date. This does not apply to part-time or temporary employees. Full-time employees receive 15 days of accrued vacation time on January 1 following the year in which they complete 10 years of employment with Newman Co.
   2. New employees — During the first calendar year of employment, those employed after January 1 will receive vacation time based on the month of employment as follows:

Number of Vacation Days

January	10 days
February	9 days
March	7 days
April, May, June	5 days
July through December	0 days

   Accrued vacation time will not be credited to you until the end of your probationary period.
   3. All officers are entitled to 15 days of vacation.
   4. Part-time and temporary employees are not eligible for paid vacations.
   5. Vacations must be taken in the year earned. Unused, accrued vacation time cannot be carried over beyond December 31.
   6. No vacation pay will be granted if the employee was dismissed for cause (misconduct or willful violation of policies) or failed to give at least two weeks notice of resignation.
   7. The department supervisor is responsible for notifying the Payroll Department in writing of employees' vacation days actually taken.

---

should be clear that compensation is also one of the ways in which organizations influence performance. A merit pay policy is one way organizations attempt to use money to motivate high performance. One organization's merit pay policy is presented in Exhibit 1.5.

   One of the major objectives of compensation systems is to motivate performance. Before compensation managers can make decisions about the compensation system's design that will motivate performance, several earlier steps are necessary. It is important first to understand what motivates people and then to understand how people are motivated — the process of motivation. These questions are the subject of Chapter 2. Finally, compensation system

---

Exhibit 1.5   *Example of a Merit Pay Policy*

Salaries

Policy
    Employees are paid twice a month, on the 15th and the last day of the month, by automatic deposits to their checking accounts. When these dates fall on weekends or holidays, employees will be paid on the preceding business day.

Comment
    1. Your employee rating is based on merit, and you are considered for a salary increase after the first year of employment and every anniversary date thereafter.
    2. Salary increases are not automatic, nor are they based on length of service. Salary adjustments are based upon a thorough review of your performance and noted improvement in performance or continued excellent performance of your actual job requirements.
    3. Salaries are confidential, and you are expected to respect and maintain this confidentiality.

---

decision makers must then be able to design components of the compensation system which put that understanding into practice. Understanding what motivates people to perform and understanding the process of how people become motivated to perform are covered in Chapters 2, 12, 15, and 16.

Constraints of the Compensation System

The first goal of the organization's compensation system is to motivate employees to behave in ways that are congruent with the organization's needs. That goal includes motivating individuals to join the organization, to stay with the organization, and to perform well for the organization. The second major goal of an organization's compensation system (summarized in Exhibit 1.6) is to accomplish the first goal within certain constraints faced by the organization. The five principal constraints are its ability to pay, legal constraints, collective bargaining, the internal labor market, and the external labor market.

Ability to Pay   Statements such as "I want to pay all of my employees as little as possible to maximize profits" and "I want to keep all of my employees in poverty" are often attributed to the early capitalists of the industrial revolution.

Exhibit 1.6   *The Second Goal of Compensation*

The Second Goal of Compensation—To achieve the first goal within a set of constraints:

1. The organization's ability to pay
2. Legislation
3. Labor unions
4. Internal labor market
5. External labor market

With the advent of the public corporation in the twentieth century, it is un-likely that managers would make such statements. It is true, however, that managers do want to hire people as cheaply as possible.

If you were to ask a typical contemporary manager what type of wages an employee in the firm should make, you might get an answer such as, "A fair wage, a living wage that allows, if not a luxurious life-style, at least a tolerably civil life-style." Yet, that same manager might actually pay minimum wages for almost all jobs. What dictates that an organization whose managers might like to pay more will not? The **ability to pay** is the determining factor, and it varies considerably from organization to organization.

Knowing that ability to pay is a strong influence on what an organization decides to pay does not provide much insight into what determines an employ-er's ability to pay. The productivity of labor and the elasticity of the organiza-tion's product demand are two critical variables that dictate an employer's ability to pay. Chapter 3 discusses these concepts and why ability to pay is such a major constraint to many organizations. However, these considerations are theoretical and do not readily translate into practice. The practical ap-proach to ability-to-pay constraints is discussed briefly in Chapter 3 and in considerable detail in Chapter 7.

Legal Constraints   Legal issues in compensation are so pervasive as to con-sume much of the time of compensation managers. For example, the board of directors of the XYZ company recently suggested that the company ought to investigate the possibility of having a private pension plan. The company's compensation director, Al Ladd, must decide several things: how large a plan should XYZ have, how should the employee and the company contributions be calculated, and what kind of legal liability does the company have? Al remem-bers from graduate school that the Employee Retirement Income Security Act of 1974 has provisions regulating vesting, funding, portability, and fiduciary standards. He starts to ask his benefits manager to investigate this when his secretary informs Al that a local attorney is in the waiting room about an employee complaint regarding pay. The attorney serves papers on XYZ on behalf of Rosie Laughlin and 246 other females who are charging XYZ with sex-related pay discrimination under Title VII of the Civil Rights Act of 1964 and the Equal Pay Act of 1963. Although the Equal Employment Opportunity Commission just investigated that issue six weeks ago and found no probable cause for a suit, they did give Laughlin a **letter of right to sue**. Concurrently Al must contend with minimum wage legislation, complex issues over when the company must pay overtime (FLSA of 1938), and provisions of the Davis Ba-con Act that will affect the wages XYZ must pay workers on a government contract in Alaska.

Where does it all end? The simplistic answer to the question is that it ends when a compensation manager knows and understands the myriad of legisla-tion and administrative law that constrains the compensation behavior of an organization. These particular constraints are enormously complex and an en-tire text could be devoted to them; the goal in this book is to give the reader a comprehensive exposure to these constraints, with further exposure left to outside readings or an advanced course on compensation. Chapter 5 deals with these complex legal constraints.

Collective Bargaining   A famous labor leader once reputedly said when asked what the union wanted, "We want more—more money, more days off with pay, more benefits—more, more, more!" The world has changed since that early labor leader's statement of union goals. While unions may still want more, there is a systematic trend that started in the 1970s and is gaining momentum in the 1980s for labor to negotiate for less; that is, pay and benefit cuts.[15] Regardless, anyone wanting to be familiar with compensation practices must appreciate the constraint imposed by labor unions. In one sense the labor union as an entity could be considered part of the legal constraint since the requirement of management to bargain over compensation is mandated by law. However, labor unions have a distinct life apart from the law. As a result, once management is required by law to bargain with the union, the union's presence provides a new dynamic to compensation decision making. Chapter 4 focuses upon this dynamic and examines the legal foundations for labor unions very briefly, examines what unions bargain for, and attempts to answer the question, "What impact does the union have on the compensation system?"

Internal Labor Market   An internal labor market can be thought of as all of the jobs within an organization and the relationships among these jobs. In organizations where an internal labor market is present, there are usually entry level jobs and then other jobs into which employees can move only after being in entry level positions. Movement to these higher level jobs is controlled by organizational rules and procedures. Internal labor markets have extremely important implications for the design of compensation systems. Chapter 4 discusses internal labor markets, how they arise, what purposes they serve, and how they influence the compensation of employees.

External Labor Market   All employers must bid for labor in the marketplace. Under the reasonable assumption that individuals would rather work for more money than for less money, employers are obligated to try to pay competitive wages. The going rate in the labor market is an additional constraint that employers must try to meet. The going rate is really an array of rates paid by employers in a given labor market area. Generally there are sound economic reasons (including ability to pay and willingness to pay) for this array. From the standpoint of trying to motivate individuals to join and stay with them, organizations in theory would want to pay at least the market rate. In reality this is often not done, and the reasons are strongly linked to the economics of the organization—while employers might want to pay at market, they may be unable to. This inherent tension between the external labor market constraint and the ability-to-pay constraint is a major theme of this text.

The Roles of Theory and Practice

It is a bias of this text that sound theory helps to understand practice. A theory can be envisioned as a conceptual framework that links two or more variables together. For example, a person might suggest a theory that the amount of pay one gets is determined solely by power. This theory says that Pay $=f$(power) — pay is a function of power. A theory is verified by testing it in the physical world. The theorist needs to find some people who vary in terms of the amount of power they have and ascertain if the more powerful get more money and if the less powerful get less money.

Suppose very little association was found between what people make as a wage and the power they have. Now, the theorist is in a position to refine this theory along several paths. Another variable could be added. For example, Pay $= f$ (power and the market value of the job.) That is, pay will be determined by the power the individual has and the market value of the job. The theorist could go to the physical world and empirically test the theory again. If the theory is still inadequate, more and more variables could be added until a theory that accurately captures reality results.

This process is the way in which theory evolves. Exhibit 1.7 depicts this process graphically. Even Einstein continually tested his theories about light, energy, and mass until he was able to refine a generalized theory of relativity. In much the same way, theories of wages have evolved. The theory of wages is less elegant and refined than a general theory of relativity. In fact, it would be more appropriate to say that there are numerous theories that explain how organization decisions about compensation are shaped. The purpose of using theory in this text is to describe general behavioral tendencies and then use that theory to show why the things that are done in compensation departments are done the way they are.

Theory and practice go hand in hand. Since theory is shaped by what occurs in the physical world, one could even argue that theory is simply an abstraction of reality and that the only reason theory exists is because it provides a rationale for practice. This text has a strong bias toward using theory to help the reader understand the practices that go on in organizations. Theory can aid in understanding the relationships between what otherwise seem like disjointed pieces of administrative practice. The theory presented here is meant to be a useful crutch for organizing facts.

The precise specifications of different theoretical frameworks presented in Chapters 2 and 3 should not be taken literally. For example, among advanced students and scholars, there is often debate over the precise specifications of a model (or theory). To the extent that alternate specifications cause different results — different behavioral conclusions or outcomes — then the alternate specifications are important. On the other hand, if alternate specifications of a model or theory result in the same behavioral conclusions, then the distinctions make little difference for the purposes to which theories are used in this text. The theories presented are taken to be generally valid or explanatory of

Exhibit 1.7   *The Relationship between the Conceptual and Physical World and the Development of Theory*

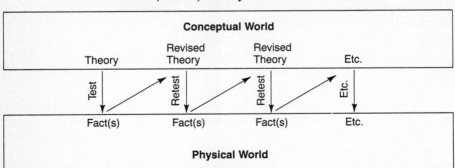

individual or market behavior. They are meant to serve as pedagogical devices with which to organize and understand the compensation world.

Every theoretical framework has behind it a set of assumptions. When it is found that the theory doesn't predict behavior, it is usually because the cases being used to disprove the theory violate one or more assumptions that are necessary for the theory to work. In that situation it would be more appropriate to suggest that the theory was misapplied than to say the theory is not valid.

Summary

This introductory chapter on compensation decision making was designed to do three things. First, the parties who have an interest in compensation decision making were introduced: individuals in society, the organizations, and society at large. The questions asked by individuals about compensation payments are also asked by organizations although from a slightly different perspective.

Second, after defining compensation, two basic goals of compensation systems were identified. The first goal is to elicit desired behaviors from potential employees and current employees; and the second goal is to accomplish the first goal within the constraints of ability to pay, the legal environment and the institutional process of collective bargaining, and internal labor markets.

Finally, this chapter presented the framework of the text and discussed how theory and practice are intimately related to each other. Theory helps in understanding why certain compensation decisions are made in particular ways, and the knowledge of practice helps us understand how certain compensation decisions are made.

Discussion Questions

1. "Theory is good for theoreticians, but it's irrelevant for the average person." Discuss.

2. Discuss the two organizational compensation goals presented. What other goals for compensation might have been included? Why do you think those goals were excluded?

3. Discuss the forces that might cause an employer like McDonald's Hamburgers to be a low-wage employer.

4. Define the following terms:

> External equity
> Internal equity
> Wage level
> Wage structure
> Ability to pay

5. Define the term *compensation*.

6. Why are organizations concerned with compensation as a managerial tool? For example, what should a compensation program accomplish?

7. Identify some of the ways in which society has influenced compensation decision making—for example, what are some of the constraints which compensation decision makers must deal with?

References

[1] In fact, the top 5 percent of income recipients in the United States receive more than two-thirds of all dividend payments and nearly half of all property income. Lloyd G. Reynolds, *Labor Economics and Labor Relations*, 6th ed. (Englewood Cliffs, N.J.: Prentice-Hall, 1974); p.308.

[2] H. G. Heneman Jr. and Dale Yoder, *Labor Economics*, 2d ed. (Cincinnati: Southwestern, 1965).

[3] "Family Income in U.S. Lagged Inflation in '81: Poverty Ranks Swelled," *Wall Street Journal*, 21 July 1982, p. 36.

[4] U.S. Chamber of Commerce, *Annual Employee Benefits Survey* (Washington, D.C., 1982).

[5] George A. Steiner and John F. Steiner, *Business, Government, and Society*, 4th ed. (New York: Random House, 1985): p. 525.

[6] Barbara Lindemann Schlei and Paul Grossman, *Employment Discrimination Law* (Washington, D.C.: Bureau of National Affairs, 1983): Chapter 13.

[7] Corning Glass Works v. Brennan, 417 U.S. 188, 9 FEP 919 (1974).

[8] The first workers' compensation law was passed in Maryland in 1902. Wendell L. French, *The Personnel Management Process*, 5th ed. (Boston: Houghton Mifflin, 1982).

[9] For a review of the wage differential over time see: Thomas J. Bergmann and Frederick S. Hills, "Internal Labor Markets and Indirect Pay Discrimination," *Compensation Review*, 4th quarter (1982): pp. 41–50.

[10] Equal Pay Act of 1963, enacted as section 6(d) of the Fair Labor Standards Act, 29 U.S.C., section 206(d), 1976.

[11] Civil Rights Act of 1964, 42 U.S.C., section 2000e, 1964.

[12] U.S. Chamber of Commerce, *Annual Employee Benefits Survey*, 1982.

[13] See, for example, Andrew D. Szilagyi, "Causal Inferences between Leader Reward Behaviour and Subordinate Performance, Absenteeism, and Work Satisfaction," *Journal of Occupational Psychology*, vol. 53 (1980): pp. 195–204.

[14] See, for example, Richard E. Walton, "Innovative Restructuring of Work," in Jerome M. Rosow, ed., *The Worker and the Job* (Englewood Cliffs, N.J.: Prentice-Hall, 1974): p. 162.

[15] John J. Lacombe III and James R. Conley, "Major Agreements in 1984 Provide Record Low Wage Increases," *Monthly Labor Review*, U.S. Department of Labor, Bureau of Labor Statistics, vol. 108 (4), April 1985, pp. 39–45.

2

The Theoretical

Framework I:

Worker Behaviors

- **Chapter Outline**
- **Learning Objectives**
- **Introduction**
- **Content Theories of Motivation**

  Maslow's Hierarchy of Needs Theory
  Murray's Theory
  Alderfer's Theory
  Herzberg's Two-Factor Theory
  McClelland's N-Achievement Theory

- **The Employment Exchange Contract**

  A Psychological Contract
  Both Parties Profit

- **Process Models of Motivation**

  The Equity Model
  Instrumentality and Expectancy Theory

Learning Objectives

To develop an understanding of both the content models of motivation and the process models of motivation.
To learn how organizations attempt to achieve external pay equity (labor market wage surveys).
To learn how organizations attempt to achieve internal pay equity (job evaluation).
To learn how an employee may decide to be a high or low performer.

Introduction

One of the basic skills needed by compensation decision makers is the ability to understand human behavior. In this chapter the focus is upon providing several conceptual frameworks for analyzing and discussing human behavior specifically as it relates to compensation. The goal of the chapter is to provide the reader with some tools to help in understanding why people behave the way that they do — why people choose to work at all, why people feel properly or improperly treated, and why people choose or choose not to expend high levels of effort at work. The frameworks employed here are not the only ones that might be used, but were selected because of their utility for understanding the behavior of people.

Content Theories of Motivation

Probably the most basic question that can be asked about people is why do they do anything? Why do they work, play golf, go to church, eat, sleep, and so on? The answer is that people have basic human needs that need to be satisfied. What needs do people have and how do these needs affect behavior? The first part of this question is answered here, and the second later in the chapter.[1]

    Content theories of motivation, theories that describe *what* motivates people, share the common feature of identifying the various needs that people have.[2] While different theorists have identified different needs, all of them are attempting to identify what motivates people to behave in particular ways. For example, a person might belong to a bowling team because of the need to affiliate with others. Or, a person might work at a job because of the need to provide food, clothing, and shelter. In this section several content theories of motivation are reviewed.

Maslow's Hierarchy of Needs Theory

One of the more popular ways to look at human needs uses a hierarchy of needs, first articulated by Abraham Maslow. According to Maslow's theory all individuals have a common set of needs that are satisfied in a hierarchical fashion, shown in Exhibit 2.1.

Exhibit 2.1   *Maslow's Hierarchy of Needs*

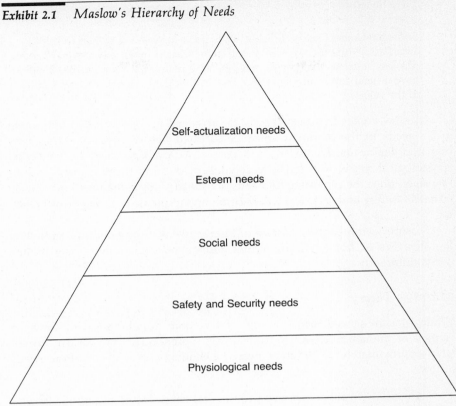

Physiological needs: The most basic human need according to Maslow is "physiological," including the need for clothing, food, and shelter. Satisfaction of these needs is essential to the maintenance of the human organism.

Safety and security needs: Once physiological needs are satisfied the individual will then be able to satisfy safety and security needs. This need is not as straightforward as the physiological need. However, it is generally taken to mean that individuals need to be free from bodily harm or injury, to be safe and secure in their environment.

Social needs: According to Maslow, all individuals need social interaction. The theory holds that people are gregarious and do not function well without social support structures around them. The particular ways in which a person tries to meet this need can range from being part of a family unit to having "buddies" at the office, but most normal people will be motivated to find and maintain social relationships.

Esteem needs: Maslow also suggests that all people have a need for esteem. This means that people need a high opinion of themselves and also want others to have a high opinion of them. Some writers even talk about a "love" need that people have — that is, people need to be loved and respected by others.

Self-actualization: Finally, Maslow argues that people are driven to self-actualize. While the concept of self-actualization may be somewhat vague, Maslow suggests that people need to become all that they can be. People have a need for accomplishment, to feel that they are using their abilities to the fullest.

Maslow argues that these needs are arranged in a prepotent order: lower order needs in the hierarchy must be satisfied before a person can satisfy higher order needs. For example, a person with a high need for satisfying physiological needs will not be very concerned about meeting social needs. However, once the physiological needs are satisfied, then the next higher level of needs (safety and security) will become important as an activator of behavior.[3]

Maslow's view of the structure of human needs is only one way to look at the structure of human needs. Other researchers and writers view human needs differently.

Murray's Theory

While Maslow's need theory is one of the more popular ways to view the content of human motives, Henry Murray, a predecessor to Maslow, articulated approximately 20 different needs.[4] Definitions of some of these needs follow:

Abasement: To submit passively to external force. To accept injury, blame, criticism, punishment. To surrender. To become resigned to fate.

Aggression: To overcome opposition forcefully. To fight.

Deference: To admire and support a superior. To praise, honor, or eulogize.

Exhibition: To make an impression. To be seen and heard.

Nurturance: To give sympathy and gratify the needs of a helpless object.

Rejection: To separate oneself from a negatively cathected object.

Understanding: To ask or answer general questions. To be interested in theory.

Murray's interpretation of the nature of human needs was purely conceptual. He identified each need not through research, but by armchair theorizing. In spite of this, his needs have face value to the extent that they make intuitive sense.

Alderfer's Theory

A third content theory of motivation was proposed by Clayton Alderfer.[5] In essence, this theory is an attempt to reduce Maslow's need hierarchy into a simpler framework. Alderfer speaks to three common needs which all people have:

> *Existence needs:* A person's desires for material things, such as clothes, money, and food.
>
> *Relatedness needs:* A person's desires for sharing feelings and thoughts with other people.
>
> *Growth needs:* A person's desire to use ability and to pursue interests to the utmost.[6]

Herzberg's Two-Factor Theory

Frederick Herzberg approached the motivation question from a slightly different direction than other writers.[7] He asked, what things in a work environment do people find satisfying and dissatisfying? Based on his work with accountants and engineers, he identified two sets of items that he called motivational (or **intrinsic**) **factors** and hygiene (or **extrinsic**) **factors.** These factors are summarized in Exhibit 2.2 and are discussed below.

Intrinsic factors:

> *Achievement:* Completing an important task successfully.
>
> *Recognition:* Being singled out for praise.
>
> *Responsibility:* Having control and authority over one's work.
>
> *Advancement:* Moving ahead through promotion.

Extrinsic factors:

> *Pay:* The money one receives for doing a job.
>
> *Technical supervision:* Having a competent supervisor.
>
> *Human relations:* Quality of supervision.
>
> *Company policy and administration:* Fair, equitable policies and their applications.
>
> *Working conditions:* The physical surroundings.
>
> *Job security:* Feeling secure in one's work.

Exhibit 2.2   *Herzberg's Two-Factor Theory*

Hygienic Factors	Motivation Factors
Company policy	Achievement
Supervision	Recognition
Salary	The work itself
Interpersonal relations	Responsibility
Working conditions	Advancement

How Factors Motivate   Herzberg maintains that intrinsic and extrinsic factors work in different ways on people. He suggests that satisfaction with work is a two-dimensional construct, and that intrinsic factors contribute to a person being motivated while extrinsic factors do not. More specifically, if intrinsic factors (recognition, achievement, and so on) are present in a job, then the worker will be motivated. If the intrinsic factors are not present, then the worker will not be motivated. Similarly, if the intrinsic factors are present the person will be satisfied with the job, but if they are not present a person will not be.[8] That is, job satisfaction will be neither positive nor negative; it will be zero.

According to Herzberg, the presence of extrinsic factors in the job assures that a person is not dissatisfied with the job. Conversely, if extrinsic factors are not present in the job then the worker will be dissatisfied with the job. In no case, however, will extrinsic factors have an impact upon motivating people to perform.[9]

Money in Herzberg's Theory   The role of money in Herzberg's two-factor theory has been a source of debate. Specifically, if money is a hygiene factor then how can it motivate? There are two partial answers. First, the fact that money is a hygiene factor is consistent with the way money is dealt with in this text. Most issues compensation managers make decisions on relate to using money to assure fair or equitable treatment. In this sense, money can only dissatisfy; it has marginal value as a true motivator. Second, money can be a motivator if it is highly valued by the employee. Even Herzberg recognizes that money can be a motivator. He specifically notes that money also has symbolic value and can be a surrogate for recognition and achievement. Thus, while money may have limited value as a motivator, the proper implementation of an economic reward system can motivate performance.[10]

McClelland's N-Achievement Theory

A final content model of motivation is worth mentioning: McClelland's *n*-achievement theory.[11] David McClelland argues that all people are driven by a need to achieve. *N* achievement is a socially learned motive, according to McClelland. This finding suggests that other kinds of motives may also be socially determined. That is, human needs may not only be innate but may also be learned. Thus, what drives behavior at one point in time may be different from what drives behavior at another point in time. For example, the desire to do socially redeeming projects may be higher in one environmental setting than in another (such as in a wealthy economy compared to a subsistence economy).[12]

Table 2.1 summarizes the various motivational theories presented above. Space does not permit a detailed discussion of the relative merits of these alternate views of the need structure. What is important is to recognize that all behavior is activated by a desire to satisfy one or more needs. Thus, a person

Table 2.1   Summary of Content Models of Motivation

Maslow's Hierarchy	Alderfer
Self-actualization	Existence
Esteem	Relatedness
Social	Growth
Safety and security	
Physiological	
	Herzberg
Murray (of 20 Needs)	Achievement
	Recognition
Abasement	Responsibility
Aggression	Advancement
Deference	
Exhibition	
Nurturance	**McClelland**
Rejection	
•	N-Achievement
•	N-Power
•	
Understanding	

eats to satisfy a hunger drive, plays golf to satisfy a need to achieve or a need to affiliate, and so forth.

Within this context of meeting needs, work plays a major role. Work satisfies many needs. It is also true that work may satisfy different needs in different people. For example, John Cheng may satisfy physiological needs by working (work enables him to buy food) as well as social needs (work allows him to interact with people he likes). Adair Link, on the other hand, may also satisfy physiological needs by working, but she satisfies achievement needs as well (work gives her a feeling of achievement). At any rate, work is a major source of need satisfaction for people who participate in the labor force.

The Employment Exchange Contract

Every individual who participates in the labor force also participates in what has been called the employment exchange contract or the inducements and contributions contract.[13] These terms mean that every individual agrees to engage in activities desired by the employer (or to make contributions and offer inducements), and the employer agrees to provide certain outcomes for the individual (or offers inducements and makes contributions).

A Psychological Contract

The employment exchange contract is a psychological contract, not an actual legal contract. While some employees do have legally binding contracts with their organizations, the employment exchange contract is an informal, unspoken agreement between the employee and the organization.

Both Parties Profit

Both parties to the employment exchange contract see themselves as better off than they were before they made the contract. From the organization's standpoint, the contributions made by the organization must be less than the inducements made by the individual. Similarly, from the individual's view, the contributions made by the individual must be less than the inducements made by the organization. How is it possible for these two views to be true at the same time? Because the contract exists only in the minds of the employee and the organization, each party has the opportunity to consider different factors as inducements and contributions. What one party sees as an inducement may not be considered relevant in the exchange by the other party.[14] In this manner, both parties see the exchange as profitable. The list of inducements and contributions in Exhibit 2.3 reflects the possible differences between the parties in making their assessments of each other.

Exhibit 2.3   *The Inducements and Contributions Contract*

Employee's perception[a]:

$$
\text{Inducements} = \begin{array}{l} \text{Money wage} \\ \text{Benefits} \\ \text{Company prestige} \\ \text{Company location} \\ \text{Challenging work} \end{array}
$$

$$
\text{Contributions} = \begin{array}{l} \text{Perform engineering tasks} \\ \text{Work from 8:00 to 5:00 each} \\ \quad \text{workday} \end{array}
$$

Employer's Perception[b]:

$$
\text{Inducements} = \begin{array}{l} \text{Perform engineering work} \\ \text{Work from 8:00 to 5:00 each} \\ \quad \text{workday} \\ \text{Candidate has degree from} \\ \quad \text{prestigious engineering school} \\ \text{Candidate has managerial potential} \\ \text{Candidate was honor student} \end{array}
$$

$$
\text{Contributions} = \begin{array}{l} \text{Money wage} \\ \text{Benefits} \\ \text{Company prestige} \end{array}
$$

[a] Employee sees inducements from employer as greater than employee contributions.
[b] Employer sees inducements from employee as greater than employer contributions.

Compensation decision makers must be aware that all behavior on the part of individuals is activated by the drive to satisfy one or more needs. Before an individual will work at a job, the individual must psychologically agree to the employment exchange contract.[15] The following example illustrates the contract between both parties.

Al Ladd has to decide whether or not to work for ABC Corporation. Al considers the contributions he must make (show up at 8 A.M. each day, offer his skills as a compensation expert, make judgmental decisions using his 20 years of experience, and so on). He also considers the inducements offered by ABC Corporation in return (the work is near his home, the salary is acceptable, the office overlooks Lake Michigan, and so on). If Al feels that he will profit from the exchange, he will decide to accept the job if it is offered. ABC Corporation goes through the same process. It looks at the contributions it will give Al (good pay, a high level of responsibility, and so on) and looks at the inducements Al is offering (20 years of experience, good verbal and writing skills, and so on). ABC Corporation may then decide that if Al is interested in the job, they will make an employment offer. In short, the two parties have arrived at an acceptable exchange.

Process Models of Motivation

Content models of motivation attempt to answer the question of *what* motivates an employee — what basic needs are present in people that motivate them toward some objective or goal. **Process** models of motivation answer a different question: how does an individual become motivated? That is, what steps does one go through in deciding to engage in a particular behavior? Two process models of motivation are presented in this chapter: the equity model and the instrumentality and expectancy model.

The equity model is presented as a heuristic model for understanding an employee's decision to join and stay with the organization. The instrumentality and expectancy model is used to understand an employee's decision to perform at particular levels.

The Equity Model

The previous sections briefly answer the questions why people work and how an employment exchange comes about. This section turns to a more detailed discussion of the exchange process. How do individuals assess the fairness of any exchange, whether it is a marriage exchange, an exchange of commodities, or an exchange of labor services? Every exchange situation must have an element of justice or fairness if it is to last over time.

The framework used here is often referred to as equity theory.[16] Exhibit 2.4 shows the model in equation form.

According to this equation, each party in an exchange relationship receives a set of outcomes (or inducements) and offers a set of inputs (or contributions).

Exhibit 2.4   *Outcomes/Input Ratios in Equity Comparisons*

$$\left(\frac{\text{Outcomes}}{\text{Inputs}}\right)_f \; \genfrac{}{}{0pt}{}{\geq}{<} \; \left(\frac{\text{Outcomes}}{\text{Inputs}}\right)_o .$$

Thus, each has a ratio of outcomes to inputs. The focal person f asks if this exchange is equitable — am I equitably treated?

Assessments of fairness are not made in a vacuum. In order to assess whether the exchange is fair, the focal person must look to some referent or relevant other o. The focal person f observes the ratio of the other's outcomes to inputs.

Three consequences are possible when the ratio of the focal person f is compared to the ratio of the other o. First, the focal person may find that the two ratios are about equal, and a state of equity exists. In this situation the focal person feels that things are satisfactory. Second, the focal person might find that the other's ratio is greater than that of the focal person. This is a condition of inequity and the focal person will feel underrewarded relative to the other. Third, the focal person's ratio may be seen by the focal person as greater than the other's ratio. This inequitable condition would be a condition of overreward relative to the other.[17]

Research on Equity Theory   Considerable research has been conducted on equity theory, particularly in the context of wage and salary payments. One subset of this research concerns what individuals do when a state of inequity exists for the focal person.

When a state of overreward exists, theoretically there are at least six actions a person might take: (1) increase inputs; (2) decrease outcomes; (3) change the referent; (4) vacate the field (abandon the present outcome and input ratio for a new one); (5) rationalize the differences in outcomes and inputs; or (6) change the referent's outcomes or inputs.

Also, in theory, there are at least six actions that a person experiencing underreward can take: (1) increase outcomes (such as by asking for a pay raise); (2) decrease the inputs (such as by not working as hard); (3) select a different referent; (4) abandon the present outcome and input ratio; (5) rationalize any differences in outcomes and inputs; or (6) change the referent's outcomes or inputs.[18]

Research generally shows that people do react to inequity in these ways. For example, one study found that if people felt overpaid, they increased their inputs.[19] This was accomplished by producing more if outcomes were expressed as an hourly rate, or by improving quality if outcomes were expressed as a piece rate.[20]

Another subset of research on equity theory focuses on the choice of the referent, or the relevant other. This research suggests an internal standard, a market referent, referents within the employing organization, and the use of family and friends as referents, among others.[21] Much more research needs to be conducted to understand these processes more completely, but it is clear that the research to date lends credence to the general validity of the equity model.

Implications for Compensation   Equity theory as developed here is useful to the compensation decision maker in understanding two important individual behaviors: the individual's decision to join the organization, and the individual's decision to stay with the organization. The first goal of a compensation system is to elicit desired behaviors from individuals, including motivating people to join and stay with the organization. Equity theory is useful in understanding how an individual is likely to assess the employment exchange (either offered or present) to make the decision to join and stay. Specifically, the individual must first feel that a potential employment exchange with the organization is equitable, and then, once the individual is a member of the organization, must perceive that the employment exchange contract remains equitable. These are minimum requirements to attract and retain people, yet they are fundamental in that if the organization is unable to attract and retain people, all other human resource activities are meaningless.[22]

External Equity and Labor Market Surveys   Two important activities commonly practiced by organizations are directly related to attracting and retaining employees: labor market surveys of wages and benefits, and job evaluation. Both are essentially concerned with assuring that the organization's compensation system is perceived as equitable. In the case of labor market surveys of wages and benefits, the concern is with external equity considerations that presumably influence the individual's decision to join the organization. That is, unless the organization's pay and benefit rates are seen as equitable relative to other firms' in the labor market, the organization may have a difficult time attracting labor.[23] It may also have a difficult time retaining labor, in some cases, if its wages and benefits are not perceived to be satisfying an external equity standard.[24]

In conducting labor market surveys, the organization asks: given a certain job with required inputs, what do other firms pay for this job? That is, are the outcomes to the organization's employees (wages and salary) relative to the employee inputs (job requirements) going to be perceived as equitable? Exhibit 2.5 shows in equation form a job in one company that requires a college education and pays $20,000 per year. The organization doing a survey is asking what a job that requires an equivalent college education should be paid so that the organization's wage rate is equitable.

Exhibit 2.5   *Labor Market Comparisons and Pay Equity*

Labor Market Other   **Employee**

$$\left(\frac{\text{Outcomes} = \$20{,}000}{\text{Inputs} = \text{College education}} \right) = \left(\frac{?}{\text{Inputs} = \text{College education}} \right).$$

Internal Equity and Job Evaluation   Organizations are also concerned that wage rates among jobs within the organization are perceived as equitable, often referred to as *internal equity*. Internal equity is traditionally achieved through job evaluation. Job evaluation can be defined as the process of establishing the relative worth of jobs within the organization. (The mechanics of conducting job evaluation is the subject of Chapters 7 and 8.) One goal of job evaluation is to achieve internal equity to influence the individual's decision to stay with the organization. Again, in equity theory terms, when the firm does job evaluation, it is trying to answer the question: given that jobs have different requirements (skill, effort, and so forth), what would be equitable pay rates for these jobs? That is, what should be the outcomes (pay) be for this job given the required inputs (skill).[25] Exhibit 2.6 shows this question in equation form.

Instrumentality and Expectancy Theory

Influencing people to join and stay are two critical parts of the overall goal of influencing individuals to behave in ways desired by the organization. Having people in jobs within the organization, however, is not enough. Organizations also would like to influence employees to work at higher than minimally acceptable performance levels. In short, the organization would like to motivate high levels of performance. This section develops the instrumentality and expectancy theory as a conceptual framework for the activities that motivate high performance.

The Instrumentality and Expectancy Model   Credit for the instrumentality and expectancy theory is usually attributed to Victor Vroom.[26] The theory is useful in understanding the process by which people are motivated to action.

Exhibit 2.6   *Job-to-Job Comparisons for Internal Equity Determination*

Job A   **Job B**

$$\left(\frac{\text{Outcomes} = ?}{\substack{\text{Inputs} = \text{0–1 years' experience} \\ \text{Strenuous work}}} \right) = \left(\frac{\text{Outcomes} = ?}{\substack{\text{Inputs} = \text{1–3 years' experience} \\ \text{Nonstrenuous work}}} \right).$$

Probably the easiest way to understand the theory is with an example. Why does Adair decide that she will expend only enough energy to be an adequate employee? Instrumentality and expectancy theory holds that effort or motivation toward a behavior is dependent upon five variables: expectancies *E*, instrumentalities *I*, valences *V*, first-level outcomes, and second-level outcomes.[27] These five variables are combined in the following way:

$$\text{Effort (motivation)} = E * \Sigma VI$$

where *E* = the expectation that a given behavior will result in
      a first-level outcome;

   I = the instrumentality, or degree of belief, that a first-
      level outcome will result in a second-level
      outcome;

   V = the valence, or value, that the individual places
      upon the second-level outcome;

First-level outcome = some immediate result associated with a behavior;

Second-level outcome = a secondary result of the first-level outcome.

An Example of Expectancy Theory   A fictional decision tree is presented for Adair, continuing the example, in Table 2.2.

Table 2.2 shows that Adair is deciding which of two behaviors she is going to engage in. Choice A is to put in 80 hours per week on her job, and Choice B is to put in 40 hours per week on her job. She first asks herself what first-level outcomes are associated with working 80 hours per week. She ascertains that there are two likely outcomes; she could be a superior performer, or she could be an average performer. Adair now asks what first-level outcomes are associated with working 40 hours per week. She determines that working only 40 hours per week she still can be an average performer.

The next step for Adair is to decide upon the probability (expectancy) of a first-level outcome occurring given her behavior. Suppose that in her mind the probability or expectancy *E* of her being a superior performer is .90 if she works 80 hours per week, and that the expectancy of her being an average performer, working 80 hours per week, is .10. She also asks what the expectancy is that she can be an average performer working 40 hours per week. Suppose that in her mind she is so confident of her abilities and the job is so unchallenging to her, that she decides that she can be an average performer with a 40-hour commitment to her job (*E* = 1.0).

What second-level outcomes are associated with each of Adair's first-level outcomes? Assume that four outcomes are associated with each second-level outcome: (1) a promotion, (2) recognition from the supervisor, (3) recognition from peers, and (4) a pay raise. It is also assumed that the same four second-level outcomes will result from each of the first-level outcomes.

Adair must now assess the likelihood of each second-level outcome occur-

Table 2.2   *An Example of Instrumentality Expectancy Theory*

Choice	E	First-Level Outcome	I	Second-Level Outcome	V
A. Work 80 hours per week	.90	Superior performance	.50	Promotion	+3
			.50	Supervisor recognition	+2
			1.00	Peer recognition	−3
			.60	Pay raise	+2
	.10	Average performance	.70	Promotion	+3
			.50	Supervisor recognition	+2
			1.00	Peer recognition	+3
			.50	Pay raise	+2
B. Work 40 hours per week	1.00	Average performance	.70	Promotion	+3
			.50	Supervisor recognition	+2
			1.00	Peer recognition	+3
			.50	Pay raise	+2

ring given the first-level outcome. That is, she must determine how instrumental (*I*) the first-level outcome is for each second-level outcome. She assumes that the degree of association between first- and second-level outcomes (instrumentalities) corresponds to the instrumentalities column in Table 2.2. She also values each of the second-level outcomes in the amounts indicated in the valences column in Table 2.2.

Given this set of *Es, Vs, Is*, and first- and second-level outcomes for Adair, applying the arithmetic of the expectancy model will show that she will elect to expend low effort. Her effort score for choice A is 1.34 units, and her effort score for choice B is 7.10 units. The calculations for determining her effort score for each choice are provided in Table 2.3.

There may be several questions about this example. Why did Adair assign a negative value to the peer recognition outcome when high performance was the first-level outcome, but assign a positive value to it when average performance was the first-level outcome? If the peer response under a high performance condition is negative (she will be viewed as making her peers look bad), then she may value it negatively. Alternately, the peer response under the average performance condition is probably positive (she will be viewed as "one of the gang"), and she may value that positively.

A second question is, why is there a greater likelihood of a promotion resulting from average performance than high performance? The answer might be that Adair is afraid that if she is too good her supervisor might try to keep her in the department. She might also feel that promotions go to people with the most seniority with little regard to variation in performance.

A third question is, do people really act this way—that is, do people actually compute all of these values? People probably do not sit down and

Table 2.3   *Calculations for Determining Behavioral Choice*

Choice A

$$.90 \times \sum \begin{pmatrix} .50 \times +3 \\ .50 \times +2 \\ 1.00 \times -3 \\ .60 \times +2 \end{pmatrix} = .63$$

$$.10 \times \sum \begin{pmatrix} .70 \times +3 \\ .50 \times +2 \\ 1.00 \times +3 \\ .50 \times +2 \end{pmatrix} = .71$$

$$1.34$$

Versus

Choice B

$$1.00 \times \sum \begin{pmatrix} .70 \times +3 \\ .50 \times +2 \\ 1.00 \times +3 \\ .50 \times +2 \end{pmatrix} = 7.10.$$

figure out a decision tree like this. However, everyone goes through this process subconsciously when they make choices. Behavior is influenced by what individuals perceive as the relationships between that behavior, the first- and second-level outcomes, and the value attached to those outcomes.[28]

Reinforcement Theory and Instrumentality and Expectancy Theory   A classical approach to human motivation (reinforcement theory) can be linked to the instrumentality and expectancy model. Reinforcement theory argues that a response that is elicited in the presence of a stimulus will be repeated in the presence of that stimulus if the original stimulus was satisfying.[29] In other words, if a person receives a favorable outcome immediately after acting in a certain way, then in the future he or she should act the same way as before if the same outcome is desired.

The role of reinforcement theory can be seen in the Adair example. Suppose Adair had never thought about whether she valued positive or negative peer response. If she is an average worker at 40 hours per week and her coworkers are nice to her, this positive response would reinforce her behavior. Further, suppose that during one week she works 80 hours, and the outcome is a negative peer response. This negative reinforcement is likely to be avoided in the future. Given the choice between a positive reinforcer (positive peer response) and a negative reinforcer (negative peer response), Adair is likely to behave in a way that will result in the positively valued outcome.

Although reinforcement theory was originally developed by psychologists in examining noncognitive animal behaviors, it has extensive application for understanding human behavior.[30] There is little doubt that employees consciously or unconsciously have their behaviors reinforced by outcomes provided by the organization. For example, money has been viewed as a secondary reinforcer in the sense that money can purchase things that satisfy basic needs.[31] In this manner managers can use money to reinforce desired behaviors (high performance).

Implications of Instrumentality and Expectancy Theory for Compensation
The instrumentality and expectancy model has several applications to compensation.

Need Satisfaction Influences Values   First, the values attached to second-level outcomes are in large part determined by how much each contributes to satisfying the needs that people bring to the work place. For example, to the extent that Adair has a strong need to achieve, then she will value a promotion more than someone with a low need to achieve. Second, not only can one second-level outcome satisfy more than one need, but different second-level outcomes may satisfy any one need. Third, instrumentalities and second-level outcomes may be controllable by the organization. For example, Adair's perceptions about the relationship between performance level and a promotion are probably learned by observing what happens where she works. If management wants its employees to believe that promotion results from high performance, it must act that way.[32] This concept is developed with the design of a pay-for-performance system in Chapter 12.

Organizations Shape Beliefs   Compensation decision makers have considerable control over shaping employee perceptions, or reinforcing employee behaviors. They can influence employees' beliefs about the expectancies, instrumentalities, and outcomes associated with performance. For example, if promotions are given only for high levels of performance, then employees learn that high performance and not something else results in promotion. If pay raises go only to those who are high performers, employees learn that performance results in more money. All of this suggests that valid performance assessment systems and pay for performance systems are an absolute necessity for employees to believe in merit pay systems and be motivated by money.[33]

Money and Motivation   Monetary outcomes are one of the major ways in which an organization can influence individual behavior. Money appeals to all of the needs that people have.[34]

There are several decisions that people make in the context of the two organizational goals of the compensation system: influencing the employees' decision to join and to stay, and influencing their decision to perform at high levels. First, the absolute level of hiring wages can influence people to join the organization. For example, if a firm offers a wage rate of $10 per hour for a given type of work and everyone else is offering $8 per hour, then a job applicant is likely to choose the higher-paying firm, all other things being equal. Second, money can influence the decision to stay. If wages in the firm fall below the **going rate,** people may start leaving the firm. Money in the form of employee benefits may also influence the decision to stay. A senior employee who is entitled to six weeks of paid vacation may be reluctant to leave for a better paying job if it means losing the vacation time. Third, organizations can use money to influence the decision to perform, as shown in the Adair example.

A series of conditions must exist before money will motivate high levels of performance. Those conditions are: (1) the person must believe that by expending the effort, he or she is capable of high performance (E is close to 1.0); (2) the person must have needs that money will satisfy; (3) the person must believe that high performance will result in money.

Summary

Chapter 2 established a theoretical framework for understanding human behavior. The compensation decision maker must understand how people behave so that the pay system will influence this behavior. This chapter discussed the employment exchange contract and the nature of human needs, and developed equity theory and instrumentality and expectancy theory.

Several administrative practices were identified that are designed to accomplish the first major goal of a compensation system. First, it is critical for employees to feel equitably treated in their wage and benefit payments. Also, there are probably at least two forms of equity that should be considered: external and internal equity. Employers are concerned about external equity because they want to influence people to join and stay with the organization. External equity is accomplished, when feasible, by conducting labor market surveys of wages and benefits. Employers are concerned about internal equity because of the compensation subgoal of influencing people to stay with the organization. Concerns about internal equity cause employers to engage in the administrative practice of job evaluation.

To understand the process of motivation of high levels of performance, the instrumentality and expectancy theory was presented in this chapter. If organizations want high levels of performance they must design the compensation system to accomplish it. Administratively, organizations must have a valid merit pay system, which requires an effective performance appraisal process, among other things.

This chapter developed several theories about human behavior, and several administrative activities were linked to those theories, to achieve the first major goal of a compensation system: eliciting desired behaviors from individuals.

Discussion Questions

1. Discuss the concepts of internal and external pay equity.

2. Think about the things that have happened to you at work (even if it's been a part-time job). How do those things relate to the needs that you may have? Relate these needs back to some of the terminology employed by the various need theorists.

3. Think about a time when you felt unfairly treated. What seemed to be unfair about that situation to you? Can you identify the comparison standard—the relevant other?

4. Most of you have had to think about spending two hours at your favorite sport or studying for that exam the next day. Which decision did you make and why? Can you recast that decision using instrumentality and expectancy theory terminology?

5. Identify a list of contributions you intend to make to your employer, and also list the inducements which you expect your employer to make to get you to work.

References

[1] S. C. Bushardt and A. R. Fowler, "Compensation and Benefits: Today's Dilemma in Motivation." *Personnel Administrator* 27 (April 1982): pp. 23–26. W. H. Franklin, "Create an Atmosphere of Positive Expectations," *Administrative Management* 41 (April 1980): pp. 32–34.

[2] See J. P. Campbell, M. D. Dunnette, E. E. Lawler, and K. E. Weick, Jr., *Managerial Behavior, Performance, and Effectiveness* (New York: McGraw-Hill, 1970): pp. 340–358, for a discussion of the distinction between content and process models of motivation.

[3] A. H. Maslow, "A Theory of Human Motivation," *Psychological Review* 50 (July 1943): pp. 370–396. J. B. Gayle and F. R. Searle, "Maslow, Motivation and the Manager," *Management World* 9 (October 1980): pp. 25–27. M. Wahba and L. G. Bridwell, "Maslow Reconsidered: A Review of Research on the Need Hierarchy Theory," *Organizational Behavior and Human Performance* 15 (1976): pp. 376–379. Lyman Porter, "Job Attitudes in Management: Perceived Deficiencies in Need Fulfillment as a Function of the Size of a Company," *Journal of Applied Psychology* (December 1963): pp. 387–388.

[4] Henry A. Murray, *Explorations in Personality* (New York: Oxford University Press, 1938).

[5] C. P. Alderfer, *Existence, Relatedness, and Growth: Human Needs in Organizational Settings* (New York: The Free Press, 1972).

[6] Benjamin Scheinder and Clayton Alderfer, "Three Studies of Measures of Need Satisfaction in Organizations," *Administrative Science Quarterly* (December 1973): pp. 489–491. Clayton Alderfer, "An Empirical Test of a New Theory of Human Needs," *Organizational Behavior and Human Performance* 4 (1969): pp. 142–175.

[7] F. Herzberg, B. Mausner, and B. Snyderman, *The Motivation to Work*, 2d ed. (New York: Wiley, 1959).

[8] Richard Steer and Richard Mowday, "The Motivational Properties of Tasks," *Academy of Management Review* (October 1977): pp. 645–658.

[9] Fred Herzberg, "One More Time: How Do You Motivate Employees?" *Harvard Business Review* (January–February 1968): pp. 56–57.

[10] Salvatore R. Maddi, *Personality Theories*, 3d ed. (Homewood, Ill.: The Dorsey Press, 1976): pp. 19–174.

[11] See, for example, D. C. McClelland, *The Achieving Society* (Princeton, N.J.: Van Nostrand, 1961), and J. W. Atkinson, ed. *Motives in Fantasy, Action, and in Society* (Princeton, N.J.: Van Nostrand, 1958) for further discussions of these needs.

[12] David McClelland, "The Urge to Achieve," *Think* (November–December 1966): pp. 19–23.

[13] The inducements and contributions contract concept is more fully developed by J. G. March and H. A. Simon in *Organizations* (New York: Wiley, 1958): Chapter 4, pp. 83–111.

[14] John Kotter, "The Psychological Contract: Managing the Joining Up Process," *California Management Review* 15 (Spring 1973): pp. 91–99.

[15] D. Yankelovich, "New Psychological Contracts at Work: Employee Incentives," *Personnel Psychology* 24 (1971): pp. 501–518. David Berlew and Douglas T. Hall, "The Socialization of Managers: Effect of Expectations on Performance," *Administrative Science Quarterly* (September 1966): pp. 207–223.

[16] E. E. Lawler III, "Job Attitudes and Employee Motivation: Theory Research and Practice," *Personnel Psychology* 23 (1970): pp. 223–237.

[17] Dennis Middlemist and Richard Peterson, "Test of Equity Theory by Controlling for Comparison Co-workers' Efforts," *Organizational Behavior and Human Performance* 15 (1976): pp. 335–354.

[18] J. S. Adams, "Toward an Understanding of Inequity," *Journal of Abnormal and Social Psychology* 67 (1963): pp. 422–435. Paul Goodman and Abraham Friedman, "An Examination of Adams' Theory of Inequity," *Administrative Science Quarterly* (September 1971): pp. 271–277.

[19] J. S. Adams, "Inequity in Social Exchange," in L. Berkowitz, ed., *Advances in Experimental Social Psychology* (New York: Academic Press, 1965): pp. 267–299.

[20] For reviews of equity theory findings, see R. D. Pritchard, "Equity Theory: A Review and Critique," *Organizational Behavior and Human Performance* (May 1969): pp. 176–211.

[21] For a review of alternative references, see F. S. Hills, "The Relevant Other in Pay Comparisons," *Industrial Relations* 19, no. 3 (Fall 1980): pp. 346–351.

[22] W. L. White and J. W. Becker, "Increasing the Motivational Impact of Employee Benefits," *Personnel* 57 (January 1980): pp. 32–37. D. Yankelovich, "New Psychological Contracts at Work: Employee Incentives," *Personnel Psychology* 24 (1971): pp. 501–518. J. S. Adams, "Wage Inequities, Productivity and Work Quality," *Industrial Relations* (October 1963): pp. 9–16. J. S. Adams and William Rosenbaum, "The Relationship of Worker Productivity to Cognitive Dissonance about Wage Inequities," *Journal of Applied Psychology* 46 (1962): pp. 161–164.

[23] Gregg Lewis, "Union Relative Wage Effects: A Survey of Macro Estimates," *Journal of Labor Economics* (January 1983): pp. 1–27.

[24] Ernest Miller, "College Recruiting Pay Practices," *Compensation Review* 11 (First quarter 1979): pp. 31–34.

[25] J. R. Andrews, "Wage Inequity and Job Performance: An Experimental Study," *Journal of Applied Psychology* 51 (1967): p. 39. J. D. Batten and Dale Stouder, "Compensation and Job Evaluation," *Personnel Journal* (December 1965): pp. 609–612.

[26] V. H. Vroom, *Work and Motivation* (New York: Wiley, 1964).

[27] J. R. Hackman and L. W. Porter, "Expectancy Theory Prediction of Work Effectiveness," *Organizational Behavior and Human Performance* 12 (1968): pp. 417–426. Herbert G. Heneman III and D. P. Schab, "Evaluation of Research on Expectancy Theory Predictions of Employee Performance," *Psychological Bulletin* 79 (July 1972): pp. 1–9. R. D. Pritchard and M. S. Sanders, "The Influence of Valence, Instrumentality, Expectancy on Effort and Performance," *Journal of Applied Psychology* 57 (1973): pp. 55–60. L. Reinharth and M. A. Wahba, "Expectancy Theory as Predictor of Work Motivation, Effort Expenditure, and Job Performance," *Academy of Management Journal* 18 (September 1975): pp. 520–537. E. E. Lawler III and J. L. Suttle, "Expectancy Theory and Job Behavior," *Organizational Behavior and Human Performance* 71 (1973): pp. 482–503. Tamao Matsui et al., "Validity of Expectancy Theory as a Within Person Behavioral Choice Model for Sales Activities," *Journal of Applied Psychology* (December 1977): pp. 764–767.

[28] Frederick Starke, "A Test of Two Postulates Underlying Expectancy Theory," *Academy of Management Journal* (December 1975): pp. 703–707.

[29] E. L. Thorndike, *Animal Intelligence* (New York: Macmillan, 1911).

[30] B. F. Skinner, *Beyond Freedom and Dignity* (New York: Knopf, 1971).

[31] Robert L. Opsahl and Marvin D. Dunnette, "The Role of Financial Compensation in Industrial Motivation," *Psychological Bulletin* 66, no. 2, (1966): pp. 94–118.

[32] Terence Mitchell, "Expectancy Models of Job Satisfaction: Occupational Preference and Effort," *Psychological Bulletin* 81 (1974): pp. 1053–1056.

[33] Robert Opsahl and Marvin Dunnette, "The Role of Financial Compensation in Industrial Motivation," *Psychological Bulletin* 66 (1966): pp. 94–118.

[34] *Ibid.*

C H A P T E R

3

The Theoretical

Framework II:

Economic Constraints

· **Learning Objectives**

· **Introduction**

· **Wage Differentials—A Technical Meaning**

· **Marginal Revenue Productivity Theory**

  Labor Demand as a Derived Demand
  An Intuitive Example of Labor's Value
  The Employer's Demand for Labor
  Labor Supply in the Marketplace

· **Marginal Revenue Productivity Theory and Ability to Pay**

  Average and Total Revenue
  Variable Costs
  Fixed Costs
  Profits
  Labor's Share

· **Labor's Productivity and Ability to Pay**

  A Caution on Labor's Productivity
  Wage Level versus Wage Structure Concepts

· **Ability to Pay and Industry Characteristics**

· **The Importance of Product Market Surveys**

  Elasticity of the Demand for the Product
  Elasticity of Demand for the Brand
  The Capital/Labor Ratio
  The Substitutability of Other Factors of Production
  The Supply Curves of Other Factors of Production

· **Consequences of Different Wage Levels**

  The Low-Wage Employer
  The High-Wage Employer

· **The Wage Level Concept**

· **Minicase: The Automobile Industry Recession**

Learning Objectives

To learn that organizations have an ability-to-pay constraint.
To learn that the demand for labor is a derived demand; that is, it is derived from the demand for the good or service that the employer produces.
To learn that marginal revenue productivity (MRP) theory is the theoretical base for understanding the organization's ability-to-pay constraint.
To learn through simple examples how MRP theory translates into ability to pay wages.
To learn the consequences associated with an organization that is a high- or low-wage employer.
To learn that the concept of ability to pay is directly related to the concept of the wage level.

Introduction

The basic issue of this chapter is to lay out the concept of ability to pay. Organizations differ in their ability to pay. To illustrate this difference, this chapter discusses the concepts of demand for labor as a derived demand, marginal revenue productivity theory, and labor supplies. The chapter concludes with a section on the significance of ability to pay in compensation practice; specifically firms conduct product market wage and salary surveys to estimate their ability-to-pay constraint.

Every labor market area has both a high-wage employer and a low-wage employer, with a large number of employers who pay a range of rates between the extremes. Restaurants and gas stations are relatively low-wage employers. On the other hand, oil firms and computer companies may be relatively high-wage employers. In the simplest case one might not expect large wage differences among employers within a labor market area. Organizations in a given labor area might be expected to pay the same rate in order to influence workers to join and stay with them (the first major goal of a compensation system). Yet there are extremely large wage differences within a given labor market area. One classic study found that for truck drivers in the Boston labor area, the highest paying firms paid 96 percent more than the lowest paying firms, even though the truck drivers were unionized.[1]

This chapter develops the theoretical framework so that the reader will understand why these wage differentials exist, by developing the concept of ability to pay. It is primarily the relative ability to pay wages among employers that causes wage differences. This chapter also deals with the consequences for an employer if its economic situation forces it to be a low-wage organization or permits it to be a relatively high-wage organization.

Wage Differentials — A Technical Meaning

The concept of a wage differential has been used in a variety of ways in compensation literature. One context concerns wage differences between particular organizations or industries. Such differences are often attributed to differences in the skill mix of employees that are used by different organizations or industries in producing a good or service.[2] In this context, a computer company, on average, will pay higher wages than a restaurant because the computer company usually uses more highly skilled workers.

Wage differentials between geographic areas have also been identified.[3] Geographic wage differentials are often attributed to the difference in the skill mix and supply of labor offered in various regions of the United States. Variation in the composition of industry among geographic regions is also a partial explanation for geographic wage differentials.

Adam Smith identified five reasons for wage differentials among workers within a given geographic area.[4] First, different kinds of work vary in terms of their agreeableness. This reason means that some work is simply cleaner, more enjoyable, or more honorable, for example. This may be partly why the banking industry pays relatively low wages, because bank work involves working in a prestigious and pleasant environment. An organization that can provide more agreeable work may be able to pay lower wages than other organizations for the same quality of employee. Second, wages for work vary as a function of the expense of learning the business. Some labor is paid more, presumably because training time is longer and workers must receive a higher wage for their training investment. Third, constancy of employment will affect wages. Employment that is stable presumably can be lower paying than unstable employment, since unstable employment requires higher wages to affect less time at work. Fourth, wages will vary with the level of trust that must be placed in the worker: a physician's pay is relatively higher than a groundskeeper's pay because of the level of trust people must have in the physician's work. Fifth, wages will vary as a function of the likelihood of success in the employment. If chances of success are low, wages should be correspondingly higher to offset the risk of failure.

These notions of wage differentials are not considered here. When high- and low-wage employers are referred to, it means that within a given labor area, holding constant the job under consideration, some organizations pay more than others for the same type of work. If an employee in one organization is paid less than an employee doing the same work in another organization, it is because different organizations have different abilities to pay.

The next sections examine the theoretical framework for understanding an organization's ability to pay and explore the implications of ability to pay.

It is also true that just because an organization has a high ability to pay does not necessarily mean that it will pay high wages. For example, a millionaire and an average wage earner have different abilities to pay someone to remove snow from their driveways, but both may pay the same. Other forces than ability to pay influence whether the millionaire will pay more than the average wage earner.

Marginal Revenue Productivity Theory

Labor Demand as a Derived Demand

Labor services, in and of themselves, have no value. That is, labor is valued only by an employing organization to the extent that the labor is combined with other factors of production to produce a good or service. Ford Motor Company and Ace Hardware want workers only because they are part of the resource mix needed to make cars or to sell nails. Therefore, the demand for labor is a **derived demand** — that is, it is derived from the demand for goods or services that an employing organization makes and sells.[5] When the demand for Ford cars is down, workers are laid off; new workers are hired by Apple Computers when demand for home computers grows. The newspaper story in Exhibit 3.1 concerns a downturn in employment caused by a downturn in the demand for the product.

An Intuitive Example of Labor's Value

The value of labor is determined, in part, by how it is applied to other factors of production, as shown in the following example. Suppose an employer is in the business of digging ditches and can sell all of the linear feet of ditch that can be dug at $1 per foot. The employer has a total of five shovels (a fixed production facility), no other tools or equipment are used, and the shovels are paid for (no capital costs). All laborers hired are interchangeable. What happens to productivity (feet of ditch dug) and revenues as the employer hires each worker?

If a typical laborer can dig 30 feet of ditch in a day, then the productivity of the first laborer hired will be 30 feet of ditch. Similarly, the second through the fifth worker hired each add 30 feet of ditch per day. The average productivity of these workers is 30 feet of ditch per day. Regardless of whether the employer uses one, two, three, four, or five workers per day, the average productivity is 30 feet of ditch, even though total productivity goes up 30 times the number of workers employed. Total productivity is 30 feet in the case of one worker, 60 feet in the case of two workers, and so forth up to 150 feet for five workers. The relationship between labor's productivity and number of workers hired in this example is summarized in Table 3.1.

What happens to marginal productivity as workers one through five are added? Marginal productivity can be defined as the increment in productivity

---

Exhibit 3.1   *Effect of Product Demand on the Demand for Labor*

GE to cut 130 white-collar by year end

By George Kegley
Business editor

About 130 managerial, professional, technical and clerical employee positions will be eliminated at the Salem General Electric plant by the end of the year.

The job reductions were caused by market conditions, plant officials said.

This is an 11 percent cut of the 1,100 salaried employees at the plant. Another 1,600 are hourly workers.

It apparently is the largest cutback of professional personnel since the plant opened almost 30 years ago.

Orders have been slow and the plant has advanced work from next year's schedule, some workers have said.

Slow orders and a highly competitive foreign market were blamed for the layoff of 400 factory workers at the plant last year.

The last change in factory forces was a recall of about 100 hourly employees in July. The company said increased orders in several business segments created a need for more hourly workers.

The plant's force has been near 2,700, down from 3,800 before the 1982 recession.

Source: "GE to Cut 130 White-Collar by Year End," by George Kegley. *Roanoke Times & World News*, November 8, 1984, p. B-8. Reprinted by permission.

Table 3.1   *Labor's Productivity and the Impact on Labor's Demand Price*

Number of Workers	Total Product (feet of ditch)	Average Product[a] (feet)	Marginal Product[b] (feet)	Price	Average Revenue Product[c]	Marginal Revenue Product[d]
1	30	30	30	$1	$30	$30
2	60	30	30	1	30	30
3	90	30	30	1	30	30
4	120	30	30	1	30	30
5	150	30	30	1	30	30
6	210	35	60	1	35	60
7	280	40	70	1	40	70
8	320	40	40	1	40	40
9	333	37	13	1	37	13
10	280	28	−53	1	28	−53

[a] Average productivity = Total productivity divided by the number of workers.
[b] Marginal productivity = The increment in total productivity realized by moving from N to $N + 1$ workers.
[c] Average revenue product = Average productivity multiplied by the unit price of the product.
[d] Marginal revenue product = Marginal productivity multiplied by the unit price of the product.

resulting from the addition of one more worker. As the employer adds the first worker, marginal productivity goes from zero (with no workers) to 30 (when the first worker is added). When the second worker is added, marginal productivity is 30 and is equal to average productivity. That is, the second worker increased total output to 60 feet of ditch, but the second worker is no more productive than the first worker. For workers one through five, then, marginal productivity is 30 feet of ditch, and average productivity is 30 feet of ditch. Each worker is using one more shovel and adding the same amount to the total productive capacity of the ditch digging company.

The company now adds a sixth worker to the work crew. This worker sharpens the shovel blades while the other five workers rest, gets water for them (and thereby shortens their breaks), and spells them periodically. With the addition of the sixth worker, total productivity goes from 150 feet of ditch (with five workers) to 210 feet of ditch. The marginal productivity of the sixth worker is 60 feet of ditch, and the average productivity of the six workers is now 35 feet of ditch. The employer is realizing an **economy of scale**; that is, workers are becoming more productive because they are more efficiently using the fixed factor of production (the five shovels).

Now the seventh worker is added to the work crew. This worker sharpens shovels even more often, spells the other workers more frequently, and drives the stakes to show where the ditch is to be dug. Workers who are digging no longer have to stop digging to plan the route of the ditch. This work crew can now dig 280 feet of ditch per day. The marginal productivity of the seventh worker is 70 feet of ditch, and average productivity is 40 feet of ditch per day. Labor is becoming more productive as it is applied to the fixed factor of production (shovels).

An eighth worker is now added to the work crew. This worker also spells other workers periodically and moves large stones out of the way of the planned ditch. Total productivity now goes to 320 feet of ditch. Marginal productivity is now 40 feet of ditch, and average productivity is 40 feet of ditch. Average productivity did not go up because marginal productivity of the eighth worker was exactly equal to the average productivity of the first seven workers. In other words, the eighth worker did not increase marginal productivity (although total productivity increased).

The ninth worker is added now. This ninth worker also helps remove obstacles from the path of the ditch and spells other workers on breaks. With this ninth worker productivity is 333 feet of ditch. Marginal productivity of this ninth worker is 13 feet of ditch, and average productivity is 37 feet of ditch per worker. Average productivity fell, even though total productivity increased slightly, because marginal productivity is falling.

The tenth worker now is added to the work crew. This tenth worker is always underfoot bumping into the other nine workers, and generally disrupting their work. Now total productivity is 280 feet of ditch. This tenth worker has a negative marginal productivity of 53 feet of ditch, and average productivity is 28 feet of ditch.

Two Important Ideas   This intuitive example demonstrates two important aspects of labor's productivity. The first is what economists call the **law of diminishing marginal proportions.**[6] This law states that as a variable factor of production (labor in the example) is added to a fixed factor of production (shovels in the example), the resulting additions to output initially increase due to economies of scale, but will eventually decrease.

The second point is that the employer's ability to pay will vary with labor's productivity. Average productivity can be translated to average revenue productivity because it is assumed that the ditch digging company can sell each foot of ditch dug for $1. When average productivity is multiplied by revenue, average revenue productivity for the work crew is $30 per day in the case of five workers, $35 per day in the case of six workers, and so on to $28 per day for ten workers. Depending upon labor's productivity at various combinations of employment, the firm's ability to pay will vary. These relationships are depicted in column six of Table 3.1. With a five-person crew of workers, the firm could pay up to $30 per day per worker; with a crew of seven the firm could pay up to $40 per day per worker; and with a crew of nine the firm could pay up to $28 per day per worker.

Limits of the Example   The ditch digging example is deficient in several respects. First, it is extremely simplistic in that there are usually several costs of production, and firms do wish to make a profit. Second, the concept of ability to pay is much richer than portrayed here. The example suggests that ability to pay varies within a fixed production technology. While this is true, it fails to make the important point that ability to pay varies across technologies. Third, the example does not adequately develop the concept of an employer's demand for labor. The demand for labor is important in understanding why firms are concerned about the wages they pay their employees. This concept is developed in the next section.

The Employer's Demand for Labor

To illustrate the employer's demand for labor, assume a small hamburger stand sells miniburgers and fries for $1 per serving. Each of these servings is called a meal. The owner of this stand figures out the amount of labor to hire by running an experiment in which one worker at a time is hired to determine how productive this labor will be. All workers hired are assumed to be equally productive, and the owner can sell all of the meals produced at $1 each.

Using the same analysis in the ditch digging example, the owner hires one worker and records the total productivity, the average productivity (*AP*), the marginal productivity (*MP*), the average revenue productivity (*ARP*), and the marginal revenue productivity (*MRP*) of that worker. The employer then adds more workers at the rate of one worker to each hourly shift to see how these five variables change. The results appear in Table 3.2, which shows that total productivity varies from zero output with no workers to 225 meals with 10 workers.

Based on these productivity figures, it can be seen that going from one to two workers will increase *ARP* from $10 to $15 and *MRP* from $10 to $20. Each additional worker, for workers one through five, results in an increase in both *ARP* and *MRP*. However, when worker six is employed, *ARP* remains unchanged, but *MRP* decreases! With the addition of workers seven through ten, both *ARP* and *MRP* decrease. These changes in *ARP* and *MRP* are due to changes in labor's productivity as a result of the law of diminishing marginal proportions as demonstrated in the ditch digging example. The *ARP* and *MRP* data from Table 3.2 can be plotted on a graph, as shown in Exhibit 3.2.

What are the profit levels of this hamburger stand at various levels of employment given an hourly wage rate of $10, $20, $30, $40, and $50 per hour respectively? The hamburger stand is most profitable at combinations of wages and employment along the portion of the *MRP* schedule from the point where *MRP* = *ARP* and to the right. All levels of employment to the left of this point are less profitable (that is, it pays to hire more workers). The firm's demand schedule for labor is equal to the *MRP* schedule for labor, and the relevant portion of this schedule is from where *ARP* = *MRP* to the right.

An employer can pay varying amounts for labor depending upon where the employer is on the demand schedule. This ability to pay wages of varying amounts is due to the fact that labor has a given productivity level at various levels of employment as it is applied to the physical plant. However, employers do not normally set wages unilaterally. That is, employers also set wages dependent upon what they must pay to attract and retain labor, which is in turn partly determined by the labor supply, which is discussed next.

Table 3.2   *Marginal Revenue Productivity Analysis (Per-Hour Basis)*

Units of Labor	Total Productivity	Average Physical Product	Marginal Physical Product	Price per Unit	Average Revenue Product	Marginal Revenue Product
0	0	0	0	$1	$ 0	$ 0
1	10	10	10	1	10	10
2	30	15	20	1	15	20
3	60	20	30	1	20	30
4	100	25	40	1	25	40
5	150	30	50	1	30	50
6	180	30	30	1	30	30
7	210	30	30	1	30	30
8	220	27.5	10	1	27.5	10
9	225	25	5	1	25	5
10	225	22.5	0	1	22.5	0

Exhibit 3.2   *Average and Marginal Revenue Productivity Curves*

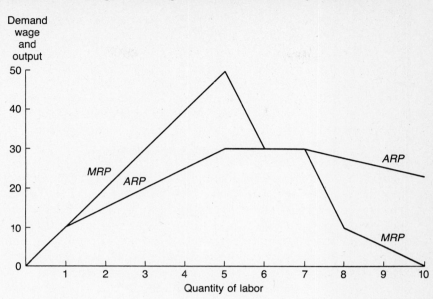

Labor Supply in the Marketplace

An example of a theoretical labor supply schedule is depicted in Exhibit 3.3. In theory, this labor supply schedule could be constructed by asking potential employees in the labor market how many of them are willing to work at different wage rates — how many would be willing to work for $4 per hour, how many would be willing to work for $5 per hour, and so forth. In general, the higher the wage offered in the marketplace, the larger is the quantity of labor willing to work. The owner in the hamburger stand example is faced with a supply schedule of labor in the marketplace and must pay (under assumptions of competition for labor) a rate that will attract sufficient labor to make the meals.

The wage that is offered is dependent upon the joint function of labor's supply wage and other employers' demands for labor. That is, if all of the labor in the market that is willing to work for $5 per hour is already employed, then the employer will not be able to hire labor at $5 per hour. In most cases, however, it is reasonable to assume that an adequate labor supply is available and that the supply of labor is highly elastic with respect to price. The hamburger stand owner can obtain all of the labor desired at the going market rate. The labor supply schedule to the hamburger stand resembles the one that appears in Exhibit 3.4. The employer here can obtain all of the labor desired at a given wage.[7]

Exhibit 3.3   *Theoretical Labor Supply Schedule*

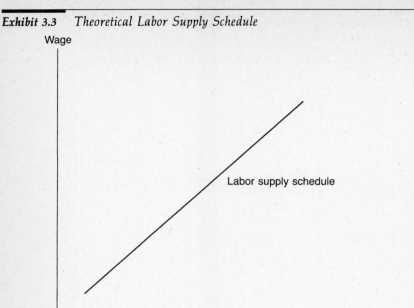

The labor demand schedule in Exhibit 3.2 and the labor supply schedule in Exhibit 3.4 can now be combined into the graph in Exhibit 3.5.

Using Exhibit 3.5, it is now possible to determine what the wage will be and what employment will be. The wage rate will be the equilibrium rate at W, and employment will be at the equilibrium level Q.

According to the graph in Exhibit 3.5, an employer has little control over wages paid. That is, wage rates presumably are a joint function of labor productivity and the labor supply's willingness to work at various wage levels. While this is partially true, it is erroneous to conclude that management has no control over wage rates. It should also be recognized that marginal revenue productivity theory as developed to this point is a theory of **employment**— given the productivity of labor (the demand schedule for labor) and the price of labor, the organization decides how many units of labor to employ.

Marginal Revenue Productivity Theory and Ability to Pay

Why is an organization constrained by its ability to pay? One of the factors that is critical in an employer's ability to pay is the productivity of labor units.[8] An organization that makes and sells a product must sell it for a price that allows the organization to cover the costs of production and make a profit. The more productive each unit of labor employed by the organization, the more valuable that labor unit is to the employer (the cheaper each unit of labor is,

Exhibit 3.4   *Labor Supply Schedule to an Organization*

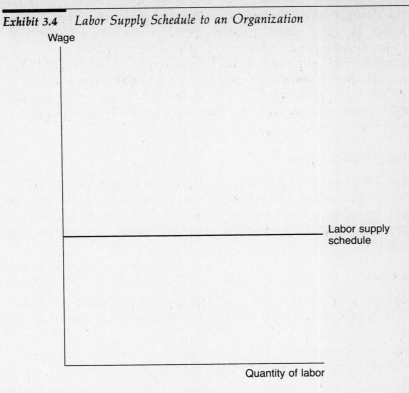

Exhibit 3.5   *Interaction of Labor Supply and Demand*

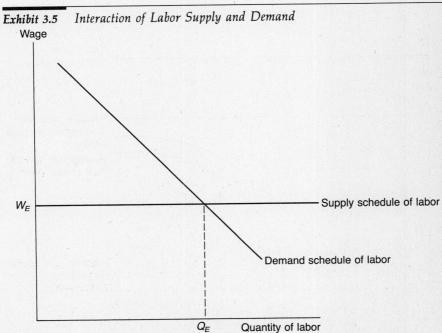

per unit of product). The following example illustrates why, using two hamburger stands. In this example, employer A has a relatively efficient labor force, and employer B has a relatively inefficient labor force.

Assume that both employers A and B are determining what hourly wage rate they could offer workers. Each employer has a targeted level of output of 220 meals per hour. These meals sell for $1 each. The amount of targeted output and the revenue associated with that output can be depicted in a graph, as shown in Exhibit 3.6.

Average and Total Revenue

In Exhibit 3.6 the line designated as *price* is the $1 per meal that the employer can charge for the product. The amount of the product to be produced is 220 meals, and the area under the curve is the total revenue to be realized: $1 × 220 meals = $220. This line also represents average revenue per unit of product.

Variable Costs

Every employer who manufactures a product must be concerned about variable costs.[9] Variable costs are the direct costs that go into the manufacture of

---

Exhibit 3.6   *Analysis of Average Net Revenue Product*

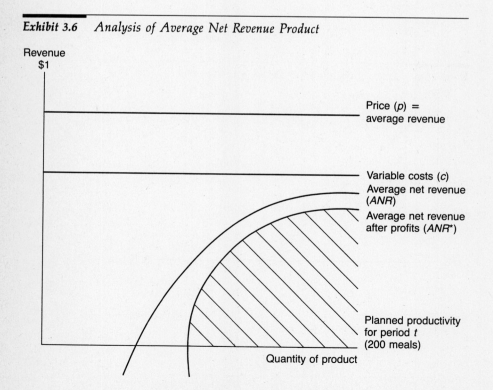

the finished good. Examples of variable costs for a meal are the cost of the hamburger, pickles, buns, potatoes, and so forth. These costs are variable with respect to the level of production (the number of units produced), but are fixed with respect to each unit produced. For example, the same amount of hamburger goes into each meal.

It is possible to represent these variable costs on the graph in Exhibit 3.6. The area between price (*P*) and line *C* represents these variable costs. In the example, variable costs represent 40¢ per unit. Total variable cost for 220 meals (output) is $88.

Fixed Costs

Every employer also has fixed costs. Fixed costs are such items as rent on the building, capital expenditures on equipment, and utilities.[10] This type of cost is fixed for a given planning cycle, but is variable with respect to output. For example, whether an employer produces 0 units of output during an hour or 220 units per hour, fixed costs remain the same. However, fixed costs per unit of output decrease as output increases in that hour.

Fixed costs in the example are constant at $30 per hour. These fixed costs can be represented on the graph in Exhibit 3.6 as the area between the curve *C* and the average net revenue (*ANR*) curve. The area remaining under the curve is the average net revenue after both variable and fixed costs have been deducted from total revenues.

Profits

All employers in the private sector desire a profit from their endeavors. It is reasonable to assume that employers would like to have a constancy of profits from their operations. An employer will express a desired level of profits with respect to a planning period (quarterly, semiannually, or annually). In the example, each employer would like to make $18 per hour profit from the hamburger stand.

The difference between the *ANR* and *ANR** curves represents profit — that is, the difference between average net revenue, and average net revenue after profits, is profits. Like fixed costs, profits are variable with respect to units produced: if a fixed profit level is desired within the planning period, then the more units produced, the smaller must be the contribution of each unit toward profitability.

Labor's Share

The remaining area under the *ANR** curve could be thought of as the pool of money from which to pay for labor's services. That is, after taking into consideration product price, output, fixed and variable costs, and profit, the employer is able to pay labor from this remaining pool of resources. In the example, the remaining pool to pay labor is $84.

Labor's Productivity and Ability to Pay

To determine a firm's ability to pay, the resources available to pay labor must be converted into an average net revenue product for labor.[11] Conceptually, the average net revenue after profits (ANR^*) is divided by the amount of labor that it took to produce ANR^*.

To continue with the example, the two hamburger stands are across the street from each other and both can sell 220 meals per hour. In spite of the identical cost structures depicted in Exhibit 3.6, their labor is not equally productive. Employer A has very modern grills, french friers, and so on, and uses only 5 workers to produce 220 meals in an hour. Employer B requires 10 workers to produce the 220 meals because of old and obsolete production processes.

Based on this analysis, employer A can afford to pay up to $16.80 per hour for each worker on average while employer B can afford to pay up to $8.40 per hour on average for its workers.

A Caution on Labor's Productivity

It would be easy to infer that labor's productivity varies with different abilities among workers (workers are not homogeneous) and differences in motivation levels among workers. Although workers do differ in these important dimensions, the differences in productivity among workers in different firms are due overwhelmingly to the technological differences among firms.

Productivity differences among employers account for large differences in ability to pay both within and across industries. For example, within an industry such as construction, a firm that digs ditches with bulldozers will have a higher ability to pay relative to a firm that digs ditches by pick and shovel, because of labor's higher productivity per unit of time when working with a bulldozer. Similarly, firms that computerize their accounting procedures are realizing greater efficiency than firms that continue to handle all accounting procedures with traditional manual systems.

Wage Level versus Wage Structure Concepts

Will an employer always pay more if it has a higher ability to pay than someone else? A relatively high ability to pay may cause an employer to pay a higher wage rate than another employer would. However, it does not mean that this will always happen.

To use the hamburger stand example, while employer A has a higher ability to pay than employer B, employer A may not pay more. In fact, employer A may choose to take the excess over actual labor costs for profit.

Employer A could, if it wanted to, pay a higher average wage than employer B. How that money will be allocated among various types of workers is a major issue for compensation decision makers.

However, employer A can afford to pay a higher *wage level* than employer B. The ability-to-pay constraint on employers influences the wage level for the firm. To be more specific, some possible decisions on the part of employers A and B can be considered. First, both owners could decide that all employees should make the same wage. If the owner works for an hour, she or he could be considered one of the employees for wage purposes. Second, the employers might decide to pay as little as they have to (minimum wages) and pocket the difference as their "managerial wage." In this case, employer A would make a higher managerial wage than employer B. Still another decision might be for employer A to pay a $1 per hour premium to its employees and still make more profit than employer B. These decision-making strategies and their influence on wages of workers and employers are summarized in Exhibit 3.7.

Ability to pay constrains the average wage that an employer can afford to pay. It does not specify how an employer will actually decide to distribute that average wage among various types of employees. That issue is the question of wage structure determination and is dealt with more deeply in future chapters.

Ability to Pay and Industry Characteristics

The previous section discussed the importance of labor productivity as it influences the amount of money available to pay labor. It is not likely that management actually calculates all of the variables that go into establishing the wage fund (it is unlikely that organizations even think in terms of a wage fund). If

Exhibit 3.7   *Strategies for Distributing the Average Wage and the Impact upon Wages for Different Employees*

	Employer A	Employer B
Pool of money for wages	$84.00 per hour	$84.00 per hour
Number of employees	5 per hour	10 per hour

Strategy A: Distribute wages equally to all employees, including owner who works for that hour.

	Employer A	Employer B
Wage rate (employees)	$16.80 per hour	$ 8.40 per hour
Wage rate (owner)	16.80 per hour	8.40 per hour

Strategy B: Pay minimum wage ($3.35/hr.) to all non-owner employees, while owner takes balance.

	Employer A	Employer B
Wage rate (employees)	3.35 per hour	3.35 per hour
Wage rate (owner)	70.60 per hour	53.85 per hour

Strategy C: Same as strategy B, but Employer A pays a $1 premium to all non-owner employees.

	Employer A	Employer B
Wage rate (employees)	4.35 per hour	3.35 per hour
Wage rate (owner)	66.60 per hour	53.85 per hour

organizations do not calculate the relative productivity of labor, how do they estimate their relative ability to pay? The most direct method is to conduct product market surveys of wages or salaries and benefits.[12]

Labor productivity is largely determined by the application of technology to units of labor. The application of technology may be highly standardized within an industry. For example, within the brewing industry there is great homogeneity of technology among Budweiser, Schlitz, and Miller. The same is true for the U.S. auto industry, the fast foods industry, dentistry, and so forth. Failure to keep up-to-date technologically can mean eventual death of a company because technologically superior firms are in a position to receive larger productivity returns from labor.[13] This increased efficiency can result in lower per-unit labor costs that allow the firm to be more competitive in the product market. The more efficient firm may then be able to sell its products more cheaply than less efficient firms, thereby driving the less efficient firms out of business.

Given the high degree of technological homogeneity within an industry, it is relatively easy for an employer to estimate its ability to pay. It determines what other firms against which it competes in the product market are paying, and then behaves in a similar manner.[14] Numerous assumptions go into this action. For one, the employer has no way of knowing that the wage level paid will result in optimal operations. All the employer knows is that if it behaves like other firms against which it competes, at least it should be able to be competitive and profitable. Second, wage comparisons should be made with relevant other firms, meaning firms with which it competes in the product market, firms with similar technology, firms of similar size (roughly equal economies of scale), and so forth.[15] The organization can then infer that if it does not behave much differently in its wage payments relative to its competitors, then it can survive and be profitable. The marginal productivity theory is crucial to understanding the importance of labor productivity as it impacts upon a firm's ability to pay. Organizations seldom actually go through the calculations of determining demand schedules for labor or their average net revenue product after profits. Instead, they rely upon a commonly accepted administrative practice known as product market surveys of wages or salaries and benefits. These surveys allow the organization to estimate its relative ability to pay, thus ensuring that they do not violate this crucial constraint.

The Importance of Product Market Surveys

Up to this point homogeneity of technology within product markets has been assumed. However, the concern over ability to pay is not constant for all firms within an industry or for firms among industries. Does the Budweiser plant in Williamsburg, Va. pay much attention to what the A-1 brewery in Arizona pays? Would the Leinenkugel brewery in Chippewa Falls, Wis. pay the same wages as the Olympia brewery in Minneapolis, Minn.? The answers reside with the importance of the ability-to-pay constraint for any given industry and firm.

Five factors affect the importance of the ability-to-pay constraint:

1. The elasticity of the demand for the product
2. The elasticity of demand for the brand
3. The proportion of labor costs to total costs
4. The substitutability of other factors of production
5. The supply curves of productive services other than labor.

The first three factors are particularly critical.

Elasticity of Demand for the Product

The demand for labor is a derived demand in the sense that labor services are demanded only after there is a demand for a good or service in the product market. The elasticity of the demand for labor is also determined in large part by the elasticity of demand for the product. Elasticity of demand for a product is defined as the ratio of the proportionate change in the demand for a product to the proportionate change in the price of the product in moving between any two points on the product demand schedule. Conceptually, there are three alternate elasticities that can occur: (1) a 1 percent unit change in price can result in a greater than 1 percent change in demand; (2) a 1 percent change in price can result in a 1 percent change in demand; or (3) a 1 percent change in price can result in less than a 1 percent change in demand. In the first case, product demand is said to be elastic with respect to price; in the third case, product demand is relatively inelastic with respect to price. The second case is referred to as unit elasticity.[16] Exhibit 3.8 illustrates these three cases.

In general, the more elastic product demand in an industry is with respect to price, the more concerned employers will be about not behaving differently from each other. For example, in one industry product demand is highly elastic with respect to price, and in another product demand is inelastic with respect to price. In the first case, assume that elasticity is equal to 20 percent (a 1 percent price increase results in a 20 percent decrease in demand). In the second case, product demand elasticity is .01 percent (a 1 percent increase in price will result in a .01 percent decrease in demand). Firms in both industries are faced with wage increases that will result in price increases of 2 percent. Firms in the first industry will be hurt more in terms of decreases in the demand for their products (40 percent versus .02 percent decreases in demand, respectively). Firms in the first industry will be much more concerned about not allowing any increases in costs, including wages, that would result in product price increases.[17] Firms in the first industry would want to pay wages that are highly consistent with their product market competitors (to assure similar cost structures for labor) and to resist wage increases.

Exhibit 3.8   *Conceptual Portrayal of Three Elasticity Conditions in Demand for the Product*

Elastic Product Demand

The percentage change in price is less than the percentage change in demand.

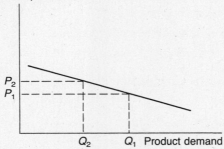

Unit Elasticity

The percentage change in price equals the percentage change in demand.

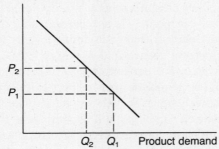

Inelastic Product Demand

The percentage change in price is greater than the percentage change in demand.

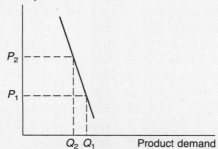

Elasticity of Demand for the Brand

Elasticity of demand for a brand also operates within an industry. In general, the more elastic brand demand is with respect to price, the more concerned an organization will be about not behaving differently in its wage payments relative to its competitors. For example, two firms in the same industry face highly elastic brand demand and currently charge the same price for their product — elasticity is 120 percent. If firm A raises wages relative to firm B so that firm A's final product is now priced 10 percent higher than firm B's, firm A would face a decrease in demand of 12 percent. If brand elasticity is only .20 percent, and firm A raises wages so that its product price goes up by 10 percent, there will be only a .02 percent decrease in brand demand.

In the first case, firm A would be very concerned that its wage payments not be much different from firm B. The more elastic the demand for the brand, the greater the concern firms in that industry will have that their wage rates (and therefore their wage level) not vary from their competitors. In the restaurant business, for example, a firm cannot afford to have its hamburgers sell for a very different price than its competitors' (brand demand is highly elastic with respect to price).

The Capital/Labor Ratio

The third major consideration in conducting a product market survey is the proportion of total costs represented by labor costs.[18] Both product demand and brand demand elasticities influence this variable. For example, two firms manufacture and sell beer. Firm A's case of beer costs it $9 to manufacture, as does firm B's. Firm A's labor costs are only 10 percent of the costs of the case of beer, while firm B's are 80 percent. Firm A is more capital intensive than firm B, so its labor costs are small relative to capital costs. The union requests a 10 percent increase in wages from both firms, and both agree to the wage increase. What is the impact of this wage increase on the two firms, and what impact will it have on the cost of beer at the grocery store?

Firm A's costs will increase by 9¢ per case: $9 × 10% (labor cost) × 10% (wage increase) = 9¢. Firm B's costs will increase by 72¢: $9 × 80% (labor cost) × 10% (wage increase) = 72¢. For both firms to still recoup their other costs of overhead, malt, hops, profits, and so on, they will have to pass the increased labor costs on to the consumer. Firm A's new price for beer will be $9.09, and firm B's will be $9.92. Under the assumption that the brand demand for beer is elastic with respect to the price, the wage increases would have a particularly harsh impact on the demand for firm B's beer. The above example is summarized in Exhibit 3.9.

Firm B will be unwilling to pay wages equal to firm A's in the first place, since unless there is an initial direct trade-off between capital and labor productivity, firm B cannot be as profitable as firm A at the same wage level. More importantly, firm B would be extremely concerned that its wage costs not rise as fast as firm A's because of the negative impact of wage increases on demand

Exhibit 3.9   *The Impact of the Capital/Labor Ratio on
Product Price When Wages Change*

	Firm A	Firm B
Total cost of product	$ 9.00	$ 9.00
Labor cost per unit of product (dollars)	.90	7.20
Labor cost per unit of product (percentage)	10%	80%
If wages go up by 10% in both firms		
New wage costs	$ .99	$ 7.92
New total costs	9.09	9.92

for its beer. Firm B would be very concerned about what its competitors are paying in wages (firm A, for example), and also that firm B would be a low-wage employer relative to firm A, even though they are both in the brewing industry.

The Substitutability of Other Factors of Production

The importance of product market surveys also rests on a fourth factor, the substitutability of other factors of production for labor. In some industries technology is very standardized and rigid, while in others there is considerable flexibility in substituting other factors of production for labor.[19]

In cases where it is difficult to substitute for labor, employers will be very concerned that their wage levels do not exceed their competitors' because of the negative impact on sales. On the other hand, if other factors of production can be substituted for labor, technological changes can be made if wages become too high, actually reducing the total wage bill. In this case the employer is less likely to be as concerned about following the wage pattern of others in the industry.

The Supply Curves of Other Factors of Production

Finally, the supply curves of other factors of production will influence an employer's concern over wage rates. For example, a firm increases wages relatively more than its competitors. Because of this wage increase and the resulting increase in the price of the product, product demand falls. The firm's demand for other resources in the production process also falls. This drop in demand for these other resources results in a decrease in the price of these other resources, which in turn offsets the relatively large increase in labor costs. In this case the employer is in a position to apply these savings against the wage increase, and it is not as crucial to follow the wage patterns of other firms in the industry.[20]

While most employers do pay very close attention to the wages paid by other firms in their industry, several factors affect the degree of concern over following the competition. The most critical of these is the elasticity of demand for the product. Second is the elasticity of demand for the brand. Third, employers whose labor costs represent a large proportion of total costs are very concerned about what the product market competition is doing with regard to wage payments. Fourth, the substitutability of other factors of production for labor, and fifth, the supply curves of other resources also affect the importance of observing wage patterns in the industry.

Consequences of Different Wage Levels

In the previous chapter we noted that employers conduct wage and salary and benefit surveys in the relevant labor market area so that they can assess the going wage rates for particular types of labor. The theoretical rationale for this is to pay a wage level for jobs that is competitive and assures that the firm can attract and retain labor.

In order to achieve external equity the employer attempts to pay a wage that will be perceived as equitable to present and potential employees. On the other hand, employers do attempt to adhere to wage levels within their industry. Because of the ability-to-pay constraint, the organization will be reluctant to pay much different wages than its product market competitors.

These two forces may yield different results.[21] The product market wage levels may be considerably lower or higher than the labor market wage levels. There are negative consequences for a firm that is at the low end of the wage distribution in a labor market, and benefits for the high-wage firm.

The Low-Wage Employer

A low-wage employer is very likely to be at the low end of a hiring queue. Within every labor market it is appropriate to think of organizations being ranked into a queue. The criterion for the queue is the relative desirability of employment with the firm in the perception of the work force. High-wage employers are at the top of the queue and are preferred by the labor force. Low-wage employers are the least preferred and, as might be expected, usually have the most difficult time attracting labor. Being on the low end of the hiring queue also means that the organization probably gets the most marginal workers in the work force since the better workers are accepted into the high-wage firms. As jobs open up at high-wage firms workers will leave low-wage firms and move up the queue. A low-wage employer thus finds it difficult to retain labor since individuals move up the queue. Low-wage employers are left with hiring the poorest qualified workers and can expect high turnover too.[22]

Faced with the ability-to-pay constraint, a low-wage employer might do a careful analysis of the costs of recruiting, selection, training, turnover, and so on. It may be possible to reduce some of these costs substantially by offering a hiring wage that is more competitive. Thus, wage costs may be offset by savings in other human resource areas. Employers also should look at all labor costs, not just the direct costs associated with wages and benefits.

The High-Wage Employer

Numerous benefits accrue to a high-wage employer, many of them the obverse of the difficulties faced by the low-wage employer. First, the high-wage employer finds itself at the top of the hiring queue. As a consequence, it has a substantially larger and more qualified labor pool from which to make selection decisions. Second, the quality of labor hired ought to be higher because of the better pool of candidates. Third, because its wages are relatively high, the employer ought to have less of a problem with external equity problems and less of a problem with turnover. It is much preferred to be a high-wage employer than a low-wage employer, although as discussed earlier the choice is not really the employer's; it is dictated by that firm's ability-to-pay constraint, which is influenced by the productivity of the employer's labor and characteristics of the product market.

Why wouldn't a firm just pay the market rate in a labor area if it is less than its product market constraint? Such a wage strategy would be highly profitable: the difference between the product market wage and the labor market wage would be pure profit. However, the employer is not likely to put the total difference between product market and labor market wages into profits because of the benefits accruing to a high-wage employer. It would be more sensible to take a middle-of-the-road course and maintain a higher place in the hiring queue and also be marginally more profitable.[23]

The Wage Level Concept

Wage level applies to the notion of an average wage, while *wage rate* refers to the actual amount of money paid for a specific job. A firm surveys a subset of jobs (often called **key jobs**) in doing a wage survey. The firm looks at the subset of wage rates paid to these jobs. Knowing the numbers of people working in each of these jobs would allow an employer to estimate the wage level for the surveyed organization.

In order for the estimated wage level obtained in wage surveys to be equal to the wage level in the surveying firm, the technologies of all of the organizations have to be highly similar. The discussion of levels and rates in this chapter holds true only where technology is standardized. The purpose of product market surveys is to make these inferences, while the purpose of labor market surveys is to satisfy equity considerations.

Summary

This chapter focused upon the economic constraints faced by an organization in making compensation decisions. The firm's ability to pay is the major economic constraint. A firm's ability to pay is influenced by labor's productivity and characteristics of the product market. Ability to pay accounts for why some employers are relatively high-wage employers within a labor market area and why other employers are relatively low-wage employers within that same labor area. High-wage employers generally have a larger and better qualified pool of applicants and can anticipate lower turnover. Low-wage employers can anticipate higher turnover and greater difficulty in attracting labor.

Discussion Questions

1. A basketball team signs six-foot, six-foot three-inch, six-foot ten-inch, seven-foot three-inch, six-foot five-inch, six-foot one-inch, and five-foot four-inch players in that order. Graph the average height and marginal height of the team as each new player is added. How is this like marginal revenue productivity analysis?

2. Major State University and Community State College are located within 20 minutes of each other in Ideal State, USA. Both employ professors, yet MSU pays, on average, 40 percent more than CSU for professors. Why?

3. Discuss the concept of the product market. How does a product market differ from a labor market? Compare and contrast these two markets — how are they alike and how are they different?

4. Major oil refining companies pay about twice as much as trucking companies for their computer programmers. Why?

Minicase: The Automobile Industry Recession

During the 1970s the U.S. automobile industry faced a severe depression in demand for cars. While Americans continued to buy cars, they generally shied away from U.S.-built cars and bought imported cars. The depression in demand was so severe that Chrysler Corporation was forced into bankruptcy.

In the early 1980s U.S. automakers took several steps to reverse this trend. First, they sought wage concessions from their employees. Second, they began to build smaller cars that more favorably met consumer preferences. Third, they modernized production plants by introducing robotics. By the mid-1980s the U.S. auto industry was once again healthy and profitable.

Using the auto industry, trace through all of the forces that threw the industry into a depression. Identify how each of these forces influenced the demand for cars and what each did to the demand for labor. Also, trace through what the auto industry recovery did to the industry's demand for labor. Relate this case to as many concepts as you can from this chapter.

References

[1] John T. Dunlop, "Suggestions toward a Reformulation of Wage Theory," in Thomas A. Mahoney, ed., *Compensation and Reward Perspectives* (Homewood, Ill.: Irwin, 1979): pp. 105–113.
[2] Melvin W. Reder, "The Occupational Wage Structure," in Campbell R. McConnell, ed., *Perspectives on Wage Determination; A Book of Readings* (New York: McGraw-Hill, 1970): pp. 199–206.

[3] H. M. Douty, "Regional Wage Differentials; Forces and Counterforces," in McConnell, *Perspectives on Wage Determination*, pp. 207–217.

[4] Adam Smith, "Wages in the Different Employments of Labour," in McConnell, *Perspectives on Wage Determination*, pp. 187–190.

[5] Lloyd G. Reynolds, *Labor Economics and Labor Relations*, 6th ed. (Englewood Cliffs, N.J.: Prentice-Hall, 1974): pp. 87–111.

[6] *Ibid.*, p. 90.

[7] Mahoney, *Compensation and Reward Perspectives*, p. 58.

[8] *Ibid.*, p. 97.

[9] Adolph E. Gruenwald and Erwin Esser Nemmers, *Basic Managerial Finance* (Philadelphia: Holt, Rinehart and Winston, 1970): p. 70.

[10] *Ibid.*, p. 70.

[11] Mahoney, *Compensation and Reward Perspectives*, p. 120.

[12] *Ibid.*, p. 123.

[13] Graef E. Crystal, "The Re-Emerging Role of Industry Pay Differences," *Compensation Review*, 3d quarter (1983): pp. 29–32.

[14] *Ibid.*

[15] Dunlop, "Suggestions toward a Reformulation of Wage Theory," p. 107. Mahoney, *Compensation and Reward Perspectives*, p. 121.

[16] Reynolds, *Labor Economics and Labor Relations*, p. 93.

[17] Mahoney, *Compensation and Reward Perspectives*, p. 122.

[18] Reynolds, *Labor Economics and Labor Relations*, p. 93.

[19] *Ibid.*

[20] *Ibid.*

[21] Crystal, "The Re-Emerging Role of Industry Pay Differences," pp. 29–32.

[22] John F. Burton, Jr. and John E. Parker, "Interindustry Variations in Voluntary Labor Mobility," *Industrial and Labor Relations Review* 22 (1969): pp. 199–216.

[23] Martin Bronfenbrenner, "Potential Monopsony Power in Labor Markets," *Industrial and Labor Relations Review* 9 (1956); pp. 577–588.

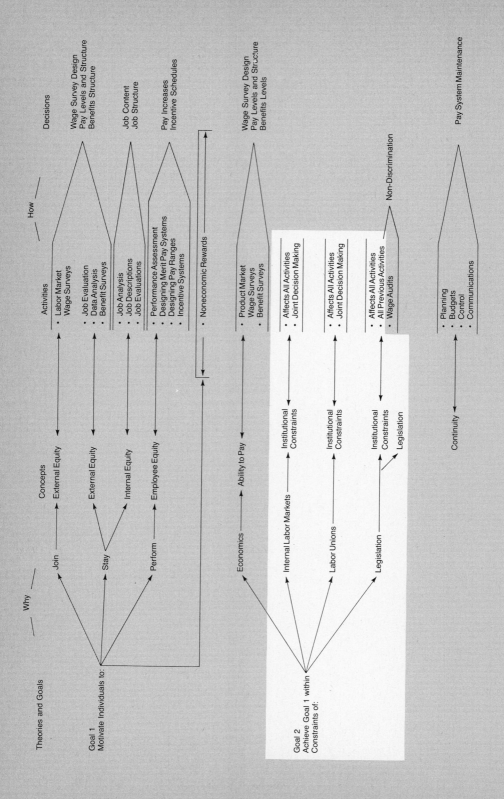

Institutional

Constraints in

Compensation

Part 2 is comprised of two chapters that focus upon several major institutional constraints that impinge upon compensation decision making. Chapter 4 deals with internal labor markets and labor unions. Chapter 5 considers the legal environment for compensation decision making.

Internal labor markets can be loosely defined as all of the employees who work in the organization. As developed in Chapter 4, the internal labor market has certain characteristics that make it more than simply a collection of employees. The chapter also identifies the major reasons why these markets have developed and the advantages of them for both employees and employers. Implications of the internal labor market concept for compensation decision making are also discussed.

Chapter 4 also deals with the institutional constraint of labor unions. Although the role of labor unions has been decreasing in the economy for the past 30 years, any employer whose employees are represented by a union must deal with this important constraint. Chapter 4 discusses the goals of labor unions, how unions and management organize for bargaining, the issues that are negotiated, and the bargaining process. The section on labor unions concludes with a discussion of how labor unions impact wages in particular, and labor costs in general.

Chapter 5 discusses the important institutional constraint of legislation. Various pieces of legislation that influence compensation decision making are discussed. Each piece of legislation is identified and discussed in terms of whom it affects. The chapter also reviews the major ways in which these statutes, or administrative rulings, impact compensation.

4

Institutional Constraints: Internal Labor Markets and Labor Unions

· **Learning Objectives**

· **Introduction**

· **The Internal Labor Market Concept**

  Organizations and Internal Labor Markets
  Implications of the Internal Labor Market for Compensation
  Pressures to Maintain Internal Labor Markets
  Emergence of Internal Labor Markets

· **Labor Unions and Compensation**

  The U.S. Labor Movement
  Issues and Process in Collective Bargaining
  General Union Impact on Compensation Decisions
  Specific Union Influence on Compensation Decision Making

· **Exercise**

Learning Objectives

To learn about the internal labor market concept.
To learn how internal labor markets influence compensation decision making.
To learn about the labor union movement in the United States.
To develop an appreciation for how unions bargain and the issues that unions bargain over.
To learn how labor unions impact compensation decisions.
To learn that unions also bargain over nonwage and nonbenefits issues that have an indirect impact on labor costs.

Introduction

This chapter explores two of the more important constraints faced by compensation decision makers: internal labor markets and labor unions. The notion of an internal labor market is important as a constraint because, as an institution, it shapes both individual and organizational perceptions of social relationships. These perceptions of social relationships translate into an institutional force that also shapes compensation decision making. Labor unions are an important institutional constraint because, as the representatives of employees, they are involved in joint labor–management decision making over compensation issues.

The concept of the internal labor market is developed first, and the significance of this market is discussed. The subject of labor unions is examined along with a discussion of their impact upon the terms and conditions of employment in general and upon wages and benefits in particular.

A number of questions are addressed: Why are entry-level jobs often the dirtiest and hardest yet also the lowest paid? When job hierarchies arise (lines of progression), what happens to an organization's pay system? An example of a line of progression is the three jobs of data entry clerk, computer programmer, and computer department supervisor. Why do job hierarchies arise in the first place? Questions are also asked about labor unions and their role in the compensation decision-making process. What do unions bargain for? How do they bargain, and do they affect the wage level of bargaining unit employees? Do they affect the wage structure?

The Internal Labor Market Concept

In a general sense the internal labor market of a firm is comprised of all of those employees who work for the organization. However, the term *internal labor market* is used with more precision in this text. Conceptually, an internal labor market can be conceived as all of the positions within an organization and the relationship of these positions to each other as well as the relationship

---

Exhibit 4.1   *A Hypothetical Labor Market for Office/Clerical Employees*

Internal Labor Market

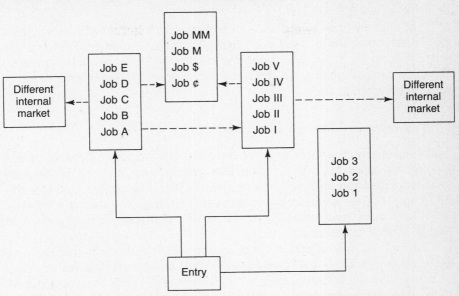

---

of those positions to the external environment of the organization.[1] Exhibit 4.1 depicts the internal labor market for an office clerical work force of a company.

Individuals enter into the internal labor market through what is often called a **port of entry**.[2] The port of entry is the job or jobs for which a new employee is hired. In Exhibit 4.1 new employees are hired into job 1, job I, or job A. These are the lowest jobs in each of three progression lines. Higher level jobs in each of the progression lines are filled by movement from lower level jobs. This movement is carried out through some set of administrative rules. Typically, these rules involve some combination of merit and seniority, although the exact combination is usually highly organization-specific and may also vary within an organization—the rules may be different for shop jobs and marketing jobs within the same company.[3]

Job A, job 1, and job I represent a number of positions. A **job** can be defined as a collectivity of tasks that can be performed by one person. A **position** is defined as a collectivity of tasks that is assigned to one person. The difference between the two is that a job is a generic grouping of tasks and duties, whereas a position is the actual assignment of those tasks or duties to a specific individual. There may be 100 people (in 100 positions) at job I, and 60 positions at job II. A company may have one job of data entry clerk (one collectivity of tasks), yet have 20 positions in that job (20 people who work as data entry clerks).

The broken lines with arrows in Exhibit 4.1 depict the points at which employees can transfer from one progression line to another. Transfers are possible from job D to job ¢. Transfers are also possible from job A to job I. Job 3, on the other hand, is a dead-end job: once an employee rises to job 3, there is nowhere to go.

Organizations and Internal Labor Markets

Every organization has one or more internal labor markets.[4] Typically, there are internal labor markets for shop jobs (maybe even separate progression lines for skilled and unskilled jobs), marketing jobs, finance jobs, and so forth. There may or may not be points of transfer from one set of jobs to another — such as transfer from unskilled to skilled jobs and transfer from personnel jobs to general management.

A common misconception about internal labor markets is that they are perfectly closed. Exhibit 4.1 depicts an internal labor market in which hiring occurs only at the bottom jobs in a progression line. While this is often true, sometimes higher level jobs are filled directly from outside of the firm. There is a **degree of openness** in the internal labor market.[5] In other words, some internal labor markets are relatively closed (they hire only into bottom jobs), while others are relatively open (they hire into all jobs). A host of factors affects the extent to which an internal labor market is closed. For example, in order to keep a perfectly closed internal labor market, the company will have to train people for advancement, plan for future human resource needs, hire people in the lower jobs who are capable of being trained, and so forth. The following chapters assume a relatively closed internal labor market, and to the extent that this assumption is invalid, many of the comments are correspondingly limited.

Implications of the Internal Labor Market for Compensation

The fact that relationships among jobs within an organization can be characterized along the concept of the internal labor market has a series of implications for compensation decision makers.[6] First, because people enter the organization and spend, in many cases, years moving into higher level jobs, it is often argued that people become isolated from the external labor market.[7] One of the benefits of this **isolation effect** for the organization is that the employer may have some latitude in setting wage rates for higher level jobs within a progression line. Since the employees who are isolated within higher level jobs have a difficult time assessing pay in other organizations, the organization is in a position to exercise discretion in pay rates.

A second reason why employees in higher level jobs become isolated is because many jobs within an organization are organization specific. Every organization combines tasks and duties into jobs in unique ways. A secretarial job in one company may be quite different from a secretarial job in another company. Given that employees in different companies are doing dissimilar work, it may be hard for them to assess what fair pay is for their job by looking to workers outside their own company. The implication of this for compensation decision making is that it is probably more critical to have pay rates that are perceived as equitable among jobs within the internal labor market than to be concerned about the equity of pay rates across internal labor markets or across companies. (Chapter 11 discusses **comparable worth,** a concern that addresses the issue of equity across internal labor markets within one firm.)

Third, employees become isolated in the sense that if they leave a high-level job in their present company they may have to start over at the bottom of the progression line with another company.[8] An employee is likely to realize that such a move will involve a cut in pay, a loss of seniority, a loss of vacation and other benefits, and so forth. With these negative outcomes, the probability that the employee will leave is likely to decrease. In one sense the employee is immobile, or locked in to the organization. The implication for the compensation decision maker is that perceptions of equity in pay (and other terms and conditions of employment) are extremely important. Given that there are many longtime employees in an organization who stand to lose a lot by leaving, it is to the organization's advantage to see that they believe they are equitably treated. Because present employees in higher jobs are somewhat immobile, relative equity among wage rates for jobs within the firm (internal equity) is probably more important than equity of wages between firms (external equity).

Finally, given that an organization tends to hire into port-of-entry jobs, the organization will be particularly concerned that these jobs pay wage rates that are competitive in the external labor market. Entry jobs are often considered key jobs and are subject to analysis of competitive wage rates when product and labor market surveys are undertaken.

Pressures to Maintain Internal Labor Markets

Why are internal labor markets maintained—why don't they eventually disappear so that all jobs are subject to purely competitive wage pricing? There are benefits to both employers and employees with internal labor markets.[9] From the organization's standpoint, internal labor markets provide a number of advantages: (1) they provide cheap training, since lower level employees can learn informally about higher jobs;[10] (2) they reduce the risk of hiring people into more responsible jobs who might fail; (3) they allow for systematic planning of human resource replacement;[11] and (4) they allow for socialization of employees into the organization's way of doing things.

Internal labor markets are also advantageous to employees, who benefit in several ways: (1) they have a career in the company if they can demonstrate competence;[12] (2) they probably will be buffered from layoffs the longer they're employed, as most organizations use a last-in, first-out layoff system; and (3) as they move up the job ladder they will earn more money.

Internal labor markets also have disadvantages for both employees and employers. From the employees' standpoint, probably one of the greatest disadvantages is that their jobs often are somewhat insulated from market forces. Therefore, their actual pay may not be comparable to what it would be under perfect competition. From the employer's standpoint, new blood is discouraged from entering the organization, thereby stifling creativity. There are also disadvantages from a societal viewpoint since internal labor markets may inhibit societal goals. For example, they can retard the rate at which women and minorities move into managerial, professional, and technical jobs within organizations.

One noteworthy example of how internal labor markets impact movement into higher jobs can be taken from a recent court case, Weber v. Kaiser Aluminum.[13] Kaiser Aluminum had an internal promotion system that allowed employees to move from unskilled to skilled jobs, after going through an apprenticeship training program, on the basis of seniority. Since mostly white males held the highest seniority, minorities would not qualify for the apprenticeship training program. In an effort to overcome this problem, Kaiser and the union agreed to an Affirmative Action Plan in which minorities qualified at a rate equal to nonminorities. One employee, Brian F. Weber, felt this was reverse discrimination and filed suit. Excerpts from the court's opinion of this case appear in Exhibit 4.2. The U.S. Supreme Court decided that Kaiser Aluminum could legally change its internal labor market system to give this type of preferential treatment to minorities.

Emergence of Internal Labor Markets

How do internal labor markets arise in the first place? Most arise out of the sociotechnical system of a specific organization.[14] For example, a large gas station sells gasoline, tires, batteries, and accessories, as well as provides tune-ups and other mechanical service. The owner of the station uses a certain technology in servicing customers. The owner at first may decide that all employees will do all of the duties, that is, be completely cross trained. In this situation the owner of the station would probably pay all of the employees the same wage rate.

Some employees may lack the skills to perform mechanical work or perform grease jobs while others have these skills. In a large station there may be enough work for employees to specialize. The employees will realize that some of them are making larger contributions to the organization than others, and they will argue that they deserve more pay. The owner may grant this pay differential so that, for example, mechanics earn more than anyone else. Over

---

Exhibit 4.2   *Kaiser Aluminum & Chemical Corporation*
v. Brian F. Weber et al.

I

In 1974, petitioner United Steelworkers of America (USWA) and petitioner Kaiser
Aluminum & Chemical Corp. (Kaiser) ⊥entered into a master collective-bargaining
agreement covering terms and conditions of employment at 15 Kaiser plants. The
agreement contained, *inter alia*, an affirmative action plan designed to eliminate
conspicuous racial imbalances in Kaiser's then almost exclusively white craft-work
forces. Black craft-hiring goals were set for each Kaiser plant equal to the percentage
of blacks in the respective local labor forces. To enable plants to meet these goals,
on-the-job training programs were established to teach unskilled production workers—black and white—the skills necessary to become craftworkers. The plan reserved for black employees 50% of the openings in these newly created in-plant
training programs.

[1] This case arose from the operation of the plan at Kaiser's plant in Gramercy, La. Until 1974, Kaiser hired as craftworkers for that plant only persons who
had had prior craft experience. Because blacks had long been excluded from craft
unions,[1] few were able to present such credentials. As a consequence, prior to 1974
only 1.83% (5 out of 273) of the skilled craftworkers at the Gramercy plant were
black, ⊥even though the work force in the Gramercy area was approximately 39%
black.

Pursuant to the national agreement Kaiser altered its craft-hiring practice in the
Gramercy plant. Rather than hiring already trained outsiders, Kaiser established a
training program to train its production workers to fill craft openings. Selection of
craft trainees was made on the basis of seniority, with the proviso that at least 50%
of the new trainees were to be black until the percentage of black skilled craftworkers in the Gramercy plant approximated the percentage of blacks in the local labor
force. See 415 F.Supp. 761, 764.

During 1974, the first year of the operation of the Kaiser-USWA affirmative
action plan, 13 craft trainees were selected from Gramercy's production work force.
Of these, seven were black and six white. The most senior black selected into the
program had less seniority than several white production workers whose bids for
admission were rejected. Thereafter one of those white production workers, respondent Brian Weber (hereafter respondent), instituted this class action in the United
States District Court for the Eastern District of Louisiana.

The complaint alleged that the filling of craft trainee positions at the Gramercy
plant pursuant to the affirmative action program had resulted in junior black employees' receiving training in preference to senior white employees, thus discriminating against respondent and other similarly situated white employees in violation
of §§ 703(a)[2] and ⊥(d)[3] of Title VII. The District Court held that the plan violated
Title VII, entered a judgment in favor of the plaintiff class, and granted a permanent
injunction prohibiting Kaiser and the USWA "from denying plaintiffs, Brian F.
Weber and all other members of the class, access to on-the-job training programs on
the basis of race." App. 171. A divided panel of the Court of Appeals for the Fifth
Circuit affirmed, holding that all employment preferences based upon race, includ-
ing those preferences incidental to bona fide affirmative action plans, violated Title
VII's prohibition against racial discrimination in employment. 563 F.2d 216 (1977).
We granted certiorari. 439 U.S. 1045, 99 S.Ct. 720, 58 L.Ed.2d 704 (1978). We reverse....

continued

Exhibit 4.2   *continued*

III

[7] We need not today define in detail the line of demarcation between permissible and impermissible affirmative action plans. It suffices to hold that the challenged Kaiser-USWA affirmative action plan falls on the permissible side of the line. The purposes of the plan mirror those of the statute. Both were designed to break down old patterns of racial segregation and hierarchy. Both were structured to "open employment opportunities for Negroes in occupations which have been traditionally closed to them." 110 Cong.Rec. 6548 (1964) (remarks of Sen. Humphrey).[8]

At the same time, the plan does not unnecessarily trammel the interests of the white employees. The plan does not require the discharge of white workers and their replacement with new black hirees. Cf. *McDonald v. Santa Fe Trail Transp. Co.*, 427 U.S. 273, 96 S.Ct. 2574, 49 L.Ed.2d 493 (1976). Nor does the plan create an absolute bar to the advancement of white employees; half of those trained in the program will be white. Moreover, the plan is a temporary measure; it is not intended to maintain racial balance, but simply to eliminate a manifest racial imbalance. Preferential selection of craft trainees at the Gramercy plant will end as soon as the percentage of black skilled craftworkers in the Gramercy plant approximates the ⊥percentage of blacks in the local labor force. See 415 F.Supp., at 763.

We conclude, therefore, that the adoption of the Kaiser-USWA plan for the Gramercy plant falls within the area of discretion left by Title VII to the private sector voluntarily to adopt affirmative action plans designed to eliminate conspicuous racial imbalance in traditionally segregated job categories.[9] Accordingly, the judgment of the Court of Appeals for the Fifth Circuit is

Reversed.

99 S.Ct. 2721 (1979).

time, the employees who grease cars and change exhaust systems may feel that they too deserve more pay than the employees who pump gas. They do not deserve as much as the engine mechanics (probably even in their own minds) but they deserve more pay than the general station attendant. Over time, three different jobs evolve in the gas station: pump attendant, mechanic, and engine mechanic. These three jobs are differentiated in the amount of pay, and over time qualified employees will be allowed to move up the progression ladder of jobs as vacancies in higher jobs occur.

Internal labor markets change over time as technology and the business change. Today a mechanic must be much more highly skilled than 30 years ago, and very often the other two jobs of attendant and mechanic are completely separate so that the internal labor market no longer exists in the old sense. There may now be three job families (a job family has been defined as a set of jobs grouped together by technology, custom, or administrative unit).

Any time there is technological change within the organization a new sociotechnical system may emerge that will restructure the internal labor market.[15] For example, the advent of the diesel engine in the railroad industry eliminated the need for the job of fireman (although this job still exists in some railroad companies). Another example is the advent of more sophisticated instrumentation in modern jet airliners that has resulted in a reduction of the flight crew from three jobs (captain, first officer, and flight engineer) to two jobs (captain and first officer).

Chapter 2 showed that equity considerations are important to workers. The gas station example above points out the fact that within organizations some jobs require more contributions than other jobs. For people to feel equitably treated relative to other employees in the organization, there must be different rates of pay for different jobs. The administrative process for determining these different rates of pay (a wage structure) requires conducting a **job evaluation** and then **pricing** the jobs. Job evaluation can be defined as "the process of determining the relative worth of jobs to the organization and its employees." Job pricing is the process of fitting the evaluated jobs to market data. Job pricing and job evaluation are important activities linked to internal and external equity considerations.[16] In terms of the internal labor market, the process of job evaluation is the process of capturing the relationships that are felt to be fair among jobs within an internal labor market.

Labor Unions and Compensation

One of the most significant institutional forces influencing compensation is labor unionism. Currently about 20 percent of the U.S. labor force is unionized. Unionism is a critical constraint in the compensation decision-making process for firms with unions. Many employers who are not unionized are also influenced by the mere presence of unions in the U.S. economy. These employers are concerned about a union coming into their organization as well as the effect of competing with unionized firms.

The U.S. Labor Movement

Development and growth of the American labor movement occurred simultaneously with the advent of the industrial revolution, which began in the seventeenth century. (Although there are those who argue that the U.S. economy has moved out of an industrial society and into a postindustrial service society, this distinction is not considered significant for purposes of this text.[17]) The industrial revolution saw the replacement of the cottage system of production with the modern factory system.

The Cottage System   The **cottage system** of production was characterized by workers producing goods in their homes. This system relied upon artisans, or craftspersons, to produce the product. Work was highly skilled, and people worked at their own pace, with considerable discretion over what work got done when and by whom. Very often whole families worked at producing the product in their home.[18] The cottage system is radically different from the **factory system** of production, which replaced it.

The Factory System   Under the factory system of production workers were brought together in a central production location. The factory system involves task specialization to the extent that what had been a craft employment often was reduced to a semiskilled or unskilled job. Large organizations, such as factories, also require coordination of functional specialties so that an administrative (managerial) labor force is imposed on the average worker. Since these managerial positions often went to the owner's relatives, an industrial caste system also developed in the economy. The owner, wishing to maximize return on the large investment in the factory, insisted upon long workdays. Work was often hard, dirty, and dangerous.[19] These forces caused workers to decide that if they were to improve their working conditions they'd have to band together into guilds or unions.[20]

Unions as Criminal Conspiracies   The history of the labor movement in the United States was not smooth and free of conflict. The labor movement was violent in its early days. One of the major problems for workers was establishing their right to organize and bargain collectively with management. It was not until Commonwealth of Massachusetts v. Hunt in 1842 that labor was permitted to organize.[21] Prior to that time labor unions were, under common law doctrine, considered criminal conspiracies in restraint of free trade.

The Right to Organize   Commonwealth v. Hunt did not give labor the right to organize; it said only that certain labor organizations were not illegal per se. It was not until the U.S. Congress passed the Wagner Act (the National Labor Relations Act) in 1935 that labor received the right to organize in the private sector.[22] Not all labor has the right to organize into a union. For example, supervisory employees cannot unionize, since they are part of management. The 90 years between the Commonwealth case and the Wagner Act was a time of extreme industrial conflict between labor and management.

In 1935 union membership was held by about 6 percent of the total work force.[23] After passage of the Wagner Act in 1935 unions began to grow substantially. In the first 10 years after the act, union membership as a percentage of the total labor force grew to about 24 percent.

Although most private sector and some public sector employees have the right to unionize today, not all groups within society have chosen to exercise this right. There is substantial variation between occupational groups in terms of their tendency to organize. Table 4.1 presents the percentage of employees within selected occupational groups that is organized and represented by a labor union.

Some industries also are more heavily organized than other industries. For example, over 75 percent of the work force in transportation, construction, and mining is unionized. In chemicals, services, and finance, less than 25 percent of the work force is organized.[24] Table 4.2 presents the proportion of employees who are organized within selected industries.

Table 4.1   Unionized Employees in Occupational Groups
as a Percentage of the Work Force

Occupation	Organized Workers (in thousands)	Employed Wage and Salary Workers	
		Number (in thousands)	Percent Organized
White-collar occupations	7,017	45,955	15.3%
Professional, technical, and kindred workers	3,272	14,436	22.7
Engineers	108	1,393	7.7
Physicians, dentists, and related practitioners	35	428	8.3
Health workers, except practitioners	342	2,085	16.4
Teachers, except college	1,688	3,271	51.6
Engineering and science technicians	209	1,109	18.0
Other professional — salaried	891	6,149	14.5
Other professional — self-employed	a	a	a
Managers and administrators, except farm	681	8,953	7.6
Salaried — manufacturing	57	1,604	3.5
Salaried — other industries	624	7,350	8.5
Clerical and kindred workers	2,857	17,507	16.3
Bookkeepers	83	1,649	5.0
Office-machine operators	145	996	14.6
Stenographers, typists, and secretaries	425	4,805	8.8
Other clerical workers	2,203	10,056	21.9
Sales workers	207	5,059	4.1
Sales workers in retail trade	125	2,646	4.7
Other sales workers	82	2,413	3.4
Blue-collar workers	11,101	28,414	39.1
Craft and kindred workers	4,308	11,083	38.9
Carpenters	276	836	33.0
Construction-craft workers, except carpenters	1,076	2,212	48.7
Supervisors, n.e.c.	288	1,705	16.9
Machinists and job setters	381	698	54.6
Metal crafts workers, except mechanics, machinists, and job setters	411	669	61.3
Mechanics — auto	208	928	22.4
Mechanics, except auto	729	1,938	37.6
All other crafts workers	939	2,097	44.8
Operatives, except transport	3,990	9,982	40.0
Mine workers	104	274	38.1
Motor vehicles and equipment	312	367	85.0
Other durable goods	1,802	4,098	44.0
Nondurable goods	1,244	3,236	38.4
All other	528	2,007	26.3

continued

Table 4.1 continued

Transport equipment operatives	1,439	3,226	44.6
Drivers and delivery workers	1,104	2,719	40.6
All other	335	507	66.1
Nonfarm laborers	1,365	4,123	33.1
Construction	254	771	32.9
Manufacturing	420	836	50.3
All other nonfarm laborers	691	2,516	27.5
Service workers, including private household	1,954	12,074	16.2
Private household workers	2	999	.2
Cleaning service	573	2,317	24.7
Food service	369	4,387	8.4
Health service	310	1,865	16.6
Personal service	134	1,092	12.3
Protective service	566	1,415	40.0

[a] Data not available.

Source: Bureau of Labor Statistics, Current Population Survey.

Table 4.2   *Unionized Employees by Industry as a Percentage of the Work Force*

Industry	Organized Workers (in thousands)	Employed Wage and Salary Workers	
		Number (in thousands)	Percent Organized
Agriculture	51	1,455	3.5%
Mining	286	892	32.1
Construction	1,574	4,982	31.6
Manufacturing, total	6,771	20,976	32.3
Durable goods, total	4,366	12,546	34.8
Ordnance	74	235	31.5
Lumber	103	539	19.1
Furniture	124	461	27.0
Stone, clay, and glass	292	618	47.2
Primary metals	686	1,176	58.4
Fabricated metals	491	1,359	36.1
Machinery, except electrical	798	2,779	28.7
Electrical equipment	599	2,230	26.9
Transportation equipment	1,038	2,031	51.1
Automobiles	582	951	61.2
Aircraft	286	676	42.4
Other transportation equipment	170	404	42.1
Instruments	79	622	12.6
Miscellaneous	82	497	16.6

continued

Table 4.2 *continued*

Nondurable goods	2,405	8,430	28.5
Food	628	1,674	37.5
Tobacco	19	60	31.6
Textiles	117	786	14.9
Apparel	326	1,298	25.1
Paper	369	751	49.1
Printing	290	1,433	20.2
Chemicals	320	1,240	25.8
Petroleum	75	220	34.1
Rubber and plastics	205	692	29.6
Leather and not specified manufacturing	58	275	20.9
Transportation, communication, and public utilities	2,903	6,048	48.0
Railroads	474	579	81.8
Other transportation	1,121	2,662	42.1
Communication	714	1,447	49.7
Other public utilities	594	1,359	43.1
Trades	1,753	17,401	10.1
Wholesale	389	3,419	11.4
Retail	1,363	13,981	9.8
Eating and drinking places	199	4,031	4.0
Other retail	1,164	9,950	11.7
Finance, insurance, and real estate	190	5,152	3.7
Banking and other finance	38	2,356	1.6
Insurance and real estate	153	2,796	5.5
Services	4,743	26,121	18.9
Private household service	7	1,214	.6
Miscellaneous services	4,735	23,909	19.8
Business and repair	293	2,902	10.1
Personal services, except private household	229	1,653	13.9
Entertainment and recreation	127	902	14.1
Professional services	4,086	18,451	22.1
Medical, except hospitals	283	2,834	10.0
Hospitals	692	3,901	17.7
Welfare and religious	207	1,541	13.4
Educational	2,767	8,062	34.3
Other professional services	137	2,114	6.5
Forestry and fisheries	12	87	13.5
Public administration	1,812	5,364	33.8
Federal, except postal	347	1,795	19.3
Postal	509	691	73.7
State	253	972	26.0
Local	703	1,906	36.9

Source: Bureau of Labor Statistics, Current Population Survey.

Partly because of structural shifts in the economy (away from heavy manufacturing and toward service) and partly because of other protective legislation (such as equal employment laws), union membership today is held by about 20 percent of the total labor force.[25] In spite of this decline in membership, unions are still a major constraint on the compensation decision-making process when workers have the right to organize and force employers to bargain collectively. Even if employees are not represented by a union, the threat of being unionized has influenced many employers' personnel policies. For example, employers may pay a wage premium to their workers to discourage them from organizing.[26] The effect of the mere presence of unions in the economy on the compensation decision-making process is discussed in a later section.

The Wagner and Taft-Hartley Acts   The Wagner Act gave private sector employees the right to organize and bargain collectively with employers over their interests. It also set up the National Labor Relations Board. This board holds certification elections in which an organization's employees vote to determine if a union (or which union) will represent them. (The board can also conduct decertification elections.) Second, the National Labor Relations Board acts as a quasi-judicial body that holds hearings to determine if national labor law has been violated by the union or by management.[27]

A companion statute to the Wagner Act is the Taft-Hartley Act of 1947.[28] Twelve years after the Wagner Act, Congress saw certain deficiencies in the law. The Taft-Hartley Act was intended to correct these deficiencies. Three specific provisions of the Taft-Hartley Act are noteworthy.

First, the Wagner Act established a set of unfair labor practices on the part of management, but did not put similar restrictions on labor unions. For example, under the Wagner Act, management was required to **"bargain in good faith"**; there was no such constraint on labor unions. The Taft-Hartley Act corrected this specific problem by requiring labor to "bargain in good faith" too.

Second, the Wagner Act did not make any provisions for what would happen if a labor and management conflict threatened the public interest. The Taft-Hartley Act attempted to correct for this deficiency with an emergency disputes clause authorizing the president of the United States to require labor to return to work (in the case of a strike) or management to reopen the plant (in the case of a lockout) when the conflict jeopardizes the national interest.

The Taft-Hartley Act also established the federal mediation and conciliation service to help the parties avoid a strike or lockout. Under the act, the parties can, without cost, request that a federal mediator help in contract negotiations.

When all employees in a bargaining unit must belong to the union, it is known as a **union shop**. The Taft-Hartley Act gives state governments the right to decide whether unions in their states can force all employees in a company to join. These **"right-to-work"** (without being forced to join a union) provisions are contained in Section 14.b of the act. Some 22 states currently exercise this right to outlaw the union shop.

Issues and Process in Collective Bargaining

When collective bargaining takes place, what is bargained over and what is the bargaining process?[29]

Issues in Bargaining   National labor law sets the framework for what can be bargained over. There are three general categories of bargaining issues: (1) **prohibited issues**, (2) **permissive issues**, and (3) **mandatory issues**.[30] Prohibited issues are prevented statutorily. For example, it is illegal for a union to negotiate an apprenticeship program that discriminates against women and minorities. Permissive issues are those issues that labor and management can negotiate if they want to, but the parties are not bound to negotiate them (bargain in good faith) by law. An example might be whether or not the union will have a say in the firm's product advertising program. Mandatory issues are those issues that the parties are required to negotiate by law. Table 4.3 lists the types of mandatory issues.

As Table 4.3 shows, nearly all terms and conditions of employment are mandatory bargaining issues. Wages and employee benefits are mandatory items, but there are also many other items that are less directly related to compensation and yet have an impact on labor costs. For example, Table 4.3 shows that the issue of prohibiting supervisors from doing the work of bargaining unit members is a mandatory issue. This issue has nothing to do with pay rates and employee benefits, but it does have an indirect effect on total labor costs. For example, prohibiting a supervisor from performing actual bargaining unit work on a shift may require the hiring of an additional worker.

A second bargaining issue is what union members want their leaders to negotiate. A recent study found that union members look to their union to bargain over wages, handling of grievances, employee benefits, and job security, and rated these four issues as the most important bargaining issues in descending order of importance.[31] Wages and employee benefits are directly related to the compensation decision-making process.

The Bargaining Committee   Once a union is certified to represent a group of employees within an organization (the bargaining unit), the members of the bargaining unit typically elect a bargaining committee. This committee is normally composed of elected rank and file members plus the union business agent or president. If the local union is affiliated with a national union organization, such as the United Auto Workers, the national union may also provide a staff person who is adept at contract negotiations. (If the contract to be negotiated is a precedent-setting contract the national union will want very much to have a person on the bargaining committee.) The local union will also

Table 4.3   *Mandatory Bargaining Subjects*

Agency shops
Arbitration
Arrangement for negotiation
Bargaining over "bar list"
Bonus payments
Cancellation of seniority upon relocation of
   plant
Change in insurance carrier and benefits
Change in operations resulting in
   reclassifying workers from incentive to
   straight time or cut work force, or
   installation of cost-saving machine
Change of employee status to independent
   contractors
Change of payment from hourly base to
   salary base
Checkoff
Contract clause providing for supervisors
   keeping seniority in unit
Cost of living increases
Discharge
Discounts on company products
Discriminatory racial policies
Duration of agreement
Employee physical examination
Employers' insistence on clause giving
   arbitrator right to enforce award
Grievance procedure
Group insurance — accident, health, life
Holidays — paid
Hours
Houses — company houses
Hunting on employer forest reserve where
   previously granted
Job posting procedure
Layoff plan
Layoffs
Leave of absence
Lunch periods
Management rights clause
Merit wage increase
Most favored nation clause
Motor carrier–union agreement providing
   that carriers use own equipment before
   leasing outside equipment

Musician price lists
Nondiscriminatory hiring hall
No strike, no lockout clause
Overtime pay
Partial plant closing
Pension plan
Piece rates
Plant closedown and relocation
Plant closing
Plant reopening
Plant rules
Price of meals provided by company
Procedures for income tax withholding
Production ceiling imposed by union
Profit-sharing plan
Prohibition against supervisor doing unit
   work
Promotions
Reinstatement of economic strikers
Rest periods
Retirement age
Safety and health
Selection of arbitrators
Seniority
Severance pay
Shift differentials
Sick leave
Stock purchase plan
Subcontracting
Superseniority for union stewards
Transfers
Truck rentals — minimum rental to be paid
   by carriers to employee-owned vehicles
Union security
Union security and checkoffs
Vacations — paid
Vended food products
Wages
Work assignments and transfers
Work loads
Work rules
Work schedules
Work sharing

Source: Adapted with permission from "Positive Collective Bargaining" by Reed C. Richardson, in D. Yoder
and H. G. Henemann, Jr. (eds.), *ASPA Handbook of Personnel and Industrial Relations*, pp. 7–120,
copyright 1979 by The Bureau of National Affairs, Inc., Washington, D.C. 20037.

Exhibit 4.3   *Conceptual Theoretical Bargaining Situation*

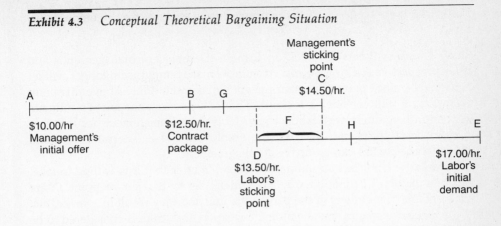

often have its lawyer on the bargaining committee, and there may be other union officials as the local union sees fit.

Management also formulates its bargaining committee. Typically, there will be a high-level member of management (such as the vice-president of production), the manager of the plant in which the union members work, the company attorney, and one or more labor relations specialists. This committee is typical in the types of members but not in terms of size. In a large company such as GE or McDonnell Douglas, the bargaining committee may consist of 25 to 30 members or more. On the other hand, at a small company the bargaining committee may consist of the president and an attorney.

Bargaining to a Settlement

Settlement Ranges   Exhibit 4.3 presents a diagram to illustrate the process of bargaining to a settlement. The dollar amounts in Exhibit 4.3 represent all labor costs — the wages, benefits, and other labor costs are expressed as an average rate for members of the bargaining unit. The points in the exhibit are not known to the opposite sides (and sometimes not to the parties themselves).

As Exhibit 4.3 shows, both labor and management have a **range of settlements** in mind. In the case of management, this range falls along a continuum from *A* to *C*. Similarly, labor has a range of acceptable settlements from *D* to *E*. As the bargaining process starts, each party presents its initial demand or offer. Labor makes the initial demand that it would like to win — point *E* in Exhibit 4.3. While it is often true that labor makes the initial demand, it is becoming more common today for management to make an initial **giveback offer**, for example, point *A*. A giveback offer can be defined as an initial offer by management that is actually below the current compensation package being received by the workers. Such giveback offers have been seen in recent bargaining in the auto industry for example, and represent situations where the organization must cut labor costs in order to stay in business.[32] Point *B* in

Exhibit 4.3 is the wage value of the present wage package for the union members.

Range Overlap Points C and D in Exhibit 4.3 represent management's and labor's respective **sticking points.** At point C management is no longer willing to negotiate, since point C is management's maximum offer. Above this point management will consider a **lockout.** The lockout is management's ultimate weapon in bargaining with labor. Under labor law, management has the right to close down its plant—lock out the employees—if it determines in good faith that the parties cannot arrive at an agreement.

Similarly, labor has a minimally acceptable offer that it is willing to take, which is point D in Exhibit 4.3. All settlements to the left of point D are unacceptable to members of the bargaining unit and may result in a **strike.** Just as the lockout is management's ultimate weapon, the strike is considered to be labor's ultimate weapon.[33] By law, labor in the private sector has the right to withhold its services—or strike against the employer—if it determines in good faith that further talks will be fruitless.

Point C in Exhibit 4.3 is to the right of point D; management's sticking point is to the right of labor's sticking point. The area of overlap between points D and C is the range of feasible settlements, as represented by the area F. There may not always be an overlap between the two parties' settlement ranges. Point D could lie to the right of point C. In this case, there would not be an acceptable settlement range for the two parties, and either a strike or lockout will occur. However, .20 percent of all work time available in the 1970s was lost to a strike or lockout, which indicates there is usually an overlap in the bargaining range.[34]

Bargaining Deadlock Using Exhibit 4.3 to illustrate the bargaining process, assume that labor opens the negotiations by making demands equal to point E. Management makes a counteroffer at point A, citing hard economic times for the organization. The two parties, if they are bargaining in good faith, now begin to concede toward agreement. This process may not be smooth or conflict-free and can take anywhere from days to months, depending on how far apart the parties were in the first place and how hard a bargain each side wants to drive. The goal of bargaining is to move toward the other side's position and at the same time to find the other side's sticking point. For example, in the process of negotiating toward agreement labor might think that management's sticking point is at point H in Exhibit 4.3. Labor will now be committed to point H and will try to convince management that the union will take a lockout or go on strike before it will move from point H. Point H is to the right of point C, however, and management will not accept a settlement at point H.

Reopening Negotiations What happens when one of the two parties gets locked into a demand or offer that is outside the range of settlement for the other party? There will be a strike or lockout unless the other party is willing to move.[35] The party who is committed to a position cannot start to bargain again because they would lose face with the other side—they'll be perceived as bluffing and they'll lose credibility in future negotiations. One solution to this problem is provided by a neutral third party, such as the Federal Mediation and Conciliation Service.[36] If labor and management agree, a representative of the Federal Mediation and Conciliation Service will enter the bargaining process to help the parties get moving again on negotiations without a loss of face for either party.

Settlement   Once the negotiations are moving again the two parties can once more attempt to find the settlement range. Management would like to find labor's minimum sticking point (point *D*) to know the best deal that management can get at the table. Labor would like to find point *C*, management's maximum sticking point, because that would give labor the best deal. Once the parties' demands and offers get between points *D* and *C*, the first one to be committed will end up with the best deal. At this point a strike or lockout will not occur since all settlements within the range are acceptable to both parties.

The bargaining process depicted in Exhibit 4.3 is simplistic in that it deals only with compensation issues. There are numerous bargaining issues that are noneconomic in nature, such as the seniority system (plantwide versus department seniority), union security provisions, and superseniority. (Superseniority awards artificial seniority to, for example, low-seniority union officials who may be let go under layoff conditions.) Regardless, Exhibit 4.3 aids in understanding the bargaining process.

The Special Case of Public Sector Unions   Unions that represent public sector employees are faced with a different situation than private sector unions. These unions, by law, are often not allowed to strike.[37] The problem created by the loss of the right to strike is serious. Without the right to strike labor will find it difficult to drive much of a bargain with management.

In many states this loss of right to strike is counterbalanced with **interest arbitration.** Under interest arbitration, if the parties cannot reach agreement they submit their final offers and demands to a neutral third party (an arbiter) who makes a decision on the merits of the positions.[38] The arbiter's decision may be **advisory** or **binding** on one or both parties depending upon that state's particular law. Interest arbitration is an attempt to rebalance the relative power of labor and management.

Interest arbitration should not be confused with **rights arbitration,** which is discussed later in this chapter. Interest arbitration involves an arbiter deciding the terms of a contract, while rights arbitration involves an arbiter deciding upon interpretation of the respective parties' rights and responsibilities within the context of an existing contract.[39]

General Union Impact on Compensation Decisions

The most important topic in this chapter from a compensation decision maker's standpoint is what impact the union has on compensation decisions.

Union Influence on Labor's Share of National Income   One way to look at the question of the impact of unions on wages is to look at the impact that unions may have had on labor's share of the national income. The data in Exhibit 4.4 suggest that labor's share of the national income has grown between 1930 and 1980, roughly the period when labor has had the most potential influence.

The data also suggest that the unionized portion of the labor force had virtually no growth during this period, while the nonunionized sector grew substantially.[40] Although labor's share of national income has grown, the proportion of workers in the economy who belong to labor unions has decreased substantially. It is difficult, therefore, to infer that the labor movement in the United States has had substantial influence on labor's share of national income.

Union and Nonunion Employees   Can the influence of the labor movement on wages be seen in the differences between union and nonunion wage rates? One of the problems with examining the wages of union and nonunion employees is that they are affected by industry and ability to pay. For example, some industries are highly unionized while others are not. At the same time, ability to pay varies among industries. The lathe operator in industry A may make more than the lathe operator in industry B; industry A may also have a higher ability to pay. Nevertheless, data from a series of studies conclude that unions raise wages of union workers in the range of 7 to 10 percent relative to the wages of nonunion workers.[41] Some of these findings are reported in Table 4.4.

Exhibit 4.4   *Labor's Share of National Income as a Percentage of GNP*

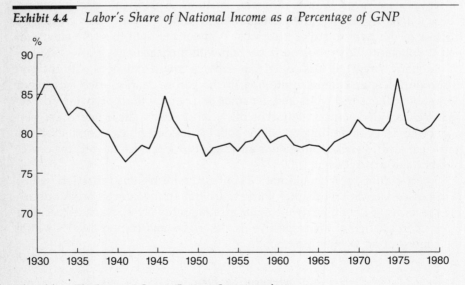

Adapted from *The Survey of Current Business Statistics*, vol. 63, p. 93.

Table 4.4   *Usual Weekly Earnings of Full-Time Wage
               and Salary Workers, May 1977.*

	Union/Nonunion Earnings Ratio			
	White Males	White Females	Nonwhite Males	Nonwhite Females
All occupations	1.06	1.29	1.30	1.34
Blue-collar occupations	1.32	1.31	1.43	1.38

Source: U.S. Bureau of Labor Statistics, *Earnings and Other Characteristics of Organized Workers,* May 1977, Report 556 (Washington: U.S. Government Printing Office, 1979): pp. 28–31.

Wage Structure Influences   Another stream of research has focused on the influence of unions upon the variation in wages within the bargaining unit and within the organization as a whole. The data suggest that unions narrow the overall wage structure within an organization and for the workers within a bargaining unit.[42] The causality of this proposition is in question, since perhaps the variation in wages in the first place caused a greater tendency for unionization. Regardless, an implication is that if a firm wishes its work force to be nonunionized it would seem that it should not let wage differences become too great.

Preventive Labor Policy   One of the major impacts unions have upon wage levels and structures in the economy is that nonunionized employers attempt to stay nonunion by being competitive with union wage rates.[43] While this argument is limited by the ability to pay, it is still a method by which unions impact wages.

Specific Union Influence on Compensation Decision Making

Unions have various impacts upon the compensation decision-making process. In addition to influencing wages and benefits and, therefore, direct labor costs, unions also influence numerous indirect labor costs. For example, a union may negotiate over the length of rest breaks. Since rest breaks are usually with pay, the results of the negotiation affect indirect costs. Labor unions will participate in decisions over virtually any issue that has an impact upon their membership.

This section discusses the major ways in which unions influence both direct and indirect costs of labor, as well as the major issues in which unions seek involvement.

Wage and Benefit Level Influences   One of the major goals of a union is to increase the average wage and benefit levels of its members. This happens in several ways. First, the union attempts to increase the **real wage** level of its members over time. Real wages can be defined as the buying power of money, and take into account the cost of living. To this end, the union will want to negotiate wage increases that are larger than the increase in the cost of living at the time contracts are negotiated.[44]

One of the ways unions protect real wages is cost of living adjustment clauses (COLAs) to wages. A COLA clause provides for an automatic increase in wages anytime the cost of living goes up by an agreed amount.[45] Exhibit 4.5 gives the history of the COLA clause. These clauses are popular with the union but are generally unpopular with management. This should not be surprising since they achieve labor's goal of maintaining real wages. The COLA clauses are also much more problematical for management since they assume that management can pass the additional costs on to the consumer. Management tends to resist COLA clauses because of the uncertain impact on labor costs and product costs.

Unions would also like to see the average wage level of their members increase relative to that of other workers in the organization. It should not be surprising that unions want to justify their existence to members, and one way to do this is to show that members of the union are better off than other employees by virtue of their membership in the union.

Unions would also like to enhance the benefits their members receive relative to other groups.[46] Thus, it is reasonable to expect unions to ask for a larger number of paid personal days off and more liberal vacation policies for union members relative to other employees. Whether unions are successful at these endeavors is likely to be dependent upon the organization's ability to pay, the history of previous settlements, and the economic outlook for the employer in the future.

Wage Structure Influences Labor unions are probably as concerned about negotiating wage and benefit structure decisions as they are about negotiating wage and benefit level decisions. Wage and benefit structure issues concern what share various union members get from the item that is bargained. In most cases, not all jobs held by union members are considered equal by the union membership, and the union may wish to negotiate a certain percentage differential in wages between particular jobs. For example, the union might represent lathe operators and machine attendants. The union might want the machine attendant to make 80 percent of what the lathe operator makes, whereas management may want the machine attendant to make only 60 percent of what the lathe operator makes. This issue must be negotiated at the bargaining table.

Just as the union wants to negotiate the distribution of wages among jobs in the bargaining unit, it will wish to negotiate the distribution of employee benefits. As an example, it is common practice to allocate the vacation time that an employee is to receive on the basis of seniority; the longer the employee works for the company, the more days of vacation will be provided. If labor and management have agreed that an additional day of vacation will be

---

Exhibit 4.5 *Unions Won't Give Up COLA, But Unit Labor Costs Could Still Fall*

Although both the inflation rate and wage gains in collective bargaining have plummetted in the last eighteen months, unions have resisted tenaciously efforts to abolish Cost of Living Adjustment (COLA) provisions that link prospective wage adjustments to changes in the Consumer Price Index. The future of these clauses will have a significant influence on wage and price stability, especially as the recovery gains momentum.

The use of COLA clauses in labor agreements dates back over sixty years but they did not become widespread until the post-World War II period. In 1948, General Motors and the United Automobile Workers entered into a multiyear agreement that provided for a fixed wage increase each year based on national productivity trends and a COLA clause that protected these gains from the erosion of inflation. This approach was acclaimed and emulated in many other industries. In fact, COLAs were a *quid pro quo* afforded the union in return for long-term contracts that insulated employers from "the guaranteed annual argument" and the threat of a strike.

These arrangements worked well through the 1950s and most of the 1960s. During this period, inflation was moderate and, by contemporary standards, fluctuated in a narrow range. Little concern was expressed over COLA clauses, and indeed many unions lost interest in extending them to new bargaining situations. However, with the onset of a prolonged period of prodigious inflation at the end of the Sixties, both the incidence—and cost—of COLA rose rapidly.

By the mid-1970s, about 60% of the larger bargaining units were covered by such provisions. Moreover, because many of the COLA clauses were "uncapped" (*i.e.*, without any specified limits on the increases they could generate), they caused wages to explode without any relation to the fortunes of the firm involved.

The durability of COLA clauses has been demonstrated by recent events. While unions have accepted wage freezes or rollbacks in autos, steel, rubber and trucking, among other industries, they have not relinquished COLA in any major bargaining situation. This persistence of COLA clauses has stirred fears that wage increases can add fuel to the inflationary embers that still smolder in the economy.

Source: "Unions Won't Give Up COLA, But Unit Labor Costs Could Still Fall," by Arnold Weber. Reprinted with the permission of *Dun's Business Month*, July 1983. Copyright 1983, Dun & Bradstreet Publications Corporation.

---

granted each year (the benefit level decision), the next issue is how will that vacation day be distributed among union members (the benefit structure decision). Management may want to allocate the additional day across the board—all union employees will get the additional day. On the other hand, the union members may want to increase the vacation time for only those union members with 10 or more years of service. The union might bargain for those with less than 10 years of service to get no extra days of vacation, those with 10 years of service to get two extra days of vacation, those with 15 years of service to get three extra days, and those with 20 years of service to get five extra days.

The total days would add up to one additional day of vacation on average for all employees in the union.

The distribution of the wage and benefit package can have considerable impact upon the direct labor costs of the firm.[47] In the vacation allocation example, since wages will be higher for more senior employees because of both their seniority and the jobs that they hold, the union's preferred distribution of the additional vacation day will result in higher labor costs than management's preferred distribution. For this reason, compensation decision makers should be concerned about both the actual apparent change in wage level negotiated and the real wage level change that results from the distribution of wages and benefits.

Income Security   In the past 20 years unions have been interested in protecting the income of their members through several mechanisms. One of these mechanisms is the Supplementary Unemployment Benefit (SUB). A SUB plan is set up to entitle employees to supplemental benefits over and above the normal unemployment benefits that they would receive should they be laid off from work.[48] The fund for a SUB is typically established by management out of current operating funds. When employees are laid off, they collect from the fund. For example, one plan allows for SUB payments to supplement unemployment insurance up to 80 percent of the employee's base pay. Benefits stop when the employee returns to work or when the fund is exhausted.

A second approach by unions to income security is the Guaranteed Annual Wage. Under this plan labor and management agree to a guaranteed annual wage (for example, 80 percent of annual base wage). In this situation, an employee who works zero hours during a year would receive 80 percent of normal pay.[49]

Both Supplementary Unemployment Benefit plans and Guaranteed Annual Wage plans are generally resisted by management. A minority of all labor and management agreements in effect have provisions for these plans. Part of the reason for this is that such plans increase income security for union members at the expense of increased financial pressure on management. Few companies are likely to be receptive to these financial burdens, especially since the burden falls at a time when the organization is itself struggling to remain healthy.

Union Influences on Process   In general, unions will wish to participate in any decisions that influence the terms and conditions of employment for their membership. The obvious decisions are wages and benefits, and often these are negotiated at the bargaining table. However, labor-management contracts cannot anticipate all of the things that might disrupt a contract over its lifetime. As a result, labor and management often establish permanent or ad hoc joint committees to deal with issues relevant for union members and the organization.[50]

Job Evaluation Committees Job evaluation is the process of determining the relative worth of jobs. (Two chapters are devoted to job evaluation later in the text.) Very often labor and management set up a job evaluation committee to reanalyze the worth of jobs.

During the course of a contract it is not uncommon for the jobs in which union members work to change. This change can result from new technology, new work processes, or both. When such changes occur there is a need to reassess the value of jobs. One way to do this would be to reopen the contract. However, many unions and organizations have adopted joint job evaluation committees to deal with job evaluation issues in lieu of a contract reopener and to avoid a strike or lockout over a dispute. Exhibit 4.6 is a union-management contract clause that provides for such a committee.

Such committees result in indirect cost increases to the firm since they are likely to consume considerable management time and require union members to be away from their work stations, thereby increasing labor costs. The impact of such committees on direct labor costs probably depends on the nature of the changes in jobs. Whether reevaluation of jobs will result in higher or lower wages is an empirical question.

Wage and Salary and Benefits Survey Committees Many times employers act unilaterally in gathering survey data for making compensation decisions. Unions often conduct their own surveys. In other cases the two parties jointly seek out survey data for comparative wage purposes. Both labor and management will initially wish to use comparative survey data that is most favorable to their position and most unfavorable (probably) to the other side's position. However, joint committees might discuss the various types of data that are available, and establish criteria for the acceptance of particular data. (A later chapter discusses the types and sources of data that are available to management and, in some cases, labor.)

As with job evaluation committees, the largest costs of such committees are likely to be the costs associated with employee time away from normal job duties, and the administrative costs for management.

Incentive Plan Committees An employer may set up an incentive plan to encourage employees to work at higher levels of productivity. Such plans are subject to negotiation at the bargaining table. Incentive plans must also be managed on a day-to-day basis, and the union may wish to participate in this process. Exhibit 4.7 presents a labor-management contract clause providing for such a joint committee.

Joint committees for the management of such plans are probably desirable.[51] In a later chapter the issue of employee resistance to incentive plans is discussed. Part of that resistance has to do with fears that management will manipulate the plan to the employees' disadvantage. Joint participation prob-

Exhibit 4.6   *Joint Labor and Management Job Evaluation Process*

Article V—Job Classifications and Incentives

Section 1.   (*a*) Each job classification now in effect or hereafter established shall remain in effect, except as changed in accordance with the provisions of this Section.

(*b*) The Union at each Plant shall designate a Plant Union Job Evaluation Committee. Such Committee shall have the exclusive right to certify the existence of disputes with respect to job classifications.

(*c*) Whenever a new job shall be established or, after the effective date of the last classification or reclassification of an existing job, the requirements of such job as to training, skill, responsibility, effort and surroundings shall have been altered to the extent of a whole numerical classification of 1.0 or more, the Management shall classify or reclassify such job, as the case may be, and the new classification shall be put into effect in accordance with the procedure set forth in this Section.

(*1*) The Management shall describe and classify such job in accordance with the Manual for Job Classification of Production and Maintenance Jobs (hereinafter referred to as the Manual) a copy of which is annexed to the agreement dated April 11, 1947, between the Company and the Union, (or as hereinafter revised by agreement between the parties) and shall present such description and classification to the Plant Union Job Evaluation Committee with a copy to a designated representative of the International Union. Thereafter, the Management may put such new classification into effect and it shall continue in effect, unless it shall be changed in the manner provided in subparagraph (*c*)(3) of this Section. The Management and the Plant Union Job Evaluation Committee shall meet, within 30 days after the description and classification shall have been presented as hereinabove provided, to review and attempt to agree on the proposed classification of such job.

(*2*) If the Plant Union Job Evaluation Committee shall agree to such proposed new classification, it shall be established for such job.

(*3*) If the Plant Union Job Evaluation Committee does not agree to such proposed new classification such Committee may, at any time within 15 days after the meeting, give written notice to the designated representative of the Management alleging that the job is improperly classified under the provisions of the Manual. Within 7 days thereafter, such Committee and the designated representative of the Management shall prepare and sign a stipulation setting forth the factors and factor codings which are in dispute and shall send it to the Manager of Industrial Relations of the Company. The parties shall make a sincere effort to set forth in such stipulation the reasons in support of their respective positions.

If the parties shall fail to agree as provided above and a request for review or arbitration is not made within the time provided, the classification as prepared by the Management shall be deemed to have been approved.

Excerpted from "Agreement between Bethlehem Steel Company and United Steelworkers of America," April 6, 1962.

Exhibit 4.7   *Illustrative Wage Incentive Plans*

Allis Chalmers Corporation, West Allis Plant and Auto Workers

Expires January 31, 1986

Section 14. An employe having a question concerning an established Incentive Standard or the revision of an Incentive Standard on a work assignment to which he has been assigned may present it to his Foreman after having worked on the assignment for a sufficient length of time to insure that the Incentive Standard has been given a reasonable trial.

If the work assignment in question is within a group of work assignments, the employe at that time may request the isolation of that work assignment in order to identify performance for purposes of investigation and resolution of the question.

If the question is not resolved by the Foreman to the employe's satisfaction, the question may be referred to the Industrial Engineering Department. If necessary, the Industrial Engineering Department shall conduct a floor review or timestudy and promptly report the results to the Steward.

If the question still remains unresolved, it may be processed as a grievance through the steps of the grievance procedure short of arbitration. A representative of the industrial engineering department will be present at second step grievance meetings where the issues being discussed require his presence. The exclusive procedure for further processing of an unresolved question which has arisen under this Article and is arbitrable shall be as provided in paragraphs 170-179.

Section 15. If the question is not satisfactorily adjusted within 10 work days after discussion in the third step of the Grievance Procedure, the Union may certify it to the Impartial Referee selected in accordance with the procedure provided in Article VIII, Section H, within 30 work days after the third step discussion for a special Impartial Referee hearing. The provisions of paragraph 235 shall apply at this point. If the assignment in question (or one sufficiently similar to make a review of it relevant) is not performed in this time period, and the Union desires to study it prior to processing the grievance further, the 30 work days shall be extended until one week, or more by mutual agreement, after there has been an opportunity for such a study. The special hearing procedure is as follows:

1. The parties shall make every effort to select an independent Industrial Engineer and notify him and the Impartial Referee of its certification of the question for a special Impartial Referee hearing.

If the parties are unable to select an independent Industrial Engineer within 2 weeks after certification of the question, they shall by joint letter request the Federal Mediation and Conciliation Service to submit to them a list of names of 7 qualified and experienced Industrial Engineers.

2. If the parties cannot agree upon one of the persons named on the list, the Company and the Union shall strike a name alternately beginning with the Company until one name remains. Such remaining person shall act as the Industrial Engineer.

3. Immediately following the selection of the Industrial Engineer or Industrial Engineering firm, a meeting among appropriate Company and Union representatives and the Industrial Engineer shall be arranged at the Plant. This meeting shall be for the purpose of presenting all necessary facts of the dispute to the Industrial Engineer.

4. In addition to hearing pertinent statements by the Union and the Company, the Industrial Engineer may make such observation and study of the operation in

continued

Exhibit 4.7   *continued*

question as is necessary to enable him to make accurate findings of fact in the case and shall have access to information pertinent to the dispute, including Standard Data and any time recording of the operation.

5. Upon completion of his study the Industrial Engineer shall send a report of his findings to the Union, the Company and the Impartial Referee.

6. Upon receipt of the Industrial Engineer's report the Union, the Company and the Impartial Referee shall meet to present their positions, including written summaries thereof, to the Impartial Referee on the question. At the instance of the Impartial Referee, the Industrial Engineer shall also be present.

7. Thereafter the Impartial Referee shall render his decision which shall be binding upon the Union, the employes and the Company, provided it is within the scope of his jurisdictional authority.

8. The jurisdictional authority of the Impartial Referee is restricted to the determination of questions which have been submitted to him by the parties concerning compliance with the provisions of this Article.

Source: Adapted from "The Era of the UnCola" by David Pauly, et al, *Newsweek*, January 6, 1986, p. 51. Copyright 1986 by Newsweek, Inc. All Rights Reserved. Reprinted by Permission.

ably helps reassure employees that the plan is fair. Joint decision making also will allow union input into daily management of the plan.

The cost to management of such joint action is, again, the time that it may require employees to be away from their normal duties.

Job Design and Redesign   It is not uncommon for organizations to design jobs in particular ways or to redesign jobs. Changes in the content of jobs can result from at least two sources: (1) desires to enrich or enlarge the job (a topic discussed in more detail in Chapter 15), or (2) technological changes in equipment or work processes. Regardless of the source of the change it is appropriate and probably desirable to have labor-management committees to deal with the change.

As Chapter 13 discusses, employees often resist change because they perceive it as threatening or misunderstand it.[52] Joint committees can alleviate this fear. They can also make the transition to the new methods easier. For example, in the 1970s the United Auto Workers and Chrysler Corporation established such committees to investigate Chrysler's redesign of work. Such efforts represent good faith action on the part of management to share decision making.[53]

As with other joint committees, probably the major cost of such a program will be time lost on normal duties.

Joint Participation and Due Process   Once a labor-management contract has been bargained at the table and ratified by the membership, the two parties must live by that agreement for its life. During the life of the contract, numerous questions as to the **rights** of the respective parties under the contract are likely to arise. Examples of questions of contract interpretation might be: Does a supervisor have the right to order an employee to work overtime? Can a pay increase be denied an employee because of poor attendance?

Even though the contract might address such issues as how overtime is to be allocated, or what standards are to be used in giving pay increases, often the wording of the contract is unclear or vague, or the parties may have different interpretations of what the words mean. When this occurs, there is a strong likelihood that the dispute could result in a strike or lockout if there is no method to deal with the dispute. Most labor-management contracts provide for a grievance procedure that allows the specific issue to be aired. An example of a grievance procedure appears in Exhibit 4.8.

Typically, if the two parties cannot agree about the issue, the grievance process ultimately requires that a neutral third party arbitrate the issue. That is, both parties will make their case to the arbitrator, and the arbitrator will make a determination for one of the parties. Usually, the arbitrator's decision is final and binding (**binding arbitration**), and the parties must live by the decision. Only if the issue is renegotiated at the next contract renewal will the decision change.

The overall grievance procedure to which the union and management agree is one more example of joint decision making between the union and management. The due process system can involve issues of compensation. For example, an employee may interpret the contract to find the total number of paid vacation days was incorrectly calculated. If this issue is grieved, which it most likely would be, the compensation decision maker should be involved in the deliberations to assure that both employees and management interpret the contract properly from the compensation expert's viewpoint. The compensation decision maker also needs to ascertain the implications of differing interpretations for the compensation cost structure. Immediate costs of grievance procedures are the cost of staff time and the lost labor costs of union members who are away from their normal duties.

Summary

This chapter addressed two important constraints on the compensation decision-making process: internal labor markets and labor unions.

Internal labor markets require organizations to focus on equity in pay relationships among jobs within the organization. The process for doing this is job evaluation. Inferences drawn from the operation of the internal labor market also suggest that organizations may have some degree of latitude in establishing the wage payments for higher level jobs, but wage payments to low-level (entry-level) jobs are probably most sensitive to competitive wage rates in the labor market. Organizations as a result are probably most concerned about being wage competitive in the market for these entry-level jobs.

Exhibit 4.8   *The Grievance Process*

ARTICLE 18
Adjustment of Grievances

Section 1. The Grievance Committee shall consist of not more than three (3) employes designated by the Union, who, at reasonable times, will be afforded such time off as may be required to visit departments other than their own only for the purpose of handling grievances after notice to the head of the department to be visited and permission from their own supervisor.

Section 2. Should disagreements arise as to the meaning and application of or compliance with the provisions of this Agreement, there shall be no cessation of work at any time but the matter shall be settled promptly in the following manner.

Any employe who believes he has a just grievance shall discuss the alleged grievance with his supervisor within twenty-four (24) hours after the occurrence in an attempt to settle same. The supervisor shall verbally answer the grievance within twenty-four (24) hours.

Step 1: In the event that no satisfactory settlement of the grievance is arrived at between the employe and his supervisor, the employe may set forth and file his alleged grievance in writing within six (6) days on a form provided by the Company. The grievance then shall be taken up by the employe and the departmental committeeperson with the departmental general supervisor who shall answer the complaint within forty-eight (48) hours from the time of presentation of such written form. The grievance form shall be dated and signed by the employe.

Step 2: In the event that no satisfactory settlement of the grievance is arrived at in Step 1 of this procedure, the written grievance may be taken up by the Grievance Committee with the Personnel Supervisor or his designee who will answer the same in writing within five (5) days of the date of presentation.

Step 3: In the event that no satisfactory settlement of the grievance is arrived at in Step 2 of the procedure, the written grievance may be taken up by the Grievance Committee with the Plant Manager or his designee, who will answer the same in writing within eight (8) days of the date of presentation.

Step 4: A grievance not satisfactorily settled in Step 3 may be appealed for discussion in an attempt to reach a mutually satisfactory settlement between the representatives of the International and Industrial Relations Director and other officials of the Company. Notice of appeal shall be served by either representative designated above on the other prior to expiration of five (5) days following the disposition of Step 3 hereof.

Step 5: If the grievance is not settled in Step 4, it may be submitted to arbitration at the request of either the International President of the Union or the Vice President and Director of Industrial Relations, and the decision of

continued

Exhibit 4.8   continued

the arbitrator will be final and binding. Notice of the request to arbitrate the grievance must be served on the other party within thirty (30) days after the termination of proceedings in Step 4 unless extended by mutual agreement. Thereafter, and as soon as possible the International President of the Union or the Vice President and Director of Industrial Relations, or both, or their designated representatives shall request Federal Mediation and Conciliation Service to submit to each a panel of seven (7) arbitrators from which panel the parties shall alternately strike one name from the panel until one remains who shall be the arbitrator to hear and decide the dispute. The right to strike the first name shall be determined by a toss of a coin. The arbitrator so selected shall have no power to add to, subtract from or modify any of the provisions of this contract. Each party shall pay one-half of the fees and expenses of the arbitrator. The decision of the arbitrator shall be transmitted in writing to the parties within thirty (30) days after the completion of the hearing.

Excerpted from "Agreement between Corning Glass Works, Blacksburg, Virginia and American Flint Glass Workers' Union, AFL-CIO including Local Union No. 1022, 1981–1984."

Internal labor markets arise out of the sociotechnical system of the organization. They persist over time because the advantages for both employees and employers apparently outweigh the disadvantages. Internal labor markets as a phenomenon hold implications for compensation decision making. The analysis of the internal labor market concept suggests that (1) organizations may have considerable discretion over wage payments for certain jobs; (2) organizations may be concerned that certain jobs (entry-level jobs) are wage competitive in the labor market; (3) there may be a greater concern about perceived fairness in wage payments between certain jobs (internal equity) than about fairness relative to the labor market (external equity).

Labor unions are also an important constraint faced by organizations. This constraint is most severe for those organizations that have a union representing some, or all, of their employees. A very brief discussion of the evolution of the labor movement was presented. The purpose of this discussion was to give the reader a sense of why employees join unions, and to develop some of the basic concepts of unionization.

This chapter discussed the major kinds of issues which unions bargain over. It presented a conceptual framework for understanding the bargaining process. The chapter noted that unions do attempt to influence the terms and conditions of employment for their members. In the case of compensation, unions attempt to influence wages and benefits through bargaining at the table. Both wage and benefit level and structure issues are bargained. Finally, the chapter discussed several of the more common ways in which unions share in joint decision making over compensation issues. These approaches range from joint decisions at the bargaining table, to standing or ad hoc joint committees, to the grievance procedure itself. In the unionized context, compensation decision makers can expect to have unions involved in the compensation decision-making process.

Discussion Questions

1. Identify how a job you have worked at fits into the internal labor market in that organization.

2. What variables would influence a person high in a firm's internal labor market not to quit a job even though he or she does not like the work?

3. Discuss the bargaining process that labor and management go through in arriving at a contract. When would it pay one side to bluff at the bargaining table?

4. Discuss the limitations faced by an employer who might want to have a preventive labor relations strategy of paying a wage premium.

Exercise

An employer has 20 union employees working in the shop. These employees are allocated among three jobs as follows:

    Machine operator: 10 employees
    Machine attendant: 5 employees
    General laborer: 5 employees

The employees currently receive the following pay rates per contract:

    All machine operators make $9.20 per hour.
    All machine attendants make $8.00 per hour.
    All general laborers make $6.00 per hour.

A. In contract negotiations the employer and the union agree: (1) to a 10 percent wage increase for machine operators, (2) that the machine attendant new wage rate will be 90 percent of the machine operator's rate, and (3) that the general laborer wage rate will be 70 percent of the machine operator's rate.

1. Calculate the current hourly wage bill for the employer.

2. Calculate the new contract hourly wage bill for the employer.

3. What effective percentage increase is the new wage bill relative to the old wage bill?

4. Calculate the current wage level (average wage) for the employer.

5. Calculate the new wage level (average wage) for the employer.

6. What effective percentage increase in the wage level (average wage) will the employer realize?

7. Is the percentage wage bill increase equal to the percentage wage level increase? Why or why not?

8. Discuss your findings in class. Does the real percentage increase in labor costs depend on how one calculates the numbers?

9. Which job got the largest percentage wage rate increase?

B. In part A, did you use the current or new machine operator wage rate in calculating the rate differential (wage structure) for the machine attendant and general laborer wage rates? Using the alternate that you did not use in Part A, reanswer questions 1 to 9.

C. Does contract language interpretation make a difference in effective costs?

References

1 For further elaboration and development of the internal labor market concept, see: Peter B. Doeringer and Michael I. Piore, *Internal Labor Markets and Manpower Analysis* (Lexington, Mass.: D.C. Heath, 1971).

2 Clark Kerr, "The Balkanization of Labor Markets," in E. Wight Bakke *et al., Labor Mobility and Economic Opportunity* (Cambridge, Mass.: Technology Press of MIT, 1954): pp. 101–102.

3 John T. Dunlop, "Job Vacancy Measures and Economic Analysis," *The Measurement and Interpretation of Job Vacancies: A Conference Report,* National Bureau of Economic Research (New York: Columbia University Press, 1966): p. 33.

4 Thomas J. Bergmann and Frederick S. Hills, "Internal Labor Markets and Indirect Pay Discrimination," *Compensation Review* 14, no. 4 (1982): p. 42.

5 Doeringer and Piore, *Internal Labor Markets and Manpower Analysis,* p. 3.

6 Herbert G. Heneman III and Marcus G. Sandvar, "Markov Analysis in Human Resource Administration: Applications and Limitations," *Academy of Management Review* 2 (1977): pp. 22–23.

7 For a general discussion of the isolation hypothesis see F. S. Hills and R. E. Hughes, "Salaries and Fringe Benefits in an Academic Labor Market: Internal/External Labor Markets and Geographic Differentials" (paper presented at the 37th annual Academy of Management meeting, Orlando, Fla., August 1977).

8 Doeringer and Piore, *Internal Labor Markets and Manpower Analysis,* p. 21.

9 *Ibid.*

10 K. M. Rowland and M. G. Sovereign, "Markov Chain Analysis of Internal Manpower Supply," *Industrial Relations* 9 (1969): pp. 88–99.

11 Janet Ford *et al.,* "Internal Labour Market Processes," *Industrial Relations Journal* (Summer 1984): p. 42.

12 *Ibid.*

13 415 F. Supp. 761.

14 Doeringer and Piore, *Internal Labor Markets and Manpower Analysis,* pp. 13–17.

15 Michael J. Piore, "On the Job Training and Adjustment to Technological Change," *Journal of Human Resources* 3 (Fall 1968): pp. 435–449.

16 Richard W. Beatty and James R. Beatty, "Some Problems with Contemporary Job Evaluation Systems," in Helen Remick, ed., *Comparable Worth and Wage Discrimination: Technical Possibilities and Political Realities* (Philadelphia: Temple University Press, 1984): pp. 59–60.

17 "The Future: How U.S. Business Will Change in the Next 50 Years," *Business Week,* September 3, 1979, p. 188.

18 Claude S. George, Jr., *The History of Management Thought,* 2d ed. (Englewood Cliffs, N.J.: Prentice-Hall, 1972): pp. 50–51.

19 *Ibid.,* p. 52.

20 Foster Rhea Dulles and Melvyn Dobofsky, *Labor in America: A History,* 4th ed. (Arlington Heights, Ill.: Harlan Davidson, 1984): p. 26.

21 Edwin E. Witte, "Early American Labor Cases," *Yale Law Journal* 35 (1926): p. 827.

[22] 49 Stat. 449, 20 USC 151.

[23] Sanford Cohen, *Labor in the United States*, 4th ed. (Columbus, Ohio: Merrill Publishing, 1975): p. 100.

[24] John A. Fossum, *Labor Relations: Development, Structure, Process*, rev. ed. (Dallas: Business Publications, 1982): p. 492.

[25] D. Seligman, "Who Needs Unions?" *Fortune*, July 12, 1982, pp. 54–56.

[26] Susan Vroman, "The Direction of Wage Spillovers in Manufacturing," *Industrial and Labor Relations Review* (October 1982): p. 102.

[27] Daniel Quinn Mills, *Labor-Management Relations* (New York: McGraw-Hill, 1978): p. 309.

[28] 61 Stat. 136, 29 USC 141.

[29] C. M. Stevens, "On the Theory of Negotiation," in *The Labor Market*, B. J. McCormick, ed. (New York: Penguin Books, 1968).

[30] Fossum, *Labor Relations*, p. 167.

[31] Thomas A. Kochan, "How American Workers View Labor Unions," *Monthly Labor Review* (April 1979): pp. 23–31.

[32] "Showdown in Detroit," *Business Week*, September 10, 1984, pp. 102–110.

[33] J. R. Hicks, *The Theory of Wages*, 2d ed. (New York: St. Martin's, 1966): p. 140.

[34] Fossum, *Labor Relations*, pp. 170–173.

[35] *Ibid.*, p. 299.

[36] John R. Stepp, Robert P. Baker, and Jerome T. Barret, "Helping Labor and Management Solve Problems," *Monthly Labor Review* (November 1982): pp. 22–28. "The Decline of Strikes," H. E. Myer, *Fortune* 104: pp. 66–84 N2 (February 1981).

[37] George H. Hildebrand, "The Public Sector," in John T. Dunlop and Neil W. Chamberlain, eds., *Frontiers of Collective Bargaining* (New York: Harper and Row, 1967): p. 126.

[38] Mills, *Labor-Management Relations*, p. 192.

[39] *Ibid.*

[40] Fossum, *Labor Relations*, p. 298.

[41] Daniel J. B. Mitchell, *Unions, Wages, and Inflation* (Washington, D.C.: Brookings Institute, 1980): pp. 80–83.

[42] For recent research on these issues, see Richard B. Freeman, "Union Wage Practices and Wage Dispersion within Establishments," *Industrial and Labor Relations Review* 36, no. 1 (October 1982): pp. 3–21; and Barry T. Hirsch, "The Interindustry Structure of Unionism, Earnings, and Earnings Dispersion," *Industrial and Labor Relations Review* 36, no. 1 (October 1982): pp. 22–39.

[43] D. Martin, "Why Unions Lose at Many Companies," *Nation's Business*, August 1982, pp. 50–51.

[44] "Talkin' Union," *Forbes*, November 26, 1979.

[45] Robert H. Ferguson, *Cost-of-Living Adjustments in Union-Management Agreements* (New York: Cornell University, 1976): p. 1.

[46] Fossum, *Labor Relations*, p. 162.

[47] "Creaky System of Collective Bargaining," *Business Week*, June 30, 1980.

[48] Jerry S. Rosenbloom and G. Victor Hallman, *Employee Benefit Planning*, (Englewood Cliffs, N. J.: Prentice-Hall, 1981): p. 371.

[49] Harvey A. Young and Michael F. Dougherty, "Influence of the Guaranteed Annual Wage upon Labor Relations and Productivity: National Sugar Refinery's Experience," *Management of Personnel Quarterly* (Winter 1971): p. 27.

[50] See "A New Partnership to Build the New Workplace," *Business Week*, June 30, 1980; and *Recent Initiatives in Labor-Management Cooperation*, National Center for Productivity and Quality and Working Life, Washington, February 1976.

[51] "A New Partnership to Build the New Workplace," *Business Week*.

[52] Edgar H. Schein, *Organizational Psychology*, 3d ed. (Englewood Cliffs, N. J.: Prentice-Hall, 1980): p. 243.

[53] "The Risk in Putting a Union Chief on the Board," *Business Week*, May 19, 1980, pp. 149–150.

C H A P T E R

5

The Legal Environment

- **Learning Objectives**

- **Introduction**

- **The Fair Labor Standards Act of 1938**

  Overtime Provisions
  Minimum Wage Provisions
  Child Labor Provisions
  Record Keeping for FLSA
  Enforcement
  The FLSA and Compensation Decision Making

- **Wage Legislation for Government Contractors**

  The Davis-Bacon Act
  The Walsh-Healy Act
  The McNamara-O'Hara Act
  The Contract Work Hours Standard Act
  Enforcement
  Contractor Wage Legislation and Compensation Decision Making

- **Workers' Compensation Laws**

  Provisions of the Laws
  Workers' Compensation and Compensation Decision Making

- **Social Security Act of 1935**

  Social Security and Compensation Decision Making
  Unemployment Insurance

- **Consumer Credit Protection Act of 1968**

- **Health Maintenance Act of 1973**

  Compensation Decision Making and HMOs

- **Employee Retirement Income Security Act of 1974**

  Fiduciary Standards
  Funding
  Vesting
  Portability
  Reporting and Disclosure under ERISA
  ERISA and Compensation Decision Making

- **Civil Rights Legislation**

  The Equal Pay Act of 1963
  The Civil Rights Act of 1964
  The Age Discrimination in Employment Act of 1967
  Executive Order 11246

- **State Legislation**

105

Learning Objectives

To review the major legislation that impacts upon compensation decision making.
To learn what each law requires and to whom the law applies.
To learn of the major provisions of each of the laws.
To learn which agency enforces each of the laws.
To learn how each of the laws affects compensation decision making.

Introduction

The previous chapter dealt with two of the major constraints that shape compensation decision making: internal labor markets and labor unions. This chapter examines major federal legislation, which also serves as a major constraint on compensation decision making. This chapter provides an overview of each piece of legislation in terms of who is affected and what the law requires. A context for each piece of legislation is also provided to show why the legislation was passed.

Societies have been regulating wage and salary payments for all of recorded history. It is possible to go clear back to the Middle Ages, when the Church and State regulated wages through the "Just Wage Doctrine." The Just Wage Doctrine was an early attempt to establish the relative pay between occupational groups. Contemporary legislation influencing wage and salary and benefit payments in the United States has a long legislative history. This chapter summarizes that history and provides a context for each piece of legislation reviewed here.

The Fair Labor Standards Act of 1938

Chapter 4 noted that union strength was consolidated and legitimatized with the passage of the Wagner Act in 1935. At this time the federal government was controlled by the Democratic Party and the U.S. political environment could be said to be pro labor. Out of this environment grew pressures for legislation to regulate one or more components of wage and benefit payments. The Fair Labor Standards Act of 1938 (FLSA) is one piece of this legislation.

The FLSA is a complex piece of legislation that has been amended numerous times. No attempt is made here to provide all of the details of the law. Some of the rulings by the Department of Labor (the enforcing agency) change so often or are so complex that a specific technical question should be addressed to the local regional office of the Wage and Hour Division of the U.S. Department of Labor. The major provisions of the FLSA are outlined here.[1]

As currently amended, the FLSA applies to all employers with two or more employees who are engaged in commerce with gross sales of $362,000 (retailing) or $250,000 (other), as well as federal, state, and local governments and their agencies, and labor unions. The FLSA distinguishes between **exempt** and **nonexempt employees.** Exempt employees are those who are exempt from the overtime provisions of the act. The four classes of employees who fall within this group are executives, administrators, professionals, and outside salespersons.[2] An employee's job title alone does not qualify him or her for exempt status. The FLSA applies a fairly rigid set of guidelines in the test of whether a job is exempt or not. An excerpt from the FLSA "short test" to determine if jobs are exempt or not appears in Exhibit 5.1.

Only if the job in question passes the FLSA test will exempt status be conferred upon it. Jobs that do not meet the exempt test are considered nonexempt.

Exhibit 5.1   *Fair Labor Standards Act Test for Exempt Administrative Jobs*

Administrative Employees

In order for an employee to be employed in a bona fide administrative capacity, all the following tests must be met:

  (a) The employee's duty must be either:

    (1) Responsible office or nonmanual work directly related to the management policies or general business operations of the employer or the employer's customers; or

    (2) Responsible work that is directly related to academic instruction or training carried on in the administration of a school system or educational establishment; and

  (b) The employee must customarily and regularly exercise discretion and independent judgment, as distinguished from using skills and following procedures, and must have the authority to make important decisions; and

  (c) The employee must:

    (1) Regularly assist a proprietor or a bona fide executive or administrative employee; or

    (2) Perform work under only general supervision along specialized or technical lines requiring special training, experience or knowledge; or

    (3) Execute under only general supervision special assignments; and

  (d) The employee must not spend more than 20 percent of the time worked in the workweek (less than 40 percent if employed by a retail or service establishment) on nonexempt work — that is, work not directly and closely related to the administrative duties; and

  (e) The employee must be paid on a salary or fee basis at a rate of not less than $155 a week (or $130 a week in Puerto Rico, Virgin Islands or American Samoa), exclusive of board, lodging, or other facilities, or in the case of academic administrative personnel in private schools, the salary requirement for exemption must be at least $155 or alternately, academic administrative personnel may be paid a salary which is at least equal to the entrance salary for teachers in the employing school system or educational establishment or institution.

Special Proviso for High Salaried Administrative Employees:

The percentage limitations on nonexempt work do not apply to an administrative employee who is paid on a salary or fee basis of at least $250 a week ($200 per week in Puerto Rico, the Virgin Islands, or American Samoa) exclusive of board, lodging, or other facilities. The employee will be exempt if:

The primary duty consists of responsible office or nonmanual work directly related to management policies or general business operations; or

continued

Exhibit 5.1   *continued*

Responsible work in the administration of a school or educational establishment or institution or department or subdivision thereof that is directly related to the academic instruction or training; and

Such primary duty includes work requiring the exercise of discretion and independent judgment.

Types of Administrative Employees include, but are not limited to:

1. Executive and administrative assistants, such as executive secretaries, assistants to the general manager, confidential assistants, and assistant buyers in the retail trade. These employees, generally found in large establishments, assist an executive in responsible duties but do not themselves necessarily have executive authority.

2. Staff employees who are advisory specialists for management. Examples: tax, insurance, and sales research experts; wage rate analysts; investment consultants, heads of one employee departments, such as credit managers, purchasing agents, buyers, safety directors, personnel directors, and labor relations directors.

3. Those who perform special assignments, often away from their employer's place of business. Examples: management consultants, lease buyers, and utility company field representatives.

4. Academic administrative personnel performing work directly in the field of education. Examples: the superintendent or other head of the system and those assistants whose duties are primarily concerned with the administration of such matters as curriculum, quality and methods of instructing, measuring and testing the learning potential and achievement of students, and other aspects of the teaching program.

In individual school establishments, the principal and the vice principals and heads of departments, such as the mathematics department, the foreign language department, and the manual crafts department are other examples.

Job Titles Insufficient as Yardsticks

The employees for whom exemption is sought under the term "administrative" have extremely diverse functions and a wide variety of titles. The exempt or nonexempt status of any particular employee must be determined on the basis of whether the duties, responsibilities and salary meet all the requirements of the appropriate section of the regulations and a title alone is of little or no assistance in making this determination.

WH Publication 1363 (Reissued March 1980). *Executive, Administrative, Professional and Outside Sales Exemptions under the Fair Labor Standards Act.* U.S. Department of Labor, Employment Standards Administration, Wage and Hour Division.

Overtime Provisions

Probably the single most significant component of the original FLSA is the requirement to pay overtime to nonexempt employees. If a nonexempt employee works more than 40 hours in any one week, the organization is required to pay that employee at a rate of pay equal to one and one-half times the normal rate of pay for each hour over 40 hours. For example, an employee who normally makes $10 per hour would be paid $15 per hour for each hour worked over 40 hours in one week. This minimum legal requirement is separate from any overtime provisions negotiated in a labor management contract or overtime provisions required by other laws (for example, the Walsh-Healy Act). Many union contracts specify that overtime will be paid for any time worked over 8 hours in a day. Some union contracts require double and even triple time to be paid for any hours worked over 40 hours in a week. These provisions are negotiated between labor and management and are beyond the minimum overtime provisions of the FLSA.

There is one important variation on the 40-hour workweek rule for paying overtime. In the case of hospitals and nursing homes, the employer may establish a system in which the employees can work up to 80 hours in a two-week period without paying overtime.[3] This option gives hospitals and nursing homes greater flexibility in scheduling workers, who frequently work rotating shifts, while minimizing the employer's obligation to make overtime payments.

Minimum Wage Provisions

The second major provision of the FLSA is the minimum wage provision. Under the act, covered employers are required to pay their nonexempt employees a wage that is at least $3.35 per hour as of 1982. As might be expected, this minimum wage rate has been changed numerous times since the passage of the act. In addition to the exempt employees, employees of certain individually owned service or retail establishments, employees of certain seasonal amusement or recreational establishments, employees of certain small newspapers, switchboard operators of small phone companies, seaworkers on foreign vessels, and employees engaged in fishing operations are not covered. Also, certain farm workers, babysitters, and companions to the elderly are not covered in this provision of the FLSA.[4]

Child Labor Provisions

A third major component of the FLSA deals with child labor. The child labor provisions of the act have two goals: (1) to protect the educational opportunities of children, and (2) to prohibit their employment in jobs that are detrimental to their health or well-being and to prohibit working conditions which are detrimental to their well-being.

The major FLSA limitations on employing youth outside of agriculture follow:

> 18 years of age and older: no restrictions regardless of hazards of the job or number of hours.
>
> 16 and 17 years old: any nonhazardous job, unlimited hours.

14 and 15 years old: various nonmanufacturing, nonmining, and nonhazardous jobs outside of school hours subject to the following provisions: no more than 3 hours on a school day, no more than 18 hours in a school week, and no more than 8 hours on a nonschool day or 40 hours in a nonschool week. Finally, work may not begin before 7 A.M. nor end after 7 P.M. except between June 1 and Labor Day, when the day is extended to 9 P.M.

Like most legislation, there are special exceptions to these rules. One special exception is for 14- and 15-year-olds who are participating in an approved Work Experience and Career Exploration Program. These teenagers can work up to 23 hours per school week, including up to 3 hours per school day (including school hours).

The above provisions of the FLSA and who is covered under the act are summarized in Table 5.1.

Record Keeping for FLSA

The FLSA requires employers to keep various records on each employee. For employees covered by both the overtime and minimum wage provisions of the FLSA, the following records are required:

1. Personal information including employee's name, home address, occupation, sex, and date of birth (if under 19 years of age).
2. Hour and day when workweek began.
3. Total hours worked each workday and each workweek.
4. Total daily or weekly straight-time earnings.
5. Regular hourly pay rate for any week when overtime is worked.
6. Total overtime pay for the workweek.
7. Deductions from or additions to wages.
8. Total wages paid each pay period.
9. Date of payment and pay period covered.

The purpose of these records is to ensure that there is adequate documentation if an investigation is necessary.

Table 5.1   *Summary of Fair Labor Standards Act*

Coverage	Provisions
Federal, state and local governments	Minimum wage ($3.35/hour)
Private employers with two or more employees engaged in commerce	Overtime after 40 hours/week (80 hours in the case of nursing homes and hospitals)
	Child labor

Enforcement

The FLSA is enforced by the Wage and Hour Division of the U.S. Department of Labor. The division has local offices throughout the United States.

The division is empowered to enforce the provisions of the law. This enforcement includes the right to investigate any complaints filed under the act, including the power to obtain the necessary records to make a determination of fact under the act. An investigator may order an employer to change its wage practices to bring that employer into compliance with the law. Employers may be ordered to pay back wages to employees under the law. The statute of limitations for back pay awards is 2 years, unless there is a willful violation of the law, in which case the statute of limitations is 3 years. Willful violation of the law may be punished by an up to $10,000 fine for a first violation and a prison sentence for subsequent willful violations.

Although the division is the enforcement agency for the FLSA, employers should not look at the division as an adversary. Most division investigators are more interested in assuring compliance than in investigating violations. As a result most division offices are extremely helpful in aiding employers in interpretation of the law. Therefore, compensation decision makers are encouraged to make full use of this resource anytime there is a question of interpretation of the FLSA.

The FLSA and Compensation Decision Making

The FLSA has several positive features in the eyes of some. For example, it is generally conceded that labor favors the overtime provisions because they foster work sharing and limit overworking a few people. That is, the act forces the organization to pay a wage premium for any employee it uses over 40 hours per week. A cost-conscious employer, therefore, may tend to allocate work time equally among all employees before overworking a few employees. The employer may tend to hire more workers when total overtime would pay an additional worker at straight time. The minimum wage provisions also presumably reduce the number of working poor, because the minimum wage is presumably above the poverty level.

Not everyone considers the FLSA a beneficial piece of legislation. Although the overtime provisions may be an inconvenience to the employer, they are relatively uncontroversial. The minimum wage provisions, however, are fairly controversial. For example, many argue that minimum wages decrease employment. That is, employers faced with a relatively expensive but marginal quality worker may choose to automate the work. The outcome of such a decision is less jobs in the economy. There is some evidence for this assertion. Recent presidential administrations have proposed that a subminimum wage for teenagers be allowed to encourage employers to hire more teenagers, who comprise one of the groups with marginal skills that tend to suffer because of the minimum wage. Such a proposal is discussed in the newspaper excerpt in Exhibit 5.2.

Exhibit 5.2   *Subminimum Wage for Youth*

The Reagan administration recently sent to Congress a proposal to lower the minimum wage for teen-agers taking summertime jobs. Under S. 2687, introduced by Sen. Percy (R-IL), and H.R. 5721, introduced by Rep. Packard (R-CA), the "Youth Employment Opportunity Wage Act of 1984" would authorize employers to pay summer workers between 16 and 19 years old $2.50 an hour minimum wage. To respond to fears that a cut-rate young worker would replace adult workers, the legislation includes penalties for employers who discharge adult workers, including a $10,000 fine, six months in jail and payment of back wages to the released worker. There are currently 13 co-sponsors of S. 2687, all Republican senators, including Orrin Hatch (R-UT), chairman of the Senate Labor and Human Resources Committee, which has jurisdiction over the bill. A hearing has been scheduled for June 18 in the Senate Committee on Labor and Human Resources. Secretary of Labor Donovan is expected to testify.

Source: "Subminimum Wage for Youth," *Resource,* July 1984, p. 4. Reprinted with permission of *Resource,* © 1984, The American Society for Personnel Administration.

A second objection to the minimum wage is that it has an impact upon the overall wage level, shifting the entire wage structure of an organization upward. That is, if the lowest paying job in an organization earns the minimum wage of $3.35, then the employer must pay the next higher job something more than $3.35, the next higher job correspondingly higher, and so forth. The result is that the impact is felt throughout the entire wage structure. It is often argued that the minimum wage provision of the FLSA is inflationary in the economy at large and has substantial impact upon total labor costs.

The FLSA establishes minimum wage and overtime provisions for employers in general. Employers that are government contractors have more stringent wage rate and overtime provisions. The major laws that establish these more stringent requirements are discussed in the next section.

Wage Legislation for Government Contractors

The four acts discussed below are summarized in Table 5.2.

The Davis-Bacon Act

Another piece of legislation growing out of early post–World War I labor pressure was the Davis-Bacon Act of 1931.[5] This act requires construction contractors who hold contracts in excess of $2,000 with the federal government to pay the **prevailing wage** rate in the area in which the contract is held. The "prevailing" wage is usually interpreted as the union wage paid in the area.

Table 5.2   *Summary of Federal Government Contractor Wage Legislation*

Davis-Bacon Act (1931)

Coverage	Provisions
Construction contractors over $2,000 annually	Prevailing wage

Walsh-Healy Act (1936)

Coverage	Provisions
Nonconstruction contractors over $10,000 annually	Prevailing wage

McNamara-O'Hara Act

Coverage	Provisions
Service contractors over $2,500	Prevailing wage

Contract Work Hours Standard Act

Coverage	Provisions
Davis-Bacon, Walsh-Healy, and McNamara-O'Hara contractors	Overtime after 8 hours a day or 40 hours a week

The Walsh-Healy Act

The Davis-Bacon Act was extended to all government contract work (not only construction) by the Walsh-Healy Public Contracts Act of 1936. This later act applies to all nonconstruction contract work where the contract is more than $10,000, and further requires time and one-half pay for all work in excess of 8 hours per day and 40 hours per week.

The McNamara-O'Hara Act

In 1965 Congress passed the McNamara-O'Hara Service Contract Act. This act extended labor standards for employees of contractors and subcontractors providing services for federal agencies.[6] The act applies to employers with service contracts of $2,500 or more.

The Contract Work Hours Standard Act

The Contract Work Hours Standard Act of 1962 established uniform overtime standards that are applied to each of the three acts discussed above. Under these provisions, all federal contractors must pay overtime to employees working on federal contracts at the rate of one and one-half times the base rate of pay for all hours worked over 8 hours in a day and over 40 hours in a week. These requirements for federal contractors to pay overtime are more stringent than those of the FLSA.

Enforcement

The four acts just discussed are all enforced by the Wage and Hour Division of the Department of Labor. The division will investigate an employer upon receiving a complaint from or on behalf of an employee. The division has the power to withhold the total payment or any portion thereof for a federal contract and to use the funds to pay any back pay that an employee might have coming under one or more of these acts. The division may also prevent an employer from holding a federal contract for up to 3 years if it is found to violate one or more of these acts.

Employers with federal contracts must post the wages of the jobs used in the contract work in a conspicuous place for their employees to see. Employers are also required under the acts to pay wages on a weekly basis. Finally, contractors must agree to allow the government to withhold accrued contract payments necessary to comply with the wage provisions of the acts.

Contractor Wage Legislation and Compensation Decision Making

The four contractor wage acts and particularly the Davis-Bacon Act have come under considerable criticism in recent years as being inflationary.[7] Specifically, critics argue that very often the federal government ends up paying an inflated wage for contract work because the acts force even nonunion employers to make bids on a union wage scale. A higher wage is paid than is necessary to construct a building or provide a service, which results in a more expensive product, which contributes to inflation. Various efforts have been made to repeal this legislation (particularly the Davis-Bacon Act) with little success. The newspaper article excerpt in Exhibit 5.3 is an example of the controversy over this act.

Exhibit 5.3   *Davis-Bacon in the Dock*

Over the 50 years the Davis-Bacon Act has existed, we've penned uncounted editorials condemning this especially flagrant example of federal economic intervention. But since the law is once again undergoing legislative scrutiny and since some of our readers may have come in late, the subject deserves review.

We'll start with the story of E.D. Plummer, a paving company located in Washington Township, Pa.—a rural community of 9,600 in Franklin County, some 130 miles from Philadelphia and 22 miles from Maryland. E.D. Plummer does a lot of road work. On private jobs, Ken Plummer Sr. pays his flagman $4 to $5 an hour: a decent wage for a flagman in Washington Township; a decent wage, too, for a flagman in Franklin County or in nearby Maryland. But when Ken Plummer Sr. does a government project, he pays the flagman $10.80 an hour. Same man, same work, same flag.

continued

Exhibit 5.3   *continued*

The difference is Davis-Bacon, a law requiring private contractors to pay something called "the prevailing wage" on federally funded construction projects. The
prevailing wage does not have to prevail in the immediate geographic area, however;
so the Labor Department usually imports it from the nearest big city. Thus, the
prevailing wage is usually a union wage and the highest wage. For Ken Plummer, the
prevailing wage is the Philadelphia wage — or twice the going rate.

This kind of thing can be pretty pricey. This year the federal budget calls for
$30 billion in construction. Over a billion of that represents the unnecessary cost of
Davis-Bacon wages.

Davis-Bacon has other, less obvious, effects. Boosting wages on federal construction makes federal construction more expensive, thus we get less of it; and it
bids labor away from private projects, thus boosting private wages and limiting
private projects. The net results, then, are less construction and less employment.
Those who do work are, of course, handsomely enriched through this sneaky redis-
tribution of income away from taxpayers.

Partly as a result, no doubt, construction workers receive wages nearly double,
on average, the level for all hourly workers. Moreover, Davis-Bacon has a rather
sordid history, passed mainly at the behest of small local contractors who wanted
protection from the competition of roving gangs of itinerant workers, many of
whom were destitute blacks, during the Depression. Also, there are a number of
other laws that protect hourly workers in the construction trades against unfair
treatment.

The times are achangin' for a law whose sole purpose is to bump up wages
wherever and whenever possible. Four states have already repealed their "mini"
Davis-Bacon and repeal is being considered in a dozen others. Congress will consider the matter after spring recess; the Senate has scheduled oversight hearings to
begin April 28. The Reagan administration, whose support is critical to any repeal
effort, has recently been talking only about tightening up the act. While we sympa-
thize with the view that attention ought not be diverted from the President's economic program, it would be a shame to skip the opportunity to remove Davis-Bacon
from the books.

Source: "Davis-Bacon in the Dock," *The Wall Street Journal,* April 22, 1981, p. 28E.
Reprinted by permission of *The Wall Street Journal,* © Dow Jones & Company, Inc., 1981.

These acts pose several potential problems for contractors. One of the
more serious is the problem of wage equity, particularly for a nonunion, low-
wage employer. For example, suppose a nonunion, low-wage employer obtains
a federal contract. This employer must pay the going rate for work performed
on the contract, and must also pay overtime after 8 hours a day and 40 hours
a week. The contractor does not have to pay these wage rates for other employees who are working on other jobs which are not involved with completion of the contract. The contractor must assess the problems this situation
might cause if two workers are doing the same job but receiving different wage
rates. Should the contractor pay all its employees the higher wage? A second
question is how the workers will feel when the contract is completed if their
wage rate reverts to the lower rate again. Will this be an incentive to unionize?

Workers' Compensation Laws

With the advent of industrialization in the United States, there was a persistent
problem with work-related injury to employees. Under common law doctrines
employees had few, if any, rights to compensation for their injuries. Beginning
with the turn of the twentieth century the individual states began to pass laws
that protected workers when they were injured on the job. These laws are
known as the workers' compensation laws. The last state to have a workers'
compensation law was Missouri, which passed its law in 1948.[8] Thus, all 50
states plus Puerto Rico have workers' compensation laws.

Provisions of the Laws

There is considerable variability in provisions of the respective states' compensation laws. However, all of the state laws share a common set of goals. These
can be summarized as follows:

1. To guarantee benefits to victims of industrial accidents, or their families, on a
no-fault basis.

2. To provide an efficient method by which claims can be processed.

3. To assure income protection through legislation, and relieve private and
public charities of the burden of providing for injured workers.

4. To reduce the administrative costs of processing claims for worker-related
injuries.

5. To encourage employer interest in safety by providing that employers pay
compensation insurance premiums on an actuarial basis.

6. To encourage investigation into the causes of accidents with the goal of
remedying any known causes to improve safety in the future.

Most state laws require that employers above a given size carry some form
of state-approved insurance to cover claims under the law. In some states it is
also possible for an employer to "self-insure" if it complies with state standards. In any event, the goal of these programs is to provide fast, efficient, and
meaningful income protection for injured workers on a no-fault basis.

Employees are entitled to initiate a claim under workers' compensation
laws for numerous kinds of accidents. For example, an employee who injures
a leg while at work could file a claim. Similarly, an employee who becomes ill
because of breathing noxious fumes could file a claim. In a recent case, an
employee filed a successful claim because of an auto accident during lunch
hour off company premises.[9] The general rule is that if an employee is injured
while performing a duty for the employer then the employee is entitled to
benefits under the company's program of insurance. The specifics of the coverage vary considerably by state and the compensation decision maker will need
to know the extent of liability within a particular state.

Under workers' compensation laws employees are entitled to several different types of payments. First, employees can usually receive some type of income protection in the short term. For example, if an employee is totally disabled for a short time up to two-thirds of the normal weekly pay for a specified period of time may be paid. Second, if the disability is not total, the employee may qualify for a disability payment in proportion to the disability up to a maximum amount of time. Third, most compensation programs provide a flat payment for certain injuries. For example, in Virginia an employee will receive up to two-thirds of the weekly pay ($253 maximum) for 150 weeks for the loss of a hand.[10] This payment will be made in a lump sum and is unaffected by other benefits or insurance that the employee may be entitled to. Fourth, most workers' compensation programs require that the insurance also pay for all medical expenses associated with the injury. Finally, the insurance program will often pay for rehabilitation expenses for the injured employee. The major provisions of workers' compensation laws are summarized in Table 5.3.

Workers' Compensation and Compensation Decision Making

Workers' compensation insurance programs are mandated by law in all 50 states. They are a true insurance program in the sense that employers must make insurance premium payments that are in line with their experience with industrial accidents and injuries. Therefore, it should be obvious that employers will become more safety conscious in an effort to keep their cost as low as possible. Compensation decision makers need to monitor these costs and bring them to the organization's attention if they seem excessive.

Beyond monitoring costs, the compensation manager will also want to determine if self-insurance (where permitted) may be more cost effective than purchased insurance. Further, there may be variation in insurance premiums even within one state. Therefore, an organization may want to shop around for the least costly plan.

Finally, the compensation decision maker will need to keep adequate records systems to keep track of injuries and reporting injuries, and to assure that employees receive their legally mandated benefits without abusing the program.

Table 5.3   *Summary of Workers' Compensation Laws*

Coverage	Provisions
Generally all private sector firms (subject to state variation)	Income protection for injury Awards for catastrophic loss Medical bills covered

Social Security Act of 1935

As part of the New Deal legislation, Congress passed the Social Security Act of 1935. One of the principal features of the Social Security Act is to provide retirement, disability, and health insurance for retired persons and those unable to work. The act is funded through a payroll deduction plan and matching contributions made by employers.[11] As of January 1, 1986, the amount of the deduction was 7.15 percent on the first $42,000 of wages each year. Each employee pays this rate and the employer matches the employee's contribution equally. The maximum wage level and the withholding rate have been changed by recent amendments and these values will no doubt be raised in the future.

Employers are obligated to pay their share and the employees' share (from payroll deductions) of social security payments to the Social Security Administration. These payments must be made quarterly, by law. The major Social Security Act provisions are summarized in Table 5.4.

Social Security and Compensation Decision Making

The social security system appears to be in financial trouble these days. Although no one specific cause can be cited for the financial problems, the federal government has raised benefits and expanded their scope without providing the financial resources to keep the system solvent. Social security has grown from a partial retirement plan to being viewed as a total retirement plan. From the compensation decision maker's standpoint one of the critical issues to be dealt with is whether the organization wants to have a private pension plan for its employees. The compensation decision maker must ask whether the organization can afford to fund two retirement plans. The issue of offering both a public retirement plan through social security and a private retirement plan will most likely grow more critical as the costs of social security continue to grow.

Unemployment Insurance

The Social Security Act also provides a mechanism whereby states can participate in a federally subsidized unemployment insurance system. Unemploy-

---

Table 5.4   *Summary of Social Security Act*

Coverage	Provisions
Private and public sector employers	Retirement and survivor insurance
	Disability insurance
	Medicare and Medicaid
	State unemployment insurance
	programs

ment insurance is not a part of the Social Security Administration but is operated through plans in the 50 states. Often referred to as **job service** in the
states, the system is funded through payroll taxes on employers on an actuarial
basis. Thus, employers who do not have stable employment pay higher premium rates than do employers with highly stable employment. The program,
therefore, encourages employers not to lay people off.

Consumer Credit Protection Act of 1968

A garnishment is a court order requiring an employer to deduct money from
an employee's paycheck to repay a bad debt that the employee has accrued.
Prior to the Consumer Credit Protection Act garnishments were covered by
state law. State laws, while highly variable, generally worked in favor of the
debt holder, who asked for the court order. For example, in some states the law
allowed the court to take 100 percent of the employee's net pay until the debt
was paid off, placing a considerable burden on the employee who relied on the
paycheck for food, lodging, and so on. Further, the employer of a person
whose wages were garnished often found it a considerable inconvenience to be
paying the court instead of issuing a paycheck to the employee. As a consequence, employers often had a policy of terminating employees whose wages
were garnished, creating even greater financial hardship for the employee.

The Consumer Credit Protection Act of 1968 was designed in part to alleviate some of these problems. The act applies to all employers in private
employment as well as state and local governments. Federal employees' wages
are exempt from garnishment. Under the act the amount of money subject to
garnishment is related to a worker's take-home pay. If a worker's take-home
pay is less than $100.50 per week, no garnishment can be made. If the take-
home pay is between $100.50 and $134.00 per week, only that portion above
$100.50 is subject to garnishment. If the worker's take-home pay is above
$134.00 per week, then the total is subject to garnishment with a maximum
limit of 25 percent.[12]

Under the act, wages can be garnished only by court order. In addition, the
employee must be given advance notice by the employer and is entitled to
appear in court to argue against the garnishment. Finally, a garnishment must
be obtained for each pay period—if one garnishment does not cover all of a
bad debt, another garnishment must be obtained. In addition, it is illegal under
the act for an employer to terminate an employee for garnishments that result
from any one bad debt.

The Consumer Credit Protection Act is enforced by the Wage and Hour
Division of the Department of Labor. Violations of the law may be reported to
the division. The provisions of this law just discussed are summarized in
Table 5.5.

Table 5.5   *Summary of Consumer Credit Protection Act*

Coverage	Provisions
Public and private sector employers	Limited withholding for garnishments Due process No termination for first bad debt

Health Maintenance Act of 1973

The Health Maintenance Act of 1973 is an amendment to the Fair Labor Standards Act. It requires all employers subject to the FLSA who have 25 or more employees and who currently provide health insurance to employees to have a health maintenance organization (HMO) option if one is available in their area.

There are two distinguishing features of an HMO. First, an HMO is essentially a form of health insurance that places primary emphasis on preventive medicine as opposed to remedial treatment. Thus, good health is encouraged by having all members have physical exams on a routine basis and by encouraging members to see their physician at an early, as opposed to a late, stage of illness.

Second, HMOs provide total health care at a fixed rate. HMOs are often set up so that a team of physicians handles the case load. Instead of having a personal doctor, the patient may go to a clinic and be treated by whoever is on duty. Often HMOs cooperate with local hospitals, and all medical services, whether on an inpatient or outpatient basis, are provided at fixed premium rates. The rationale behind HMOs is that in the long run medical services are cheaper if preventive rather than corrective medicine is practiced. The HMO provisions are summarized in Table 5.6.

Compensation Decision Making and HMOs

The Health Maintenance Act of 1973 requires certain employers to provide an HMO option if one is available in their area. The required option feature means that an employer's employees may be split between two insurers for

Table 5.6   *Summary of Health Maintenance Act*

Coverage	Provisions
Employers with 25 or more employees who currently provide health and medical insurance and have health maintenance organizations in their area	Provide an HMO option if available

health benefits, which may increase total benefit costs. As a result, the compensation decision maker must be concerned about determining the benefits of such a health insurance package.

Employee Retirement Income Security Act of 1974

By the 1970s there was concern over an employee's rights to funds in a private pension plan and the employee's ability to collect from private pension plans. An employee's rights to a private pension fund were assured only by an employer's willingness to follow through on the promise to pay. Often private pension plans were unfunded or only partially funded, so that benefits were paid out of current revenues. Further, an employer could sidestep its obligation to pay an employee by retiring the employee early or by forcing the employee to quit. These and other problems culminated in the Employee Retirement Income Security Act of 1974 (ERISA).

In general, the act regulates private pension plans and establishes standards that private plans must meet. There is nothing in ERISA that requires an employer to have a pension plan. The act only stipulates that if an employer has a pension plan, then it must meet the standards of the act. The principal features of the act are: (1) fiduciary standards, (2) funding, (3) vesting, and (4) portability.

Fiduciary Standards

Historically, there had been considerable conflict of interest on the part of the person who managed the retirement fund. For example, should retirement funds be reinvested in the company to help with cash flow problems, or should they be invested in an independent portfolio to minimize risk? The issue of fiduciary standards addresses this conflict. The law is very strict in assuring that the person in charge of the pension fund acts in the best interests of the fund and its members. Because of the fiduciary standards nearly all plans are now managed by outside parties (for example, insurance companies, banks, and investment houses).

Funding

Prior to ERISA most pension plans were not fully funded. That is, current obligations under a plan were at least partially funded with current revenues since the employer had made no historical commitment to set aside funds as obligations accrued. The major problem with such a strategy is that if the company starts to lose money there may be no revenue to use for pension payments. The author is aware of one situation where 3,000 employees lost all of their rights under a pension plan when the company went bankrupt. To solve this type of problem, Congress required employers who have pension plans to fund the plan in the same fiscal year in which obligations are incurred.

One of the major concerns was what to do with plans in effect at the time the law was enacted but that were not yet funded fully. The act specifies that such employers would have to immediately begin fully funding new obligations and also to begin working toward full funding of historical obligations. An employer could have up to 20 years to accomplish full funding of historical commitments.

Vesting

One problem employees had with private pension plans prior to ERISA was collecting from the fund if they left their employer prior to retirement. When does an employee have a right to money in the retirement plan? First, an employee is always entitled to money that he or she has paid into a plan, plus any interest earned by that money. What about the employer's contribution to the plan? Vesting has to do with the question of when the employee has a right to the employer's contribution to the plan. ERISA provides three different formulas for vesting in a pension plan. The employer is free to choose from these options; however, ERISA requires that an employee be fully vested by the end of 15 years. At that time the employee is entitled to 100 percent of the employer's contributions to the pension plan.

Portability

The issue of portability deals with whether or not an employee can take money from one pension plan and transfer it to another plan. ERISA does not require an employer to make an employee's share portable. The act does allow the employee to transfer money from one employer's fund to another without incurring tax liability if the two plans are ERISA-approved. Employers are free to decide if they wish to have portability provisions. Even if an employee is not allowed to transfer funds from one fund to another, the employee always has a right to his or her contributions and a right to the employer's contributions once vested. Usually, an employee is entitled to take either the cash value of the vested rights at termination with the organization, or to leave the money with the employer and draw a reduced pension from that employer at retirement. These various provisions are summarized in Table 5.7.

Table 5.7   *Summary of Employee Retirement Income Security Act*

Coverage	Provisions
Organizations with private pension plans	Fiduciary standards
	Funding
	Vesting
	Portability
	Insurance

Reporting and Disclosure under ERISA

The reporting and disclosure requirements under ERISA are numerous enough to fill an entire book.[13] In this chapter these requirements are only briefly discussed. Probably the two most important agencies to inform are the Department of Labor and the Internal Revenue Service. The Department of Labor's Pension and Welfare Benefits Programs unit is responsible for overseeing the administration of qualified retirement plans. This agency requires the filing of a summary plan description that outlines the benefits of the plan. The Internal Revenue Service must also receive information about the plan. The IRS is concerned about retirement plans because they must satisfy certain legal requirements if they are to qualify as tax-exempt. Failure to meet filing requirements of the Department of Labor and the IRS can be serious. At the least it can result in fines and penalties. At the extreme it could mean that an employer's pension plan will not receive tax-exempt status. From a practical standpoint this means that the employer may not be able to shelter from taxes any earnings that the plan realizes. Since most pension plans rely on investment income to help offset future liabilities, this could have considerable impact on the solvency of a pension plan.

ERISA and Compensation Decision Making

There are penalties for violations of the filing requirements for ERISA. The compensation decision maker will need to be sure that all appropriate forms are filed with the Department of Labor and the IRS. This is also important to assure that the pension plan will receive favorable treatment under tax law.

Beyond these concerns, the compensation decision maker's major concern with respect to ERISA probably is deciding on the level of private pension benefits that will be provided. Since employers are required to contribute to the retirement component of the social security program, the best general rule is to integrate social security and the private pension plan so that total retirement benefits are roughly equal to the net take-home pay of a person ready to retire. If an employee makes $1,500 per month net pay at the time of retirement, social security plus private pension plan payment should equal about $1,500. This strategy enables employees to retire on a stable income rather than take an income loss at retirement. There is not much justification for higher retirement payments since such a strategy would reward retired workers more than those actually on the job.

An organization's ability to fund a retirement plan at the level described in the preceding paragraph is limited by its ability to pay. Firms with low ability to pay may not be able to fund at a level to assure postretirement income equal to preretirement income. On the other hand, firms with high ability to pay may be able to afford a higher level of funding than a simple income replacement level. Even if it could afford higher funding, however, it probably would not want to do so.

Civil Rights Legislation

The legislation reviewed so far in this chapter either has been supported by organized labor or has been a response to problems introduced by previous labor legislation. Early limitations on minimum wage, prevailing wages, overtime, and maximum workweeks are all factors that labor supported in its interest. Similarly, HMOs support labor's position for better benefits.

In spite of the labor movement's championing of certain wage and benefit issues, other issues did not gain legislative support until after the peak of the labor movement's influence in the American political experience. These legislative initiatives involve civil rights gains on the part of certain special interests in society. In the next sections the major legislative gains by these special interest groups and their importance for compensation decision makers are discussed.

The Equal Pay Act of 1963

One of the realities about wage payments in the late 1950s and early 1960s was the fact that the average woman worker earned only about 60 percent of the average male worker's wage. In response to this fact and political pressures from women's groups, Congress passed the Equal Pay Act of 1963 (EPA).[14]

The EPA stipulates:

> No employer having employees subject to [the minimum wage provisions of the FLSA] shall discriminate, within any establishment . . . between employees on the basis of sex by paying wages to employees in such establishment at a rate less than the rate at which he pays wages to employees of the opposite sex in such establishment for work on jobs the performance of which requires equal skill, effort, and responsibility, and which are performed under similar working conditions. . . .[15]

The act also provides for four affirmative defenses:

> Wages may be different if they are paid pursuant to: I) a seniority system, II) a merit system, III) a system which measures earnings by quantity or quality of production, or IV) a differential based on any factor other than sex.[16]

Employers covered by the EPA are those covered by the minimum wage provisions of the FLSA. The EPA is an amendment to the FLSA and until January 1, 1979, was enforced by the Department of Labor. As of that date, the Equal Employment Opportunity Commission (EEOC) assumed the enforcement.[17]

Under the EPA, it is illegal for an employer to discriminate on the basis of sex in wage payments. The overriding limitations are that the jobs must be substantially equal in terms of skill, effort, and responsibility, and must be performed under similar working conditions. The above language has specific meaning to the industrial relations practitioner. Further, the four exceptions also have precise limitations based on court interpretation, as can be seen from the excerpt from a U.S. Supreme Court decision in Exhibit 5.4.

One of the more sobering statistics today is that in spite of 23 years of compensation decision making under the EPA, females on average still make only 60 percent of what the average male makes. The law has been less than

---

Exhibit 5.4   *Corning Glass Works v. Brennan,*
417 U.S. 188, 9 FEP 919 (1974)

Mr. Justice Marshall delivered the opinion of the Court, in which Douglas, Brennan, White, and Powell, J.J., joined. Burger C.J., and Blackmun and Rehnquist, J.J. dissenting.

These cases arise under the Equal Pay Act * * *. The principal question posed is whether Corning Glass Works violated the Act by paying a higher base wage to male night shift inspectors than it paid to female inspectors performing the same tasks on the day shift, where the higher wage was paid in addition to a separate night shift differential paid to all employees for night work.

We agree with Judge Friendly, however, that in this case a better understanding of the phrase "performed under similar working conditions" can be obtained from a consideration of the way in which Congress arrived at the statutory language than from trying to reconcile or establish preferences between the conflicting interpretations of the Act by individual legislators or the committee reports. * * *

The most notable feature of the history of the Equal Pay Act is that Congress recognized early in the legislative process that the concept of equal pay for equal work was more readily stated in principle than reduced to statutory language which would be meaningful to employers and workable across the broad range of industries covered by the Act. As originally introduced, the Equal Pay bills required equal pay for "equal work on jobs the performance of which requires equal skills." There were only two exceptions — for differentials "made pursuant to a seniority or merit increase system which does not discriminate on the basis of sex. * * *"[14]

In both the House and Senate committee hearings, witnesses were highly critical of the Act's definition of equal work and of its exemptions. Many noted that most of American industry used formal, systematic job evaluation plans to establish equitable wage structures in their plants.[15] Such systems, as explained coincidentally by a representative of Corning Glass Works who testified at both hearings, took into consideration four separate factors in determining job value — skill, effort, responsibility and working conditions — and each of these four components was further systematically divided into various subcomponents.[16] Under a job evaluation plan, point values are assigned to each of the subcomponents of a given job, resulting in a total point figure representing a relative objective measure of the job's value.

Congress' intent, as manifested in this history, was to use these terms [skill, effort, responsibility and working conditions] to incorporate into the new federal act the well-defined and well-accepted principles of job evaluation so as to ensure that wage differentials based upon bona fide job evaluation plans would be outside the purview of the Act. The House Report emphasized:

"This language recognizes there are many factors which may be used to measure the relationships between jobs and which establish a valid basis for a difference in pay. These factors will be found in a majority of the job classification systems. Thus, it is anticipated that a bona fide job classification system that does not discriminate on the basis of sex will serve as a valid defense to a charge of discrimination." H. R. Rep., *supra*, at 3.

It is in this light that the phrase "working conditions" must be understood, for where Congress has used technical words or terms of art, "it [is] proper to explain them by reference to the art or

continued

Exhibit 5.4   *continued*

science to which they [are] appropriate." *Greenleaf v. Goodrich,* 101 U.S. 278, 284 (1879). *See also National Labor Relations Board v. Highland Park Mfg. Co.,* 341 U.S. 322, 326 (1951) (Frankfurter, J., dissenting). This principle is particularly salutary where, as here, the legislative history reveals that Congress incorporated words having a special meaning within the field regulated by the statute so as to overcome objections by industry representatives that statutory definitions were vague and incomplete.

While a layman might well assume that time of day worked reflects one aspect of a job's "working conditions" the term has a different and much more specific meaning in the language of industrial relations. As Corning's own representative testified at the hearings, the element of working conditions encompasses two subfactors: "surroundings" and "hazards."[20] "Surroundings" measure the elements, such as toxic chemicals or fumes, regularly encountered by a worker, their intensity, and their frequency. "Hazards" take into account the physical hazards regularly encountered, their frequency, and the severity of injury they can cause. This definition of "working conditions" is not only manifested in Corning's own job evaluation plans but is also well accepted across a wide range of American industry.[21]

Nowhere in any of these definitions is time of day worked mentioned as a relevant criterion. The fact of the matter is that the concept of "working conditions," as used in the specialized language of job evaluation systems, simply does not encompass shift differentials.

---

successful in eradicating pay differentials based on sex. In a later section some of the reasons why the differential still exists will be explored. The provisions for the EPA are summarized in Table 5.8.

The EPA and Compensation Decision Making   The EPA is a mandate by the federal government not to discriminate in wage payments between men and women. From a compensation decision-making standpoint this means that the organization should study jobs through job analysis (the subject of the next chapter) very carefully to assure that there are true differences between jobs. Further, decision makers should audit the pay system to determine if there are differences in pay that cannot be justified by the four exceptions under the law.

To highlight the pay system audit, suppose that an organization has a data entry clerk job, in which both men and women work. Men in the job earn on average $250 per week, while women in the same job earn on average $200 per week. Would this be an example of illegal pay discrimination under the EPA? There are legitimate reasons for the difference in average pay. For example, the organization might find that when it began hiring people into the job, it hired

---

Table 5.8   *Summary of Equal Pay Act of 1963*

Coverage	Provisions
Employers with 20 or more employees as under Fair Labor Standards Act	Equal pay for equal jobs

more men than women. If this were the case and the organization gave pay increases as a function of length of service, then the difference in average pay may be justified. However, without an ability to articulate a legitimate reason for the difference, the organization would probably be guilty of illegal pay discrimination under the EPA. Foresighted organizations will want to conduct such audits on all jobs so as to be sure they are not liable in wage discrimination suits.

The Civil Rights Act of 1964

Congress, responding to considerable social pressures in the early 1960s, passed the Civil Rights Act of 1964, a complex law.[18] Of particular interest to the compensation manager is Title VII of the Civil Rights Act. Title VII applies to all employers with 15 or more employees, plus state and local governments and their agencies, plus employment agencies and labor unions.[19] Title VII prohibits discrimination "in the terms and conditions of employment on the basis of race, color, creed, sex, or national origin." Any employer who is found guilty of discrimination against one or more of these groups in a court of law will incur considerable expense.

A showing of intent is not necessary in establishing a case of discrimination under Title VII of the Civil Rights Act. The two most commonly discussed discrimination doctrines under Title VII are **adverse treatment** and **adverse impact.** Adverse treatment discrimination occurs when two people of different race, ethnic, or sex groups are treated unequally. For example, requiring women to pay more into a retirement fund than men has been determined to be adverse treatment discrimination because the two groups are not treated the same way. A case of adverse treatment discrimination can be seen in the excerpt of a court case in Exhibit 5.5.

Adverse impact discrimination occurs when an employer treats two people of different race, ethnic, or sex groups equally, but the treatment has different outcomes for each.[20] The most stereotypical example of this is in the selection area where both blacks and whites are required to pass a test for employment. If that test screens out a larger proportion of blacks than whites then it has adverse impact and would be illegal without a business necessity or job-relatedness defense for using the test.[21] Title VII requirements of the Civil Rights Act are summarized in Table 5.9.

Enforcement   Title VII of the Civil Rights Act is enforced by the Equal Employment Opportunity Commission (EEOC). Upon receipt of a complaint, the EEOC will investigate it. If the agency does not find **probable cause** for the complaint, it will normally issue a letter of right to sue to the person bringing the complaint. This means that a person can pursue a private lawsuit. If the EEOC finds that there is probable cause then it will try to mediate or conciliate the complaint. This means that the EEOC will attempt to arrive at an out-of-court settlement with the employer. However, if the employer disagrees that there is a legitimate complaint or disagrees with the EEOC's solution and

---

Exhibit 5.5   *City of Los Angeles v. Manhart,*
435 U.S. 702, 17 FEP 395 (1978)

Before BURGER, Chief Justice, and STEWART, WHITE, MARSHALL, BLACKMUN, POWELL, REHNQUIST, and STEVENS, Justices

MR. JUSTICE STEVENS delivered the opinion of the Court.

As a class, women live longer than men. For this reason, the Los Angeles Department of Water and Power required its female employees to make larger contributions to its pension fund than its male employees. * * *[1]

Based on a study of mortality tables and its own experience, the Department determined that its 2,000 female employees, on the average, will live a few years longer than its 10,000 male employees. The cost of a pension for the average retired female is greater than for the average male retiree because more monthly payments must be made to the average woman. The Department therefore required female employees to make monthly contributions to the fund which were 14.84% higher than the contributions required of comparable male employees.[4] Because employee contributions were withheld from pay checks, a female employee took home less pay than a male employee earning the same salary.[5]

An employment practice which requires 2,000 individuals to contribute more money into a fund than 10,000 other employees simply because each of them is a woman, rather than a man, is in direct conflict with both the language and the policy of the Act. Such a practice does not pass the simple test of whether the evidence shows "treatment of a person in a manner which but for the person's sex would be different."[21] It constitutes discrimination and is unlawful unless exempted by the Equal Pay Act or some other affirmative justification.

---

conciliation fails, the EEOC can file suit in court. Filing suit does not mean the EEOC will win. Only about 50 percent of all EEOC cases actually result in victory for the plaintiff. Regardless, the enforcement mechanisms are present to make Title VII effective.

Title VII and Compensation Decision Making   Title VII affects compensation decision makers directly since compensation is a "term or condition" of employment. As a consequence all compensation decisions must be made without regard to race, color, creed, sex, or national origin. For example, paying one set of jobs less because they are held predominately by females would be illegal under the law. This example is, in fact, much more technically com-

---

Table 5.9   *Summary of Civil Rights Act of 1964*

Coverage	Provisions
All employers with 15 or more employees, state and local governments, employment agencies, labor unions	No discrimination in the terms and conditions of employment on the basis of race, color, creed, sex, or national origin

plex, and the complexity is discussed in detail in Chapter 11. Nonetheless, this would be an example of **direct pay discrimination.**

Another form of pay discrimination is **indirect pay discrimination.**[22] This would occur if an employer discriminated against a person because of race, color, creed, sex, or national origin in promotion opportunities, for example. The result of such discrimination in promotions would be that the affected individual or group would be paid less as a secondary outcome associated with promotional discrimination. This form of discrimination is of concern because if the employer loses a lawsuit, back pay plus interest will be awarded. Thus, other forms of discrimination besides direct pay discrimination have an impact on compensation and labor costs under Title VII. The magnitude of this impact can be seen from the case excerpted in Exhibit 5.6.

The Age Discrimination in Employment Act of 1967

The Age Discrimination in Employment Act of 1967, as amended prohibits discrimination on the basis of age for people between the ages of 40 and 69 inclusive. The act applies to employers engaged in commerce who have 20 or more employees, unions, employment agencies, and state and local governments and their agencies. The act is enforced by the EEOC and prohibits discriminating "with respect to the terms and conditions of employment." Since compensation is a term or condition of employment, any compensation decisions with respect to age would be illegal.

The 1978 amendments to the act increased the age at which employers could mandatorily retire employees from 65 to 70. This change has potential impact on labor costs to the extent that the firm is required to retain older, more expensive employees for an additional 5 years. Further, since these employees will continue to pay into the private pension fund (if there is one) for longer periods at higher wages, an employer's pension obligations will also continue to grow. Thus, the act is not without potential cost implications for an employer. The provisions of the Age Discrimination in Employment Act are summarized in Table 5.10 and an example of a case is excerpted in Exhibit 5.7.

Executive Order 11246

Executive order 11246, 1965, as amended, is not a piece of legislation but an order issued by President Johnson under presidential executive power.[23] The order requires all employers who are government contractors and subcontractors and have 10 or more employees and $10,000 worth of contracts not to discriminate on the basis of race, color, creed, sex, or national origin. Further, such employers must also engage in **affirmative action.** If the employer has 50 or more employees and $50,000 or more in federal contracts, it must have an approved **written affirmative action plan.** The executive order is summarized in Table 5.11.

Exhibit 5.6   *Bing v. Roadway Express, Inc.,* 485 F.2d 441,
                6 FEP 677 (5th Cir. 1973)

V. Back Pay

The back pay issue in this case is narrow and relatively simple. Are William Bing, John T. Johnson, and Wess Shorty, Jr. entitled to back pay, and if so, how much? At oral argument Bing's counsel clearly expressed his demand that these three class members, and only these three, should receive back pay.

The Government, as amicus, seeks to broaden the issue by framing it as whether or not the trial court should have awarded back pay to all members of the affected class. We have already determined that the trial court's notice effectively brought forth all class members who deserved individual relief in this proceeding. Of the five who were entitled to road jobs, only Bing was blocked by discrimination from entering the OTR unit. The other four are not entitled to back pay because they were hired by Roadway in a period when no road drivers were hired; even if Roadway had not been discriminatory, they could not have obtained road jobs earlier than they did. Therefore they suffered no financial loss from Roadway's discrimination.

Calculating Bing's back pay is made difficult by his "moonlight earnings" and by a road unit layoff that would have reduced his earnings as a road driver to nothing for a nineteen-month period extending from August 1969 through March 1971. The district court approached the problem by first calculating the amount a road driver would have made, less his expenses, during the period when discrimination relegated Bing to a city driving job. The trial court allowed no earnings for the period August 18, 1969, to March 28, 1971, because it found that Bing would have been laid off. Counting the layoff and a road driver's expenses Bing, the court found, would have made $52,980. As a city driver during the same period of time Bing actually made $43,649, and he "moonlighted" at various driving jobs to make an additional $11,238. The trial court found that as a road driver Bing would have had to work sixty to one hundred hours per week and thus would not have had time to work extra hours at odd jobs. The court found he would have had to forgo the extra $11,238 if he had been a road driver; it therefore subtracted that amount, plus his earnings as a city driver, from the $52,980 he would have made as a road driver. In other words, with his city driving job, extra jobs, and the layoff of road drivers, Bing was better off financially as a city driver than as a road driver during the pertinent period. Accordingly the trial court awarded Bing no back pay.

While the trial court was correct in deducting all of Bing's moonlight earnings from the amount he would have earned as a road driver, it calculated his protected OTR earnings incorrectly. As we understand the trial court's calculations, it allowed no earnings for the nineteen-month layoff period. It seems blatantly unfair to subtract Bing's supplementary earnings, which continued through the layoff period, from his hypothetical road earnings, which had been reduced by the assumption that he would have earned nothing during the layoff period. It seems quite possible to us that he may have moonlighted during the period when road drivers were laid off. Any such earnings he would have made should be added to the trial court's estimate of his road driver earnings. Accordingly, on remand we direct the trial court to determine whether Bing could and would have made supplementary earnings during the layoff period. If the trial court finds that he would have had supplementary earnings during the layoff period, it must recalculate his back pay to take them into account.

Before THORNBERRY, AINSWORTH, and RONEY, Circuit Judges. THORNBERRY, Circuit Judge: [Only Section V is reproduced.]

Exhibit 5.7   *Geller v. Markham*

MANSFIELD, Circuit Judge:

Miriam Geller, a 55-year-old teacher, brought a class action in the District Court for the District of Connecticut under the Age Discrimination in Employment Act of 1967 (ADEA), 29 U.S.C. §§ 621, *et seq.*, claiming that defendants–appellants violated her rights by denying her employment as a teacher because of her age. She sought damages, equitable relief (including reinstatement, pension rights, benefits and seniority) and attorney's fees. A jury trial before Judge M. Joseph Blumenfeld resulted in an award of $15,190 damages. Following the trial, Judge Blumenfeld denied her application for equitable relief but awarded attorney's fees. From this denial she appeals.

[10] Judge Blumenfeld viewed reinstatement as inappropriate because he interpreted the jury's decision granting damages equal to one year's salary at Bugbee School as a factual conclusion that Ms. Geller was deprived of only one year's employment by the defendants' discriminatory action. We agree with this conclusion. Ms. Geller had never formally been hired as a permanent teacher during the time she was working but had merely been told to get started. Permanent reinstatement therefore is unwarranted.

[11,12] On the other hand, we disagree with the trial judge's refusal to consider Ms. Geller's request for lost pension benefits on the ground that "[d]amages for lost pension benefits are one component of the overall damages suffered by a plaintiff, which a jury may assess in ADEA actions." Despite some case law that supports viewing lost pension rights as an aspect of damages, see *Fellows v. Medford Corp.*, 431 F.Supp. 199, 201 (D.Or.1977), the better view is that these rights fall within the category of equitable relief, see *Cleverly v. Western Electric Co.*, 450 F.Supp. 507, 510 (W.D.Mo.1978), *affd.*, 594 F.2d 638, 640 (8th Cir. 1979). As distinguished from damage awards, which are payable to the plaintiff, pension benefits are paid into pension annuity funds. They merely replace the benefits that would have accrued during the year of employment wrongfully denied to Ms. Geller. Because a judge exercising his equitable power over a discrimination action should afford "make-whole" relief to wronged plaintiffs, *Rodriguez v. Taylor*, 569 F.2d 1231, 1238 (3d Cir. 1977), we remand to the district court with directions to award pension rights to plaintiff for the 1976–77 year, to be paid into the Connecticut Teachers' Pension Fund. Plaintiff's application for reasonable attorney's fees in prosecuting this appeal is granted in the sum of $500 plus her costs in prosecuting the appeal and defending against defendants' cross appeal.

Miriam E. Geller, Plaintiff-Appellant, Cross-Appellee, v. Walter Markham et al., Defendants-Appellants, Cross-Appellees. Docket Nos. 80–7087, 80–7089. United States Court of Appeals, Second Circuit. Argued Sept. 5, 1980. Decided Dec. 8, 1980.

Table 5.10   *Summary of Age Discrimination in Employment Act*

Coverage	Provisions
Employers with 20 or more employees	No discrimination in terms and conditions of employment based on age Protects those 40 through 69 inclusive

Table 5.11   *Summary of Executive Order 11246*

Coverage	Provisions
Government contractors and subcontractors with contracts over $10,000 and with 10 or more employees	No discrimination on the basis of race, color, creed, sex, or national origin

Special Written Plan

Coverage	Provisions
Employers with 50 employees and $50,000 in contracts	Practice affirmative action

The executive order is enforced by the Office of Federal Contract Compliance Programs (OFCCP) or its designated agency, which is within the Department of Labor. The office is empowered to conduct compliance reviews of federal contractors and subcontractors. As a result of such reviews it is possible that an employer would be found guilty of pay discrimination (either direct or indirect) and consequently subject to back wage payments, interest, and modification of the present compensation program. Just as with other civil rights legislation, the compensation decision maker must be familiar with the constraints placed on organizational decision making by the executive order.

State Legislation

Previous sections reviewed the major federal legal constraints placed on the compensation decision maker. Virtually every state also has its own set of laws that constrain wage and salary payments. Even if an employer is not subject to the federal law it may be subject to state and even local regulation.

Although it is beyond the scope of this text to articulate the various laws in each of the respective states, there are certain types of state laws that an employer will likely encounter. Workers' compensation laws and unemployment insurance laws have already been discussed. Compensation decision makers need to be sure they are in compliance with these laws. Most states also have their own minimum wage laws. In most cases state minimum wage levels are lower than federal minimum wage levels. For those employers not covered by the federal laws a knowledge of state laws is important to be sure the organization is in compliance. Most states also have some form of child labor protection.

Most states have one or more laws dealing with discrimination in employment. It is difficult to generalize about such laws since in some states there is one law, whereas in other states there may be numerous laws prohibiting discrimination. Examples of these would be laws that prohibit discrimination on the basis of race, color, creed, sex, and national origin. Also, numerous states have laws regulating age discrimination.

Readers interested in the specific laws within a given state should contact the state government for information. Typical state agencies for this purpose include State Human Rights Commission, Department of Industry, Department of Commerce, Labor Department, and Department of Human Resources.

Summary

This chapter reviewed the major federal legislation that impacts upon the compensation decision-making process. The Fair Labor Standards Act is important principally because of its overtime, minimum wage, and child labor provisions. Federal contractors must be concerned about the Walsh-Healy Act, the McNamara-O'Hara Act, the Davis-Bacon Act, and the Contract Work Hours Standard Act. These acts require certain federal government contractors to pay prevailing wages, and they set more rigid overtime standards than the FLSA for these contractors. Workers' compensation laws, the Social Security Act, state unemployment insurance laws, and the Consumer Credit Protection Act add more constraints to compensation decision making.

Two federal laws with a direct impact upon the employee benefits component of compensation were identified. These were the Health Maintenance Act and the Employee Retirement Income Security Act.

In the last decade or so, the federal government has enacted legislation to prohibit various forms of discrimination. Laws in this area include the Equal Pay Act, the Civil Rights Act, and the Age Discrimination in Employment Act. In addition, Executive Order 11246, as amended, places restrictions on employers and requires them to practice affirmative action.

This chapter focused on the major ways in which these laws and the executive order constrain compensation decision making. Some discussion also focused on the reporting requirements under these various laws.

Discussion Questions

1. Compare and contrast the FLSA, EPA, and Title VII of the Civil Rights Act—what does each attempt to do, who is covered, and what are the enforcement agencies?

2. Identify and discuss the concepts of direct and indirect pay discrimination. Identify examples of each.

3. Distinguish between adverse impact discrimination and adverse treatment discrimination in the context of wage and salary payments.

4. Some organizations have all-salaried plants. This means that all workers, regardless of their jobs, are paid a salary. Given your knowledge about the FLSA, comment on all-salaried plants.

5. Discuss the notion that certain wage and salary legislation is inflationary—for example, which legislation contributes to inflation and how does it do so?

References

[1] Most of the details about the FLSA were taken from various government documents dealing with this piece of legislation. A good summary document is U.S. Department of Labor, *Handy Reference Guide to the Fair Labor Standards Act* (Washington, D.C.: U.S. Government Printing Office, 1981): 8 pp. Also see Brent E. Zepke, "The Fair Labor Standards Act," *Supervisory Management* 22 (February 1977): pp. 30–36.

[2] U.S. Department of Labor, *Handy Reference Guide to the Fair Labor Standards Act*, p. 4.

[3] U.S. Department of Labor, *Hospitals under the FLSA*, WHD Publication 1326 (Washington, D.C.: U.S. Government Printing Office, 1971).

[4] U.S. Department of Labor, *Handy Reference Guide to the Fair Labor Standards Act*, p. 5.

[5] Donald Elisburg, "Wage protection under the Davis-Bacon Act," *Labor Law Journal* 28: pp. 323–328. E. I. Manger, "Administration of the Davis-Bacon Act," *Construction Review* 11 (August 1965): pp. 4–6.

[6] Steven C. Kahn, Barbara A. Brown, and Brent E. Zepke, *Personnel Director's Legal Guide* (Boston: Warren, Gorham & Lamont, Inc., 1984): pp. 3–13.

[7] Robert S. Goldfarb and John F. Morrall III, "The Davis-Bacon Act: An Appraisal of Recent Studies," *Industrial and Labor Relations Review* 34, (January 1981): pp. 191–206.

[8] Sanford Cohen, *Labor in the United States*, 4th ed. (Columbus, Ohio: Merrill, 1975): p. 456.

[9] See *Resource*, October 1983, p. 1. (A monthly publication of the American Society for Personnel Administration, Berea, Ohio.)

[10] The Virginia Workmen's Compensation Act, Industrial Commission of Virginia, 1982.

[11] Robert M. McCaffery, "Benefits and Services-Statutory," in *Motivation and Commitment*, ed. Dale Yoder and Herbert G. Heneman, Jr., *ASPA Handbook of Personnel and Industrial Relations*, vol. II (Washington, D.C.: Bureau of National Affairs, 1975), pp. 6-157—6-184.

[12] U.S. Department of Labor, *The Federal Wage Garnishment Law*, WHD Publication 1324 (Washington, D.C.: U.S. Government Printing Office, 1978): p. 5.

[13] Barbara B. Creed, *ERISA Compliance: Reporting and Disclosure* (New York: Practicing Law Institute, 1981): 477 pp.

[14] "Equal Pay Act of 1963," *Monthly Labor Review* 86 (August 1963): p. 947.

[15] 29 U.S.C. 206(d)(1).

[16] U.S. Department of Labor, *Equal Pay*, WHD Publication 1320 (Washington, D.C.: U.S. Government Printing Office, 1971). John E. and Katherine G. Burns, "Analysis of the Equal Pay Act," *Labor Law Journal* 24 (February 1973): pp. 92–99.

[17] Harry Sangerman, "Look at the Equal Pay Act in Practice," *Labor Law Journal* 22 (May 1971): pp. 259–265.

[18] *The Civil Rights Act of 1964: What It Means to Employers*, A BNA Operations Manual (Washington, D.C.: BNA, Inc., 1964).

[19] Morag MacLeod Simchak, "Equal Pay in the United States," *International Labor Review* 103 (June 1971): pp. 541–557.

[20] The adverse impact doctrine was first established in the Griggs v. Duke Power case [401 U.S. 424, 3 FEP 175 (1971)], which involved the selection of employees into the organization. The adverse impact doctrine, however, could certainly be applied to a pay situation.

[21] Job relatedness and business necessity are not the same concepts. For a discussion on this point see Frederick S. Hills, "Job Relatedness vs. Adverse Impact in Personnel Decision Making," *Personnel Journal* (March 1980): pp. 211–216.

[22] Thomas J. Bergmann and Frederick S. Hills, "Internal Labor Markets and Indirect Pay Discrimination," *Compensation Review* (4th quarter 1982): pp. 41–50.

[23] 3 CFR 339.

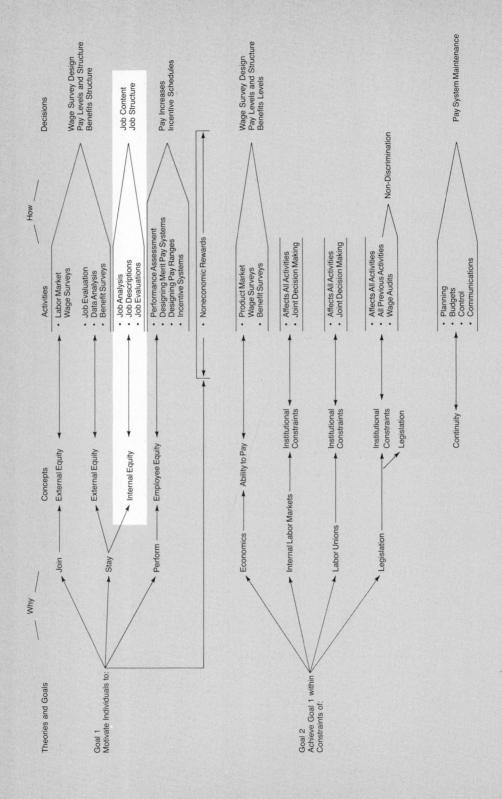

Internal Equity

Determination

Parts One and Two set the stage for a discussion of actual compensation administration. In Part One the discussion focused on the goals of a compensation system in Chapter 1, the important constraints placed on compensation decision making by individuals in Chapter 2, and the economics of business enterprise in Chapter 3. Part Two focused upon three important institutional constraints: internal labor markets and labor unions in Chapter 4, and legislation in Chapter 5.

Part Three moves into the realm of actual compensation decision making. An important first step in designing a compensation system is understanding the jobs that an organization has and the methods that exist for studying those jobs. This subject, job analysis, is the topic of Chapter 6. Chapter 6 also discusses the uses of job analysis data, including the documentation of job analysis findings into job descriptions and job specifications.

Chapters 7 and 8 discuss establishing internal pay equity within organizations. From an administrative standpoint, organizations attempt to achieve internal equity in wage payments through a process of job evaluation.

There is a considerable amount of literature on job evaluation, and there are numerous methods of conducting job evaluation. Chapters 7 and 8 are devoted to this important compensation activity. Chapter 7 focuses upon what are called nonquantitative approaches to job evaluation. Included in this discussion is the development of compensable factors (what factors the organization wants to pay for), and the ranking method and the job classification method of job evaluation. The relative advantages and disadvantages of these methods are also discussed.

Chapter 8 deals with quantitative approaches to job evaluation. The two general types of quantitative methods discussed are the factor comparison method and the point method. The advantages and disadvantages of these methods are also discussed.

Because Part Three introduces not only the concepts in compensation administration but also the tools of compensation administration, Chapters 7 and 8 include exercises and activities at the end of them. These should be completed for a good grasp of the processes involved in job evaluation. Completion of the exercises also aids in understanding some of the difficulties of conducting job evaluation.

6

Job Analysis and

Job Descriptions

- **Chapter Outline**
- **Learning Objectives**
- **Introduction**
- **Tasks, Jobs, and Positions**
- **Job Analysis**

  Uses of Job Analysis Data
- **Steps in Conducting Job Analysis**

  *Determining the Use of the Data
  and Information*
  Selecting a Method of Analysis
  Informing Other Managers of the Study
  Informing Job Incumbents of the Study

Carrying Out the Study
Validating the Study
Summarizing the Results

- **Job Analysis Techniques and Methods**

  Direct Observation
  Interviewing Techniques
  *Standardized Structured Approaches
    to Job Analysis*

- **Custom-Designed Job Analysis**
- **Job Analysis Outcomes**

  The Job Description
  Job Specifications
  Performance Standards

Learning Objectives

To learn that the job is the basic unit of analysis in compensation decision making.
To learn that job analysis is a fundamental activity for compensation decision making.
To learn the process or steps in conducting job analysis.
To learn the commonly accepted approaches and techniques that organizations use in conducting job analysis.
To learn how to build a job analysis program for compensation decision making.

Introduction

Chapters 1 through 5 identified the subject of compensation decision making and addressed some of the major theoretical concerns surrounding compensation decision making. This chapter begins the transition from the theoretical framework into the administrative practices that compensation decision makers use and begins to develop the basic skills of the compensation specialist. In this chapter the focus is upon job analysis and job descriptions, including the meaning of these terms, the purposes of job descriptions and job analysis data, and methods of conducting job analysis and writing job descriptions.

Tasks, Jobs, and Positions

Any discussion of jobs and job analysis assumes a knowledge of certain definitions. What are tasks, jobs, and positions; how are they alike and how are they different? A task can be defined as an activity that a person performs. For example, washing a wall, typing a letter, and starting an engine are all tasks that an employee might perform. A job is a collectivity of tasks performed by one worker. For example, the job of movie projectionist might include the tasks of unpacking the film, adjusting the carbon arc light, mounting the film on the projector, threading the film, showing the film, focusing the projector, and so on. A position refers to the person performing one job. For example, a company may have 100 truck drivers who operate semitrailer rigs. This company has one job of truck driver, but there are 100 positions for this job, assuming one driver per truck.

In talking about a job, it is important to distinguish between collections of tasks that are substantially similar and those that are substantially different. A trucking company may have several different jobs titled "driver." For example, a company might employ *over the road drivers, short haul drivers,* and *dispatch drivers.* The distinction between these three jobs might be made on the size of the equipment used (semitrailer trucks, regular trucks, and vans), or on the basis of differences among the jobs in terms of working conditions. (Over the road drivers may be gone from home regularly for a week at a time, short haul drivers may be out usually no more than one night per week, and dispatch drivers may never have to be gone from home.)

In this example the company has three types of driver jobs and a series of positions for each job. Each job has a slightly different set of tasks. One of the major issues in studying jobs is deciding when two jobs are alike enough to be considered the same job and when they are different enough to be considered distinct jobs.

The issue of similarity and differences among jobs is important from several standpoints. First, organizations engage in job evaluation. *Job evaluation* can be defined as the process of determining the relative worth of jobs. A key element in determining the relative worth of jobs is to identify how jobs differ from each other. Second, differences and similarities among jobs hold legal implications under the Equal Pay Act of 1963, the Civil Rights Act of 1964, and the Fair Labor Standards Act of 1938. Under each of these acts the employer must be able to meet certain legal requirements to insure that the compensation system does not violate the law. For example, under the Equal Pay Act the employer must show that men and women earn equal wages if the jobs they perform are *substantially equal in terms of skill, effort, responsibility,* and are performed under *similar working conditions.* The Civil Rights Act imposes similar requirements in wage payments regardless of race, color, creed, sex, or national origin. Under provisions of the Fair Labor Standards Act, employers must study jobs to determine which of those jobs must be paid overtime (nonexempt jobs) and which jobs do not require overtime payments (exempt jobs).

Job Analysis

Job analysis is the process of gathering information about the job. The job information normally gathered will include things such as (1) the activities performed in that job, such as what tasks are performed; (2) to which job the analyzed job reports; (3) the tools, materials, and equipment required for the job; (4) the outcomes of the job, for example, nails driven, walls built, engines assembled, or reports written; (5) the knowledge, skills, and abilities needed to perform the job; (6) the job environment, such as the working conditions; and (7) what constitutes good, poor, and superior performance on the job.

Uses of Job Analysis Data

The data obtained from the job analysis process is usually codified in several documents, one of which is a job description. A job description can be defined as a narrative essay that details what the job is all about in terms of the previous paragraph. Frequently, these data are used to construct other documents as well, for example, job specifications. A job specification is a statement of the job requirements: for example, the job requires typing skills, a college degree, or legal training. The data may be used to set performance standards (discussed later in the text). Exhibit 6.1 shows the relationship between job analysis and job descriptions, performance standards, and job specifications.

Exhibit 6.1 *The Relationship between Job Analysis and Other Human Resource and Compensation Activities*

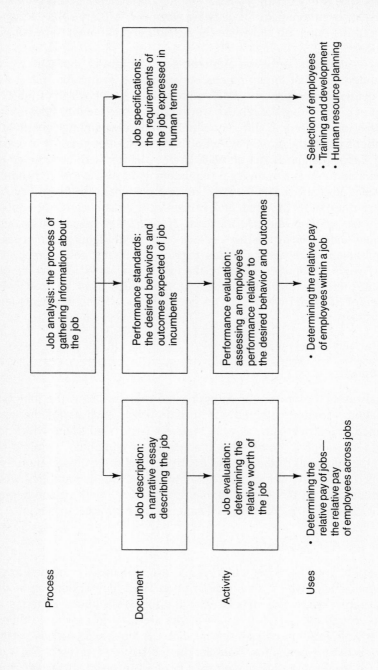

Process

Job analysis: the process of gathering information about the job

Document

Job description: a narrative essay describing the job

Job specifications: the requirements of the job expressed in human terms

Performance standards: the desired behaviors and outcomes expected of job incumbents

Activity

Job evaluation: determining the relative worth of the job

Performance evaluation: assessing an employee's performance relative to the desired behavior and outcomes

Uses

• Determining the relative pay of jobs— the relative pay of employees across jobs

• Determining the relative pay of employees within a job

• Selection of employees
• Training and development
• Human resource planning

Job analysis is usually designed for a specific purpose. That is, a systematic job analysis project is seldom undertaken within an organization. Typically, job analysis is done to accomplish only a limited set of objectives. The organization may do job analysis to clarify reporting relationships, to clarify responsibilities among jobs, or for other reasons, but seldom for all possible uses of such data. The multitude of uses for job analysis data is revealed in Table 6.1.

Job Analysis and Job Evaluation   To the compensation decision maker the two most important reasons for conducting a job analysis are to gather performance standards information and to have information for conducting job evaluation. Establishing performance standards is the subject of Chapter 12. Job evaluation is briefly discussed here and discussed in more detail in Chapters 7 and 8.

Job evaluation is the process of establishing the relative worth of jobs. In order to decide if some jobs should ultimately be paid more than others, the organization needs to have information about each of the jobs in question so that it can establish the relative value of jobs to each other.

Job Analysis and Compensable Factors   To establish the relative worth of jobs, it is absolutely critical that the information collected about jobs allows the analyst to make meaningful distinctions between jobs. Making these distinctions is based on the compensable factors that are important to the organization.

A **compensable factor** can be defined as any standard or criterion that the firm wishes to use in distinguishing among jobs for pay purposes. Examples of compensable factors are: (1) the degree of responsibility, as measured by the number of subordinates supervised; (2) the amount of education required, as measured by the years of schooling needed to do the job; and (3) the working conditions, as measured by the degree of physical discomfort (such as heat, cold, and noise) associated with the job. In the next chapter the types of compensable factors used by organizations are developed more completely. For now, however, compensable factors and their identification are important for job analysis when the purpose is job evaluation.

Steps in Conducting Job Analysis

The procedures for conducting a job analysis are examined here in a step-by-step process, which is summarized in Exhibit 6.2.

Determining the Use of the Data and Information

There are many uses for job information that may be related only incidentally to compensation decision making. What the information is to be used for is critical, since the use may dictate the job analysis technique employed. For example, direct observation of jobs to identify the interfaces among jobs may

Table 6.1   *Various Uses of Job Analysis Results*

	Frequency of Use	
	Salaried **(n = 638)**	**Hourly** **(n = 430)**
Job evaluation	98	95
Setting wage and salary levels	92	88
Appraising personnel	59	44
Establishing incentives	11	14
Determining profit sharing	6	2
Other	2	1
Recruiting and placing	95	93
Making job specifications	74	75
Promoting, transferring, rotating	72	67
Constructing tests	14	18
Indicating sources of employees	18	16
Counseling (vocational)	25	26
Matching workers with jobs	65	61
Placing the handicapped	17	25
Structuring jobs	58	54
Diluting jobs	19	19
Enriching jobs	26	25
Other	3	4
Conducting labor and personnel relations	83	79
Developing performance standards	48	42
Establishing responsibility	70	56
Establishing authority	64	44
Establishing accountability	66	46
Handling grievances	17	44
Conducting labor negotiations	8	34
Establishing channels of communication	32	24
Organizing personnel records	35	36
Other	1	1
Utilizing workers	72	67
Organizing and planning	56	47
Engineering jobs	17	16
Controlling costs	22	29
Controlling quality	14	16
Predicting changes	13	11
Avoiding excess task duplication	45	40
Other	1	1
Training	61	63
Developing courses	33	36
Selecting trainees	34	34
Orienting employees	36	36
Programming teaching machines	2	2
Other	1	1

Source: Cited by Ernest J. McCormick in Job Analysis: Methods and Applications (New York: AMACOM, 1979).

Exhibit 6.2 *Summary of Steps in Job Analysis*

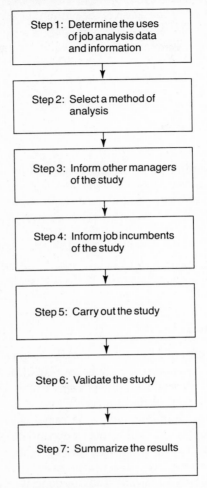

be useful for identifying work flow knowledge, but it may tell nothing about which jobs are worth more, or what it takes to perform well in each of the jobs studied.

Compensation decision makers will most frequently be involved in a job analysis when the data are to be used in some way for pay decision. To this end, the job analyst will be interested in an analysis technique that allows distinctions among jobs or distinctions among performance levels within jobs.

Selecting a Method of Analysis

Once the purpose of the analysis is known, the analyst is in a position to decide upon a technique for analysis. One consideration in selecting the technique is the purpose of the analysis. A second consideration is the nature of the jobs being studied. For example, routine jobs that have clearly defined indicators of success are more amenable to study using a **work methods approach** than jobs that require nonroutine work with less clearly defined indicators of success. A third consideration is the amount of time and money that the organization is willing to commit to the job analysis program. Cost considerations may constrain the quality of the job analysis activity.

A later section in this chapter is devoted to the techniques of job analysis. An extensive discussion of analysis techniques follows the steps of job analysis.

Informing Other Managers of the Study

Carrying out the job analysis requires careful planning on the part of the analyst. The analyst should set up an analysis schedule with department managers.[1] Work processes go on even while the analysis must be done. If the analyst wants to interview an employee or wants an employee questionnaire completed, for example, it should be coordinated with department managers to alleviate conflicts.

Communication to managers should include the purpose of the analysis, who will conduct the analysis, and the amount of time that will be involved. The analyst should pave the way for the analysis to receive maximum cooperation.[2]

Informing Job Incumbents of the Study

People generally are wary of job analysis studies. Two reasons may be distrust of management and a general tendency to be fearful of things which are not understood. Whenever possible, employees should be clearly informed of the job analysis and the purpose of the analysis.[3] Effective communications should enhance the probability of gaining employee cooperation in the study.

The immediate supervisor is the most appropriate person to inform job incumbents of the analysis.[4] In most cases communication between the organization and employee about any subject goes through the supervisor. The supervisor will probably insist that the study is done when work flow permits, making participation easier for the job incumbent.

Carrying Out the Study

The analyst is now ready to conduct the job analysis using the methods and procedures determined in the previous steps. This step is discussed in detail in the next section of this chapter.

Validating the Study

Job analysis may be incomplete if some aspect of the job is not studied, or information is inaccurately recorded. The analyst should attempt to validate the information collected. This might be accomplished by reviewing the results of the analysis with departmental supervisors or conducting the analysis on several incumbents who perform the same job, which would provide information as to consistency among what a set of incumbents do in any given job.

Summarizing the Results

The final step in job analysis is to summarize the data. The last section of this chapter discusses this step in detail.

Job Analysis Techniques and Methods

The objective of job analysis is to gather information about jobs for use in making other human resource decisions. Whatever job information is collected should be relevant for the purpose for which it is intended. One of the major problems with job analysis is that there is no good taxonomy for studying jobs. In spite of the importance of job analysis information, there exists no single framework for understanding jobs. Marc J. Wallace notes that job analysis is a series of fragmented and diverse approaches and definitions. He notes that the "unit of analysis" at which a job is defined varies considerably with the approach taken. Wallace identifies at least four levels of analysis: (1) the organization function served by the job, (2) the tasks accomplished on the job, (3) the worker behavior or task elements required to accomplish the job, and (4) the worker attributes required to perform the job. He suggests the need for understanding the meaning and implications of the various approaches and determining the relationships among the various levels of analysis.[5]

Until more research is conducted the decision maker must work with what is available to make human resource decisions. At least in the short run, job analysis must be tailored for the purpose for which the data will be used. In the case of job analysis data that are used for job evaluation purposes, it would seem to be important to analyze jobs in terms of dimensions which distinguish between jobs. With job analysis data used in performance assessment, the data ought to make distinctions between relative levels of performance within each job.

The whole issue of what information should be collected is often called the "criterion problem" in psychology.[6] What standard does the organization want to use, and how is that standard measured? Different job analysis techniques often seek out different types of information. The organization must decide what it is going to use the information for, and what criteria to use for assessing performance or the relative worth of jobs.

Ultimately, there are only three ways in which job analysis is conducted: (1) the analyst can watch people do their jobs and document the activities; (2) the analyst could actually do the job to learn about the job; and (3) the analyst can ask the job incumbent what the job entails. Every method of job evaluation uses these basic approaches. Some of the common techniques are reviewed in detail in this section.

The discussion is broken down into two parts. The first part discusses observational techniques of job analysis, and the second part discusses interviewing techniques of job analysis. No discussion is presented on techniques in which the analyst does the job. In that approach the analyst records what he or she did—the analyst can be seen as interviewing or observing herself or himself.

Direct Observation

To conduct a job analysis by direct observation the analyst might start with a basic recording form like the one in Exhibit 6.3.

Exhibit 6.3   *Recording Form for Direct Observation Job Analysis*

Job title: _____

Job reports to: _____

Job interfaces with (other jobs) _____ _____ _____

Tools/equipment/materials used: _____ _____ _____

Tasks performed in the job: _____

_____

_____

Outcomes expected: _____

_____

_____

Skills required of job incumbents: _____

_____

Job environment: _____

_____

The analyst would then gather the job information data at the work area. In the case of a job with a short cycle time (all tasks are performed within an hour or so), the analysis might take only a few hours. If the cycle time of the task is very long (it takes several days before all of the tasks in the job can be observed) then the amount of time required for analysis is longer.

The direct observation method of job analysis may be useful for identifying health and safety hazards of jobs, but it also has certain limitations.[7] First, direct observation does not capture the mental aspects of jobs, including such things as decision making or planning, and second, observation provides little information on the personal requirements for performing jobs. A third problem with direct observation is that the behaviors observed may not be the total set of behaviors that should be performed on the job. The worker may not perform all of the tasks that should be performed. A check against this happening should be built into the job analysis system. Two potential checks are to observe more than one employee at the same job, and to review the observed results with the supervisor or job incumbent to be sure that all activities were included in the analysis.

A fourth limitation of many observation methods is the problem of rater bias. Most people have perceptual biases, and analysts can disagree on what they think they saw in observing workers. One way around this type of bias is to have several analysts observe each job and then discuss their results. Collectively they may be able to arrive at a more accurate picture of what the job entails.

Several of the more common direct observation techniques follow.

Work Methods Analysis Work methods analysis is a direct observation technique for studying jobs. A job analyst watches the employee perform the job in the work setting.

The analyst may be an industrial engineer who times the employee in various phases of the job. For example, a work methods analyst studies the job of lathe operator. The analyst first identifies all of the various physical activities that go into processing a part on a lathe—obtaining a piece of unprocessed metal, mounting the metal in the lathe, starting the lathe, turning down the part, turning off the lathe, loosening the part from the lathe, and placing the part in the finished products bin. After identifying each step in the process of producing a finished part, the analyst then uses a stopwatch to record the amount of time to complete each discrete step in the process. Based on large numbers of observations, the analyst could arrive at an average time for each discrete step in the production process, and an average time for producing a finished product.

The type of information obtained from the work methods approach to job analysis is often used for job redesign by determining if there is a better or more efficient way of doing the job and for establishing the production standards for a piece rate incentive system. A **piece rate incentive** system is a pay system based on the number of units made. If the job analyst finds that an average worker could make 20 units of product per hour, then the piece rate might be set at 40¢ per unit. An average employee could make $8 per hour, while above- and below-average employees would make more or less per hour. Work methods analysis is an important job analysis technique where the employer wants to pay on a piece rate system.[8]

Work methods analysis is also appropriate where the employer wishes to establish a performance evaluation system. For example, the analyst, by studying large numbers of employees performing in the same job, could arrive at production levels for superior performance, average performance, and below average performance. Work methods, on the other hand, are not concerned with studying differences between jobs, and are not useful for job evaluation purposes.

Critical Incident Techniques   Critical incident techniques are another type of direct observation.[9] In the critical incident approach the job analyst observes the actual behavioral incidents exhibited by an employee on the job and records them. For example, in a critical incidence analysis of the job of carpenter, it would be possible to identify those behaviors that are particularly good or poor. The analyst identifies positive behaviors (driving a nail straight, making a square cut on a board, and erecting a straight wall) and negative behaviors (damaging the wood while driving a nail, ruining a board because of an incorrect cut, and not having a level wall).

After deciding what the desired and undesired work outcomes are, the analyst looks at the behaviors that are critical in attaining those desired and undesired outcomes. In the carpenter example, if a smoothly finished wooden wall is desired, then one of the critical incidents that go into the desired outcome is to "strike squarely the head of each nail with the hammer"; the critical incident associated with the undesired outcome is to miss the head of the nail and hit the board itself. Considerable time and effort go into the job analysis to identify all of the critical incidents that are likely to result in desired and undesired outcomes. Once each of the outcome's dimensions and the critical incidences are identified, then the analyst goes over the information with those who are to use the data to make sure that employees know what the incidences mean. The purpose of this step is to be sure that the incidences are expressed in terms of the users' language.

In recent years there has been a growth in the number of variations of critical incidence methods. Techniques such as behaviorally anchored rating scales and behavioral observation scales have been suggested.[10] The data indicate that when these techniques are used for assessing performance, they are probably no more accurate than other, more traditional performance appraisal techniques.[11]

Critical incidents techniques probably have their greatest utility in the personnel area of performance appraisal, since the techniques focus on important incidents within a job and not across jobs. With regard to pay decisions, this method is probably useful in establishing wage differences between job incumbents within a given job, but is probably less valuable for establishing wage differences between jobs. This method would be appropriate for input into performance evaluations, but not useful for input into job evaluation.

Because of the need to study numerous incumbents to assure that all job components are observed, the need to use multiple analysts to get analyst reliability, and the need to observe the entire job cycle, observation methods are time-consuming and costly. For this reason many employers resort to interview methods of job analysis.

Interviewing Techniques

The second major method of job analysis is to ask people what they do. The job analyst interviews one or more job incumbents to find out what activities and so forth go on in the job. There is wide variation in how structured these interviews are. The interview may be very informal, or the analyst may undertake the interview with a detailed and highly structured questionnaire. The structured interview has a greater likelihood of assuring that all components of the job will be discussed and that there will be common information across all jobs being analyzed, and it is generally preferable to the informal interview.

The interview process and some of the standardized structured interview procedures are discussed in this section.[12]

The Interview Process

Opening the Interview   A job incumbent may consider the analyst a stranger in the work environment. The employee is likely to be unsure of the analyst and the motives for studying the job. The analyst should work to overcome these apprehensions.

First, the analyst should make an effort to develop rapport with the employee by calling the employee by name when meeting for the first time. The analyst should also allow for a "warm-up" period of 5 to 10 minutes to talk about something of interest to the employee and put the person at ease.

Second, the analyst needs to make clear to the employee the purpose of the interview, what the analyst expects to accomplish, and how the interview will help in determining fairer personnel practices. It should not be assumed that the employee's immediate supervisor has informed the employee of any of these points. This second step allows the analyst to reinforce the supervisor's message if the supervisor did communicate with the employee.

Third, the analyst should encourage the worker to talk by listening intently, not interrupting but allowing the employee to finish a line of thought. This will also facilitate putting the employee at ease.

Directing the Interview   The analyst should direct the interview so that minimal time is used to gain maximal information. First, the interviewer should consider the best procedure for getting job information from the incumbent. If the worker normally performs a routine task or set of tasks, it is probably appropriate to have the worker describe it, beginning with the first task in the work cycle and moving to the last task. The worker will then be able to describe the natural flow of tasks in the work cycle. On the other hand, a worker may perform a nonroutine job, or a job in which duties are not performed in any regular order. In this case the analyst would probably want the worker to describe the tasks, beginning with the most important task performed and moving to the least important task performed. The employee should also be asked to describe those nonroutine but nonemergency duties that are performed. For example, an employee may only occasionally set up a machine or handle finished inventory. All of the dimensions of the job may then be discovered.

Second, the worker should be asked only one question at a time and allowed time to answer each question completely before moving on. Third, questions that can be answered yes or no should be rephrased to require more explanation by the employee. Fourth, the worker should be allowed to answer questions in his or her own words.

Fifth, as the interview proceeds, the interview questionnaire should be followed to keep the interview on track. If the incumbent strays from the subject at hand, the analyst might summarize the point up to where the employee strayed and then continue.

Sixth, language that is easily understood should be used. For example, the analyst may be interested in identifying the amount of a certain compensable factor in a job. The term *compensable factor* may not mean much to the incumbent in the interview. The incumbent can be asked how much time it takes to become competent to perform the job without excess supervision, for example, without identifying this as one compensable factor.

Seventh, there may be unease or nervousness in the job incumbent during the interview. If some portion of the interview makes the employee nervous, the analyst should gently lead him or her through that portion and allow adequate time to answer. The employee should never feel pressured by the analyst.

Suggestions for Interviewing   It is difficult to anticipate everything that may arise during the course of an interview, but some suggestions to smooth the interview follow.

1. Do not become argumentative with the employee. Take statements at face value. If there is a question as to the accuracy of a statement, check out the facts later with another employee or with a supervisor.

2. Do not show partiality to statements made by the employee that concern the employee and employer relationship. For example, an employee might protest that a required duty is unfair or inappropriate. Do not take sides on this type of issue. Explain that your job is to find out what is done, not whether it should or shouldn't be done.

3. Do not discuss the wage classification of the job.

4. Be polite and courteous during the interview. Always afford complete respect for the employee and his or her statements.

5. Don't talk down to an employee. Say nothing to denigrate the employee or the job.

6. Don't permit notes or responses to be influenced by personal likes or dislikes. Be as neutral and objective as possible.

7. Talk to the worker only with permission of the immediate supervisor.

8. Verify the information that is obtained by interviewing more than one job incumbent, by checking the responses with supervisors, or both.

9. Take notes in as nondisruptive a fashion as possible.

10. Don't assume that the worker will know all of the information that is requested. For example, a worker may not know all of the job titles of the jobs that his or her job interfaces with. The worker may also not know the training times for the job. It may be necessary to interview several people (including the supervisor) to get a completed interview schedule.

11. Do not assume that employees can follow a written questionnaire. It is better for the analyst to ask the questions verbally.

12. Don't assume that all employees have good verbal skills and can readily describe their jobs. Patience is critical in helping many employees describe their work.

Standardized Structured Approaches to Job Analysis

Over the years a number of fairly standardized approaches to job analysis have been developed. Several of the more commonly accepted approaches are discussed below.

Functional Job Analysis Functional job analysis is a method of analyzing jobs which was developed by the Training and Employment Service of the U.S. Department of Labor. It is a combination of observation and interview methods.[13]

In functional job analysis the analyst is concerned about collecting job information in five categories: (1) worker functions, (2) work fields, (3) machines, tools, equipment, and work aids, (4) materials, products, subject matter, and services, and (5) worker traits. The first category, worker functions, refers to how people relate to three aspects of work: data (mental aspects), people (social aspects), and things (physical aspects), as shown in Exhibit 6.4.

A job might carry a code of Data=4 (computing), People=8 (taking instructions—helping) and Things=0 (setting up).

Work fields consist of 99 categories encompassing use of tools, equipment, and machines, or techniques designed to fulfill the job. An example of a category is "drafting, riveting, and sawing." A job is also identified by the particular machines, tools, equipment, and work aids required to perform the job. Fourth, jobs are coded into one or more of 580 categories for materials, products, subject matter, and services. Finally, worker traits are recorded for each job. The dimensions of worker traits recorded are: (1) training time for the job, (2) aptitudes needed for the job, (3) interests tapped by the job, (4) tempera-

Exhibit 6.4   *Worker Functions*

Data	People	Things
0 Synthesizing	0 Mentoring	0 Setting up
1 Coordinating	1 Negotiating	1 Precision working
2 Analyzing	2 Instructing	2 Operating-controlling
3 Compiling	3 Supervising	3 Driving-operating
4 Computing	4 Diverting	4 Manipulating
5 Copying	5 Persuading	5 Tending
6 Comparing	6 Speaking-signaling	6 Feeding-offbearing
	7 Serving	7 Handling
	8 Taking instructions–helping	

Source: U.S. Department of Labor, Manpower Administration, *Handbook for Analyzing Jobs* (Washington, D.C.: U.S. Government Printing Office, 1972): p. 73.

ments necessary for the job, (5) physical demands of the job, and (6) the working conditions of the job.[14]

The functional job analysis approach is incorporated into the *Dictionary of Occupational Titles*.[15] From the compensation decision maker's viewpoint, probably one of the best features of this type of analysis is that it is extremely comprehensive, although some of the dimensions it measures are probably not useful for job evaluation purposes. Regardless, it is an approach to job analysis that should be reviewed when designing a job analysis system since it can provide ideas as to what one would want to look for in jobs. Some of the dimensions are very consistent with the types of compensable factors used by some employers. For example, two of the worker trait dimensions—training time for the job and working conditions of the job—are standard compensable factors used in job evaluation plans. Unfortunately, the breakdown of these factors in functional job analysis may not provide the level of refinement needed for job evaluation. Functional job analysis is not very useful for performance evaluation systems since it provides for a taxonomy (classification) of jobs rather than distinguishes between good and poor performers within a job.

Position Analysis Questionnaire   The position analysis questionnaire approach uses an extremely lengthy and sophisticated standardized questionnaire designed by Ernest J. McCormick and his associates.[16] It identifies 187 job elements related to six major divisions of work. These major divisions and examples of the job elements associated with them are depicted in Table 6.2.

The position analysis questionnaire is probably the most well-known standard questionnaire and was used to analyze thousands of jobs in McCormick's research program.[17] An organization can obtain the questionnaire from PAQ Services, Inc. along with a training manual and computer packages to analyze the large volume of data generated with the questionnaire.[18]

Table 6.2   *Job Elements from the Position Analysis Questionnaire*[a]

1. Information input (where and how the worker gets information used in performing the job)
   a. written materials
   b. behaviors
   c. touch
   d. estimating speed of moving objects

2. Mental processes (reasoning, decision making, planning, and information processing activities involved in performing the job)
   a. reasoning in problem solving
   b. analyzing information or data
   c. using mathematics

3. Work output (physical activities the worker performs and the tools or devices used)
   a. precision tools
   b. foot-operated controls
   c. assembling/disassembling
   d. finger manipulation

4. Relationships with other persons (relationships with other persons required in performing the job)
   a. entertaining
   b. coordinates activities
   c. supervision received

5. Job context (physical and social contexts in which the work is performed)
   a. indoor temperature
   b. noise intensity
   c. frustrating situations

6. Other job characteristics (activities, conditions, or characteristics, other than those described above, relevant to the job)
   a. specific uniform/apparel
   b. irregular hours
   c. working under distractions
   d. travel

---

[a] PAQ further specifies job elements in questionnaire.
Source: Ernest J. McCormick, P. R. Jeanneret, and R. C. Mecham, *Position Analysis Questionnaire,* © 1969 Purdue Research Foundation.

Information from this questionnaire probably has little value to the compensation decision maker for performance evaluation. The information collected is again designed more as a taxonomic (classification) device for jobs rather than to determine variations in performance within a job. On the other hand, the position analysis questionnaire may have considerable utility for the compensation decision maker in the job evaluation context. McCormick reports one study that found compensation rates could be predicted with considerable accuracy by using specific job elements in the questionnaire.[19] These results were also observed by another researcher.[20] These findings suggest that the position analysis questionnaire holds considerable promise in job evaluation programs.

Job Analysis Questionnaire The job analysis questionnaire is another lengthy questionnaire that analyzes jobs along three dimensions: job tasks, job environment, and job knowledge. In a study conducted by Newman and Krzystofiak the questionnaire yielded 60 underlying factors among 1,700 jobs.[21]

Like other standardized job analysis questionnaires, the job analysis questionnaire holds promise for job evaluation purposes.[22] However, it probably has limited utility for performance evaluation purposes.

Job Inventories Another common type of questionnaire is a job inventory. Job inventories typically measure job characteristics and worker characteristics. Table 6.3 displays information from an inventory that assesses job characteristics.

A worker-oriented inventory measures worker attributes such as skills needed, education required, strength needed, manual dexterity, and so forth.

Job inventories also probably have utility for job evaluation purposes, but little utility for performance evaluation purposes.

Custom-Designed Job Analysis

From a compensation decision maker's viewpoint, no one standard approach seems to adequately satisfy the data requirements for compensation purposes (job evaluation and performance evaluation). Job analysis is usually undertaken with some specific purpose in mind; for example, to understand reporting relationships in the organization, or to set performance standards. Different analysis procedures collect different types of data. Some approaches look at good or poor behaviors, while others look at good or poor performance outcomes, and still others look at what is done, not how well it is done.

Because of the limitations of any one approach, the most practical resolution is either to combine numerous approaches and adapt them to the organization or to design a job analysis program tailored to the needs of the organization. Designing a plan comes back to the purpose for which it is intended. The organization will probably never do one comprehensive job analysis. A number of different job analyses, each adapted to the needs at the time, will probably be undertaken.

From a compensation perspective the data obtained from a job analysis must have two characteristics. First, it must gather information about jobs that distinguishes between jobs. For this characteristic a standardized procedure such as the position analysis questionnaire might be used. Conversely, the organization might design a job analysis system that is developed only after the organization decides which compensable factors it wishes to use. The second characteristic is that information must distinguish between various per-

Table 6.3 *A Task-Oriented Job Checklist*

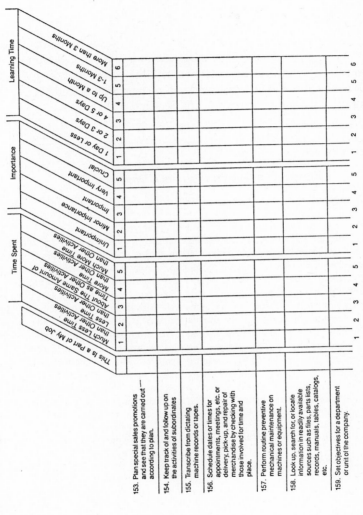

Source: M. D. Dunnette, L. H. Hough, and R. L. Rosse, "Task and Job Taxonomies as a Basis for Identifying Labor Supply Sources and Evaluating Employment Qualifications," *Human Resource Planning 2* (1979), p. 1. Used for describing nonexempt level clerical, maintenance, warehousing, selling, and foreman jobs in a retail organization. Copyright by Personnel Decisions Research Institute, 1977. All rights reserved.

formance levels within the job. This information is necessary for performance evaluation. Again, the organization might elect to use one of the approaches discussed here to capture performance differences after the goals of the system are established.

Job Analysis Outcomes

The Job Description

Regardless of the information collected in a job analysis, the data is usually codified in one or more documents, most commonly a job description. A **job description** can be defined as a narrative essay that communicates information about the job. The information collected will dictate what is said about a job in the description. Two job descriptions are depicted in Exhibit 6.5.

Exhibit 6.5   *Two Job Descriptions*

Job Description from the *Dictionary of Occupational Titles*

Title: Keypunch Operator
DOT: 213582010

Operates alphabetic and numeric keypunch machine, similar in operation to electric typewriter, to transcribe data from source material onto punchcards, paper or magnetic cards, and to record accounting or statistical data for subsequent processing by automatic or electronic data processing equipment: attaches skip bar to machine and previously punched program card around machine drum to control duplication and spacing of constant data. Loads machine with decks of tabulating punchcards, paper or magnetic tape, or magnetic cards. Moves switches and depresses keys to select alphabetic or numeric punching, and transfer cards or tape through machine stations. Depresses keys to transcribe new data in prescribed sequence from source material into perforations on card, or as magnetic impulses on specified locations on tape or card. Inserts previously processed card into card gauge to verify registration or punches. Observes machine to detect faulty feeding, positioning, ejecting, duplicating, skipping, punching, or other mechanical malfunctions and notifies supervisor. Removes jammed cards, using prying knife. May tend machines that automatically sort, merge, or match punchcards into specified groups. May verify accuracy of data, using verifying machine. May perform general typing tasks.

Job Description from the Position Analysis Questionnaire

A. Title: Keypunch Operator
   DOT: 213582010

B. Duties:
   General description

Under general direction, performs clerical and/or related activities, has a non-typical schedule and/or optional apparel style, operates machines and/or equipment. To a lesser extent, performs routine and/or repetitive activities, works other work schedules.

Source: PAQ Users Manual (System II), p. 43. Copyright by PAQ Services, Inc. Purdue Research Foundation, *Layfette,* Indiana. Reprinted with permission.

The first job description in Exhibit 6.5 is taken from the *Dictionary of Occupational Titles*; the second description was established using the position analysis questionnaire. They demonstrate the difference in job descriptions that can result from different approaches to job analysis and different ways of summarizing the data.

Job Specifications

A **job specification** can be defined as the statement of the job in human terms. A job specification might note that a job requires typing at a minimum of 60 words per minute, the ability to maintain an accounting ledger, and so forth. Sometimes the specification will be more general and indicate that job incumbents ought to have 2 years of business school training or equivalent experience, for example. Sometimes the job specifications are included as part of the job description. An example of a job specification appears in Exhibit 6.6.

Performance Standards

Performance standards can be defined as the desired employee behaviors or performance outcomes. A set of performance standards, expressed in terms of performance outcomes, is presented in Exhibit 6.7. Performance standards are

---

Exhibit 6.6 *Job Description and Specification for a Personnel Manager*

Job Description

General description

Performs responsible administrative work managing personnel activities of a large state agency or institution. Work involves responsibility for the planning and administration of a personnel program which includes recruitment, examination, selection, evaluation, appointment, promotion, transfer, and recommended change of status of agency employees, and a system of communication for disseminating necessary information to workers. Works under general supervision, exercising initiative and independent judgment in the performance of assigned tasks.

Example of work performed

Participates in overall planning and policymaking to provide effective and uniform personnel services.

Communicates policy through organization levels by bulletin, meetings, and personal contact.

Interviews applicants, evaluates qualifications, classifies applications.

Recruits and screens applicants to fill vacancies and reviews applications of qualified persons.

Confers with supervisors on personnel matters, including placement problems, retention, or release of probationary employees, transfers, demotions, and dismissals of permanent employees.

Supervises administration of tests.

Initiates personnel training activities and coordinates these activities with work officials and supervisors.

Establishes effective service rating system, trains unit supervisors in making employee evaluations.

Maintains employee personnel files.

Supervises a group of employees directly and through subordinates.

Performs related work as assigned.

continued

Exhibit 6.6   continued

Job Specification

General qualification requirements

Experience and training
Should have considerable experience in personnel administration
Education
Graduation from a four-year college or university, with a major in education and personnel administration.
Knowledge, skills, and abilities
Considerable knowledge of principles and practices of personnel administration; selection and assignment of personnel, job evaluation.

Exhibit 6.7   *Performance Standards for Salesperson*

Quantity of Sales

Superior performance: $50 thousand gross/month
Above average performance: $40 to $49 thousand gross/month
Average performance: $30 to $39 thousand gross/month
Below average performance: $20 to $29 thousand gross/month
Unacceptable performance: less than $20 thousand gross/month

Sales Quality

Superior performance: 95 percent repeat business from first-time accounts
Above average performance: 90 percent repeat business from first-time accounts
Average performance: 85 percent repeat business from first-time accounts
Below average performance: 80 percent repeat business from first-time accounts
Unacceptable performance: Less than 80 percent repeat business from first-time accounts

---

important for assessing the performance of employees in their jobs, and Chapter 12 is devoted to performance assessment.

Summary

This chapter focused on the process of job analysis and the outcomes associated with job analysis. The terms job analysis, task, job, position, job evaluation, job description, and job specification were defined.

Job analysis is the process of studying jobs. While job analysis is an important activity for human resource management in general, it is particularly important to the compensation decision maker, since it serves as the cornerstone for job evaluation and performance evaluation.

There are three ways to conduct a job analysis: observing, performing the job, or asking the job incumbents what they do. Job data is usually collected by recording observations or by interviews.

Most job analysis approaches use some combination of observation and interviews. It is important to conduct a thorough and complete job analysis, and to get cooperation of others in the organization. The steps in job analysis and how to conduct an interview were discussed.

There are numerous job analysis approaches. Among these are work methods analysis, critical incidence, functional job analysis, position analysis questionnaires, job analysis questionnaires, and job inventories. The discussion focused on the utility of these for the compensation decision maker. No one standard approach to job analysis seems to collect the data necessary for a good job evaluation system and a good performance evaluation system. A custom-designed job analysis system would seem to have the most overall utility.

The major outcomes of a job analysis are a written job description, performance standards, and job specifications. The first two of these are particularly important to the compensation decision maker because they serve as inputs into job evaluation and performance evaluation, respectively.

Discussion Questions

1. Define the terms job analysis, job description, job specification, and performance standard. What is each of these used for; how are they related to each other?

2. What is a job; a task; a position?

3. Some job analysis techniques seem to be more useful for performance evaluation purposes than other techniques. Which ones are these, and why are they better?

4. Suppose a job analyst only collected information on how jobs related to each other; that is, horizontal and vertical relationships among jobs were identified. Would this data be useful in conducting a job evaluation? Why or why not?

5. Discuss the steps in conducting a job analysis.

6. Refer to the suggestions for job analysis interviewing. Why is each of these important?

References

[1] Ernest J. McCormick, "Job Information: Its Development and Application," in *ASPA Handbook of Personnel and Industrial Relations* (Washington, D.C..: Bureau of National Affairs, 1974): pp. 4-50–5-53.

[2] *Ibid*, p. 4-53.

[3] U. S. Department of Labor, Manpower Administration, *Handbook for Analyzing Jobs* (Washington, D.C.: Government Printing Office, 1972).

[4] McCormick, *Job Information*, p. 4-53.

[5] Marc J. Wallace, Jr., "Methodology, Research Practice and Progress in Personnel and Industrial Relations," *Academy of Management Review* 8, no. 1 (January 1983): pp. 6–13.

[6] For a general discussion, see Patricia C. Smith, "Behavioral Results and Organizational Effectiveness: The Problem of Criteria," in M. D. Dunnette, ed., *Handbook of Organizational and Industrial Psychology* (Chicago: Rand-McNally, 1976): pp. 745–776.

[7] Thomas H. Stone, *Understanding Personnel Management* (Hinsdale, Ill.: The Dryden Press, 1982): p. 122.

[8] Methods study evolved out of the scientific management movement, of which Frederick W. Taylor is considered to be the father. For a development of this subject and its contribution to human resources management, see: Daniel A. Wren, "The Origins of Industrial Psychology and Sociology," in Thomas H. Patten, Jr., ed., *Classics of Personnel Management* (Oak Park, Ill.: Moore Publishing, 1979): pp. 4–12.

[9] J. C. Flanagan, "The Critical Incident Technique," *Psychological Bulletin* 51 (1954): pp. 28–35.

[10] For examples of these techniques, see: H. John Bernardin and Patricia Cain Smith, "A Clarification of Some Issues Regarding the Development of Behaviorally Anchored Rating Scales (BARS)," *Journal of Applied Psychology* 66, no. 4, (1981): pp. 458–463; and Kevin R. Murphy, *et al.*, "Do Behavioral Observation Scales Measure Observation?" *Journal of Applied Psychology* 67, no. 5 (1982): pp. 562–567.

[11] Donald P. Schwab *et al.*, "Behaviorally Anchored Rating Scales: A Review of the Literature," *Personnel Psychology* 28 (1975): pp. 549–562.

[12] These are adapted from U.S. Department of Labor, Manpower Administration, *Handbook for Analyzing Jobs* (Washington, D.C.: Government Printing Office, 1972): pp. 342–343.

[13] *Ibid.*

[14] *Ibid.*

[15] U.S. Department of Labor, *Dictionary of Occupational Titles*, 4th ed. (Washington, D.C.: Government Printing Office, 1977).

[16] Ernest J. McCormick *et al.*, *Position Analysis Questionnaire* (West Lafayette, Ind.: Purdue University, 1969).

[17] *Ibid.*

[18] Ernest J. McCormick *et al.*, *PAQ: Job Analysis Manual* (Logan, Utah: PAQ Services, 1977).

[19] Ernest J. McCormick, "Job and Task Analysis," in M. D. Dunnette, ed., *Handbook of Industrial and Organizational Psychology* (Chicago: Rand-McNally, 1976): pp. 651–696.

[20] *Ibid.*, p. 688.

[21] Jerry Newman and Frank Krzystofiak, "Quantified Job Analysis: A Tool for Improving Human Resource Management Decision Making." Paper presented at the Academy of Management Meeting, Orlando, Fla., August 15, 1977.

[22] *Ibid.*

Nonquantitative

Job Evaluation

- **Chapter Outline**

- **Learning Objectives**

- **Introduction**

- **Job Evaluation and Relevant Theory**

- **An Overview of Job Evaluation**

  The Comparison Standard
  Quantitative and Nonquantitative Dimensions
  The Evolution of Job Evaluation
  Job Assessment and People Assessment
  Compensable Factors

- **The Ranking Method of Job Evaluation**

  Steps in the Job Ranking Method
  Advantages and Disadvantages of the Ranking Method
  The Whole Job Method of Job Evaluation

- **The Job Classification Method**

  Steps in the Classification Method
  Advantages and Disadvantages of the Classification Method

- **Exercises**

Learning Objectives

To learn what job evaluation is and to review the reasons for conducting job evaluation.

To learn the evolution of job evaluation.

To learn what compensable factors are and how and why they are used in job evaluation.

To learn the ranking method of job evaluation, including the steps an organization follows.

To learn the job classification method of job evaluation and the steps to follow.

To understand some of the more important advantages and disadvantages of these two approaches to job evaluation.

Introduction

Chapter 6 discussed job analysis as an important step prior to conducting a job evaluation. Chapters 7 and 8 discuss the major types of job evaluation. These two chapters also discuss the strengths and weaknesses of the various types of job evaluation, identify the steps required in conducting job evaluation, explain compensable factors, and show how to conduct a job evaluation. Job evaluation is also discussed as it relates to compensation theory.

Job Evaluation and Relevant Theory

Chapter 2 discussed equity theory and the importance of equity in motivating employees to stay with the organization. Chapter 2 argued that job evaluation is an administrative technique to maintain feelings of internal equity by assessing the relative worth of jobs. Different jobs have characteristics that require employees to make different contributions to the organization. For example, jobs differ in terms of responsibility and in terms of the skills they require. The amount of pay that different jobs should earn also differs.[1]

Job evaluation is intertwined with this concern over internal pay equity. In general, job evaluation attempts to answer the basic question: In what important ways do jobs differ, and how should those differences in jobs be reflected in the wage rates for those jobs?

An Overview of Job Evaluation

In this chapter and the next, four common types of job evaluation are discussed. Job evaluation techniques can be seen in two dimensions: what comparison standard is used to assess relative worth, and whether the technique is quantitative or nonquantitative in its approach.[2] Exhibit 7.1 presents a classification table of these two dimensions.

Exhibit 7.1   *Job Evaluation Methods Classified in Two Dimensions*

	Nonquantified	Quantified
	Quantification	
Job to job	Job ranking method	Factor comparison method
Job to predetermined standard	Job classification method	Point method

Comparison standard

The Comparison Standard

The comparison standard is based on whether the job evaluation method compares jobs to other jobs or to a predetermined standard. For example, an organization has two jobs (groundskeeper and lathe operator) and wants to determine their relative worth. First, compensable factors—criteria or standards the organization wishes to use for paying jobs—must be chosen.[3] The organization considers responsibility for equipment as the sole compensable factor. The organization might rank the two jobs in terms of which job has the most responsibility for equipment. The lathe operator job is determined to have more responsibility for equipment and would be worth more to the organization.

When jobs are compared to a predetermined standard, job classes or grades are established that carry predetermined narrative statements about the amount of responsibility for jobs that fall in that grade. For example, Grade I might be defined as including jobs that involve responsibility for equipment of up to $500 in value. Grade II might cover responsibility for equipment valued at $501 to $1,000. Grade V might encompass jobs that involve responsibility for equipment valued from $5,000 to $50,000. The job descriptions for lathe operator and groundskeeper would probably indicate that the former should be classified Grade V, and the latter as Grade I. The jobs are compared not to each other but to a preestablished grading scheme.

The distinction between job-to-job comparison and job-to-predetermined standard is highlighted in Exhibit 7.2.

Exhibit 7.2   *Comparison Standards in Job Evaluation*

Job-to-Job Comparison

Jobs	Compensable Factor
Groundskeeper Lathe operator	Responsibility for equipment

Since the lathe operator carries more responsibility for equipment, it is ranked higher.

Job-to-Predetermined Standard Comparison

Jobs	Compensable Factor
Groundskeeper Lathe operator	Predetermined scaling standard for compensable factor of responsibility for equipment
	Grade 1: $0–$500 for equipment Grade 2: $501–$1000 for equipment Grade 3: $1001–$2500 for equipment Grade 4: $2501–$5000 for equipment Grade 5: $5001–$50,000 for equipment

Since the groundskeeper uses a $400 mower, that job is classified in Grade 1. Since the lathe operator uses a $35,000 lathe, that job is classified in Grade 5.

In Exhibit 7.2, the job-to-job comparison rates the lathe operator job higher than the groundskeeper. In the job-to-predetermined standard comparison, predetermined job grades are set up. These grades vary in terms of the amount of responsibility for equipment. Since the groundskeeper job requires responsibility for equipment in the $400 range, the job is classified in Grade 1. The lathe operator job, on the other hand, has responsibility for equipment of $35,000 in value, and according to the preestablished grading scheme, is classified into Grade 5.

Quantitative and Nonquantitative Dimensions

The other dimension in which job evaluation techniques can be categorized is quantitative or nonquantitative, as illustrated in Exhibit 7.3. To continue with the example of groundskeeper and lathe operator jobs, the job ranking method is nonquantitative in that numeric values are not established—no attempt is made to distinguish how much more one job is worth relative to another, only that one is worth more than another. This nonquantitative approach is shown in the first part of Exhibit 7.3.

In the point method of job evaluation, a weighting scheme is used to assign points for each amount of a compensable factor, which are then added. The point method is shown in the second part of Exhibit 7.3.

Exhibit 7.3   *Nonquantitative and Quantitative Job Evaluation*

Nonquantitative Evaluation

Jobs	Compensable Factors
Lathe operator	Responsibility for equipment
Groundskeeper	Training time

Since the lathe operator job carries more responsibility for equipment and requires more training time, it is worth more than the groundskeeper job.

Quantitative Evaluation

Jobs	Compensable Factors
Lathe operator	Responsibility for equipment:
Groundskeeper	
	$0–$50: 10 points
	$501–$1000: 25 points
	$1001–$2500: 50 points
	$2501–$5000: 75 points
	$5001–$50,000: 100 points
	Training time:
	0–2 weeks: 5 points
	3–8 weeks: 10 points
	9–26 weeks: 15 points
	½–1½ years: 25 points
	1½–3 years: 35 points
	Greater than 3 years: 50 points

Since the lathe operator has responsibility for a $35,000 piece of equipment and the job takes over 3 years to learn, the job carries 150 points. Since the groundskeeper's job has responsibility for a $400 piece of equipment and is learned in less than 2 weeks, the job carries 15 points.

In Exhibit 7.3, two factors used to evaluate jobs are responsibility for equipment and training time. Using the quantitative approach, the employer might determine that if responsibility for equipment was in the range of $0 to $500, the job would get 10 points for that factor, and if it was between $5,000 and $50,000 the job would get 100 points. Training time points might be assigned so that if the job could be mastered in less than 2 weeks it would get 5 points, and if the job required 3 or more years of training it would carry 50 points. In the earlier example, the groundskeeper job might receive 15 points and the lathe operator job 150 points.

The point method compares the relative magnitude of differences between jobs across the compensable factors used—in this example, the lathe operator job is worth considerably more than the groundskeeper job. The point method is complex and is covered in detail in Chapter 8. It is considered a quantitative approach to job evaluation because it assigns numeric values for compensable factors.

The Evolution of Job Evaluation

Job evaluation has been traced back to the early 1900s when Frederick W. Taylor conducted a systematic study of jobs to establish piece rate pay systems for jobs. The scientific management movement gave job evaluation its first great push. Subsequently, job evaluation became part of the pay system in American industry.

Two other important factors reinforcing the use of job evaluation were the wage-price freezes during World War II and the growth of labor and management relations in general. During World War II the federal government was concerned about inflation in the economy and instituted wage and price freezes. However, employers were concerned about wage adjustments to alleviate inequities in pay that existed prior to the implementation of the freeze. The federal government permitted employers to adjust wages where the employer could demonstrate an inequity—employers were required to justify differences in jobs if they wanted to adjust wages. The administrative vehicle for adjusting pay rates was job evaluation.

The other major factor contributing to job evaluation growth is the growth of labor and management relations.[4] A labor contract between labor and management typically has a no-strike and no-lockout clause. Problems may emerge during existing contracts over how to settle **rights disputes**. Rights disputes arise over interpretation of the parties' rights under an existing contract.[5] A grievance procedure may be established to resolve these disputes. Often, one component of that grievance system is a labor and management job evaluation committee that evaluates jobs. An example of such a contract clause is presented in Exhibit 7.4. This committee is most likely to be needed when jobs change during the period of the contract and need reevaluation.

Although many labor and management situations use job evaluation to solve rights disputes under the terms of a contract, not all unions support job evaluation.[6] Sometimes labor views job evaluation as a management ploy to manipulate wages. Job evaluation may also not be consistent with the union's philosophy about wage rates. For example, some unions believe that all workers in the bargaining unit should make the same wage regardless of the work performed. Under this philosophy of equal pay for a day's work, a union is likely to be resistant to management's attempts to distinguish among jobs in terms of pay rates, and is also likely to resist job evaluation.[7] Labor unions may also be resistant to job evaluation programs if they do not see themselves as having meaningful input into the decisions that are made. Some managements may structure the job evaluation process to give the union only a rubber stamp role in the decision process. Without meaningful joint decision making, unions can be expected to resist the program.

Exhibit 7.4   *Labor-Management Contract Clause for Job Evaluation*

Article V—Job Classifications and Incentives

Section 1.   (*a*) Each job classification now in effect or hereafter established shall remain in effect, except as changed in accordance with the provisions of this Section.

(*b*) The Union at each Plant shall designate a Plant Union Job Evaluation Committee. Such Committee shall have the exclusive right to certify the existence of disputes with respect to job classifications.

(*c*) Whenever a new job shall be established or, after the effective date of the last classification or reclassification of an existing job, the requirements of such job as to training, skill, responsibility, effort and surroundings shall have been altered to the extent of a whole numerical classification of 1.0 or more, the Management shall classify or reclassify such job, as the case may be, and the new classification shall be put into effect in accordance with the procedure set forth in this Section.

(*1*) The Management shall describe and classify such job in accordance with the Manual for Job Classification of Production and Maintenance Jobs (hereinafter referred to as the Manual) a copy of which is annexed to the agreement dated April 11, 1947, between the Company and the Union, (or as hereinafter revised by agreement between the parties) and shall present such description and classification to the Plant Union Job Evaluation Committee with a copy to a designated representative of the International Union. Thereafter, the Management may put such new classification into effect and it shall continue in effect, unless it shall be changed in the manner provided in subparagraph (*c*)(*3*) of this Section. The Management and the Plant Union Job Evaluation Committee shall meet, within 30 days after the description and classification shall have been presented as hereinabove provided, to review and attempt to agree on the proposed classification of such job.

(*2*) If the Plant Union Job Evaluation Committee shall agree to such proposed new classification, it shall be established for such job.

(*3*) If the Plant Union Job Evaluation Committee does not agree to such proposed new classification such Committee may, at any time within 15 days after the meeting, give written notice to the designated representative of the Management alleging that the job is improperly classified under the provisions of the Manual. Within 7 days thereafter, such Committee and the designated representative of the Management shall prepare and sign a stipulation setting forth the factors and factor codings which are in dispute and shall send it to the Manager of Industrial Relations of the Company. The parties shall make a sincere effort to set forth in such stipulation the reasons in support of their respective positions.

If the parties shall fail to agree as provided above and a request for review or arbitration is not made within the time provided, the classification as prepared by the Management shall be deemed to have been approved.

Excerpted from "Agreement between Bethlehem Steel Company and United Steelworkers of America," April 6, 1962.

The events that led to job evaluation discussed in this section are based on specific cases of internal equity. Job evaluation is an administrative activity to determine equitable pay relationships among jobs. One recent survey found that 86 percent of the firms responding to the survey used some form of job evaluation.[8]

Job Assessment and People Assessment

Job evaluation is the process of assessing the relative worth of jobs. The selection of compensable factors is tied to differences among jobs. There is no assessment of people at this point. This may sound obvious, but confusion may occur when one is attempting to assess the requirements for a job and then confuses the job requirements with the attributes of the job incumbent.

For example, a job evaluator assesses the amount of training time a job requires. The job requires a training time of from three days to one month. The evaluator may consider the employee who works in that job who has three years of experience at the job, and assign the job a higher grade. This would be incorrect, since the employee's amount of experience has nothing to do with the value of the job. The actual experience of the employee is distinct from the normal training time that the job requires. Similarly, if the skill level of the job were being assessed, some employees might be overqualified for the job, but that is separate from the skill a given job requires.

The job evaluator must always think in terms of the average time it would take an average employee to learn the job. If the compensable factor being assessed is potential damage to equipment, for example, damage incurred in the normal course of the job should be considered. For example, a janitor has the potential to destroy the entire plant by accidentally breaking a steam line or pouring water into a main electrical circuit. However, in the normal course of the job, a reasonably diligent janitor would cause neither of these accidents. It would be more appropriate to think in terms of a reasonably diligent janitor possibly breaking a floor finishing machine ($500 value).

This chapter and the next chapter on job evaluation are concerned about determining the relative worth of jobs. The focus is on the assessment of differences in jobs. The assessment of people and how well they are performing relative to their job is covered in Chapter 12.

Compensable Factors

Several references have been made to the use of compensable factors in job evaluation. This section discusses common compensable factors and how an organization chooses compensable factors.

Common Compensable Factors   Table 7.1 lists compensable factors that an organization might choose. It is not intended to be an exhaustive or restrictive list, but it contains some of the more common factors that are used by organizations.

Some of the factors listed in Table 7.1, such as education, might suggest that one assess attributes of employees. The compensable factor actually is how much education the job requires. Organizations must be careful to express the amount of a compensable factor in a realistic way. Failure to do so can result in legal charges that the job evaluation system is biased.[9] Either undervaluing or overvaluing educational or other aspects of jobs may work for majority employees or against minority employees.[10]

Table 7.1   *Compensable Factors*

Skill

Education
Education or mental development
Education or trade knowledge
Schooling
Experience
Previous experience
Experience and training
Training time
Time required to become 80% efficient
Training required
Time required to learn trade
Time required to adapt skill
Job knowledge
Knowledge of machinery and dexterity with tools
Knowledge of materials and processes
Knowledge
Mentality
Accuracy
Ingenuity
Initiative and ingenuity
Judgment and initiative
Mental capability
Intelligence
Resourcefulness
Versatility

Job skill
Degree of skill and accuracy
Manual accuracy and quickness
Physical skill
Details
Aptitude required
Difficulty of operation
Ability to do detailed work
Social skill
Mental requirement
Mental application
Creative ability
Analytical ability
Skill requirements
Complexity of duties
Personal qualifications needed for the job
Personal requirements
Ability to make decisions
Managerial techniques
Character of supervision given
Capacity for getting along with others
Capacity for self-expression
Ability to do routine work
Office machine operation
Manual dexterity
Dexterity

Effort

Mental effort
Mental application
Mental or visual demand
Concentration
Visual application
Physical application
Physical demand
Physical or mental fatigue
Muscular or nerve strain
Fatigue due to eye strain

Fatigue
Honesty of effort
Monotony of work
Monotony and comfort
Physical requirement
Manual effort
Pressure of work
Volume of work
Attention demand

Responsibility for:

Executive responsibility
Personnel
Monetary responsibility
Commitments, property, money, or records
Company cash
Records
Confidential data

Methods
Determining company policy
Market
Contact with others
Contact with public, customers, and personnel
Goodwill and public relations

continued

Table 7.1   *continued*

Responsibility for:

Cooperation and personality	Time span of discretion
Safety of others	Spoilage of materials
Material or product	Protection of materials
Equipment or process	Equipment
Machinery and equipment	Product
Quality	Physical property
Material and equipment	Plant and services
Work of others	Cooperation and personality
Supervision of others	Dependability
Supervision exercised	Adjustability
Cost of errors	Coordination
Effect on other operations	Details to master
Necessary accuracy in checking, counting and weighing	

Working Conditions

Unavoidable hazards	Job conditions
Hazards involved	Difficulty in locating work elsewhere
Exposure to health hazard	Attendance
Exposure to accident hazard	Job stress
Occupational hazard disease	Disagreeableness
Danger—accident from machinery or equipment	Tangible surroundings
Danger—from lifting	Intangible conditions
Surroundings	Monotony
Dirtiness of working conditions	Attention to details
Environment	Out-of-town travel

Source: Adapted from Jay L. Otis and Richard H. Leukart, *Job Evaluation,* © 1984, pp. 90–91. Reprinted by permission of Prentice-Hall, Englewood Cliffs, New Jersey.

Criteria for Choosing Factors   The compensable factors that an organization should select is a complex subject.[11] The following criteria for selecting compensable factors are general; the final decision must be organization specific.

First, compensable factors ought to be acceptable to the parties involved. They must be acceptable to management, employees, and union leaders if there is a union. This constraint is crucial since the heart of job evaluation is to establish an internal pay system that is perceived as equitable. Only if the compensable factors are perceived as relevant will the job evaluation plan itself be perceived as equitable.

A second criterion for compensable factors is that they must be valid as distinguishers among jobs.[12] The compensable factors must capture important differences among jobs. This criterion is important for the job evaluation to be valid and to assure that the compensable factors satisfy legal requirements so that they are not challenged in court.[13]

Third, compensable factors must be present in all jobs. If the amount of a factor is zero in all jobs then the factor will not distinguish among those jobs.

For example, if the factor working conditions is applied to all clerical jobs and there is no difference in working conditions among those jobs, then this factor is actually irrelevant for these jobs.

Fourth, and related to the above point, jobs must vary on the factors chosen. Different jobs must possess different amounts of the compensable factor.

Fifth, the compensable factors must be measurable.[14] If physical conditions is chosen as a factor, the organization must be able to measure the differences in physical conditions within jobs. It might be applied as "length of time exposed to extreme temperatures," or "length of time exposed to noxious fumes." If the factor cannot be measured, then it will not be useful for establishing the relative worth of jobs.[15]

Sixth, compensable factors should be independent of each other. Two factors should not measure the same thing. If they do then double weight is given to the same construct. Either one alone would give the relative worth of the jobs. These six criteria should be considered when selecting compensable factors to give the organization a better opportunity of ending up with a meaningful job evaluation system.

Who Selects Compensable Factors Intimately related to the criteria for selecting compensable factors is the issue of who selects the compensable factors. Since the job evaluation plan will ultimately result in a hierarchy of jobs within the organization, management will want to have a say as to what criteria jobs will be compensated for. In addition, first line managers and rank and file employees should be included in the factor selection process. There are sound reasons for including both of these groups of people.

Supervisors have an intimate understanding of the jobs they supervise, and will probably have insight into the important ways that these jobs differ. Supervisors are a potentially rich source from which to identify useful compensable factors.

Employees are the ones who perform the jobs, and have feelings about equitable pay among jobs. It makes sense to determine what employees see as the important criteria that distinguish among jobs. In spite of the apparent theoretical importance in considering employee views in the selection of compensable factors, it is seldom done. One recent study found that only 7.5 percent of all job evaluation plans in existence within the surveyed companies involved employee committees.[16]

Finally, if a labor union has representational rights over the jobs that are to be evaluated, union representatives should also be included in the factor selection process. Since the determination of wages for jobs will rest in part upon the result of the evaluation, management will by law need to negotiate with the union over the compensable factors.

The Ranking Method of Job Evaluation

The ranking method of job evaluation is the simplest of the job evaluation approaches.[17] It is nonquantitative, and compares one job to another. The steps in conducting job evaluation with the ranking method are summarized in Exhibit 7.5.

Steps in the Job Ranking Method

Obtain Job Information   As with all job evaluation methods, the first step is to obtain job information. As noted in Chapter 6, this involves conducting a job analysis and then writing up the results of the job analysis into a job description.

Select Raters   The raters in every job evaluation program are the job evaluation committee. Those who serve on the committee should satisfy the following criteria. First, they should be familiar with the jobs in question. As the ranking exercise at the end of this chapter shows, it is difficult to evaluate jobs if one does not know what the job is about. Good job descriptions help solve this problem.

   Second, committee members should be selected from management and from the employees whose jobs are being evaluated. Employees should feel that the important job attributes are included and that they have input into the evaluation process.

Exhibit 7.5   *Steps in the Job Ranking Method*

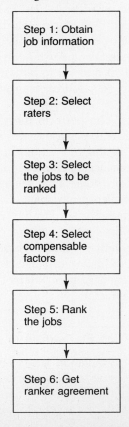

Step 1: Obtain job information

Step 2: Select raters

Step 3: Select the jobs to be ranked

Step 4: Select compensable factors

Step 5: Rank the jobs

Step 6: Get ranker agreement

Third, raters should be trained in the concept and objectives of job evaluation. They should have a good grasp of what job evaluation is about and what they will be doing in their committee work.

Often compensation decision makers rely on outside consultants to assist in the implementation of a job evaluation program. One study found that this is done about 55 percent of the time.[18] The use of outside consultants does not negate the importance of having managers and employees involved in the job evaluation committee. Reliance on outside consultants places even greater importance on the need for the organization to assure that managers and employees know the system and how it works. Management needs to be sure that the consultants' program is understood.

Select the Jobs to Be Ranked   Several items must be considered in selecting the jobs to be ranked. First, because the job ranking method can be difficult to work with if there is a large number of jobs, it may be useful to conduct ranking within departments. This method sometimes is called the **departmental order of importance method.**[19] Conducting rankings within departments is similar to evaluating by job cluster (by job families). A **job cluster** can be thought of as a set of jobs that are linked together by administrative unit, by technology, or by custom.[20] For example, within a factory the jobs of lathe operator, machine attendant, stock handler, and maintenance mechanic may all be located within one department and be considered a job cluster. Within a hospital, the jobs of nurse, nurse's aide, orderly, and housekeeping aide may all be linked together by geographic proximity (a hospital wing), even though several of these jobs report to different functional units: housekeeping aide to the housekeeping department, orderly to the admissions department, and so on. These jobs may all be considered part of one group or cluster for wage determination purposes.

If a subset of jobs is ranked then there is the problem of getting an overall ranking for all jobs. This can be done in one of two ways. The first approach is to simply ignore inter-job family relative worth. This is often done and is one reason for the fact that some organizations have more than one job evaluation system.[21] There may be an evaluation system for each job family within the organization. There is no problem with this so long as job families are anchored to different labor markets—job pricing is carried out within job families.

A different approach is needed if the organization wishes to integrate the departmental rankings and develop an overall ranking scheme. In this case it may be necessary to conduct a second ranking among dissimilar jobs across organizational units to find out the relative value of those jobs.

Select Compensable Factors   The committee members must now determine the criteria upon which the relative worth of jobs will be based. In the ranking method, only one or two compensable factors are usually chosen. The evaluation process becomes unwieldy if there are too many factors in the ranking method. Once the factors are chosen the committee must then decide how to measure each of them. If responsibility is the compensable factor, it must be defined so that all members know what responsibility means as a compensable factor. Responsibility could be defined as the dollar cost of errors in workmanship, dollar value of equipment used on the job, supervision of others, or some other way. It is probably less important how the factor is defined than it is that committee members agree and apply the same definition consistently. If the committee does not agree and apply the same definition across jobs, it is unlikely that they will get the same relative ranking for the jobs.

Rank the Jobs   There are numerous techniques to rank the jobs. Two of the most common are the deck of cards method and the paired comparison method. In the deck of cards method, the ranker starts with the job title of each of the jobs to be ranked on a separate card. The ranker then goes through the entire deck to identify the most highly ranked job. This card is set aside, and the balance of the deck is gone through a second time until the next highest ranked job is identified. This card is then set aside and the deck is gone through again. This process continues until the original deck is exhausted, and should give the ranker the relative ordering of the jobs.

The paired comparison method of ranking is probably the most commonly used approach. In this method the ranker compares each job to all other jobs. One way to do this is with a comparison table, such as the one in Table 7.2.

To use the paired comparison method as shown in Table 7.2, the ranker compares a job title from column one with each job title in each column. If the job is worth more than a job in the column, an X is made in the cell. If the job is worth less than a job in the column, the cell is left blank. This process is continued for each job in the first column. After all of the jobs have been compared to all other jobs, the evaluator adds up the Xs for each job across the row. The total number of Xs for a job will establish its worth relative to other jobs. In Table 7.2, the mailroom clerk job is worth the least, and the data processing manager job is worth the most.

Get Rater Agreement   After the committee members have conducted independent assessments of the jobs, they should discuss their rankings and seek agreement on the overall relative rankings.[22] If members of the committee disagree on the relative rankings, discussion will reveal different perceptions of the job or different applications of the compensable factors. If discussion does not resolve the discrepancy, one approach is to average the rankings of the committee members. Unless there is extreme disagreement on one or more jobs, this approach should provide a relative ranking of jobs.

Advantages and Disadvantages of the Ranking Method

The ranking method is the simplest of the job evaluation methods. This simplicity is one of the major advantages of the technique. The ranking method is

Table 7.2   Paired Comparison Ranking Table

Columns / Rows	Mailroom Clerk	Data Processing Manager	Data Entry Clerk	Executive Secretary	Computer Operator	Systems Analyst	Control Clerk	Programmer	File Clerk	Assistant Manager	Total
Mailroom Clerk	-										
Data Processing Manager	X	-	X	X	X	X	X	X	X	X	9
Data Entry Clerk	X		-						X		2
Executive Secretary	X		X	-	X		X	X	X		6
Computer Operator	X		X		-		X		X		4
Systems Analyst	X		X	X	X	-	X	X	X		7
Control Clerk	X		X				-		X		3
Programmer	X		X		X		X	-	X		5
File Clerk	X								-		1
Assistant Manager	X		X	X	X	X	X	X	X	-	8

Place X in box where job in row has more responsibility than job in column.

also the fastest method to implement because of its simplicity, and requires very little time to develop a committee, define factors, and rank the jobs. It is also without a doubt the least costly method in terms of staff time and involvement.

In spite of these advantages, there are numerous disadvantages to the ranking method. First, if there are large numbers of jobs involved it can be extremely difficult to compare all jobs to each other. For example, 15 comparisons need to be made if there are 6 jobs, whereas 66 comparisons need to be made if there are 12 jobs.[23] As a result, the method is limited to smaller organizations, or organizations in which smaller numbers of jobs are ranked in job families.

A second disadvantage is that because only a few compensable factors are chosen, the method may not capture important differences among jobs. Third, since the method does not require careful specification of the factors and careful documentation of the procedures used, it can appear to be arbitrary to those not involved in the original evaluation process. Finally, and perhaps most importantly, the ranking method does not allow one to determine how much more one job is worth than another. While one might know that job L is more valuable than job C, the magnitude of the differences between these jobs is not known.

The Whole Job Method of Job Evaluation

The whole job method of job evaluation is a special case of the ranking method. In this case the compensable factor is very loosely defined. For example, evaluators may be asked to rank the jobs in terms of their importance to the organization, or in terms of their value to the organization. In this situation committee members are asked to consider the job as a *whole* and to rank the jobs, all things considered, in terms of their importance to the organization.

One obvious difficulty with this method is that it is possible for different committee members to conceive of different standards (operational measures of the compensable factors) for importance, or for value. If this is the case, then different members will very likely arrive at different relative rankings for the jobs. On the other hand, if committee members have a shared *norm* or value system about what is important then this may not happen.

The whole job method is most useful where there are very few jobs and gross differences between jobs in terms of content. One example is a small production plant where there are skilled machine operator jobs, unskilled operator jobs, and attendant jobs. The whole job method yielded these three job groups and there was no attempt to distinguish between them in content. The whole job method seemed to be appropriate in this case since both management and the employees were satisfied with the job rankings. However, the system would likely have been unsuccessful had, for example, skilled operators perceived important differences in job content among the various skilled jobs.

The Job Classification Method

The job classification method is another nonquantitative job evaluation technique that compares the job to a predetermined standard.[24] The job classification method establishes broad job grades, and based on the descriptions of those grades, jobs are slotted into them. This approach is like a ladder: each rung represents the base of a grade (the space between one rung and another is the grade range), and jobs must then be slotted onto one rung only. This is one of the more popular job evaluation methods and is used by the federal government for assigning civil service jobs to pay grades.

Steps in the Classification Method

The steps for implementing this method are discussed in this section. The steps are summarized in Exhibit 7.6.

Exhibit 7.6   *Steps in the Job Classification Method*

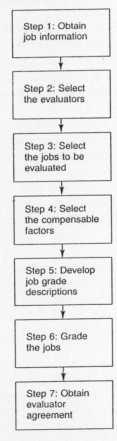

Obtain Job Data   The first step in using the classification method is to obtain job data through a job analysis and job descriptions. As usual, this data should be collected and documented with an eye toward the compensable factors in jobs that either can be made explicit or can be inferred from the job.

Select the Evaluators   The job evaluation committee needs to be selected, as discussed earlier.

Select the Jobs to Be Evaluated   The jobs that are to be included in the job evaluation program are normally apparent. The determination of jobs will have been decided by management and reflected in the instructions given to the job evaluation committee. The job evaluation committee at this point must decide whether the jobs will be treated as one family of jobs or if they will be broken down into narrower job families. This decision must be made to facilitate step five of the procedure, developing job grade descriptions. There may be enough diversity among the jobs to be evaluated that grade descriptions could be expressed in the language of the job or occupational family.

Exhibit 7.7 presents both a general and occupational-specific factor degree description from the federal government's job evaluation plan.

Exhibit 7.7 shows the primary description for the first two degrees of the factor "knowledge required by the job." Exhibit 7.7 also shows the same two degrees for that same factor worded for the occupation of mail and file clerks.

This concern over expressing compensable factors in job family-specific language is important only if the organization wishes to use one job grade system for all jobs.

When job evaluation is conducted across job families, the job grade structure encompasses several job families. An example of combining jobs across families into one classification system appears in Table 7.3.

In Table 7.3 a fire chief and director of nursing both fall within Grade 20, while fire captain, ward director, and administrative assistant are in Grade 19.

If the decision is made to keep job families separate, separate job grading systems are made for each job family, which means multiple job evaluation systems within the organization.

Select Compensable Factors   The job evaluation committee must decide which factors are to be used. It is possible to use one or many factors in the classification method. The more factors that are utilized, the more lengthy each grade description will be. The compensable factors should be clearly defined and each factor necessary for each grade.

Develop Job Grade Descriptions   Once the compensable factors are known it is important to attach a grade level to each amount of a compensable factor for grading purposes. For example, responsibility for equipment valued at from $500 to $2,000 may cause a job to be graded to Grade III. The requirement to know company procedures may require the job to be graded to Grade III also. If only one or the other of these requirements is necessary for a Grade III

Exhibit 7.7   *General (Primary) and Occupational-Specific*
Factor Degree Descriptions

Primary[a]

Factor 1 measures the nature and extent of information or facts which the worker must understand to do acceptable work (steps, procedures, practices, rules, policies, theory, principles, and concepts) and the nature and extent of skills/abilities necessary to apply these knowledges.

Degree A

Knowledge of simple, routinized, or repetitive tasks, processes, or operations which typically includes following step-by-step instructions; operating simple equipment (e.g., date stampers and mailing machines) or equipment which operates repetitively (e.g., reproduction machines); or equivalent knowledge.

Degree B

Knowledge of basic or commonly used rules, procedures, or operations which typically require some previous training or experience; basic knowledge of keyboard or switchboard equipment; or equivalent knowledge.

Occupational Specific: Mail and File Grade-Level Standard[b]

This series grade-level standard shows the application of the Primary Grade-Level Standard to the Mail and File Series. It describes degrees of factors typically found in the mail and file occupation. There may be some positions, however, which do not fall into the typical pattern.

Knowledge Required by the Job

Degree A

Knowledge of filing or sorting in alphabetical, numerical, chronological, or other logical sequence. Skill in operating simple equipment such as date or time stampers or equipment which operates repetitively such as copy machines and power mail openers.

Degree B

In addition to knowledges described at Degree A, positions at Degree B of this factor require knowledge of functions or work flow of operating units; knowledge of classified categories and security precautions or regulations; extensive knowledge of modes of transportation and related schedules; extensive information concerning postal regulations; or similar knowledges.

[a] Primary factor degree descriptions are from C.H. Anderson and D.B. Corts, *Development of a Framework for a Factor Ranking Benchmark System of Job Evaluation,* U.S. Civil Service Commission, December, 1973, p. 77.
[b] U.S. Civil Service Commission, *Report of Project to Develop, Test and Evaluate an Improved Approach to the Evaluation of Non-Supervisory Positions at GS1 through GS15;* July, 1974, p. 122.

Table 7.3   *An Example of Job Grade across Job Families*

		Job Families	
Grade	Fire Department	Nursing	Secretarial
20	Fire chief	Director of nursing	–
19	Fire captain	Ward director	Administrative assistant
18	–	–	Legal secretary
17	–	Registered nurse	Department secretary

slotting, and if the two in combination do not qualify a job to be moved to a higher grade, then this must be stated explicitly. Thus, consistent with the example, the Grade III grade description might read in part: "Jobs that require responsibility for $500 to $2,000 of equipment or which require knowledge of company procedures . . . are assigned to this grade."

A second approach to the grading scheme in the classification method is to use **grading rules.** In this approach a series of grading rules is established, based on the compensable factors, that results in a job being assigned to only one grade. The exercise at the end of this chapter uses grading rules. Whether actual job grade descriptions are written or grading rules are written, both are predicated on the same compensable factors and should yield identical results.

It is not an easy task to write clear grade descriptions that are mutually exclusive and collectively exhaustive of all the combinations of compensable factors, as the classification exercise at the end of this chapter shows. It is partly because of this difficulty of writing grade descriptions that grading rules are developed. However, it is also difficult to write grading rules that are readily interpretable by individuals not involved in their development. New employees involved in grading should be well trained in how the job evaluation scheme was developed, what each grading rule means, and how it was arrived at.

Grade the Jobs In this step committee members grade the jobs to be evaluated. It is recommended that individual members initially conduct independent evaluations. Part of the reason for this is to determine if the grade descriptions or grade rules are sufficiently clear to assure accurate classification of jobs.

Obtain Agreement among Evaluators Evaluators may not agree on the grade to which a job should be assigned. The grades or grading rules may not be clear. It is also possible that important compensable factors were omitted, or that the process does not yield distinctions among jobs that are known to exist. Rater agreement serves to check on the validity of the job classification approach. Finally, if there is not major disagreement over the grade assignment, one way to resolve any discrepancies is to allocate the job to the grade most commonly assigned by the evaluation committee members.

Advantages and Disadvantages of the Classification Method

Probably the greatest advantage of the classification approach to job evaluation is that it causes both managers and employees within the organization to think in terms of job groupings. A hierarchy of jobs is considered as soon as the method is introduced to the organization. A second advantage of the classification method is that often jobs are graded even if some other more elaborate and costly method of job evaluation is initially used. For example, if the point method is used and jobs carry point values of between 400 and 1,000 points, the organization may assign jobs of point values 400 to 460 to Grade I, jobs with point values of 461 to 520 to Grade II, and so on. It is, therefore, argued that one can skip all of the steps involved in developing a point system and just work directly with the job classification method.

There are two major criticisms of the classification method. First, job grades tend to combine factors in ways that are not readily apparent based on reading the grade description. It may appear that a job fits into more than one grade. This typically happens because the amount of a factor required in a job to qualify for a particular grade may not be clear in the grade description. A second related disadvantage of the classification method is that it is extremely time-consuming and difficult to construct clear grade descriptions. Some organizations deal with this problem by constructing grading rules instead of grade descriptions. A grading rule system specifies the grade value a job will carry for having certain amounts of a compensable factor.

In spite of these disadvantages, the job classification method is very popular. It is used by the federal government in its job evaluation system for civil service employees. It is also the most common method used by state and local governments.[25]

Summary

This chapter has examined two job evaluation methods: the ranking method and the job classification method. Both are nonquantitative. The ranking method compares one job to another, while the job classification method compares jobs to a predetermined standard.

The concept of compensable factors was discussed. Compensable factors should be chosen to reflect what management, employees, and labor leaders want as distinguishing characteristics between jobs. Examples of compensable factors were presented. Finally, this chapter discussed the steps to use in developing the ranking and classification method, discussed strengths and weaknesses of each, and cautioned the compensation decision maker to not confuse jobs with people in the evaluation process.

Discussion Questions

1. Identify the steps in conducting both the ranking and job classification methods of job evaluation.

2. Why is it important to have employees or their representatives involved in the job evaluation process?

3. Discuss the relative advantages and disadvantages of the ranking and classification methods.

4. Distinguish between job assessment and people assessment as it was discussed in this chapter. Why is this distinction important?

5. Develop three operational measures for each of the following compensable factors: (a) working conditions, (b) skill level, (c) responsibility.

Exercises

1. Using one of the techniques identified in this chapter, use the ranking method to establish the relative worth of the following jobs:

Floor Finisher: Operates 19-inch floor scrubbing machine. Uses various chemicals to remove old finishes from floors and to clean carpets. Must have ability to examine old finishes, identify their type, and mix chemical solutions to desired strength so as not to ruin floor surfaces when removing old finishes. Must be able to identify various types of terrazzo and tile flooring composition and use appropriate cleaning agents. Must know several types of polymeric floor finishes and appropriate application to floor surfaces. Uses mops and buckets to clean up residue from stripping floor and to apply new finishes.

Checkout Aide: Cleans patient's room after the patient checks out of the hospital. Must know procedures for properly cleaning patient room. Must know procedures for stripping off old linen, cleaning bed frame, and remaking patient bed. Must coordinate cleaning with check-in desk so that rooms are ready for next scheduled patient. Must be able to use routine germicidal products to ensure safe patient environment.

Housekeeping Aide: Must know procedures and germicidal products for cleaning patient rooms. Works on a routine schedule established by Department Supervisor.

Projects Aide: Major job duties are to engage in nonroutine labor tasks within hospital. Incumbent must be capable of working under general supervision. Typical projects are: move furniture, clean up nonrecurring messes (e.g. water puddle due to broken water pipe), move equipment.

Flatiron Attendant: Works at finishing end of flatiron in hospital laundry. As pressed sheets and other flat linen emerge from flatiron, folds linen and places on laundry cart. Pushes full carts to linen wareroom.

Washer/Extractor Operator: Operates commercial washers of up to 3,000-pound capacity, and extractors of up to 1,000-pound capacity. Must know how to load and unload washer and extractor. Centrifugal force extractor requires judgment in loading so that loads are not out of balance, thereby causing damage to equipment or hazards to employees. Must know appropriate washing formulas to assure that linens are clean. Must know special procedures for assuring that difficult-to-clean stains are handled so as to salvage the linens. Oversees work of Assistant Washer/Extractor Operator.

2. From the job descriptions below, extract the basic abilities required and use the job classification method to evaluate the jobs. The basic abilities system to be used as the basis for the job classification follows the job descriptions.

Job Descriptions

Mail Clerk: Sorts mail and runs postage meter. Takes mail to post office. Picks up supplies from supply houses. Picks up and delivers mail within the office. Takes photostats to photographer. Drives mail truck. Reports to Mailroom Supervisor.

IBM Clerk: Operates IBM machines to perform tabulating, sorting, bookkeeping, and reproducing functions. Wires control panels from diagrammed instructions. Performs miscellaneous clerical duties. Reports to Data Processing Supervisor.

Keypunch Operator: Operates keypunch to record written and typed information on IBM cards. Verifies work of other keypunch operators. Reports to Data Processing Supervisor.

File Clerk: Sorts, arranges, and files documents and correspondence. Finds and pulls needed information and documents from files. Picks up and delivers filing from and to other departments. Reports to Department Secretary.

Clerk-Typist: Types, files, and performs miscellaneous clerical duties. Reports to Department Secretary.

Advertising Manager: Meets salespersons and advertising solicitors. Escorts visitors through office. Composes, edits, and prepares layout for copy. Assists in preparing newspaper, radio, and magazine advertising. Acts as chairman of annual supervisors' meeting. Prepares weekly bulletin for supervisors. Answers correspondence. Composes letters and ads for agents. Supervises department in the absence of Department Head. Formulates advertising policy. Meets with advertising agency representatives. Attends policymaking meetings. Reports to Marketing Department Head.

Assistant Purchasing Agent: Supervises supply and service department. Keeps inventory of supplies. Processes orders from departments. Orders office supplies. Provides for service calls from suppliers of office equipment. Supervises mailroom. Reports to Purchasing Agent.

Secretary: Takes and transcribes dictation on confidential matters. Sets up and maintains necessary files and records. Relieves superior of minor administrative details such as reports and requisition. Makes appointments. Meets and directs callers. Answers routine correspondence. Reports to Department Manager/Head.

Grading Rules Used in the Basic Abilities System

1. Classifications that require a basic skill or knowledge that can be acquired in only three to six months shall originally be graded to salary grade III, while classifications that require a basic skill or knowledge that takes a year or more to acquire shall originally be graded to salary grade V.

2. Classifications that do not require the ability to exercise independent judgment shall be moved up one salary grade if in addition to basic skills or knowledge they require one of the following:

    a. Knowledge of department or company procedures.

    b. Ability to work under unpleasant conditions.

    c. Ability to act as a group leader directing two to four employees.

    d. Ability to get along with people and meet people.

3. Classifications that do not require the ability to exercise independent judgment shall be moved up two salary grades if in addition to basic skills and knowledge they require one of the following:

    a. Knowledge of company procedures and products.

    b. Ability to work under hazardous conditions.

    c. Ability to organize and direct the work of four or more employees.

4. Classifications that because of some combination of grading rules 1, 2, and 3 are in salary grade V shall be moved up two salary grades to grade VII, whenever the requirement to exercise independent judgment is added. No job classification shall be graded to VII or above unless it requires the ability to exercise independent judgment and no classifications in the first six salary grades can possess this requirement.

5. Classifications that are in salary grade VII, because of rule 4, shall be moved up one salary grade if in addition to basic skills or knowledge and independent judgment they require one of the following:

    a. Knowledge of company procedures and products.

    b. Ability to work under hazardous conditions.

    c. Ability to plan, organize, and direct the work of others.

    d. Ability to create or design company procedures or products.

6. Supervisory classifications must be graded at least one salary grade above the majority of the classifications supervised. For purposes of this rule, the lead worker who is ordinarily the senior member of a group of three to five workers is not considered a supervisor. With this elimination, the three supervisory classifications are:

    a. Group Leaders, who direct the work of from two to four employees engaged in the same type of work as their own.

    b. Group Supervisors, who organize and direct the work of from four to eleven employees engaged in the same general type of work.

    c. The Supervisors, Department Heads, and Assistant Department Heads, who plan the work of other employees as well as organize and direct it. All employees in this group must exercise independent judgment.

As a result of the operation of rules 2 through 5, group leaders will commonly be graded one grade above the employees supervised, and higher supervisory classes two or more grades above the employees supervised. Rule 6 has an independent effect only in those cases where the condition that it states is not already met as a result of rules 2 through 5.

Source: Ralph W. Ellis, *The Basic Abilities System of Job Evaluation* (Madison, Wis.: University of Wisconsin, Bureau of Business Research and Service, 1951).

3. Using the grading rules from problem 2, write grade descriptions that reflect the compensable factors. Hint: you might want to draw a decision tree to reflect all of the branches in the decision process for moving a job to a particular grade.

References

[1] Richard I. Henderson and Kitty L. Clark, *Job Pay for Job Worth: Designing and Managing an Equitable Job Class and Pay System* (Atlanta, Ga.: Business Publications Division, College of Business Administration, Georgia State University, 1981).

[2] N. G. Dertien, "The Accuracy of Job Evaluation Plans," *Personnel Journal* 60 (July 1981): pp. 566–570.

[3] Herbert G. Heneman III *et al., Personnel/Human Resource Management*, rev. ed. (Homewood, Ill.: Irwin, 1983): p. 392.

[4] John Zalusky, "Job Evaluation: An Uneven World," *American Federationist* 88 (April 1981): pp. 11–20.

[5] For a discussion of the distinction between rights arbitration and interest arbitration see: John A. Fossum, *Labor Relations Development, Structure, Process*, rev. ed. (Dallas: Business Publications, 1982): p. 387.

[6] H. D. Janes, "Union Views on Job Evaluation: 1971–1978," *Personnel Journal* 58 (February 1979): pp. 80–85.

[7] Thomas A. Mahoney, *Compensation and Reward Perspectives* (Homewood, Ill.: Irwin, 1979): p. 169.

[8] Sara Rynes, B. Rosen, T. Mahoney, "Comparable Worth: Summary Report of Survey," paper presented to the American Compensation Association, 1983: p. 1.

[9] Elaine Wegener, "Does Competitive Pay Discriminate?" *Personnel Administrator* 25 (May 1980): pp. 38–43.

[10] For a discussion of potential sex bias in undervaluing compensable factors and statistical approaches to adjust for this bias see: Donald J. Treiman and Heidi I. Hartmann, eds., *Women, Work, and Wages: Equal Pay for Jobs of Equal Value* (Washington, D.C.: National Academy Press, 1981): pp. 87–89; David J. Tomsen, "Eliminating Pay Discrimination Caused by Job Evaluation," *Personnel* 55 (1978): pp. 11–22.

[11] E. Jaques, "Taking Time Seriously in Evaluating Jobs," *Harvard Business Review* 57 (1979): pp. 124–32.

[12] J. A. Lee and J. L. Mendoza, "Comparison of Techniques Which Test for Job Differences," *Personnel Psychology* 34 (Winter 1981): pp. 731–758.

[13] The analogy to selection settings is inevitable. We know of no cases challenging the validity (or job relatedness) of compensable factors in a compensation setting. However, for a review of the problem in selection settings see: Griggs v. Duke Power Co. (401 U.S. 424, 3FEP 175, 1971) for a case dealing with educational requirements, and Weeks v. Southern Bell Telephone & Telegraph Co. (408 F.2d 228, 1 FEP 656, 5th Cir. 1969) for a case dealing with weight lifting requirements.

[14] J. T. Brinks, "The Comparable Worth Issue: A Salary Administration Bombshell," *Personnel Administrator* 26 (November 1981): pp. 37–40.

[15] K. E. Foster, "Measuring Overlooked Factors in Relative Job and Pay," *Compensation Review* 15, no.1, pp. 44–55.

[16] Rynes, *Comparable Worth*, p. 3.

[17] J. D. Bexson, "A System for Job Ranking," *Personnel Management and Methods* 30 (March 1964): pp. 28–29, 38.

[18] Rynes, *Comparable Worth*, p. 3.

[19] J. S. McCleod, "Dual Job Evaluation Systems: EEO Hazard," *EEO Today* 6 (1979): pp. 45–48.

[20] John T. Dunlop, "The Task of Contemporary Wage Theory," in *New Concepts in Wage Determination*, George W. Taylor and Frank C. Pierson, eds. (New York: McGraw-Hill, 1957): pp. 127–139.

[21] Rynes, *Comparable Worth*, p. 3.

[22] R. D. Arvey, *et al.*, "Detecting Job Differences: A Monte Carlo Study," *Personnel Psychology* 34 (Winter 1981): pp. 709–730.

[23] The general formula for determining how many comparisons must be made is $[N(N - 1)] \div 2$, where N is equal to the number of jobs to be compared or ranked.

[24] Robert B. Pursell, "R&D Job Evaluation and Compensation," *Compensation Review*, 2nd quarter, 1972, pp. 21–31.

[25] Philip M. Oliver, "Modernizing a State Job Evaluation Plan," *Public Personnel Management*, (May/June 1976): pp. 168–173.

8

Quantitative

Job Evaluation

· **Learning Objectives**

· **Introduction**

· **The Theoretical Basis of Job Evaluation**

· **Factor Comparison Method of Job Evaluation**

Steps in the Factor Comparison Method
Advantages and Disadvantages of the Factor Comparison Method

· **The Point Method of Job Evaluation**

Steps in the Point Method
Advantages and Disadvantages of the Point Method

· **Other Job Evaluation Techniques**

Single Factor Job Evaluation Methods
Employee Attribute Techniques
Maturity Curves
The Hay Guide Chart Profile Method
Direct Market Method
Position Analysis Questionnaire

· **Exercises**

Learning Objectives

To review the theoretical reasons for conducting job evaluation.
To learn the factor comparison method of job evaluation and the steps used by
organizations to implement the method.
To learn the major advantages and disadvantages of the factor comparison method
of job evaluation.
To learn the point method of job evaluation including the steps to follow in
implementing the method.
To learn the major advantages and disadvantages of the point method of job
evaluation.
To compare other job evaluation methods used by organizations.

Introduction

Chapter 7 reviewed nonquantitative job evaluation methods. In this chapter
two quantitative methods of job evaluation are discussed: the factor comparison method and the point method. These methods are called quantitative because they assign specific point values to jobs based on the compensable factors utilized.

The objectives of this chapter are to explain these two quantitative job
evaluation methods, review the steps involved in conducting each method,
review the strengths and weaknesses of each method, and briefly discuss other
quantitative approaches to job evaluation. By the end of this chapter the reader
should be able to design a job evaluation program using the content of this
chapter and Chapter 7.

The Theoretical Basis of Job Evaluation

Job evaluation can be used to establish internal equity in pay rates among jobs
within the organization. It does this by establishing the relative worth of jobs to
the firm. Relative worth is determined by comparing jobs on one or more
compensable factors. Compensable factors normally measure worker inputs
into the job (different jobs require different amounts of skill, effort, responsibility, and so forth). These different job requirements should be rewarded with
different rates of pay if people are to feel equitably treated with respect to one
another within the organization.

Nonquantitative methods of job evaluation, as discussed in Chapter 7,
attempt to establish a relative ordering of jobs (job X is worth more than job
L). Quantitative methods of job evaluation attempt to establish how much
more one job is worth than another on a continuum (scaling system). Quantitative approaches attempt to refine the job evaluation process. Whether or not
quantitative approaches achieve this objective is not clear from the literature.
Some authors suggest that this is the case.[1] Others conclude the opposite.[2]

About the safest thing that can be said for quantitative approaches over nonquantitative approaches is that they give the illusion of being more precise. This is probably one of the main reasons for the extreme popularity of quantitative methods, particularly the point method of job evaluation. Given the illusion of precision in measurement, quantitative approaches are probably more easily defended (rationalized) to both employees and managers.

Factor Comparison Method of Job Evaluation

The factor comparison method of job evaluation is a refinement of the ranking method. The method uses a process of comparing and ranking jobs to each other (the standard of comparison, therefore, is job to job). Two aspects of the process make the factor comparison system more complex than the ranking method. First, the method almost always entails a set of universal factors for defining jobs.[3] In a later section the types of universal factors used by some of the more common factor comparison methods are identified.

Second, the method begins with the assumption that key jobs, which are evaluated first, have a fair price already assigned to them. Job pricing for key jobs is therefore done before the internal relationships among all other jobs are established.[4] Other job evaluation methods price the jobs after the internal job structure is determined (after job evaluation is completed).

Steps in the Factor Comparison Method

The steps to implement the factor comparison method are summarized in Exhibit 8.1 and are discussed in this section.

Obtain Job Information   This step is the same as in other job evaluation methods, and was discussed in detail in Chapter 6 on job analysis. The only additional point that should be stressed is that often the job descriptions are written in terms of the compensable factors utilized in the job evaluation plan. Sets of compensable factors appear in Table 8.1. Because of the high degree of acceptability of these factors and their frequent use in job evaluation plans, they are sometimes referred to as *universal factors*. (Table 8.1 is provided so that the reader can see the high overlap in factors between different plans.)

The universal factors identified in Table 8.1 come from job evaluation plans established by consultants and industry trade associations over the last 60 or so years. Many of these sets of compensable factors are similar. Part of the reason for this is that some plans have borrowed from earlier plans. In the case of the Equal Pay Act factors, the U.S. Congress accepted these factors because they were common in industry.

> Most of American industry used formal, systematic job evaluation plans to establish equitable wage structures in their plants. Such systems . . . took into consideration four separate factors in determining

Exhibit 8.1   *Steps in the Factor Comparison Method of Job Evaluation*

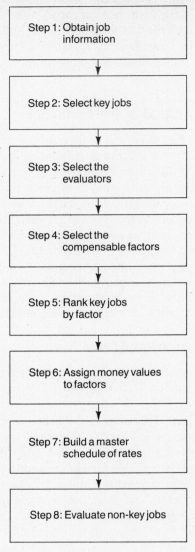

job value—skill, effort, responsibility and working conditions—and each of these four components was further systematically divided into various subcomponents.

Under a job evaluation plan, point values are assigned to each of the subcomponents of a given job, resulting in a total point figure representing a relative objective measure of the job's value.

In comparison of the rather complex job evaluation plans used by

---

Table 8.1   *Commonly Used Universal Compensable Factors*

Bass	Benge	NEMA-NMTA
Skill	Mental requirements	Skill
Responsibility	Skill requirements	Effort
Working conditions	Physical requirements	Responsibility
	Responsibility	Job conditions
	Working conditions	

FES	Hay and Purves	Equal Pay Act
Knowledge required by the position	Know-how	Skill
Supervisory controls	Problem solving	Effort
Guidelines	Accountability	Responsibility
Complexity		Working conditions
Scope and effect		
Personal contacts		
Physical demands		
Work environment		

---

industry, the definition of equal work used in the first drafts of the Equal Pay Act was criticized as unduly vague and incomplete. Industry representatives feared that as a result of the Act's definition of equal work, the Secretary of Labor would be cast in the position of second-guessing the validity of a company's job evaluation system. They repeatedly argued that the bill be amended to include an exception for job classification systems, or otherwise to incorporate the language of job evaluation into the bill.

Congress' intent, as manifested in this history, was to use these terms [skill, effort, responsibility and working conditions] to incorporate into the new federal act the well-defined and well-accepted principles of job evaluation so as to ensure that wage differentials based upon bona fide job evaluation plans would be outside the purview of the Act. . . .

Source: Data from Corning Glass Works v. Brennan, 417 U.S. 188, 9 FEP 919 (1974).

Select Key Jobs   The selection of key jobs is important in both the factor comparison method and the point method of job evaluation, discussed next. Key jobs will be priced in the market before other jobs are priced. Because of their importance, key jobs should satisfy a number of criteria. The seven criteria of key jobs are shown in Exhibit 8.2.

First, key jobs should be selected from the range of all jobs to be evaluated. The key jobs should constitute a sample of all jobs from high to low in the hierarchy of jobs. The evaluation committee can rank key jobs and then interpolate the relative position of nonkey jobs. The importance of this crite-

---

Exhibit 8.2   *Criteria for Key Jobs*

1. Key jobs should be selected from the total range of jobs to be evaluated.
2. Key jobs should be important (they should have large numbers of employees in them or contribute substantially to organizational goals).
3. Job content should be relatively stable in key jobs.
4. Key jobs should be comparable in content across organizations and industries so that a correct wage can be established.
5. Key jobs should be clearly defined in terms of job descriptions and job specifications.
6. Key jobs should be common to many firms.
7. Key jobs should be acceptable to labor and management.

---

rion for proper interpolation of nonkey job rankings is shown in step eight, evaluating nonkey jobs.

A second criterion for key jobs is that they be important. Importance can be assessed in several ways. For one, key jobs may have relatively large numbers of employees working in them, which means they contribute substantially to labor costs. A second way key jobs may be important is in terms of the contributions that their incumbents make to the organization. There may be particular concern that these jobs are paid equitably to compensate for their contributions.

A third criterion for a key job is that the content of the job should be fairly stable over time. If this criterion is present, the job evaluation system itself should remain stable, and the job is probably stable in other organizations as well.

Fourth, the wage or salary paid to key jobs should be considered to be correct by whatever criteria are used to determine correctness. Normally, the organization will have conducted a wage and salary survey for the key jobs and determined the pay rates considered correct for those jobs. This criterion also means that the same key jobs in other organizations can be surveyed to determine fair wages.

Fifth, key jobs should also have clear and well-defined job descriptions and performance standards written for them. This again is important since market rates for these jobs must be determined, and the organization must be able to clearly identify the job and its contents to compare it to a nearly identical job in other organizations.

Sixth, key jobs should be common jobs in the sense that many employers have them, which means that there will be numerous other organizations for comparison in wage surveys.

Finally, key jobs should satisfy the criterion of acceptability. Management, employees, and the labor union must believe that these are important jobs that are useful in setting the pay of other jobs in the organization. Without this criterion the parties are not likely to have much faith in the results of the job evaluation process.

Select the Evaluators   The job evaluation committee should be selected as outlined in Chapter 7.

Select the Compensable Factors   The job evaluation committee has a wide range of choices in selecting compensable factors. The committee may create factors or it might use compensable factors that have been developed by others for job evaluation systems. Table 8.1 summarized some of the more common universal factor systems.[5] The factors developed by Benge[6] are used in the factor comparison exercises at the end of this chapter.

Rank Key Jobs by Factor   The factor comparison method is a refinement of the ranking method, which can be seen at this step. The job evaluation committee members rank the key jobs on each compensable factor. Table 8.2 is an example of the ranking scheme applied to several jobs.

Each of the key jobs is ranked on one factor at a time. That is, there should be an independent ranking of jobs for each of the compensable factors. Since different factors are likely to result in different rank orderings of jobs, if the evaluator does not rank jobs on each factor independently there is a chance that the ranking on one factor will bias the ranking on another factor. Therefore, ranking of jobs within factor is important to reduce this potential bias.[7]

Once all members of the committee have ranked the jobs on each of the factors independently, the results should be compared. The committee will need to agree where there are different results among members. One method is to take the average ranking on a factor across committee members. Another approach is to take the modal ranking. Probably the best approach in case of a dispute is for the committee to first discuss the reasons for their rankings, which may explain the disparity and lead to reconciling the differences.

Disagreement on the rankings of key jobs within factors can usually be attributed to one or more of the following causes. First, the job descriptions or specifications may be ambiguously written so that it is difficult to reach con-

Table 8.2   Ranking of Key Jobs by Factor

Key Job	Mental Require- ment	Skill Require- ment	Physical Require- ment	Responsi- bility	Working Conditions
Patternmaker	1	1	7	2	9
Machinist	3	2	5	3	7
Pipe fitter	4	4	4	4	4
Poleman	8	8	2	8	2
Painter	5	5	6	6	5
Substation operator	2	3	10	1	10
Drill-press operator	6	6	9	5	6
Rammer	10	9	1	9	1
Carpenter helper	7	7	8	7	8
Laborer	9	10	3	10	3

sensus on how much of a compensable factor is present in a job. Second, the compensable factors may be written so that there is ambiguity in the application of a factor. Third, committee members may not understand the job evaluation process and what is being done. For example, committee members, through lack of good training, may confuse the credentials of job incumbents with the requirements of the job. Finally, the committee might be made up of the wrong people. For example, committee members should have some firsthand knowledge of the job—no matter how good the job descriptions or compensable factor definitions, there is no substitute for firsthand knowledge of the job and what is required of incumbents.

Assign Money Values to Factors   Once the relative rankings within all factors have been assigned, the committee must determine the wages to be paid to a job. This step involves deciding the relative contributions or weighting of compensable factors for total pay for each job. In the process of allocating the wage rate among factors, two constraints must be satisfied. First, the total wage for a job must be allocated among the factors. Table 8.3 shows allocation of wages to the jobs ranked in Table 8.2. For example, in Table 8.3 the pattern-maker job carries a wage rate of $8.40 per hour and is divided up as follows:[8] Second, the dollar amounts allocated among factors for jobs must also be consistent within factor rankings. That is, since the patternmaker job is ranked highest on mental requirements and receives $2.46 for this factor, no other job in the key job group could receive more than $2.46 for mental requirements since no other job is ranked as high. If the numeric rankings and the dollar allotments are not consistent, then the process needs to be repeated until there is internal consistency.

Table 8.3   *Wage Allocation by Factor and Job*

Key Job	Mental Require- ment	Skill Require- ment	Physical Require- ment	Responsi- bility	Working Conditions	Total Wage
Patternmaker	$2.46	$3.04	$ .94	$1.44	$ .52	$8.40
Machinist	1.50	2.26	1.28	1.34	.72	14.20
Pipe fitter	1.18	2.08	1.40	1.18	1.12	13.92
Poleman	.74	1.18	2.48	.90	1.60	6.90
Painter	1.12	2.04	1.26	1.12	1.06	6.60
Substation operator	1.80	2.10	.24	1.62	.24	5.90
Drill-press operator	1.04	1.86	.76	1.16	.98	5.80
Rammer	.34	.50	2.52	.56	1.68	5.60
Carpenter helper	.94	1.72	.88	1.04	.62	5.20
Laborer	.64	.36	2.10	.50	1.40	5.00

Each committee member should allocate the wage independently, then the committee as a whole should compare individual results to agree on the wage allotments. Failure to reach agreement will most likely be attributable to one or more of the reasons identified in step five.

Build a Master Schedule of Rates Once internal consistency has been achieved among jobs and within factor ranks, the committee can build a master schedule of rates for the key jobs. The master schedule lists the jobs as they are ranked within compensable factor and the associated monetary value assigned to the job.

Two types of master schedules can be constructed that differ only in the way the information is presented. One master schedule is portrayed in Table 8.3, which lists the jobs in the left column, the compensable factors at the top, and the wage allocated for each factor and each job in the body of the schedule.

A second way to arrange the data is portrayed in Table 8.4. Here the wage values appear in the left-hand column, the compensable factors across the top, and the jobs within the body of the schedule. In this method the jobs are entered into the schedule according to their ranking within each compensable factor. This type of master schedule shows the relative ordering of jobs within compensable factors.

Evaluate Other Jobs The master schedule of key jobs and their wage values by factor now allows the job evaluation committee to evaluate the nonkey jobs. The committee slots each of the remaining jobs into the master schedule. For example, the nonkey job of tool crib attendant can now be evaluated. The committee first decides where this job ranks relative to the other jobs on each of the compensable factors and then assigns a monetary amount for each factor. The factor monetary values total to the wage rate for that job. If the tool crib attendant job ranks lower in mental requirements than the pipefitter job but higher in mental requirements than the painter job, it might be assigned a dollar value for mental requirements of $1.15, between those of the two key jobs. This process is repeated for the tool crib attendant job for each of the compensable factors. Once the dollar value is established for each factor, then the total across all factors is the total wage for the tool crib attendant job. In Exhibit 8.3 the tool crib attendant job is evaluated using the data in the master schedule in Table 8.4. By adding up the dollar value across factors, Exhibit 8.3 shows that the job will be paid $5.09.

This slotting process continues for all nonkey jobs, and they are slotted into the master schedule as they are evaluated. Subsequent jobs are compared not only against key jobs but also against previously evaluated nonkey jobs. When all jobs have been evaluated, then all jobs will be recorded in the master schedule.

Table 8.4   *Master Schedule*

Rates	Mental Requirement	Skill Requirement	Physical Requirement	Responsibility	Working Conditions
3.04		Patternmaker			
2.52			Rammer		
2.51					
2.50					
2.49					
2.48			Poleman		
2.47					
2.46	Patternmaker				
2.26		Machinist			
2.10		Substation operator	Laborer		
2.09					
2.08		Pipefitter			
2.04		Painter			
.65					
.64	Laborer				
.63					
.62					Carpenter helper
.56				Rammer	
.55					
.54					
.53					
.52					Patternmaker
.51					
.50		Rammer		Laborer	
.36		Laborer			
.35					
.34	Rammer				
.24					Substation operator

Advantages and Disadvantages of the Factor Comparison Method

Advocates of the factor comparison method argue that a custom-made job evaluation plan results since the master schedule reflects only the jobs in the organization. It is also argued that the method is relatively easy to use once it

---

Exhibit 8.3   *Slotting in the Tool Crib Attendant Job*

Factor 1: Mental Requirements

Tool crib attendant (TCA) job demands more mental requirements than pipe fitter (ranked 4 = $1.18), demands less mental requirements than machinist (ranked 3 = $1.50). Therefore, allocate $1.48 to TCA: $1.48

Factor 2: Skill Requirements

TCA job requires more skill than rammer job (ranked 9 = $.50) and less than poleman job (ranked 8 = $1.18). Therefore, allocate $1.10 to TCA: 1.10

Factor 3: Physical Requirements

TCA job requires more physical effort than drill-press operator (ranked 9 = $.76) but less effort than carpenter's helper (ranked 8 = $.88). Therefore, allocate $.80 to TCA: .80

Factor 4: Responsibility

TCA job requires more responsibility than drill-press operator (ranked 5 = $.98) but less than pipefitter (ranked 4 = $1.12). Therefore, allocate $1.11 to TCA: 1.11

Factor 5: Working Conditions

TCA job has better working conditions than carpenter's helper (ranked 8 = $.62) but poorer conditions than patternmaker (ranked 9 = $.52). Therefore, allocate $.60 to TCA: .60

Total pay for tool crib attendant $5.09

---

is set up. That is, even relatively untrained evaluators can slot jobs into the master schedule and come up with the total wage for a job. Third, it is suggested that the relative value of a job is expressed in terms that everyone can understand.

Critics of the approach suggest that the use of dollar values can bias the assessment of jobs. Because evaluators may know the relative wage of a job, they may assign more money to a factor than the job is actually worth. A second major criticism focuses on the assumption that key jobs are available throughout the total range of jobs to be evaluated. Often key jobs are entry-level jobs, and there are no good benchmark jobs at higher levels. As a consequence, the fairness of the wage rates assigned to higher level jobs is in question. Third, while the method is relatively easy to use, it is not easily set up. Some critics assert that because of the complexity of establishing the master schedule many employees will not understand how the plan was conceived and operationalized. Employees may have little faith in an evaluation approach which they do not understand. If this happens, the purpose in conducting job evaluation in the first place is defeated. Finally, it is often argued that when actual dollars are used to assess jobs, the master schedule becomes more obsolete every time wage rates change for key jobs. As inflation or other factors cause the value of the dollar amounts in the master schedule to change, the organization will need to change the master schedule itself. This is one reason some organizations use a measurement scheme independent of dollars.[9]

The Point Method of Job Evaluation

In the point method of job evaluation the organization breaks the compensable factors down into subfactors. The organization first decides the weighting of the factors, and then, the subfactors are weighted. The number of steps or scales for each subfactor are determined and assigned points. The result is that the evaluator assigns a numeric score to a job for each factor and subfactor based on how much of that factor or subfactor appears in the job. The job's total worth is then determined by adding up the numeric scores across all factors and subfactors. This procedure, when conducted across all jobs, will result in a relative ordering of jobs based on the number of points that each job earns.

Although the point method allows an organization to develop one job evaluation scheme for all jobs in the organization, this is rarely done for several pragmatic reasons. First, it is difficult to identify one set of compensable factors that is valid for distinguishing among all jobs. For example, the use of working conditions may distinguish among shop jobs, but there is not likely to be any variance among office jobs on that compensable factor. Second, factor definitions should be written in language easily understood by the employees. Different operational definitions would be needed for the same compensable factor for different clusters of jobs. Third, different job groups are often anchored to different labor markets.[10] In an equity sense, comparisons may be less relevant between job families within an organization than to the relevant labor market for a job family.

Even with point methods of job evaluation, organizations usually have a series of job evaluation plans. For example, there may be one plan for skilled shop jobs, another plan for unskilled assembly work, and still a third plan for office and clerical employees. The discussion that follows is valid regardless of the employee population on which the point method is used.

Steps in the Point Method

The steps for implementing the point method of job evaluation are summarized in Exhibit 8.4 and are discussed below.

Obtain Job Data As with all job evaluation approaches, the jobs must be analyzed and job descriptions prepared.

Select the Evaluators The job evaluation committee must be appointed as outlined in Chapter 7.

Select Compensable Factors Types of compensable factors were identified in Chapter 7, and some of the universal factors were identified in Table 8.1.

Exhibit 8.4 *Steps in the Point Method of Job Evaluation*

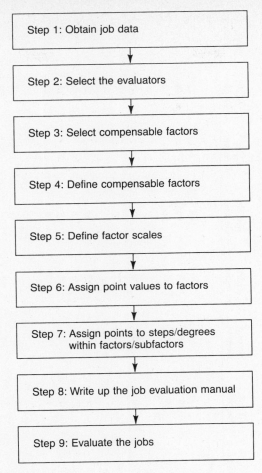

Basically, the job evaluation committee should select those factors that are viewed in its organization as most important in rewarding work and distinguishing among jobs.

Just as with the factor comparison method, the point method often uses a set of universal factors that have been developed by others. An organization can purchase a plan from a consultant, adapt an existing plan, or generate a whole new set of compensable factors. The maximum number to use is probably restricted only by complexity; after eight or nine factors are chosen, additional factors will probably be redundant.[11]

Define Compensable Factors In this critical step, once factors are chosen, there should be a clearly written definition of what each factor will mean in the context of the job evaluation plan. Table 8.5 presents several factor definitions from one point method job evaluation plan.

Table 8.5   *Factors, Degrees, and Weighted Point Values for Hourly Employees*

Factors and Subfactors	Percent	Points						Weight in Percent
		First Degree	Second Degree	Third Degree	Fourth Degree	Fifth Degree	Sixth Degree	
Skill	50%							
Education and job knowledge		12	24	36	48	60	72	12%
Experience and training		24	48	72	96	120	144	24
Initiative and ingenuity		14	28	42	56	70	84	14
Effort	15							
Physical demand		10	20	30	40	50	60	10
Mental or visual demand		5	10	15	20	25	30	5
Responsibility	20							
Equipment or tools		6	12	18	24	30	36	6
Material or product		7	14	21	28	35	42	7
Safety of others		3	6	9	12	15	18	3
Work of others		4	8	12	16	16	20	4
Job Conditions	15							
Working conditions		10	20	30	40	50	60	10
Unavoidable hazards		5	10	15	20	25	30	5
Total	100	100	200	300	400	500	600	100%

Source: Wage and Salary Administration, Second Edition by Herbert G. Zollitsch and Adolph Langsner, p. 234. Copyright © 1970 by South-Western Publishing Co.

Table 8.5 shows that the factor **skill** in the context of this job evaluation plan has three subfactor definitions: education and job knowledge; experience and training; and initiative and ingenuity. The factor **effort** is defined in this plan as physical demand and mental or visual demand. Other plans might define skill and effort differently.

The more specific a factor is the narrower the definition tends to be, and, the author finds, the easier the factor is to use. One of the important criteria as to whether factors are broadly or narrowly defined is related to the types of jobs covered. If the jobs are from a narrow job family then the factor might be correspondingly narrow. However, if the jobs are from a range of job families, then factors will need to be correspondingly broader to capture variability in all the jobs.[12]

As an example of this point, suppose an organization is defining the factor of **working conditions** for a narrow job family of shop jobs. In this case the subfactor definitions might include only noise and temperature. If the firm wishes to use one job evaluation plan to cover office workers as well, then another subfactor for working conditions might be necessary, such as visual stress (to cover staring at video terminals).

The subfactors of the compensable factor of skill in Table 8.5—education and job knowledge; experience and training; and initiative and ingenuity—now need to be operationally defined in specific terms. These three subfactors for skill might be operationally defined as in Exhibit 8.5, which shows education, for example, measured in terms of years of education needed to perform the job.

Exhibit 8.5   *Operational Definitions for Compensable Factors*

Education and Job Knowledge

This factor considers the education and job knowledge the worker must have. It is measured by the number of months or years of education needed to perform the job and the knowledge of company and department procedures needed to perform the job.

Experience and Training

This factor considers the experience and the training the worker must have. It is measured by the number of days, weeks, or months it will take a worker to become proficient in the job and by the number of weeks of on-the-job or formal technical training it will take a worker to be able to perform the job.

Initiative and Ingenuity

This factor considers the requirements of a job concerning the exercise of judgment and ingenuity in dealing with problems arising from normal work assignments. It is measured by the importance of decisions made and the ingenuity required in planning one's work. It is limited by the degree of supervision received and the instructions available.

Define Factor Scales   The committee must decide how many degrees should be on the scale for a given factor, or how many rungs on the ladder. There should be enough degrees to make meaningful distinctions among jobs. If there are too many degrees, the distinctions may be meaningless. In addition, if no job falls within the degree, then the steps are probably too narrowly defined. Table 8.6 shows one method of defining factor degrees.

Assign Point Values to Factors   The process for assigning point values to factors begins with a decision as to how many total points the job evaluation plan will have. There is no magic number of points that a plan should have. A good general rule is to have enough total points in the plan to adequately differentiate among the jobs to be evaluated. One way to arrive at this number is to take the highest paid job covered by the job evaluation plan and divide its wage rate by the wage rate of the lowest paid job. This value is then multiplied by 100.

To illustrate this formula, suppose that the annual wage for the highest paid job is $70,000 and the annual wage for the lowest paid job is $7,000. Dividing the highest wage by the lowest results in 10 ($70,000 ÷ $7,000). Multiplying this value by 100 results in a total of 1,000 points for the job evaluation plan. Under normal conditions this should be enough points to adequately distinguish among the jobs in the organization.

After determining the total number of points that will go into the job evaluation plan, the committee must determine how the points will be divided up among the factors. Points may be assigned to factors based on committee judgment or based on statistics. Statistical assignment of points is less common partly because of its complexity. One recent study found that about 40 percent of the plans used by responding organizations used statistical weighting, and the balance used judgmental weighting.[13] Nonetheless, a number of plans do use regression techniques to find which factors best predict pay rates for jobs.[14]

The assignment of points to the various factors is equivalent to weighting the factors as to what the organization considers the most important compensable factors.

Table 8.6   *Degree Definitions for Training Time Required*

Degree	Training Time
1	One month or less
2	Greater than 1 month but less than 3 months
3	At least 3 months but less than 6 months
4	At least 6 months but less than 1 year
5	One year or more

As an example, suppose that an organization has a skill factor in its plan and considers it a very important factor, weighting it 50 percent. In this case, assuming that the plan carries a maximum of 1,000 points, the skill factor is assigned 500 points. In this same fashion, points are assigned to subfactors. If skill is composed of several subfactors (such as education and job knowledge; and experience and training) then the points are divided among them. If the organization decides that the education and job knowledge subfactor should be weighted 60 percent, while experience and training should be weighted 40 percent, then these subfactors would receive 300 and 200 points respectively.

Assign Points to Degree Levels within Factors and Subfactors   Once the total number of points and the weight of a factor or subfactor are established, the next step is to assign points to the degrees within the factors and sub-factors. Exhibit 8.6 illustrates one procedure for assigning points, which is explained here. First, the highest degree of a factor is assigned the maximum points for the factor. Using the education and job knowledge subfactor in the above example, the highest degree of this subfactor is assigned 300 points. Second, the number of factor degrees is determined and 10 percent of the maximum points is assigned to the lowest degree.[15] In the above example the education and job knowledge subfactor received 300 points; the lowest degree is assigned 30 points (10 percent of the total points). Third, the lowest degree points are subtracted from the highest degree points (300 points − 30 points = 270 points), and this quantity is divided by the number of factor steps minus 1. This value plus the points assigned to the lowest degree (30, in this case) gives the number of points to be allocated to each factor degree. For example, if the lowest factor degree is 30, the highest 300, and there are seven factor degrees, the scaling is 30, 75, 120, 165, 210, 255, and 300—(300 − 30) ÷ (7 − 1) = 270 ÷ 6 = 45.

The above procedure assumes that factor degrees are equidistant from each other. Usually this procedure gives an adequate distinction between jobs. However, if the committee feels that equidistances between degrees are not satisfactory since the definitions are not equidistant from each other, points can be assigned to factor degrees in a manner that is consistent with committee judgments about differences between degrees. Finally, it should be noted that some point plans use a geometric progression in assigning points to degrees. Points may be assigned on the basis of 2, 4, 8, 16, 32, and 64. When geometric progressions are used, the committee will need to do log transformations of the point scale to assign degrees. The use of geometric progressions does not alter the relative rank of jobs, it only creates a perception of greater distances between jobs.[16]

Having developed the weighting scale for factors and degrees within factors, the committee must then check the validity of the results by evaluating several key jobs to determine if the point plan as developed results in the expected job hierarchy. This step is critical if the points were developed judgmentally.[17]

Exhibit 8.6   *Allocating Points to Factor Degrees*

Total points in job evaluation plan:	1,000 points
Weight of the factor *skill:*	50%
Points assigned to *skill:*	1,000 × .50 = 500
Weights assigned to *skill* subfactors of education and job knowledge, experience and training:	
education and job knowledge: 60%	
experience and training: 40%	
Points assigned to education and knowledge:	500 × .60 = 300

Number of degree steps for subfactor *education and knowledge:*	7
Assign 10 percent of total subfactor points to lowest step (step 1):	30 points
Highest point value (300) minus the point value for the lowest step (30) = 300 − 30:	270 points
Divide the remaining steps (6) into the remaining points = 270 ÷ 6:	45 points

Therefore: Step 1 = 30 points

Step 2 = 45 + 30 = 75 points

Step 3 = 120 points

Step 4 = 165 points

Step 5 = 210 points

Step 6 = 255 points

Step 7 = 300 points

Write Up the Job Evaluation Manual   The results of the committee's activities must now be written up in a job evaluation manual. Without a well-documented job evaluation plan, the plan will not be usable except by the original committee. Documentation of the committee's work should include the rationale for the factors chosen, the rationale for the weighting of the factors, the rationale and procedures for assigning points to factor degrees, and finally, a description of the factors, subfactors, and the degrees assigned to each.

It may be useful for committee members to remember that other employees who were not involved in development of the plan may have to use it. The documentation of the committee's work should be clear enough so that other employees could retrace the decisions with the job evaluation manual.

Evaluate the Nonkey Jobs   Once the manual is complete and all of the documentation is in place, the committee must evaluate all of the jobs. The outcome of this process will be a numeric value assigned to each job.

As with all job evaluation methods it is quite possible for the committee members to disagree on the points to be assigned for a given factor. As with other methods, the committee members should compare their independent assessments of the job and seek agreement. Discussion should resolve any discrepancies among evaluators. Significant amounts of disagreement and an inability to resolve differences suggest that the factor definitions and degree definitions are not precise enough, or that individual evaluators perceive the job in radically different ways. In either case, efforts must be made to clarify the cause of the discrepancies.

Advantages and Disadvantages of the Point Method

Probably the greatest single advantage of the point method is that once factors and degrees are defined the job evaluation plan should be highly stable over time. The compensable factors should be valid for several years unless there is radical change in the way the organization does business. Second, given the amount of work that goes into a carefully defined job evaluation manual, the plan is likely to be perceived as valid by the users, thus enhancing employee perceptions of equitable treatment. Third, because factors and degrees are carefully defined, if job descriptions are equally accurate there is likely to be high agreement within the committee in assessing jobs. A final advantage of the point method is that it provides ample data as to why a job is evaluated at a certain point amount, which can be used to explain to employees why their jobs fell where they did in the overall pay structure.

Probably the greatest disadvantage to the point plan is the time, effort, and money required to set up the plan. Implementation of the point method requires careful definition and weighting of factors, careful definition and assignment of degrees to factors, and careful development and documentation of the evaluation manual. The compensation decision maker must weigh the benefits of this approach against the costs associated with it. A second disadvantage is that the organization will typically end up building pay grades even after going through the point method. For example, an organization with a 1,000-point plan may end up with ten pay grades, each 100 points in width. If the organization is going to revert to a job classification method anyway, why should it go to the trouble and expense of developing a point method? Finally, as with the factor comparison method, the point method relies heavily upon key jobs for which valid wage rates can be determined. Unless such key jobs and correct pay rates exist, the point method may not be valid.

Other Job Evaluation Techniques

The four methods of job evaluation reviewed in this chapter and Chapter 7 are the most commonly used methods. However, there are other approaches to job evaluation.

Single Factor Job Evaluation Methods

One of the more intriguing job evaluation methods is suggested by Elliott Jaques.[18] Jaques argues that all jobs can be evaluated in terms of their **time span of discretion.** Time span of discretion to Jaques is defined as the longest period of time an employee is permitted to exercise discretion without review of his or her actions by a supervisor.

While this approach is interesting, there is not a great deal of empirical work to substantiate it. Where research has been conducted, there has been difficulty administering such a program. The principal problem seems to be getting an accurate description of the time span for any given job. Another problem is that time span of discretion amounts to a single factor method of job evaluation, and most employees would probably want to have several important job dimensions reflected in the evaluation process.

There are other single factor job evaluation methods besides Jaques's approach, such as the popular problem-solving compensable factor method.[19] This approach amounts to a ranking method using the problem-solving factor as the criterion for ranking jobs. A third single factor method is the broad-banding method, which uses decision making as the compensable factor.[20] In this method six levels or bands of decision making are identified, and jobs are slotted into one of these bands. The bands amount to job classes or grades.

Employee Attribute Techniques

The text up to this point has focused on job-oriented techniques, since it is the job and not the individual being evaluated. At the same time, there are special situations where job evaluation is conducted on attributes of employees rather than job attributes themselves. These distinctions seem to be relevant in work groups composed of professional employees, such as law firms, accounting firms, and universities. An example of an employee attribute approach to job evaluation is provided in Exhibit 8.7. For instance, in a research and development laboratory, there are many scientists, most with advanced degrees. In this setting it is not uncommon to have job and pay levels differentiated on the educational degree held rather than on the actual work performed. Distinctions may be made between scientist, junior scientist, associate scientist, and research associate. In situations where the actual work does not vary significantly, the only rationale for pay or job distinctions is that the employees expect these differences based on educational qualification.

A similar situation occurs in elementary and secondary education with schoolteachers. All schoolteachers do the same things in terms of educating

---

Exhibit 8.7   *Employee Attribute–Based Job Structure*

Position	Requirements
Senior scientist	Ph.D. and 15 plus years experience
Associate scientist	Ph.D. and 5–15 years experience
Assistant scientist	Ph.D. and 0–5 years experience
Laboratory assistant	M.S. in appropriate scientific field
Laboratory aide	B.S. in appropriate scientific field

students; however, the pay system for these educators has adjustments for seniority and education. Starting pay varies by number of graduate credit hours earned past the bachelor's degree. Typically, a scale is set up with gradations from a base pay rate for a bachelor's degree up to a base pay rate for a doctorate. Number of years of service is then added in. An example of such a pay system is presented in Exhibit 8.8.

Pay distinctions on the basis of educational attainment are not job based, yet teachers seem to agree that education is a valid criterion for distinguishing among pay rates.

One or a combination of three criteria is usually used in employee attribute methods. First, such pay systems may be rationalized on the basis of the changing nature of work. For example, in the research and development setting it might be argued that some scientists work on projects while others supervise projects. Higher pay would accrue to scientists who are supervising projects.

Often it is impossible to distinguish between the person and the job. Pay in these situations may be based on the unique contributions of people rather than the job. For example, in a law firm, a particular attorney may be highly valued for presenting and winning a specialized type of case before the bar. This person may be paid well out of line for these services in a market sense, but is compensated for unique contributions to the law firm. Finally, custom may dictate rates among jobs. For example, in most university settings it is difficult to find real differences in the jobs of assistant, associate, and full professors. However, most universities have a pay structure for these jobs based on tradition or custom as much as anything.

Maturity Curves

Maturity curves have been popular in the past for establishing the pay of professional employees.[21] The basic rationale behind a maturity curve is that performance is probably in part a function of experience (or maturity) in the profession. For example, a newly trained physicist is not perceived as capable as a physicist with a number of years of experience. It is also assumed that beyond a certain number of years these professionals will become obsolete, and pay is expressed as a function of years of employment, degree, or age. (If age is used the employer should be careful not to violate the Age Discrimination in Employment Act.)

A maturity curve may express a base pay for each year or range of years of experience plus a pay range. Very marginal performers would earn near the base rate, while the top 10 percent of performers would be in the 90th percentile of the pay range for their years of experience.

Maturity curves appear to be similar to seniority pay raises, in which pay rises as a function of years since a degree was earned. However, the rationale is quite different. Seniority implies that pay raises are given to reward long tenure. Maturity curves are based on hypothesized changes in proficiency as a function of experience. From a policymaking standpoint it should be stressed

Exhibit 8.8   *Teacher Salary Scale*

1	2	3 B.A. Plus 20 Semester Hours	4	5 M.A. Plus 20 Semester Hours
Years Experience	Bachelor Degree		Master's Degree	
0	$11,826	$12,176	$12,826	$13,176
1	11,934	12,284	12,934	13,284
2	12,042	12,392	13,042	13,392
3	12,150	12,500	13,150	13,500
4	12,420	12,770	13,420	13,770
5	12,798	13,148	13,798	14,148
6	13,176	13,526	14,176	14,526
7	13,554	13,904	14,554	14,904
8	13,932	14,282	14,932	15,282
9	14,364	14,714	15,364	15,714
10	14,796	15,146	15,796	16,146
11	15,336	15,686	16,336	16,686
12	15,876	16,226	16,876	17,226
13	16,416	16,766	17,416	17,766
14	16,956	17,306	17,956	18,306
15	17,496	17,846	18,496	18,486
16–21	18,144	18,494	19,144	19,494
22+	18,792	19,142	19,792	20,142

(Salary paid for 10-month, 200-day contract)

A. Columns 3 and 5, $350 is added to the B.A. and M.A. scale for completion of 20 semester hours of credit leading to advanced degree approved by an accredited college or university.

B. In Column 4, $1,000 is added to the B.A. degree scale for a M.A. degree.

C. $1,500 is added to B.A. degree scale for teachers holding a Ph.D. or Ed.E. from an accredited college or university.

D. For explanation A, qualifications include a transcript and a letter from the university certifying that the teacher is enrolled in a *graduate program leading toward an advanced degree* and submitted to the Personnel Office by October 1 for teachers to be eligible for payment for the current school year; for explanation B a transcript indicating completion of the degree shall be submitted by October 1 if a teacher is to be eligible for payment for the current school year.

that these relationships are *hypothesized,* and caution is urged before adopting such a pay system.

The Hay Guide Chart Profile Method

The Hay method of job evaluation is probably the most popular proprietary job evaluation system around.[22] The system was developed for use on predominantly white-collar, managerial, and professional jobs. The system is actually a variation on the point and factor comparison methods of job evaluation. As developed by Hay and Associates the Hay plan uses three universal factors to compare jobs: **know-how, problem solving,** and **accountability.** Where appropriate, a fourth factor—working conditions—can be added.[23] Know-how is the total of all skills and knowledge required to do the job.

Problem solving is the amount of original thinking required by the job for arriving at decisions. Accountability is the answerability for actions taken on the job.

These three factors are in turn divided into subfactors.[24] For example, the know-how factor is broken down into substantive know-how, managerial know-how, and human relations know-how.

To use this method the evaluator needs the Hay guide chart for each of the three factors. The job will be assigned a point value for each factor/subfactor. The total of points across all of the factors is the point value for the job.

Direct Market Method

The direct market method of job evaluation is not a job evaluation method at all as defined in this text. The method requires that an organization survey wage rates in the labor market for jobs and then pay the market rate.[25] Typically, the organization sets the midpoint of the pay grade for a job at the average rate revealed by a wage and salary survey. This approach calls for the market pricing of nearly all jobs in the organization. A major disadvantage of this approach is that it can result in internal inequity problems among jobs. Since the midpoint for jobs is purely a market phenomenon, pay rates for jobs across all types of organizations and the desired internal hierarchy of jobs within the firm may not correspond. Further, since this method treats as many as 40 to 60 percent of the jobs in an organization as key jobs, it is not always clear that the organization is in fact comparing its jobs with similar jobs in the market. To the extent that internal jobs are not similar in content to jobs in other organizations in the market, organizational pay rates may not accurately reflect the true market value of the job.

Position Analysis Questionnaire

The position analysis questionnaire is yet another method of job evaluation.[26] As discussed in Chapter 6, the questionnaire is a method of job analysis; however, in combination with known key job market wage rates, it has also been used for job evaluation. This method relies upon a statistical association between the various jobs' scores on the questionnaire's dimensions and known equitable market rates for those key jobs (obtained from a market survey of key job rates). This policy-capturing approach is not unique to this method but has been used to capture pay and point associations in other quantitative job analysis systems as well.[27]

Summary

This chapter reviewed the quantitative approaches to job evaluation. The factor comparison method uses known market rates for key jobs in constructing a master schedule to allocate money to jobs. This process involves the simultaneous process of weighting factors and jobs within factors. Advantages and disadvantages of the factor comparison method were discussed.

The point method, the most sophisticated of the job evaluation methods, was also discussed. Emphasis was placed on defining factors, weighting factors, and assigning degrees to factors. Advantages of this approach were discussed, as were disadvantages. Several other methods of job evaluation were also briefly discussed.

Discussion Questions

1. Why is the factor comparison method of job evaluation also called the job pricing method?

2. A job evaluation plan has a maximum of 750 points. Factor A is to be weighted 20 percent and will have 6 degrees. Assign the point values to each degree.

3. Identify the steps in the factor comparison method and the point method of job evaluation.

Exercises

A set of job descriptions and job specifications follows the Exercises, along with the known fair wage rate for the key jobs in this group.

1. Using the factor comparison method, evaluate the key jobs and construct a master schedule. Evaluate the remaining jobs and assign a final pay rate to them.

2. Develop a job evaluation plan using the point method. After developing the job evaluation manual, evaluate all of the jobs using the manual and write up a final report.

The report is to contain:

Factors selected for compensation.

Rationale for these factors.

Factor definitions.

Degrees within each factor defined.

Total points to the plan stated.

Weights assigned to the factors and the reason the weights were assigned as they were.

Points distributed to the factors and the factor points to the degrees within each factor.

The final point value assigned to each job.

Job Specifications

1. *Universal Teller.* This job requires occasional direction and checking of work. The employee does not have to exercise independent judgment often. Although there is substantial public contact, infrequent intrabank contact is demanded. There are few physical demands and few

continued

unpleasant working conditions, but a high degree of concentration is required. This job requires two to three months of on-the-job training. The employee uses general banking equipment, pneumatic units, and teller machines, and typing, finger dexterity, and human relations skills are needed.

2. *Deposit Services Representative.* This job requires occasional independent judgment. Some direction and checking of work is needed. Substantial public contact is demanded, but there is infrequent intrabank contact. Although a high degree of concentration is required, there are few physical demands and few unpleasant working conditions. About two to three months of on-the-job training is needed. The employee uses general banking equipment and needs typing and human relations skills.

3. *File Clerk.* This job requires little independent judgment, and the employee needs infrequent direction and checking of work. Little public or intrabank contact is made. A high degree of concentration is required, but there are light physical demands with little or no unpleasant working conditions. One week of on-the-job training is needed. The employee uses general banking equipment, and finger dexterity skills are important.

4. *Coin Processor.* The employee exercises little independent judgment. Although this job requires infrequent direction, the work is frequently checked. There is little public or intrabank contact. A moderate degree of concentration is required, with moderate physical demands and few unpleasant working conditions (some machinery noise). One month of on-the-job training is needed to perform the job at an acceptable level. The employee operates general banking equipment, coin wrapper, and postage machines.

5. *Document Sorter.* The job requires occasional direction, but work is infrequently checked. The employee infrequently exercises independent judgment. There is little public or intrabank contact. A high degree of concentration is needed with light physical demands (occasional heavy lifting) and moderate amount of unpleasant working conditions (machine noise). One to three months of on-the-job training is needed to perform the job at an acceptable level. The employee needs finger dexterity skills using the document sorter, proof machine, and general banking equipment.

6. *Statement Bookkeeper.* The employee needs occasional direction and checking of work. There is, however, infrequent independent judgment on the part of the employee. There is not much public or intrabank contact. A moderate degree of concentration is required with little physical demand or unpleasant working conditions. Training period is from one to three months. The employee must have typing skills and uses general banking equipment and teller machines.

7. *Secretary (Trust).* The employee exercises infrequent independent judgment, and the work needs occasional direction and checking. There is some public and intrabank contact. This job requires a moderate degree of concentration, few physical demands, and it offers few or no unpleasant working conditions. Two to three months of on-the-job training is required. This job involves the use of general banking equipment and transcribing equipment. General secretarial skills are important, including shorthand.

8. *Switchboard Operator.* The job requires little independent judgment on the part of the employee. Little direction is needed, and the work is infrequently checked. There is substantial public contact but infrequent intrabank contact. The job demands little or no extraordinary concentration. There are few physical demands with little or no unpleasant working conditions. Less than a month of training is required. General banking equipment and the PBX are used. Telephone communication skills are necessary.

9. *Supervisor, Universal Tellers.* This job requires occasional independent judgment and needs occasional direction and checking of work. Although there is frequent public contact, there is not much intrabank contact. A high degree of concentration is required, but there are few physical demands and little or no unpleasant working conditions. Training takes about two to three months. The employee works with general banking equipment, pneumatic units, and teller machines. Typing, finger dexterity, and human relations skills are important.

10. *Staff Accountant.* This job requires occasional independent judgment and needs occasional direction and checking of work. There is little public or intrabank contact. The job demands a high degree of concentration, but there are few physical demands and little or no unpleasant

continued

working conditions. Training takes from about three to six months. General banking equipment is used, and typing skills are needed.

Job Descriptions

Position title: Universal Teller   Market Rate: $4.21/hr.
Division: Deposit Services
Department: Main Office, Drive-In, Bloomington Branch
Title of immediate supervisor: Branch Manager, Branch Supervisor
Date Issued: 9-1-80

1. Provide banking services to all customers in a friendly, efficient, and professional manner.
2. Verify and control the payment and receipt of cash assigned to you.
3. Balance all cash assigned to you and prepare a balance sheet.
4. Accept and verify demand deposit, savings, and time deposit transactions.
5. Accept and verify installment, charge card, ready reserve, and real estate loan transactions.
6. Process night depository and bank by mail transactions.
7. Process armored car transactions.
8. Process Series E Bonds, travelers' checks, and bank money order transactions.
9. Accept and issue receipts for collection items.
10. Process loose coin and verify coin machine totals.
11. Prepare cash item report.
12. Accept and verify miscellaneous payments such as federal taxes, utilities, etc.
13. Prepare volume and activity reports.
14. Assist other employees within the department whenever possible.
15. Perform other duties that are approved or assigned by your superiors.

Position title: Deposit Services Representative
Division: Deposit Services
Department: Main Office, Drive-In, Minneapolis
Title of immediate supervisor: Deposit Services Supervisor (Main Office), Drive-In Manager
Date issued: 9-1-80

1. Provide banking services to all customers in a friendly, efficient, and professional manner.
2. Open all types of demand deposit accounts.
3. Open all types of savings and time deposit accounts.
4. Issue travelers' checks and Series E Bonds.
5. Open night depository accounts.
6. Provide general information pertaining to bank services available in other departments and banking locations.
7. Process and sell bank promotional and premium items.
8. Process check and deposit ticket orders and reconcile billings.
9. Distribute and explain Ready Reserve and charge card applications.
10. Establish file for the proper follow-up on missing social security numbers, incomplete account resolutions, and unsigned signature cards.
11. Process special agreement forms for such services as direct deposit, IRA accounts, funeral trusts, etc.
12. Approve specific savings withdrawals, checks, cash paybacks, and cash advances.
13. Process volume and activity reports.

continued

14. Assist other employees within the department whenever possible.
15. Perform other duties that are approved or assigned by your superiors.

Position title: File Clerk   Market Rate: $3.82/hr.
Division: Deposit Services
Department: Deposit Accounting, Main Office, Minneapolis
Title of immediate supervisor: Deposit Accounting Supervisor
Date issued: 9-1-80

Minimum responsibilities:
1. Provide banking services to all customers in a friendly, efficient, and professional manner.
2. File checks and deposit tickets.
3. Review items on specified accounts for proper signatures, endorsements, dates, etc.
4. File bank money orders and payroll and interest checks.
5. File signature cards on closed accounts.
6. Assign numbers to new accounts.
7. Assist other employees within the department whenever possible.
8. Perform other duties that are approved or assigned by your supervisor.

Additional responsibilities that may be assigned:
1. File daily computer reports.
2. File corporate resolutions.
3. Balance and maintain files for payroll account monthly.
4. Maintain money order audit sheets.
5. File money orders daily and balance weekly.
6. Relieve other desks as needed.

Position title: Coin Processor
Division: Deposit Services
Department: Main Office–Customer Services, Main Office, Minneapolis
Title of immediate supervisor: Customer Services Supervisor
Date issued: 9-1-80

1. Provide banking services to all customers in a friendly, efficient, and professional manner.
2. Operate the coin wrapping machine.
3. Balance all processed coin.
4. Deliver documents to and from other banks.
5. Deliver daily transactions to the proof department from all bank locations.
6. Assist in opening the main office cash vault.
7. Deliver coins to all bank locations.
8. Assist as a teller.
9. Check the security cameras and record the frame numbers daily.
10. Deliver specified commercial account statements.
11. Assist the Internal Services Department whenever possible.
12. Assist other employees within the department whenever possible.
13. Perform other duties that are approved or assigned by your superiors.

continued

Position title: Document Sorter Operator
Division: Deposit Services
Department: Proof and Adjustments, Main Office, Minneapolis
Title of immediate supervisor: Proof and Adjustments Supervisor
Date issued: 9-1-80

1. Provide banking services to all customers in a friendly, efficient, and professional manner.
2. Microfilm all transactions and cash letter tapes.
3. Operate document sorters and proof machines.
4. Prepare and deliver cash letters.
5. Prepare proof balance worksheets and appropriate entries.
6. Prepare recap totals and deliver all items for application updates.
7. Assist other employees within the department whenever possible.
8. Perform other duties that are approved or assigned by your superiors.

Position title: Statement Bookkeeper
Division: Deposit Services
Department: Deposit Accounting, Main Office, Minneapolis
Title of immediate supervisor: Deposit Accounting Supervisor
Date issued: 9-1-80

1. Provide banking services to all customers in a friendly, efficient, and professional manner.
2. Microfilm all processed items.
3. Review items on specific accounts for proper signatures, endorsements, dates, etc.
4. Organize and prepare demand deposit account statements.
5. Prepare all computer reports for distribution.
6. Balance item counts for demand deposit accounts with list postings.
7. Review all processed microfilm.
8. Assign numbers to new accounts.
9. Assist other employees within the department whenever possible.
10. Perform other duties that are approved or assigned by your superiors.

Position title: Secretary—Trust Department
Division: Trust
Department: Trust, Main Office, Minneapolis
Title of immediate supervisor: Vice President and Senior Trust Officer
Date issued: 9-1-80

1. Provide trust services to all customers in a friendly, efficient, and professional manner.
2. Perform general secretarial duties such as typing, taking shorthand, acting as receptionist, filing, etc.
3. Prepare all checks and deposits for trust customers.
4. Prepare and verify computer entries.
5. Maintain all paying agency accounts.
6. Prepare month end computer filing and mail customer statements.
7. Maintain all authentication accounts.
8. Post and balance debenture and corporate accounts.
9. Maintain all files.

continued

10. Assist other employees within the department whenever possible.
11. Perform other duties that are approved or assigned by your superiors.

Position title: Switchboard Operator   Market Rate: $3.72/hr.
Division: Financial Services
Department: Internal Services, Main Office, Minneapolis
Title of immediate supervisor: Internal Services Officer
Date issued: 9-1-80

1. Provide banking services to all customers in a friendly, efficient, and professional manner.
2. Operate the switchboard.
3. Open incoming mail and disperse to the proper departments.
4. Maintain the copy machine and record daily usage.
5. Coordinate the usage of the bank-owned vehicles.
6. Receive information for the daily bulletin.
7. Receive and deposit all rental income.
8. Maintain petty cash and prepaid postage funds.
9. Receive and deposit milk machine money.
10. Verify and record Internal Services time cards and attendance records.
11. Provide specific copy machine reproductions for all bank locations.
12. Assist other employees within the department whenever possible.
13. Perform other duties that are approved or assigned by your superiors.

Position title: Supervisor, Universal Tellers—Main Office   Market Rate: $5.27/hr.
Division: Deposit Services
Department: Universal Tellers—Main Office, Minneapolis
Title of immediate supervisor: Vice President and Cashier
Date issued: 9-1-80

1. Supervise and coordinate all daily functions of the tellers and safe deposit receptionists.
2. Organize and prepare work and vacation schedules and approve requests for days off.
3. Review, discuss, and explain all operational policies, procedures and related changes to all department personnel through scheduled meetings.
4. Review, approve, and maintain employee time cards and attendance records.
5. Review, approve, and complete reports for all teller variations within the department.
6. Prepare all salary increases, requests for additional staff, terminations, promotions, demotions, transfers, and employee grievances.
7. Assist in planning and developing training and cross training programs for all employees in the department.
8. Provide relief for peak periods, lunch breaks, vacations, and absentees.
9. Manage the collection function including land contracts, sight drafts, bonds, coupons, checks, and any other transactions requiring special handling.
10. Process all foreign currency, coin, and travelers' check transactions.
11. Daily balance of the collection desk for travelers' checks, issued and redeemed U.S. Series E Bonds, credit card cash advances, and Treasury, tax, and loan deposits.
12. Approve checks, savings withdrawals, cash back on deposits, cash advances, cashed certificates, and closed accounts.
13. Prepare reports for all phases of the collection functions.

continued

14. Assist other employees within the department whenever possible.
15. Perform other duties that are approved or assigned by your supervisor.

Position title: Staff Accountant I—General Accounting
Division: Financial Services
Department: General Accounting
Title of immediate supervisor: Senior Staff Accountant
Date issued: 9-1-80

1. Provide banking services to all customers in a friendly, efficient, and professional manner.
2. Prepare reconciliation of various accounts.
3. Verify and obtain approvals on all invoices and review all accounts payable.
4. Verify purchasing orders and maintain expense control ledgers.
5. Prepare annual closing entries for all income and expense accounts.
6. Prepare requisitions for major recurring expenditures.
7. Prepare Branch and Trust Profitability Reports.
8. Perform a physical inventory of all fixed assets.
9. Verify and process changes and generate current listing of fixed assets.
10. Prepare inventory listings and returns for personal property taxes.
11. Assist bank examiners and auditors.
12. Assist other employees within the department whenever possible.
13. Perform other duties that are approved or assigned by your superiors.

Wage Data (Product Market)

Hourly rates are converted to monthly rates using 173 hours in an average work month.
Rate ranges are calculated using 30 percent.
1. Universal Teller
   Averages calculated using 40 employees:

Number of Employees	Hourly Rate	Monthly Rate
4	$4.00	$692.00
4	4.05	700.65
10	4.15	717.95
15	4.25	735.25
4	4.40	761.20
3	4.55	787.15

Average hourly rate: $4.21
Average monthly rate: $728.33 ($4.21 × 173)
Hiring rate: $4.00/hr., $692.00/mo.
Rate range: $4.00/hr.–$5.20/hr. ($4.00 × 1.30 = $5.20)
$692.00/mo.–$899.60/mo.

2. File Clerk
   Averages calculated using 40 employees:

Number of Employees	Hourly Rate	Monthly Rate
10	$3.65	$631.45
9	3.75	648.75

continued

4	3.80	657.40
12	3.95	683.35
4	4.00	692.00

Average hourly rate: $3.82
Average monthly rate: $660.80 ($3.82 × 173)
Hiring rate: $3.65/hr., $631.45/mo.
Rate range: $3.65/hr.–$4.75/hr. ($3.65 × 1.30 = $4.75)
          $631.45/mo.–$821.75/mo.

3. Switchboard Operator
   Averages calculated using 33 employees:

Number of Employees	Hourly Rate	Monthly Rate
12	$3.65	$631.45
8	3.70	640.10
4	3.75	648.75
4	3.82	660.86
5	3.87	669.51

Average hourly rate: $3.72
Average monthly rate: $643.56 ($3.72 × 173)
Hiring rate: $3.65/hr., $631.45/mo.
Rate range: $3.65/hr.–$4.75/hr. ($3.65 × 1.30 = $4.75)
          $631.45/mo.–$821.75/mo.

4. Supervisor, Universal Tellers
   Averages calculated using 10 employees:

Number of Employees	Hourly Rate	Monthly Rate
3	$5.15	$890.95
2	5.23	904.79
1	5.28	913.44
2	5.35	925.55
1	5.40	934.20
1	5.45	942.85

Average hourly rate: $5.27
Average monthly rate: $911.71
Hiring rate: $5.15/hr., $890.95/mo.
Rate range: $5.15/hr.–$6.70/hr. ($5.15 × 1.30 = $6.70)
          $890.95/mo.–$1,159.10/mo.

References

[1] R. C. Mecham, "Quantitative Job Evaluation Using the Position Analysis Questionnaire," *Personnel Administrator* 28, no. 6 (1983): pp. 82–88, 124.

[2] R. M. Madigan, "Job Evaluation as a Determinant of Job Worth: A Conceptual and Comparative Analysis." Unpublished doctoral dissertation, Michigan State University, 1982.

³ The reader should not be overly concerned with the concept of a universal factor. The term is used because the factors employed in factor comparison plans are commonly accepted factors. That is, they have widespread acceptability among those who design and implement job evaluation plans. Table 8.1 presents some of the more common universal factor job evaluation plans. Some of the factors are so universally accepted that they have even been written into the Equal Pay Act of 1963.

⁴ In recent years some firms have attempted to separate the pricing of key jobs from the design of the factor comparison system by substituting arbitrary units in the place of dollars. This has been done partly to eliminate problems in keeping master schedules up to date during inflationary times. For ease of discussion, however, the factor comparison method is discussed as it was originally developed.

⁵ Discussion of the universal factors listed in Table 8.1 can be found in the following sources: A. W. Bass, Jr., "Applying the Point Method of Job Evaluation," *Iron Age*, October 8, 1936, pp. 58–60; Eugene J. Benge, *Job Evaluation and Merit Rating* (New York: National Foreman's Institute, 1946); American Association of Industrial Management, *Job Rating Manual (Shop)*, (Melrose Park, Penn.: AAIM, 1969); U.S. Office of Personnel Management, *Factor Evaluation System* (Washington, D.C.: Government Printing Office, 1977); Edward N. Hay and Dale Purves, "The Profile Method of High-Level Job Evaluation," *Personnel*, September 1951, pp. 162–170; *Equal Pay Act of 1963*, 29 U.S.C. Sec. 206(d) (1).

⁶ Benge, *Job Evaluation and Merit Rating*.

⁷ David J. Chesler, "Reliability and Comparability of Different Job Evaluation Systems," *Journal of Applied Psychology*, October 1948, pp. 465–475.

⁸ The reader should not forget where this wage rate came from. The job of patternmaker is a key job. The wages that the organization is going to pay key jobs are *a priori* determined. These wage rates were established through some process that usually involves a wage survey of other organizations. The factor comparison method assumes that fair wage rates for key jobs have already been determined.

⁹ For two different computational methods see: William D. Turner, "The Percent Method of Job Evaluation," *Personnel*, May 1948, pp. 476–492, and Edward N. Hay, "Creating Factor Comparison Key Scales by the Percent Method," *Journal of Applied Psychology*, October 1948, pp. 456–464.

¹⁰ The practice of using more than one job evaluation plan and anchoring each plan to separate labor markets is part and parcel of the comparable worth pay discrimination debate currently raging in the public sector. For implications of these practices see: David J. Thomsen, "Eliminating Pay Discrimination Caused by Job Evaluation," *Personnel*, September–October 1978, pp. 11–22.

¹¹ One recent study examined this issue and suggested that as few as two or three factors may be adequate for capturing the major variances across jobs. See Madigan, "Job Evaluation as a Determinant of Job Worth: A Conceptual and Comparative Analysis."

¹² See for example J. A. Lee and J. L. Mendoza, "Comparison of Job Evaluation Techniques Which Test for Job Differences," *Personnel Psychology* 34 (Winter 1981): pp. 731–758.

¹³ Sara Rynes, B. Rosen, T. Mahoney, "Comparable Worth: Summary Report of Survey," American Compensation Association, unpublished manuscript, 1983, p. 3.

¹⁴ In the simplest case, multiple regression could be used to weight the factors. This procedure calls for the investigator to know acceptable pay rates for key jobs, and then to regress each job's relative standing on each factor onto the pay rates for the key jobs. Through approximation (exploring alternate weighting schemes) the weighting scheme that best predicts the desired pay rates for key jobs could be discovered and used. For a contemporary article that examines the weighting of factors, see Luis R. Gomez-Mejia *et al.*, "Development and Implementation of a Computerized Job Evaluation System," *Personnel Administrator*, February 1979, pp. 46–54.

¹⁵ There is nothing magical about this procedure. The allocation of points to factor degrees is inherently judgmental, unless one of the more elaborate statistical approaches is used. The rule of assigning 10 percent of the total possible factor points to the lowest degree is used simply because most employees probably will feel better knowing that their job received some points, even though it has the least amount of a factor, rather than zero points. Using this rule means

that the effective range of points used in the job evaluation system will be the maximum minus 10 percent. In the example developed here, the maximum usable points is $1,000 - 100 = 900$.

[16] On this point and on the general observation that the relative ranking of jobs depends less on the weighting of factors than the variability of the distribution of factor scores, see Donald P. Schwab, "Job Evaluation and Pay Setting: Concepts and Practices," in E. Robert Livernash, ed., *Comparable Worth Issues and Alternatives* (Washington, D.C.: Equal Employment Advisory Council, 1980): pp. 51–77.

[17] If statistical weighting is done, the weights for factors will by definition capture the market rates of key jobs and reflect the desired hierarchy. See Schwab, "Job Evaluation and Pay Setting: Concepts and Practices."

[18] Elliot Jaques, *Time-Span Handbook* (London: Heinemann Educational Books, 1964).

[19] A. W. Charles, "Installing Single-Factor Job Evaluation," *Compensation Review* (1st quarter 1971): pp. 9–17.

[20] T. T. Paterson and T. M. Husband, "Decision Making Responsibility: Yardstick for Job Evaluation," *Compensation Review* (2nd quarter 1970): pp. 21–31.

[21] See George W. Torrence, "Maturity Curves and Salary Administration," *Management Record,* January 1962, pp. 14–17; Edward A. Shaw, "The Maturity Factor as an Aide in Administering Professional Salaries," *Personnel,* September–October 1962, pp. 37–42; Ralph Kulberg, "Relating Maturity Curve Data to Job Level and Performance," *Personnel,* March–April 1964, pp. 45–50.

[22] Hay Associates, "The Guide Chart Profile of Job Evaluation," 1981.

[23] Edward N. Hay and Dale Purves, "A New Method of Job Evaluation," *Personnel,* July 1984, pp. 72–80.

[24] Hay and Purves, "The Profile Method of Job Evaluation."

[25] Richard C. Smyth and Matthew J. Murphy, *The Guide Line Method of Job Evaluation* (Rhinebeck, N.Y.: Smyth and Murphy Associates, 1974).

[26] Ernest J. McCormick, "Job and Task Analysis," in M. D. Dunnette, ed., *Handbook of Industrial and Organizational Psychology* (Chicago, Rand-McNally, 1976): pp. 651–696.

[27] See, for example, Walter Tornow and Patrick Pinto, "The Development of a Managerial Job Taxonomy: A System for Describing, Classifying, and Evaluating Executive Office Positions," *Journal of Applied Psychology* 61 (1976): pp. 410–418.

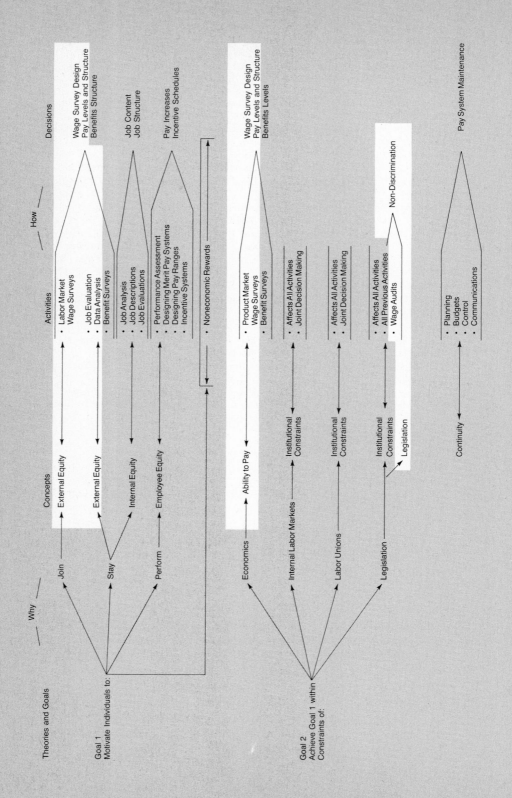

Pay Structure Decisions

The study of jobs and the process of job evaluation were the subjects of Chapters 6 through 8 in Part Three. Part Four deals with the determination of an overall wage structure for jobs, the considerations involved in the wage level decision, and considerations involved in setting pay ranges for jobs.

Chapter 9 is concerned with the pricing of jobs. Job evaluation establishes the relative worth of jobs, but it does not actually price these jobs. Chapter 9 deals with the logical next step in this process, job pricing. For simplicity, one can think of pricing jobs against two separate criteria: labor market standards that focus upon external equity considerations, and product market standards that focus upon ability to pay constraints. In order to price its own jobs, the organization must have some mechanism to assess wage payments in other organizations. This mechanism is the wage and salary survey. The nature of survey data, sources of survey data, and how to collect survey data are also covered in Chapter 9.

Once the organizations has collected wage data from other organizations, it must integrate these data with job evaluation data to make decisions about the actual wage level. This process of integrating external wage data with data from the organization is the subject of Chapter 10. In some senses Chapter 10 is the most important chapter in the text since everything which has preceded comes together in a pay structure that the organization can live with. Being able to live with the pay system means that the system can motivate people to join, stay, and perform, and the jobs are also affordable. Considerable time is spent in Chapter 10 dealing with the decisions that must be made to assure that this happens. Chapter 10 also focuses upon pay ranges for jobs, including the design of ranges and the purposes to which these ranges can be put.

Wage discrimination is not discussed until Chapter 11 for several reasons. First, wage discrimination is a technical concept and the reader needs to have a relatively sophisticated understanding of the compensation subject before it can be discussed. Second, an understanding of how a pay system is designed and what the law requires have been developed in earlier chapters. Chapter 11 is a logical place to deal with wage discrimination since this material should still be fresh in the reader's mind.

Job Pricing: Surveying Labor and Product Markets

· **Learning Objectives**

· **Introduction**

· **Labor and Product Market Constraints**

Organizations Included in a Labor Market Wage and Benefits Survey
Organizations Included in Product Market Surveys
Wage and Benefit Survey Data and Antitrust Law

· **Who Conducts Wage and Benefits Surveys?**

Third-Party Surveys
Custom-Designed Surveys

· **Summarizing Survey Data**

Benefits Data
Wage Data
Summary Statistics and Wage Data
Reporting Data to Management

· **Exercises**

Learning Objectives

In general, to learn about how organizations price jobs in the marketplace.
To learn that labor market surveys are conducted with external equity
considerations in mind.
To learn how to decide on which organizations to include in a labor market
survey.
To learn that product market surveys are conducted with ability to pay constraint
considerations in mind.
To learn how to decide which firms should be included in a product market
survey.
To learn about third-party sources of labor and product market data.
To learn how to design a survey for wages and benefits.
To learn about the more commonly used methods of summarizing survey data.

Introduction

In Chapters 7 and 8 the subject of job evaluation was covered. The purpose of
job evaluation is to determine the relative worth of jobs to the organization,
and job evaluation should result in a structure of jobs, from high to low, that is
internally equitable. That is, the job structure should be perceived as equitable by employees and management within the company.

The next step in establishing a wage system is to price the jobs that have
been evaluated. Job pricing is the subject of this chapter. Job evaluation does
not establish the absolute wage rates paid to jobs. It only establishes the relative position of jobs with respect to each other. Job pricing is a decision as to
absolute wage rates for specific jobs in the job structure. When all jobs are
priced, the wage structure that results should reflect the job structure.

Job pricing involves conducting wage and salary and benefit surveys.
These surveys are normally conducted in labor or product markets. The organization uses survey data to achieve external equity with respect to the labor
market,[1] and uses product market data to price jobs within the economic constraint of the organization's ability to pay.[2] These purposes are elaborated on in
this chapter. Job pricing, then, is the process of attempting to achieve external
pay rate equity within the organization's ability to pay constraint. Job pricing,
is carried out with labor market data in order to elicit the desired behaviors
from individuals: to motivate them to join and to motivate them to stay. These
behaviors must be achieved, however, within the organization's ability to pay.

Labor and Product Market Constraints

Chapter 2 discussed equity theory as it relates to compensation decision making. Organizations must have pay systems that are perceived as equitable if
they are going to be able to accomplish the goal of attracting and retaining

employees. Organizations usually conduct wage and salary and benefit surveys to assure that they are competitive in their wage and benefits payments to employees. In one sense, then, the wages paid in the labor market are indicators of what any single organization will have to pay to foster perceptions of equity. These rates operate as one constraint in compensation decision making.

In Chapter 3 marginal revenue productivity theory as it relates to compensation decision making was discussed. Organizations are constrained by their ability to pay. If an organization is going to survive in the long run, its costs (including labor costs) must not be so high that they put that employer at a competitive disadvantage in the product market.[3] Employers, especially labor-intensive employers whose product demand is elastic with respect to price, should conduct wage and salary and benefits surveys among the firms with which they compete for consumers of their good or service. Ability to pay is another constraint faced by the organization.

The distinct goals of labor and product market wage and benefit surveys are summarized in Exhibit 9.1.

Chapter 3 also considered what happens when these two surveys give conflicting results. That is, wages in the product market may be above or below wages in the labor market, and this fact constrains compensation decision making. Chapter 3 reviewed the employer's options under varying combinations of these constraints. The reader may wish to refer back to the discussion on page 63 and 64.

Labor market and product market surveys are management tools to accomplish different purposes. Understanding the nature of labor and product markets will aid in designing a wage and salary and benefits survey.

Organizations Included in a Labor Market Wage and Benefits Survey

The question of which organizations should be included in a labor market survey is best answered by considering the nature of labor markets and the purpose of conducting such a survey in the first place. The purpose of conducting a labor market survey is to assure that the organization is paying a competitive wage so that there are not perceptions of pay or benefit inequity. In other words, the objective is to pay a wage that is competitive in the labor

Exhibit 9.1   *Summary of Goals for Labor and Product Market Surveys*

Type of Survey	Goals
Labor market wage and benefit survey	To assure equitable wages and benefits so that individuals are motivated to join and stay with the organization.
Product market wage and benefit survey	To assure that wage and benefit costs do not exceed the firm's ability to pay.

market, thereby allowing the organization to successfully attract and retain labor. Organizations from the **relevant labor market** should be surveyed.

Geographic Scope of Labor Markets   Labor markets have a definable geographic scope. That is, any given organization is considered to be located at the center of a specific labor market. If an employer were to analyze the percentage of people who work as office and clerical employees, it might discover that 50 percent of those employees come from a 10-mile radius of the office complex, that 75 percent come from a 20-mile radius, and that fully 95 percent come from a 30-mile radius. In this case, the geographic scope of the relevant labor market for office and clerical employees would be 30 miles or less, as depicted in Exhibit 9.2.

Actually, it is a misconception to think of an employer as located at the

---

Exhibit 9.2   *Conceptual Analysis of Relevant Labor Area for Office and Clerical Employees*

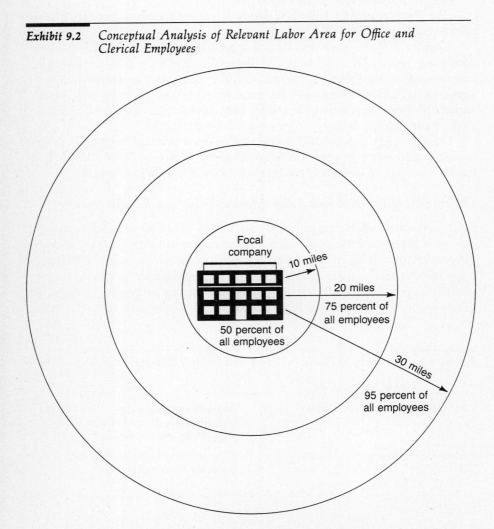

geometric center of a labor area, since most employees may come from only one direction—from the north, southwest, or so on. Because of this phenomenon, some labor market analysts have suggested that employers use isobar analysis. Isobars (lines of equal distance) are like the contour lines on a map that show changes in elevation. Exhibit 9.3 is an example of isobar analysis.

To use isobar analysis for a labor market, the employer might draw a continuous line around a plant (or other operating site) to represent the area from which 20 percent of the employees come. A second line is drawn around the area from which 30 percent of the employees come, a third line for 40 percent, and so forth until a line is drawn to show the area from which 95 percent of all employees come. The areas within the concentric lines define the geographic labor area for a given group of employees. Isobar analysis shows more precisely where employees come from, and in what concentrations. This type of analysis has also been supported as valid in a court of law where there was concern over possible discrimination in hiring of minorities.[4]

Occupational Level and Labor Markets   Geographic area is one dimension of

---

Exhibit 9.3   *Isobar Analysis of Relevant Labor Area for Office and Clerical Employees*

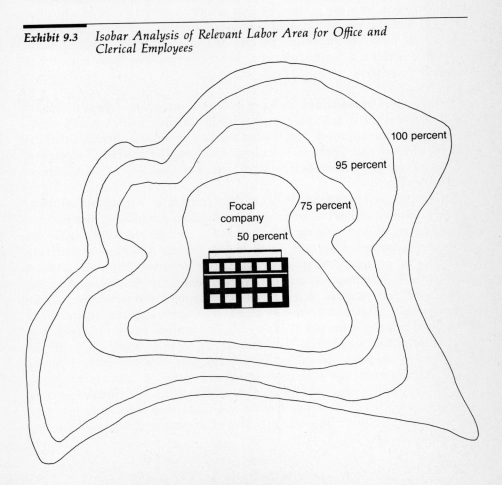

a relevant labor market. Another dimension of the relevant labor market is occupation.[5] Different occupational groups have different labor markets. As a general rule, the geographic area for the relevant labor market varies directly with the skill level of the occupation. For example, the relevant labor area for unskilled laborers may be a 20-mile radius; the relevant labor area for highly skilled employees, such as middle managers, may be regional, or even national. The precise relevant labor area for any given occupational group is an empirical question subject to study. It can vary from organization to organization, and compensation decision makers should study the labor areas for occupational groups for their organizations. In general, it is worth asking if the organization's present human resource policies and programs (pay levels, recruiting efforts, training and development, and so on) allow the organization to attract an adequate quantity and quality of applicants. What geographic areas do these employees come from?

The fact that labor markets have a geographic dimension and an occupational dimension suggests that it is inappropriate to think of the labor market survey just as "a" survey. The labor market survey is really a series of surveys. In other words, since the geographic area of labor markets varies as a function of occupational level, the organizations to be surveyed will vary also. For example, the subset of organizations included in a survey of wage rates for operatives will be different from the subset of organizations in a survey of wages for managers.

Selecting the Organizations to Survey   The compensation decision maker must decide which organizations to include in the labor market survey. Probably the simplest approach uses a labor markets analysis to identify all of the organizations in each of the relevant labor markets. The number of employers in the relevant labor markets may be so large, however, that it is not practical to survey all of them.

One approach to reducing the number of firms is to do a random sampling of organizations within the labor markets. Random sampling allows the surveying organization to assume that the mean or average wage obtained in the survey is reflective of average wages in the market. A second approach to selecting the organizations to survey is first to determine the organization's position in the labor queue through exit interviews, for example (asking the future employment plans of employees who leave the organization). If the organization can determine this position, then surveying the organizations above and below it in the labor queue will allow it to price its jobs to remain at the same relative standing in the labor queue. A third approach is for the employer to use wage and salary and benefits data gathered by third parties (such as government agencies, professional associations, or consultants) to establish a pay policy relative to the median. Although this last approach is often followed, it has the disadvantage that the wage data often is not from a particular employer's relevant labor market. This disadvantage is discussed the section on third-party data.

Organizations Included in Product Market Surveys

Just as with labor market surveys, compensation decision makers must make a series of decisions as to whom to include in the product market wage and benefits survey.

Firms surveyed in the product market ought to satisfy three criteria. First, they must be in the relevant product market; second, they should utilize the same technology; and third, they should be the same size as measured by number of employees. Ideally a compensation decision maker would conduct a survey among those firms that meet these criteria. Unfortunately, it is not always easy to attain this ideal. For example, an organization may use one technology to produce a series of products, some of which the surveying organization may not make. These two firms are not totally similar in terms of products made and the allocation of labor costs to those products. Further, costs outside the production process may not be similar. For example, differences in shipping costs may offset labor savings. A brewery in Eden, North Carolina, with a lower wage rate will incur large shipping costs to send its product to Detroit, whereas a brewery in Detroit that has higher labor costs will incur low shipping costs to sell its product there. These additional costs must be considered.

The ideal product market surveys should be worked for; however, the compensation decision maker must be creative as well as analytical in analyzing survey data, since seldom will competitors be surveyed under the ideal conditions outlined here.

Geographic Scope of the Product Market   Like labor markets, the product market also has a geographic scope. That is, an organization typically markets its product in a particular geographic area. To determine which organizations to survey in the product market, the first general rule is to determine which organizations are competed with in the product market. Which companies' products are next to the organization's on the supermarket shelf, at car dealerships, in hardware stores, and so forth? For example, a brewery in Eden, North Carolina, would be interested in knowing wage rates paid by a brewery in Detroit and a brewery in Williamsburg, Virginia, which sell beer in the same market. However, it would not need to know the wages paid at a brewery in Phoenix, Arizona, which, even though it is in the same industry, does not compete in the product market for beer in the Atlantic coast area. The relevant product market can be seen in the same sense as the relevant labor market, in that both have a definable geographic scope.

Technology and Product Market Surveys   Product markets also have a second dimension for determining which firms should be included in the survey. That dimension is technological. Specifically, the surveying organization will particularly want to include those competitors who have similar technologies and are of about the same size.[6] The organization is trying to assure that its labor costs will not vary significantly from its competitors' so as not to be at a competitive disadvantage in the product market. To state it another way, the surveying organization wants to be sure that its wage level is not substantially different from its competitors' in the product market. An employer can estimate the wage level of the production unit of its competitors if the competitor uses the same technology.

Exhibit 9.4 is a diagram that illustrates this dimension. The organization depicted in the diagram is assumed to make a product with a given technology. The production unit of this firm has three job levels as depicted in Exhibit 9.4. The weighted average of the wage rates across job levels for this production unit is $6.46 per hour. The organization also has a key job at each of the three job levels. If the organization wants to know the wage level paid by its competitors, it could survey the three key jobs among its competitors. Assuming that its competitors use the same technology (and apply labor to technology in roughly the same ratio), the employer will have a good estimate of the wage level of these competing firms. Exhibit 9.4 shows at the bottom that given the wage rate for the three key jobs and the job level of each key job relative to total employment, the wage level in the product market is $6.53 per hour. This is a favorable comparison to the organization's rate of $6.46.

Exhibit 9.4   *Theoretical Production Organization and Associated Key Job Product Market Rates*

Average Key Job Rate (Product Market)	Job Level as Proportion of Total Weighting	
Job 3 = $11.00	5/255 = 2.0%	$ .22
Job 2 = $ 7.80	50/255 = 19.6%	1.53
Job 1 = $ 6.10	200/255 = 78.4%	4.78
		WAGE LEVEL $6.53

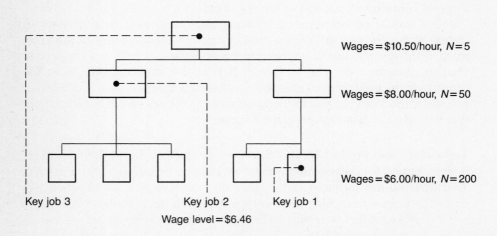

Wages = $10.50/hour, N = 5

Wages = $8.00/hour, N = 50

Wages = $6.00/hour, N = 200

Key job 3   Key job 2   Key job 1

Wage level = $6.46

Since managers, support staff, and so on, tend to be employed in roughly similar ratios to production employees for employers of the same size, similar estimates can be made for the wage levels of these groups, and finally the organization as a whole.

The Purpose of a Product Market Survey   The purpose of a product market survey is implied in the criteria used for including a firm. Employers within an industry are constrained by their ability to pay wages. While optimal behavior might suggest a complex marginal revenue productivity analysis, such analyses are not undertaken for numerous technical and pragmatic reasons. Surveys of other organizations in the product market will enable an organization to estimate the wage level of the product market competition. The surveying organization is then in a position to compare its own wage level against this estimate.

Other things being equal, paying higher wages than the product market competition is likely to result in lower profitability and threaten long-term success. Product market wage and benefits surveys are important as estimates of the employer's ability to pay constraint. Estimates of wages and benefits paid in the product market generally should not be exceeded unless the organization can identify sizable offsetting cost savings from other components of operations. For example, if the employer can determine that it saves considerable money relative to its competitors on transportation costs for the product, then this additional revenue could go toward higher wages without increasing total costs relative to its competitors' total costs. Although these variables are important to compensation decision making, pursuing them would take this text from the main thread of analysis.

Wage and Benefit Survey Data and Antitrust Law

One potentially serious concern with compiling and using wage and benefit data is whether or not the data lead to setting wages at a specified level. If organizations act in a way that could be regarded as a **conspiracy** to restrain the free pricing of labor, this behavior would likely be looked at as a violation of antitrust law. At least one employer association has signed a consent decree with a court after a labor union in the Boston area raised questions about the antitrust implications of conducting wage surveys.[7]

Employers can probably best protect themselves from such charges by not collectively agreeing to set wages at a particular level; doing so would almost certainly be considered a violation of antitrust law. On the other hand, the employer is perfectly free to collect and use wage and benefit data from other employers so long as the collecting organization makes independent judgments in using the data. In other words, to collect such data and to make decisions on such data is legal as long as the organization does not act in concert with other organizations.

Surveys of the product market seem most likely to be challenged on an antitrust basis because of the implications for labor costs and the pricing of the final product. It is possible, however, that an organization could follow the behavior of its product market competitors and make independent decisions about wage rates based on their behavior. This employer may appear to be colluding with other firms in the product market when in fact it is acting alone and is concerned only with remaining competitive in the product market. There are some things the organization can do to protect itself from appearances of collusion.

First, if the organization has face-to-face encounters with other organizations while sharing survey data, it would be prudent to have an independent third party at the meeting to monitor the discussions to assure that they do not involve anything that could be considered collusion. Second, the organization should not imply in any way that its behavior is contingent upon a specific behavior of other survey participants. For example, to imply that the organization will not raise wages more than 5 percent if other survey participants do not raise their wages by more than a specified percentage would probably be considered illegal. Third, organizations may want to collect and report the data in such a way that individual employee pay rates cannot be identified.[8] For example, it is not important to the survey what a specific labor relations director makes; what is important is what a company pays for labor relations directors in general.

Who Conducts Wage and Benefits Surveys?

Wage and benefit survey data are available from numerous sources. A distinction is made here between third-party data and custom-designed data. Third-party data may be provided by three sources: government agencies, professional associations, and consultants. Custom-designed surveys are developed by the surveying organization.

Third-Party Surveys

Federal Government Surveys   The U. S. government conducts a number of surveys that are available to private and public sector organizations. Of the four major federal government surveys discussed here, three are conducted by the Bureau of Labor Statistics. The fourth survey is conducted by the Federal Reserve System.

Area Wage Surveys   Area wage surveys are conducted throughout the United States in the largest of the standard metropolitan statistical areas. The surveys cover numerous clerical and operative occupations in both manufacturing and nonmanufacturing sectors of the economy. The results are presented in the form of pay data for classes of jobs and indicate mean, median, and pay range data for the jobs. There is also information on employee benefits, such as vacation practices, health insurance and pension plans, shift differentials, and weekly work schedules. An example of the results of an area wage survey is presented in Exhibit 9.5.

Industry Wage Surveys   Industry wage surveys cover 50 manufacturing and 20 nonmanufacturing industries within the economy. The surveys provide data on wages for select jobs and also on hours worked per week and employer contributions to insurance and pension plans. Many of the industries in the survey are relatively low-wage industries, suggesting that the government is subsidizing product market surveys for certain firms in the economy. The partial results of an industry wage survey appear in Exhibit 9.6.

Professional, Administrative, Technical, and Clerical Surveys   The professional, administrative, technical, and clerical survey is conducted in metropolitan areas among employers with 2,500 or more employees. Types of occupations surveyed include accounting, legal services, personnel management, engineering, chemistry, buying, clerical supervisory, drafting, and clerical. The survey data report straight-time earnings, bonuses, commissions, and cost-of-living increases. The partial results of a survey appear in Exhibit 9.7.

Federal Reserve System   The Federal Reserve System conducts wage surveys in each of its respective districts to ensure that its employees' pay is at market within the district. These data are generally available to survey participants in return for their cooperation in the survey.

Professional Association Surveys   Numerous professional associations at both the local and national level conduct one or more wage and benefit surveys of their membership. For example, the American Society of Personnel Administrators in conjunction with a private firm conducts wage and salary surveys for personnel and industrial relations executives. Many local chapters of this association also conduct wage and benefit surveys for select key jobs within their local labor areas.

Table 9.1 presents a partial list of professional associations that conduct wage and benefits surveys. As the table shows, there are many sources of wage and salary information available to the compensation decision maker from professional associations. In many cases the professional association data is crucial for determining market rates. For example, in engineering the professional association survey is conducted regularly, and many engineers look to these surveys to determine whether they are equitably paid. In short, these surveys define equitable pay in some cases.

Consultants   Another major source of data for compensation decision makers is consulting firms. A number of the large consulting firms conduct wage and benefit surveys that are made available to clients and others wishing to purchase the data. They are often a rich source of information for the compensation decision maker. Many of these firms operate exclusively within an industry. Others specialize in a particular occupational segment. For example, Table 9.2 shows that Towers, Perrin, Forster and Crosby specialize in top and middle management surveys.

Exhibit 9.5

Exhibit 9.5 *Hourly Earnings of Material Movement and Custodial Workers in Richmond, Virginia, June 1984*

Occupation and Industry Division	Number of Workers	Hourly Earnings (in Dollars)			$3.30 and under $3.50	$3.50 – $3.70	$3.70 – $3.90	$3.90 – $4.10	$4.10 – $4.30
		Mean	Median	Middle Range					
Truckdrivers	1,503	9.19	9.10	7.40–10.15	–	–	6	5	2
Manufacturing	121	8.98	8.56	7.10–11.10	–	–	–	–	–
Nonmanufacturing	1,382	9.21	9.32	7.45–10.15	–	–	6	5	2
Transportation and utilities	806	9.60	9.85	7.35–13.21	–	–	6	3	–
Truckdrivers, light truck	136	8.47	9.66	8.00– 9.85	–	–	–	2	–
Nonmanufacturing	129	8.40	9.75	7.30– 9.85	–	–	–	2	–
Truckdrivers, medium truck	348	9.26	8.36	7.10–12.02	–	–	–	–	2
Manufacturing	72	7.23	7.10	5.48– 8.36	–	–	–	–	–
Nonmanufacturing	276	9.79	10.15	8.10–13.46	–	–	–	–	2
Truckdrivers, heavy truck	260	8.37	8.44	8.06–10.00	–	–	6	3	–
Nonmanufacturing	258	8.36	8.44	8.06–10.00	–	–	6	3	–
Truckdrivers, tractor-trailer	689	9.67	10.06	7.45–11.07	–	–	–	–	–
Nonmanufacturing	662	9.56	10.06	7.40–11.07	–	–	–	–	–
Transportation and utilities	382	9.09	7.65	6.80–13.21	–	–	–	–	–
Shippers	151	9.92	11.31	8.47–11.55	–	–	–	–	–
Manufacturing	114	10.71	11.55	11.31–11.55	–	–	–	–	–
Receivers	140	7.99	8.35	5.86– 9.00	–	–	–	–	–
Manufacturing	42	10.09	11.55	8.31–11.55	–	–	–	–	–
Nonmanufacturing	98	7.10	8.00	5.73– 8.44	–	–	–	–	–
Shippers and receivers	102	9.09	8.99	8.34– 9.96	–	–	–	–	–
Manufacturing	47	8.59	7.37	7.37– 8.99	–	–	–	–	–
Warehousemen	569	7.49	8.00	6.15– 8.50	–	–	–	–	–
Manufacturing	77	8.65	8.94	8.35– 9.22	–	–	–	–	–
Nonmanufacturing	492	7.31	7.51	5.95– 8.27	–	–	–	–	–
Order fillers	335	8.20	8.38	8.23– 9.04	–	–	–	–	25
Manufacturing	60	8.57	9.01	7.34–10.07	–	–	–	–	9
Material handling laborers	456	7.31	6.40	5.79– 8.96	–	–	1	1	6
Manufacturing	238	7.24	6.11	5.79– 9.37	–	–	–	–	–
Nonmanufacturing	218	7.38	7.80	5.96– 8.90	–	–	1	1	6
Transportation and utilities	148	8.25	8.30	7.70– 9.50	–	–	–	–	4
Forklift operators	725	9.16	9.61	6.72–11.12	3	6	6	5	10
Manufacturing	529	9.93	10.79	6.94–12.42	–	–	–	2	2
Nonmanufacturing	196	7.08	8.34	5.11– 8.49	3	6	6	3	8
Guards	1,296	4.30	3.75	3.50– 3.90	318	262	375	121	25
Manufacturing	98	9.74	10.12	9.29–11.50	–	–	5	–	–
Nonmanufacturing	1,198	3.86	3.71	3.46– 3.76	318	262	370	121	25
Guards I	1,206	3.91	3.75	3.46– 3.80	318	262	375	121	25
Manufacturing	42	8.65	7.16	6.43–12.70	–	–	5	–	–
Nonmanufacturing	1,164	3.74	3.71	3.46– 3.75	318	262	370	121	25
Guards II: Nonmanufacturing	34	7.87	8.13	7.32– 8.34	–	–	–	–	–
Janitors, porters, and cleaners	3,411	4.24	3.35	3.35– 4.00	2,281	138	112	68	87
Manufacturing	438	8.52	8.16	6.15–12.08	1	2	3	1	16
Nonmanufacturing	2,973	3.61	3.35	3.35– 3.45	2,280	136	109	67	71
Transportation and utilities	25	7.61	7.19	6.65– 7.51	–	–	–	–	–

Area Wage Survey—Richmond, Virginia, Metropolitan Area June 1984 (Washington, D.C.: Bureau of Labor Statistics, 1984): p. 9.

(continued)

Exhibit 9.5 continued

Number of Workers Receiving Straight-time Hourly Earnings (in Dollars)

$4.30 – $4.70	$4.70 – $5.10	$5.10 – $5.50	$5.50 – $5.90	$5.90 – $6.30	$6.30 – $6.70	$6.70 – $7.10	$7.10 – $7.50	$7.50 – $7.90	$7.90 – $8.30	$8.30 – $8.70	$8.70 – $9.10	$9.10 – $9.50	$9.50 – $9.90	$9.90 – $10.90	$10.90 – $11.90	$11.90 – $12.90	$12.90 – $13.90
28	28	50	15	91	36	46	81	50	146	107	12	74	82	303	75	50	216
–	–	21	–	3	–	–	13	–	13	18	2	11	–	–	15	25	–
28	28	29	15	88	36	46	68	50	133	89	10	63	82	303	60	25	216
16	2	10	4	80	11	37	43	47	19	33	4	59	73	143	1	–	215
12	–	12	–	–	4	1	2	–	6	10	2	14	69	1	–	1	–
12	–	12	–	–	4	1	2	–	6	10	2	8	69	1	–	–	–
–	24	22	3	9	18	–	14	2	64	30	2	–	1	67	2	3	85
–	–	21	–	3	–	–	13	–	13	18	2	–	–	–	2	–	–
–	24	1	3	6	18	–	1	2	51	12	–	–	1	67	–	3	85
–	2	6	8	2	8	8	8	–	67	50	4	8	4	76	–	–	–
–	2	6	8	2	8	8	8	–	67	50	4	6	4	76	–	–	–
–	–	–	–	80	6	33	57	48	9	17	4	52	8	159	59	46	111
–	–	–	–	80	6	33	57	48	9	17	4	49	8	159	59	22	111
–	–	–	–	80	5	33	41	47	7	11	–	48	–	–	–	–	110
7	–	14	–	–	–	–	10	2	–	28	2	2	–	–	58	9	19
7	–	2	–	–	–	–	10	2	–	5	–	2	–	–	58	9	19
2	14	–	26	2	6	1	2	1	7	37	15	1	1	3	20	1	1
–	–	–	–	–	5	–	2	–	4	–	4	1	1	3	20	1	1
2	14	–	26	2	1	1	–	1	3	37	11	–	–	–	–	–	–
–	–	–	–	–	–	9	16	–	–	19	14	–	–	29	9	6	–
–	–	–	–	–	–	8	16	–	–	4	8	–	–	5	–	6	–
24	42	42	13	30	21	25	20	60	114	81	42	14	11	14	–	16	–
–	1	4	–	–	1	2	6	2	–	21	18	5	8	5	–	4	–
24	41	38	13	30	20	23	14	58	114	60	24	9	3	9	–	12	–
8	–	–	–	–	–	9	26	4	91	83	9	6	58	4	9	3	–
–	–	–	–	–	1	7	4	3	3	9	6	2	4	9	3	–	–
11	20	31	99	50	24	3	12	26	32	11	25	38	39	–	–	27	–
–	13	26	76	34	3	1	3	19	–	–	–	36	–	–	–	27	–
11	7	5	23	16	21	2	9	7	32	11	25	2	39	–	–	–	–
–	–	4	4	4	6	2	9	6	32	11	25	2	39	–	–	–	–
21	5	3	11	59	19	77	15	2	9	101	1	–	28	95	73	176	–
3	–	–	6	54	8	63	12	1	7	22	–	–	5	95	73	176	–
18	5	3	5	5	11	14	3	1	2	79	1	–	23	–	–	–	–
28	9	10	6	9	15	7	11	5	10	5	2	23	3	17	14	18	3
–	–	–	–	5	9	1	2	2	–	–	–	20	2	17	14	18	3
28	9	10	6	4	6	6	9	3	10	5	2	3	1	–	–	–	–
28	9	7	6	9	15	5	5	3	–	–	–	–	–	3	3	12	–
–	–	–	–	5	9	1	2	2	–	–	–	–	–	3	3	12	–
28	9	7	6	4	6	4	3	1	–	–	–	–	–	–	–	–	–
–	–	3	–	–	–	2	6	2	10	5	2	3	1	–	–	–	–
171	90	28	37	46	29	26	18	32	7	25	22	1	9	56	2	126	–
30	9	18	18	36	24	24	9	25	3	7	22	1	9	56	–	124	–
141	81	10	19	10	5	2	9	7	4	18	–	–	–	–	2	2	–
–	–	4	–	–	3	1	6	7	–	–	–	–	–	–	2	2	–

Area Wage Survey—Richmond, Virginia, Metropolitan Area June 1984 (Washington, D.C.: Bureau of Labor Statistics, 1984): p. 9.

Exhibit 9.6   *Occupational Earnings Distribution: Data Librarians*

Weekly Earnings	Northeast			South		North Central	West	
	Boston	New York	Phila-delphia	Dallas–Fort Worth	Wash-ington	Chicago	Los Angeles–Long Beach	San Jose
Number of workers	17	16	35	44	28	42	51	36
Average weekly earnings	$233.50	$242.50	$213.50	$229.50	$260.50	$236.50	$266.00	$292.00
Average weekly hours	38.0	36.5	39.5	40.0	40.0	40.0	40.0	40.0
Total	100.0	100.0	100.0	100.0	100.0	100.0	100.0	100.0
$150 and under $160	–	–	–	–	7.1	–	–	–
$160 and under $170	–	–	11.4	–	–	–	–	–
$170 and under $180	–	–	11.4	–	7.1	–	–	–
$180 and under $190	5.9	–	11.4	–	7.1	–	–	–
$190 and under $200	11.8	–	22.9	4.5	3.6	2.4	–	–
$200 and under $210	5.9	–	–	4.5	–	38.1	3.9	8.3
$210 and under $220	11.8	–	2.9	22.7	–	4.8	3.9	–
$220 and under $230	5.9	25.0	2.9	38.6	17.9	4.8	7.8	–
$230 and under $240	29.4	25.0	–	–	–	7.1	11.8	–
$240 and under $250	–	31.3	2.9	–	3.6	7.1	13.7	5.6
$250 and under $260	–	–	–	15.9	10.7	9.5	7.8	11.1
$260 and under $270	–	–	34.3	4.5	–	7.1	3.9	–
$270 and under $280	29.4	–	–	9.1	–	–	–	33.3
$280 and under $290	–	18.8	–	–	–	4.8	19.6	–
$290 and under $300	–	–	–	–	–	7.1	7.8	5.6
$300 and under $310	–	–	–	–	7.1	–	7.8	–
$310 and under $320	–	–	–	–	10.7	2.4	7.8	–
$320 and under $330	–	–	–	–	–	–	3.9	11.1
$330 and under $340	–	–	–	–	17.9	4.8	–	–
$340 and under $350	–	–	–	–	–	–	–	–
$350 and under $360	–	–	–	–	–	–	–	25.0
$360 and under $370	–	–	–	–	7.1	–	–	–

(Percent distribution of data librarians by straight-time weekly earnings[1] in computer and data processing services establishments, selected metropolitan areas, October 1982)

[1] Excludes premium pay for overtime and for work on weekends, holidays, and late shifts. Average weekly hours relate to standard workweeks and average weekly earnings correspond to these hours. Weekly earnings are rounded to the nearest half dollar; weekly hours to the nearest half hour.

Note: Because of rounding, sums of individual items may not equal 100. Dashes indicate that no data were reported. Distributions are not provided for work levels with fewer than 15 incumbents.

Industry Wage Survey: Computer and Data Processing Services, October 1982 (Washington, D.C.: Bureau of Labor Statistics, 1983), p. 15.

Exhibit 9.7 *Employment Distribution by Salary: Clerical Occupations*

Monthly Salary	Secretaries					Stenographers		Typists	
	I	II	III	IV	V	I	II	I	II
$600 and under $625	–	–	–	–	–	–	–	8.2	–
$625 and under $650	–	–	–	–	–	–	–	1.0	–
$650 and under $675	–	–	–	–	–	–	–	.5	–
$675 and under $700	–	–	–	–	–	–	–	1.6	–
$700 and under $725	–	–	–	–	–	–	–	2.4	–
$725 and under $750	–	–	–	–	–	–	–	3.1	–
$750 and under $775	–	–	–	–	–	–	–	4.3	–
$775 and under $800	–	–	–	–	–	–	–	5.7	–
$800 and under $825	–	–	–	–	–	–	–	6.7	(2.0)
$825 and under $850	(2.1)	–	–	–	–	–	–	5.8	2.4
$850 and under $875	1.3	–	–	–	–	–	–	6.4	2.3
$875 and under $900	1.7	–	–	–	–	(3.2)	–	5.0	2.0
$900 and under $925	1.7	–	–	–	–	1.0	–	5.7	2.7
$925 and under $950	1.4	–	–	–	–	1.3	–	6.5	1.9
$950 and under $975	3.3	–	–	–	–	1.7	–	6.8	4.8
$975 and under $1,000	2.9	(3.1)	–	–	–	1.5	(1.2)	3.6	2.7
$1,000 and under $1,050	5.6	2.5	(1.3)	–	–	3.8	1.0	8.2	8.3
$1,050 and under $1,100	6.9	3.8	1.2	–	–	3.8	1.4	6.1	8.4
$1,100 and under $1,150	8.0	4.7	2.1	(0.3)	–	6.4	1.8	4.1	7.0
$1,150 and under $1,200	8.3	6.5	2.6	1.2	–	4.1	1.4	3.7	5.9
$1,200 and under $1,250	10.4	8.3	4.1	1.1	–	6.4	1.5	1.9	7.2
$1,250 and under $1,300	9.2	9.5	5.2	1.6	–	3.4	1.9	1.5	5.8
$1,300 and under $1,350	7.5	8.1	6.2	2.1	–	3.7	2.6	2.5	6.8
$1,350 and under $1,400	5.5	8.2	6.9	3.8	–	6.5	3.2	.5	3.4
$1,400 and under $1,450	4.8	7.1	7.3	3.5	(4.0)	5.1	3.0	.6	3.6
$1,450 and under $1,500	3.3	6.7	7.1	4.0	2.4	4.0	3.7	1.2	2.7
$1,500 and under $1,550	3.2	6.6	6.9	5.3	1.9	4.8	4.6	.6	2.1
$1,550 and under $1,600	1.7	4.6	6.6	6.1	2.3	4.5	7.6	.4	3.6
$1,600 and under $1,650	2.2	4.5	6.3	5.6	2.1	7.9	9.3	.3	1.5
$1,650 and under $1,700	1.2	2.9	4.9	5.9	4.7	4.8	6.3	1.0	3.3
$1,700 and under $1,750	(7.5)	2.4	5.3	6.7	4.6	4.6	11.2	(2.1)	2.6
$1,750 and under $1,800	–	1.7	4.4	6.9	4.7	7.8	7.7	–	1.4
$1,800 and under $1,850	–	1.3	3.9	4.8	5.2	1.4	2.8	–	1.5
$1,850 and under $1,900	–	1.4	2.7	5.6	3.5	.6	1.5	–	.6
$1,900 and under $1,950	–	.8	2.4	5.2	5.3	.9	2.6	–	1.4
$1,950 and under $2,000	–	.9	1.8	5.8	5.4	2.9	5.3	–	1.0
$2,000 and under $2,050	–	.6	1.4	4.8	5.8	.2	5.2	–	1.2
$2,050 and under $2,100	–	.4	2.1	3.3	5.9	.4	.9	–	(1.5)
$2,100 and under $2,150	–	2.4	1.3	2.7	3.7	2.1	5.2	–	–
$2,150 and under $2,200	–	(0.8)	1.3	3.1	4.1	(1.2)	2.7	–	–
$2,200 and under $2,250	–	–	.9	2.0	4.7	–	1.3	–	–

(continued)

Exhibit 9.7   *(continued)*

Monthly Salary	Secretaries					Stenographers		Typists	
	I	II	III	IV	V	I	II	I	II
$2,250 and under $2,300	–	–	1.8	1.6	3.6	–	(3.2)	–	–
$2,300 and under $2,350	–	–	(2.0)	1.2	4.4	–	–	–	–
$2,350 and under $2,400	–	–	–	2.2	3.6	–	–	–	–
$2,400 and under $2,450	–	–	–	1.0	2.9	–	–	–	–
$2,450 and under $2,500	–	–	–	(2.2)	2.0	–	–	–	–
$2,500 and under $2,600	–	–	–	–	5.1	–	–	–	–
$2,600 and under $2,700	–	–	–	–	2.4	–	–	–	–
$2,700 and under $2,800	–	–	–	–	2.0	–	–	–	–
$2,800 and under $2,900	–	–	–	–	1.0	–	–	–	–
$2,900 and under $3,000	–	–	–	–	.8	–	–	–	–
$3,000 and under $3,100	–	–	–	–	1.1	–	–	–	–
$3,100 and under $3,200	–	–	–	–	(0.7)	–	–	–	–
Total	100.0	100.0	100.0	100.0	100.0	100.0	100.0	100.0	100.0
Number of employees	58,242	55,132	114,459	47,241	18,627	10,012	6,831	24,405	13,951
Average monthly salary	$1,275	$1,410	$1,588	$1,794	$2,058	$1,437	$1,698	$983	$1,262

(Percent distribution of employees in selected clerical occupations by monthly salary, United States, except Alaska and Hawaii, March 1984)

Note: To avoid showing small proportions of employees scattered at or near the extremes of the distribution for some occupations, the percentages of employees in these intervals have been accumulated and are shown in the interval above or below the extreme interval containing at least 1 percent. The percentages representing these employees are shown in parentheses. Because of rounding, sums of individual items may not equal 100.

National Survey of Professional, Administrative, Technical, and Clerical Pay, March 1984 (Washington, D.C.: Bureau of Labor Statistics, 1984), p. 34.

Table 9.1   *Professional Associations Conducting Wage and Benefit Surveys*

Administrative Management Society—Maryland Road, Willow Grove, PA 19090; (215) 659-4300; clerical, management and electronic data processing compensation; regional breakdown; $100 each.

American Association of Engineering Societies—345 East 47th Street, New York, NY 10017; (212) 705-7840; engineering salaries including government and education; $55–$225.

American Chemical Society—1155 16th Street, NW, Washington, DC 20030; (202) 872-4600; members' salaries and starting salaries for chemists and chemical engineers; geographical and industrial breakdown; $20–$75.

American Compensation Association—P.O. Box 1176, Scottsdale, AZ 85252; (602) 951-9191; management compensation, salary budget survey; geographical breakdown; Free–$10.

Table 9.1   *continued*

Bank Administration Institute— 60 Gould, Rolling Meadows, IL 60008; (312) 228-6200; compensation for all positions in banking; geographical breakdown; $50 for members, $75 for nonmembers.

Battelle Institute— 505 Kings Avenue, Columbus, OH 43201; (614) 424-6424; research and development, salary and compensation; across industries; price varies, available to participants or government contractors.

Chamber of Commerce— 1615 H Street, NW, Washington, DC 20062; (202) 659-6000; manufacturing and nonmanufacturing benefits; geographical breakdown; $17.50.

College and University Personnel Association— 11 Dupont Circle, Suite 120, Washington, DC 20036; (202) 462-1038; compensation for administration and faculty in higher education; geographical breakdown; $25 for participants, $75 for nonparticipants.

College Placement Council, Inc.— 65 East Elizabeth Avenue, Bethlehem, PA 18018; (215) 868-1421; starting salaries of all college graduates; industrial and geographical breakdown; free to members, $150 per year to nonmembers.

The Conference Board, Inc.— 845 Third Avenue, New York, NY 10022; (212) 759-0900; compensation of top executives and outside directors; breakdown by industry and company size; $25–$150.

The Dartnell Institute— 4660 Ravenswood Avenue, Chicago, IL 60640-9981; (312) 561-4000; sales personnel compensation; industrial breakdown; $115.50.

The Endicott Report— Northwestern University, Evanston, IL 60201; (312) 492-3709; salaries offered to college graduates; $10.

Executive Compensation Service, Inc.— Two Executive Drive, Fort Lee, NJ 07024; (201) 585-9808; top, middle and supervisory management, professional and scientific, clerical and sales compensation; industrial and regional breakdown; $110–$495.

Health Insurance Institute— 1850 K Street, NW, Washington, DC 20006; (202) 862-4000; health insurance benefits; free.

International Foundation of Employee Benefits Plans— P.O. Box 69, Brookfield, WI 53005; employee benefits; regional and asset size breakdowns; free.

National Association of Mutual Insurance Companies— P.O. Box 68700, Indianapolis, IN 46268; (317) 875-5250; executive salaries in insurance industry; geographical breakdown; free to participants, $20–$30 for nonparticipants.

National Society of Professional Engineers— 1420 King Street, Alexandria, VA 22314; (703) 684-2800; salaries of engineers; breakdowns geographically and by industry; $30 to members, $55 to nonmembers.

National Telephone Cooperative Association— 2626 Pennsylvania Avenue, NW, Washington, DC 20037; (202) 298-2300; all telephone jobs; breakdown by region; $20 to members, $40 to nonmembers.

New York Chamber of Commerce— 200 Madison Avenue, New York, NY 10016; (212) 561-2020; salaries and benefits for all office jobs in New York City; $165 for members, $196 for nonmembers.

Scientific Manpower Commission— 1776 Massachusetts Avenue, NW, Washington, DC 20036; (202) 223-6995; salaries of scientists, engineers, and technicians; industrial and regional breakdown; $30.

Tool and Die Institute— 77 Busse Highway, Park Ridge, IL 60068; (312) 825-1120; trade compensation in the Chicago area; some by industry; free to members, $75 for nonmembers.

Table 9.2   *Consulting Organizations Providing Wage and*
                 Benefit Survey Data

Abbott, Langer and Associates—548 First Street, Crete, IL 60417; (312) 672-4200; wage surveys of numerous occupations; geographical and industrial breakdowns; $55–$175.

Arthur Young and Company—277 Park Avenue, New York, NY 10017; (212) 407-1500; executive compensation and compensation for board of directors; industrial breakdowns; $95–$195.

Cole Survey—100 Summer Street, Boston, MA 02110; (617) 547-3341; compensation in financial organizations; geographical breakdown; $300–$5,000.

Compass International—338 Beacon Street, Boston, MA 02116; (617) 536-2333; worldwide compensation; $1,000/year.

D. Dietrich Associates, Inc.—P.O. Box 511, Phoenixville, PA 19460; (215) 935-1563; technical compensation and compensation of some others; geographical breakdown; $60–$130.

Educational Research Services, Inc.—1800 Kent Street, #1020, Arlington, VA 22209; (703) 243-2100; salaries and compensation for professionals in teaching; geographical breakdown; three volumes at $30/volume.

Hay Associates—229 South 18th Street, Philadelphia, PA 19103; (215) 875-2300; both exempt and nonexempt wages; all industries and some by geographic region; price varies by client.

Heidrick and Struggles—125 South Wacker Drive, Chicago, IL 60606; (312) 867-9876; outside director and committee service compensation; breakdown by industry and company size; $20.

Hewitt Associates—100 Half Day Road, Lincolnshire, IL; (312) 295-5000. Top and middle management compensation; geographical breakdown; free for participants, $25 for nonparticipants.

Hospital Compensation Services—115 Watchung Drive, Hawthorne, NJ 07506; compensation for all positions in nursing homes and salaries for executives in hospitals; regional breakdowns; $105.

Reggio and Associates, Inc.—547 West Jackson Boulevard, Suite 505, Chicago, IL 60606; (312) 236-1840; numerous salary surveys covering various occupations; dependent on survey, geographical and industrial breakdowns; price varies with survey.

Robert Half International—552 Fifth Avenue, New York, NY 10036; (212) 221-6500; financial and data processing starting salaries; free.

Towers, Perrin, Forster and Crosby—600 Third Avenue, New York, NY 10016; (212) 309-3400; top and middle management and some nonexempt positions; $500–$1,200.

Advantages and Disadvantages of Third-Party Surveys   There are both advantages and limitations to the use of third-party surveys. One of the major advantages is that the data can be obtained relatively cheaply. This is particularly true of government data, and may be true if data from consultants are provided as part of a larger package in which the consultant is involved in implementing a comprehensive compensation system. A second advantage of third-party surveys is that data is often provided in summary form. The organization does not have to manipulate the data into usable form. Third, these data are usually based on large numbers of organizations and jobs. From a statistical sampling standpoint, the user can put greater faith in the data as being truly representative of prevailing wage practices.

In spite of the above advantages, there are several drawbacks to third-party data. First, the user has no way of knowing that the wage and benefit data reported in the survey are relevant for the key jobs of the organization. Since many of the data are obtained from mailed surveys of organizations, it may not be clear whether the jobs for which pay rates are reported are the same jobs that the organization would like pay data for.

Second, since the data are usually reported in summary form, it may be difficult for the user to determine if the pay rates reported are relevant for the organization's labor area or industry. If, for example, data are reported for a job only by organization size and broad industry groupings, there is no way to be sure that the data are the appropriate reference base for the user organization's pay system.

Third, especially in the case of government survey data, often the data may be out of date by the time they are made available to an organization.

Finally, the user is subject to the reporting system of the provider. This often restricts the relevancy of the data in several ways. On the one hand, the data reported may not be from the user's labor area. For example, the survey may report a job's wage data for the state as a whole, or for a region within a state. If the data are not available for a user's particular labor area or product market, then the data have little utility for assessing pay equity or checking pay constraints. Further, the ready-made survey results may not inquire into the important issues from the user's standpoint. For example, the survey data may give no information on health insurance or retirement plans. In short, users of ready-made surveys are in the position of taking whatever data is given them.

Custom-Designed Surveys

If custom-designed surveys are designed properly, the compensation decision maker can articulate the relevant organizations for inclusion in the labor and product market surveys and can also control the types of data which are collected.

A Sample Survey   An example of a custom-designed survey appears in Exhibit 9.8. The sample survey here has five parts. Each part is discussed separately.

Letter of Transmittal   Each survey questionnaire should have a letter of transmittal attached to it. This letter should include:

> A statement of purpose
> A desired response date
> An overview of the survey content
> An assurance of anonymity, if desired
> A commitment to share the results with the surveyed organization
> The name of the specific contact person at the surveying organization

(continued)

Exhibit 9.8   *Example of a Custom-Designed Survey*
Letter of Transmittal

Ms. Compensation Manager
XYZ Corp.
Anytown, USA ZIP

Dear Ms. Jones:

Thank you for agreeing to participate in ABC Companies' wage and benefits survey. The data are very important to us for our annual survey of key jobs and as we agreed on the phone, I will look forward to a return of the information in the enclosed self-addressed stamped envelope no later than February 15, 19___.

I would like to take just a second to acquaint you with the survey itself. The survey has four basic parts. First, we would like information on general policy issues. Second, since benefits are becoming such a major component of pay we ask that you provide benefits information to us. Third, we have included a separate sheet for each of _____ key jobs. Please provide us with information on the jobs that seem (based on the enclosed descriptions) to be most like our key jobs. The fourth and final section asks for information on merit and bonus systems in your organization.

I also want to reiterate our assurances to you that we will not identify your company individually in reporting the survey results. As is true of all our surveys, we are interested in assessing wage payments across a number of employers. However, we would like your permission to use your name as one of the respondents to the survey. Thus, while your individual pay practices will not be identified, we would like participants who receive the results to know which firms were included in the survey. If you would agree to allow us to use your company name, please indicate so at the appropriate place on the survey form. If you do not wish your company name identified with the survey, of course, we will not do so.

As has been our policy for the past 15 years, we continue to provide the results of this survey to all of those who participate free of charge. If you would like a copy of these results please indicate so at the appropriate place on the survey form.

Finally, you might note that we are providing you with our current pay practices for each of the key jobs. While this may not be as useful as summary data, we feel that you may be interested in knowing OUR pay practices at the present time for these key jobs.

Ms. Analyst is coordinating this survey for our company. She will be contacting your company on December _____, to determine if you have any questions on the survey. If, prior to that time, you have questions on the survey please call her at (XXX) YYY-ZZZZ.

Thank you again for your participation in the survey. If you can have your results back to us by February 15, 19___we should be able to share these results with you by April 1.

Sincerely,

Organizational Policy

I. Staff and Hours

Exempt=E and Nonexempt=NE

Number of employees?   E _____   NE _____

How many hours per week do your employees normally work?
E _____   NE _____

How much time allotted for lunch?   E _____   NE _____

(continued)

Exhibit 9.8   *continued*

Organizational Policy—continued

How much time allotted for breaks? E_____ NE_____

How much daily time allotted for them? E_____ NE_____

Do you have a 4-day week? E—Yes No;   NE—Yes No

Do any of your employees work on shifts?   (E only)   Yes No
If "Yes," answer below:

SHIFT	Shift hours	% premium pay
Evening (2nd)	_____	_____
Late (3rd)	_____	_____
Other	_____	_____

Do you have any form of flextime (allows employees to choose working hours)?
Managerial—Yes No;   Other Exempt—Yes No;   NE—Yes No.
If "Yes," please provide a sheet explaining how your flextime system works.

II. Salary Payment Policies

If your standard number of hours worked per week is less than 40, do you pay overtime
for hours in excess of the normal workweek but less than 40?   Yes No

If certain groups within the organization have less than a 40-hour workweek, please list
them.

GROUP	HOURS
_____	_____
_____	_____

What is overtime rate for individuals required to work on regularly scheduled holidays?
_____None _____1½ _____Double time _____Other

Have you granted any general across-the-board adjustments in wages or salary within the
past 24 months? Yes No.   If "Yes":

	Date	Approximate % Adjustment
1.	_____	_____
2.	_____	_____

Are these adjustments linked to the Bureau of Labor Statistics Consumer Price Index?
Yes No. If linked to any other price index, please indicate. _____

III. Starting Salaries of College Graduates

What is your average starting salary for a college graduate with a Bachelor's degree in
Business Administration, Accounting, Finance, Economics, Management, etc., pursuing a
nontechnical occupation in your firm? $_____.

What is your average starting salary for a college graduate with a Bachelor's degree in
Engineering, Mathematics, Statistics, etc., pursuing a technical occupation in your firm?
$_____.

(continued)

Exhibit 9.8   *continued*

Organizational Policy—continued

IV. Employment Policies

Do you pay employment agency fees for noncollege graduates?   Yes   No.
If "Yes," do you pay the fee at the time of employment?   Yes   No.   If "No"
when? _____.

Do you require aptitude tests be passed prior to employment?   Yes   No.
If "Yes," for which jobs do you require those tests?

Employee Benefits

I. Paid Vacations

What paid vacations are allowed?

Years of service inclusive:	Weeks of Vacation Allowed		
	Nonexempt	Exempt	Executive
0–1			
1–4			
5–9			
10–15			

Can unused vacation time be carried over to the following year?   Yes   No.   If "Yes,"
how many days? _____.

II. Paid Holidays

How many paid holidays do you grant? _____.

Christmas Day	E___	NE___	Independence Day	E___	NE___
New Year's Day	E___	NE___	Labor Day	E___	NE___
Washington's B'day	E___	NE___	Veterans' Day	E___	NE___
Good Friday	E___	NE___	Thanksgiving Day	E___	NE___
Memorial Day	E___	NE___	Employee's B'day	E___	NE___
Other (specify)					
_____	E___	NE___			
_____	E___	NE___			

III. Sick Leave

Do you have an official sick leave plan?   Yes   No.

How many days sick leave are granted per year?   E_____   NE_____

Do you have a waiting period before an employee is eligible for sick leave?
E—Yes   No.   NE—Yes   No.

(continued)

Exhibit 9.8   *continued*

Employee Benefits—continued

IV. Other Leaves

Do you grant leave with pay for any of the following reasons? (If yes, please indicate the number of days.)

Jury Duty	E_____	NE_____	Death (Family)	E_____	NE_____
Marriage	E_____	NE_____	Dental Appt.	E_____	NE_____
Family Illness	E_____	NE_____	Other_____	E_____	NE_____

V. Insurance Benefits

Do you have a group hospitalization or surgical plan?   Yes   No.   If "Yes," what % is paid by the employer?_____.

What is the monthly cost to the employee?   Single Plan $_____
Family Plan $_____

Is there a major medical addition to the regular insurance plan?   Yes   No
If "Yes," what is the one-time illness maximum? $_____
What is the lifetime illness maximum? $_____

At what amount of "out-of-pocket" employee cost per illness does the major medical plan assume full responsibility? $_____

Do you have a group dental plan?   Yes   No.   If "Yes," what % is paid by the employer?_____.

Do you have a group life insurance plan?   Yes   No.
If "Yes," is it contributory?   Yes   No
If "Yes," what % does the employer pay? _____.
Is the amount of insurance made available as a percentage of annual salary? (circle appropriate figure). 1.5   2.5   3.5   other_____
Is there a base to your insurance plan?   Yes   No
If "Yes," what is that base? $_____
Is there a cap to your insurance plan?   Yes   No
If "Yes," what is that cap? $_____

VI. Pension Plan

Do you have a pension plan?   Yes   No
Does it include all employees?   Yes   No
If "No," which groups are excluded?

Is it integrated with Social Security?   Yes   No

How do you determine average salary for pension purposes? (Please circle your method.)
Salary, final 3 years,   5 years,   10 years,   career average,   other_____.
Is it a defined benefit plan?   Yes   No.
If "Yes," what formula do you use for determining final pension benefits?

Is it a defined contribution plan?   Yes   No.
If "Yes," how do you determine contributions?

(continued)

Exhibit 9.8   *continued*

Employee Benefits—continued

Which ERISA vesting plan are you using?

What is your normal retirement age?_____
Do you have an early retirement eligibility?   Yes   No.
If "Yes" how do you determine it? Age, service, age and service, other_____

Have you provided a pension plan supplement for retirees in the past five years?
Yes   No.
Do you provide death benefits for retirees?   Yes   No.
Do the retirees contribute to the death benefit premiums?   Yes   No.

VII. General

Do you provide a cafeteria service for your employees?   Yes   No.
If "Yes," % subsidization?_____
Do you provide parking for all employees or subsidize parking fees?   Yes   No.
Are your clerical employees represented by a labor union?   Yes   No.
Are your nonclerical employees represented by a labor union?   Yes   No.
Do you have an education benefit?   Yes   No.
If "Yes," for what employee groups? E_____   NE_____   Exec_____
If "Yes," for what programs?   G.E.D.   Undergraduate   Graduate   Vocational
Other _____.
If "Yes," what % of tuition is reimbursed?_____

Does your organization calculate the total cost of fringe benefits as a percentage of payroll
or base pay?   Yes   No.
If "Yes," what is the %?_____
What components go into this percentage?   (Check all that apply.)
Employer contributions to Social Security_____
Employer contributions to private pension plan_____
Employer contributions to group health insurance_____
Employer contributions to group dental plans_____
Unemployment compensation insurance_____
Workers' Compensation Insurance_____
Other_____

Merit Review Plan

Do you have a merit pay plan?   E—Yes   No;   NE—Yes   No;   Exec—Yes   No.
Briefly describe:

Do you have an annual bonus plan?   E—Yes   No;   NE—Yes   No;   Exec—Yes   No.
For each group indicate: date of last bonus,
                                    % of salary

Job Data

Job Title: Switchboard Operator

Thumbnail Job Description:

   1. Provide banking services to all customers in a friendly, efficient, and professional
manner.
   2. Operate the switchboard.

                                                                    (continued)

Exhibit 9.8   *continued*

Job Data—continued

3. Open incoming mail and disperse to the proper departments.
4. Maintain the copy machine and record daily usage.
5. Coordinate the usage of the bank owned vehicles.
6. Receive information for the daily bulletin.
7. Receive and deposit milk machine money.
8. Verify and record internal services time cards and attendance records.
9. Provide specific copy machine reproductions for all bank locations.
10. Assist other employees within the department whenever possible.
11. Perform other duties that are approved or assigned by your superiors.

Job Specifications: Switchboard Operator
The job requires little independent judgment on the part of the employee. Little direction is needed, and the work is infrequently checked. There is substantial public contact but infrequent intrabank contact. The job demands little or no extraordinary concentration. There are few physical demands with little or no unpleasant working conditions. Less than a month of training is required. General banking equipment and the PBX are used. Telephone communication skills are necessary.

Please complete this form for your comparable job:

Job Title: _____
Minimum Pay: _____ (or entry-level hiring rate)
Median Pay: _____ (or average of the range)
Maximum Pay: _____ (or maximum longevity rate)

Total Number of Employees in This Job:_____
Minimum Actual Pay: _____ Number of Employees: _____
Maximum Actual Pay: _____ Number of Employees: _____
Average Actual Pay: _____ Number of Employees: _____
Median Actual Pay: _____ Number of Employees: _____

A specific date that the contact person will telephone to clarify any items on the survey

An expression of appreciation for participation.

The last item is desirable, not just from a courtesy standpoint, but to ensure as high a response rate as possible. The commitment to share survey results will also enhance response rates, as will the assurance of anonymity. It is also desirable to contact each company by phone, in advance of sending out the survey, to verbally solicit its participation.

Organizational Policy   There is considerable variance among employers on general policies.[9] This variability seems to be greatest across industries; responses in a labor market survey would probably vary more than in a product market survey.[10]

Organizational policies should be solicited for different groups of employees. In the sample survey form in Exhibit 9.8, the breakdown is provided for exempt and nonexempt jobs. Further breakdowns may be desirable. For example, office and clerical nonexempt jobs are typically treated the same as managerial jobs for workweek periods and hours of work. However, in some settings they may not be treated the same. Similarly, usually nonexempt union and nonunion employees are treated the same for overtime purposes, but this is not always the case. There seems to be no sure way of knowing where these exceptions occur except to have a firsthand knowledge of employee practices in one's industry and geographic area. Where these differences are known they should be allowed for in the wage survey form.

Employee Benefits Employee benefits have grown over the years until today they represent over 40 percent of base pay.[11] Employee benefits are a major component of the total compensation package, and failure to obtain employee benefits data could threaten the validity of the survey data. One industry study found that benefits and wages tend to vary together.[12] High-paying firms within the industry also had higher benefit levels. This study, in addition to demonstrating the importance of employee benefits in general, also found that both employee wages and benefits are determined by ability and willingness to pay. These results are consistent with a major theme of this textbook, that wages are constrained by a firm's ability to pay.

A major problem associated with surveying organizations about benefits data is that the formulas used for computing the employers' contributions to such things as the group health insurance plan vary considerably from one plan to another. A second problem is that the absolute benefits vary considerably from one plan to another.[13] Knowing the percentage rate an employee contributes to a plan says nothing about the relative costs of this benefit for the employer. Since, particularly in the case of a product market survey, the surveying organization is basically interested in the contribution of benefits to labor costs, it may be more appropriate to ask the surveyed organizations to report the cost of all benefits as a percentage of payroll or as a percentage of base pay. Many organizations are now doing this, and in the future this information should be more readily available in most firms.[14] A firm that is concerned over compensation in the product market is less concerned about the structure of benefits (such as paid holidays off versus longer vacations) and more concerned about the total costs of the benefits package.[15] The sample survey in Exhibit 9.8 in the employee benefits section asks for the cost of benefits as a percentage of total labor costs or base pay.

On the other hand, if the organization is concerned about benefits from an employee equity standpoint, then the earlier questions in the employee benefits section are most crucial. Since employees may compare their pension, vacation, or paid holiday schedule to those offered by other organizations, the surveying organization will be concerned about how the structure of its benefits package compares to the structure of benefits packages of other firms within the relevant labor market.[16]

Merit Review Data The surveying organization will want to know how employees qualify for pay increases within their jobs. Are pay raises based on merit, on seniority (such as time in grade), or on a combination of merit and seniority? Also, it is important to know if employees qualify for annual bonuses. It is not uncommon for an employer to offer slightly lower wages, but to provide an annual bonus of 5 to 10 percent. For pay purposes, such bonuses ultimately increase the rate of pay accordingly.[17]

Job Data   The job data section of the survey form asks the responding organization to provide data about the specific key jobs. In Exhibit 9.8 the form is for only one job. There would be as many of these forms as there are key jobs being surveyed. In general, it is worthwhile to provide the job title in use, alternate job titles, and a brief job description and job specifications. The responding organization can then determine which of its jobs is closest to the key job in the survey.

   In addition to providing this information, it is recommended that the surveying organization also provide wage data about its own organization to the respondent. This is one more way to increase the likelihood of a response.

   Finally, the job data section asks for both wage information as it might appear in policy statements, and wage behavior actually engaged in by the firm. This distinction is an important one. Often an employer's pay behaviors are different than its stated policy. To the extent that an employer is paying more or less than stated policy, using only the stated policy data will place the surveying organization at a disadvantage when it makes its own pay decisions. If, for example, the responding organization's pay is actually higher than its policy but the surveying organization follows the policy statement, then the surveying organization has underpriced its jobs relative to the responding organization. In the case of wage behavior relative to the product market, underpricing may result in wage savings. However, if the data is from the labor market, then the employer may be hurt in its ability to compete for employees. Overpayment relative to the product market will result in a cost disadvantage for the organization, whereas overpayment relative to the labor market should work to the organization's advantage in attracting labor supplies. In any event, it is critical to obtain information on actual pay practice as well as stated pay practice so that valid data is obtained for compensation decision making.[18]

Comprehensive and Abbreviated Surveys   The survey form in Exhibit 9.8 is a comprehensive survey form used to ascertain considerable information from the surveyed organization. In all likelihood, an organization will not regularly ask for all of this information in every survey, for several reasons. First, one of the problems of custom surveys is obtaining cooperation. While there may be numerous reasons for a lack of willingness to participate in surveys, one major reason is the length of the survey. The shorter the survey form is, the greater the likelihood that others will cooperate in filling it out.[19]

   A second reason for using a shorter survey questionnaire is that many employment policies do not change rapidly over time. For example, there are rarely changes in vacation policy or number of paid holidays.[20] Benefits data probably do not have to be surveyed more than every four or five years, and the same is probably true for general policies and for merit policies. Only the questions dealing with wage rates for key jobs need be sent to respondents on a regular annual basis. This will reduce the length of the survey considerably, and may increase the probability of respondents returning the completed questionnaire.

Telephone Surveys   Exhibit 9.8 presented a comprehensive custom-designed survey format. Mailed surveys are generally much briefer in format. For the active compensation decision maker there may be infrequent use of mailed surveys.

The compensation decision maker may use the telephone to solicit specific information from several organizations. For example, the organization may be concerned about the wage rate for a particular entry-level job, or the number of paid holidays provided by other firms. In these cases the compensation manager may call a number of labor or product market competitors to find out their current practices. If this process is repeated often enough (it frequently is in many firms) and the information is properly maintained, then a mail survey may never be undertaken because the data have been collected piecemeal through time.

Information collected in this manner is perfectly acceptable so long as it is collected and recorded systematically. That is, such data should not come from a haphazard survey. Valid data will result only when there is careful selection of organizations based on the intended use of the information.

Selecting Organizations for the Survey   Previous sections discussed how to identify which organizations qualify for inclusion in either a product market or labor market wage and salary and benefits survey. After all of the possible firms that might be included in a survey have been identified, the number may be so large that it is impractical to survey them all. In this case the surveying organization may wish to survey a subset of these firms. There are two common methods of determining a subset of firms: the random sample and the stratified random sample.

Random Sample   For the wage and benefits survey, random sampling involves selecting a sample of organizations from a larger population. If the sample is to be a true random sample, then each organization should have an equally likely probability of being selected for the sample. If the sampling procedure does not assure that each organization is equally likely to be chosen, then the sample is said to be biased.[21] Biases in sampling are important to the extent that they cause mistakes in inferring attributes of the larger population of organizations. For example, to make an inference about the average height of student athletes, it would be unwise to sample only those people observed playing basketball in an NCAA tournament.

In the context of wage and salary surveys, an organization should obtain the survey data from an unbiased sample so that an inference can be made about the average wage for a job. It is important that firms are chosen for the survey on a random basis. To do so the organization could use very simple to very complex procedures. For example, suppose that there are 500 possible firms in the labor market. Perhaps the organization wishes to have 50 firms in the final sample (for a 10 percent sampling rate). The organization could write the names of all 500 firms on cards, and draw 50 cards out of a barrel. Alternately, the firm could assign each firm a number and then use a table of random numbers to identify the 50 firms.[22]

Stratified Random Sampling   There may be times when an organization would want to intentionally bias the survey data. For example, if an employer considered it important to sample by size of firm, or if an employer wished to place particular weight on firms with a particular technology, then it could introduce this known bias into the sample using stratified random sampling.[23]

As an example, the organization might have identified 500 firms within the population to be surveyed. Half of those firms have fewer than 250 employees, 25 percent have 251 to 500 employees, and another 25 percent have more than 500 employees. If the surveying organization places heavy emphasis on being competitive with the firms which have 251 to 500 employees, then the survey sample could be weighted accordingly. The organization might want 50 percent of the responding firms to be from this group, and 25 percent of the respondents from each of the other two groups. If the total sample is to be 50 organizations, the composition of that sample will be: 12.5 firms with 1 to 250 employees, 25 firms with 251 to 500 employees, and 12.5 firms with more than 500 employees. (The fractions could constitute a 26th firm in the 251 to 500 employee size group.) If the employer wanted this ratio of firms from all firms identified, it could then determine the sampling rate by firm size. The calculations for doing this are shown in Exhibit 9.9.

Conscious bias should be well grounded in some rationale. Conscious bias might be used to assure that one type of company that is a small percentage of

Exhibit 9.9   *Calculations for Determining the Sampling Rate of Firms to Survey in a Stratified Sample*

	Number of Firms in Labor Area	Desired Weighting of Firms in Survey	Number in Desired Final Sample[a]	Sampling Rate by Firm Size
Less than 251 employees	250	25%	12	$12 \div 250 = 4.8\%$
251 to 500 employees	125	50	26	$26 \div 125 = 20.8\%$
More than 500 employees	125	25	12	$12 \div 125 = 9.6\%$
Total	500	100%	50	

[a] Rounding adds 1 firm to the 251 to 500 employee group and deletes .5 from the other two groups.

the total labor market gets extra weight so as to accurately assess wages in that industry; to place extra emphasis on one geographic area of the market; or to place more or less stress on companies that use certain types of equipment (such as video terminals as opposed to card punch machines).

Summarizing Survey Data

There are almost as many ways to summarize wage data as there are people who summarize the data.[24] The general rule to use in summarizing the survey data is use a format that is useful for the surveying organization. This issue, of course, is a moot one for those organizations that rely on third-party data. Those organizations will find that they must use the data as it is summarized for them. This discussion pertains to data collected in a custom designed survey.

Benefits Data

There are numerous ways to summarize benefits data from the survey. Only an example is presented here. In the case of numbers of holidays granted with pay, several questions may be of interest. First, the organization may wish to know the total number of holidays with pay provided by surveyed organizations. In this case the appropriate summary of data would be a distribution of the number of holidays with pay, along with relative and cumulative frequency distributions. The data table might show that 15 firms (30 percent) provide 8 paid holidays per year; 10 firms (20 percent) provide 9 paid holidays per year; 15 firms (30 percent) provide 10 paid holidays per year; 25 (50 percent) of all firms provide either 9 or 10 paid holidays per year; and so forth. An example of how these data may be presented is shown in Exhibit 9.10.

A second question may be which holidays are granted with pay each year. Thus, the data may show that 100 percent (all 50) of the firms grant the Fourth of July off with pay, but that only 50 percent (25 firms) grant the employee's birthday off with pay, and so forth. One way of presenting the data is displayed in Exhibit 9.11.

The data collected on benefits in the sample survey form in Exhibit 9.8 can provide answers for various questions. The data itself should be summarized in a way that is consistent with the questions to be answered.

Wage Data

It is easier to be more precise about how to summarize wage data. Since the purpose of this data is to find out going rates in the labor or product market, data should be summarized in terms of minimum, maximum, mean, and median actual pay rates. An employer may also be interested in the averages of these pay rates. By examining the average of the minimum rates, maximum rates, mean, and median rates, the compensation decision maker can identify the parameters surrounding the organization's own pay practice to make decisions about changes in current pay rates.

Exhibit 9.10   *Relative and Cumulative Frequency Distributions for Paid Holidays among Firms Surveyed*

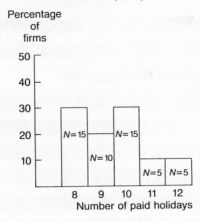

Relative Frequency

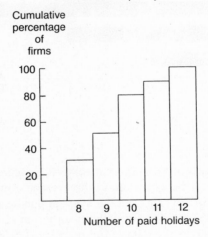

Cumulative Frequency

Summary Statistics and Wage Data

The reporting of wage rate data can take numerous forms. As noted above, means, medians, and modes are one set of summary statistics. The mean of a set of wage rates is the arithmetic average of all the wage rates reported. The modal wage rate is the most common wage rate reported, while the median wage rate is the middle wage rate reported. Each of these may be important in its own right, and they will be equal only in the case where the distribution of wage rates is normal.

More often than not, what is more interesting than the simple mean wage or modal wage is the mean, median, or mode of other characteristics of the wage data. For example, 20 employers might report the minimum pay, the median pay, and the maximum pay for a given job. It may be of interest to

Exhibit 9.11   *Frequency Distribution of Firms Providing Select*
Holidays with Pay

ᵃ Some organizations provide other holidays with pay, such as Hanukkah, Lee-Jackson Day, or the employee's
spouse's birthday.

look at the mean of each of these three measures. Specifically, the compensation decision maker may be interested in the average minimum wage rate for the job, the average median rate, and the average maximum rate. These three wage rate values would provide for stability in the statistics being analyzed.

Another way to report the data is by quartiles. This summary would include the wage rate below which 25 percent of the reported rates fall, the rate below which 50 percent of the reported rates fall, and the wage rate below which 75 percent of the wage rates fall. From these data the interquartile range can be reported. The **interquartile** range is the range between the 25th percentile wage rate and the 75th percentile wage rate. This is a commonly accepted indicator of central tendency.

Still another way to summarize the data is to examine **weighted average** wage rates. That is, the analyst could take the actual wage rate paid to employees, multiply it by the number of employees at each rate, sum this value, and divide by the total number of employees working in the job. This weighted average provides information about the average actual pay level in the survey group, a figure that could be different than the average wage rate across surveyed companies. A number of these summary statistics can be seen in Exhibit 9.12 (page 258), which reports survey results from a local government survey for the job of clerk steno II.

Reporting Data to Management

It is easy to overkill with numbers and to confuse rather than clarify. A good way to report data to management is by job. A summary sheet might look something like the one in Exhibit 9.13.

Exhibit 9.13 (page 259) shows the wage data from 14 organizations that participated in a survey. The top of the figure contains the raw data reported by the responding organizations. If the number of participants is very large, this information should be left off the report. The information at the bottom of Exhibit 9.13 is most relevant. It shows the average minimum wage, average median wage, average maximum wage, and the weighted average wage in these organizations. As presented, the data are relatively easy to understand and could be presented clearly to management.

Wage data are perceived here as being used as micrometers rather than yardsticks to assess an organization's pay practices relative to other organizations'. Some sources argue that survey data are a yardstick.[25] Because of sampling problems, sample sizes, and lack of participation, survey data are considered too unstable for making fine distinctions about wage payments, and should be used only to make rough comparisons about relative pay equity. These arguments have considerable validity, but if the data are well collected from the appropriate organizations, the author feels they can be used for fine tuning the pay system. Results that can be used to fine tune wages can generally be obtained only from custom-designed surveys.

Summary

This chapter focused on wage and salary and benefits surveys. The first part of the chapter reviewed the importance and nature of labor and product market surveys to identify characteristics of labor and product markets for designing wage and salary and benefit surveys.

The second portion of this chapter examined survey data sources. There are three main sources of third-party survey data: government agencies, professional associations, and consulting firms. Strengths and weaknesses of third-party data were discussed. Custom-designed surveys were then discussed, along with the attendant strengths and weaknesses of these surveys. A sample survey form was presented and discussed to show the importance and purpose of each of the components of a wage and salary and benefits survey. Finally, summarizing survey results was discussed.

Discussion Questions

1. Discuss the relative advantages and disadvantages of third-party and custom-designed survey data.

Exhibit 9.12   Summary Analysis Sheet: *Clerk Steno II*

Minimum			Midpoint			Maximum			Average/Actual		
Rate	Number Employed	Agency	Rate	Number Employed	Agency	Rate	Number Employed	Agency	Rate	Number Employed	Agency
$15,048	14	V	$18,150	14	V	$21,252	14	V	$19,728	14	V
13,624	2	S	16,224	2	S	18,824	2	S	16,102	11	U
12,792	21	T	15,600	11	U	18,720	11	U	15,652	2	S
12,480	11	U	14,900	4	M	17,772	4	M	13,865	21	T
12,028	4	M	14,394	21	T	16,046	1	N	13,520	4	D
11,690	0	L	13,520	4	D	15,995	21	T	13,454	1	N
10,962	15	C	13,454	0	L	15,964	9	P	13,262	4	M
10,861	1	N	13,454	1	N	15,620	4	D	13,137	2,414	R
10,816	9	P	13,130	9	P	15,350	0	L	12,871	15	A
10,706	8	J	12,606	2,414	R	14,639	4	I	12,810	9	P
10,656	2,414	R	12,515	4	I	14,556	2,414	R	12,802	15	C
10,580	15	A	12,383	8	J	14,196	15	A	12,383	8	J
10,566	4	D	12,256	15	A	14,060	8	J	12,102	4	I
10,440	4	Z	12,086	15	C	13,991	15	C	11,972	32	H
10,391	4	I	11,972	32	H	13,673	32	H	11,785	2	Z
10,271	32	H	11,764	4	Z	13,468	13	B	11,690	0	L
10,072	7	E	11,463	7	E	13,128	4	Z	11,572	13	B
9,776	13	B	11,076	13	B	12,853	7	E	11,457	7	E
8,189	1	G	9,320	1	G	10,451	1	G	9,953	1	G

Respondents	19	
Mean range	$11,155–$15,293	
Mean midpoint	$13,172	
Q1 range	$10,416–$13,832	
Median range	$10,706–$14,639	
Q3 range	$11,859–$16,021	

Respondents	19
Mean	$13,164
Q1	$11,972
Median	$12,841
Q3	$13,520
No. emp.	192
Weighted average actual	$13,412

Clerk Steno II

This is responsible clerical work involving the performance of a variety of secretarial and office manager duties. The Clerk Steno II exercises considerable judgment in establishing or adapting work procedures to new situations. Work is reviewed upon completion, but frequently no check is made of the data compiled or the records prepared. May exercise supervision over the general operations of an office and over other clerical personnel. Requires graduation from high school and considerable experience (usually two to five years) in clerical and stenographic work.   (Grade 23)

Exhibit 9.13 *Summary of Wage Survey Data*

Organization	Pay Policy Rates			Average/Actual Rate	
	Minimum	Midpoint	Maximum	Rate	Number of Employees
D	$12,251	$15,620	$18,096	$14,913	15
P	11,908	14,482	17,602	14,144	2
H	11,848	13,814	15,783	13,814	4
K	10,780	13,004	16,439	13,628	40
A	11,112	12,871	14,909	14,549	26
C	11,510	12,690	14,690	14,306	16
I	10,391	12,515	14,639	14,249	3
M	9,896	12,259	14,621	10,911	5
G	10,451	11,895	13,339	12,598	3
N	9,960	11,544	13,128	12,557	28
E	10,072	11,463	12,853	12,029	9
J	9,692	11,203	12,714	11,203	4
R	8,911	10,543	12,175	11,451	2,268
B	8,476	9,776	11,648	10,526	14

Average of minimum = $10,518
Average of midpoint = $12,406
Average of maximum = $14,474
Weighted average for actual = $11,579

Interquartile range for midpoint is $11,463 − $13,004.

2. A college wants to conduct a labor market survey for (a) office clerical employees; (b) maintenance employees; (c) administrators; and (d) faculty. Identify the relevant labor market for each of these occupational groups.

3. Is a college concerned about relevant product market surveys? Might it be concerned about such surveys for one or more occupational groups but not others? If so, which groups and why?

4. What are the relevant dimensions of a labor market and a product market?

5. Explain why product market surveys are intended to reflect the wage level of product market competitors.

6. Why is it important to collect actual wage and benefits data as opposed to stated wage and benefits policies?

7. After conducting a labor market survey, a truck manufacturer in rural Virginia finds that it is paying about $4 per hour above the going market rate, but about $1 per hour below the product market rate (employees are unionized and represented by the UAW). Discuss this phenomenon. What do you suspect led to this situation, and what advantages and disadvantages would you associate with this wage position in the marketplace?

8. A hospital in a small university-dominated community (population 35,000, with 23,000 students) pays at the bottom of the wage rate range for all occupational groups except doctors relative to other hospitals in the area and relative to other firms in the area. Total population in the relevant labor and product market area is 300,000. This hospital has no trouble attracting qualified applicants. Why?

Exercises

1. The Busti National Bank has just decided to open a branch in Bemus Bay, an exclusive resort located about 20 miles from Arkwright, a large city. There is no bank there at present.

Busti is anxious to determine the appropriate wage for the clerical staff it expects to hire. Clerks in the bank's offices in Arkwright receive a starting wage of $150 a week, but through promotions they can work up to $200. As a matter of company policy, these wage rates have been set at the midpoint of the other banks' rates in Arkwright.

A survey of the local businesses at Bemus Bay, primarily realty and insurance offices for local stores, indicates that the going rate for qualified clerical personnel is $225 to $250 a week. The higher rates in Bemus Bay may be attributed in part to the higher cost of living in this resort town, the limited number of young people seeking employment, and the fact that there are no other banks in Bemus Bay. Banks in Arkwright have traditionally paid lower wages than other businesses, on the grounds that banks offer better working conditions and higher prestige.

 a. What should the Busti Bank establish as its hiring rate for clerical personnel? What factors should be considered in making the decision?

 b. Could the bank justify to its Arkwright employees the fact that it was paying higher wages in Bemus Bay?

Exercise 2

Survey of Labor Market Wages

Organization	Minimum	Midpoint	Maximum	Rate	Number of Employees
S	$16,432	$19,552	$22,672	$19,344	2
U	15,200	19,000	22,800	20,300	2
V	15,444	18,909	22,374	19,728	14
T	13,832	15,564	17,295	16,328	18
M	12,028	14,900	17,772	13,262	6
W	11,336	14,200	17,056	14,200	2
D	10,566	13,520	15,620	13,520	5
N	10,861	15,454	16,046	13,454	1
P	10,816	13,130	15,964	12,974	5
A	11,112	12,871	14,909	13,518	13
H	11,022	12,854	14,686	12,854	10

Survey of Product Market Wages

Organization	Minimum	Midpoint	Maximum	Rate	Number of Employees
L	$11,157	$12,837	$14,644	$13,328	2
K	10,286	12,408	15,686	13,004	21
Z	10,920	12,324	13,728	12,431	18
J	11,115	12,105	13,094	12,105	2
C	10,962	12,086	13,991	13,455	20
Y	9,588	11,988	14,388	15,444	1
I	9,888	11,916	13,944	9,888	2
R	9,749	11,529	13,309	11,808	1,509
G	9,953	11,329	12,704	12,099	1
E	9,605	10,914	12,222	9,890	1
B	8,476	9,776	11,648	9,343	14

Source: Leonard R. Sayles, George Strauss, *Managing Human Resources*, ©1977, p. 390. Reprinted by permission of Prentice-Hall, Inc., Englewood Cliffs, N. J.

2. On the preceeding page are the results of labor and product market survey data for one job.

    a. Calculate summary statistics for these data.

    b. Recommend a pay rate for this job.

References

[1] John F. Burton and John E. Parker, "Interindustry Variations in Voluntary Labor Mobility," *Industrial and Labor Relations Review* 22 (January 1969): pp. 199–216.

[2] David G. Brown, "Expected Ability to Pay and Interindustry Wage Structure in Manufacturing," *Industrial and Labor Relations Review* (October 1962): pp. 45–62.

[3] Ibid.

[4] See Howard R. Bloch and Robert L. Pennington, "Measuring Discrimination: What Is a Relevant Labor Market?" *Personnel*, July/August 1980, pp. 21–30.

[5] Walter Fogel, "Occupational Earnings: Market and Institutional Influences," *Industrial and Labor Relations Review* (October 1979): pp. 24–35.

[6] Richard Lester, "Pay Differentials by Size of Establishment," *Industrial Relations*, October 1967, pp. 57–67.

[7] See In the Matter of the Boston Survey Group, Superior Court of Massachusetts, C.A. No. 56341, August 2, 1982.

[8] Ibid.

[9] Herbert Heneman III *et al.*, *Personnel/Human Resource Management* (Homewood, Ill.: Irwin, 1983).

[10] Thomas A. Pugel, "Profitability, Concentration and the Interindustry Variation in Wages," *Review of Economics and Statistics*, May 1980, pp. 248–253.

[11] U.S. Chamber of Commerce, *Employee Benefits 1979* (Washington, D.C.: U.S. Chamber of Commerce Survey Research Center, 1980).

[12] Frederick S. Hills and R. Eugene Hughes, "Salaries and Fringe Benefits in an Academic Labor Market: Examining Internal and External Labor Markets, Explaining Geographic Differentials," presented at National Academy of Management Meetings, National Academy of Management, San Francisco, Calif., 1978.

[13] Eddie C. Smith, "Strategic Business Planning and Human Resources: Part 1," *Personnel Journal* (August 1982): pp. 606–610.

[14] Jerry Rosenbloom and G. Victor Hallman, *Employee Benefits Planning* (Englewood Cliffs, N.J.: Prentice-Hall, 1981).

[15] Robert W. McCaffery, *Managing the Employee Benefits Program* (New York: American Management Association, 1972).

[16] Robert Otteman, "Employee Preference for Various Compensation and Benefit Options," *Personnel Administrator*, November 1975, pp. 31–36.

[17] Robert E. Sibson, "Executive Pay—The Long Term Is Where the Action Is," *Nation's Business*, November 1971, pp. 29–33.

[18] Barbara L. Fielder, "Conducting a Wage and Salary Survey," *Personnel Journal* (December 1982): pp. 879–890.

[19] S. Avery Raube, "Pay Surveys in Perspective," *Business Management Record*, May 1963, pp. 11–16.

[20] U.S. Chamber of Commerce, *Employee Benefits 1980* (Washington, D.C.: U.S. Chamber of Commerce Survey Research Center, 1981).

[21] Russell L. Ackoff, *Scientific Method* (New York: Wiley, 1962): pp. 223.

[22] Ibid., p. 224.

[23] Ibid., p. 225.

[24] D. W. Belcher *et al.*, "Analysis and Use of Wage Survey Data," working paper, San Diego State University, 1982.

[25] Graef S. Crystal, "The Reemergence of Industry Pay Differentials," *Compensation Review* (third quarter, 1983): pp. 29–32.

10

Pay Structure Design:

Integrating Job

Evaluation and Pay

Structure Data

· **Learning Objectives**

· **Introduction**

· **Theoretical Objectives of a Wage Structure**

· **Multiple Wage Structures**

Reasons for Multiple Structures
Multiple Wage Structure Relationships

· **Job Evaluation Data and Pay Grades**

Establishing Pay Grades
Administrative Convenience
Other Factors
Determining the Number of Grades

· **Determining Internal Equity**

Internal Equity Using a Freehand Line of Best Fit
Internal Equity with a Regression Line
Internal Equity as a Sole Criterion

· **External Equity Determination**

Wage Rates
Slotting in Nonkey Jobs

· **Product Market Constraints**

· **Labor Costs and Decision Making**

· **Nonlinear Wage Lines**

· **Designing Pay Ranges**

Ranges for Merit
Ranges for Seniority
Examples of Merit and Seniority Pay Ranges
Flat Rate Systems
Range Overlap

· **Implementing a Systematic Pay Structure**

Communication with Employees
Initial Adjustment of Rates
Pay Structure Maintenance
Training of Managers

· **Exercise**

Learning Objectives

In general, to learn how to integrate information from job evaluation with information from wage surveys so as to build a wage policy line.
To learn the theoretical objectives of building a wage structure with market data (balancing internal and external equity).
To learn how to develop a wage policy line with the freehand method and with the multiple regression method.
To learn why and how to construct pay grades.
To learn about pay ranges and how they can be used in compensation decision making.
To learn how to go through a decision process which will result in a comprehensive pay structure.
To learn how to implement a comprehensive pay structure.

Introduction

This chapter is in some senses a summary and integration of the efforts of compensation decision makers discussed in the previous three chapters. Chapters 7 and 8 concerned job evaluation and how to conduct job evaluation. Chapter 9 discussed labor and product market wage and benefits surveys. Having collected all of this information, the compensation decision maker must now act upon the data. That is, these data must now be combined into the pay structure for the job group under analysis.[1]

This chapter discusses the activities involved in building the pay structure. The objectives are to identify why these activities are undertaken, to present techniques used in setting a wage structure, and to show the reader how to use these techniques. Finally, this chapter deals with the topic of designing pay ranges. By the end of this chapter the major compensation goal of building a pay structure that is internally equitable (to motivate staying) and externally equitable (to motivate joining and staying), and that allows for performance rewards (to motivate high performance) will have been completed.

Theoretical Objectives of a Wage Structure

When conducting a job evaluation, the compensation decision maker is attempting to establish a hierarchy of jobs in terms of their relative worth. Chapters 7 and 8 noted that this relative worth is partially a function of what management wishes to base pay on, and partially a function of what employees wish their pay to be based on. As a consequence compensable factors are chosen in the context of a job evaluation committee that has both employees and management as members. This committee, through job evaluation, establishes the relative value of jobs. Job evaluation determines that one job is worth more than a second job, which in turn is determined to be worth more than a third job—but how much more has not been determined. Job evaluation establishes an internal relationship among jobs that is perceived as equitable by members of the organization. Enhanced equity feelings may result in high motivation to remain with the organization.

Not everyone views job evaluation as a pure process of establishing internally equitable pay relationships among jobs. For example, some authors suggest that job evaluation is a process of rationalizing going rates in the marketplace. They argue that firms select and weigh compensable factors in a way that will capture current labor market rates.[2] This is one reason for policy capturing and statistical approaches to weighting factors discussed in Chapter 9.[3] To the extent that this argument is valid, job evaluation is not a purely internal rationalization of relative job worth as suggested by others.[4]

Chapter 9 developed the notion of wage surveys. Although there are both labor market and product market surveys the labor market survey is most relevant for determining external pay equity. Through labor market surveys the organization can determine the extent to which it is paying equitable wages relative to other employers of labor in its recruiting area.[5] If its wage rates are equitable relative to the labor market, then the firm should be competitive for labor resources, thereby motivating employees to join the organization. Similarly, perceived equity relative to the labor market should encourage employees to stay with the firm. An organization's decision to pay labor market competitive wages will be constrained by its ability to pay. Assuming that an organization must compete against other firms in the product market, the organization is constrained by wages paid by its product market competitors.

Analysis of wage survey data can be thought of as the process whereby the organization establishes the absolute wages for jobs in the evaluated hierarchy. While job evaluation determines the relative ranking of jobs in terms of worth, the use of market data to anchor key jobs at certain wage rates establishes the absolute pay rate that jobs will carry. The resulting wage structure reflects both internal and external equity considerations, and can be seen as the balancing of internal and external wage equity.

Having established the absolute wage rates for jobs in the internal job hierarchy, organizations typically will establish a wage range for a job. A **wage range** can be defined as the variation in pay that is available in a job. This wage range gives the organization three options, or a combination of the three.

First, wage ranges for a job can be used to pay different amounts of money to different employees in the same job depending upon their relative performance levels. The use of pay ranges for this purpose allows the organization to reward performance. The establishment of pay ranges can be thought of as an administrative mechanism to motivate performance.

Second, pay ranges allow for salary growth based on differences in seniority. When wage ranges are used for this purpose an employee will typically move up in pay for each fixed interval of time on the job. For example, an employee might receive a $0.25 raise at the end of the first six months of employment, another $0.25 raise at the end of one year of employment, and

$0.25 at the end of each subsequent year of employment, up to the maximum of the range. Use of the pay range in this fashion will probably not motivate performance, but such seniority-based raises should motivate employees to stay with the organization.

A third reason to have pay ranges is to allow for variation in pay among employees during probationary employment. For example, it may take time for employees to become minimally proficient in their jobs. The organization may wish to pay lower wages during the time employees are learning the job and to increase wages once they are proficient at the job.

Some pay plans use some combination of merit increase, seniority increase, and probationary or proficiency increases, and these will be discussed later in the chapter.

Multiple Wage Structures

Although an organization may occasionally develop one wage structure for the entire organization, it is more realistic to think in terms of an organization having multiple wage structures.

Reasons for Multiple Structures

Organizations employ numerous types of labor, such as managerial talent, clerical talent, operative talent, and sales talent. For a number of reasons, the organization may not want to or be able to integrate all of these occupational job families into one wage structure. One reason why this may not be practical is that it is difficult to find compensable factors that are appropriate for distinguishing among jobs across job families, such as working conditions as a factor to distinguish among managerial jobs, or decision-making authority to distinguish among operative jobs.

A second reason for having numerous wage structures is that jobs are usually anchored to a specific labor market. Wage structures across job families may pose problems when it comes time to price those jobs.

A third reason for multiple structures is the labor union. Unions are more concerned about equity for jobs in the bargaining unit (the jobs held by union members) than about equity for jobs in general. Where wage structure considerations are under the joint decision of management and labor, only the union jobs are usually considered.[6]

Fourth, technology may influence which jobs are included in a given wage structure. While it is true that technology tends to be constant within an industry, there is also variation in technology to some extent. For example, there is considerable variation in technology between a fast food hamburger stand and the neighborhood deli. One might also expect these differences to influence the relationships among jobs within these respective organizations.[7]

Given these forces that impact the way jobs are combined and organized, it should not be surprising that it may be administratively convenient to have multiple wage structures. The compensation decision maker may decide to have one wage structure for the operative jobs (production jobs), another for jobs in the warehouse, another for the engineering staff, and a fourth wage structure for the managerial and office staff, for example.

Multiple Wage Structure Relationships

If an organization utilizes multiple wage structures, an important compensation decision-making issue has to do with balancing equity perceptions among the various wage structures. An obvious situation that challenges interstructure equity is when the union is able to negotiate a wage increase for bargaining unit members. Nonunion employees in the other wage structures may wonder why they too are not eligible for more money. Organizations will often adjust the wage structure upward for these other groups too, particularly if there is strong concern about interstructure equity.

Wage adjustments between union and nonunion wage structures have been referred to as **tandem** wage adjustments. The same problem exists for any two wage structures. For example, the firm may adjust the wage structure of engineers. If it does so, it has the problem of deciding whether to adjust the other wage structures as well to eliminate perceptions of inequity.

In many regards the comparable worth issue discussed in Chapter 11 is related to multiple wage structure equity questions. Many job families are female (usually clerical) or male (usually maintenance) dominated. Since there are often large differences between wage rates for clerical and maintenance jobs (maintenance jobs generally pay higher), questions arise as to the fairness of these differences. This inequity is being challenged by comparable worth advocates.

Job Evaluation Data and Pay Grades

In Chapters 7 and 8 the techniques used in evaluating jobs were discussed. Once jobs are evaluated one of the first concerns is whether or not a series of pay grades should be established. This concern over pay grades is less relevant in the ranking method and the factor comparison method, is determined *a priori* with the job classification method, and is a primary policy question with the point method. Since the point method of job evaluation is the one most commonly used and is used as an example in this chapter, it is necessary to discuss the determination of pay grades.[8]

Establishing Pay Grades

In point method job evaluation, it is not at all uncommon to have a continuum of points associated with various jobs. An example appears in Table 10.1.

The organization must decide to leave these jobs arrayed along a continuum or to clump jobs together into grades. One is not really preferable to the

Table 10.1   *Jobs and Their Associated Job Evaluation Points*

Job Number	Points	Midpoint Wage	Job Number	Points	Midpoint Wage
1	306	$5.50	61	456	$7.60
5	312	5.65	62	462	7.80
8	318	5.65	65	468	7.80
10	324	5.80	67	474	8.00
13	330	5.70	69	480	8.20
14	336	6.00	70	486	8.00
17	342	6.20	73	492	8.15
20	348	6.15	74	498	8.35
21	354	6.30	77	504	8.50
24	360	6.40	78	510	8.40
26	366	6.50	80	516	8.60
29	372	6.55	81	522	8.65
30	378	6.65	84	528	8.65
33	384	6.80	87	534	8.90
35	390	6.65	90	540	8.85
38	396	6.70	92	546	9.00
39	402	7.00	93	552	9.00
41	408	7.05	95	558	9.15
45	414	7.15	98	564	9.05
47	420	7.30	99	570	9.45
50	426	7.20	103	576	9.30
51	432	7.35	104	582	9.50
53	438	7.50	107	588	9.60
56	444	7.60	110	594	9.70
59	450	7.55	117	600	9.75

other, although it is generally conceded that jobs of different point values should be lumped together. There are several suggested reasons for this.

Administrative Convenience

First, the continuum of points may be too refined a measurement system, and the differences between jobs may have been overmeasured. While two jobs may vary from each other by three or four points, when the jobs themselves are examined it is difficult to actually distinguish between them.

A second argument suggests that since jobs must be reevaluated whenever their duties change, considerable administrative effort can be saved by forming broad groups of jobs. Jobs can then be changed in minor ways without continually having to reevaluate them.[9]

A third suggested reason for forming job grades is to allow for meaningful differences for rates of pay. If each point is worth 4 cents, and one job is worth 100 points and another is worth 101 points, then presumably the first job would be paid $4.00 per hour and the other job would be paid $4.04 per hour. This point distinction may be meaningless, and the organization may just as well pay both jobs at the same rate. Broader grades would allow larger pay differences between grades.

All of these arguments ultimately come back to the fact that it is administratively more convenient to collapse jobs within a range of point values into a reduced set of grades. If this were done for the jobs in Table 10.1, a series of grades would be established such as that in Table 10.2.

Other Factors

The arguments for using pay grades focus on administrative convenience. Other considerations may also go into the determination of grades. One of the most important of these is the desired relationship among jobs. Specifically, the decision maker needs to take into account the natural breakdown of jobs.[10] Within a job family both management and employees may distinguish between a subset of jobs such as clerk typist, file clerk, and typist. If there is a

Table 10.2   *Pay Grades Based on Job Evaluation Point Ranges*

Grade	Job Number	Points	Midpoint Wage	Grade	Job Number	Points	Midpoint Wage
	1	306	$5.50		61	456	$7.60
	5	312	5.65		62	462	7.80
1	8	318	5.65	6	65	468	7.80
	10	324	5.80		67	474	8.00
	13	330	5.70		69	480	8.20
	14	336	6.00		70	486	8.00
	17	342	6.20		73	492	8.15
2	20	348	6.15	7	74	498	8.35
	21	354	6.30		77	504	8.50
	24	360	6.40		78	510	8.40
	26	366	6.50		80	516	8.60
	29	372	6.55		81	522	8.65
3	30	378	6.65	8	84	528	8.65
	33	384	6.80		87	534	8.90
	35	390	6.65		90	540	8.85
	38	396	6.70		92	546	9.00
	39	402	7.00		93	552	9.00
4	41	408	7.05	9	95	558	9.15
	45	414	7.15		98	564	9.05
	47	420	7.30		99	570	9.45
	50	426	7.20		103	576	9.30
	51	432	7.35		104	582	9.50
5	53	438	7.50	10	107	588	9.60
	56	444	7.60		110	594	9.70
	59	450	7.55		117	600	9.75

perceived meaningful distinction between these jobs, then the grade system should be designed to reflect these distinctions, even though there may not be much difference among these jobs on a point basis.

A further consideration is the internal labor market for promotion. If employees and the organization perceive a set of jobs as related in a promotional sequence, then it would be inappropriate to consider all of these jobs as falling in the same grade. If this is the case then the job evaluation system may be ineffective if it has not assigned this set of jobs to different grades.

The above points might seem to be circular reasoning—if the job evaluation system did not make distinctions among jobs, then maybe the jobs are the same. What is important is the perceived relationship among jobs. In any event, decision makers will want to be aware of these considerations in establishing pay grades.

Determining the Number of Grades

There are no absolute answers to how many pay grades will suffice for a pay structure. However, several guidelines are suggested.

First, as noted earlier, one very important consideration is the number of pay grades it will take to achieve perceived internal equity in pay among jobs. Employees and management may perceive meaningful differences among jobs even though those differences are not large from a job points perspective. These differences should be reflected in the job grade system.

A second guideline is more mechanical in nature.[11] This view suggests that only three variables are needed to establish the number of grades. First, the company must know the midpoint wage rate for the lowest paid job in the structure. Second, it needs to know the midpoint wage rate for the highest paid job. Third, the desired percentage increase from grade to grade must be determined. The decision maker then looks at the total percentage increase from lowest to highest paid job and asks: How many times must the lowest paid job's rate be compounded at the given percentage rate between grades to achieve the highest wage rate?

For example, suppose the lowest paid job in the structure receives $10,000 per year and the highest paid job receives $20,000 per year. The desired midpoint difference between grades is 5 percent. Since the grade system will result in a wage structure with 100 percent increase in pay from lowest to highest job, and since the midpoint difference between grades is 5 percent, there will need to be about fifteen grades. The way to solve for the number of grades is to take the value of 1.00 plus the known percentage increase between grades (in this case 5 percent) and raise this value (1.05) to the power that will equal the ratio of the highest to lowest wage rate. That is: 1.05 raised to the 15th power will give a value of about 2.0, which is equal to the ratio of the highest to lowest paid job ($20,000/$10,000 = 2). In this case, it would take about 15 pay grades with midpoint increments of 5 percent to move smoothly from a grade with a $10,000-a-year job to a grade with a $20,000-per-year job.

These automatic calculations should never replace sound judgment based upon considerations noted in previous paragraphs.

Determining Internal Equity

The first step in establishing an equitable pay structure is to examine internal wage relationships. The data are the jobs that have been evaluated and the relative relationships among those jobs. A stereotypical example of this appears in Exhibit 10.1.

Exhibit 10.1 depicts a bivariate plot of present midpoint wage rates of jobs against the evaluated number of points that each of these jobs carries. Examination of the relationship between current pay rates and the job evaluation points in Exhibit 10.1 indicates that there is considerable inequity among current pay rates. For example, an examination of jobs carrying 200 points shows that midpoint wage rates for these jobs range from about $3.95 to $4.30. These data suggest that there is an internal equity problem; all jobs worth 200 points should carry the same pay rate. Further examination of Exhibit 10.1 shows that while one job evaluated at 200 points is currently paid at $4.30, another job evaluated at 205 points is currently carrying a pay rate of $3.95. Examining the relative pay rates of jobs of different point values shows there also appears to be internal inequity.

Exhibit 10.1 *Bivariate Plot of Current Midpoint Wage Rates and Job Points*

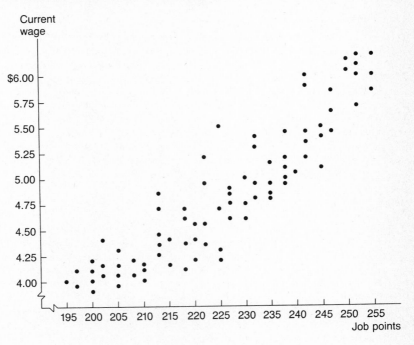

Internal Equity Using a Freehand Line of Best Fit

The compensation decision maker's need to make judgments shows up at this stage when an effort is made to determine what the wage rate ought to be for jobs of varying points. One way to achieve equity within jobs of equal point value and across jobs of different point values is to find a line of fit that best captures the central tendency or trend among all of these data points on the figure. Several approaches are used in practice. One is to inspect the data points and draw a line to capture the relationships among and within jobs. An example of such a freehand line is in Exhibit 10.2.

A freehand line of best fit requires the decision maker to go through a four-step process. First, the decision maker draws a two-dimensional graph. The y axis signifies wage rates. The x axis signifies the point value of jobs (these are stated midpoint wage rates for each job, not actual rates of pay given to individuals). The second step in determining a freehand line is to plot onto the graph the location of each job indicating the wage (y) and job points (x) coordinates for the job. This process is repeated for all jobs under consideration. In the third step, a line is then drawn that expresses the general upward trend in wages relative to job points. The line in Exhibit 10.2 was drawn using this three-step procedure. It is the trend line that captures the jobs' wage and points combinations.

Exhibit 10.2 *Freehand Trend Line of Central Tendency among Wage Rates and Job Points*

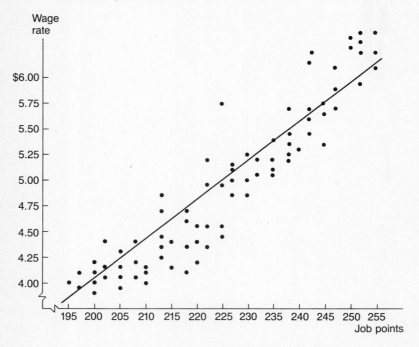

The final step is to find the equation for this trend line using simple algebra. Using the data in Exhibit 10.2, a job worth 205 points that is paid at the trend line receives $4.25 per hour. A job having 225 points receives $5.00 per hour, if paid on the trend line. Algebraically the trend line can be found by using the equation for a straight line and solving these two equations simultaneously. The equation for a straight line is: y (wage) $= a$ (y intercept) $+ b$ (slope of the line) $* x$ (job points). The two equations are:

$$\$5.00 = a + 225b;\ \text{and}$$
$$\$4.25 = a + 205b.$$

Solving these simultaneously reveals that the slope of the line is equal to .0375. In other words, according to this freehand line, jobs are paid 3.75 cents per hour for each job evaluation point. The y intercept in this case is $-\$3.43$, and the full wage equation for this freehand trend line is:

$$y\ (\text{wage}) = -\$3.43 + .0375 * x\ (\text{job points}).$$

Internal Equity with a Regression Line

A second, commonly used method of determining a line of best fit is to use least squares regression methods.[12] This is the approach used in this text. The least squares method for a line of best fit involves the use of a statistical procedure known as regression analysis. In regression analysis the investigator, in this case the compensation decision maker, uses the equation for a straight line to empirically derive a line of best fit between the ordering of the jobs and the wage rates for the jobs. Just as with the freehand method of establishing a trend line, the decision maker begins the equation for a straight line. Formally stated, the equation for a straight line is:

$y = a + bx,$

where
y is the wage rate for a job,
a is the y intercept,
b is the slope of the line, or the money value per point, and
x is the number of points which the job carries.

An Example   As an example, a firm wants to pay a job a constant amount plus so many cents per job evaluation point. The firm decides to pay every job the equivalent of $1.50 (the constant is equal to $1.50), plus $0.05 per point (the slope of the line is .05). With these data actual pay for jobs of different point values can be found. For example, a job worth 200 points would then carry a pay rate of:

$$y = a + bx,\ \text{or}$$
$$\text{Wage rate} = \$1.50 + .05\ \text{points, therefore,}$$
$$\text{Wage rate (at 200 points)} = \$1.50 + .05 \times 200,\ \text{or}$$
$$\text{Wage rate (at 200 points)} = \$11.50.$$

Similarly, a job worth 240 points would be paid $13.50 per hour, and a job worth 190 points would be paid $11.00 per hour. This pay line is depicted in Exhibit 10.3.

The geometrical relationship between pay rates and job evaluation points also can be expressed with the equation of $y = \$1.50 + .05$ points. In working with the equation for a straight line, the y intercept (where the line crosses the y axis) is $1.50, and the slope of the line is $0.05 (for each one-unit increase in points x there is a 5-cent increase in pay).

How does the compensation decision maker decide upon the equation for the pay line? Estimating the equation for the pay line is what regression analysis is used for. In fact, using the data in Table 10.1 shows that the equation is:

$$y = \$1.197 + .014x.$$

This line can be plotted on the data from Table 10.1 as shown in Exhibit 10.4.

The Regression Equation   With computers, pocket calculators, and more recently the advent of miniprocessors of various types, using (and misusing) regression has become relatively easy. The computational equations for determining the constant a and the slope b of a line are:

$$b = \frac{N(\Sigma xy) - (\Sigma x)(\Sigma y)}{N(\Sigma x^2) - (\Sigma x)^2},$$

$$a = \frac{(\Sigma y) - b(\Sigma x)}{N}.$$

The regression procedure treats the data as though a straight line is the best way of expressing the relationship between the y and x variables (in this case, between pay rates and job evaluation points). The procedure minimizes the sum of squared deviations around the line. The computer calculates an infinite array of equations with the goal of finding a line of best fit for the data with the minimum (least) sums of squared deviations. This line, when derived, is the best expression of a linear relationship between pay rates and job points. Once the equation is derived, if the organization adjusts wage rates to the line (bringing all deviations to zero), then there would be a theoretically equitable and continuous array of job and pay rate combinations.

Internal Equity as a Sole Criterion

The calculations to derive the wage rate and job point combinations in Exhibit 10.4 are based on data that reflect current wage rates in the organization. The first step in balancing internal and external equity is to examine present wage

Exhibit 10.3   *Hypothetical Pay Line*

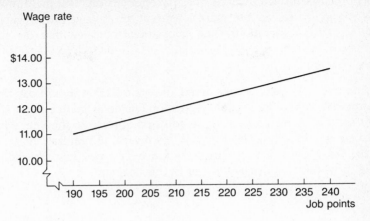

Exhibit 10.4   *Regression Line for Line of Best Fit*

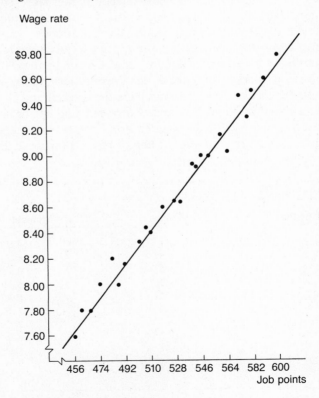

rates against the evaluated job points. This process says nothing about external equity but focuses instead upon the internal equity issue. This preliminary step gives the wage line for an internally consistent set of wage rates regardless of external equity considerations. The calculations revealed that the pay line should be:

$$y = \$1.197 + .014x.$$

If only internal equity is considered, the organization should pay the wage rate and point combinations on the regression line depicted in Exhibit 10.4. Pay rates for some jobs would need to be adjusted upward to the line, while pay rates for other jobs should be adjusted downward. (Organizations rarely decrease the wage rates of jobs that carry too high a pay rate. Procedures for handling these jobs are discussed later in this chapter.)

External Equity Determination

The analysis of present wages relative to job points has so far focused on the internal equity question. A second important question is how current wage rates for jobs in the organization compare to labor market rates. The procedure for determining external equity is similar to that for internal equity. The wage rates used in the analysis of pay rate and job point relationships are the market rates obtained from the labor market survey of key job wage rates. Each of these key jobs has a predetermined point value. Creating a trend line for these key jobs relative to market rates allows the organization to infer what its pay structure should look like if market rates were the determining factor. A set of key job rates appears in Table 10.3, and a corresponding line of best fit superimposed on a bivariate plot of the wage rate and points combinations appears in Exhibit 10.5. The regression line (or line of best fit) for these data is:

Table 10.3   *Labor Market Key Job Rates*

Job Number	Points	Midpoint Wage
1	306	$6.25
8	318	6.30
14	336	6.52
24	360	6.82
29	372	6.90
47	420	7.29
62	466	7.73
80	522	8.26
93	552	8.44
107	588	9.01

Exhibit 10.5 *Bivariate Plot and Regression Line for Labor Market Wage Rates*

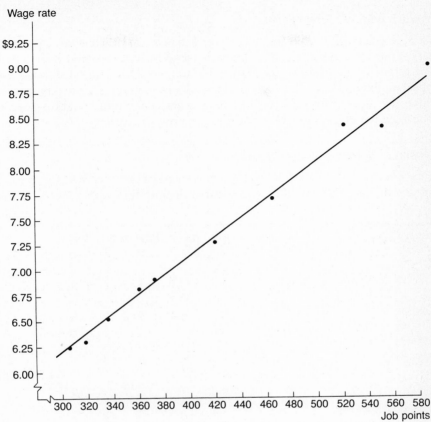

Wage rate (y) = \$3.54 + .0089 job points (x).

Wage Rates

The wage rate data in Table 10.3 and Exhibit 10.5 need to be questioned. The rates reflect the actual average current pay per key job for each of the ten firms surveyed. The calculated regression line is a reflection of labor market rates across a diverse group of organizations with which the surveying organization competes for labor. If the organization pays according to this line of best fits, its wages will be reflective of rates for key jobs in the market, and still maintain an internally equitable wage structure.

Slotting in Nonkey Jobs

If the organization decides to pay according to the wage line in Exhibit 10.5, then it can use the wage line equation to slot in other, nonkey jobs. The organization will calculate the pay rate for jobs of various point values using the regression equation based on external labor market rates.

Product Market Constraints

Just as a wage line can be calculated for key jobs and their associated labor market rates, a wage line can also be calculated for key jobs and their associated rates in the product market. Sample data and an associated wage line appear in Exhibit 10.6. Once again, the compensation decision maker can examine the association between key job points and product market rates to determine the wage line with respect to the product market.

Labor Costs and Decision Making

To be effective, compensation decision makers must be concerned about motivating employees to join and stay with the organization within the economic

Exhibit 10.6 *Bivariate Plot and Regression Line for Product Market Wage Rates*

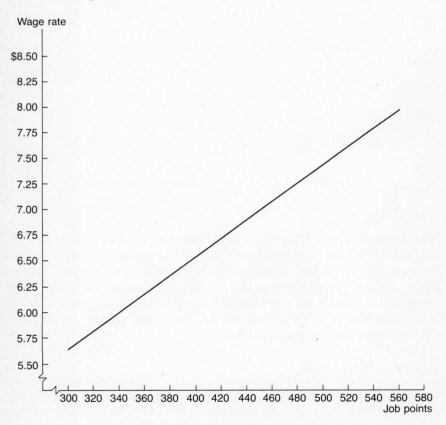

constraints faced by their organization. In one sense, the purpose of pay structure calculations is to assess the impact of alternatives upon labor costs, and to determine what the organization can achieve within its economic constraints.[13] The decision maker must examine the wage lines based on current rates, labor market rates, and product market rates to determine the impact each would have on the organization's labor costs.

What will be the wage bill cost if the organization attempts to achieve internal equity by establishing a systematic pay line among its current internal rates? The cost is the difference between the current wage bill and the wage bill that would result if the organization would pay to a standard line. What would be the wage bill if the organization uses a wage line reflective of labor market rates? The compensation decision maker can compare this wage cost both to its present pay practice and to a wage bill based on internal equity alone.

An estimated wage bill can also be calculated with the product market data. This information is critical since it represents the wage bill constraint that the organization does not want to exceed under normal assumptions of product market competition.

Using these calculations, the decision maker can recommend or take action on the organization's pay structure. For example, if the current wage bill and the projected wage bill using the labor market wage line are both below the wage bill calculated with product market data, the organization can choose to adjust its wage rates upward to stay competitive with the labor market. However, if calculations reveal that the wage bill is above the product market line but below the labor market line, the decision maker may discover that the organization is not competitive in either the labor or the product market.

Nonlinear Wage Lines

Most organizations that have a systematic job evaluation system do rely on a linear model, but this practice is reflective more of custom than any scientific reason or rationale. A firm may use nonlinear wage lines for many reasons. Two reasons are to conform with market practice, and to allow for compatibility among job families. Two hypothetical examples of nonlinear wage lines sometimes used in designing a pay structure appear in Exhibit 10.7.

Curve *A* in Exhibit 10.7 is an exponential curvilinear wage line. This curve might result from the actual wage relationships in the labor or product market. That is, this curvilinear relationships may more accurately capture the relationship between job points and wage rates than a straight line. If so, then an organization using a trend line established with linear regression would tend to overpay jobs in the midrange of the distribution of jobs, and underpay jobs at the high and low ends of the distribution of jobs. Use of the curvilinear line may reduce the total wage bill relative to the wage bill under a linear trend line, since wage rates will rise more slowly for jobs of lower point values, which typically have the most job incumbents.

Curve *B* in Exhibit 10.7 may result from a pay structure when wage pres-

Exhibit 10.7   *Two Nonlinear Pay Lines*

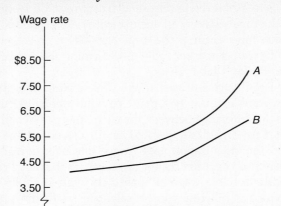

sure is exerted from another job family below the lower jobs in the evaluated job group.[14] For example, this family of jobs in the curve may be managerial, technical, and professional, with the 100-point jobs held by first-line supervisors. The supervisors lead unionized workers, and the union pushes its wages up for highly skilled bargaining unit members (the top jobs in a separate job hierarchy). In order to provide compatibility between the two job families and not have supervisors' pay below that of the employees being supervised, the supervisory jobs may pay higher than what the market dictates. This would result in a more gradually sloped pay line for the first series of jobs in the managerial, professional, and technical job family.

Designing Pay Ranges

Once the wage trend line is determined, the next step in building the pay structure is to establish the pay range for jobs. Important considerations for determining the width of pay ranges are expected length of service of job incumbents, and whether the increases are large enough to be meaningful. The precise use of ranges (merit, seniority, training steps, or combination) is dependent upon management policy and philosophy. Decisions about pay ranges should reflect these considerations.

Wage ranges for a job are used for several purposes, such as to allow for merit- and performance-based pay increases, to allow for wage increases based on seniority, to allow for training steps as newly hired workers move towards minimum proficiency, or a combination of these three purposes.

Ranges for Merit

To use pay ranges to reward employees for differential performance on jobs requires several considerations. First, the organization must determine if there is ample opportunity for performance variance within a job for merit to be used as a criterion for pay allocations. Many jobs have little room for performance variation. For example, an assembly line worker who mounts a seat in a car either does or does not install the seat correctly. There is little room for superior performance in terms of doing an excellent installation. There is also no opportunity for this worker to install extra seats, since the speed of work is dictated by the movement of the line.[15] If there is little room for performance variance, there is little sense in distinguishing between performance levels.

Second, the performance variance of jobs must be measurable if the organization hopes to pay for performance. It is extremely difficult to measure differences in performance in many jobs. In these cases, the organization may be better off not using performance as a pay criterion since if it is not measured properly the system itself may not work properly or may be perceived as inequitable.

Third, employees should want to be assessed on the basis of relative or absolute job performance.[16] Even if performance variance exists and can be measured, employees must accept performance as a valid pay criterion. If the employees do not want pay for performance, then it will be resisted, as often happens when "soldiering" occurs on some production line jobs.[17] This is also why unions often negotiate a single rate for their members.[18]

Policy Considerations for Merit Ranges   Although merit pay ranges are typically in the range of 25 to 30 percent[19], pay policy decisions about pay ranges should be consciously made to reflect several considerations. An important consideration is the expected length of service for employees in these jobs. For example, if the organization expects employees to stay in a job for eight to ten years, then ranges need to be relatively wide for the organization to continue to reward high performance. Without reasonably wide ranges high performers will reach the top of the range early and there will not be room for future salary growth. Range width is also influenced by the size of the annual increases that the firm wishes to grant to employees. For example, if superior performance can result in a 10 percent pay raise, then a high performer will be at the top of a 30 percent range within three years, and a 20 percent range in two years. This may be acceptable if it is expected that high performers will be promoted within these time frames, but it would be unacceptable if promotions come at a slower rate.

Ranges for Seniority

Because the criteria for pay ranges based on merit are often not met, many organizations use pay ranges only for seniority. It is typical for ranges to reward seniority when performance is not a consideration or when employees want seniority pay. Seniority pay ranges may be desirable as a matter of policy. One example of this would be a situation where management knows that job performance varies with length of service but performance itself is extremely costly to measure. In this situation it may be desirable to reward on seniority because performance is assumed to increase with seniority.

A second situation where seniority pay may be appropriate as a matter of policy is when it is highly desirable to encourage employees to stay with the company. For example, turnover may be extremely costly to the organization, and it may be cheaper in the long run to reward for seniority and realize reduced turnover costs.[20] This is especially true for jobs that require long and costly training times, or other extensive investment in labor resources.

Examples of Merit and Seniority Pay Ranges

An example of three pay ranges—a merit range, a seniority range, and a combination range—is presented in Exhibit 10.8 (A training step range design is not presented because it is a special case of a seniority pay range policy.)

Exhibit 10.8   *Pay Ranges and Their Uses*

A. Pay Ranges for Performance Rewards

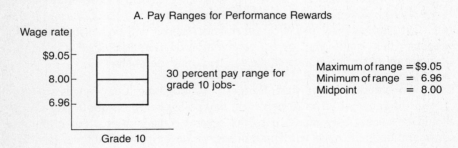

Wage rate

$9.05

8.00

6.96

Grade 10

30 percent pay range for grade 10 jobs-

Maximum of range = $9.05
Minimum of range =   6.96
Midpoint   =   8.00

B. Pay Ranges for Membership Reward (Seniority)

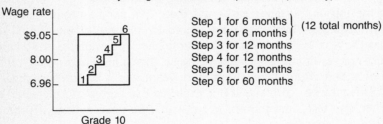

Wage rate

$9.05

8.00

6.96

Grade 10

Step 1 for 6 months ⎫ (12 total months)
Step 2 for 6 months ⎭
Step 3 for 12 months
Step 4 for 12 months
Step 5 for 12 months
Step 6 for 60 months

C. Pay Ranges for Rewarding Membership and Performance

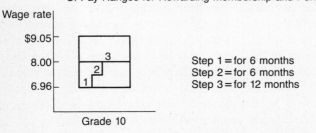

Wage rate

$9.05

8.00

6.96

Grade 10

Step 1 = for 6 months
Step 2 = for 6 months
Step 3 = for 12 months

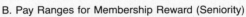

Ranges for Performance   Part A in Exhibit 10.8 depicts a pay range established to reward performance. One of the primary considerations in setting pay ranges for merit is how wide the pay range should be. From a decision-making standpoint, two primary variables in setting the range are the average length of time an employee remains in a job in that range, and the size of the pay increases which are expected to be granted. In terms of length of tenure, the concern is with how many pay increases will have to be allowed for the typical employee. Actual increases may vary from the average, but an average increase for the average employee should allow the employee to reach the top of the range at about the end of the expected tenure period for the job. If the organization wishes to give pay increases that average 5 percent, and average tenure is about five years, the organization would need to establish a pay range slightly greater than 25 percent (to allow for the compounding effect of adding one increase onto the other).

The second variable of considerable importance is the size of the increase. Some literature suggests increases that are not large enough may not even be perceived by the employee.[21] For wage increases to have any value in rewarding performance, they should at least be between 5 and 6 percent, which requires a pay range of 25 to 30 percent if average tenure is five years.

One formula for setting the minimum and maximum pay rates is to divide the wage rate from the trend line (the midpoint rate for the range) by 100 percent plus one-half the desired percentage range. The midpoint of $8.00 would be divided by 1.15 percent in part A of Exhibit 10.8. The base wage for this range is $6.96, and 30 percent above this is $9.05.

Ranges for Seniority   A typical pay range for rewarding long membership is displayed in part B of Exhibit 10.8. This pay system provides for a pay increase at fixed intervals of tenure with the job. In the example in Exhibit 10.8 employees would start at the minimum rate, move up a step after six months, move up another step at the end of one year, and move up in consecutive steps until they reach the top of the grade after five years in the job.

Ranges for Performance and Seniority   Organizations may combine seniority with merit as shown in part C in Exhibit 10.8. Here the organization allows for seniority increases after six months, one year, and two years. One philosophy behind this approach might be that all employees who are capable of performing the job at an average performance level should make the average pay for the job. The steps from the starting rate to the midpoint correspond with the length of time it takes to become an average employee. The example assumes an employee should be able to perform at average levels after two years in the job. Beyond the midpoint salary increases are allotted on the basis of performance.

Flat Rate Systems

In a flat rate pay system there is only one pay rate for a job in a given grade. There are no pay ranges, and everyone makes the same rate regardless of seniority or performance variance among job incumbents. The wage rates for job grades are the wage rates on the trend line. Flat rate systems are typically used for jobs covered by labor union contracts where the wage structure is renegotiated at each contract renewal date.

Range Overlap

In an integrated pay structure there is an overlap in the ranges from one job grade to another. Such overlap is generally considered to be no threat to internal equity since it allows incumbents in lower jobs to make as much as or more than incumbents in higher jobs under conditions of greater seniority or higher performance. These conditions are generally considered valid reasons for pay differences and are accepted by employees. It is possible to have a set of jobs highly linked through internal promotions, however, in which too much overlap is dysfunctional. For example, if there is 70 percent overlap between two jobs, and an incumbent in the lower grade job at the top of the range is promoted to the higher job, then there is only a small opportunity to continue to reward that person on the new job. When jobs in one grade are feeder jobs for the next higher grade, the organization may want the jobs to have no more than a 50 percent overlap in ranges.

Implementing a Systematic Pay Structure

Beginning with the discussion of job analysis in Chapter 5 and ending with the discussion of pay ranges in this chapter, this text has traced through the administrative activities and elements of a comprehensive wage structure. These activities and elements can now be put together for the pay structure to emerge. Exhibit 10.9 is a graphic representation of a completed pay structure. Once the pay structure is completed, other considerations deal with its implementation, as discussed in this section.

Communication with Employees

Communication with employees at each stage of the pay structure process is critical. At the time the decision is made to proceed with a program to design a new pay system employees should be informed that a reanalysis of current pay policies is under way. This communication should be both written and verbal. It should stress the goals of a new pay structure (including the organization's continued concern over fairness of wage payments), and assure employees that no one's pay will be reduced by a new pay structure. This is important to overcome possible resistance to the new program.

Communication should continue, both verbally and in writing, as to the status of the project as it progresses. Employees are going to expect change, and it is helpful and settling to know when the changes are likely to occur.

At the time the program is put into place, employees should be told where

Exhibit 10.9   *A Pay Structure and Its Elements*

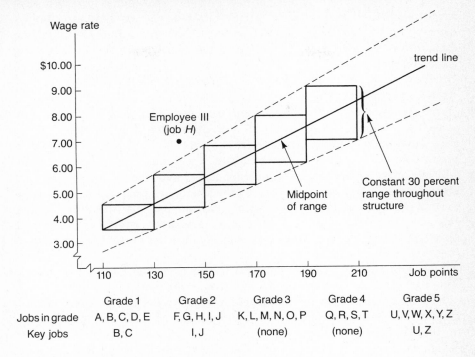

	Grade 1	Grade 2	Grade 3	Grade 4	Grade 5
Jobs in grade	A, B, C, D, E	F, G, H, I, J	K, L, M, N, O, P	Q, R, S, T	U, V, W, X, Y, Z
Key jobs	B, C	I, J	(none)	(none)	U, Z

their individual jobs fit into the new program (which grade). It is also appropriate to educate employees on how certain decisions were arrived at, such as the methods employed in arriving at the median wage rate for the grades (such as, set at the 50th percentile of the labor or product market). The criteria (merit, seniority, and so on) for moving through the grades should also be clearly explained.

Employees should also be told if their individual pay rate is above their job's pay grade and the policy the company will follow to deal with this: to freeze the wage in the future or to transfer the employee to more highly valued work. The process of "red circling" these jobs is discussed in the next section.

In general, it is desirable to keep employees as informed as possible about the new program. If the objective of the program is a more equitable wage system, both in an internal and external sense, then the value of the program is not likely to be appreciated unless it is communicated effectively.

Initial Adjustment of Rates

When a new pay plan is introduced there are likely to be a considerable number of employees whose wages are below the rates dictated by the new program. These employees are said to have **"green circle"** pay rates. In theory these employees' rates would be increased to the minimum of their grade immediately upon implementation of the new plan. However, this may not be practical. For example, an employer may find itself locked into long-term contracts for products whose cost is based on lower wages. In these cases implementation of the new wage program might be delayed until the organization can afford to bring all green circle rates to the minimum of the new structure.

A problem arises when jobs or incumbents are above the pay range for the job. For example, in Exhibit 10.9 the employee's pay rate is above the range for job *H* given the job's pay grade. What should be done in this situation?

Numerous solutions to this problem have been suggested. The most practical one is known as **"red circling"** the job incumbent's pay. Red circling means that the incumbent's pay is kept at its present level, but the job itself is brought into line within the pay structure. Thus, while the incumbent's pay will stay at the higher rate, all new individuals hired into the job will be paid according to the pay policy dictated by the internal wage structure—the range for that job. Red circling the incumbent's pay rate may also mean that further pay raises will not be granted until the wage structure overtakes the current rate. This will gradually happen over time as inflation causes the entire wage structure to shift upward.

A slight variation to this policy is to red circle the rate of incumbents whose jobs are out of line, and attempt to transfer them to jobs whose wage rates are consistent with the employees' current pay. If an employee refuses the transfer, the current pay will be reduced in accordance with the pay range for the job.

These approaches are preferred over direct pay reduction, which will generate employee resistance to a new systematic wage structure. Management usually communicates to employees at the start of the process of designing a pay system that no one's pay will be reduced as a result of the new pay policies to allay fears of the new program, and it would be extremely unwise to then behave differently.

Red circling concerns job incumbents and not jobs. That is, the red circle applies to the rate that an incumbent is paid, not to the job itself. This distinction is important because new entrants into the job are paid the rate as established by the new pay structure.

Pay Structure Maintenance

After the new wage structure is in place, several procedures should be implemented to maintain it. The organization should conduct periodic labor and product market surveys to assure that the wage structure does not fall behind current practice in other organizations. Normally it is sufficient to resurvey key jobs every 12 to 24 months. The higher the rate of inflation, the more frequently surveys should be conducted.

A second important procedure to maintain the pay structure is to have an ongoing job evaluation committee. While this is common in labor union and management settings, it is much less common in nonunion settings. The purpose of such a committee is to reevaluate those jobs that have changed substantially since the implementation of the program. Changes in jobs occur as technology changes, work processes change, and management decides to redesign jobs. It is more accurate to have a committee evaluate the effect of changes since individual analysts may make less reliable decisions than a collection of decision makers. For a more elaborate discussion of this point the reader may want to review the section of Chapter 7 that discussed the design of the job evaluation committee.

Training of Managers

Ultimately managers and supervisors throughout the organization are the people who will use the new wage structure. If they fail to implement the system properly on a day-to-day basis, the system is likely to fail regardless of how well it is designed.

Managers should be trained in a number of areas. First, they should understand the new pay system in terms of how it was developed and what it is attempting to achieve. Second, if merit pay is to be a part of the plan, managers need to know the goals of the merit pay plan and how it was developed (performance assessment is the subject of Chapter 12). They also need to be trained in how to conduct effective performance appraisals, which includes awareness training for bias, the legal considerations in performance appraisal, the purposes and workings of the organization's performance appraisal system, and the importance of accurate appraisal. Failure to train managers in these important areas can result in useless appraisals, which in turn may mean that the organization's goal of rewarding merit may not be realized.

Summary

This chapter focused on designing an integrated pay structure. Job evaluation data and labor and product market data on key jobs were combined to develop a trend line of wage rates to reflect both internal and external equity. In addition, wage ranges were discussed as tools to reward either seniority or performance.

By this point in the text all the necessary tools and skills to implement a systematic wage structure into an organization have been discussed. In addition, the goals of a compensation system and the theoretical foundations for the administrative practices that are a part of the compensation decision maker's job have been presented in detail. In subsequent chapters the remainder of the components of a total compensation program are discussed.

Discussion Questions

1. Suppose an organization finds that the wage structure in its product market is less steeply sloped than the wage structure in its labor market. What implications would this have for designing a wage structure, and how will this impact the wage bill? (Assume that the two trend lines intersect about halfway through the job hierarchy.)

2. Discuss the concept of a red circle rate and discuss why red circling is preferable to other approaches of adjusting wages.

3. What are pay ranges used for, and what influences the percentage spread in the range?

4. Discuss the concept of a flat rate pay system. Why might an organization use a flat rate system?

Exercise

1. Following are information and data about the current pay practices of the Olson Company, along with labor and product market wage data, job evaluation data, and limited financial information. Based on these data, design a comprehensive wage structure for the Olson Company that is consistent with the goals and objectives of a compensation program as outlined in this text. Be sure to make recommendations and support each recommendation with the appropriate reasoning consistent with the known parameters that are critical for shaping a wage structure. Also, demonstrate your mastery of the techniques used in designing a wage structure. Do one analysis with A data for turnover and product market information, then repeat the analysis with B data.

Exercise 1

The Olson Company, located in a large metropolitan area, is a distributor of sand and gravel. The company employs 140 unskilled laborers and 20 exempt employees.

The Olson Company is an old and venerated supplier to individual home owners and major construction companies. The company provides sand and gravel to home owners doing self-repair work on driveways and self-built garages and other buildings. This was their major business until 1961. After 1961 the company's principal market was major construction companies. They provide sand and gravel to these companies for driveways and foundations, and occasionally they provide extensive concrete contracts on large commercial buildings.

During the early 1970s, the company's wage level was competitive in the labor market. As the general wage level began to rise, the Olson Company failed to adjust its wage level accordingly. The company soon found that it was paying only the minimum federal wage, which resulted in a heavy turnover of personnel, but management was not worried because the labor market was fairly loose, and they were able to keep an adequate work force.

As the labor market got tighter, management experienced increasing problems with maintaining a work force of sufficient quality and quantity to operate the company. With great reluctance, management adjusted the wage level enough to reduce turnover to about 45 percent.

Years passed, during which management made no additional wage adjustments. General wage levels increased considerably, and although the labor market is currently quite loose the company has considerable turnover and is experiencing an inability to attract new workers.

In response to these problems the company hired a dynamic personnel manager with particular expertise in compensation. The personnel manager immediately undertook a systematic analysis of the problems faced by Olson, spending long days and weeks amassing data to guide recommendations to the president. Some of this data is contained in the following tables. In addition, the following personnel policies were already in effect.

(continued)

Exercise 1 (continued)

The company has a single flat rate system of pay for each job; hiring rates and any pay changes are negotiated by the individual employee with management.

All jobs throughout the unskilled job family tend to be filled from outside the company through newspaper ads or walk-ins.

Some turnover is good (as a matter of policy) since it discourages too stable a work force and, therefore, unionization.

On average, it costs $400 to recruit, train, and process onto the payroll one nonexempt employee.

The company has a modest profit-sharing plan (10 percent net profit) but no other employee benefits.

The new personnel manager was stricken with a heart attack after collecting all the data and was completely incapacitated for eight months. The Olson Company, not wanting to let their turnover problem deteriorate further, has retained you as a consultant to analyze and make recommendations on the data gathered by the personnel manager.

Revenues from Sources of Business

Year	Individuals	Contractors
1950	$.12 million	$.01 million
1955	.16 million	.09 million
1960	.22 million	.22 million
1965	.30 million	.42 million
1970	.48 million	.72 million
1975	.72 million	1.30 million
1980	.90 million	1.44 million

Results of Job Evaluation

Job Number	Points	Current Flat Hourly Rate
1	195	$3.30
2	200	3.30
3	200	3.40
4	205	3.60
5	205	3.40
6	210	3.20
7	210	3.50
8	210	3.60
9	215	4.00
10	215	4.35
11	215	4.45
12	220	4.15
13	220	4.15
14	220	4.55
15	230	4.65
16	235	4.65
17	240	4.75
18	240	4.95

(continued)

Exercise 1 (continued)

Results of Job Evaluation

Job Number	Points	Current Flat Hourly Rate
19	250	4.85
20	250	5.05
21	250	5.15
22	255	5.05
23	255	4.95
24	260	5.45
25	260	5.15
26	270	5.25
27	270	5.50
28	280	5.70
29	280	5.80
30	290	6.00

Results from Labor Market Wage and Salary Survey ($N = 15$ Firms)

Job Number	Low[a]	Median[a]	High[a]
1	$3.20	$3.40	$3.60
3	3.50	3.70	3.90
7	3.80	3.90	4.00
13	3.90	4.25	4.55
15	4.45	4.85	5.30
17	4.65	4.95	5.30
20	4.85	5.15	5.50
24	5.30	5.70	6.10
26	5.70	6.10	6.50
29	6.00	6.50	7.00

[a] The average of the five lowest, five median, and five highest wage rates for each job.

"A" Data for Product Market Wage and Salary Survey

Job Number	Average Hourly Rate
1	$3.35
3	3.44
7	3.87
13	4.07
15	4.58
17	4.65
20	5.25
24	5.40
26	5.96
29	6.08

(continued)

Exercise 1 (continued)

"A" Data for Analysis of Turnover for Olson Company Jobs

Job Number	Number of Positions	Annual Number of Voluntary Quits
1	10	13
2	10	14
3	5	7
4	5	8
5	6	8
6	6	11
7	6	9
8	6	9
9	6	8
10	6	3
11	5	1
12	5	7
13	5	6
14	5	1
15	5	2
16	5	2
17	5	2
18	5	2
19	4	3
20	4	0
21	3	0
22	3	1
23	3	1
24	3	0
25	3	3
26	3	4
27	2	0
28	2	1
29	2	0
30	2	0

"B" Data for Product Market Wage and Salary Survey

Job Number	Average Hourly Rate
1	$3.65
3	3.90
7	4.00
13	4.40
15	4.50
17	4.70
20	5.05
24	5.15
26	5.50
29	5.60

(continued)

Exercise 1 (continued)

"B" Data for Analysis of Turnover for Olson Company Jobs

Job Number	Number of Positions	Annual Number of Voluntary Quits
1	10	7
2	10	5
3	5	3
4	5	2
5	6	5
6	6	6
7	6	4
8	6	3
9	6	2
10	6	0
11	5	1
12	5	3
13	5	3
14	5	0
15	5	1
16	5	0
17	5	2
18	5	0
19	4	3
20	4	7
21	3	5
22	3	7
23	3	12
24	3	5
25	3	6
26	3	12
27	2	5
28	2	5
29	2	5
30	2	7

References

[1] Lloyd G. Reynolds, *The Structure of Labor Markets* (Westport, Conn.: Greenwood Press, 1951).

[2] Donald P. Schwab, "Job Evaluation and Pay Setting: Concepts and Practices," in E. Robert Livernash, ed., *Comparable Worth Issues and Answers* (Washington, D.C.: Equal Employment Advisory Council, 1980): pp. 51–77.

[3] Luis R. Gomez-Mejia *et al.*, "Development and Implementation of a Computerized Job Evaluation System," *Personnel Administrator*, February 1979, pp. 46–54.

[4] E. Robert Livernash, "The Internal Wage Structure," in George W. Taylor and Frank C. Pierson, eds., *New Concepts in Wage Determination* (New York: McGraw-Hill, 1957): pp. 143–172.

[5] David Peterson, "Defining Local Labor Markets," in *Perspectives on Availability* (Washington, D.C.: EEAC, 1977).

6 Richard B. Freeman, "Union Wage Practices and Wage Dispersion within Establishments," *Industrial and Labor Relations Review* 36, no. 1 (October 1982): pp. 3–21.

7 Livernash, "The Internal Wage Structure."

8 John A. Patton, *Job Evaluation in Practice: Some Survey Findings*, AMA Management Report no. 54 (New York: American Management Association, 1961).

9 Herbert G. Heneman III et al., *Personnel/Human Resource Management* (Homewood, Ill.: Irwin, 1983).

10 Livernash, "The Internal Wage Structure."

11 Richard C. Smyth and Matthew J. Murphy, *The Guide Line Method of Job Evaluation* (Rhinebeck, N.Y.: Smyth and Associates, Inc., 1974).

12 Bruce R. Ellig, "Salary Surveys, Design and Application," *Personnel Administrator*, October 1977, pp. 41–48.

13 Graef S. Crystal, "The Reemergence of Industry Pay Differentials," *Compensation Review* (third quarter 1983): pp. 29–32.

14 Frederick S. Hills, "Comparable Worth: Implications for Compensation Managers," *Compensation Review* 14, no. 3 (1982): pp. 33–43.

15 Task Force to the Secretary of Health, Education, and Welfare, *Work in America* (Cambridge, Mass.: MIT Press, 1973).

16 Chris Berger, Craig Olson, and John Boudreau, "The Effects of Unions on Work Values, Perceived Rewards and Job Satisfaction," presented at the National Academy of Management Meetings, August 1980.

17 L. S. Festinger and K. Back, *Social Pressures in Informal Groups* (New York: Harper and Row, 1950).

18 Brewery Malt and Beverage Workers Local #1081 and G. Heileman Brewing Co., Inc., Articles of Agreement, April 1, 1984, to April 1987, pp. 34–36.

19 "How Companies Set Top and Middle Management Salaries . . . A Compensation Review Symposium," *Compensation Review* (first quarter 1977): pp. 32–46.

20 Dan R. Dalton, W. D. Todor, and D. M. Krackhardt, "Turnover Overstated: The Functional Taxonomy," *Academy of Management Review*, 7, no. 1 (1982): pp. 117–123.

21 See for example, Linda A. Krefting and Thomas A. Mahoney, "Determining the Size of a Meaningful Pay Increase," *Industrial Relations* 16 (February 1977): pp. 83–93.

11

Wage

Discrimination

- **Learning Objectives**
- **Introduction**
- **Basic Concepts of Wage Discrimination**

  Fair versus Unfair Discrimination
  Legal versus Illegal Discrimination
  Components of Illegal Discrimination
  Examples of Discrimination

- **Doctrines of Illegal Employment Discrimination**

  Disparate Treatment Discrimination
  Adverse Impact Discrimination
  Present Effects of Past Discrimination
  Reasonable Accommodation
  Discrimination

- **Compensation Audits for Pay Discrimination**

  Direct Pay Discrimination
  Indirect Pay Discrimination

- **Comparable Worth Pay Discrimination**

  Examples of Alleged Comparable Worth
  Discrimination
  Comparable Worth Court Cases
  Evolution of the Concept

Learning Objectives

To learn about wage discrimination as a technical concept.
To learn about various forms of illegal discrimination.
To learn how to audit an organization's pay system to check for possible wage discrimination.
To learn about direct and indirect forms of pay discrimination.
To learn about comparable worth wage discrimination.

Introduction

Chapter 5 discussed the legal environment for wage and benefits payments. An understanding of several of the concepts and methods developed in Chapters 6 through 10 is essential before the complex issue of wage discrimination is introduced. This chapter summarizes earlier material, examines wage discrimination in greater detail, and applies many of the concepts developed earlier.

The 1980s brought a new set of opportunities and challenges to the field of compensation decision making. Probably the most profound impact in the 1970s and early 1980s has been the civil rights legislation discussed in Chapter 5; specifically, the Equal Pay Act of 1963 and Title VII of the Civil Rights Act of 1964. Under these two pieces of legislation an employer can be found guilty of wage discrimination. Three types of wage discrimination are possible within the evolving body of civil rights law. Employers might be guilty of indirect pay discrimination, direct pay discrimination, or comparable worth pay discrimination. Comparable worth pay discrimination is the least well developed of the three, and yet it is potentially the most challenging to the organization. This chapter explores the three forms of pay discrimination and discusses what the organization must do to assure that it is not guilty of illegal wage discrimination.

Basic Concepts of Wage Discrimination

Discrimination is a confusing concept for many people. In a technical sense, discrimination has a prescribed meaning.

Fair versus Unfair Discrimination

In a sense all employment decisions involve discrimination. For example, a wage increase on the basis of seniority discriminates among people on the basis of seniority. Some discrimination is considered to be fair, other discriminatory treatment is considered to be unfair. Fair discrimination implies that the discriminatory treatment uses a valid standard, perceived as fair. To the extent that there are differences in performance levels of people, for example, and the organization awards pay increases on the basis of performance, then merit discrimination would be considered fair.

In contrast to fair discrimination is unfair discrimination. Unfair discrimination occurs when the standard for the discriminatory treatment is not considered legitimate or valid. For example, many people feel that quota hiring on the basis of race or sex under an affirmative action plan is unfair discrimination. They argue that race or sex quotas do not take into account other more sensible standards such as merit, ability, and seniority. Many people suggest that using race or sex as a factor in hiring means that qualified white males will be replaced by less qualified minority or female candidates, an assumption that is usually incorrect.

Legal versus Illegal Discrimination

Fair and unfair discrimination must be distinguished from legal and illegal forms of discrimination. For discrimination to be illegal it must be proscribed by law: other forms of discrimination would be legal. The best example of illegal discrimination is found in the Civil Rights Act of 1964. Under that act it is illegal to discriminate in the terms or conditions of employment on the basis of race, color, creed, sex, or national origin. Any employment decision made on the basis of one of these categories (such as a wage increase based on race) is illegal. However, an employment decision based on any other area is legal, according to the act (although other legislation prohibits some other forms of discrimination).

Components of Illegal Discrimination

Illegal discrimination has five components. First, there must be a prohibition under law. For example, Title VII of the Civil Rights Act prohibits discriminating on the basis of race, color, creed, sex, or national origin in the terms and conditions of employment. Second, there must be a respondent, which is the person or organization that carries out the alleged discrimination. Under Title VII a respondent could be an employer engaged in commerce who has 15 or more employees; an agency of a state, county, or local government; an employment agency; or a labor union. Third, there must be an aggrieved person. The person discriminated against could be someone of Title VII status (such as a male or a female, on the basis of sex), or the discrimination could have occurred because of the aggrieved person's actions on the part of someone else with Title VII status (for example, a white may be discriminated against for representing the interests of blacks). Fourth, there must be an action taken or alleged to have been taken; for example, a discriminatory increase in wage payments. Fifth, there must be a causal nexus between the action taken and the prohibited status. That is, there must be a demonstration that the discriminatory action was taken because of the aggrieved party's Title VII status.

Examples of Discrimination

The distinctions between fair and unfair employment discrimination and legal and illegal employment discrimination are not always clear. Exhibit 11.1 depicts the various forms of discrimination.

Exhibit 11.1   *The Four Types of Discrimination*

	Legal	Illegal
Fair	A (discrimination is fair and legal).	B (discrimination is fair but illegal).
Unfair	C (discrimination is unfair but legal).	D (discrimination is unfair and illegal).

The first combination, in cell A, is discrimination that is both fair and legal. To most people this form of discrimination is perfectly acceptable. An example of this would be the decision to give larger pay increases to females than to males because the females performed at higher levels. Cell B in Exhibit 11.1 is the situation where the discrimination is fair but also illegal. A contemporary example of this combination is that it is currently illegal to require women to contribute more to a pension plan, or to reduce the pension benefit level of women. In an actuarial sense it would be fair to have women contribute more to the pension plan or receive a reduced benefit (since they have a longer life expectancy and would receive benefits over a longer period of time, on average). However, by court decision it is illegal to have women contribute more or to receive a reduced benefit.[1]

Cell C of Exhibit 11.1 presents the situation where the discrimination is unfair but perfectly legal. For example, the decisions of a manager to give a subordinate a pay raise because they are good fishing buddies and to penalize an uncared-for employee in pay are unfair in a meritorious society, yet they are not illegal in and of themselves. Many employer decisions fall in this category, and while employees may be unfairly treated they have no legal grounds for recourse.

Cell D in Exhibit 11.1 is the case where the action is both unfair and illegal. An example of unfair and illegal discrimination would be to fail to give a deserving black employee a pay raise when nondeserving white employees received a pay raise. This form of discrimination is easy to understand, and is the form that most people think about when they say that discrimination has occurred.

Doctrines of Illegal Employment Discrimination

The concept of illegal employment discrimination has gone through an evolution since passage of civil rights legislation. The courts use four discrimination doctrines when looking for illegal discrimination: (1) disparate or adverse treatment discrimination; (2) adverse impact discrimination; (3) present effects of past discrimination; and (4) reasonable accommodation discrimination. The first two doctrines are the major ones for compensation decision makers to be aware of since most issues of discrimination in compensation involve one or both of these doctrines.

Disparate Treatment Discrimination

From a legal viewpoint, the original definition of employment discrimination dealt with unequal treatment and intent of the employer. In fact, when Congress passed Title VII of the Civil Rights Act of 1964, the only form of discrimination recognized was unequal treatment based on intent. This type of discrimination is known as disparate treatment discrimination (or adverse treatment discrimination).[2] This definition of discrimination means that the employer treated blacks differently than whites, for example, and that the action was intentional: employers, under this doctrine, knowingly treated one group of employees in an inferior way based on their Title VII status.

Adverse Impact Discrimination

Early experience with disparate treatment discrimination was that it was very difficult to prove. In particular, it was hard to show that the discrimination was intentional. The courts soon endorsed a new concept of illegal discrimination, adverse impact discrimination. Under the concept of adverse impact discrimination the courts no longer had to find intent to discriminate. The impact of the employment practice was considered instead. If the impact of the employee practice was to adversely affect employees of a particular Title VII status, then an employee (or group of employees) of that status would have a *prima facie* case of employment discrimination, meaning that on the surface discrimination appeared to have taken place. Once an aggrieved party demonstrates to a court of law that there is a *prima facie* case, then the employer is presumed to be guilty of illegal employment discrimination, unless the employer can show that there was no discriminatory intent and that the policy or practice in question is grounded in business necessity.

While the process of proving or refuting a charge of discrimination is more complex than this, it should be apparent that the burden clearly falls on the employer once the *prima facie* case is made. Intent is not necessary under this doctrine of discrimination, and the employer must be able to show a legitimate business purpose for a discriminatory policy once a *prima facie* case is made.

As an example of adverse impact discrimination, suppose that females earn less than males on the same job. These females could argue a *prima facie* case of wage discrimination under Title VII of the Civil Rights Act of 1964, under the Equal Pay Act of 1963, or both. Once the court agrees that women earn, on average, less than men for the same work, the *prima facie* case is made. Now the employer must show justification for this pay differential. How an employer does this is discussed much more extensively in the next section of this chapter.

Present Effects of Past Discrimination

Another court-determined doctrine of discrimination is known as present effects of past discrimination, or present effects discrimination.[3] Present effects
discrimination occurs as a result of a discriminatory employment practice that
was in effect before the act was passed. If the discriminatory practice is perpetuated into the present, then the employer would be guilty of the discrimination
that occurred since the law was changed. Present effects discrimination applies
only to discrimination that might have occurred since the law was changed.
That is, pre-act discrimination is not covered.[4]

For example, suppose an employer intentionally paid women less than
men prior to passage of the Equal Pay Act of 1963. By the effective date of the
act the organization does not make the wages of men and women equal (a
violation of the law for other reasons) but keeps the average wage differential.
However, from the date of the act onward the organization does give men and
women equal dollar increments when the wage level is adjusted. In this example the organization no longer discriminates against women, since they now
get the same dollar wage increment as men. However, historical discrimination
is perpetuated into the future because the original discrimination was never
corrected.

Reasonable Accommodation Discrimination

A final kind of illegal discrimination as interpreted by the courts is reasonable
accommodation discrimination. This form of illegal discrimination is most often observed in the area of accommodation of an individual's religious beliefs.
Because this form does not usually affect wages, it is not considered here.

Compensation Audits for Pay Discrimination

Inevitably an organization will be challenged over the legality of its compensation system. This text takes the view that it is better to conduct audits of the
compensation system and correct known deficiencies than to wait for a lawsuit.
This section discusses auditing the compensation system in terms of two separate, although related, forms of possible pay discrimination: direct pay discrimination and indirect pay discrimination. These categories are divided for
conceptual clarity, but in fact, are highly related.

Direct Pay Discrimination

Direct pay discrimination as discussed here refers to discrimination that occurs
when the focus of the decision process is the compensation of employees.
Examples of direct pay discrimination are paying a female employee less than
a male employee even though they are equally qualified, or paying black employees less than white employees.

Direct pay discrimination is illegal under both the Equal Pay Act and Title VII of the Civil Rights Act in the case of women, and under Title VII of the Civil Rights Act in the case of other protected classes of people. Nevertheless, many cases of direct pay discrimination still go to court each day. How do such cases arise, and how can the organization audit itself to prevent or to refute such charges? Two types of discrimination lawsuits are identified and discussed separately here: individual lawsuits and class action lawsuits. Individual lawsuits are brought by an individual employee. The charge will usually be made on the basis of disparate treatment; however, adverse impact discrimination might also be chosen as a basis. Class action lawsuits are brought by a class of employees (such as women or blacks). Class action lawsuits usually rely on an adverse impact doctrine of discrimination, although present effects discrimination might also be alleged. These distinctions are used here primarily for pedagogical purposes in that these separate treatments help focus on the necessary steps in understanding discrimination.

Individual Cases of Direct Pay Discrimination   The most obvious charge of illegal pay discrimination is for an employee to charge that decisions about pay were the result of a discriminatory process. For example, an employee might simply argue that a smaller pay increase was received than that given to another employee. The five components of discrimination must be present for a charge of discrimination to be valid—there must be a respondent, an aggrieved party, an illegal action, and a person with a protected status, and the action must have been because of the person's protected status (the causal nexus).

Investigation of Charges   In an example of an individual case of pay discrimination, suppose that a black male employee complains that his pay is less than that of a white male employee. The probable basis for the charge is disparate or unequal treatment between the black male employee and other employees. Once this allegation is made, it is of paramount importance for the organization to investigate the facts in the situation.

Fact-finding should proceed along the following lines. First, the organization will want to find other nonblack employees who are **similarly situated** to the black employee. These other employees work in the same job as the black employee, were hired at about the same time, have had similar seniority and merit increases, and so forth. Each of these variables suggests legitimate reasons why the black employee might make less than the white employee; for example, he might be in a different job grade, he might be in the same job grade but hired at a time when the organization paid less for new workers, or he might be in the same job grade but be a lower performer than the white employee. In theory the organization would want to find a nonblack employee who started at the same time, had equal starting pay, worked in the same job grade, and had equal merit increases. Because organizations are often relatively small, it may be impossible to find a similarly situated nonblack, but the effort should be made.

These steps are one way to refute the employee's claim of discrimination. The organization may be able to demonstrate that there are other nonblack employees at the company who resemble the black employee in work-related ways (same job, same starting date, same performance evaluations) and who make the same amount of money. The ability to demonstrate this fact would refute the allegation of pay discrimination.

Establishing proof for the individual case of direct pay discrimination is difficult. First, it may be hard for the organization to find someone similarly situated to another employee. Second, even if the organization presents such proof, the employee may not believe the data. From the employee's standpoint making the charge stick is also difficult. Unless there is evidence of the organization's intent to discriminate, most courts would allow any employer's evidence that pay was not discriminatory. Even if the employee feels mistreated, only a court of law can make the final determination.

Correcting the Problem When an allegation of discrimination is made it is in the employer's interest to investigate the case along the above lines. The employer should also have a procedure for discrimination grievances to be filed before the employee sees a lawyer or contacts the Equal Employment Opportunity Commission. The employee cannot be required to use a grievance procedure, but complaints that are handled expeditiously reduce the possibility of discrimination suits. Once the employer has investigated the case, it should be prepared to take corrective action if it agrees with the employee's allegation, such as an adjustment in pay. If the employer finds it has a defensible pay policy, this should be communicated to the employee. It is also advisable for the company to share the data it used in making the determination with the employee. Some employers may resist this last step. However, if the employee files a lawsuit during the fact-finding process the employee will learn the data anyway, so it might as well be shared early when it might convince the employee there are no grounds for a lawsuit.

Class Action Suits of Direct Pay Discrimination Class action suits of direct pay discrimination are likely to be charged as adverse impact discrimination. A group of women employees, for example, may observe that its wages on average are less than some other group's wages, and believe that it is discriminated against in pay. The group of women may argue that compensation policies result in adverse impact on its wages. In the simplest situation, the women employees may take the average pay for their group organizationwide and compare it to the average pay of another group organizationwide. If this broad general comparison is enough to establish a *prima facie* case of discrimination, how would the organization defend itself?

Variables to Analyze The charge that a protected group of employees receives less, on average, in wages may be enough to establish a *prima facie* case of discrimination. At the same time, there may be legitimate reasons for the difference in average wages between two groups. The two groups may differ significantly on important dimensions. The Equal Pay Act requires equal pay for members of both sexes for jobs that are "substantially" equal in terms of skill, effort, and responsibility and that are performed under similar working conditions.[5] A class of employees alleging discrimination may be comparing itself to another class of employees whose jobs are not the same. One of the variables to control for in an analysis of discrimination is the job grade of employees. As an example, if men and women work in jobs that are not equally distributed throughout the wage structure, then there is a need to control for the value of different jobs so that the effects of job worth are removed from the comparison.

As discussed in Chapter 5, four affirmative defenses are written into the Equal Pay Act. An employer may pay different wages to men and women for substantially equal jobs if pay is based on a merit system; pay is based on a seniority system; pay is based on a system that measures earnings in terms of quantity or quality of production; or if pay is based on any factor other than sex. While the act pertains strictly to sex-related discrimination suits, the standards are appropriate in any alleged pay discrimination suit.[6] As these provisions show, differences in pay may exist among groups of employees that are attributable to these positive defenses. For example, if men, on average, are higher performers than women, then one would expect pay, on average, to be higher for men than for women. The same would be true for differences between the groups in terms of seniority, quantity or quality of production, or any factor other than sex. These variables permitted by law that may account for pay differences also need to be controlled for in an analysis of discrimination.

Human capital variables are a third category of variables that might be used to justify differences between groups in pay.[7] Although related to job differences and Equal Pay Act exceptions, these variables may also lead to legitimate pay differences. Human capital variables recognize that people differ in the attributes they bring to the organization. For example, more educated workers are more productive and valuable to organizations than less educated workers. Organizations pay higher wages to educated workers than to uneducated workers. Education is one human capital variable. Other examples of human capital variables are labor force experience and the discipline in which a degree is earned (for example, natural science degrees may be more valuable to an organization than social science degrees). These variables may not be independent of other variables. For example, differences in job pay reflect to some extent differences in education among workers.

Statistical Analysis Once the organization determines the legitimate variables that might account for differences in pay (the factors used in making pay decisions), then some method must be found to control for these variables to see if the original pay differential disappears. If the differential can be explained away, then presumably there is no discrimination. If only a portion of the differential can be explained away, then that portion not explained away is inferred to be pay discrimination.

There are a number of statistical approaches for statistically controlling for legitimate variables.[8] Most of these approaches rely on some variation of multiple regression analysis. One of the most common approaches is presented here as an example. Other statistical approaches yield slightly different conclusions.[9] Because of possible variations, caution should be exercised in the use of these methods. One method is discussed here to illustrate the basic process of examining pay differentials statistically.

To set up a hypothetical situation, suppose a group of employees complains to the organization as a class that they are underpaid relative to another group of employees. To support their claim they present the fact that members of their class earn on average $17,566 per year, while other people in the organization earn on average $23,940 per year. The employees are a protected group under the law (by race, sex, or some other definition), and they wonder why their average pay is $6,374 less than the other group's pay.

If these facts are correct the organization is faced with a *prima facie* case of direct pay discrimination. Wanting to be proactive and investigate this allegation before the Equal Employment Opportunity Commission is involved, the organization might try to explain away this difference in pay. First, the organization realizes that the group is comparing pay across a large group of jobs, and jobs must be controlled for in an analysis. Second, the organization uses a merit pay system and pay varies based on performance evaluation scores. Third, the organization also uses a seniority pay system, which may capture two components of pay: straight seniority pay, and differences in performance as a function of experience.

The organization identifies these three variables that influence pay and that account for differences in pay among people (including differences between the groups in question). The differences between the two groups in pay, job evaluation points (job worth), tenure (length of service on the job), and performance evaluation scores are presented in Table 11.1.

To analyze the pay difference, the employer might first ask what would happen to the pay differential if it treated the discriminated group (group B) the same as the other group (group A)? That is, group B believes the organization discriminates against it, but since tenure, job worth, and performance may explain the difference in pay they must be controlled for. To do so the organization might ask two questions: first, what explains pay for the group that it is not discriminating against (the higher paid group—group A), and second, if it then treats employees in group B the same way it treats employees in group A, will the difference in pay disappear?

To find why group A is paid more, the organization would use multiple regression to regress the wages of group A employees on their scores for job points, performance, and tenure. Using our data to do this, pay for group A employees would be: Wages (group A) = $2,909.69 + $105.08 Tenure +

Table 11.1 Descriptive Statistics for a Hypothetical Pay Audit

Variable		Mean	S.D.	
Salary:	Overall group	$21,342	$6,281	N = 211
	Group A	23,940	6,344	N = 125
	Group B	17,566	3,295	N = 86
Tenure:	Overall group	10.11 years	8.27 years	
	Group A	10.40	8.04	
	Group B	9.70	8.64	
Performance:	Overall group	3.19 points[a]	.62 points	
	Group A	3.26	.61	
	Group B	3.09	.62	
Points:	Overall group	520.4 points[b]	184.0 points	
	Group A	594.5	186.0	
	Group B	412.7	115.5	

a. Measured in performance appraisal points (1–5).
b. Measured in Hay job evaluation points.

$214.71 Performance + $32.36 Job points. This regression equation explains 94 percent of the variation in group A pay, the regression equation is statistically significant at the p less than .0001 level, and all of the variables are statistically significant in the equation except performance (this fact is ignored here). According to the regression line, to determine the pay for a group A member one needs to allot $2,909.69 for being with the organization, plus $105.08 for each year of tenure which they have on the job, plus $214.71 for each point received on the last performance evaluation, plus $32.36 for each point the job carries in the job evaluation plan. The pay for a group A employee who has five years of service on the job, earned a merit rating of 3, and whose job is worth 500 points would come to $20,259.22, using these data.

The second question still needs to be answered. To get the answer to that question, the organization might do the following. It might take the values assigned to each of the legitimate variables that were determined by the regression with group A and apply those values to all of the employees in group B. If the organization did this it would have determined a **predicted pay rate** for all of the employees in group B. For each person in group B the employer would calculate a predicted wage based on the weights assigned to the legitimate variables in the previous analysis. Now the employer is in a position to compare the predicted pay rate of each employee in group B with his or her **actual pay.** When the difference between predicted and actual pay for all employees is totalled, and then divided by the number of employees in group B, the average difference between actual pay and predicted pay is $382.31 per group B employee.

After controlling for the variables accounting for pay differentials in the organization and after treating group B employees by the same standards as group A employees, group B employees are found to be underpaid by $382.31 each on average. This amount is statistically significant from zero (it does not occur by chance), so the conclusion is that there is discrimination in the treatment of group B employees with respect to pay. Some writers suggest that the analysis is incomplete at this point.[10] However, for purposes of illustration, the above analysis shows how regression would be used in a class action context.

Correcting the Problem   At this point, the organization would conclude that group B employees were underpaid, on average, by $382.31 per person per year. The wages of individuals in this group need to be adjusted to correct this average underpayment in wages.

Organizations should conduct wage audits to determine if their pay system is defensible. There are sound pragmatic reasons for doing so. Sooner or later there is likely to be a suit filed over wages. By taking a proactive stance and discovering the discrimination in advance the employer can limit the cost of remedy to the average dollar difference revealed by the analysis. If the employer waits until a court of law rules on the matter, the settlement costs may be the wage difference, plus back pay with interest, plus legal fees. A proactive stance is probably the soundest stance in the long run.

Indirect Pay Discrimination

Indirect pay discrimination occurs any time decisions are made with respect to other terms or conditions of employment that have a secondary effect on wage payments.[11] Examples include discrimination in promotion or discrimination in training opportunities. To the extent that protected group members do not receive promotional opportunities, then their pay will be correspondingly lower.

Numerous decisions have an indirect influence on pay. The variables in the previous discussion on accounting for differences in pay among groups may indirectly influence pay. For example, the use of performance appraisal scores assumes that the performance appraisal scores are unbiased. However, to the extent that such scores are biased, then pay decisions based on those performance scores will also be biased. This would result in indirect pay discrimination.

The Individual Case   As with direct pay discrimination, individual employees might charge that they were discriminated against in the performance appraisal process or in some other personnel decision. Employers should investigate any allegations, have a complaint process, and correct the problem where necessary. As with investigation of direct pay cases, it is desirable to communicate directly with employees on any findings during the investigation.

The Class Action Case   A group of employees that has decided to bring a lawsuit over one part of the pay system is likely to sue on other grounds as well. If the class believes it has reasonable grounds to sue the organization over direct pay discrimination, it will likely sue over other components of the pay system as well. To continue with the performance appraisal example, if employees of a protected group observe that there is an average difference between their performance appraisal scores and those of another group, then there is a *prima facie* case of discrimination in performance appraisals. The employer will then be obligated to come forward with a defense of this fact, and show that the performance scores reflect true performance differences. Failure to do so will result in a finding of illegal discrimination. Discussions on performance assessment in Chapters 12 and 16 advise the organization to monitor these programs.

Findings of indirect pay discrimination will have wage and salary costs associated with them. For example, once discrimination is shown to have occurred in performance assessment, then as part of the remedy the organization will have to adjust wages to make up the difference between what wages actually are and what they would have been had discrimination not occurred in the first place. This can also mean back pay with interest. Again, it is in the interest of employers to be proactive in auditing human resource programs in general and taking corrective action as is necessary.

Comparable Worth Pay Discrimination

The concept of comparable worth pay discrimination is still emerging. As a result, any definition is tenuous at best. Definitions range all the way from comparable worth discrimination as a catchall for all forms of discrimination to the more traditional definition of equal pay for jobs of comparable worth. Comparable worth discrimination is more than discrimination in jobs of *equal worth*. The equality of jobs issue was addressed in part with the Equal Pay Act, which requires equal pay for jobs that are substantially equal in terms of skill, effort, and so forth. Over 20 years of the Equal Pay Act and Title VII of the Civil Rights Act, however, have not even reduced the pay differential between men and women.[12] In part, comparable worth discrimination, which is championed particularly by women's groups, is the latest assault on the resistance to solution of this 40 percent pay differential between the sexes.

Examples of Alleged Comparable Worth Discrimination

Similar Job Titles   One of the most vocal proponents of the concept of comparable worth discrimination is the American Federation of State, County, and Municipal Employees (AFSCME). AFSCME represents many public sector employees who are also largely female. AFSCME points out that within certain states jobs that are essentially equal are paid different wage rates; "women's jobs" are paid less than "men's jobs." AFSCME has found that in the state of Wisconsin the job of upholsterer (predominantly male) is paid about 20 percent more than the job of seamstress (predominantly female). Similarly, the job of chef is paid substantially more than the job of cook. These jobs are also segregated by sex. These facts lead AFSCME to conclude that there are jobs that are comparable, but that carry different pay rates. Further, in almost all cases, the jobs that are female dominated are the lower paid.

Comparable worth discrimination from the above viewpoint sounds very much like bias in the job evaluation system of these employers. More specifically, employers may have adverse impact discrimination in their job evaluation plans that cannot be defended.[13]

The Wisconsin example cited above points up one of the problems of comparable worth discrimination when examined from a layperson's perspective versus the compensation professional's perspective. To a layperson the jobs of chef and cook may sound the same. However, from a compensation professional's perspective the jobs may not be the same. For example, in the hospitality industry (restaurants and hotels) there is a clear difference between the jobs of chef and cook. Often a chef job is an executive job requiring complete management of the restaurant (ordering food, menu planning, staffing, and so on) while the job of cook involves cooking from a recipe. In this situation the jobs of chef and cook are not the same.

This example points again to the importance of job analysis for determining if jobs are substantially equal. The only way that any organization can know if jobs are equal is to do a thorough analysis of the jobs in question.

Dissimilar Job Titles   Another form of alleged comparable worth discrimination is when the jobs are not at all similar in title or content, yet it is argued that the lower paid female jobs carry equal or greater amounts of some compensable factor, such as responsibility. The case of Lemons v. City and County of Denver makes this point.[14]

In the Lemons case nurses complained that their job was worth more to the employer than other jobs for which the employer paid more (tree trimmers and sign painters). The employer argued that wages for nurses and tree trimmers were all based on market wage surveys for each of those occupations. The nurses argued that since labor market rates reflected historical discrimination in those markets that the employer was therefore discriminating in their wage payments.

The court in the Lemons case as well as in another case rejected the comparable worth doctrine put forward.[15] The courts specifically accepted the market rate defense as legitimate. In the case of Briggs v. City of Madison, the court accepted a market defense where nurses (predominantly female) and city sanitarians (mostly male) were in the same job classification but were paid different wage rates because the city had difficulty attracting sanitarians and had to pay a higher labor market rate.[16] In short, a market rate differential even within job class or grade is apparently legal where it can be demonstrated that the employer has difficulty attracting employees at anything other than the going rate.

Comparable Worth Court Cases

In recent years a number of other cases have been brought under the comparable worth banner. The courts have not addressed the issues about bias in job evaluation plans directly, and they shed little light on comparable worth discrimination as a concept. For example, one of the major cases was the Gunther decision, which deals with the issue of discrimination between male and female guards.[17] The County of Washington's job evaluation system identified that female jobs were worth about 80 percent of male jobs, yet the county knowingly paid them less than 80 percent of the male wage rate. The court sidestepped the issue of comparable worth discrimination in this case by noting that the organization intentionally discriminated and finding a direct case of unequal treatment discrimination.

A second major comparable worth discrimination case is in the courts as of this writing. The case of AFSCME vs. State of Washington is still under appeal.[18] In this case, the state had conducted numerous job evaluations over the years that showed that predominantly female jobs were paid less than comparable jobs held predominantly by males. The state had conducted these studies over several years, all with the same results, but had failed to remedy the differences in pay. The judge's opinion was that this was tantamount to intentional discrimination since the state knew the problem existed but did not move to solve it. This case too was not decided on the issue of the comparable worth concept but on the fact that the state knowingly was underpaying females. Most recently an appeals court overturned the trial judge's decision. The United States Supreme Court may well decide the issue.

Evolution of the Concept

The National Academy of Sciences commissioned a study to examine whether job evaluation as a tool can be used to remedy comparable worth discrimination.[19] Its study found that job evaluation systems could be biased against women and that these biases can be controlled for statistically.[20]

The author's view, which is certainly debatable, is that the comparable worth discrimination issue will ultimately emerge as a form of discrimination attributable to adverse impact discrimination in job evaluation systems. Organizations, as noted in Chapters 7 and 8, often conduct job evaluation within job families within the organization. There may be separate job evaluation plans for different occupational groups. This process is usually done because organizations hire from different labor markets and wish to price jobs to their respective labor markets. In this fashion, a firm might have numerous wage structures, each tied to a different sub–labor market.

Pegging internal wage structures to different sub–labor markets is acceptable to employees so long as two conditions exist: they view this mechanism for pricing as legitimate, and they don't make comparisons across job families. The comparable worth issue seems to the author to be tied to this second condition. That is, in the last 10 years some employees (mostly female) have started to examine wages across job families and to ask why they aren't paid more. As an example, a female clerk typist may observe that she has responsibility for accurately entering data on reports and preparing summaries of reports for the boss to sign, yet she is paid only 60 to 70 percent of what the male groundskeeper makes. She might correctly argue that her job carries much more responsibility than the groundskeeper's.

This example points up a problem and a challenge with job evaluation plans. Job evaluation establishes the relative worth of the job in terms of factors that the firm wishes to pay for. Compensable factors can be defined to give male-dominated jobs a decided edge. For example, working conditions are usually defined in terms of heat and dirt, noise, and the like. Seldom are they defined in terms of tedium, boredom, or inability to move from the work station. Under such constraints female-dominated jobs invariably come out more poorly paid. Ultimately, compensable factors are defined the way the organization wants to define them. If the organization's decision makers are out of touch with what workers view as legitimate standards for rewarding work, then the job evaluation system will break down. It is the author's view that this is precisely what is happening with job evaluation. Comparable worth discrimination can be seen as a direct challenge to job evaluation systems per se.

Summary

This chapter focused on wage discrimination. The differences between fair and unfair discrimination and legal and illegal discrimination were first discussed. Distinctions were also made between direct and indirect forms of wage discrimination. It was suggested that employers audit their pay systems to proactively head off discrimination suits. Audit strategies for both individual and class action suits were identified. Finally, comparable worth pay discrimination was discussed as a concept and as an emerging issue for compensation decision makers.

Most of the activity in comparable worth discrimination cases is currently in the public sector. However, the prediction is that private sector firms will be sued in adverse impact discrimination cases in the near future. For example, can an employer defend paying a file clerk who has decision-making responsibility over information flow only 60 percent of what unskilled laborers are paid? Proactively, employers might decide to examine biases in their own job evaluation systems. On the other hand, at this time no one knows how the comparable work discrimination issue will be shaped. Most employers will probably wait to see how the issue is resolved before taking action, when the response may not fit the problem.

Discussion Questions

1. Distinguish between fair and unfair and legal and illegal discrimination in wage and salary payments. Can you think of other examples of each of these beyond those presented in the chapter?

2. Distinguish between the four types of illegal discrimination doctrines. Can you identify other examples of these besides those noted in the chapter?

3. What does it mean to discriminate in wage payments in a direct way? In an indirect way?

4. Discuss comparable worth discrimination. Based on outside readings can you make a case for the fact that comparable worth pay discrimination is not related to adverse impact in job evaluation?

References

[1] Manhart vs. City of Los Angeles, Dept. of Water and Power, 553 F.2d 581, 13 FEP 1625, (9th circuit, 1976); Norris vs. Arizona, Governing Comm., 486F Supp. 645, 22 FEP 1059 (D. Ariz. 1980).

[2] Barbara Lindemann Schlei and Paul Grossman, *Employment Discrimination Law*, 2d ed. (Washington, D.C.: Bureau of National Affairs, 1983); Chapters 4 and 5, pp. 80–205.

[3] *Ibid.*, Chapter 3, pp. 23–79.

[4] Teamsters vs. The United States, 431 U.S. 324, 14 FEP 1514, 1977.

[5] Equal Pay Act, 29 U.S.C. 206d, 1976.

[6] Gunther vs. County of Washington, 602 F.2d 882, 20 FEP 792 (9th circuit, 1979).

[7] A. S. Blinder, "Wage Discrimination: Reduced Form and Structural Estimates," *Journal of Human Resources* 8 (1973): pp. 436–455.

[8] See, for examples of other approaches, Kevin Mossholder *et al.*, "An EPA Exceptions Model—Cracking the Sex Based Wage Differential," *Compensation Review* (first quarter, 1979): pp. 42–51.; and George T. Milkovich, "The Emerging Debate," in E. Robert Livernash, ed., *Comparable Worth Issues and Answers*, (Washington, D.C.: Equal Employment Advisory Council, 1980): pp. 23–48.

[9] Frederick S. Hills and Thomas J. Bergmann, "Alternate Regression Models in Analyzing Sex Based Pay Discrimination," paper presented at the National Academy of Management Meetings, August 1982.

[10] Harry V. Roberts, "Statistical Biases in the Measurement of Employment Discrimination," in Livernash, *Comparable Worth Issues and Answers*, pp. 173–196.

[11] Thomas J. Bergmann and Frederick S. Hills, "Internal Labor Markets and Indirect Pay Discrimination," *Compensation Review* (fourth quarter, 1982): pp. 41–50.

[12] U.S. Department of Labor, "The Female-Male Earnings Gap," Report no. 673., September 1983.

[13] Bureau of National Affairs, *The Comparable Worth Issue* (Washington, D.C.: The Bureau, 1983): p. 21.

[14] 620 F.2d 228 (10th circuit) cert. den. 449 U.S. 888 (1980).

[15] *Ibid.*; Christiansen v. State of Iowa, 563 F.2d 353 (8th circuit, 1977).

[16] 536 F. Suppl. 435 (1982).

[17] *Ibid.*

[18] AFSCME vs. State of Washington, 33 FEP Cases, 808, 1983.

[19] Donald J. Trieman and Heidi I. Hartman, eds., *Women, Work, and Wages* (Washington D.C.: National Academy of Science Press, 1981).

[20] *Ibid.*, p. 87.

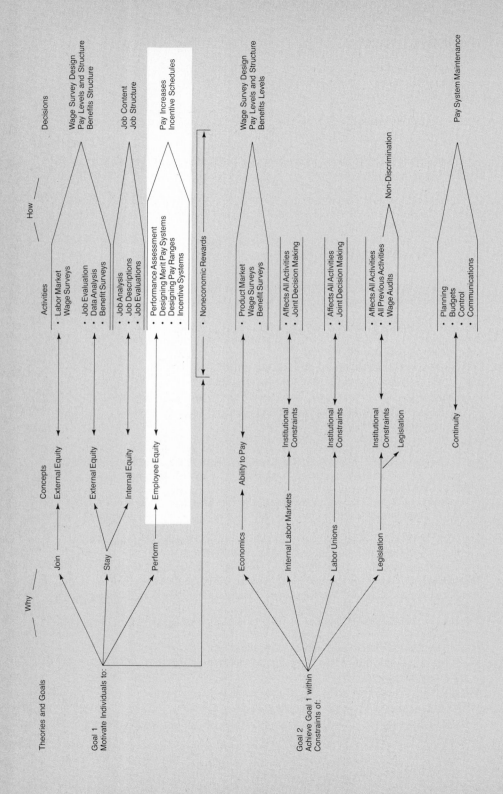

PART · FIVE

Individual Equity

Part Five is comprised of two chapters that focus upon individual performance pay. Any organization that wishes to design a subjective merit pay system must wrestle with the design of a performance assessment system. Chapter 12 discusses subjective performance assessment, including how to design a performance assessment system, problems in performance assessment, and legal concerns about performance assessment.

Chapter 13 completes Part Five with a discussion of individual and group incentive plans. Over the years organizations have come up with an array of schemes to try to motivate employees to high levels of performance. Some of these plans have been geared to individuals while others have been aimed to motivating groups. Some incentive schemes are used to motivate operative employees, while others are geared to motivating managers. Further, some plans seek to share profits while others seek to share cost savings. This tangle of incentive schemes is discussed systematically in Chapter 13.

CHAPTER

12

Performance Assessment

· **Learning Objectives**

· **Introduction**

· **Performance Assessment and Compensation**

Instrumentality and Expectancy Theory and Performance
The Performance Appraisal Paradox

· **What Is Performance Assessment?**

Work Rules versus Job Outcome Compliance
Job Outcome versus Behavioral Outcome Dimensions
People Assessment versus Job Assessment Revisited

· **Who Conducts Performance Assessment?**

Immediate Supervisors
Peer Evaluations
Subordinate Evaluations
Other Evaluators
Multiple Evaluations

· **Problems with Performance Standards**

Criterion Contamination and Deficiency
Measurability of the Criteria
Combining Performance Dimensions

· **Rater Biases and Errors in Performance Assessment**

"Halo or Horns" Bias
Excessive Strictness or Leniency

Central Tendency
Recency Tendency
Primacy Bias
Similarity or Difference Bias
Order Effect and Contrast Bias

· **Other Factors Influencing Performance Assessment**

Unwillingness to Discriminate
Poor Training
Superordinate Goals

· **Legal Considerations in Performance Assessment**

Adverse Impact Discrimination under Title VII
Equal Pay Act Considerations
Age Discrimination in Employment Act of 1967

· **Performance Assessment Techniques**

Ranking Methods
Graphic Rating Scales
Behaviorally Anchored Rating Scales
Management by Objectives

· **Performance Assessment and Compensation Decision Making**

The Departmental Unit Problem
Allocating Percentage Pay Increase Budgets
Percentage Increases to a Department
Guidecharts

· **Exercises**

317

Learning Objectives

To learn the relationship between merit pay and subjective performance assessment systems.

To learn the process of conducting employee performance reviews.

To learn the major types of errors and biases and problems that enter into the performance review process.

To learn the major ways in which performance assessment systems will come under legal scrutiny.

To learn some of the more common approaches to performance assessment.

To learn how performance assessment information is linked to pay decisions.

Introduction

This chapter deals with the process of performance assessment. The purposes of this chapter are to review the objectives of performance assessment; to discuss the major methods for conducting performance assessment; to review the legal parameters surrounding performance assessment; to discuss the role of performance assessment in the compensation system; to identify some of the more important biases that interfere with accurate performance assessment; and to discuss performance assessment techniques in the context of pay determination.

This chapter should provide an appreciation for performance assessment, an understanding of the assessment techniques available, and the means to design a performance assessment system to accomplish compensation objectives.

Performance Assessment and Compensation

For organizations to tie pay to performance they must have some method of assessing performance. Several other boundary conditions must also be met before a pay for performance system will be effective. First, the performance assessment system must accurately assess performance. Second, the organization must be willing to assess performance. There may be numerous situations where an organization is not willing to assess performance. As a matter of philosophy or policy the organization may want seniority pay, or it may be so costly to measure performance that it is not considered worth the time and effort.

Instrumentality and Expectancy Theory and Performance

Performance assessment as an activity can be linked to theory developed earlier. Chapter 2 discussed instrumentality and expectancy theory and showed that before a pay system is likely to motivate high levels of performance, numerous conditions must be met.[1] Employees must have the ability to perform at high levels, must believe that they have the ability, and must value more money relative to less money, and the organization must show employees that sizes of pay increases are systematically associated with relative levels of performance. In other words, employees must expect an association between performance levels and pay levels. In a later section of this chapter threats to this expectation on the part of employees are examined in more detail. Finally, employees must value money outcomes relative to other outcomes. For example, the monetary outcomes associated with higher performance must be valued more than peer acceptance. These conditions that are necessary for a merit or performance pay system to succeed are summarized in Exhibit 12.1.

Like many human resource activities, performance appraisal is used for other purposes besides pay determination. For example, performance assessment information is often used for developmental purposes, training needs purposes, feedback, discipline, discharge, and promotability assessment. Further, just as with other human resource activities, performance assessment needs will often dictate what information should be collected in the assessment process. For present purposes performance assessment is examined strictly from a compensation decision-making standpoint. Certain issues are not discussed as they relate to performance assessment, such as how to conduct developmental performance assessment sessions.

The Performance Appraisal Paradox

One of the major difficulties with performance assessment has to do with the use of performance assessment information for pay purposes and developmental purposes.

Some years ago researchers at General Electric observed that performance appraisal systems used for both pay determination and for developmental purposes seemed to break down.[2] It was observed that these two goals did not seem to be successfully achieved with one appraisal system. The problem seems to be that the goals are so radically different that one appraisal system is insufficient. For example, if the performance review is to be used for both

---

Exhibit 12.1   *Conditions for a Successful Merit or Performance Pay System*

1. Employees must have the ability to perform at high levels.
2. Employees must believe they have the ability to perform at high levels.
3. Employees must value more money more than less money.
4. Employees must value more money relative to other outcomes.
5. Employees must believe that level of pay is associated with level of effort.
6. There must be a method to measure performance.
7. The organization must be willing to discriminate on the basis of performance.
8. The performance assessment method must capture real and meaningful differences in performance.

---

development of employees and for determining pay, then an employee is not likely to be very open to discussion of weaknesses because the employee knows that pay is also an outcome of the performance assessment. The employee is apt to find external reasons for poor performance and may not be responsive to suggestions for performance improvement.

Based on the research at General Electric, it is suggested that organizations operate two separate performance assessment programs: one for employee development purposes and the other for pay determination purposes. The assessment process used for development can be less formal, involve more frequent feedback sessions, and focus on goal setting. The assessment procedure used for pay purposes has a clear judgmental aspect to it. That is, the assessor reviews performance over a fixed period of time to determine performance during that period. It may be appropriate to think of this assessment as a judgment about actual performance over the whole period of time. The assessor is attempting to take a snapshot of behavior for the review period.

This text is primarily concerned about performance assessment for pay determination purposes and pays particular attention to the judgmental aspects of assessment. Performance assessment is done for other purposes besides pay determination, and the assessment procedure should be designed for the purposes for which the assessment is to be used. The differences between performance assessment in a developmental setting and performance assessment for pay purposes are summarized in Exhibit 12.2.

What Is Performance Assessment?

Most people would say that performance assessment is determining how well the employee is doing on the job. The question is more complex, however. There are two parts to performance assessment in practice: how well a person performs relative to the general work rules of the organization, and how well a

---

Exhibit 12.2 *Performance Assessment for Developmental and Pay Purposes*

Goal	Characteristics
Development	Ongoing
	Can be informal
	Emphasis on growth and change
	Forward looking (what is wanted to happen)
Performance pay	Set intervals
	A snapshot of performance over the period
	Formal
	Judgmental
	Backward looking (what has happened)

person performs relative to the performance standards of the job. Each of these components is discussed here.

Work Rules versus Job Outcome Compliance

Work rules are defined as the general rules of conduct that apply to all employees. Examples of work rules are rules governing absenteeism, rules about consumption of alcoholic beverages on the job, rules of dress and grooming, rules for tardiness, and so forth. Most organizations have explicit or implicit work rules governing the conduct of employees over numerous subject areas.[3] It is often the case that employees are assessed on performance on these rules for pay purposes, but it is the position of this text that this should not be the case. Employees should meet minimum standards for work rules to qualify to hold their employment, and pay should not be dependent upon these criteria. Many organizations do in fact use attendance and absenteeism as criteria in allocating pay increases. This is often done simply because employees have come to expect pay increases to be based on work rule compliance. It is suggested here that this should not be done, especially if pay is intended to reflect relative job performance. If performance is assessed on work rules, then a seniority pay increase system should be used. In this way the organization has the opportunity to terminate employment if the person does not perform to the work rules. On the other hand, if the employee does continue to adhere to the work rules, then seniority will be rewarded.

When wage payments are involved the performance criterion of relevance should be the performance standards of the job itself. Examples of job-related performance standards are numbers of dowels turned on a lathe per hour, number of dollars of insurance policies sold, and percentage of parts made that pass quality control tests. Performance standards can be defined as the relative levels of performance variation that exist within a job.[4] A specific example of performance standards follows:

> Superior performance: 90 units built per hour
>
> Above average performance: 80 units built per hour
>
> Average performance: 70 units built per hour
>
> Below average performance: 60 units built per hour
>
> Unacceptable performance: 50 units or less built per hour

Pay raises based on relative performance levels communicate to employees that their relative productivity will influence their relative pay. In other words, those who perform highly relative to the standards established will receive more pay accordingly.

One criticism of the distinction between pay increases based on work rules versus performance standards is that an employee may be a superior performer relative to job performance standards but may exhibit terrible attendance behavior. In this case, distinguishing between the two means the employee deserves a large wage increase for performance but deserves to be terminated because of poor attendance behavior. In spite of this apparent con-

flict these two concerns should be dealt with as distinct decisions. In the remainder of this chapter the discussion on performance assessment relates specifically to job-related performance standards, and not to work rule behaviors.

Job Outcome versus Behavioral Outcome Dimensions

The above discussion on performance assessment focuses on performance
standards that could be defined as **job outcome** dimensions. Job outcome dimensions of performance are those that measure performance in terms of
some product. Examples of job outcome dimensions are number of units produced and error rates per number of units produced. Job outcome dimensions
tend to measure a tangible outcome of performance.

For many jobs it is not easy to express performance in terms of some
tangible outcome. When this is the case organizations assess behaviors of employees that are thought to be associated with acceptable or high levels of
performance. This type of performance assessment focuses on behavioral outcomes, or employee behaviors.

The following example distinguishes between job outcomes and behavioral outcomes. An organization wishes to establish performance standards for
a lathe operator. For this job it may be relatively easy to specify job outcomes.
Job outcomes that might be identified include number of units turned out in an
hour and percentage of units passing quality control. Both of these measures
are readily observable. It would also be relatively easy to establish behavioral
outcomes for this job. Examples of behavioral outcomes might be properly
inserting raw material onto the lathe bench, selecting the appropriate cutting
tool for the job at hand, periodically checking the tolerances on the machine,
and reporting machine wear to maintenance staff in a timely way. As this
example shows, job outcome measures are a more direct and more objective
assessment of performance. Job outcome measures are preferable to behavioral measures in performance assessment.

It may be that job outcome measures are not readily observable or measurable. When this is the case behavioral dimensions are secondary measures
that might be used instead. In the lathe operator example above, it would be
inferred that if the lathe operator did all of the behavioral things which good
lathe operators do, then she or he too should be a good lathe operator. That is,
if lathe operators who produce large numbers of units with low error rates are
also operators who properly fit raw material into machines, select the correct
cutting tool, routinely check machine tolerances, and so forth, then when these
behaviors are observed in a worker it is reasonable to conclude that the employee is a high performer.

People Assessment versus Job Assessment Revisited

In Chapters 7 and 8 job evaluation was shown as a process in which the
relative worth of jobs is established. The outcome of job evaluation is a hierarchy of jobs. Job evaluation does not deal with a person's worth, but with job
worth.

Performance assessment is the process of determining the relative worth of employees within a job. Performance assessment, therefore, deals with assessing the relative worth of people. It is also important to recognize that performance assessment is with respect to a given job. That is, performance assessment determines how well a person is doing in a job. In other words, performance assessment considers which people who work in a certain job are superior performers, which people are average performers, and which people are poor performers.

Job evaluation and performance assessment differ in their purposes. Both are important in pay determination. Job evaluation establishes job pay, while performance evaluation establishes relative pay within jobs (i.e., individual equity). This chapter deals with assessing people relative to their jobs.

Who Conducts Performance Assessment?

Immediate Supervisors

The responsibility for evaluating employee performance is most often delegated to the employee's immediate supervisor.[5] This makes sense from several perspectives. First, an employee's supervisor is the person who is most directly responsible for assuring that the employee is performing at an acceptable level. Therefore, it makes sense to give the supervisor a tool for assuring performance.[6]

Second, and probably more important, the employee's immediate supervisor is usually the person most familiar with an employee's performance level and the job that the employee is supposed to perform. It is highly desirable that the supervisor with the firsthand knowledge of what the job requires and the knowledge of the employee's performance conducts the evaluation.[7]

Peer Evaluations

Not all performance assessment is carried out by immediate supervisors. There are cases where peers conduct the evaluations. Peer evaluations have been used in situations where it is difficult for a supervisor to observe the exact contributions of individuals.[8] For example, loosely supervised team projects might necessitate peers evaluating each other's performance.

A second situation where peer evaluations are used is in cases where peers have greater technical knowledge of performance. For example, in universities faculty peers evaluate other faculty for promotion and tenure. It is assumed that faculty are better informed of a colleague's academic performance than are administrators.

Subordinate Evaluations

Another approach to performance assessment is to have an employee's subordinates evaluate performance. In university settings a departmental faculty may evaluate the performance of the department head. It is sometimes done in business and industry as well when top management wishes to know if lower level and middle managers are performing well in the eyes of their subordinates.

Subordinate assessments of performance seem to be appropriate under at least two conditions. First, subordinate evaluation can be useful in situations where a great deal of importance is placed on voluntary compliance with the supervisor's directives. In this case, the supervisor must be looked upon positively by subordinates before they will comply with orders. A second situation where subordinate evaluation may be useful is where top management wants to be sure that supervisors are being fair to their employees. In this case, getting subordinate input into the evaluation is important. However, rarely do subordinate evaluations of an employee constitute the sole performance assessment. Normally they would only be input into a much larger assessment.

Other Evaluators

There may be cases in which an employee's immediate supervisor has too little information on actual performance to make a sound judgment about performance. For example, in the sales field it may be difficult for a sales manager to spend much time watching a salesperson close a deal. Furthermore, when this behavior is observed, it may not be the typical behavior for the salesperson (who may know he or she is being observed). In these cases it may be appropriate to query customers of the salesperson to see if the closing was handled well from their perspective.

Using customers for evaluating performance is also done in the hotel and restaurant industry, where they may be encouraged to fill out evaluation forms on cleaning staff and food servers to determine if they are pleased with the performance levels of employees. As with subordinate evaluations, customer evaluations are likely to be used as one form of input into a larger assessment.

Multiple Evaluations

Accurately assessing employee performance is a monumental task. Because performance assessments are subject to many biases (as discussed in the next section), it is often desirable to have multiple assessments.

In many work organizations employee performance assessment is the principal responsibility of the immediate supervisor. The immediate supervisor's evaluation must also be acceptable to the evaluator's superior. Similarly, in universities, faculty members may evaluate other faculty for promotion and tenure; this peer evaluation must then be agreed to by several levels of university management. Multiple reviews have several advantages. First, they assess performance more accurately because several assessors are involved. Second, they provide for checks and balances in the review system so that no one person can bias the evaluation. Of course, multiple assessor systems add considerably to the cost of assessment, in both time and money.

Most performance assessment systems used for pay purposes have at least one check against the immediate supervisor. This is desirable for the two reasons noted above. The remainder of this chapter discusses performance assessment from the immediate supervisor's perspective, although the issues are valid for any kind of assessment.

Problems with Performance Standards

It is easy to think in terms of assessing employee performance relative to job-related standards. However, in the performance assessment process, problems become immediately apparent. For example, evaluating performance in one dimension (such as number of units produced) is not difficult, but as a practical matter performance is usually multidimensional.[9] For a lathe operator, performance is more than turning out a certain number of dowels; it is turning out that number of dowels that also meet quality control standards a given percentage of the time, with a minimally acceptable materials waste rate, and with acceptable levels of wear and tear on the lathe itself. A major objective in designing a performance appraisal system is to identify the important performance dimensions for the job through job analysis.

Criterion Contamination and Deficiency

Proper identification of performance dimensions can eliminate or at least reduce two common biases that enter into performance assessment: **criterion contamination** and **criterion deficiency.** Criterion contamination and criterion deficiency are illustrated in the diagram in Exhibit 12.3.

In Exhibit 12.3, the circle on the left, area *A*, can be thought of as the true domain of job performance. This area is unmeasured job performance. To the extent that the performance assessment system fails to measure area *A*, the

---

Exhibit 12.3 *Criterion Contamination and Criterion Deficiency*

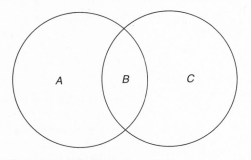

A = True performance
B = Criterion relevance
C = Measured performance

assessment device is deficient. Area A, known as criterion deficiency, can be defined as true job performance which is unmeasured. Or, to state it another way, the performance assessment device is deficient because it did not measure area A.

The circle on the right depicts the measured domain of job performance. There is some overlap between true job performance and measured job performance, which is area B in the exhibit (sometimes called **criterion relevance**).

Area C in the exhibit results in criterion contamination. That is, there are aspects of performance that are measured but that do not overlap with the true domain of performance. To the extent that a performance assessment device has dimensions that do not overlap with the true domain, there is criterion contamination.

An example of criterion contamination is assessing a lathe operator on typing speed. Since typing performance has nothing to do with performance as a lathe operator, this criterion is contaminated. Criterion deficiency occurs when an important performance standard is omitted in the process of conducting a performance assessment on an employee.[10] For example, if a lathe operator's performance is based on an evaluation that does not consider the number of units produced on the lathe in some period of time, then the assessment has criterion deficiency.

Job analysis is the major method of guarding against both deficiency and contamination problems. Job analysis is also a necessary requirement for a performance appraisal system to withstand a legal challenge under equal employment opportunity litigation.[11]

Measurability of the Criteria

A second and related problem in establishing performance standards is the issue of their measurability. It may be relatively easy to determine performance standards for many operative employees for example, but it can be extremely difficult to establish performance standards for a director of marketing or a labor relations specialist. Thus, measurement is often a problem for many jobs. In a later section some techniques are discussed that attempt to assess performance standards in behavioral rather than job outcome terms for jobs of this latter sort.

Combining Performance Dimensions

A third problem with performance standards is how the standards should be combined into a total overall score for an employee. That is, given the multidimensionality of performance, how are the various dimensions weighted into a composite score for the employee? This decision relates directly to the final decision on an employee's pay raise. One writer suggests three bases for combining various standards into one overall measure.[12] The three bases are judgmental (what individuals think is the relative importance of the criteria); statistical (depending upon whether dimensions are correlated or not); and economic (which dimensions are most important in terms of economic contribution to the organization). From a purely pragmatic standpoint the last approach is probably best since it links individual rewards most directly to organizational success.

Rater Biases and Errors in Performance Assessment

Two important types of performance assessment errors were noted in the preceding section: criterion contamination and criterion deficiency. Numerous other errors and biases that arise in performance assessment can be directly attributable to the rater.

Performance assessment problems identified in this and the previous sections and recommended procedures for reducing the problems are summarized in Exhibit 12.4.

All performance evaluators are potentially guilty of biases and errors in the performance assessment. Some of the more common biases are reviewed in this section. Many of these are mutually exclusive. For example, an evaluator cannot be guilty of excessive strictness and excessive leniency at the same time. Also although suggestions for reducing biases and errors are made there are no known methods to completely eliminate them in performance assessment.

Exhibit 12.4 *Problems and Solutions of Performance Appraisal*

Problem	Solutions
Criterion deficiency	Job analysis Clearly defined performance dimensions
Criterion contamination	Job analysis Performance appraisal form with no extraneous performance dimensions included
Halo or horns bias	Evaluator training for bias Clearly defined performance dimensions
Excessive strictness or leniency bias	Evaluator training for bias Clear performance standard
Central tendency bias	Evaluator training for bias Clear performance standards for each dimension
Recency tendency bias	Employee performance log over time
Primacy bias	Employee performance log over time
Similarity or difference bias	Reference to clearly defined performance dimensions
Order effect or contrast bias	Reference to clearly defined performance dimensions for each employee

"Halo or Horns" Bias

The halo or horns bias occurs when an evaluator allows one positive or negative performance dimension to influence the assessment of the employee on
other performance dimensions.[13] For example, if the assessor is guilty of the
halo bias in evaluating a secretary, then good typing performance influences
the evaluator to give the secretary a high score on filing performance as well,
even though the secretary actually does poorly on the filing performance dimension. The horns effect would result in a poor score on typing performance
based on the poor score on the filing dimension. The halo or horns bias can be
reduced by training assessors so they are aware of the potential bias, and by
designing assessment techniques that specify clearly the separate performance
dimensions.[14]

Excessive Strictness or Leniency

A second type of rater bias is the tendency of some evaluators to rate all
employees either too leniently or too strictly. A manager who rates all employees leniently might rate all employees as above average in performance. Conversely, a manager who evaluates all employees too strictly might rate their
performance as below average. Probably the best way to reduce this bias is to
make the standards extremely clear for what is above, below, and average
performance. Evaluators should also be trained to be aware of this bias.

Central Tendency

Just as some managers are guilty of excessive leniency or strictness in evaluating employees, other managers have a tendency to evaluate everyone the same
and in the middle. In this type of bias, called central tendency, a manager
might assess all employees as having average performance regardless of their
actual performance levels. Again, the two best methods to reduce this bias are
performance standards expressed in behavioral or job outcome terms, and
training to raise evaluator awareness of the problem.

Recency Tendency

Another major rater bias is the tendency of assessors to remember the most
recent performance behaviors and to forget performance behaviors that occurred earlier. Recency bias can influence the performance assessment because
it prevents a fair assessment of the employee's performance over the entire
evaluation cycle, not just the recent past. One effective way to reduce this bias
is to keep a log of employee behaviors or performance outcomes over the
entire assessment period. When it is time to conduct the assessment the assessor can then refer to the log to determine a weighted overall performance level
during the period of each performance dimension.

Primacy Bias

Many people are guilty of allowing first impressions to taint their judgments. This phenomenon is known as primacy bias. As an example, an employee might perform some part of a job exceedingly well or poorly the first time he or she attempts the task, and this first impression may be carried by the evaluator into future assessments of performance. In some ways this bias is the reverse of the recency bias. A performance log is also useful in guarding against primacy bias.

Similarity or Difference Bias

In similarity or difference bias, an evaluator may use a stereotyped good or poor performer to compare other employees. The evaluator makes judgments of the person being assessed relative to that stereotype. In some cases, this stereotype may be the evaluator. The assessor may say that an employee is unlike or like the stereotype. Depending on whether the stereotype is a good or poor performer, the employee's performance will be judged to be good or poor correspondingly. Probably the best way to avoid this bias is to use the job requirements when assessing performance and not other employees.

Order Effect and Contrast Bias

In the process of evaluating the performance of one employee the assessor may be influenced by the performance assessment of another employee. This phenomenon is known as order effect and contrast bias. In this type of bias, a superior performer may be evaluated first. When the performance of other employees is assessed, it seems poor in comparison with the superior performance. A prior assessment of a poor performer may also make later assessees appear superior. In other words, the evaluator allows the assessment of one employee to influence the assessment of another employee. This effect works against an employee if the previous employee was superior in performance and for the employee if the previous employee was an inferior performer. Bias caused by order and contrast can be reduced by evaluating employees against predetermined standards rather than against each other.

Other Factors Influencing Performance Assessment

The two general categories of variables that threaten the validity of performance assessment are problems with the standards and evaluator biases. Beyond these considerations is another set of variables that contributes to invalid performance assessment. These variables concern additional problems with the evaluator.

Unwillingness to Discriminate

While evaluators may be found to discriminate on the basis of race, color, creed, sex, and national origin, they may also seem to be reluctant to discriminate on the basis of performance. Assessments by managers who do not like to discriminate on performance are often biased and invalid.

Numerous factors contribute to unwillingness to discriminate on the basis of performance. One reason is that managers may not want to have to justify different performance ratings to the employees. The manager may find it easier to give all employees similar evaluations. Managers may also not want to have to defend their decisions about people to their own supervisors. For example, if pay is based on performance, then a superior evaluation should result in more money. A manager's supervisor may not want to spend extra money unless the superior rating is valid, and the manager may then have to develop additional documentation to support the rating. This manager may find it easier to give the employee a slightly above average rating to save the additional work involved in defending a superior rating.

A third reason why managers don't discriminate on performance is an unwillingness to play God, so to speak. Many managers don't like being put in the position of judging others and resist doing so. Managers with this attitude are likely to evaluate all employees at least average, and to give similar evaluations to all employees.

Poor Training

Few managers actually understand their organizations' performance appraisal system, including how the system was developed, what the system is to accomplish, and how it works. Because managers do not understand the performance appraisal system in many cases, it should not be surprising that their appraisals are biased.

Better training of managers should result in more valid appraisal systems. Every organization should develop a training program to teach managers five fundamentals:

1. The organization's policy on performance appraisal.
2. The purposes of the organization's performance appraisal system.
3. How the performance appraisal system was developed.
4. How to conduct an appraisal interview.[15]
5. The biases that each manager is likely to bring to the appraisal interview and ways to reduce them.[16]

Superordinate Goals

Many managers do not view themselves as managers of people, but as managers of sales, marketing, production, and so forth. These managers may place more emphasis on activities in their jobs other than people assessment. To these managers, balancing the budget or meeting production goals, for example, may be more important than valid performance assessment. This type of manager usually views the performance review as some silly report that the personnel department insists on having filled out, and sees the performance review as a waste of valuable time. Under these conditions it should not be surprising that performance assessments are inaccurate. Training of assessors is a potential method of reducing this problem.

Legal Considerations in Performance Assessment

Adverse Impact Discrimination under Title VII

Adverse impact occurs whenever a performance assessment system used by an organization results in lower performance assessment scores for one protected group under the Civil Rights Act of 1964 compared to the scores for other protected groups. If those scores are then used for determining employment outcomes (in this case pay outcomes), an organization would be subject to a discrimination suit under Title VII of the Civil Rights Act. The presence of adverse impact does not mean that the organization actually is discriminating against particular protected groups, since the lower performance assessment scores could be due to actual differences in performance between the groups. In this case, the organization may be able to successfully defend itself against a lawsuit. However, if adverse impact is present, the organization should investigate the differences to determine if they are truly performance differences, or if they are caused by intended or unintended illegal discrimination on the part of managers who are conducting the performance assessments.

A Defense for Adverse Impact Allegations   While there are no hard and fast rules for determining the properties of a performance assessment system that will survive legal challenge when there is adverse impact, at least one court has given some guidance on the subject. In the case of James v. Stockham Valve and Fittings Co., the court found that the performance evaluation system used for pay determination was not discriminatory, even though black employees earned less than white employees.[17] The evidence showed that:

1. Each of the jobs in the plant had been studied and evaluated in terms of job functions (job analysis).
2. The defendant's procedure allowed an employee to file and simultaneously maintain applications on any number of jobs in the plant regardless of whether a vacancy existed.
3. When a vacancy occurred, all pending applications were reviewed.
4. The performance evaluation was undertaken by the manager having firsthand knowledge.
5. The standards for ratings were defined in written terms.

6. The evaluative instrument was of fixed content and called for the recording of discrete judgments.

7. Each employee's performance was rated on seven factors: quality, quantity, job or trade knowledge, ability to learn, cooperation, dependability, and industry and attendance.

8. The evaluations were graded under standardized conditions.

9. The rating form was weighted according to a predetermined numerical table. The rating manager was unaware of the weights assigned.

10. An employee who did not receive a pay increase because of the merit rating could ask for a meeting with the manager, the superintendent, and a committee member to discuss the failure to qualify for an increase.

The Stockham case has several interesting features. First, job analysis was critical to identify the important job components upon which performance was determined. Second, the factors were weighted, not arbitrarily, but beforehand, and the manager doing the rating did not know the weights so that there was no opportunity to bias the scores. Third, the manager who knew the employee's performance did the evaluating.[18] Fourth, the evaluations were conducted under standardized conditions, which meant that every employee was assessed by an identical process. Finally, the employee had several levels of appeal to resolve a disagreement with the manager's assessment. This last point is particularly important in public sector organizations where failure to provide due process to an employee can be a violation of the employee's 14th Amendment rights to due process.[19]

Equal Pay Act Considerations

Chapter 5 discussed the major legal considerations for designing a compensation system. One of the important pieces of legislation is the Equal Pay Act of 1963. The act provides for specific exceptions to an equal pay policy that are related to performance assessment.

The act allows for differences in pay between men and women in similar jobs if the difference is attributable to a merit system, a system that measures earnings by quantity or quality of production, a seniority system, or any factor other than sex. The first exceptions are directly applicable to performance evaluation.

First, the act permits employers to pay men and women different wages on similar jobs if the differences result from a merit pay system. However, if the merit system is discriminatory, then such a pay system would be illegal. Stated another way, it is permissible to have differences in pay caused by a merit pay system if the merit system is not designed to, nor does it in fact, illegally discriminate on the basis of sex. The excerpt from one court case presented in Exhibit 12.5 concerns discrimination both legal and illegal.

For example, suppose that an employer uses a merit pay system that bases pay increases on supervisors' judgments of relative performance. Women, on average, score poorer on the performance appraisal form than men, on aver-

---

Exhibit 12.5 *Legitimate Differences in Performance Level*

Maureen S. Bullock
v.
PIZZA HUT, INC. and Pizza Hut
of Louisiana, Inc.
Civ. A. No. 75–176.
United States District Court,
M. D. Louisiana.
March 30, 1977.

[5–7]   Defendant argues that the higher salaries paid to the male Unit Managers were based upon characteristics which these men possessed that made them more valuable as managers. With one exception, we do not agree. The defendants established that Paul Grace had seven years experience in Florida and Texas as a Pizza Hut Unit Manager and Area General Manager. He was also personally known to Gerald York, defendants' Area General Manager for Baton Rouge. We think that these facts justified the wage differential between plaintiff and Grace. As to the other two managers in the Baton Rouge area, defendants argue that Clyde Martin's higher salary was based upon his three years of college education and extensive experience in dealing with the public. However, we note that plaintiff's application for employment with defendants shows she had at least as much experience in dealing with the public as did Martin, having occupied positions as either manager or manager trainee in other food service establishments at least as far back as 1965. Furthermore, while not discounting the value of a college education, we do not believe it justifies the wage differential in this instance.

While we might have found the evidence of a broader educational background as justifying a disparity in wages during an initial period of employment, we think that in light of plaintiff's repeated high performance in profitability it cannot provide justification for her wage differential during the entire period prior to the standardization of wages. We derive support for this position from the fact that Charles Naquin, the manager who was hired at almost exactly the same time as plaintiff, at all times prior to the standardization of wages earned as much as $150.00 per month more than plaintiff. No justification is offered for this other than defendants' assertion that this disparity was due to Gerald York's personal assessment of Naquin's worth as a manager. We have previously discussed the factors that York used in evaluating the salaries of potential employees. We can see no justification for the difference in salaries other than the plaintiff's gender. The defendant argues that plaintiff's sex was important only to the extent that it played a part in her performance. It is argued that plaintiff's gender was a valid consideration because of cultural distinctions which would inhibit the plaintiff's development in learning leadership qualities and mechanical skills. A short answer to this contention is that this was not shown to be the case here. Defendants' stereotyping plaintiff in this manner is merely a round-about way of saying that the plaintiff is being paid less because in our society women are willing to work for less. This is clearly an inappropriate factor under the law. *Brennan v. Prince William Hospital Corp.*, 503 F.2d 282 (4th Cir. 1974); *Hodgson v. Brookhaven General Hospital*, 436 F.2d 719 (5th Cir. 1970).

---

age. If pay is based on merit, women would be expected to be paid less than men, on average. This pay system would be legal so long as there were true differences in merit between men and women. However, if the difference in average scores between men and women is due to one or more biases (perhaps some of the biases identified earlier), then the merit system itself would be discriminatory. In turn, the pay system would also be discriminatory.

The second exception relevant to this discussion permits a pay system based on quantity or quality of production. If an employer establishes pay on one or both of these criteria, then the pay plan is permissible under the act, subject to the requirement that such a pay plan is not designed to, nor does in fact, discriminate against one sex or the other.

As an example, suppose that an employer pays employees 10 cents for each 100-pound bag of material taken from a loading dock and stacked in a storeroom. Both men and women work at this job. Men, on average, can move 60 bags per hour, while women, on average, can move 40 bags per hour. In this situation men earn, on average, $6.00 per hour, while women earn $4.00 per hour. This difference in pay is legitimate since it is based on true differences in productivity. On the other hand, if there were errors in measuring productivity such that women were in fact equally as productive as men, but the assessment method systematically shorted women on the productivity report, then this pay difference would be illegal.

Age Discrimination in Employment Act of 1967

Employers must continually be alert to the possibility of discrimination charges under the Age Discrimination in Employment Act of 1967 in addition to Title VII of the Civil Rights Act and the Equal Pay Act. Very few managers may consciously make pay decisions on the basis of age; however, built-in biases about age and productivity may cause an organization to discriminate on the basis of age. For example, some managers assume that you "can't teach old dogs new tricks." Such a belief is apt to result in older employees receiving lower scores in a judgmental performance rating.

There is nothing wrong with paying older employees less than younger employees if the differences in pay are legitimate. That is, older employees must in fact be less productive than younger employees. To be sure that the pay system does not discriminate illegally against older workers, the merit ratings of older employees should be compared to those of younger employees to determine if older employees systematically receive lower evaluations. If so, the organization should make sure that the ratings are in fact valid and defensible.

Performance Assessment Techniques

Ranking Methods

Over the years a number of performance assessment techniques have been suggested. Some of the earliest methods of assessment were ranking systems. Ranking systems compare employees to each other rather than to precisely defined performance standards.

The simplest of the ranking approaches is the **rank order** method. In this approach the assessor ranks all of the employees working in a job from best to poorest. An alternative to the rank order approach is the **alternate ranking** method. In this method the assessor identifies the best performer, then the poorest performer, then the second best, the second poorest, and so forth. The basic idea behind this approach is to make distinctions by constantly contrasting good and poor performance.

Most ranking methods, although not all, use a single performance dimension, such as quantity or quality of work. Often the performance criterion is not defined by the organization but is left to the discretion of the assessor. If this is done, the ranking system is subject to the biases of criterion contamination and deficiency. Further, if individual performance dimensions are not identified and each is ranked separately, there is a real possibility of halo or horns bias entering into the assessment.

Another problem with simple ranking approaches is that while the process gives a distribution of employees from best to poorest, it does not address the question of how well employees perform relative to absolute performance standards. In other words, the poorest employee might actually be performing well above average, or the best might be well below average.

Another ranking method is the **forced distribution** method. In this method the assessor assigns a predetermined percentage of the employees to each of several categories, such as superior, above average, average, and so on. This approach is predicated on the assumption that employee performance varies according to some predetermined distribution, which of course may not be true. Further, just as with the rank order and alternate ranking methods, very often only one performance dimension is identified, if any. This approach is subject to many of the biases noted earlier.

A third approach to ranking is the **paired comparison** method. In this approach each employee is compared to every other employee and receives a point for each time she or he is ranked higher than another employee. After all comparisons have been made, the ranking is determined by totalling the points. Again, the approach does not really address the question of how well an employee performs relative to absolute performance standards, but only how well the employee performs relative to other employees.

A fourth ranking approach is the **forced choice** method. In this method the assessor is required to choose between a positive and negative performance statement to describe the employee and assign points. After assigning points for an extensive list of paired statements, the assessor adds the points to determine a performance score for the employee. All employees can then be ranked according to their total scores.

Graphic Rating Scales

The most frequently used performance assessment technique is the graphic rating scale method. An example of a graphic rating scale appears in Exhibit 12.6.

Several features of Exhibit 12.6 are important. The Factors column, which outlines performance dimensions, identifies five important factors: job knowledge, technical skills, quality of work, work volume, and initiative. Although

Exhibit 12.6 *A Graphic Rating Scale*

Nonexempt Performance Review

Name	Employee number	Date of hire

Department name		Job title

Salary grade	Time on present position	Years	Months	Date of review	Date of prior review

Performance Appraisal Statement and Comments: This form provides a suggested format in which to comment on the employees' performance against job requirements. Please consider all statements carefully. You should check one of the suggested comments on the scale and write in your own statement or status of the incumbent's performance within the "Remarks" section. This will enable you to provide an overall rating on each factor, as well as comment on specific characteristics of the position of the individual evaluated.

Factors	Evaluations	Remarks
Job knowledge Consider knowledge of own job and department's function; the understanding of principles, methods, or processes used.	☐ 5. Exceptional understanding of all phases of the job. ☐ 4. Full knowledge of all job duties; exceptional understanding of some phases of the job. ☐ 3. Full knowledge of the job. ☐ 2. More knowledge is needed for fully effective performance. Knowledge is adequately improving. ☐ 1. Lacks adequate comprehension of job; adequate improvement is not observed.	
Technical skills Consider degree of proficiency and strengths or weaknesses in such technical skills as clerical, secretarial, technician, or paraprofessional.	☐ 5. Exceptionally proficient in all technical skills. ☐ 4. Fully competent technical skills; exceptionally proficient in some technical skills. ☐ 3. Fully competent technical skills. ☐ 2. More skills are needed for fully effective performance. Skills are improving adequately. ☐ 1. Lacks adequate job skills; adequate improvement is not observed.	

(continued)

Exhibit 12.6 *(continued)*

Factors	Evaluations	Remarks
Quality of work Consider accuracy, thoroughness, neatness of work, and ability to make improvements.	☐ 5. Work quality is consistently excellent. ☐ 4. Work quality consistently meets job standards; in some areas work quality is excellent. ☐ 3. Work quality generally meets job standards. ☐ 2. Work quality is below acceptable standards, but is improving adequately; work must be regularly checked. ☐ 1. Work quality is not a - quate; errors are exc. - sive; adequate improvement is not observed.	
Work volume Consider the quantity of acceptable work accomplished and promptness in completing assignments.	☐ 5. Unusually high work output; consistently exceeds job standards. ☐ 4. Work output consistently meets job standards; in some areas, work output exceeds job standards. ☐ 3. Work output generally meets job standards. ☐ 2. Work output is adequate; adequate improvement is observed. ☐ 1. Work output is not adequate; adequate improvement is not observed.	
Initiative Consider ingenuity, self-reliance, ability to originate ideas and actions, degree of supervision required.	☐ 5. Consistently performs job duties independently; initiates improvement which increases in job performance. Also, makes sound recommendations which improve departmental effectiveness. ☐ 4. Consistently performs normal duties without detailed instruction; initiates work improvements which increase effectiveness in job performance.	

(continued)

Exhibit 12.6 *(continued)*

Factors	Evaluations	Remarks
	☐ 3. Consistently performs normal duties without detailed instruction. ☐ 2. In some cases, must be given detailed, repeated instruction. Adequate improvement is observed. ☐ 1. Must consistently be given detailed instruction even on repeated assignments; adequate improvement is not observed.	

Overall Performance Level

☐ Outstanding — Far above competent performance—a high degree of excellence (approximately five (5) percent of all people perform at this level). Overall rating is "5."

☐ Commendable — Noticeably better than competent (required) job performance (approximately ten (10) to fifteen (15) percent of all people perform at this level). Overall rating is "4."

☐ Competent — At or somewhat above required job performance (approximately sixty (60) percent of all people perform at this level). Overall rating is "3."

☐ Learning/competent — Learning the job assignment; in training and performance is consistently improving (most persons recently assigned to a new job perform at this level). Overall rating is "2."

☐ Satisfactory improvement/ marginal — Below competent (required) job performance; however, improvement to meet job requirements is expected (approximately fifteen (15) percent of all people perform at this level). Overall rating is "2."

☐ Unsatisfactory — Unacceptable job performance, improvement is unlikely and transfer or termination should be considered (approximately five (5) percent of all people perform at this level). Overall rating is "1."

Plans for Future Action

(What action do you plan to take to continue this employee's development?. For example, cross-training, transfer, education.)

(continued)

Exhibit 12.6   (continued)

Supervisor Comments	**Employee Comments**

Employee's signature ———————————————

Supervisor's signature ——————————————— Title ————————————————————

Approval signature ——————————————— Title ————————————————————

Personnel manager approval ——————————— Title ————————————————————

the example is a good first attempt to identify the important performance dimensions, the factor degrees as listed in the Evaluations column are not defined in clear detail to identify the standard employed. For example, for the job knowledge factor, the highest possible evaluation is a 5: "exceptional understanding of all phases of the job." This evaluation is likely to result in considerable bias since there is no operational definition of what exceptional understanding consists of. That is, what are the job behaviors or performance outcomes that result if an employee exhibits exceptional understanding of the job? None of the evaluations possible for the individual factors are anchored in employee behaviors or job outcomes.

The next section of the form in Exhibit 12.6 is for evaluating overall performance levels. Several features of this section are also worth commenting on. There are six possible levels of performance that are again not anchored in job behaviors or job results. Each assessor must determine what outstanding, commendable, and so forth should mean. The example in Exhibit 12.6 also attempts to combine a forced distribution technique with the overall rating: only 5 percent of the employees can be outstanding, only 5 percent unsatisfactory, and so forth. As noted earlier, one should be very careful about making assumptions about the distribution of employee performance.

The remaining sections of the form provide space for any employee development plans (meaning that this appraisal is used for more than pay purposes), for both supervisor and employee comments, and for the signatures of the assessor and assessee (these last two sections protect the company legally).

The graphic rating scale method is the most commonly used performance assessment system. In spite of its popularity, there are numerous problems with the system: (1) a lack of job outcome or job behavior anchors for the degrees within dimensions; (2) a failure to combine the various performance dimensions into a global assessment; and (3) the opportunity for various forms of bias to enter the assessment process. Partly because of these problems with graphic rating scales, other approaches have been suggested. One of these approaches is behaviorally anchored rating scales.[20]

Behaviorally Anchored Rating Scales

The behaviorally anchored rating scales approach to performance assessment is actually an outgrowth of the **critical incidence** method. Under a critical incidence method of assessment, assessors keep track of job behaviors that are exceptionally good and lead to high performance, or exceptionally bad and lead to exceptionally poor performance.[21]

The evolution of the critical incidence method into a behaviorally anchored rating scale involves five steps. First, individuals with firsthand knowledge of the job describe specific examples of exceptional, good, poor, and average performance. Second, these individuals cluster the behavioral descriptions into five to ten performance dimensions that are considered important for overall job success. Third, a second group of individuals that also has firsthand knowledge of the job allocates the behavioral descriptions among the performance dimensions. This step acts as a check on the reliability of the behavioral descriptions for capturing a performance dimension. Any behavioral descriptions or incidents over which there are major disagreements are then dropped. Fourth, the second group of individuals assigns the behavioral descriptions along a continuum in terms of how well the descriptions or incidents contribute to performance variation. Fifth, based on this assignment of descriptors or incidents, a final instrument is developed to assess employees. An example of one dimension for a behaviorally anchored rating scale appears in Exhibit 12.7.

Because of the enormous time involvement on the part of many individuals to successfully develop behaviorally anchored rating scales, they are quite expensive to develop. This fact has caused some to inquire into their economic feasibility. At least one set of writers, after reviewing the literature on this approach against other performance assessment techniques, has concluded that it is not sufficiently more accurate to make it worth the additional cost. It has also been suggested that regardless of the assessment method used, the reliability and validity of assessment scores are determined by the assessor, the assessee, and the intent of the assessment. Thus, apparently, there is no such thing as a bias-free assessment.[22]

In spite of these limitations, behaviorally anchored rating scales are developed using individuals with firsthand knowledge of the job and are based on observed job behaviors, so they are in essence based upon a thorough job analysis. Thus, they should withstand legal scrutiny. Further, and perhaps more importantly, the process of developing a scale in the first place is advantageous in that individuals come to appreciate the importance of accurate performance assessment. Performance assessment standards are written in language that both job incumbents and assessors readily understand.[23] Finally,

---

Exhibit 12.7   *An Example of a Behaviorally Anchored Rating Scale*

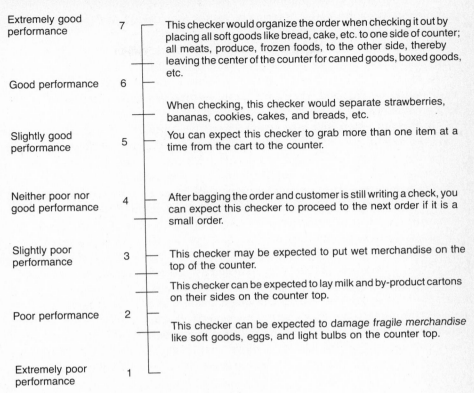

Extremely good performance	7	This checker would organize the order when checking it out by placing all soft goods like bread, cake, etc. to one side of counter; all meats, produce, frozen foods, to the other side, thereby leaving the center of the counter for canned goods, boxed goods, etc.
Good performance	6	
		When checking, this checker would separate strawberries, bananas, cookies, cakes, and breads, etc.
Slightly good performance	5	You can expect this checker to grab more than one item at a time from the cart to the counter.
Neither poor nor good performance	4	After bagging the order and customer is still writing a check, you can expect this checker to proceed to the next order if it is a small order.
Slightly poor performance	3	This checker may be expected to put wet merchandise on the top of the counter.
		This checker can be expected to lay milk and by-product cartons on their sides on the counter top.
Poor performance	2	This checker can be expected to damage fragile *merchandise* like soft goods, eggs, and light bulbs on the counter top.
Extremely poor performance	1	

Source: Lawrence Fogli, Charles Hulin, and Milton R. Blood, "Development of First-Level Behavioral Job Criteria," *Journal of Applied Psychology* 55, no. 7 (February 1971). Copyright 1971 by the American Psychological Association. Reprinted by permission of the author.

behaviorally anchored rating scales are not likely to be cost-effective unless large numbers of job incumbents are involved.

Management by Objectives

Management by objectives is many things to many people. To some it is a total management philosophy, while to others it is a performance assessment process.[24] Since the concern here is the more narrow topic of performance assessment, those features of management by objectives most relevant to performance assessment are discussed.

The Management by Objectives Process   The management by objectives process involves several steps. First the subordinate and the superior agree upon a set of objectives to be completed at certain dates. This step of establishing objectives can be thought of as a negotiating and role clarification process in which both parties understand more clearly what the subordinate's job is and what needs to be accomplished in the job. These objectives should have completion dates, be stated in terms of results (outcomes), and wherever possible be expressed quantitatively.

In the second step the subordinate works on the established objectives. As time passes, the superior and subordinate communicate with each other in terms of how much progress is being made and if the target date or the objectives should be changed. As events modify objectives, new objectives should be immediately set.

In the third step, the assessment stage, the superior and subordinate review the extent to which the earlier objectives have been completed. At this stage, the level of performance would tie back into the merit pay system to determine the pay increase for the person. After the assessment stage, the process is repeated with a new objectives-setting stage and so on.

Management by objectives is very difficult to implement. For example, employees must trust their supervisors. Lack of trust will cause subordinates to set easy objectives so that they will look good at the assessment stage. Another difficulty is that it takes a long time for employees to identify and commit to objectives. There is a tendency for managers to assign employees their objectives. This goes against one of the fundamental goals of management by objectives, to have employees participate in establishment of their objectives.

At the same time, management by objectives can be an effective performance assessment technique, especially for jobs where it is difficult to define performance in the first place. In those jobs, it can be helpful in obtaining agreement among levels of management on what performance levels (objective attainment) are acceptable.

Management by Objectives and Compensation Decision Making   One of the major problems with management by objectives as it relates to compensation is that it sets objectives for individual employees. This causes problems for compensation purposes when it comes time to allocate money based on the performance review.

For example, suppose that a manager has two subordinates: subordinate A is a superior performer in all regards, and subordinate B is average in all respects. The manager works with both employees on setting goals. Subordinate A sets goals that will result in a very small improvement in performance but that require high levels of ability and effort (subordinate A is already a superior performer). Subordinate B sets objectives that will result in a considerable improvement in performance, but since subordinate B is an average performer presently, little effort is required to meet these objectives. At the end of the assessment period subordinate A has failed in the objectives, but subordinate B has succeeded. Even so, subordinate A is still a better performer than subordinate B. According to the assessment, the manager should recommend a larger pay increase to subordinate B than to subordinate A. On the other hand, subordinate A is the one who deserves a larger increase.

The above example points out the problem of using objectives designed for individuals as a basis for pay. Unless the organization is able to translate each person's achievements back into a common metric across all employees, inequities are likely to result. Therefore, while management by objectives can be highly useful for the development of employees, its use in a compensation context is problematical at best.

Performance Assessment and Compensation Decision Making

Once the performance assessment process is complete, the results must be translated into pay increases for employees. Regardless of the performance appraisal system used, the appraisal data must be translated into dollar increases. Like performance assessment itself, this process becomes difficult in practice. This section discusses this subject and also identifies some of the more common problems in achieving fair treatment in performance rewards.

The performance appraisal process should achieve two objectives simultaneously. First, every employee within a given job should be ranked with respect to all other employees within that job. Second, all employees should be ranked absolutely relative to the standards for the job. Both of these rankings should be achieved across all of the standards used. That is, if multiple performance dimensions are used, the evaluation should be a composite across all dimensions. Few organizations actually use such a systematic appraisal system which is not heavily value laden, for several reasons.

The Departmental Unit Problem

The theoretical ideal identified in the previous paragraph may not be achieved for numerous reasons. One of the most obvious reasons is that not all employees in a given job (for example, operatives, data entry clerks, or machinists) work in the same organizational unit. Therefore, assessments of all employees within a given job may be noncomparable across organizational units because different people did the appraising.

Allocating Percentage Pay Increase Budgets

The common organizational method of equalizing assessment is to allocate an average percentage of money to each department for distribution among employees within a job group. There are problems with this approach. For example, such action assumes that performance among a group of employees within a department is average. This may be an invalid assumption. Acting on such an assumption could mean that a superior group of employees in one department will share the same average raise as a group of marginal employees within another department. Some organizations allocate a larger percentage increase to some units relative to others when there are clear unit performance differences.

Another problem is that a given employee within a department may be the only one performing that job. Should this employee receive the average increase for the job, or should the manager plead for a larger or smaller than average raise based on merit?

Percentage Increases to a Department

If a fixed percentage pay increase budget is allocated to each department, the manager must grant increases to employees without exceeding the average percentage increase available. Administrative complications emerge here. For example, some organizations review all employees for a pay increase at a given time in their fiscal year. Other organizations review employees for pay increases on the employees' individual anniversary dates of employment. In the latter case the budgeting of pay increases is a bit more complicated. This complication and the administrative mechanism for handling it are discussed in Chapter 16.

Once the performance level of employees relative to the job standards and the average percentage increase available for distribution are known, then the manager can make recommended pay increases for subordinates. Assuming that merit is the only criterion for a pay increase, then the manager needs to translate the performance appraisal outcome into a dollar outcome. This is usually done by deciding upon the percentage or dollar increase that the manager wishes to recommend based on performance.

Although the manager recommends the pay increase to be allocated, he or she usually does not have unilateral authority to make this decision. Normally the decision must be reviewed by the manager's superior, and typically the compensation manager will also have to agree on the recommendation. This process is important as a check in the compensation control system. The role of line managers and compensation specialists is discussed in more detail in Chapter 16.

Guidecharts

Most recommendations for pay increases are subject to one more constraint. The recommended increase should not bring the employee's total pay rate above the maximum rate for that employee's job. This is one reason why the compensation manager may have to agree on the recommended rate. Some organizations use guidecharts in assisting managers in making pay decisions. A typical guidechart appears in Exhibit 12.8.

The guidechart in Exhibit 12.8 might be used for pay increases based on merit. Using the guidechart, the pay increase is dependent upon two variables: the employee's current status within the pay range, and the performance rating. According to the guidechart, the higher the employee moves up the pay range, the smaller the pay increase that is available while holding performance constant. Further, the poorer is performance, the smaller the increase. Most perplexing is the fact that two employees (or the same employee at two different points in time) can earn different percentage increases for the same level of

---

Exhibit 12.8   *Guidechart for Merit Increases*

Performance Rating

Current Pay Quartile	Superior	Above Average	Average	Below Average
Maximum[a]				
4th	4%	2%	0%	0%
3rd	6	4	2	0
2nd	8	6	4	0
1st	10	8	6	0
Minimum				

[a] Percent increase cannot put the employee above the maximum for the job.

---

performance, or the same percentage increase for different levels of performance.

Guidecharts are necessary because maximum pay rates for jobs cannot be exceeded if the organization hopes to achieve a consistent pay policy. However, guidecharts probably contribute substantially to the confusion about whether there is any association between pay and performance levels. It is quite difficult to convince an employee that there is a pay for performance system in effect when another employee who is paid less and is no higher a performer receives a larger increase because there is more room in the pay grade. In short, the administrative necessity of guidecharts threatens the perception of a pay for performance system. Some writers have suggested that pay increases not be built into the base pay but rather that they be one-time allocations. Under such a system an employee may qualify for up to a 30 percent performance pay bonus each year, but the following year would earn only the base rate and would have to qualify for performance-based pay.[25]

Summary

This chapter focused on performance assessment for pay increases. The traditional ranking and rating methods of performance appraisal often fall short of being good assessment methods because they often require only comparisons of one person to another, they fail to establish predetermined job-related performance dimensions, and as a result they are often quite biased. Different types of errors and biases enter the assessment process, including criterion contamination, criterion deficiency, halo or horns bias, excessive strictness or leniency bias, central tendency bias, and recency bias. Approaches to reducing these biases were discussed.

Concerns about adverse impact discrimination were also discussed as they relate to performance assessment. One court case gives some guidance as to the characteristics of performance assessment systems that are likely to withstand court challenge.

It was also noted that accurate performance assessment based on job performance variance is fundamental to an effective merit pay system. Unless employees believe that different performance is rewarded differently they are not likely to be motivated by the promise of differential monetary increases. The chapter concluded by discussing how performance assessment data translates into pay increases.

Discussion Questions

1. Distinguish between the simple ranking, alternate ranking, paired comparison, and forced choice methods of performance assessment.

2. Describe the graphic rating method of performance assessment and discuss the limitations of this method.

3. Discuss behaviorally anchored rating scales as a performance assessment method along with their strengths and weaknesses.

4. Describe the management by objectives process as it relates to performance assessment and its utility for making pay decisions.

5. Identify a set of performance dimensions for any job. Once you have identified the important performance dimensions, develop a scaling system for each dimension. Repeat this exercise for the job using (a) job outcome dimensions, and (b) behavioral outcome dimensions.

6. Discuss the characteristics of a performance assessment system that is likely to withstand legal challenge. Why are each of these components necessary in defending the system?

7. Discuss the rationale as to why merit pay ought to be based on performance variation within a job rather than on work rule behavior.

8. Identify the sources of bias that tend to disrupt the link between actual performance and measured performance.

9. Discuss how performance appraisal data are translated into pay increases for employees. What are the problems in this process? How are these problems likely to influence the employee's perceptions of a pay for performance system?

Exercises

1. Below are some data on employees from two departments within a textile firm. Based on the information, make recommendations for pay increases to these employees. How would you justify your decisions to your boss? To the employees? Were you fair? Note: Assume all information is valid—there is no bias in performance assessment, etc.

2. Rework exercise 1, except this time use as your allocation guidelines the guidechart from Exhibit 12.8. Again, make your recommendations and defend your decisions both to your boss and to the employees. What do you think the conversation would be like if Bob Scott and Linda Nelson discussed their current pay and your recommended increase for them? What would the conversation be like if Steve Hooper and Sally Boone discussed their current pay and recommended pay increases? How about Sheila Rowe and Moe Hill? Tina Lund and Michelle Gowan?

Exercise 1

Job Titles	Name	Current Pay	Company Seniority	Job Seniority	Performance Evaluation Score
Department A					
System analyst	Joe Hage	$37,600	14	8	4
System analyst	Sally Boone	38,100	23	12	8
System analyst	Billy Carper	34,500	6	5	8
Programmer	Linda Nelson	32,200	21	1	7
Programmer	Karl Figgs	34,000	10	5	5
Programmer	Tina Lund	28,500	8	7	3
Data entry clerk	Moe Hill	13,700	2	2	6
Data entry clerk	Phyllis Hardy	11,000	3	3	8
Department B					
System analyst	Steve Hooper	38,700	18	14	4
Programmer	Mike Veil	32,800	9	3	8
Programmer	Al Marks	33,600	3	1	7
Programmer	Michelle Gowan	30,000	10	7	6
Programmer	Bob Scott	36,500	14	12	8
Data entry clerk	Mabel Kavid	12,500	4	4	6
Data entry clerk	Sheila Rowe	12,500	8	8	6
Data entry clerk	Allison Wade	12,500	6	6	6
Data entry clerk	Becky Stone	12,500	1	1	6

Merit increase budget for the current year is 6 percent based on the total department labor budget.

Wage Data

Job	Pay Range
System analyst	Maximum: $40,000 Midpoint: 35,000 Minimum: 30,000
Programmer	Maximum: $36,000 Midpoint: 32,000 Minimum: 28,000
Data entry clerk	Maximum: $14,000 Midpoint: 12,500 Minimum: 11,000

References

[1] V. H. Vroom, *Work and Motivation* (New York: Wiley, 1964).

[2] Herbert H. Meyer, Emanuel Kay, and John R. P. French Jr., "Split Roles in Performance Appraisal," *Harvard Business Review* 43 (January-February 1965): pp. 123–129.

[3] Joseph Wollenberger, "Acceptable Work Rules and Penalties," *Personnel* 40 (July 1963): pp. 23–29.

[4] Thomas Alewine, "Performance Appraisal and Performance Standards," *Personnel Journal* 61 (March 1982): pp. 210–213.

[5] Edward Lawler, "Managers' Attitudes towards How Their Pay Is and Should Be Determined," *Journal of Applied Psychology* 50 (1966): pp. 273–279.

[6] Allan H. Lochner and Kenneth S. Teel, "Performance Appraisal—A Survey of Current Practices," *Personnel Journal* (May 1977): pp. 245–254.

[7] Harry Levinson, "Appraisal of What Performance," *Harvard Business Review* 54 (July 1976): pp. 30–36.

[8] Edward Lawler III, *Pay and Organizational Effectiveness: A Psychological View* (New York: McGraw-Hill, 1971).

[9] For a discussion of the multidimensionality of criteria, see Patricia C. Smith, "Behaviors, Results, and Organizational Effectiveness: The Problem of Criteria," in Marvin D. Dunnette, ed., *Handbook of Industrial and Organizational Psychology* (Chicago: Rand-McNally, 1976): pp. 745–775.

[10] For a more detailed discussion of criterion contamination and deficiency, see Milton L. Blum and James C. Naylor, *Industrial Psychology: Its Theoretical and Social Foundations* (New York: Harper and Row, 1968): pp. 176–177.

[11] Barbara L. Schlei and Paul Grossman, *Employment Discrimination Law* (Washington, D. C.: Bureau of National Affairs, 1976): Chapter 6, pp. 166–181.

[12] Smith, "Behaviors, Results, and Organizational Effectiveness," pp. 746–747.

[13] Robert M. Guion, *Personnel Testing* (New York: McGraw-Hill, 1965): p. 99.

[14] S. N. Stevens and E. F. Wonderlic, *Personnel Journal* 13 (1934): pp. 125–134.

[15] Larry L. Cummings and Donald P. Schwab, *Performance in Organizations* (Glenview, Ill.: Scott Foresman, 1973).

[16] Steven J. Carroll and Craig E. Schneir, *Performance Appraisal and Review Systems* (Glenview, Ill.: Scott Foresman, 1981).

[17] James V. Stockham Valves and Fittings Co., 394 F. Supp 434 (N. D. Ala. 1975).

[18] Gary Lubben *et al.*, "Performance Appraisal: The Legal Implications of Title VII," *Personnel* 57 (May 1980): pp. 11–14.

[19] Schlei and Grossman, *Employment Discrimination Law*, p. 625.

[20] John P. Campbell, "The Development and Evaluation of Behaviorally Based Rating Scales," *Journal of Applied Psychology* 57 (1978): pp. 15–22.

[21] Walter C. Borman and Marvin D. Dunnette, "Behavioral Based versus Trait-Oriented Performance Ratings: An Empirical Study, " *Journal of Applied Psychology* 60 (1975): pp. 561–565.

[22] D. P. Schwab, H. G. Heneman III, and T. A. DeCotis, "Behaviorally Anchored Rating Scales: A Review of the Literature," *Personnel Psychology* 28 (1975): pp. 549–562.

[23] H. John Bernardin and Patricia Cain Smith, "A Clarification of Some Issues Regarding the Development and Use of Behaviorally Anchored Rating Scales (BARS)," *Journal of Applied Psychology* 66, no. 4 (1981): pp. 458–463.

[24] Mark L. McConkie, "A Clarification of the Goal Setting and Appraisal Processes in MBO," *Academy of Management Review* 4, no. 1 (1979): pp. 29–40.

[25] Frederick S. Hills, "The Pay for Performance Dilemma," *Personnel* (September-October 1979): pp. 23–31.

13

Individual and

Group Incentives,

Compensation of

Special Groups

· **Learning Objectives**

· **Introduction**

· **Incentive Plans and Theory**

Instrumentality and Expectancy Theory
  Assumptions
Work Environment Assumptions

· **Individual versus Group Plans**

· **Merit Pay versus Incentive Pay**

· **Individual Incentive Plans for Production
  Employees**

Piece Rate Plans
Standard Hour Plans
Problems with Individual Incentive Plans

· **Individual Incentive Plans for Salespersons**

Salary plus Commission
Draw plus Commission
Sales Commission Plans
Special Sales Incentive Plans
Problems with Sales Incentive Plans

· **Individual Managerial Incentive Plans**

Bonus Plans
Executive Bonuses

· **Group Incentive Plans**

Small Group Incentive Plans
Plantwide Group Incentive Plans

· **Exercises**

Learning Objectives

To reinforce that all incentive plans are efforts to motivate high levels of job performance.

To learn in some detail about individual incentive plans for production employees, salespersons, and managers.

To learn to distinguish between individual and group incentive plans.

To appreciate the ways that incentive plans can be mismanaged, including problems with setting standards and attitudinal problems on the part of both employees and management.

Introduction

This chapter focuses upon individual and group incentive plans and upon the compensation of two special groups, executives and salespersons.

This chapter reviews the basic incentive plans used in organizations. After studying the chapter the reader should be able to discuss the major forms of incentive plans, discuss the conditions under which incentive plans are likely to work, and design an incentive plan. The sections on executive and salesperson compensation stress that these groups have special incentive plans because of the unique nature of the groups.

Incentive Plans and Theory

As the term *incentive* implies, incentive plans share the common objective of motivating high performance in employees.[1] Whether they accomplish this goal is partially dependent upon a set of boundary conditions. These boundary conditions are the underlying assumptions necessary for instrumentality and expectancy theory to predict high performance when money is used as a reward, and the assumptions about human motivation and the work environment.

Instrumentality and Expectancy Theory Assumptions

As discussed in Chapter 2, in order for monetary rewards to motivate high performance, a number of conditions must be satisfied. Among these are that employees must value money, money must be valued more than other rewards, employees must see a link between behaviors (high performance) and money, employees must be able to perform at high levels, and they must believe that they can perform at high levels if they expend the effort.

All incentive pay plans are based on these and other assumptions. These assumptions are summarized in Exhibit 13.1, and are discussed in the context of incentive plans.

The first assumption that all incentive plans make is that employees are

---

Exhibit 13.1   *Assumptions of an Incentive System*

1. Employees must be capable of performing at high levels.
2. Employees must believe they can perform at high levels.
3. Employees must believe that performance will result in more money.
4. Employees must value money.
5. Money must be valued relative to other rewards.
6. Jobs must allow for performance variation.
7. Performance must be measurable.
8. The plan must be compatible with the nature of work (individual vs. group output).

---

capable of performing at high levels. Unless the work force has the capability to perform at high levels there will be no potential for high performance. A second assumption is that employees believe that they can perform at high levels. Even if individuals have the capability to perform at high levels, they are unlikely to do so unless they also believe that they can perform highly. In other words, without a belief about ability to perform well, actual high performance will probably not be realized.

A third assumption is that individuals believe that high performance will be rewarded. There must be a strong demonstration that the level of reward varies directly and systematically with the level of performance. A fourth assumption is that individuals value money as a reward. Not all individuals value money equally, but money must have enough value to motivate behavior. Fifth, money must be valued more than other rewards. Most people value money, but other rewards may be valued more highly. For example, people may value acceptance from peers more than they value money. In this case money alone is not likely to be adequate incentive for encouraging high performance because of the possibility of antagonizing peers in the process.[2]

Work Environment Assumptions

Two basic assumptions are made with respect to the work environment, as shown in Exhibit 13.1. First, incentive systems assume that there is room for performance variation in the job.[3] That is, the job must allow for differences in performance level. Second, the performance variation must be measurable in a relatively objective way.[4] Unless the organization can assess differential performance, an incentive plan will not likely work because the organization will not be able to isolate the contributions of individuals or groups.

Individual versus Group Plans

One final boundary condition must be considered when designing an incentive plan. The organization must determine whether successful performance is a group or an individual effort. Does high performance result from the contribution of the work unit as a whole, or is high performance a result of individual effort?[5]

An example of individual contribution to success would be number of insurance policies sold. This outcome can usually be attributed to one person, and an individual incentive plan would be appropriate. An example of group-determined success might be where a team of eight people constructs a building. In this case the success is a function of every one of the eight contributing his or her best. A group plan would be more appropriate in this situation.

All individual incentive plans rest on seven basic assumptions about motivation and the work environment. Individual incentive plans also rest on the assumption that individual performance and not group performance can be assessed. To this extent all incentive plans, whether for salespersons or for production or managerial personnel, must satisfy the same assumptions.

Merit Pay versus Incentive Pay

In a technical sense any time the organization attempts to pay for merit there is incentive pay involved. In this sense, discussions in Chapter 12 about pay ranges for performance pay increases also qualify for incentive systems. Chapter 13 will not discuss this topic again, but focuses on incentive pay plans that determine an employee's total compensation (such as salesperson commissions) or that provide for compensation in addition to normal compensation (such as profit sharing). This distinction is somewhat arbitrary and is used for the convenience of dividing the subject matter of this text.

Individual Incentive Plans for Production Employees

There are two basic types of incentive plans for production employees: piece rate plans and standard hour plans.

Piece Rate Plans

In the piece rate incentive plan the employee is paid a given rate for each unit produced. Pay is based on level of output.

Steps in Designing a Piece Rate Plan   This section discusses the steps in establishing a piece rate incentive system. These steps are summarized in Exhibit 13.2.

Establishing a Standard   Every piece rate system must establish the production standards for a job. This first step usually requires industrial engineering input. An industrial engineer will study the job in minute detail, often using **time and**

Exhibit 13.2 *The Piece Rate Incentive Plan Process*

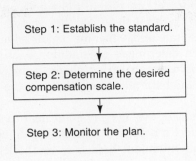

motion study methods to determine the average amount of time it will take a fully trained average employee with average ability to complete the task.

In discussing time and motion study work it is normally the case that writers gloss over the time and motion parts of the analysis and treat them as equivalent.

Time and motion study involves two distinct although highly related parts. Motion study analyzes different ways to do the same task or activity. This analysis identifies the most efficient movements for completing the task or activity. Time study determines the average time to perform a task or activity when a particular motion is used. Time study is based on the assumption that raw materials are always available and that finished goods are removed so as not to interfere with future production.[6] A simplified example of the process that industrial engineering uses to design a piece rate plan of compensation is presented in Exhibit 13.3.

As a result of time and motion study, a production standard is set for a given unit of time. This production standard is the average production rate per hour (or some other unit of time) for all of the employees on the job.

Determining the Compensation Rate   Several considerations go into establishing the incentive rate for a piece rate system. These include: desired base pay, desired maximum pay, and whether fixed or variable incentive rates will be

Exhibit 13.3 *IE Process for Arriving at a Standard Time*

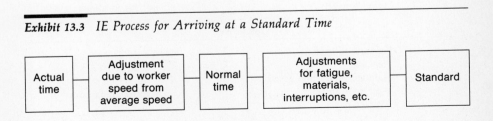

used. These three issues are interrelated, but they are discussed separately to highlight the key decisions in each issue.

Base pay rate: Every piece rate system must determine the desired base pay. One popular way to do this is to equate the average production standard with the minimum or base rate of pay that the organization wishes to pay. This base pay may have been determined by traditional job evaluation and job pricing procedures as discussed in earlier chapters. In this approach, every employee is guaranteed the base rate whether or not the average production standard is met.

A second approach makes average pay equivalent to the average production standard but guarantees a base rate to those who do not meet the average production standard. This minimum base may be the legal minimum wage rate. In this approach, the pay rate at the average production standard is the midpoint of an imaginary pay range. The average producer (at the average production standard) will make average pay for the job.

Examples of these two approaches are highlighted in Exhibit 13.4.

In the first approach (option A in Exhibit 13.4), the employer may want average wages to be $5.00 per hour. If the production standard is 100 units per hour, then the piece rate would be $.05, and the average worker would earn $5.00 per hour. An employee who does not meet the production standard will still be guaranteed the $5.00 minimum. Not meeting the production standard could be due to employee problems or to other problems (such as a shortage of raw material or machine downtime).

In the second approach (option B in Exhibit 13.4), the employer might set the equivalent wage at $5.00 and use a separate minimum or base wage of the legal minimum wage. The piece rate would remain at $.05 and the average worker could earn $5.00 for meeting the production standard of 100 units per hour. Employees who do not meet the average standard in any given hour

---

Exhibit 13.4 *Setting Base Pay in an Incentive Plan*

	Option A
Guaranteed base	$5.00
Piece rate	$ .05
Standard production based on time study	100 units/hour
Average pay	$5.00/hour

	Option B
Guaranteed base	$3.35
Piece rate	$ .05
Standard production based on time study	100 units/hour
Average pay	$5.00/hour

receive the minimum wage of $3.35 for that hour.[7] Option B in Exhibit 13.4 results in lower labor costs across all employees who cannot meet the standard.

Maximum pay rate: A second major consideration is the maximum pay an employer is willing to pay an employee under a piece rate incentive system. While in theory there is no limit to how much an employee can earn under a piece rate system, practicality does limit the amount. For one thing, if piece rate workers earn too much relative to other employees in the plant, including their supervisors, feelings of inequity may result.[8] Thus, some practical limit on the total amount that can be earned must exist.

One way to limit incentive pay is related to the rate scale (discussed next). The employer decides the percentage above the average pay rate equivalent that will be allowed, and scales the piece rate along a continuum that corresponds to this maximum. Administratively this could be done as follows. First, the organization decides the maximum pay for the job. Next it determines the maximum production rate that could be achieved by no more than 95 percent of the employees, for example. The piece rate is then scaled accordingly. For example, an employer may decide that employees can earn up to 35 percent of base pay. An incentive scale is then determined that takes into account the productivity opportunities of technology and is compatible with the above goals.

Incentive rate scales: The incentive rate scale is the pay rate per unit produced over the entire productivity schedule. That is, what will the piece rate be for each unit produced? There are four variations on incentive rate scales: fixed rates, increasing rates, decreasing rates, and fixed plus variable rates. Examples of the first three variations appear in Table 13.1.

The data in Table 13.1 demonstrate several features of incentive rate scales. For example, if overhead is $100 per hour (for machine maintenance, electricity, and so on), any increases in productivity will reduce the hourly overhead costs per unit of output in column 4. Overhead per unit produced goes down as productivity goes up.

A second feature is that fixed, increasing, and decreasing rate scales allow employees to share in these cost savings in some cases. Under the fixed rate schedule, employees do not share in the cost savings; they are paid the same per unit of output regardless of the productivity level. With increasing rate scales employees share in the savings caused by their greater productivity. At the same time that employees are sharing the productivity gains, per unit production costs are still decreasing for the employer.

With decreasing rate scales employees do not share in productivity gains. In this case, employees are wealthier only because of their own productivity increases, because the rate scale is decreasing as a function of productivity. Employees still make more per hour, and decreasing rate scales result in the greatest decrease in per unit costs.

Under the decreasing rate scale in Table 13.1, employees can make up to 35 percent of the standard pay rate (assuming a standard rate of $.05 per unit at 100 units per hour = $5.00 per hour). At 150 units of output per hour, and

Table 13.1   *Fixed, Increasing, and Decreasing Incentive Scales*

Fixed Incentive Rate Scales

(1) Number of Units	(2) Rate	(3) Total Earnings	(4) Overhead/Unit	(5) Total Unit Cost
100	$.050	$ 5.00	$1.00	$1.05
110	.050	5.50	.91	.96
120	.050	6.00	.83	.88
130	.050	6.50	.77	.82
140	.050	7.00	.71	.76
150	.050	7.50	.67	.72

Increasing Incentive Rate Scale

Number of Units	Rate	Total Earnings	Overhead/Unit	Total Unit Cost
100	$.050	$ 5.00	$1.00	$1.050
110	.055	6.05	.91	.965
120	.060	7.20	.83	.890
130	.065	8.45	.77	.835
140	.070	9.80	.71	.780
150	.075	11.25	.67	.745

Decreasing Incentive Rate Scale

Number of Units	Rate	Total Earnings	Overhead/Unit	Total Unit Cost
100	$.050	$ 5.00	$1.00	$1.050
110	.049	5.39	.91	.959
120	.048	5.76	.83	.878
130	.047	6.11	.77	.817
140	.046	6.44	.71	.756
150	.045	6.75	.67	.715

a standard rate of $.045, a worker can make $6.75 per hour, which is a 35 percent increase over the desired base pay rate.

Decreasing rate scales do not always result in this relationship. The precise relationships are a function of the range in performance variability, the magnitude of the overhead costs, and the interaction of the two. The organization will need to know its own productivity variability potential and overhead rates and experiment with the two to determine the precise rate scale which would allow for a 35 percent growth opportunity in wages while still controlling costs.

An increasing rate scale should be more motivating than either a fixed or decreasing rate scale, and a fixed rate scale should be more motivating than a decreasing rate scale.[9] The marginal reward for additional effort is directly related to increasing, fixed, and decreasing rate scales. No data is known to exist to support this point, however.

Monitoring the Plan   Successful piece rate plans must have a good administrative system behind them to accurately tabulate performance levels of employees and to provide wage payments on a timely and routine basis. One of the problems with piece rate systems is that incentive pay may lag behind performance. For example, the employer may pay the standard rate for the current period but delay the performance pay by one or more periods. This procedure is likely to result in confusion among employees about whether they are paid relative to their productivity level, and weakens the link between effort and performance.

Quantity of production for pay determination purposes is not all that the organization needs to monitor. It is also important to monitor quality of production. In situations where pay is determined by quantity of output alone, there may be a strong tendency on the part of employees to ignore quality issues. The organization needs to establish quality standards to back up the quantity standards. For example, an organization may specify that productivity levels must be achieved with less than 2 percent of the parts produced rejected by quality control, or less than .05 percent waste of raw materials. (This point reinforces the point made in Chapter 12 that even under a piece rate system, performance is multidimensional.)

Examples of Piece Rate Plans   Over the years a number of organizations have developed piece rate incentive plans. Such plans are common in the rubber, textile, and apparel industries. In this section a few of the better-known plans are discussed.

The Taylor Plan   Frederick W. Taylor developed a piece rate plan at the end of the 19th century that provided for two different piece rates for the same work.[10] The criterion used to determine which rate applied was the employee's productivity level. An employee who performed below the predetermined standard was paid at the lower rate. An employee who performed at or above the predetermined standard received the higher rate. This higher rate was normally about 20 percent more than the lower rate.

The Merrick Plan   The Merrick plan, developed by D. W. Merrick in the early 20th century, is similar to the Taylor plan. The major difference between the two is that the Merrick plan uses three different pay rates.[11] The highest rate is used for employees who meet the predetermined standard. These employees receive 120 percent of the lowest rate. A middle rate is used for employees who achieve 83 percent of the standard. These employees receive 110 percent of the lowest rate. The lowest rate is paid to those below 83 percent of the standard.

Both the Taylor and Merrick plans vary the pay rate as a function of productivity level. This relationship is direct so that in effect both plans have an increasing rate scale that permits employees to share in their productivity gains.

Straight Piecework   Straight piecework plans are common. For example, truck farms often use piecework plans to pay employees so many cents for each pint of strawberries picked. Straight piecework plans are also used in the textile industry, where employees may be paid a certain amount for each towel they fold and package, for example. Piecework plans also are common in the apparel industry, where some employees are paid a certain amount for sewing pieces of a garment.

Piece rate plans for production employees are popular in industries that have highly competitive product markets and are labor intensive. These firms must keep labor costs at a minimum because of the impact of labor costs on total costs and the competitive nature of product markets. Piecework systems allow for this; employees who do not produce may not be paid, subject to minimum wage limitations.

Standard Hour Plans

Standard hour plans are very similar to piece rate incentive plans. The major difference is that in standard hour plans the production standard is expressed in time units. Under this type of plan a job is analyzed with industrial engineering time study methods, and a fixed unit of time is established for the completion of the job. The employee who is assigned to the job receives the standard rate of pay for the job, whether he or she finishes the job in the standard time frame or takes a shorter or longer time.

An example of a standard hour plan is a task that is determined through time study to carry a standard time of .40 hours (24 minutes). If the standard pay rate is $5.00 per hour, then the employee receives $2.00 (.40 $\times$ $5.00 = $2.00) for completing the task, whether it required .40 hours or .20 hours or .50 hours.

In most cases the actual time to do the job is expressed relative to the standard time. In the above example, if the employee completed the job in .20 hours, the employee is working at 200 percent of standard time (.40 hours divided by .20 hours $\times$ 100% = 200%). Expressing actual output as a percentage of standard output tells the employee how much of the standard hourly rate is earned. In this example, if the employee performs five tasks at the above rate, she or he has worked at 200 percent of standard time for one full hour, and the actual pay would be twice the standard time rate, or $10.00 (2 $\times$ $5.00 standard rate).

The steps for establishing a standard hour plan are identical to setting up a piece rate system. First, industrial engineering establishes what the standard times are for each task or job; second, the organization decides the desired standard hour rate of pay; and third, the organization must monitor the plan and the quality of work.

Examples of Standard Hour Plans   The preceding discussion is based on the assumption that standard hour plans use a fixed rate schedule of pay for standard time units. Just as a piece rate incentive rate may vary with output, so can a standard hour rate. The following discussion considers three of the more well-known standard hour plans in which the rate varies with production level.

The Halsey Plan   The Halsey plan, established by Frederick Halsey at the end of the 19th century, allows both employees and management to share in any direct labor savings.[12] Under the Halsey plan employees are guaranteed a predetermined hourly wage. When the worker performs the task, the amount of time it took to perform the task is compared to the standard time. Any savings are shared by employees and management.

   For example, an employee who is paid $5.00 per hour (the minimum rate) performs a task with a standard time of eight hours, but completes the task in only six hours. For this task the worker is 25 percent more productive than the standard. Under the Halsey plan, the employee receives a bonus for the savings as a percentage of the base pay. The employee may be entitled to a 10 percent bonus for each hour saved and would receive a $1.00 bonus.

The Rowan Plan   The Rowan plan is similar to the Halsey plan.[13] The basic difference is that whereas management and labor share in the labor cost savings at a fixed rate in the Halsey plan, in the Rowan plan the employees realize a larger proportion of the savings as their productivity increases.

   To use the previous example, the employee might receive 20 percent of the direct labor savings for completing the job within 85 percent of standard time, but 30 percent of the labor savings if the task is completed within 70 percent of standard time. The bonus percentage applied to base pay is a direct function of the percentage of time saved under the Rowan plan.

The Gantt Plan   A third version of a standard hour plan is the Gantt plan, which is a variation of the Halsey and Rowan plans.[14] The Gantt plan sets the initial standard time quite high. All employees are guaranteed a base wage, and a bonus is paid at the rate of 120 percent of time saved for employees who meet or exceed the standard.

Problems with Individual Incentive Plans

There are a host of problems associated with installing and operating incentive plans, ranging from engineering problems to problems with managerial and employee attitudes and behaviors. These problems are summarized in Exhibit 13.5 and discussed in this section.

Engineering Standards   The first step in an incentive plan is for an industrial engineer to conduct a time and motion study of one or more employees to determine the average number of pieces that can be produced per unit of time, or the average time to complete a job or task. This process can be difficult. Numerous factors contribute to the problem of setting standards.

Exhibit 13.5   *Problems with Incentive Plans*

Engineering Related

Are typical employees studied?
Are observed performance rates actually typical?
Are work conditions normal during the study?
Are allowances made for set-up time and machine adjustment?
Are standards changed as conditions change?

Employee Related

Fears that standards will be tightened.
Fears that jobs will be lost.
Fears attributable to failure to understand the plan.
Resistance to constant pressure to produce.
Employees value equal pay for equal work.

Managerial Related

Assuming that only money motivates.
Failure to understand employee values.
Failure to develop trust between employees and management.

For example, the employee being studied by the industrial engineer may not be a typical employee. One way to combat this would be to study many employees doing the same task or job and to average the results. There is also a question of whether or not employees are performing at their normal work rate in the study, or if they are working more slowly so that a low standard will result.[15] Employees may also work faster than average to impress management during the study. To combat this problem the rate structure may be varied to reflect the industrial engineer's assumptions about the employees. If employees seem to slow down during the study, the standard rate may be adjusted upward, or a larger premium paid above standard, or a lower premium paid for below-standard output (as provided by the Taylor and Merrick plan rates discussed above).

Another engineering difficulty is that no matter how carefully the study tries to establish the standard time or standard rate per hour, individual work situations rarely conform to standard conditions. In the short run there may be spot shortages of raw materials inventory, shortage of storage for finished goods, uneven quality of raw materials, and uneven machine performance, to name a few. Standard times may also assume long production runs of the same units and not allow for set-up time or adjustment times for machinery needed for frequent changeovers. These forces mean that in the short run it may be nearly impossible for an employee to operate at standard. To the extent that these factors are not stable, they cause employees to doubt the validity of the established standards, and also weaken their beliefs that high levels of performance can result in more pay.[16]

A third major engineering problem is that organizations may not adequately monitor and change the standards as necessary. In almost every production process there are continual ongoing changes in the production process. Each change may be small in and of itself. Examples are switching a bolt system for two parts from a four-bolt to a five-bolt assembly, using a new and more pliable raw material, or modifying a machine so that the release mechanism works faster. Each change in the production process may have a minute impact upon the standards, but collectively they can cause considerable deviation from standard.[17]

When the collective changes result in extended work cycles, employees will have difficulty meeting the standard and may become resentful of the now unrealistic standards. In cases where work becomes easier, the standards will be easily exceeded, resulting in excessive employee bonuses that can destroy internal pay equity relationships.

The only cure for changes is to make time and motion analysis a perpetual process that never ceases. As soon as a job or some component of a job changes, the job should be reanalyzed to set a new fair standard rate. Incentive systems require an enormous commitment to industrial engineering if they are to have validity.

Employee Attitude Problems   Employees who work under piece rate systems may often distrust such systems and react negatively towards them. Often this distrust results in peer pressure to conform to certain output levels (the group norm).

Employees have natural and sometimes real fears that if they produce at too high a level, management will raise the standard or lay off some employees. These fears may result from historical experience if management has raised the standards or laid off employees in the past. Both of these fears can result in **soldiering**, or working to standard. The best although not necessarily an easy approach to the first concern is to establish meticulously equitable standards in the first place. Employee distrust of management is not easy to overcome.[18] Management must establish over time by example a belief on the part of employees that they will be dealt with fairly and equitably. This means extensive communication of plan content, intent, how it will work, and why changes must be made if they must be made. Management must also be willing to consider the impact of changes in plans as employees see them to be able to understand why there might be employee resistance and to counter it.

Employees may also resist incentive plans that they do not understand, and it is natural to distrust something that is not understood. The plans may not be well communicated to employees to show how and why the standards are set.[19] The solution to this resistance is clear and precise communication of plan content and operations. (If management has no credibility in the first place, however, such messages are not likely to be received in the manner intended.)

Employees may also resist the constant pressure of production standards. It is sometimes argued that even under piece rate systems employees will work only up to a desired income level and then squander time. This might be predicted under an assumption that employees want more from their jobs than money.[20] At many organizations, for example, employees may take care of a football pool or set up a surprise birthday party during work hours, satisfying needs other than money. Employees satisfy multiple needs at work, and money alone may not elicit higher performance on a day in, day out basis.

Some employees also have different attitudes toward work and the rewards associated with work.[21] While many people hold the attitude that different levels of productivity should result in different levels of pay, this is not universally true. Some employees think that equal work regardless of performance differences should result in equal pay. While new job candidates may have the opportunity to self-select themselves in or out of an organization based on their views about what is fair pay, incumbent employees do not. Employee acceptability of an incentive plan in terms of their views about fairness should be considered when the plan is contemplated.

Managerial Attitude Problems   Attitude and behavioral problems of management have been discussed indirectly. Management itself may contribute to the failure of incentive plans.

Probably the greatest single mistake that management makes is to assume that money alone will motivate high levels of performance. Employees value many things from work other than money.[22] Managers must also remember that not all employees share the individual performance and reward values of management but may believe in equal pay for equal work (an equal job). Employees may even share their output so that it appears that all of them are working at the same rate.

Third, managers must realize that employees do not see the work world the same way as managers. For example, management may see the need to change the standard because it has become too easy as a result of better work methods. Employees may see this change as an attempt to manipulate them to get higher output or to decrease their pay. Incentive plans must rest on a trust relationship between labor and management. Worker involvement and understanding are necessary for plans to be maximally effective. This is true whether there is a labor union involved or not.[23]

Individual Incentive Plans for Salespersons

Salesperson incentive plans are established in much the same way as incentive plans for production employees. However, this is a different group of employees and the reasons for implementing an incentive plan are different. Also, the standard used for determining the incentive differs between sales and production employees.

One of the major reasons for paying salespersons on an incentive basis is that it is difficult to supervise these employees. Unlike production employees who are at a work station, most salespersons spend extended periods away from their company, making it difficult for management to observe their behaviors.

A second important reason for incentive pay in the sales field is that many salespersons see themselves as independent employees or entrepreneurs. People with this orientation are highly motivated to perform, and money is important to them. Further, at the extreme many salespersons are in fact independent agents (such as independent insurance agents) and the only way the organization can entice them to sell its product is with an incentive system.

Third, as with production employees, compensating salespersons with incentive pay ties pay directly to performance. If employees produce they are paid; if they don't produce they are not paid. Such a system is convenient for controlling labor costs.

Sales incentive systems usually use product price as the basis for setting commissions. A salesperson will get a certain percentage of the premium value of an auto insurance policy, for example, or of the selling price of a Caterpillar tractor, or of the retail price of a dress. This criterion is different from that used for production employees, where the standard is usually the labor savings realized by the employee.

There are many types of sales incentive plans. Some plans operate for special promotions while others operate for specific periods of time. Still others are used in the normal course of sales compensation. This latter type of incentive plan is discussed first, followed by specific plans.

Salespersons are typically paid on some variation of four basic plans: straight salary, salary plus commission, draw plus commission, or straight commission. The first of these plans is a standard wage and salary plan, which was the subject of earlier chapters and is not discussed here.

Salary plus Commission

A salary plus commission compensation plan amounts to a guaranteed minimum wage level (the guaranteed salary) plus the commission rate. Commission rates in such a plan are usually lower than in other plans because they take into account that sales personnel are guaranteed a minimum salary.

Draw plus Commission

Many organizations that pay salespersons on a commission basis also allow for a draw against future commissions. The basic philosophy behind a draw is that there might be considerable variation in sales over time. This could occur because the employee is still learning how to be an effective salesperson, or because of seasonal variation in demand for the product. The salesperson can draw against an account up to a specified limit each week or month (with a maximum total amount). All draws made against the account are repaid from sales commissions as they are realized. Draws operate to smooth out salesperson income in the short run. As they become experienced, salespersons may become proficient enough to be completely off the draw.

Sales Commission Plans

Sales incentive plans typically operate on a commission-basis. A commission-based compensation plan for salespersons is usually based on a percentage of sales made. Thus, a salesperson might make 3 percent on the total premium value of sales. Examples of sales commission schedules for two different occupations appear in Exhibits 13.6 and 13.7.

Just as with piece rate incentive plans for operative employees, sales commissions may be based on an increasing, decreasing, or fixed scale. As with piece rate systems, the commission scale will be a function of decisions about the desired base pay and decisions about the desired maximum pay. Maximum salesperson compensation is less sensitive to equity challenges than in a production incentive plan. One reason is that salespersons do not usually interact with other employees on a regular basis, and so there is less awareness of possible pay inequities. Another reason is that salespersons are often viewed as independent contractors or independent agents and other employees may not consider them a relevant comparison in pay equity terms. Nevertheless, even though equity perceptions may not be sensitive to high salesperson compensation, the organization will be concerned about the maximum pay for the typical salesperson.

Inside and Outside Sales   The arguments about the sensitivity of other employees to high commission levels assume that salespersons are physically distant from other employees. Inside salespersons (such as shoe salespersons and department store salespersons), however, work in close physical proximity to other employees, and large pay discrepancies between them and other employees will likely result in substantial feelings of inequity in pay. Concern over the maximum rate of pay is undoubtedly higher for inside salespersons than for outside salespersons.

Special Sales Incentive Plans

Periodically organizations may stress some particular product or service over others. The organization may put on a sales promotion specifically for that product or service. Reasons for a special promotion include clearing out inventories of one product line, increasing market penetration for a particular product, rebalancing the sales mix, and introducing new products. Sales incentives programs usually run for a specified time period. An example of a special sales promotion for an insurance sales staff appears in Exhibit 13.8.

Specific sales promotion incentives operate very much like regular incentive programs. When they are added to already established incentive programs, the organization should make sure that they add to total sales and do not detract from other sales areas. The special incentive rewards programs

Exhibit 13.6 *A Sales Commission Schedule for Insurance*

Schedule of First-Year Commissions

Contract Update (Agent)

This Update will be effective as of _____, 19_____.

I. Commissions

A. First-Year Commissions

Kind of Policy	Rate of Commissions
Health Policies & Riders	40
Adjustable Life—Term Plans	50
Convertible Annual Renewable Term	25
Adj. Life (nonrepeating premium)	4

Premium Paying Period	Kind of Policy and Rate of Commission Adjustable Life—Life Plans	Premium Paying Period	Kind of Policy and Rate of Commission Adjustable Life—Life Plans
20 yrs. or more	50	12	37
19	48	11	36
18	46	10	35
17	44	9	32
16	42	8	29
15	40	7	26
14	39	6	23
13	38	5	20

Modified first-year commissions on large premium policies:

We will modify first-year commissions on all policies with annual premiums of $100,000 or more. The modification will apply to any excess over $100,000 as set forth in our rules.

We will credit you with all renewal commissions which would regularly be payable under the contract.

First-year commissions on large premium policies: Below explains how commissions are paid on policies that pay more than $100,000 in premiums. On these types of policies, your commission will be spread out over a three-year period.

You'll be paid 30 percent the first year, 15 percent the following year, and 10 percent in the third year for a total of 55 percent. Production points, however, will be credited to you in the first year. The following table shows how commissions on a large adjustable policy would be paid.

Premium	Commission	First Year 30%	Second Year 15%	Third Year 10%
$100,000	$50,000	$50,000 × .30 = $30,000	$50,000 × .15 = $15,000	$50,000 × .10 = $10,000

Total Commission = $55,000

Source: Adapted from various insurance companies' commission schedules.

Exhibit 13.7 *A Sales Commission Schedule for Electronics*

$3.35/hour $\times$ number of hours = Draw[a]
Retail sales $\times$ 5.5% = Commission paid[a]

[a] Actual weekly pay is the larger of the two figures.

Exhibit 13.8 *Example of a Special Sales Incentive Schedule in Insurance*

The purpose of this contest is to stir up interest in our fall business. It has been our history that almost every year for the past 33 years, we have done as much business from September 1 to December 31 as we do the other eight months. We do not want this year to be an exception to that.

Rules for the Contest

1. Prize for this contest is a suit of clothes purchased at XYZ clothing store.
2. Requirements: applications secured on September 1 to December 31, 1977. If you have 16 paid and delivered new applications during this time, you will be entitled to a suit of your choice not to exceed $150 at the above named store.
3. If you do not have 16 cases written and delivered in this period, but have 20 applications applied for with money on the applications, you will be entitled to the suit.
4. If you have $600,000 of paid volume you will be entitled to this suit provided this amount is paid for between September 1 and December 31, 1977.
5. If you have 16 paid applications and $600,000 of volume that has been paid for between September 1 and December 31, you will be entitled to two suits or a suit and a top coat.

---

should be large enough to have value to the sales staff, but not be so large that salespersons ignore other lines of business. No research was discovered which addressed the size of incentives that satisfy these two constraints, but the problem is a potentially serious one.

Problems with Sales Incentive Plans

The same problems that plague piece rate and standard hour incentive plans exist with sales incentive plans. These problems were discussed in a previous section.

A traditional problem unique to salespersons concerns setting standards and balancing territory opportunity. As with setting production standards in a factory, performance standards need to be set by sales territory. Sales territories may vary considerably in their potential for customers, and the same standard can be too high in one territory and too low in another territory. One territory may be so lucrative that the salesperson by acting only as an order taker can easily reach 150 percent of quota. On the other hand, in a difficult territory the salesperson may have to work 60 hours a week to reach 80 percent of quota. This inequity can be incredibly demoralizing to salespersons. Probably the best solution is to set different standards based on the territory rather than reassigning territories.

Individual Managerial Incentive Plans

Bonus Plans

Beyond any performance pay that may be built into pay ranges, the most common individual incentive plan for managerial employees is a bonus plan. Bonus plans tie managerial pay to performance for a time frame (typically one year), and are usually formula driven. Managers can earn up to a predefined percentage of base salary as a bonus depending on their contribution to organizational success. The percentage limit usually averages about 80 percent of base salary for top level managers and about 20 percent for lower level managers.[24]

A bonus fund usually is established by allocating a percentage of profits to the fund. The bonus fund is separate from profit sharing, however. Once the bonus fund is established, the money is allocated by senior managers to individual managers. Very often the bonus fund is defined as a portion of total organization profits, not of division or regional profits. Because of this, bonus plans are questionable motivators of high performance. Specifically, because the bonus is more a function of overall organization success than of individual managers' contributions to the organization's success, the link between contribution and reward is tenuous. Since the relationship between individual contribution and reward level is so vague, some have questioned whether bonuses operate as incentive pay at all.

Bonus plans are subject to all of the problems of other types of incentive plans. It may be even harder to measure managerial contributions than the contributions of any other group of employees. It is questionable whether bonuses achieve what they are intended to achieve—to motivate and reward high performance in managers.

Executive Bonuses

A major form of performance motivation in corporations is the bonus system for chief executive officers. Decisions about these bonuses are usually made by the compensation committee of the company's board of directors and rarely fall under the purview of the organization's compensation manager.

In theory, executive bonuses are designed to motivate high levels of performance and are tied to corporate success. Assessing corporate success is highly judgmental. For example, if a company loses $10 million during a fiscal year, whether or not this loss reflects bad performance depends on what would have happened had the CEO not been in charge. As Exhibit 13.9 shows, depending on the alternative outcome, actual performance may be high or low.

It may be difficult to know what would have happened to the organization's performance without the executive's behavior. Thus, judgment is required in CEO bonus decision making.

Executive bonuses may be in forms other than cash, such as stock options,

Exhibit 13.9   *Corporate Performance and Chief Executive Officers*

Actual Performance with CEO	Theoretical Performance without CEO	CEO Assessed Performance
$10 million loss	$80 million loss	High
10 million loss	20 million profit	Low
10 million profit	20 million loss	High
10 million profit	80 million profit	Low

to defer the tax liability and allow for estate planning. As one company president said to the author, "Once my salary reached $100,000, I was interested in tax sheltering as much of my income over that amount as I could. At [my company] we try to defer tax liability for senior executives as best we can."

Short-Term Bonuses   Many executives receive a large proportion of their annual compensation in the form of bonuses. Data showing average annual bonus in dollar amounts and as a percentage of annual salary by salary level appear in Exhibit 13.10. Data showing the percentage of firms in select industries that provide bonuses for CEOs appear in Exhibit 13.11. Annual bonuses are important to total compensation for this group.

In theory, short-term annual bonuses should cause the executive to focus on short-term financial health of the organization. However, as noted earlier, it may be difficult to attribute success to the executive in many cases, and the true motivational value of short-term bonuses is highly suspect.

Exhibit 13.10 *Bonus as a Percentage of Total Compensation*

Salary	Average Bonus	Average Long-Term Award	Average Total Pay[a]	Annual Bonus as a Percentage of Total Compensation
$ 30,000	$ 7,000	$ 5,000	$ 42,000	16.67%
40,000	10,000	9,000	59,000	16.95
50,000	14,000	15,000	79,000	17.72
75,000	18,000	22,000	115,000	15.65
100,000	35,000	42,000	177,000	19.77
150,000	48,000	70,000	268,000	17.91
200,000	90,000	130,000	420,000	21.43
250,000	127,000	190,000	567,000	22.40

[a] Excluding benefits and perquisites.

Source: Adapted from "The Million Dollar Manager" by Robert E. Sibson, *Nation's Business*, November 1979.

Exhibit 13.11 *Percentage of Companies in Select Industries with Executive Bonus Plans*

Type of Business	Total Companies	May 1984 Percent with Bonus Plan	May 1980 Percent with Bonus Plan
Manufacturing	478	92%	90%
Construction	67	92	89
Retail trade	73	78	81
Commercial banking	203	73	55
Insurance	138	64	52
Gas and electric utilities	94	37	13

Source: *Top Executive Compensation: 1985 Edition* (New York: The Conference Board, 1984) by Harland Fox, p. 2. Reprinted with permission.

Long-Term Bonuses Organizations are also concerned that executives not make decisions that are good in the short run at the expense of long-term success. The organization may tie executive pay to long-term indicators of success to motivate high levels of performance in the long run.

Stock Option Plans Stock option plans are designed to tie the executive's interests (future stock value) to present behavior (making sound long-run decisions). In practice, such programs are often little more than vehicles for tax deferral and estate planning.

Stock option plans are one of the oldest forms of long-term incentives for executives and managers. Stock option plans continually change as tax laws change and are described only generally here.[25]

Under stock option plans executives are given the right to purchase a fixed number of shares of stock at a fixed price (usually market price on the offering date) as long as they remain with the organization, and they have a certain number of years to exercise the option. Any growth in the market value of the stock during the purchase period is realized by the executive.

For example, an executive might be offered the option to purchase 1,000 shares of stock at $50 per share any time during the next five years. In year 4, the stock may be worth $200 per share. The executive could then exercise the option and realize a financial gain of $150,000—$200,000 current value — $50,000 (cost). The executive may choose to hold the stock or sell it (and pay taxes on the proceeds). The executive realizes a financial gain based on the organization's improved performance (as reflected in the increased stock price), which presumably is a result of the executive's performance.

Employee Stock Ownership Plans Employee stock ownership plans (ESOPs) were originally designed for top managerial personnel. Today they are often offered to all employees who wish to participate. With an ESOP the organization sets aside money in an employee trust that purchases organization stock on behalf of the employees. These payments are treated as a business expense for tax purposes and serve as a source of investment capital for the organization. From a motivational standpoint it is believed that ESOPs will keep employees interested in high productivity and profitability. ESOP proceeds cannot be touched by the employee until retirement or severance from the organization.

Group Incentive Plans

Group incentive plans operate under the same five assumptions about individuals and work as do individual incentive plans. In addition, group plans are most effective in situations where productivity is a function of collective group output. Group incentives fall into two general categories: small group incentive plans and plant- or companywide group incentive plans.

Small Group Incentive Plans

As the term implies, small group incentive plans are restricted to small production groups. These plans are usually most effective in situations where there is high interdependence among workers so that productivity is predominantly determined by the contribution of the team as a whole. An example of this might be the construction of a building by a team of equally qualified carpenters. These carpenters may specialize in one part of the building, such as roofers, wall builders, finishing carpenters, bricklayers, and so on. On the other hand, if they all work together cooperatively and help with all of the different functional tasks, they may be much more productive. If this cooperation were desired, the contractor could use a group incentive plan whereby the carpenters could make extra money as a team for high production.

Just as with individual incentive plans, the two key steps in establishing a group plan are determining the standard production rate and determining the incentive rate. In the case of production standards, the organization must study the work processes and determine the rate to be considered normal (the standard). In the case of the incentive rate, the organization must decide upon a minimum rate, a maximum rate, and the rate scale. Each of these, as in individual incentive plans, calls for decisions by compensation decision makers.

Plantwide Group Incentive Plans

Plantwide group incentive plans are predicated on the basic philosophy that an organization is successful only when everybody is contributing to organizational goals. Employees are considered as members of a larger team of workers and in spite of their various specialized jobs, no one is considered successful unless everybody is successful.[26] There are two basic types of plantwide incentive plans: cost reduction plans and gain-sharing plans.

Cost Reduction Plans   Cost reduction plans are designed so that employees share in cost savings caused by group effort. A key feature is that all employees share in the cost savings to encourage teamwork. A number of different cost reduction plans exist, including the Scanlon and Rucker plans.

To focus strictly upon the incentive nature of these plans is probably erroneous. Successful cost savings plans are supported by an elaborate suggestion mechanism for employee input and to process recommendations. These plans also exist in an environment where there is a strong commitment on the part of both management and labor to make the organization more efficient. Further, this commitment is reinforced behaviorally: often the trappings of status (such as separate employee and management washrooms, or executive cafeterias) are notably absent. In short, successful incentive plans may be more successful because they are only one component of an overall management philosophy of a true belief in a company team as opposed to a primary manipulative device to use money to motivate high performance.[27]

The Scanlon Plan   The Scanlon plan is named for Joseph Scanlon of the U.S. Steelworkers, who devised it.[28] Under a Scanlon plan a formula determines the employees' share of all cost savings. Exhibit 13.12 contains an example of a Scanlon plan, devised as follows. First, the employer determines the ratio of payroll costs to the value of production. For example, suppose that it took $500,000 of payroll to produce $2 million worth of sales. The ratio of payroll to sales value is 25 percent. Second, the employer determines the amount of savings that results from increased efficiency. For example, if the payroll drops from $500,000 to $400,000 on sales of $2 million, then the savings is $100,000. Third, the employer allocates to a bonus fund the employees' share of this savings. For example, if the employees are to realize 75 percent of the cost savings, then $75,000 would be paid into the bonus fund. Normally the bonus is paid out at the end of the year, after setting aside a reserve for periods in which labor is less efficient. The bonus is paid to employees as a proportion of their wage to the total wage bill.

Scanlon plans rely upon an elaborate suggestion system for employee

---

Exhibit 13.12 *Example of a Scanlon Plan Cost Saving Group Bonus*

Sales value of production	$2,000,000
Standard labor costs	$500,000
Labor ratio	25% (500,000/$2,000,000)
Current labor costs	$400,000
Actual savings	$500,000 − $400,000 = $100,000
Reserve for deficit	25% = $25,000
Management share	(25% of $75,000) = $18,750
Labor share[a]	(75% of $75,000) = $66,250

[a] This is allocated to each worker based on that worker's earnings as a percentage of total payroll for the period.

recommendations for improved efficiency. Usually a departmental committee of one or more workers and one or more managers reviews cost savings suggestions and has the power to act on suggestions below a certain dollar cost. A suggestion with a cost above a certain minimum is forwarded to a higher level committee, also composed of managers and workers, and the suggestion is reviewed at this higher level. All suggestions are reviewed, and all decisions are communicated to employees whether the suggestions are implemented or not. If the suggestion is not implemented the reasons why are also communicated.

Like all incentive systems, the integrity of Scanlon plans is rooted in the determination of an accurate standard (the current payroll to sales value ratio) and in good labor management relations.[29] Unless accurate base levels are determined, the actual value of cost savings suggestions cannot be computed. Unless employees trust management they are likely to see the plan as an attempt on the part of management to manipulate them.

Not many organizations have adopted Scanlon plans. One reason may be that like all incentive plans, Scanlon plans take a considerable commitment on the part of management to establish the standards and maintain the system.[30] They also require considerable trust between labor and management. If these conditions are not present, an organization is probably wise not to implement such a plan. At the same time, the early 1980s have seen a renewed interest in these types of plans to combat the profit squeezes which many firms have felt as a result of the recession.

The Rucker Plan   Another group incentive plan is the Rucker plan. The Rucker plan is quite similar to the Scanlon plan. The principal difference is in the method of arriving at the labor ratio, which is called the *economic productivity index* in this plan.

The economic productivity index is determined by dividing the value added by labor's efforts (the sales value of production minus the costs of materials, supplies, and so on) by the costs of labor (payroll for the period). An example of these variables, their definitions, and their relationships is shown in Exhibit 13.13.

Of the $100,000 savings attributable to labor in Exhibit 13.12, one-third might go into a reserve fund and two-thirds be distributed on a monthly basis. At the end of the accounting period, any reserve not used up by labor cost overruns or accounting adjustments is distributed to the employees.

Gain-Sharing Plans   Many organizations have profit-sharing plans for their employees. Profit-sharing plans motivate performance or membership. On the one hand, profit sharing implies that because employees will reap the benefits of high profits, they should want to produce at high levels. In this sense, profit sharing is oriented toward performance motivation. Most profit-sharing plans, however, probably do not motivate performance because of their design.[31]

Several features of profit-sharing plans work at cross purposes with moti-

---

Exhibit 13.13 *Example of a Rucker Plan Bonus Calculation*

Historical Data

Sales value of production	$2,000,000
Cost of material, etc.	1,000,000
Value added (VA)	$1,000,000
Standard cost of labor for $2,000,000	500,000
Labor's contribution to value added (LCVA)	$\dfrac{500,000}{1,000,000} = 0.5$

Economic productivity index (EPI) $\dfrac{1}{LCVA} = 2.0$

Bonus Period Data

Sales value of production	$2,000,000
Cost of material	1,000,000
Value added (VA)	$1,000,000
Cost of labor (COL)	400,000

Actual value of production (AVP) = Sales value of production − (Cost of material + Cost of labor)

= $2,000,000 − ($1,000,000 + $400,000).

Expected value of production = EPI × COL (for bonus period)

= 2.0 × $400,000

= $800,000.

Saving or loss = EVP − AVP

= $800,000 − $600,000

= $200,000.

Labor's share = Labor's contribution to value added × Savings

= 0.5 × $200,000

= $100,000.

---

vating performance.[32] First, most profit-sharing plans pay out on the basis of total net profit for a given period of time (usually the organization's fiscal year). Employees do not see immediate rewards for high performance. Second, because the payout is a percentage of overall profits, there is no direct relationship between individual performance level and the payout level. Third, profit levels may be a function of variables beyond employee control. For example, in recessionary periods employees may work doubly hard simply to keep the company solvent. More employee contributions may be made than when the organization can ride the crest of an economic recovery. Profits may not correspond to actual levels of performance.

Because of these and other limitations, profit-sharing plans may be more successful at motivating membership for several reasons. First, employees may not receive the cash value of their profit-sharing accounts immediately after they earn their credit. Companies often deposit the funds into a trust, and the employee may be entitled to withdraw the money only under certain emergency conditions or when leaving the company. Second, numerous firms use profit-sharing contributions as a part of an employee's retirement program. In other words, profit sharing becomes a form of deferred compensation that is realized only at retirement or termination. This fact tends to seriously jeopardize the performance and reward relationship in the employees' perceptions and to mitigate strong pay and performance links.

Summary

This chapter focused on individual and group incentive plans. For incentive plans to be effective the employer must be able to meet the assumptions of the instrumentality and expectancy model developed in Chapter 2: employees must believe they can perform at high levels, they must see that high performance results in more pay, they must value money, and they must prefer more money to other employment outcomes. In addition, there must be performance variability potential in the jobs, and employers must develop systems that measure that variability.

The principal distinction between using a group or an individual incentive plan is whether performance is a group phenomenon or whether performance can be attributed to specific individual behaviors.

Individual incentive plans for production employees are of two basic types: piece rate incentives and standard hour plans. Similarities between the two were noted. Individual incentive plans for managerial and sales employees were also discussed. Group incentive plans can be applied to either small groups or on a plantwide basis.

Numerous problems were discussed that tend to mitigate the effectiveness of incentive plans. These include engineering problems as well as attitudinal problems of both employees and managers. Incentive plans require enormous commitment in time and money to be kept current and relevant.

Finally, profit sharing was briefly discussed. While profit sharing plans are intended to motivate high performance, they probably do not do so because of their design.

Discussion Questions

1. Discuss the assumptions that must be satisfied for instrumentality and expectancy theory to influence employee behavior in desired ways.

2. Identify the problems that make employees resist piece rate pay systems, and discuss solutions to these problems.

3. Discuss the steps in designing an individual incentive system. Are the considerations the same for operative employee plans and for sales force plans— how are such plans alike? How are they different?

4. Compare and contrast Scanlon and Halsey plans. Discuss why they might not motivate high performance.

5. Discuss why profit-sharing plans are not likely to motivate high performance.

Exercises

1. Do not read this case until directed to do so by your instructor. It has been set up as a prediction case so that you can test your analysis by answering questions before reading the entire case.[33]

Part I: The Hovey and Beard Company manufactured wooden toys of various kinds: wooden animals, pull toys, and the like. One part of the manufacturing process involved spraying paint on the partially assembled toys. This operation was staffed entirely by girls.

The toys were cut, sanded, and partially assembled in the wood room. Then they were dipped into shellac, following which they were painted. The toys were predominantly two colored; a few were made in more than two colors. Each color required an additional trip through the paint room.

For a number of years, production of these toys had been entirely handwork. However, to meet tremendously increased demand, the painting operation had recently been reengineered so that the eight girls who did the painting sat in a line by an endless chain of hooks. These hooks were in continuous motion, past the line of girls and into a long horizontal oven. Each girl sat at her own painting booth so designed as to carry away fumes and to backstop excess paint. The girl would take a toy from the tray beside her, position it in a jig inside the painting cubicle, spray on the color according to a pattern, then release the toy and hang it on the hook passing by. The rate at which the hooks moved had been calculated by the engineers so that each girl, when fully trained, would be able to hang a painted toy on each hook before it passed beyond her reach.

The girls working in the paint room were on a group bonus plan. Since the operation was new to them, they were receiving a learning bonus which decreased by regular amounts each month. The learning bonus was scheduled to vanish in six months, by which time it was expected that they would be on their own—that is, able to meet the standard and to earn a group bonus when they exceeded it.

Prediction question: What will the new hook-line do to productivity and satisfaction?

Part II: By the second month of the training period trouble had developed. The girls learned more slowly than had been anticipated, and it began to look as though their production would stabilize far below what was planned for. Many of the hooks were going by empty. The girls complained that they were going by too fast and that the time study man had set the rates wrong. A few girls quit and had to be replaced with new girls, which further aggravated the learning problem. The team spirit that the management had expected to develop automatically through the group bonus was not in evidence except as an expression of what the engineers called "resistance." One girl whom the group regarded as its leader (and the management regarded as the ringleader) was outspoken in making the various complaints of the group to the foreman: The job was a messy one, the hooks moved too fast, the incentive pay was not being correctly calculated, and it was too hot working so close to the drying oven.

Part III: A consultant who was brought into this picture worked entirely with and through the foreman. After many conversations with him, the foreman felt that the first step should be to get the girls together for a general discussion of the working conditions. He took this step with some hesitation but took it on his own volition.

The first meeting, held immediately after the shift was over at four o'clock in the afternoon, was attended by all eight girls. They voiced the same complaints again: The hooks went by too fast, the job was too dirty, the room was hot and poorly ventilated. For some reason, it was this last item that they complained of most. The foreman promised to discuss the problem of ventilation and temperature with the engineers, and he scheduled a second meeting to report back to the girls. In the next few days the foreman had several talks with the engineers. They and the superintendent felt that this was really a trumped-up complaint and that the expense of any effective corrective measure would be prohibitively high.

The foreman came to the second meeting with some apprehensions. The girls, however, did not seem to be much put out, perhaps because they had a proposal of their own to make. They felt that if several large fans were set up as to circulate the air around their feet, they would be much more comfortable. After some discussion, the foreman agreed that the idea might be tried out. The foreman and the consultant discussed the question of the fans with the superintendent, and three large propeller-type fans were purchased.

Prediction question: What will be the impact of the fan decision on morale, and relations with the foreman?

Part IV: The fans were brought in. The girls were jubilant. For several days the fans were moved about in various positions until they were placed to the satisfaction of the group. The girls seemed completely satisfied with the results, and relations between them and the foreman improved visibly.

The foreman, after this encouraging episode, decided that further meetings might also be profitable. He asked the girls if they would like to meet and discuss other aspects of the work situation. The girls were eager to do this. The meeting was held, and the discussion quickly centered on the speed of the hooks. The girls maintained that they would never be able to reach the goal of filling enough of them to make a bonus.

The turning point of the discussion came when the group's leader frankly explained that the point wasn't that they couldn't work fast enough to keep up with the hooks but that they couldn't work at that pace all day long. The foreman explored the point. The girls were unanimous in their opinion that they could keep up with the belt for short periods if they wanted to. But they didn't want to because if they showed they could do this for short periods they would be expected to do it all day long. The meeting ended with an unprecedented request: "Let us adjust the speed of the belt faster or slower depending on how we feel." The foreman agreed to discuss this with the superintendent and the engineers.

The reaction of the engineers to the suggestion was negative. However, after several meetings it was granted that there was some latitude within which variations in the speed of the hooks would not affect the finished product. After considerable argument with the engineers, it was agreed to try out the girls' idea.

With misgivings, the foreman had a control with a dial marked "low, medium, fast" installed at the booth of the group leader; she could now adjust the speed of the belt anywhere between the lower and upper limits that the engineers had set.

Prediction question: What will be the impact of the dial control decision on productivity and satisfaction?

Part V: The girls were delighted and spent many lunch hours deciding how the speed of the belt should be varied from hour to hour throughout the day. Within a week the pattern had settled down to one in which the first half of the shift was run on what the girls called a medium speed (a dial setting slightly above the point marked "medium"). The next two and one-half hours were run at high speed; the half hour before lunch and the half hour after lunch were run at low speed. The rest of the afternoon was run at high speed with the exception of the last 45 minutes of the shift, which was run at medium.

In view of the girls' reports of satisfaction and ease in their work, it is interesting to note that the constant speed at which the engineers had originally set the belt was slightly below medium on the dial of the control that had been given the girls. The average speed at which the girls were running the belt was on the high side of the dial. Few, if any, empty hooks entered the oven, and inspection showed no increase of rejects from the paint room.

Production increased, and within three weeks (some two months before the scheduled ending of the learning bonus) the girls were operating at 30 to 50 percent above the level that had been expected under the original arrangement. Naturally the girls' earnings were correspondingly higher than anticipated. They were collecting their base pay, a considerable piece rate bonus, and the learning bonus which, it will be remembered, had been set to decrease with time and not as a function of current productivity. The girls were earning more now than many skilled workers in other parts of the plant.

Prediction question: How will other personnel react and why?

Part VI: Management was besieged by demands that this inequity be taken care of. With growing irritation between superintendent and foreman, engineers and foreman, superintendent and engineers, the situation came to a head when the superintendent revoked the learning bonus and returned the painting operation to its original status: the hooks moved again at their constant time-studied designated speed, production dropped again, and within a month all but two of the eight girls had quit. The foreman himself stayed on for several months but, feeling aggrieved, then left for another job.

a. What parallels can you see between the case and chapter discussion?

b. What conclusions can be drawn from this case about piece rate incentive systems?

c. Review the problems introduced by the new system and discuss how they might have been avoided.

2. The Henley Brothers Machine shop performs batch drilling for numerous organizations in its area. Skilled drill press operators at the shop currently earn $8.00 per hour. Donald Henley, vice-president of production, is considering putting drill press operators on a piece rate incentive system when they work on these large batch drilling operations (other work would be straight hourly work).

As a skilled tool and die maker and a trained engineer, Donald Henley has undertaken a time study for these large batch drilling operations. He has observed that his two slowest employees average 60 drilling operations per hour and his two fastest employees average 72 drilling operations in an hour. The average across all employees is 66 drilling operations. If he goes to a piece rate system, Henley would not want maximum pay to exceed $9.20 per hour because of equity considerations for other employees.

a. Design at least two different piece rate incentive plans that Henley might use. Which do you recommend? Why? Which would keep labor costs at a minimum?

b. Would you recommend to Henley that he use or not use a piece rate incentive plan? Why or why not?

c. How would you administer the piece rate plan? Are the costs and troubles worth it?

d. What do you think employees will think of the new plan you propose?

3. Donald Scalzo is a bread truck delivery route driver for the Howard Bread Company. The company pays him a guaranteed weekly draw plus commission. The draw allows Donald to make a guaranteed weekly wage of $280. His commission is a flat 3 percent of gross sales. Last year he earned $27,000 driving the bread truck (on gross sales of $900,000).

Because his route is in a tourist area, 60 percent of sales occur from June 1 to September 1 each year. The other 40 percent are realized the rest of the year. The Howard Bread Company is concerned about the size of the income delivery route drivers like Donald make. For one thing, annual earnings of $27,000 put driver wages out of line with other company employees, including the semitruck drivers who bring bakery products to the delivery route drivers during the night. Second, the guaranteed minimum is more reflective of the true value of the delivery driver's worth, and the $27,000 per year is almost twice this amount. Third, the bakery thinks that delivery drivers are simply order takers (especially during the peak tourist season) and are enjoying an undeserved earnings windfall that has nothing to do with their performance.

Because of these factors Howard Bread is considering one of two courses of action. First, it is considering implementing a new incentive policy that would reduce the commission from 3 percent to 1 percent for the three summer months. The commission rate would remain unchanged for the remainder of the year. The second option is to hire additional part-time drivers (at straight hourly wages) during the summer and take away certain chunks of territory from Donald and other regular drivers during the summer.

a. What do you recommend that Howard Bread do?

b. How are Donald and other delivery drivers likely to respond to your recommendation?

c. If you changed the policy how would you implement the change? Why? Hint: think about an earlier chapter's discussions on red circle rates.

4. Generic Services Inc. is a small company of employees with no fringe benefits other than a two week paid vacation policy after one year of service. The owner is considering offering a profit-sharing plan to these employees. Five percent of net profits would be distributed to employees as a percentage of their salary to total payroll.

The five-year history of payroll costs and net (after tax) profits appears below.

Year	Number of Employees	Payroll	Net After-Tax Profit
19___	4	$40,000	$60,000
19___	4	42,000	(3,000)
19___	4	43,500	81,000
19___	5	55,000	42,000
19___	5	56,500	96,000

a. What do you recommend to the owner?

b. In the absence of prior employee benefits, would you recommend initiating some benefits before profit sharing? Why or why not?

References

[1] F. Bartlett, "Incentives," *British Journal of Psychology* 41, numbers 3,4 (1950): pp. 122–128.

[2] D. Belcher, "Pay and Performance," *Compensation Review* (third quarter, 1980). S. Shimmin, "Workers' Understanding of Incentive Payment Systems," *Occupational Psychology* 32, number 2, pp. 106–110.

[3] F. Hills, "The Pay-for-Performance Dilemma," *Personnel* 56, number 5, pp. 23–31. E. Lawler, *Pay and Organizational Effectiveness: A Psychological View* (New York: McGraw-Hill, 1971).

[4] *Ibid.* L. Bentley, "Conversion from Piece Rate to Time Rate Pay for Production Workers," *Compensation Review* 11, number 4, pp. 31–35.

[5] L. Miller and R. Hamblin, "Interdependence, Differential Rewarding, and Productivity," *American Sociological Review* 28 (1963): pp. 768–778.

[6] Historically, piece rate plans used the concept of "task" in designing the standard. "Task" has to do with various assumptions about how hard employees who are studied are working. That is, are they working at a high, average, or low level of productivity? For a further discussion of task, see Thomas H. Patten, Jr., *Pay: Employee Compensation and Incentive Plans* (New York: The Free Press, 1977): pp. 406–409. In this text, the assumption is made that industrial engineering can determine the average productivity of the average worker under normal work conditions.

[7] Employers using incentive systems for nonexempt employees must be sure that such plans do not violate overtime and minimum wage provisions of the FLSA. See, for example, Michael Schuster and Gary Florkowski, "Wage Incentive Plans and the Fair Labor Standards Act," *Compensation Review* 14, number 2 (Second quarter, 1982): pp. 34–46.

[8] E. Lawler, "Equity Theory as a Predictor of Productivity and Work Quality," *Psychological Bulletin* 70, number 6, pp. 596–610. R. Opshal and M. Dunnette, "The Role of Financial Compensation in Industrial Motivation," *Psychological Bulletin* 66, number 2, pp. 94–118.

[9] Lawler, *Pay and Organizational Effectiveness*.

[10] F. W. Taylor, "A Piece Rate System," *Transactions of the American Society of Mechanical Engineers* 16, (1895): pp. 856–905.

[11] D. W. Merrick, "Time Studies as a Basis for Rate Setting," *The Engineering Magazine*, 1920.

[12] Frederick A. Halsey, "The Premium Plan of Paying for Labor," *Transactions of the American Society of Mechanical Engineers* 12 (1891): pp. 755–780.

[13] Sir William Rowan Thomson, *The Rowan Premium Bonus System of Payment by Results*, 2d ed. (Scotland: McCorquedale and Co., 1919).

[14] H. L. Gantt, "A Bonus System of Rewarding Labore," *Transactions of the American Society of Mechanical Engineers* 12 (1891): pp. 755–780.

[15] Lawler, *Pay and Organizational Effectiveness*. William F. Whyte, *Money and Motivation* (New York: Harper and Row, 1955).

[16] Shimmin, "Workers' Understanding of Incentive Payment Systems." P. Daly, "Selecting and Designing a Group Incentive Plan," *Personnel Journal* (June 1975): pp. 322–356. Bentley, "Conversion from Piece Rate to Time Rate Pay for Production Workers." C. Mace, "Advances in the Theory and Practice of Incentives," *Occupational Psychology* 24, number 4 (1950): pp. 239–244.

[17] Shimmin, "Workers' Understanding of Incentive Payment Systems." Bentley, "Conversion from Piece Rate to Time Rate Pay for Production Workers."

[18] Mace, "Advances in the Theory and Practice of Incentives."

[19] Bentley, "Conversion from Piece Rate to Time Rate Pay for Production Workers." E. Lawler and R. Olson, "Designing Reward Systems for New Organizations," *Personnel* 54, number 5, pp. 48–60.

[20] H. Rothe, "Does Higher Pay Bring Higher Productivity?" *Personnel* 37, number 4, pp. 20–27.

[21] J. Schuster, "A Spectrum of Pay for Performance: How to Motivate Employees," *Management of Personnel Quarterly* (Fall 1969): pp. 35–38.

[22] Rothe, "Does Higher Pay Bring Higher Productivity?"

[23] Schuster and Florkowski, "Wage Incentive Plans and the Fair Labor Standards Act."

[24] Graef S. Crystal, *Financial Motivation for Executives* (New York: American Management Association, 1970): p. 137.

[25] *Ibid.*

[26] L. Baytos, "Nine Strategies for Productivity Improvement," *Personnel Journal* 58, number 7, pp. 449–456.

[27] Rothe, "Does Higher Pay Bring Higher Productivity?"

[28] B. Moore and T. Ross, *The Scanlon Way to Improved Productivity* (New York: John Wiley & Sons, 1978).

[29] A. Geare, "Productivity from Scanlon-Type Plans," *Compensation Review* 9, number 3, pp. 53–58; from the *Academy of Management Review*, July 1976.

[30] Moore and Ross, *The Scanlon Way to Improved Productivity.*

[31] William F. Whyte, "The Scanlon Plan," in Thomas A. Maloney, ed., *Compensation and Reward Perspectives* (Homewood, Ill.: Irwin, 1979): pp. 350–362.

[32] Rothe, "Does Higher Pay Bring Higher Productivity?"; O. Dalaba, "Misuses of Compensation as a Motivator," *Personnel* (September–October 1973): pp. 30–37.

[33] The following case is abridged from pp. 90–94 "Group Dynamics and Intergroup Relations" (under the title "Hovey and Beard Company") by Alex Bavelas and George Strauss in *Money and Motivation* by William F. Whyte. Copyright © 1955 by Harper & Row, Publishers, Inc. By permission of Harper & Row, Publishers, Inc.

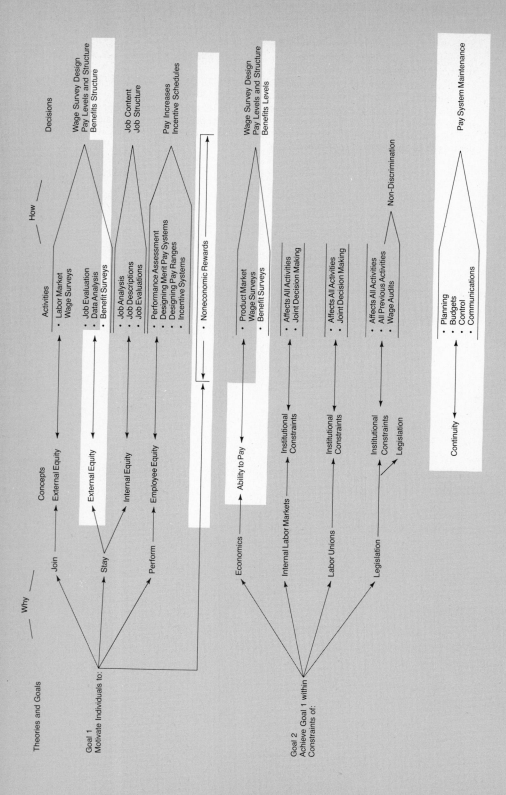

Completing the

Compensation Package

Part Six completes the discussion of compensation decision making. Chapter 14 covers the important topic of employee benefits, which have continued to grow as a percentage of total compensation. The reasons are detailed in this chapter. The chapter also focuses upon the types of benefits employers offer and discusses important decision-making issues in the benefits area.

Chapter 15 is a relatively nontraditional chapter that deals with the noneconomic rewards available to employers and why they might be offered, and suggests how the organization can assess which noneconomic benefits are likely to be valued by employees. One important message of this chapter is that employees work for rewards other than money.

The concluding chapter, Chapter 16, deals with compensation administration and control. The chapter assumes that the organization has carried out the decision processes discussed in Chapters 6 through 14. This chapter then discusses how the organization can keep its compensation system current and up to date.

Further, the chapter deals with communication of the compensation system to employees, and also focuses upon integrating compensation decisions into ongoing operating budgets.

CHAPTER

14

Employee Benefits

· **Learning Objectives**

· **Introduction**

· **Employee Benefits Defined**

· **Employee Benefits versus Perquisites**

· **Theoretical Foundation for Employee Benefits**

· **Growth in Employee Benefits**

Societal Attitudes
Favorable Tax Treatment
Employer Self-Interest
Group Coverage Effects
Employer Paternalism
Income and Leisure Preferences
Changing Philosophies about People and Work
Indirect Returns from Benefits
Union Pressures
Bandwagon Effect

· **Types of Benefit Programs**

· **Pension Plans**

Issues in Designing Pension Plans
Types of Pension Plans
Pension Plan Costs

· **Pay for Time Not Worked**

Vacation Time
Holiday Pay
Other Paid Time
Indirect Costs of Pay for Time Not Worked

· **Insurance**

Health Insurance
Life and Accident Insurance
Long-term Disability Insurance
Other Insurance

· **Other Benefits**

Discounts on Goods and Services
Subsidized Meals
Moving Expenses
Severance Pay

· **Legally Required Benefits**

Social Security
Workers' Compensation
Unemployment Compensation

· **Benefits Decision Making**

Benefit Level and Product Market
   Benefit Surveys
Benefit Structure and Labor Market Benefit
   Surveys
Benefit Structure and Survey of Current
   Employees
Benefit Structure and Goals
Contributory versus Noncontributory Benefits

· **Future Trends in Employee Benefits**

Cafeteria Benefit Plans
Retirement Plans
Taxation of Benefits

· **Exercise**

Learning Objectives

To introduce the subject of employee benefits.
To learn the reasons for the growth in employee benefits.
To learn the types of employee benefits that are offered by organizations.
To learn the benefits that are legally required.
To learn the important variables that influence the employee benefits decision process.
To learn about several important future events that may have a major impact on benefits decision making.

Introduction

This chapter deals with the topic of employee benefits. The objectives of the chapter are to discuss the growth in employee benefits; to identify the major types of benefits that employees receive; to discuss the role of employee benefits in influencing individual employee behaviors; and to discuss future trends in benefits.

Employee Benefits Defined

Employee benefits can be defined as all of the indirect economic rewards that the employee receives.[1] Common employee benefits are pension plans, pay for time not worked, and group insurances.

Employee Benefits versus Perquisites

Some types of benefits in organizations go to a select group of employees. Examples of these benefits are keys to executive washrooms and lunchrooms, company cars, and the privilege of having mahogany paneling in one's office. These types of benefits (going to a privileged few) are considered perquisites, and should not be confused with employee benefits that accrue to nearly all employees of an organization by virtue of their status as employees. Employee benefits are generally made available to all full-time employees of the organization.

Theoretical Foundation for Employee Benefits

As Chapter 1 noted, a major goal of an organization's compensation system is to influence individuals to behave as desired by the organization. Organizations want to motivate individuals to join and stay with the organization, and to perform at high levels. How do employee benefits contribute to influencing individual behavior? Since benefits accrue to employees by virtue of membership in the organization, it is doubtful that they contribute to motivating performance. Stated another way, since employees receive benefits regardless of their performance levels, even if the benefits are highly valued, it is unlikely that they will motivate anything other than minimally acceptable performance (performance adequate to retain a job).

It is also unlikely that employee benefits motivate joining, for several reasons. First, most benefit programs are fragmented, and are difficult to compare between organizations. Individuals may not be able to compare the benefits packages of two firms where the list of benefits provided is noncomparable. One recent trend among employers is to express benefits as a proportion of direct pay, thereby informing employees of the total economic value of the employee benefit package. To the extent that this becomes standard practice, individuals may become more sensitive to the economic value of the benefits package, and perhaps make employment decisions on the basis of relative benefit package worth. However, one study demonstrated that wage levels and benefits levels tend to vary directly with each other.[2] Thus, high-wage employers tend to be high-benefit employers as well.

A second reason why benefits probably do not motivate joining is that very often they are noncomparable, although similar on the surface. For example, two organizations may each have a group health insurance plan that will cost an employee the same monthly premium, but one plan may be vastly superior in terms of the coverage. Even though the benefit provided is the same in one sense (health insurance coverage), the plans are noncomparable in terms of the quality of the coverage. In this situation an individual making a decision to join one of these organizations would probably see the two organizations as equal (both have a health plan) and overlook the qualitative differences in the two plans. The considerable variation in the quality of benefits plans can be seen in Exhibit 14.1.

Probably the major role employee benefits play in influencing individual behavior is to motivate staying. In fact, employee benefits have been referred to as "golden handcuffs" because they tend to tie the employee to the organization. This effect is particularly true for benefits that appreciate in value as a function of employment seniority, such as vacation time and pension benefit levels. The role of benefits in achieving compensation's goal of influencing individual behaviors is summarized in Exhibit 14.2.

Growth in Employee Benefits

There has been tremendous growth in benefits over the past 20 years. The data in Table 14.1 indicate that benefits have grown from 24.7 percent of payroll in 1959 to 41.4 percent of payroll in 1980. These data are based on large employers and are not indicative of the average benefits level across all employers in the United States; rather they are skewed toward large employers' benefits

Exhibit 14.1 *A Comparison of Two Health Plans*

Plan Attribute	Plan A	Plan B
Deductible	None	$400
Surgery	100%	80% after deductible
Maternity	100%	80% after deductible for the following procedures only: 1. Caesarean section 2. extrauterine pregnancy 3. complications requiring surgery after pregnancy termination.
Hospitalization	100%, unlimited days, semiprivate or private room, if medically necessary	80% after deductible for usual and customary rate
Dental	100% of preventive care for children, treatment for injuries except for lab charges	80% after deductible for injury or surgery
Maximum coverage	No maximum	$20,000 per illness

levels. Since employee benefits do not likely motivate performance or joining behavior, why has there been such rapid growth in benefit levels? There are numerous causes for this growth.

Societal Attitudes

One of the prime contributors to continued benefits growth is the attitudinal change that began with the Great Depression of the 1930s. Prior to the Depression, both individuals and employers felt that it was the responsibility of the individual to face economic adversity.The severity of the Great Depression, however, showed both parties that economic circumstances could be completely beyond the individual's control. Out of this grew a desire to insulate employees from the most severe forms of economic dislocation.

These attitudinal changes resulted in government intervention in some areas (for example, unemployment insurance programs and workers' compensation insurance), and also resulted in labor and management responding to

Exhibit 14.2 *Role of Benefits in Achieving Compensation Goals*

1. Do benefits motivate joining?
   Answer: Probably not, because they are fragmented and noncomparable, and there are qualitative differences across organizations.
2. Do benefits motivate staying?
   Answer: Yes, because they act as "golden handcuffs," and some benefits grow with seniority.
3. Do benefits motivate superior performance?
   Answer: No, because they accrue because of membership, not performance.

Table 14.1 Comparison of 1959 to 1980 Employee Benefits for 186 Companies

	1959	1961	1963	1965	1967	1969	1971	1973	1975	1977	1979	1980
As percent of payroll, total	24.7%	26.6%	27.4%	27.7%	29.2%	31.1%	33.1%	35.3%	37.9%	40.0%	41.3%	41.4%
a. Legally required payments (employer's share only)	3.5	4.0	4.5	4.2	4.9	5.3	5.6	6.6	7.0	7.6	8.1	8.1
b. Pension, insurance, and other agreed-upon payments (employer's share only)	8.5	8.9	9.1	9.4	9.7	10.4	11.5	12.2	13.4	14.5	15.1	15.2
c. Paid rest periods, lunch periods, etc.	2.2	2.6	2.6	2.6	2.9	3.1	3.2	3.3	3.8	3.8	3.8	3.8
d. Payments for time not worked	8.4	8.9	9.1	9.3	9.5	10.1	10.6	10.8	11.3	11.6	11.8	11.9
e. Profit-sharing payments, bonuses, etc.	2.1	2.2	2.1	2.2	2.2	2.2	2.2	2.4	2.4	2.5	2.5	2.4
As cents per payroll hour	62.0¢	70.8¢	79.2¢	85.9¢	100.6¢	118.4¢	141.4¢	174.0¢	219.7¢	260.4¢	330.6¢	355.2¢
As dollars per year per employee	$1,282	$1,461	$1,637	$1,782	$2,084	$2,467	$2,927	$3,640	$4,553	$5,368	$6,871	$7,633

Source: Copyright 1981 U.S. Chamber of Commerce. Reprinted with the permission of the U.S. Chamber of Commerce from *Employee Benefits 1980*, p. 27.

the challenge in other areas (such as supplementary unemployment benefit insurance).[3] Employer participation in these types of programs, whether required by law or voluntary, contributes to the costs of employee benefits.

Favorable Tax Treatment

Another reason benefits have grown significantly is the favorable tax treatment that indirect forms of compensation receive.[4] A good example is the favorable treatment received by a health insurance plan. A typical family coverage health insurance plan would cost about $200 per month for an employee in 1985. If an employer wished for its employees to have such coverage, the employer could just increase the employees' pay and let them buy the insurance. However, since any increase in the employee's paycheck is taxed, the employer would have to pay each employee more than $200 so that the employee would net $200 to buy the insurance. The actual cost to the employer would be considerably greater than the $200 individual premium. In recent years there has been considerable pressure to tax employee benefits as direct income. Should this happen, it is unlikely that benefits programs will be as attractive to individuals or organizations.

Employer Self-Interest

The above example demonstrates the clear economic benefit to the employer of providing a health plan under a group system. The employer might also provide the group health plan out of self-interest. For example, in the above case the employer would have no way of knowing if the employees actually use the additional $200 for the health insurance. An employee might use the money toward a new car, for example. Providing the coverage directly for the employee limits the actual cost to the actual premium rate. By providing for the health plan directly the employer protects its own self-interest of having a healthy work force.

Group Coverage Effects

It is also possible for the organization to take advantage of lower rates for programs because of the pooled risk associated with groups of people. In the above example of health insurance, the premium rate for family coverage under a group plan would probably not be $200 as for an individual family policy, but would be more in the range of $125. The group plan reduces the cost to the employer even further.

Employer Paternalism

It is unpopular to talk about organizations that are paternalistic to their employees, acting as father figures. Some organizations do feel a paternal need to take care of their employees, and this alone may be a reason for providing certain benefits.

Income and Leisure Preferences

As America has become a relatively more affluent society, individuals prefer more free time from work. Employees enjoy time off from work, whether for paid vacation time or paid holidays. This preference is another reason for the increase in benefits in recent years.

Changing Philosophies about People and Work

Just as attitudes have changed about who should shoulder the responsibility for economic hardship, attitudes are changing about the nature of people and work itself. With respect to people, if organizations believe that people are not lazy, that work is as natural as play, and that people want to contribute to organizational goals, then tying money to performance is not necessary since people will want to perform to the maximum regardless of whether money is an associated outcome. Stated another way, if people receive intrinsic rewards from doing well, there is no reason to think that money is the only vehicle for obtaining high levels of performance.

There are two important features of jobs in this regard. First, on many jobs either there is little room for performance variation or the variation is not measurable. Given these conditions, reward for membership may be the most logical for these jobs. Second, employee turnover can be extremely expensive in and of itself. For example, turnover costs may run as high as 68 percent of first year salary for a senior engineer.[5] Faced with this economic fact, it would make sense to undertake employee benefit programs that motivate retention.

Indirect Returns from Benefits

While benefits motivate employees to stay with the organization, at the same time many organizations believe they receive an indirect return from providing certain benefits. Health plans are an example for this point. In theory at least, employers who provide a group health plan might expect to have a healthier work force than employers without such plans, presumably receiving an indirect return on performance and productivity. Similarly, many organizations believe that vacation time should be used not just for recreation, but also for re-creation. These organizations require employees to use vacation time to refresh and rejuvenate themselves. How much of an indirect return firms get from employee benefits is poorly understood, but firms do believe that they receive such benefits.

Union Pressures

Labor unions have multiple goals for their members. It is often thought (erroneously) that unions only want larger paychecks for their members. However, unions also wish to provide for security of members during retirement and in times of unemployment. To these ends unions often bargain for mandatory retirement programs (after 30 years of service, for example), and for Supplementary Unemployment Benefits, as discussed in Chapter 4. In addition, unions have pushed for a four-day workweek for years. One way to achieve this indirectly is to increase the number of days off with pay (holidays, personal days, and so on).

Bandwagon Effect

Finally, some organizations provide benefits simply because everyone else seems to be doing it. Under an assumption that employees do compare organizations on benefits, their employers may wish to have competitive benefits to attract and retain labor.

Types of Benefit Programs

There are numerous ways to categorize benefits. For convenience this text discusses employee benefits in terms of their relative cost to the organization. The discussion is divided into pension plans, pay for time not worked, insurances, and a catchall category of other benefits. The next section covers legally required benefits. Legally required benefits must be factored into each of the categories discussed here for each category to be properly ordered in terms of relative cost. For example, pension plans are generally the most costly benefit to the employer; however, this is only the case when Social Security, a federally mandated retirement plan, is considered in conjunction with the private pension plan.

These benefit components are discussed in terms of a typical organization's relative contribution to costs. The cost structure may vary considerably among employers since employee benefit plans vary from one employer to another.

Pension Plans

Issues in Designing Pension Plans

Pensions are clearly a significant cost component in the employee benefits package. Pension plans vary so much in operational detail that a specialist in pension plans should be consulted by any organization considering introducing such a plan. In this text only the basic features of pension plans are discussed.

All pension plans must deal with the issues summarized in Exhibit 14.3, which are discussed in this section.

Pension Plan Objectives   Before implementing a pension plan the compensation decision maker must ask what the objectives of the plan are. For example, is the plan to provide for all of the retirement needs of an employee and the

Exhibit 14.3 *ERISA-Related Issues in Establishing a Pension Plan*

Issue	Consideration
Benefit level	How large will the pension benefit be?
Retirement age	What is the earliest age at which employees can retire under the plan?
Vesting	When does the employee have a right to the employer's contribution to the plan?
Funding	When must money be set aside to cover the pension liability?
Fiduciary standards	Is the fund managed in the interest of the participants?
Pension Benefit Guaranty Corporation	How does the Pension Benefit Guaranty Corporation become involved in private pension plans?
Pension plan objectives	What are the goals for income replacement, partial replacement, and so on?
Who qualifies?	Who is eligible to participate in the plan?

dependent spouse, or is it intended only to supplement other income? Most pension plans today are not designed to stand alone as the sole income of a person in retirement. At a minimum, most plans are integrated with Social Security. One typical approach to determining benefit levels under a pension plan is to make postretirement income from Social Security and the pension plan equal to a percentage of preretirement pay.[6] The funding scheme would require adequate funds be set aside to realize this percentage.

Who Qualifies?   One important question in developing a pension plan is to determine who will be eligible to participate in the pension plan. In general, under the Employee Retirement Income Security Act (ERISA), if a pension plan is offered an employee must become eligible for a pension after one year of service or at age 21 (under 1984 amendments), whichever comes later. This requirement applies only to employees who work more than half-time (defined as more than 1,000 hours in a calendar year). An employer wishing to avoid pension liability should be careful that its part-time employees do not exceed the ERISA standard. At the same time, the employer must make employees eligible for a pension when they work more than 1,000 hours in a year.

Benefit Level   While pension plan goals determine benefit levels, other factors influence benefit levels as well. The percentage of the preretirement income (sometimes referred to as the replacement ratio) is used to calculate the pension level.[7] Also of concern is whether the plan is based on a single employee or if it takes into account an employee and a dependent spouse. Today experts suggest the use of the single employee criterion, which results in higher benefit levels and higher costs.[8] Costs are higher under a single employee criterion because the employee is not assumed to realize the economies of scale of a two-person household or the spouse's Social Security benefit.

Retirement Age   Every pension plan must specify a retirement age. Traditionally age 65 has been used as the standard retirement age for private pension plans, although there are pressures both to reduce and eliminate the retirement age. Unions, for example, have pushed for 62, 60, and even 55 years of age in some cases, and in other cases they have also pushed for a 30 years and out (mandatory retirement after 30 years of service) rule. At the same time that unions have been pushing to reduce the retirement age, amendments to the Age Discrimination in Employment Act (1978) have moved the minimum mandatory retirement age to 70 years. Thus, while an employer may still specify age 65 (or a younger age) as its standard retirement age, the employer cannot force employees to retire until age 70.

While there must be a standard retirement age, many pension plans make provisions for early retirement. There is considerable variability in practice, but a standard approach is to allow employees to retire at age 60 or 62 at reduced benefit levels. The reduced benefit levels are based on the fact that younger employees will have paid into the plan for a shorter period of time and also are expected to draw against the plan for a longer period of time.

Vesting   Vesting refers to the rights that an employee has to benefits that have accrued in a pension fund. In the case of contributory plans (plans in which employees contribute part of their salaries), the employee is always entitled to the individual share. However, when does the employee have a right to the company-contributed share in noncontributory or contributory plans? Under ERISA the employer has three minimum options for vesting employees: (1) the employer can provide 100 percent vesting after 10 years of service; (2) the employer can provide 25 percent vesting after five years of service, then 5 percent per year to 50 percent vesting in 10 years, and then 10 percent per year so that at the end of 15 years the employee is 100 percent vested; or (3) the employer can vest 50 percent after five years if the employee's age and years of service total 45, or after 10 years of service if less, and at the rate of 10 percent per year thereafter.[9]

Funding   Under ERISA, pension plans must also be funded. Liabilities incurred in a given year by a pension plan must be funded in that same year. Expert accounting and actuarial advice are needed in order to arrive at realistic estimates of the employer's future expected liability under a pension plan. If the plan meets the ERISA standards, then these liabilities can be treated as a business expense for tax purposes.

Fiduciary Standards   Compensation decision makers must be concerned that the fiduciary standards of ERISA are met. The funds placed in the pension plan must be managed by an individual or institution that acts only in the interests of the participants in the plan. Normally, an organization will choose a bank, insurance company, or other financial institution to act as the fiduciary of the fund.

Pension Benefit Guaranty Corporation   The Pension Benefit Guaranty Corporation (PBGC) is managed by the Department of Labor and administers insurance programs for private pension plans that conform to ERISA standards. In the event that a private pension plan ceases to exist, the PBGC guarantees that an employee will be able to collect accrued benefits under the plan.

The PBGC also allows an employee to transfer funds from an employer's pension fund if the employer agrees. An employee may be able to transfer funds from one employer to another without incurring tax liability on the funds. Any transfer is contingent upon the former employer being willing to release the funds and the new employer being willing to accept the funds. If the former employer releases the funds, the individual can also leave the monies with PBGC and draw against those benefits at retirement age.

Types of Pension Plans

It is a misrepresentation to consider all pension plans as being the same. There is almost an unlimited array of options in setting up a pension plan for employees. This section discusses several categories of the more common types of pension plans.

Defined Benefits Plans   The distinguishing feature of a defined benefits pension plan is, as the title implies, that a participant in the plan will be entitled to a defined benefit level at retirement. From the organization's standpoint this plan is probably the most costly. The burden of assuring that the funds are in the plan resides with the employer. As yield rates on the investments in the retirement fund change, or as the demographics of the work force change, the employer must be sure that the funds are available to meet the obligations of the defined benefit level.

Defined Contribution Plans   A less costly pension plan is a defined contributions plan. In defined contribution plans, as the name implies, the employer contributes a fixed amount into a retirement plan, however, there is no guarantee of a fixed benefit level when the employee retires. This method is less risky and costly to the employer because the major commitment is to the initial level of funds. The employer carries no responsibility for the yield rate on the investments. The benefits under such a plan may be highly variable. The employee, on the other hand, loses on this plan since it is harder to plan for retirement.

Salary Reduction Plans   Salary reduction plans are special types of defined contribution plans. In this case, the employee contributes some portion of current earnings to the pension plan. Two types of salary reduction plans are extremely popular today: thrift plans and 401K plans (the latter take their name from the legislation enacting them).

Salary reduction plans are of relative low cost to the organization since the funds are typically from employee salaries. Further, there is no liability for yield rates on investments, nor is there a defined benefit.

Thrift Plans   Thrift plans allow employees to contribute from current income into a pension plan that is invested on their behalf. The advantage to the employee is that the contributions are made before taxes are paid on them, therefore sheltering the contributions from taxes until they are paid back out of the plan. Typically, thrift plans involve an employer contribution as well. For example, the employer may contribute on a one-for-one basis with the employee—the employer matches each dollar the employee puts into the plan up to a prescribed limit (such as 6 percent of total pay).

401K Plans   401K plans allow an employee to defer current income into the future and to shelter the money from taxes until it is withdrawn. A typical 401K might work in conjunction with a profit-sharing plan. Once a year an employee may be entitled to a share of the company profit-sharing plan. The employee may decide to invest this money in a pension fund, which means that the employee can defer the taxes on this money.[10]

Simplified Pension Plans   A simplified pension plan might resemble an individual retirement account (IRA). The employer might agree to put aside a fund of money into an IRA for each employee. This type of arrangement provides the least long-term financial commitment of the four types of plans discussed here. The employer's only involvement is the initial cash outlay. The employee is free to leave the money in the account or to withdraw it (and pay the tax).

Stock Purchase Plans   Employee stock ownership plans (ESOPs), tax reduction act stock ownership plans (TRASOPs), and payroll stock ownership plans (PAYSOPs) are all stock purchase plans that are used to fund pension programs. More formally they are considered profit-sharing plans. The common theme that they share is enabling an employer to take advantage of tax law in granting stock to employees. The law also gives favorable tax treatment to employees when they redeem the stock at retirement.

Pension Plan Costs

Pensions are the largest single component in the cost of employee benefits, but this is true only if the costs of Social Security are included as part of the package. A later section discusses in more detail Social Security payments. In 1986 the organization paid 7.15 percent of an employee's gross pay (up to a maximum gross pay of $42,000) into the Social Security program. This 7.15 percent contribution plus the cost of a private pension plan cause this benefit to be the largest single cost component to the benefits package. For example, if an employer had a private pension plan in which it contributed 8 percent of an employee's base pay to the plan, then a total of 15.15 percent of base pay goes into pensions. This amount is nearly 37 percent of the total value of benefits identified in Table 14.1.

Pay for Time Not Worked

The second largest category of benefits is pay for time not worked. Several different components go into this category. Paid lunch breaks and other breaks that employees receive are not discussed further here. A second and major category is vacation time.[11] A third category is holiday time, and a fourth category considers other paid time off.

Vacation Time

Most organizations have some policy governing vacation benefits. A typical vacation policy allows an employee two weeks off with pay after one complete year of service to the organization. In more liberal vacation policies the length of time off with pay varies with seniority. For example, an employer might have a policy of two weeks off for employees with 1 to 5 years of service, three weeks off with pay for employees with 6 to 10 years of service, four weeks off with pay for employees with 11 to 15 years of service, five weeks off with pay for employees with 16 to 20 years of service, and six weeks off with pay for employees with more than 21 years of service. Obviously, the more liberal the vacation policy, the more costly it will be to the organization. An example of two vacation policies appears in Exhibit 14.4.

Holiday Pay

Holidays are another major benefit that results in pay for time not worked. One survey found that the average number of holidays that employees receive off with pay is ten.[12] The most common holidays are Christmas, New Year's Day, Memorial Day, July 4th, Labor Day, and Thanksgiving. Holidays with pay and the proportion of employers who grant each day off are presented in Exhibits 14.5 and 14.6, respectively.

Including only vacation and holiday time, an employee normally receives one month per year off with pay.

Other Paid Time

A large number of components go into the other time off with pay. Examples of these are:

1. Jury duty
2. Serving as an election official
3. Serving as a witness in court
4. Civic duty
5. Military duty (such as the National Guard)
6. Funeral leave
7. Maternity or paternity leave
8. Sick leave
9. Time off to vote

Exhibit 14.4   *Two Vacation Policies*

Company A

Nonofficer employees

Through the fifth year of continuous service	10 days
January 1 following the year in which they complete five years of continuous service	15 days
January 1 following the year in which they complete ten years of continuous service	20 days

Officers—vice-president and below

Through the eighth year of continuous service	15 days
January 1 following the year in which they complete eight years of service	20 days

Officers—senior vice-president and above

January 1 following the date of employment	20 days

Company B

Employees with 6 months or more service are eligible for paid vacation based on this schedule:

Service	Vacation
6 months	1 week
1 year	2 weeks
5 years	2 weeks plus 3 days
10 years	3 weeks
15 years	3 weeks plus 3 days
20 years	4 weeks

10. Time off for regular attendance
11. Personal leaves
12. Sabbatical leave
13. Time off for exercise

Specific time off with pay varies partly as a function of organizational philosophy. Two examples should make the point. In one case an insurance company gives employees up to 90 minutes per day off with pay to use the company-operated physical fitness facility. This policy would be consistent with a belief that employees who are in better physical condition will perform better and also be better actuarial risks. In the second case, a pharmaceutical company, believing that managers should be good citizens in the larger society, will give employees a sabbatical for one year at half-pay to serve in local political office. The philosophy seems to be to encourage participation in local political affairs without penalizing the employee economically.

Exhibit 14.5   *Number of Paid Holidays*

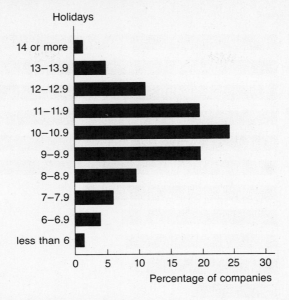

Source: Adapted from *Profile of Employee Benefits:* 1981 Edition, by Mitchell Meyer (N.Y.: The Conference Board, 1981), p. 55. Used with permission.

Indirect Costs of Pay for Time Not Worked

The direct costs associated with pay for time not worked are normally the hourly wage costs that are incurred plus the cost of other benefits (pension contributions, social security, and so forth). However, there are numerous potential indirect costs that are much less obvious. For example, the work of an employee who is granted vacation time needs to be done by someone else. Unless careful planning goes into scheduling vacations the employer may have to pay other workers overtime, to increase staffing levels, or to run at reduced production levels.

Because these indirect costs can be substantial, careful administration of time off is necessary, including planning vacation and holiday schedules.

Insurance

Organizations usually provide an array of insurance benefits for employees on either a contributory or noncontributory basis. These include health insurance, life insurance, dental insurance, and all other forms of insurance. The more important of these are discussed in this section.

Health Insurance

Almost three-fourths of the employees in the private sector, and about 80 percent of public sector employees, are covered by some type of group health

---

Exhibit 14.6　*Percentage of Companies Granting Specific Holidays*

Holidays

Holiday	
Thanksgiving Day	██████████████████████████ 100+
Christmas Day	██████████████████████████ 100+
New Year's Day	██████████████████████████ 100+
Independence Day	██████████████████████████ 100+
Labor Day	██████████████████████████ 100+
Memorial Day	██████████████████████████ 100+
Friday after Thanksgiving	████████████████ 62
Christmas Eve	█████████████ 50
Good Friday	█████████████ 49
Washington's Birthday	███████████ 42
Veteran's day	████████ 29
New Year's Eve	███████ 25
Columbus Day	██████ 23

10　20　30　40　50　60　70　80　90　100

Percentage of companies

Source: Adapted from Profile of Employee Benefits: 1981 Edition, by Mitchell Meyer (N.Y.: The Conference Board, 1981), p. 55. Used with permission.

insurance program.[13] Health insurance programs usually consist of two parts. One part is a plan to provide for basic medical services. Usually, this component has a deductible level ($50 to $500 per year) that the employee must pay, and the plan covers all other reasonable expenses up to some maximum. The second part of a typical plan is a major medical component. This component is designed to provide for catastrophic medical expenses, so that when the benefits under the first plan are exhausted, the employee has continued coverage up to some maximum (for example, $250,000). Normally major medical costs are shared on an 80 to 20 percent split between the organization and the employee, respectively. An example of one employer's health insurance plan is depicted in Exhibit 14.7.

When health insurance plans were first introduced, they were generally **contributory plans**—employees usually contributed to the cost of the plan. Increasingly, these plans have become **noncontributory** in that the employer pays the entire cost of the plan. Many plans today are designed so that all of

---

Exhibit 14.7   *A Health Insurance Plan*

Diagram of Your $100,000 Comprehensive Medical Insurance

Type A (Hospital)	Type B (Surgical)	Type C (All Other)
Hospital room and board: Standard semiprivate room rate	Surgery: In or out of the hospital	Doctor calls—hospital, home, or office
		Nurse's fees—L.P.N. or R.N.
		Dental charges—due to accident
Hospital extras	Anesthetist	X-rays
		Radiological and laboratory
Ambulance (up to $30.00 round trip)		Oxygen, blood, plasma
		Artificial eyes and limbs
		Casts, splints, trusses, braces
Emergency room within 72 hours following injury		Crutches and surgical dressings
		Rental of wheelchair, hospital bed and iron lung
		Rental of equipment for treatment of respiratory paralysis
		Prescription drugs and medicines
80% reimbursed up to $2,000, then 100% for balance of calendar year.	80% reimbursed up to $2,000, then 100% for balance of calendar year.	80% reimbursed up to $2,000, then 100% for balance of calendar year.
No deductible	No deductible	$100 calendar year deductible for all causes each year per person (maximum of three deductibles per family), 12-month accumulation.

Note: Maternity benefits are payable as any other illness.

---

the individual employee's costs are covered by the employer, but the employee contributes to the cost of family and dependent coverage.[14]

Health Insurance Cost Growth   The cost of health insurance coverage has grown substantially over the years, as shown in Exhibit 14.8.

This growth is attributable to at least three factors. First, health care costs have grown because of the increasingly comprehensive nature of coverage. As noted above, early plans often provided base care with few extras, whereas today's plans often cover many extras for which hospitals charge. For example, many early plans did not cover surgical procedures performed in the doctor's office (such as removal of warts). For the insurance to cover the procedure, the procedure would have to be performed in the hospital. Today many plans do cover surgical procedures performed in the doctor's office.

Second, health care coverage has grown partly because of doctors' fears over malpractice charges. Because doctors are sued much more frequently today they tend to order diagnostic tests that in the past they may not have ordered. This extensive diagnostic testing is billed back to the insurance carrier.

Exhibit 14.8 *Growth Rates of Gross National Product and National Health Expenditures*

| | Gross National Product | | National Health Expenditures | | |
Calendar Year	Amount in Billions	Annual Rate of Growth	Amount in Billions	Annualized Percentage Change	NHE as Percent of GNP
1950	$ 286.5	11.1%	$ 12.7	12.2%	4.4%
1955	400.0	6.9	17.7	7.0	4.4
1960	506.5	4.8	26.9	8.7	5.3
1965	691.0	6.4	41.7	9.2	6.0
1970	992.7	5.2	74.7	13.6	7.5
1971	1,077.6	8.6	83.3	11.5	7.7
1972	1,185.9	10.1	93.5	12.3	7.9
1973	1,326.4	11.8	103.2	10.3	7.8
1974	1,434.2	8.1	116.4	12.8	8.1
1975	1,549.2	8.0	132.7	14.0	8.6
1976	1,718.0	10.9	149.7	12.8	8.7
1977	1,918.3	11.7	169.2	13.1	8.8
1978	2,163.9	12.8	189.3	11.9	8.7
1979	2,417.8	11.7	215.0	13.5	8.9
1980	2,631.7	8.8	249.0	15.8	9.5
1981	2,954.1	12.3	286.6	15.1	9.7
1982	3,073.0	4.0	322.4	12.5	10.5
1983	3,310.5	7.7	362.3[a]	12.4	10.9

[a] Estimated

Source: U.S. Department of Health and Human Services, Health Care Financing Administration, *Health Care Financing Review*, March 1983.

Third, health costs have grown because both labor and capital costs have increased in hospitals. The cost of equipment has increased dramatically because of its greater sophistication, and is passed on to the consumer. Similarly, health care is labor intensive and it is necessary to pass these costs on to the consumer. The consumer in this case is the health insurance carrier, which then increases the premiums.

One of the major issues of national debate in the 1980s is the containment of health care costs. Some suggested remedies are pressuring doctors to keep fees down, increasing the deductible to discourage overuse of health care, and introducing more competition into the field (for example, by allowing doctors to advertise their fees). Any one of these approaches is likely to be only partially successful since the causes of the growth of health care costs are numerous.

Health Maintenance Organizations As noted in Chapter 5, health maintenance organizations (HMOs) are designed to provide comprehensive medical coverage for employees at fixed premium rates, and to optimize the presumed benefits associated with preventive medicine. If an HMO is available in the employer's area and the employer already provides health insurance, the employer is required to provide an HMO option to its employees. The employer is obligated to provide coverage equal to the cost of conventional health insurance provided. The coverage does not have to be equal.

Often the coverage under an HMO can be substantially larger for the same dollar cost than under more traditional health insurance programs. While it is hard to attribute this fact to a precise cause, it may be due in part to at least three factors. First, HMOs have fixed labor costs—doctors agree to work for a salary. Second, HMOs stress preventive features (it is presumably cheaper to cure someone at an early stage of illness). Third, some HMOs may use paramedical personnel (doctors may delegate some duties to narrowly trained specialists).

Dental Insurance   Early health insurance programs provided for rather limited coverage, and the trend is to broaden the coverage. One way in which coverage is expanding is by considering dental coverage as part of the basic health plan. One study found that dental coverage increased from 8 percent of the firms surveyed in 1974 to 41 percent of the firms surveyed in 1981. In the survey, dental plans were noncontributory about two-thirds of the time.[15]

Life and Accident Insurance

Many employers provide life insurance. Under a typical plan, the employee's life is insured up to double the annual wage or salary. Life insurance plans can be contributory or noncontributory, but all of them have the advantage of lower group rates.

A second type of plan provides accidental death and dismemberment insurance. These plans typically have a fixed scale of benefits so that an employee or a beneficiary receives a fixed amount in the event of accidental death or dismemberment. Such plans can also be contributory or noncontributory, and premium structures take advantage of group rates.

Long-Term Disability Insurance

Employers typically cover short-term disability through their sick leave policy, discussed as pay for time not worked. There is also concern over long-range disability coverage when an employee is sick or injured and out of work for long periods of time. This situation is often covered through some form of long-term disability insurance. For example, an employee off the job for more than six months could draw against the disability insurance plan. These plans provide for coverage of up to 100 percent of a person's net pay.

Employers often make an effort to integrate the short-term and long-term disability plan. An example of one employer's plan is depicted in Exhibit 14.9.

Other Insurance

Just as health-related insurances have become more comprehensive over time, so have the types of group insurance offered in general. Today, some employ-

---

Exhibit 14.9   *A Disability Insurance Plan*

If you become disabled, the Company will continue your salary based on your length of service.

At full salary: 3 months
At one-half salary: 3 months

Should total disability extend beyond 6 months, you will receive a monthly income from the long-term disability (LTD) plan.

Your monthly income would be $X,XXX.XX

The benefits from the LTD plan are adjusted according to received benefits from governmental and other company-sponsored disability plans such as social security and workers' compensation.

Additional Disability Benefits If Totally Disabled

Your basic group life insurance will continue (after 12 months of total disability) to age 65, or to age 70 if disability occurs after age 65, at no cost to you.
If you enrolled, Permaplan premiums will be waived up to age 65.
The long-term disability plan makes your contributions to the retirement system for as long as you are disabled up to age 65.
After one year of disability, you may elect to withdraw all or part of your profit sharing or all of your retirement system accounts or both. The total value of your accounts was:

Profit sharing as of 10/1/83: $XX,XXX.XX
Retirement system as of 9/30/83: $ XXXX.XX

---

ers offer auto insurance, legal insurance, and liability insurance. Other examples of this trend are group home insurance and bond insurance.

Other Benefits

Other employee benefits include:

1. Discounts on goods and services
2. Subsidized employee meals
3. Moving expenses
4. Severance pay

These benefits are discussed below.

Discounts on Goods and Services

Numerous employers allow their employees to purchase company products or services at reduced rates. A gas station owner may sell gas to employees at cost, or auto manufacturers may allow employees to purchase cars at a fixed discount. These programs stimulate demand for the organization's products or services, as well as allow the employee to obtain cheaper goods and services. A related benefit is when an employer arranges with other producers of goods and services to provide their output at reduced rates. For example, an employer may arrange with a local amusement park to give its employees a 50 percent discount on admission.

Subsidized Meals

Numerous organizations provide for full or partially funded cafeterias. One reason may be a conviction on the part of the organization that employees who are well fed will work better. Another reason may simply be that there are inadequate meal facilities off premises. Still another reason may be that the company does not want employees to stray off for three-beer or martini lunches. Regardless of the motivations, these programs can be extremely costly. In one situation the organization subsidizes 65 percent of the cost of lunches in the company cafeteria.

Moving Expenses

Employers with multiple operating sites often provide employees with relocation expense coverage. This benefit may be necessary to encourage employees to relocate without penalty. (Even with relocation expenses covered, however, employers are finding it harder to get employees to relocate.)[16]

Severance Pay

Very often an employer will provide an employee with the equivalent of two weeks of pay upon termination (whether voluntary or not). This benefit is designed to aid the employee in the transition from one job to another.

Other companies provide severance pay to employees only if they are involuntarily terminated. Usually such severance pay is designed to help employees during the transition from one employer to another. An example of a severance pay policy schedule is depicted in Exhibit 14.10.

Exhibit 14.10 *A Severance Pay Policy*

Time with Employer	Severance Pay[a]
Probationary period	None
Postprobationary period–2 years	2 weeks base pay
2–5 years	3 weeks base pay
5–10 years	5 weeks base pay
10–15 years	6 weeks base pay
15–20 years	7 weeks base pay
Greater than 20 years	8 weeks base pay

[a] Severance pay is paid only when the termination is company initiated.

Legally Required Benefits

As noted in Chapter 5 in the discussion on legal constraints, employers are required to pay into certain mandatory programs. The major compulsory programs are Social Security, unemployment compensation, and workers' compensation. Each is discussed briefly below. The reader should refer back to Chapter 5 for more detail.

Social Security

Just as individuals pay a portion of their wages or salaries into Social Security, employers too must contribute to the Social Security funds. Social Security funds (formally titled Old-Age, Survivors', Disability, and Health Insurance) are provided by individual contributions and matching contributions from organizations. The Federal Insurance Contribution Act (FICA) imposes the tax. As of 1986 the amount required by an employer is 7.15 percent to match the individual's contribution of 7.15 percent of the first $42,000 dollars in wages. Recent amendments to Social Security legislation call for substantial increases in both the percentage rates and the total dollar amount subject to taxation.[17] After 1986, the percentage rate will remain at 7.15 percent; but it will increase to 7.51 percent in 1988 and 1989. The maximum dollar amount for Social Security is tied to the average national wage, which cannot be determined years in advance.

Employers typically integrate their private pension plans with Social Security so that employees can be assured of a living income after retirement.[18] Since 1979 employers have had the option of paying not only their share of the FICA tax, but also the employee's share. If the employer pays the employee's share, reducing the employee's gross pay by this amount, it costs the employer less in total wages and taxes on an annualized basis and may also put the employee in a lower tax bracket.[19]

Workers' Compensation

Workers' compensation is required under state laws and requires the employer either to purchase workers' compensation insurance or to insure itself. As noted in Chapter 5, the premium rates are directly a function of claim experience. As a result, organizations are often motivated to keep claims to a minimum by stressing employee safety.

Unemployment Compensation

Just as with workers' compensation, organizations are required to pay state unemployment tax premiums on the basis of actuarial experience. To some extent employers have a motive to maintain stable employment and save on payments.

Benefits Decision Making

Of central concern to compensation decision makers is the question of which benefits to offer. It is useful to think along two separate dimensions in answering this question. The first dimension is the **benefit level** (analogous to a wage level). Second is the dimension of the **benefit structure** (analogous to a wage structure). Benefit level is constrained by product market considerations, just as the wage level is constrained. The benefit structure is constrained by labor market considerations and employee preferences.

Benefit Level and Product Market Benefit Surveys

The chapter on wage and salary surveys suggested that organizations ought to survey their product market for benefits. The purpose of this survey is less to determine the actual components of the benefits package than to estimate the actual costs of such benefits. Just as ability to pay constrains wage levels, benefits levels are also constrained by ability to pay. The concern in product market surveys of benefits is the cost of those benefits, regardless of the composition of benefits.

Benefit Structure and Labor Market Benefit Surveys

On the other hand, a survey of benefits in the labor market is particularly concerned with the structure of benefit packages. This concern stems from an assumption that benefit packages are compared when individuals make employment decisions. Under this assumption it would be important for an organization to provide benefit packages of similar composition to its labor market competitors. However, if benefits are not used by employees in making decisions to join the organization, then such surveys are less critical.

Because of the fragmented nature of benefits, it is probably more important to offer roughly similar benefits than identical ones. For example, if the preponderance of firms in a labor market area offer dental coverage, then a low-wage firm might want to offer this too, although it may make the plan contributory on the part of employees. Whether the organization can afford the plan at all, however, is a function of ability to pay constraints.

Benefit Structure and Survey of Current Employees

A second way to assess which benefits the organization might offer is to survey present employees. Such a survey is particularly useful if the employer is considering increasing the benefits package. The rationale behind surveying present employees is that not all benefits are valued equally by all employees. The organization should spend the money on increased benefits in areas that will get the most recognition from employees.

Benefit Structure and Goals

It should go without saying that the structure of the benefits package should reflect the goals of the organization (as constrained by the firm's ability to pay). The organization should question its values and goals and decide what it wants its benefits program to achieve. For example, some organizations may want to stress retirement programs, while other organizations may want to stress both short-run and long-run disability programs.

Contributory versus Noncontributory Benefits

An important decision-making issue centers on whether or not the benefit programs will be contributory or noncontributory. Will employees pay part or all of the costs, or will the employer pay the entire cost? This decision has an impact upon both the level of benefits and the benefit structure, since a higher level and a wider variety of benefits may be possible if employees share in the costs.

Another important consideration in deciding between contributory and noncontributory programs is that of having employees recognize the value of their benefits. One employer requires employees to pay 10 percent of the costs of all benefit plans where contributions are feasible. This employer's rationale is that employees have a greater appreciation of the true cost of benefits (and, therefore, realize their true value) when 10 percent of the cost is deducted from their paycheck each month.

Future Trends in Employee Benefits

Future trends in employee benefits are less than clear-cut. On the one hand, societal values seem to suggest that there will be a continued growth in benefit levels caused by continuing efforts to make benefit programs more comprehensive. For example, the recent trend to provide dental benefits can be viewed as one step in making health care coverage more comprehensive.

Organizations may also make a more systematic and sensible package out of their short-term disability plans and their long-range disability plans. Today, many firms' sick-pay plans cover an employee only for two to four weeks. These firms' long-term disability plans do not begin until the employee has been off the job for six months. This gap in benefits is a natural one to fill, and benefit levels may continue to grow.

On the other hand, the serious structural changes in industry experienced during the early 1980s, along with the attendant world recession, have made organizations more fiscally conservative, and as a consequence, they may be less likely to continue to increase benefit levels. Further, if benefits programs are taxed as direct income in the future, they may be less desirable to both employers and employees. Which of these forces will dominate in the future is not clear.

Cafeteria Benefit Plans

One trend in benefits packages has been a cafeteria approach to benefits. Under this approach, an employee is provided with a core set of benefits, and then may choose among other benefits.[20] For example, the employee with a very sick dependent might prefer more health care coverage, while an employee who has a large number of dependents may elect to carry more life insurance. There is a maximum total dollar amount to the benefits an employee may choose, and the employee can select a benefits package that fits his or her needs at a point in time.

Cafeteria benefits plans have not enjoyed widespread use for at least two reasons. First, the Internal Revenue Service considers the cash/noncash options feature of cafeteria plans as placing the dollar value of those benefits in the wage/salary component of pay. (Some plans allow an employee the option of choosing between cash or benefits.) The dollar value of those benefits may not be tax-sheltered, and the employer and employee may lose the tax-sheltered advantage of traditional benefit packages.

A second and perhaps more important reason why cafeteria plans are not offered more often is that they require both a solid core of benefits and optional benefits. A firm that can afford to provide a cafeteria plan must have a relatively high ability to pay in the first place. Not many employers can afford such affluent benefit levels.

Other concerns about the feasibility of cafeteria plans are the administrative costs of constantly changing benefits levels for individual employees, and the impact of self-selection of benefits on actuarially based costs. To deal with the first problem, organizations typically allow employees to change their benefit plan structure only once each year. The second problem is not well defined as of this date, but it makes intuitive sense, for example, that unhealthy workers would prefer higher health benefit levels. If enough unhealthy employees acted this way, the cost of the group plan would increase to provide the benefits. However, no good data are available on this point. It is unlikely that cafeteria plans will grow substantially in the next decade.[21]

Retirement Plans

Another area in which there may be change on the horizon is private retirement plans. As the concept of Social Security has changed over the years from providing partial retirement income to providing full retirement income, and as its costs have soared correspondingly, it would not be surprising if employers with private plans freeze their benefit levels, and if employers without pension plans increasingly decide not to implement private plans. There are no good data to support or refute these suggested trends.

Taxation of Benefits

In the 1980s one of the major issues is likely to be the taxation of employee benefits. To combat mounting federal deficits Congress and the executive branch of government are looking for new ways to raise revenues. One approach is to take away the tax-sheltered status of employee benefits. Given that benefits have grown substantially due to this preferred status, it would not be surprising to see a cessation in benefit growth and perhaps even a decline if they lose this status.

Summary

This chapter has focused upon employee benefits. Links between theory and practice were discussed. Benefits in all likelihood do not influence performance, and they probably do not influence joining behavior, but their major impact is probably motivating retention.

Various forms of employee benefits were discussed. The major benefits, in terms of costs, are pensions, pay for time not worked, and insurances. Reasons for the growth in employee benefits are employer and employee attitudes toward income maintenance, and preferential tax treatment of benefits.

Recent trends in benefits were discussed. Cafeteria benefit plans will probably not become commonplace. There may actually be a decrease in the number of firms providing private pension plans if Social Security evolves into a comprehensive retirement plan.

Discussion Questions

1. Compare and contrast a defined benefit pension plan with a pension plan funded by profit sharing.

2. Benefits do not motivate employees—discuss this proposition.

3. Why have benefits grown so much as a percentage of base pay?

4. List the major types of employee benefits. Which type has the greatest growth potential? Why?

5. Discuss an employer's concern with employee benefits from both a labor market and product market perspective. What strategies might be available to an employer whose benefits package is noncompetitive with other labor market firms but competitive with product market firms?

Exercise

1. As a class project, each student is to identify five people who work full time. Develop a list of all of the benefits discussed in this chapter. Ask each full-time worker which four of these benefits he or she prefers and why. In class, discuss and make some generalizations about your findings.

References

1 "Benefit Boosts: Most Firms Expand Health Coverage to Keep Pace with Inflation," *The Wall Street Journal,* February 23, 1982, p. 1. J. M. Burcke, "Benefit Bounty: Offerings Range from Vacations to Free Lunch," *Business Insurance* 16 (July 5, 1982). "Big Changes in Employee Benefits Seen," *National Underwriter* 86 (August 27, 1982): p. 32.

2 Frederick S. Hills and R. Eugene Hughes, "Salaries and Fringe Benefits in the Academic Labor Market: Internal/External Labor Markets and Geographic Differentials," paper presented at the National Academy of Management meetings, Orlando, Florida, August 1977.

3 J. McCroskey, "Work and Families: What Is the Employer's Responsibility?" *Personnel Journal* 61 (January 1982): pp. 30–38.

4 "Stock-Options Are Offered to More Employees, due to Favorable 1981 Tax-Law Change," *The Wall Street Journal,* May 25, 1982, p. 1.

5 Robert Sibson, "The High Cost of Hiring," *Nation's Business,* February 1975, pp. 85–88.

6 Robert D. Paul and Jack M. Elkin, "Principles of Plan Design," in Fred K. Foulkes, ed., *Employee Benefits Handbook,* (New York: Warren, Gorham, and Lamont, 1982): pp. 2–8.

7 B. Densmore, "More Firms Self-Funding Benefit Plans," *Business Insurance* 16 (April 26, 1982): pp. 14–15. K. F. Maldonado, "Special Qualification Requirements for Defined Benefit Plans Covering Self-Employed Individuals or Shareholder Employees," *Taxes* 59 (November 1981): pp. 784–796.

8 *Ibid.,* p. 786.

9 Robert A. Bildersee, "Minimum Vesting Standards for Qualified Plans," in Fred K. Foulkes, ed., *Employee Benefits Handbook* (New York: Warren, Gorham, and Lamont, 1982): pp. 14–31, 32.

10 "Profit Sharing Arrangements in Cafeteria Plans," *CPA Journal* 52 (August 1982): pp. 58–59.

11 Burcke, "Benefit Bounty: Offerings Range from Vacation to Free Lunch."

12 Mitchell Meyer, *Profile of Employee Benefits* (New York: Conference Board, 1981): p. 55.

13 *Daily Labor Report,* Bureau of National Affairs, Washington, D.C., September 11, 1981, p. 1.

14 "HMO's Flourish as an Alternative Form of Health Care Coverage for Workers," *The Wall Street Journal,* December 14, 1982, p. 1. L. Palmer, "Survey Finds Employees Happy with HMO Treatment," *Business Insurance* 16 (August 9, 1982): p. 3.

15 Meyer, *Profile of Employee Benefits,* p. 13.

16 American Management Association, *Compensation Review* 12, number 3 (third quarter, 1980): pp. 11–13.

17 "Families Paying the Price of Social Security: An Editorial Page Article Highlighting the Necessity for Social Security," *The Wall Street Journal,* April 2, 1982, p. 22.

18 "Offbeat Benefits Multiply as a Way to Keep Workers Happy Inexpensively," *The Wall Street Journal,* July 7, 1982, p. 1.

19 J. L. Martin, "A Payroll Tax Alternative Using FICA 2," *Compensation Review* (third quarter, 1979): pp. 30–38.

20 J. Geisel, "Bill Would Limit Types of Benefits Offered in Cafeteria Plans," *Business Insurance* 17 (August 1, 1983): p. 1.

21 M. Zippo, "Flexible Benefits: Just the Beginning," *Personnel* 59 (July/August 1982): pp. 56–58. R. B. Cockrum, "Has the Time Come for Employee Cafeteria Plans?" *Personnel Administrator* 27 (July 1982): pp. 66–72. "Profit-Sharing Arrangements in Cafeteria Plans," *CPA Journal* 52 (August 1982): pp. 58–59.

C H A P T E R

15

Noneconomic Rewards

· **Learning Objectives**

· **Introduction**

· **Noneconomic Rewards**

Economic versus Noneconomic Rewards
Noneconomic Rewards and Human Needs
Work Adjustment Theory

· **Job-Related Rewards**

Intrinsic Job Rewards
Extrinsic Job Rewards

· **Non-Job-Based Rewards**

Organization Status
Geographic Location

· **Organizational Responses**
   to Noneconomic Rewards

Job Design and Redesign

Flexitime
Professional Development Programs
Job Posting and Bidding Systems
Supervisory Training
Organizational Due Process
Quality Circles
Management by Objectives
Company-Sponsored Events

· **Noneconomic Reward Decision Making**

Employee Attitude Surveys
The Minnesota Satisfaction Questionnaire

· **Impact of Noneconomic Reward Programs**
   on Economic Rewards

Indirect Impact
Direct Impact

· **Exercise**

Learning Objectives

To reinforce the concept that noneconomic rewards can be powerful motivators of individual behaviors.

To develop a theoretical framework (the work adjustment theory) that integrates both economic and noneconomic rewards into worker motivation.

To identify some of the more common types of noneconomic rewards.

To discuss how organizations respond to employee needs for noneconomic rewards.

To learn how organizations can assess employee desires for noneconomic rewards.

To learn the impact of noneconomic rewards on employee behavior.

To learn the relationship between economic and noneconomic rewards.

Introduction

Employees often make employment decisions on criteria other than economic compensation, or wages and benefits. This chapter discusses in some detail the types of noneconomic rewards that employees seek in employment. The chapter also examines some of the programs employers engage in to enhance the noneconomic aspects of employment.

The objectives of this chapter are to identify types of noneconomic rewards, discuss programs operated by employers to meet employees' desire for noneconomic rewards, and evaluate the relative merits of these programs.

Noneconomic Rewards

Noneconomic rewards are defined in this text as employment outcomes that do not directly affect the employee's wage or benefits. Many types of rewards flow from employment. Examples are power and status, geographic locale, and friendships. The numbers and types of noneconomic rewards are enormous. Examples of the types of noneconomic rewards obtained from employment are shown in Exhibit 15.1.

For purposes of discussion this text will use two categories of noneconomic rewards: job-based and non-job-based. (This distinction is arbitrary, and other categories might be established.)

Economic versus Noneconomic Rewards

There is little doubt that individuals work, in large part, to provide for themselves and their dependents. To this extent work can be looked at as an instrumental activity. That is, individuals work because work is one way to earn the economic outcomes needed to satisfy their needs for food, clothing, and shelter, among other things.

To assume that other types of rewards from work are not important to individuals is a mistake. A worker who dislikes the duties of a job may leave it for that reason. Another employee may decide to stay with an employer

---

Exhibit 15.1 *Noneconomic Rewards*

The work flow system
Optimum information flows
The number of operations
Complexity of the work
Skill requirements
Attention required by the work
Predictability
Knowing in advance what the tasks are
Job status and prestige
Job importance and level
Opportunity to think of other things while
   working
Interruptions in the work
Having enough time for personal needs
Safety of the job
Cleanliness of the work
Pleasant working conditions
The quality of tools and equipment
Making a quality product
Value of product or service
Usefulness of the product
Clear authority symbols
Well-defined rules
Knowing how my work fits in
Opportunity to teach new people
Compatibility of interactions required by the
   job with preferred interaction pattern
Dominance over other people
Authority over other people
Power
Opportunity to compete with others
Low-pressure supervision
Democratic supervision
Competent supervision
Representation by supervision
General supervision
Nonpunitive supervision
Fair supervision

Pleasant co-workers
Cooperative job atmosphere
Consideration by supervision
Opportunity to develop friendships
Acceptance by other people
Emotional significance of the task
The job as "a cause"
Job familiarity
Enjoyment of the activity
Enjoyment of energy expenditure
Amount of physical work
Keeping busy
Feeling of contribution
Feeling of having a purpose in life
Feeling of completion
How the work pulls me along
Flexibility of movement while working
Pride in work results
Seeing the results of my work
Knowing exactly how my equipment works
How fast time goes
Compatibility of work requirements with
   other roles
Compatibility of work requirements with self-
   image
Opportunity for promotion (advancement)
Status
Recognition (appreciation and praise)
Power
Influence on decisions
Participation in problem solving
Setting performance goals
Variety
Responsibility
Autonomy
Freedom
Independence

---

because of the colleagues in the department, or because of the influence he or she has. Still another person may choose a lower paying job in order to stay in a particular geographic area. Noneconomic rewards are important aspects of work that shape individual behavior.

Noneconomic Rewards and Human Needs

The human needs models presented in Chapter 2 are useful in considering noneconomic rewards, especially Maslow's hierarchy of needs.

According to Maslow's model, individuals have a range of needs to satisfy, from physiological needs (food, water, shelter) to self-actualization needs (to live to one's potential). Money may satisfy some of these needs; however, others are satisfied in other ways.

Work environments provide more or less satisfaction for some of the individual's needs. For example, some employees may value large amounts of social interaction. Some jobs provide considerable social interaction (such as secretary or salesperson), while other jobs provide very little social interaction (such as night watchman or auditor). Individuals who value social interaction would be expected to be more satisfied with jobs that provide for this need. These individuals would also be more likely to stay with the organization. Provision for noneconomic rewards in this case should have particular impact upon influencing the individual's decision to join and stay with the organization.

One of the major problems with noneconomic rewards management is that since there is so much variability in individuals' needs, it is often hard to know which programs will influence which individuals. However, organizations are able to design programs to attempt to satisfy these needs, and this process is discussed in a later section.

Work Adjustment Theory

The noneconomic rewards and employee satisfaction that result from employment can be more easily explained in terms of work adjustment theory. A graphic model of work adjustment theory is presented in Exhibit 15.2.

Although this theory has much broader applications, the comments here are restricted to only the rewards derived from work. The portion of the model in Exhibit 15.2 below the dashed line is pertinent here.

One of the circles in Exhibit 15.2 is labelled "Individual," and the other is labelled "Job." Every time an individual accepts a job in an organization, a job and individual dyad is formed. Individuals bring needs to the work environment that they would like to have satisfied. Similarly, each job has a **reinforcer system,** also shown in Exhibit 15.2. Jobs provide such things as autonomy (or lack of), good and poor co-workers, a sense of task completion, and so forth. The predominant focus of this chapter is to identify and discuss both the needs people bring to the job and the attributes of jobs which satisfy those needs.

Exhibit 15.2 indicates that individuals investigate if the reinforcer system of the job is compatible with their needs. In work adjustment theory this compatibility is referred to as **correspondence**. That is, is there a correspondence between the individual's needs and the reinforcer system? Correspondence is a continuous variable, and can range from extremely high to completely nonexistent.

According to work adjustment theory, the degree of correspondence will predict the degree of employee satisfaction with the job. For example, suppose an employee has a need to interact with people. If this employee is put into a small cubicle that prohibits interacting with others and is told to assemble parts, there will be a mismatch (or a lack of correspondence) between the

Exhibit 15.2 *Prediction of Work Adjustment*

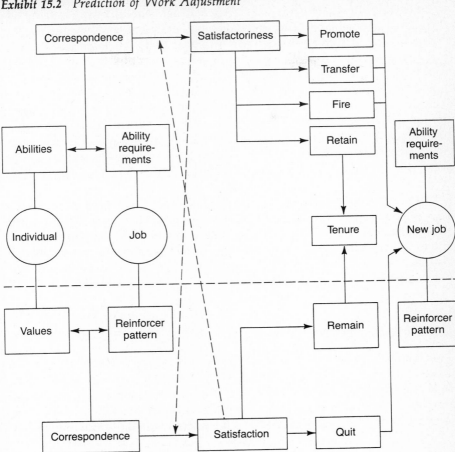

Source: From *A Psychological Theory of Work Adjustment,* by Rene V. Dawis and Lloyd H. Lofquist (University of Minnesota Press, 1984). Used with permission.

employee's needs and the reinforcer system of the job. On the other hand, if this same employee is put at a large work table with a large number of other assemblers at the same table, there is likely to be a relatively high level of correspondence between the employee's need for interaction and the reinforcer system. In the former case the employee is likely to be dissatisfied with the job, while in the latter case the employee is likely to be satisfied.

This example is overly simplistic in that employees have many needs to satisfy at work, and jobs have many different dimensions for reinforcement. It is more appropriate to think in terms of satisfaction as a weighted average of all needs balanced against all reinforcer dimensions.

Job satisfaction in this model is a person's affective orientation to the job—

that is, how the worker feels about the job. Satisfaction in Exhibit 15.2 predicts whether a person will remain in the job (reach high tenure), or will quit the job and seek a new job. This inverse relationship between employee satisfaction and turnover has been established empirically as well.[1] It is important to try to maintain a correspondence between employees' needs and the reinforcer system of jobs if the organization hopes to motivate membership.

Some writers suggest that the work adjustment theory is too narrow a focus for understanding rewards in organizations since it focuses directly upon the job itself. For example, the reinforcer properties of work are larger than just the job (i.e., organizational prestige is not necessarily a job characteristic). Some writers prefer the concept of organizational climate. Organizational climate is a much broader grouping of variables that potentially provide reinforcement to people.[2]

In fact, many of the potential noneconomic rewards identified in Exhibit 15.1 extend beyond the characteristics of the immediate job. However, the work adjustment theory is still valid in that it identifies the reinforcer system, and the correspondence between employee needs and the reinforcer system. It also shows that turnover is an important negative consequence of low employee satisfaction.

Job-Related Rewards

Two types of job-related noneconomic rewards are particularly important to individuals: intrinsic and extrinsic rewards. Intrinsic rewards are associated with characteristics of the job itself, such as status, autonomy, and sense of accomplishment. Extrinsic rewards are associated with the immediate job environment, such as supervisory feedback (or recognition) and social interaction.[3]

Intrinsic Job Rewards

There is almost an unending list of intrinsic job rewards.[4] Only a few of the more common ones are discussed here.

Job Autonomy Job autonomy has to do with the amount of discretion or freedom that an employee has in carrying out the duties of the job. Jobs vary tremendously in this reward. In some cases the employee has a wide range of discretion, and in other cases the job may be highly routinized with little room for autonomous action.[5]

Some types of employees prefer more autonomy than others. For example, highly trained employees would likely prefer more autonomy than unskilled operative employees. At the same time, there are likely to be differences within the unskilled operative group as well, so that some of these employees may prefer more autonomy than others. Because there is considerable variation both within and between employee groups on desires for autonomy, organizations should survey employee attitudes to determine what employees want, as discussed in a later section. (The comment about preferences for autonomy can also be made with regard to other types of noneconomic rewards as well.)

Task Completion Task completion refers to whether the job allows the incumbent to observe the product of the incumbent's efforts, or if the job outcomes are so vague as to never be seen. For example, a painter in a paint room might only spray a primer coat of paint and never see the finished product. The employee may never know what the final paint job looks like. On the other hand, a painter may be responsible for applying not only the primer coat but the finish coat too, and can see the completed paint job. It is often argued that task completion is important in order for employees to identify with their work.[6]

Power and Influence Another variable in which jobs differ is the amount of power or influence the job incumbent exercises. Power and influence vary from having control over others to simply having the ability to make a financial decision. Power and influence are related to job autonomy, however, the term as used here means that an employee has an impact upon activities outside of the job domain. Individuals are probably motivated to obtain power and influence for numerous reasons, including the need for power, the need to control others, and the need to control their environments.[7]

Achievement Achievement can be thought of as the need to accomplish something worthwhile. What is worthwhile to one employee may not be worthwhile to another, and how the employee looks at a job can to a large extent determine how much achievement is felt. The proverbial distinction between two masons—one who is "laying bricks," and the other who is "building a cathedral"—is appropriate here. At the same time, depending on the way jobs are structured, there may be more or less opportunity to find achievement in a job.[8] It should also be noted that high levels of intrinsic job rewards in general not only can result in employee satisfaction with the job, but can also have an impact on motivational level and, therefore, performance level.[9]

Extrinsic Job Rewards

Extrinsic job rewards are those job-related rewards external to the work itself. Money and employee benefits are extrinsic rewards, but, since they are economic rewards, and this chapter focuses upon noneconomic rewards, they are not discussed here. This section discusses just a few of the extrinsic job rewards associated with employment.

Supervisory Recognition One of the most common, and least recognized extrinsic rewards is recognition from the supervisor. Supervisory recognition accomplishes several things. It provides feedback so that the employees know how well they are doing. It also provides extrinsic satisfaction in that good performance and work behaviors are recognized as such.[10]

Insensitive supervisors argue that people get paid to do their job, so they should do it right. These supervisors are assuming that money alone motivates or is the most powerful motivator. They forget that supervisory recognition is a powerful motivator in its own right and may be the most powerful motivator on a day-to-day basis.

Congruent Leadership Styles   There is a considerable body of literature which deals with contingency theories of leadership.[11] This literature notes that some leaders are authoritarian while others are democratic, for example. Leaders can be directive or participative and have high or low position power. There is also some evidence that jobs differ in the degree to which one particular leadership style is effective. In addition, some employees may prefer one leadership style and others prefer yet other leadership styles.[12] The superior and subordinate relationship can be a source of reward or frustration for an employee depending upon whether or not there is a congruence between the style an employee prefers or expects, and the style actually used by the supervisor.

Social Interaction   The Hawthorne studies of the 1930s showed that individuals receive extensive satisfaction from social interaction on the job. The need for social interaction varies across individuals, yet all individuals value some minimum level of social interaction. This need can be met both through informal associations on the job, or through formal activities (such as picnics or company-sponsored sports teams) at the work environment.

Non-Job-Based Rewards

Non-job-based rewards can be defined as rewards associated with belonging to the employing organization but not associated with the actual work performed. These are discussed next.

Organization Status

Just as jobs within organizations carry different levels of status and prestige, organizations within industries and geographic areas carry different levels of status and prestige in the eyes of employees and job candidates. Within a particular labor market a truck assembly plant may carry greater employment prestige than a local trucking firm, which in turn may carry greater prestige than a local machine shop. Organizational prestige may vary systematically with other variables (for example, wage level or employment stability), but there is no good empirical data to support this point. The case of banks is contrary to this point. That is, often banking is a relatively low wage occupation within a labor area, yet it carries considerable prestige by the nature of the work.

Geographic Location

There is little doubt that geographical preferences operate as a reward for employees. This preference may not be true for all employees or potential employees, however, many cases can be cited where individuals wish to live in specific areas. One person may want to live in Denver, another in Sleepy Eye, Minnesota, and still another in Houston. Having made the choice to live in a particular geographic locale, the individual is then restricted in the employment search to that area.

The empirical evidence is too sketchy to show clearly the dynamics of geographic choice. However, a number of factors probably shape this decision process. A chief factor may be a person's social network, including family ties and friendships. Also, some individuals probably feel more comfortable within some subcultures than others (urban versus rural, for example) and make decisions on that basis. Still others may prefer one climate to another, or one topographic environment to another. In any event, such preferences will affect the rewards received from employment. Congruence between preferences and actual outcomes should enhance rewards; lack of congruence should decrease rewards.

Organizational Responses to Noneconomic Rewards

Noneconomic rewards are valued differently by different individuals, and as a result it is extremely difficult for organizations to manage these rewards efficiently. Regardless, organizations attempt to provide noneconomic rewards to employees. A number of the more common programs are described in this section.

Job Design and Redesign

One of the more systematic ways in which organizations provide for noneconomic rewards is through job design or redesign. In job redesign the organization attempts to find the most efficient way to design jobs. The most efficient design of a job is not necessarily the most effective design. Besides the most efficient design, the organization should consider the tradeoffs between productivity gains (or increased revenue) and operating costs (including materials waste, turnover, error rates, and so on). Job design or redesign involves finding the best set of tradeoffs between productivity and costs.[13]

In a historical context, job redesign has gone through two stages. In the first stage, prior to the Hawthorne experiment era, the primary concern of job design was the greater and greater simplification of jobs. During this time the jobs were made as routinized and productive as possible. The Hawthorne experiments revealed that jobs could be oversimplified and that very often human costs were not factored into the analysis of what was the most efficient. In stage two of job redesign the human element in the design of jobs was considered.

Job Enlargement   Job enlargement is a method of job redesign that increases the number of tasks in a person's job. Job enlargement is represented in Exhibit 15.3, in which the original job shown in part A is enlarged in part B.

Exhibit 15.3   *Job Enlargement and Job Enrichment*

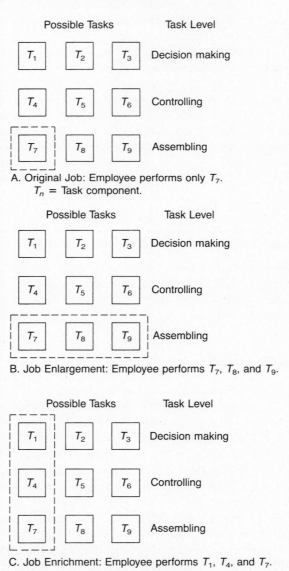

A. Original Job: Employee performs only T_7.
T_n = Task component.

B. Job Enlargement: Employee performs T_7, T_8, and T_9.

C. Job Enrichment: Employee performs T_1, T_4, and T_7.

For example, an assembler originally may fit two wheels on an axle assembly. After job enlargement, the assembler may put the two wheels on the axle assembly and also attach the entire wheel and axle system to the chassis. The principal idea behind job enlargement is that jobs that are narrowly defined provide no sense of task completion and boredom is excessively high. Adding more tasks to the job was thought to relieve the boredom by increasing the job's cycle time, and to increase the incumbent's sense of achievement. A later section shows that job enlargement does not seem to work as well as its proponents claim.

Job Enrichment   Job enrichment is a second approach to redesigning jobs and is meant to increase the job's discretion. Job enrichment is pictorially presented in part C of Exhibit 15.3. Using the previous example of an assembler who originally attaches two wheels to the axle, after job enrichment the assembler still attaches two wheels to the axle but also is responsible for quality control checks. This type of vertical enlargement of a job is thought to enhance the job in terms of autonomy, pride, sense of accomplishment, and decision making.[14] Job enrichment alone or in combination with job enlargement has been shown to enhance productivity and employee satisfaction, which in turn should result in less turnover and absenteeism.[15]

Job redesign can be an effective technique for providing job-based noneconomic rewards. Whether this technique will work in a particular organization is an empirical question. That is, whether or not any given organization will realize gains from job enrichment is a question that can be answered only by experimentation.

Job redesign also means a change in the economic reward system. If jobs are enriched so that all employees are exercising discretion on their jobs and are working as skilled workers, then the economic value of these jobs will be enhanced. The jobs will need to be reanalyzed and reevaluated within the job evaluation system. At the extreme, this could mean a common and higher pay rate for all jobs.[16]

Flexitime

A flexible work schedule, called flexitime, spreads the workday over a longer period of time than the regular eight-hour day, and allows the employees to decide which hours they will work. An example of a flexitime schedule appears in Exhibit 15.4.

A workday in a typical flexitime program might extend from 6:00 A.M. to 6:00 P.M. During this time there will be a **core** work time (such as from 9:00 to 12:00 and from 1:00 to 3:00) when all employees are required to be at their jobs.[17] The employees can then select the remaining three hours they wish to work, to make an eight-hour day.

A number of factors go into deciding the core work time. The most important factor is the need to have adequate staff to cover the work flow. Also, for

Exhibit 15.4   *Use of Flexitime in Work Scheduling*

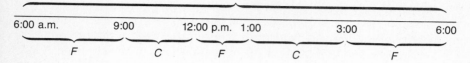

C = Core hours—all employees must be present for these five hours each day.

F = Flexitime hours—employees may complete their eight hours per day by
     working any three of these seven hours.

jobs that are interdependent the employer will have to be concerned that adequate numbers of people are on duty so that bottlenecks do not develop.

Flexitime programs have been introduced in organizations in part because
of employer recognition that employees need some flexibility in their workday
for personal business. For example, flexitime allows the employee to visit the
dentist without being absent from work.[18] A dual career family would be able
to get children off to school and to meet them by 3:30 P.M., using flexitime to be
home at that time. In short, flexitime is thought to be one mechanism to reduce
absenteeism and tardiness when employees must be away from work. Research suggests that flexitime may not reduce absenteeism in the long run.[19]
Flexitime should also enhance the amount of autonomy that an employee feels
in the job. Since the employee establishes the daily work schedule some discretion is put back into the job.[20]

Professional Development Programs

Many companies operate professional development programs for employees.
An example of one organization's professional development program policy
appears in Exhibit 15.5.

The structure and content of these programs vary tremendously. In some
cases the organization operates in-house training and development programs;
in other cases the employer offers a tuition refund program for employees.
These programs are usually conducted because the employer has a continuing
need for scarce talent. At the same time, such programs should contribute to
the satisfaction of employee needs for growth and development.[21]

Job Posting and Bidding Systems

Numerous employers operate job posting and bidding systems.[22] An example
of a job posting and bidding system is presented in Exhibit 15.6.

In a typical job bidding or posting system the employer routinely posts all
job vacancies within the company. Employees are then permitted to apply for
these vacancies. Posting systems exist for numerous reasons, including a recog-

---

Exhibit 15.5 *Professional Development Policy Statement*

Educational Assistance Policy

The company encourages employees to continue to develop their skills and effectiveness on the job. The company will provide partial reimbursement for the cost of tuition and books for work-related study programs offered by accredited organizations as described below:

1. American Institute of Banking—Twice a year, beginning in January and again in September, the AIB offers a number of 15-week courses directly related to banking. At the time of registration, the company will pay the tuition, which includes the textbook.

2. Undergraduate and Graduate Work—Full-time employees who have completed six months of employment are eligible for tuition assistance for work-related courses or study programs taken through a nationally recognized correspondence school, junior college or university. Prior to registration, the officer to whom the employee is responsible must approve each course.

After registration in the course is completed, the company will pay 80 percent of the registration fee, other processing fees, and the cost of required texts. Reimbursement will be reduced by the amount of any veterans benefits or other outside assistance received. The employee is required to provide the personnel department with a copy of the final grade report upon completion of the course or courses.

Comment

Failure to receive a grade of C or to otherwise complete a course makes you ineligible for company educational assistance until you successfully complete a course or AIB class with a grade of C or better at your own expense.

---

nition that sometimes the organization overlooks talent, legal requirements under EEOC/AA programs, and a desire to let individuals self-select into jobs. It is this last objective that probably comes closest to satisfying noneconomic needs of employees.

Individuals vary in terms of their need levels and interests. To the extent

---

Exhibit 15.6 *A Job Posting and Bidding Policy*

Advertising the Vacancy

1. When the vacancy card is received in the Employee Relations Office it is assigned to one of the employment representatives who will be responsible for filling the vacancy.
2. The Employee Relations Office will advertise the vacancy for a minimum of five working days.
   a. Advertising deadline is 5:00 p.m. Tuesday for the listing on the following Monday.
   b. Vacancies are routinely advertised on the Job-Line recordings, the Employment Opportunities notebooks in the Employee Relations Office, the VEC, the *Spectrum*, and campus bulletin boards, and are mailed to several local community groups for affirmative action recruitment. All classified salaried positions are also advertised on the statewide RECRUIT system.
3. If a department wishes to advertise a position in a professional journal, newspapers, or any other publication, the ads must be approved in advance by the Employment Representative. These ads are placed by the department at its expense.

that employees can bid on internal job vacancies, they are self-selecting for consideration of work to satisfy their needs. Job posting can result in employee and job matches that are good from the employee's perspective.[23] This should contribute to need satisfaction in numerous ways. For example, the employee has an opportunity for growth (a more responsible job), autonomy (some control over their career), and recognition (when transfer or promotion is based on past performance).

Supervisory Training

Since the Hawthorne studies of the 1930s organizations have increasingly recognized the importance of effective supervision and its contribution to noneconomic rewards.[24] Today, many organizations provide for human relations training of supervisors. Human relations training covers a wide range of topics, from supervisory leadership style, to understanding individual motivation, to simple training in how to treat employees with dignity. Such training is important since employees look to their supervisors for support, approval, and recognition for a job well done. Effective supervision can lead to satisfaction of noneconomic needs.[25]

Organizational Due Process

Organizational due process is used here to describe the organization's grievance system, as well as any other appeals system for employees when they feel that they are treated unfairly.[26] Traditionally, grievance systems have been associated with union and management relationships. However, progressive employers without labor unions are now introducing grievance systems into their organizations as well. An example of a nonunion grievance procedure is presented in Exhibit 15.7.

Such programs are designed to ensure that employees are treated fairly by the organization. Due process systems can meet employees' security needs and their needs for feeling justly treated.[27]

Quality Circles

A quality circle is a work group that routinely meets to discuss work quality problems. The group usually identifies problems and then seeks solutions to the problems from members of the quality circle. The basic idea of a quality circle is predicated on the assumption that employees have much more to contribute to their jobs than is normally tapped by the organization. To enable employees to contribute all that they can, they are encouraged to give input into solving organizational problems.

Quality circles may be offered as a vehicle to improve quality.[28] At the same time, they have the potential to satisfy noneconomic needs for achievement, autonomy, and responsibility.[29]

Exhibit 15.7   *A Nonunion Grievance Procedure*

Faculty Grievance Procedures

The Governor of the Commonwealth in 1972 by Executive Order and then the General Assembly by legislative action in 1978 and in later amendments ensured that classified employees in the Commonwealth have an effective procedure by which grievances could be fairly and objectively reviewed and resolved. These grievance procedures excluded academic employees of State-supported colleges and universities. Therefore, the following procedure is provided to serve as the means for effective resolution of grievances experienced by any employee who is a member of the faculty of Virginia Polytechnic Institute and State University.

2.10.1 Grievable Issues:

A grievance shall be defined as a complaint alleging a misinterpretation, incorrect application, or violation of a policy, procedure, or practice of the University, not pursued by the faculty member in some other forum. Some examples of "grievable issues" are the following: the application of policy, salary levels, or salary adjustments, teaching load/work load, reprisals, discriminatory actions, EEO complaints, and facilities/space.

1. Nongrievable issues: While it shall be the intent of the University grievance policy to see that most faculty disputes may be resolved by means of this procedure, not all issues may be grieved. The following issues may *not* be grieved:

   a. determination of policy (which is the domain of the governance system);

   b. those items falling within the jurisdiction of other University appeal procedures;

   c. the contents of personnel policies, procedures, rules, regulations, ordinances, and statutes;

   d. promotion and tenure.

2. Timeliness of grievance: The faculty member shall identify the grievance verbally to the immediate supervisor (i.e., the department or division head or the dean/director responsible for the performance appraisal of the aggrieved faculty member) in an informal meeting within fourteen (14) calendar days after discovery of the event or action which is the basis for the grievance. No grievance need be accepted for processing under this procedure after this fourteen (14) day period.

3. Collegial communications: Most faculty concerns or complaints can be resolved informally through normal colleague communications. Accordingly, faculty members are encouraged to take their complaints to their immediate supervisor in the normal spirit of faculty problem solving. Should these efforts be unsuccessful, the faculty member may request the assistance of the Faculty Senate Committee on Reconciliation in fashioning an equitable solution. If the faculty member has requested assistance of the Faculty Senate Committee on Reconciliation, that Committee must invoke a postponement of the time limits indicated in the following procedure. If the assistance of this Committee has not been requested, or if this Committee determines that it cannot provide assistance in the matter, within the time limits indicated, the faculty member may pursue the issue through the following procedure. Department/division heads, deans/directors and other administrative faculty shall assist the faculty member in the processing of the grievance.

continued

Exhibit 15.7 *continued*

The Procedure:

1. Step One: The faculty member shall identify the grievance verbally to the immediate supervisor in an informal meeting within fourteen (14) calendar days after discovery of the event or action which is the basis for the grievance. The supervisor shall provide a verbal response to the faculty member within five (5) weekdays following the meeting. If a resolution is not reached at this point, the faculty member shall within five (5) weekdays submit to the supervisor, on the Faculty Grievance Form, the nature of the grievance and the specific relief requested. The supervisor, in turn, shall give the faculty member a written response on the Faculty Grievance Form within five (5) additional weekdays.

2. Step Two: If the first step written response is not found acceptable, the faculty member may advance the grievance to the second step by indicating this desire on the Faculty Grievance Form. The Grievance Form must be submitted to the next direct level of University administration within five (5) weekdays following the receipt of the Step One reply. (The next direct level of administration for collegiate faculty will normally be the college dean). Following receipt of the Grievance Form, the Step Two administrator or designee shall meet with the faculty member within five (5) weekdays. The Step Two administrator may request the immediate supervisor to be present; the faculty member may similarly request that a representative of his/her choice be present. The Step Two administrator shall give the faculty member a second step written response on the Grievance Form within five (5) weekdays after the meeting.

3. Step Three: If the second step written response is not acceptable, the faculty member should send the Grievance Form with the appropriate Step Three request checked, indicating to the Step Two administrator the desire to advance the grievance; the Step Two administrator will direct it to the attention of the appropriate Vice President or Provost immediately. The faculty member shall give the form to the Step Two administrator within five (5) weekdays after the Step Two decision has been reached. The Vice President or Provost, or appropriate designee, shall contact the faculty member directly within five (5) weekdays after receipt of the Step Three grievance. A meeting shall be held within the next ten (10) weekdays. The faculty member and the Step Three administrator shall determine if other than those present in the previous step hearing should be present. The administrator herein referred to shall respond to the grievance within five (5) weekdays of the hearing.

4. Impartial Panel Hearing: If the faculty member is not satisfied with the resolution of the grievance as determined by the management steps, the faculty member may petition the President of the University within ten (10) calendar days to review the facts, findings, and proceedings of the management steps. The purpose of the President's review would be to determine if the case warrants a review by an impartial panel.

If the President decides that the matter should be reviewed by an impartial panel, this step of the procedure will be structured in the following manner. A three-person panel will be constituted. The aggrieved faculty member and the President will each select one faculty member from the University. These two persons thus selected will choose a third University faculty member who shall then serve on the three-member panel as its chair. All faculty members so chosen shall not have had any prior involvement in the instant grievance. Every reasonable effort will be made to assure that the impartial panel hearing will be held within thirty (30) calendar days of the receipt of the request by the President. The panel shall submit its decision within thirty (30) days after the close of the hearing.

5. Panel Findings: The three-person panel will make a recommendation to the President on their findings and the President's decision will be final.

From *The Faculty Handbook,* Virginia Polytechnic Institute and State University, September 1983, pp. 54–56.

Management by Objectives

Management by objectives is described in the chapter on performance appraisal. This system, like other participative management systems, assumes that individuals want to contribute as much as they can to the organization, that people are not lazy, and that work is as natural as play or rest. Under these assumptions, individuals will feel truly satisfied in their work environments only if they have the opportunity to contribute their utmost to the organization. The system assumes people look for satisfaction of noneconomic needs as well as economic needs in their work. Management by objectives and other participative programs can meet many of the noneconomic needs of employees.[30]

Company-Sponsored Events

Company-sponsored events include a multitude of activities, such as traditional events like the annual company picnic and company-sponsored sporting events. On the other hand, sponsorship to annual professional meetings also is a company-sponsored event. This latter type of event may be as valuable to a professional employee as a picnic might be to someone else. Such programs are designed to satisfy social and belonging needs by encouraging the employee to be involved with fellow employees in non-job-related settings.

Noneconomic Reward Decision Making

The previous sections discussed some of the more common approaches used by management in enhancing noneconomic job rewards for employees. Which of these rewards should an employer attempt to provide? There is no clear and satisfactory answer to this question. There is little systematic evidence that employees have particular needs that are not satisfied.

Rather than speculate upon what employees within a particular enterprise find lacking in the way of noneconomic rewards, employers can survey their members to solicit their desires for such programs. Employers who are seriously interested in the noneconomic rewards that are present or absent in their organization can construct attitude surveys.

Employee Attitude Surveys

Attitude surveys (sometimes called job satisfaction surveys) measure employees' cognitive orientations toward their jobs and employer. There are numerous employee attitude surveys. While many of these surveys measure aspects of work other than noneconomic rewards, they can be adapted to capturing employees' interests for noneconomic rewards. For example, If an employer is interested in whether employees would like to have company-sponsored sporting or cultural events, a series of questions could be designed to assess the desire and willingness of employees to participate in such events. Similarly, employers can ask attitudes about the amount of challenge in jobs. High levels of dissatisfaction could cause the employer to attempt job redesign.[31]

The Minnesota Satisfaction Questionnaire

The Minnesota Satisfaction Questionnaire (MSQ) is an instrument designed for other purposes that could be adapted to assessing the presence or absence of noneconomic rewards. Several MSQ standard questions to assess noneconomic rewards appear in Exhibit 15.8.

The first category in the exhibit concerns the extent to which employees feel that their abilities are being utilized. The second category considers whether or not employees feel they have opportunities to advance, the third asks employees whether their work is challenging, and the last two categories focus on whether employees receive adequate feedback and how they feel about their supervisors' competency level.

Exhibit 15.8   *Sample Questions from the Minnesota Satisfaction Questionnaire*

Ability Utilization

The opportunity to develop my talents.
The opportunity to make use of my past experience.
The opportunity to do work that is well suited to my abilities.
The way my abilities and potential are utilized here.

Advancement Opportunities

The opportunities for advancement on this job.
My chances for advancement.
The amount of mobility I have for advancing into a better job.
The way the company publicizes what jobs are available for advancement.

Work Challenge

The way my work challenges me to develop new skills.
Being able to find challenge in my work as the organization expands.
Being able to do work that challenges my skills and abilities.
Being able to avoid jobs that are routine and boring.

Feedback

Being told how I am doing.
Being told where I stand.
Being told what my superior thinks of me.
Being told what others think about my ideas.

Supervision I (Competence)

The way my superior provides competent and consistent supervision.
The effectiveness with which my efforts are directed.
The way my boss provides help on problems relating to my job.
The supervisory competence of my superiors in making decisions.

Using a companywide survey, the organization would have a feeling for how employees at large felt about these and other issues. In the event that there is concern over these issues, the employer could conduct an in-depth analysis of one or more areas and assess what strategy should be adopted to provide for employees' need satisfaction. The categories in Exhibit 15.8 do not exhaust the list of questions that an employer might ask, but they are indicative of the types of data that could be collected for decision making.[32]

For example, suppose that survey results indicated that employees feel they are being passed over for promotion. To counteract these negative feelings, the organization institutes a job bidding system. When a position opens up the employees can bid for the job. All employees who bid for a job are considered, and those who do not receive the job are informed as to why they did not receive the job. A subsequent survey one year later indicates that the negative feelings that employees had toward advancement opportunities had been reduced substantially.

In a second case, the results of a survey indicate serious dissatisfaction with the quality of supervision in several departments. As part of a more general supervisory development effort the organization begins to upgrade the technical skills of supervisors. Subsequent survey results show an improvement in attitudes of employees in the focal departments.

Impact of Noneconomic Reward Programs on Economic Rewards

Earlier sections of this chapter discussed noneconomic rewards as though they are independent of economic compensation. Noneconomic rewards have both an indirect and direct impact on economic compensation.

Indirect Impact

The introduction of many programs that provide noneconomic rewards often has an indirect effect upon the wage costs of the organization. For example, organizational sponsorship of company picnics, bowling teams, and so on involves costs associated with such programs. These costs can be viewed as indirect labor costs. Even programs such as job bidding and posting systems can be costly to operate. The overhead costs to operate these programs can be viewed as an indirect cost of motivating retention. Given these indirect costs an organization may be reluctant to implement such programs unless there is some evidence of a direct economic payoff.

Human resource management as a field of knowledge and study has done a relatively poor job of demonstrating the financial benefits of such programs. This failure to demonstrate the value of such programs is probably attributable to more than a lack of sophistication on the part of practitioners and others in the field. For one thing, in field settings it is hard to isolate the cause and effect relationships necessary to conclusively demonstrate the impact of a given program. For example, does the incidence of a job bidding system improve employee satisfaction? A simple before and after measure of satisfaction is inadequate to determine this factor, since a large number of other variables could have intervened to improve attitudes.

The establishment of a program to enhance noneconomic rewards from employment is not an all or nothing decision. The quality of the program can vary tremendously with the people implementing and operating the program. In one unit of the company a very good implementation may result in a meaningful program, whereas in another unit the implementation and follow-through may be extremely poor. This type of problem plagues human resource research.

Direct Impact

A second and perhaps more important way that noneconomic reward programs are related to economic compensation is the direct impact that they have on wage and salary payments. To illustrate this potential impact, several programs are discussed in terms of how they may impact upon wage payments.

Job Design and Redesign   Any time that job redesign is introduced into an organization with an established pay structure, the pay structure will have to be changed. Job redesign implies that the content of jobs will change, which means that to restore equity in pay, jobs with an increase in inputs will have to be upgraded in pay. Enriching jobs can result in an increase in labor costs to the organization.

Another program sometimes used to make work more meaningful is to have all employees cross-trained. When employees within a work unit are completely cross-trained, they are capable of performing any of the jobs in that unit, even if they continue to work at only one job. This program has a potential direct impact upon wage and salary payments since unless there is some type of a learning bonus employees may not be motivated to learn the various jobs. An employer might pay for "capacity" to perform a job rather than for the actual job performed. In this case direct wage rates would go up and so would labor costs.

Flexitime   Flexitime systems also imply a need to cross-train employees to cover for each other. Flexitime may result in generally higher wage rates and labor costs.

An organization considering flexitime will also want to be sure that such a policy is consistent with requirements for overtime provisions under appropriate laws or under collective bargaining agreements. For example, if the collective bargaining agreement requires a continuous eight hours of work in a 24-hour period, an employer may have to pay wages for time not worked (the breaks in continuous work) or for overtime if the flexitime hours overlap the 24-hour period from one day to the next. The organization will need to coordinate the flexitime program and the union contract. Overtime will increase the effective wage rate of employees and also labor costs.

In a similar vein, some organizations that do not offer flexitime may provide for employee free time with a four-day workweek where employees work 10 hours per day for each of the four days. Firms operating under a four-day workweek must be sure that employees work on government contracts for only eight hours per day to not be liable for overtime wages (under Davis-Bacon, Walsh-Healy, or McNamara-O'Hara government contract requirements). This workweek also needs to be coordinated with the union contract.

Quality Circles   Quality circles require employees to be away from their work stations to discuss productivity issues. Production in the work unit can be halted for these meetings. If this strategy is employed, the organization is giving up productivity, at least in the short run. An alternate way to allow time for the discussion meetings is to have employees report to work early or stay after hours. In either case, these hours will contribute to overtime wage payments for nonexempt employees. Therefore, the costs of such a program should be considered when installing the program.

Employee Training and Development   Many benefits accrue to the organization from training and developing employees. These include preparing people for future jobs which can reduce the organization's reliance on external selection, as well as having more up-to-date employees performing their jobs.

At the same time, careful consideration needs to go into coordinating these training efforts with future needs. Failure to do so can result in increased costs. For example, suppose an organization trains a group of low-level managers for promotion into middle-management positions. Unless the positions are available for these people, the organization may lose these employees to other organizations that have an immediate need for their services. One option is for the organization to pay these employees a higher wage (perhaps the wage rate for the job they are qualified to assume). This would solve the turnover problem; however, it would also result in an increase in labor costs in the short run. The prevalence of this practice is not known, but there can be direct costs in compensation associated with training and development programs.

Summary

This chapter focused upon the noneconomic rewards of employment. The first section discussed the nature of human needs and the types of needs that individuals attempt to satisfy on the job. The second section discussed some of the programs that companies operate to enhance noneconomic reward satisfaction of employees. The third section briefly noted one strategy for identifying the unsatisfied needs of organization members.

Overall, it was stressed that the noneconomic rewards that people look for in the job environment are highly variable. Thus, there is a need to assess what each particular employee group in a company finds desirable or lacking.

Discussion Questions

1. Do a salesperson and a research scientist have the same needs? Would they look for different things to satisfy their needs? Speculate on the basic needs that each person has and speculate on how those needs might be satisfied on the job.

2. What are job enlargement and job enrichment? Compare and contrast the two.

3. Consider a firm that allows managers to take a year sabbatical at half-pay to participate in political activities. Discuss the types of human needs that this program might satisfy. What are the ramifications for organizational performance?

Exercise

1. Blueridge Manufacturing specializes in the manufacture and distribution of household appliances in a regional eastern market. It is organized functionally with formal departments in manufacturing, marketing, finance, industrial relations, and research and development. During the past five years, the corporation's share of the market has declined from 20 to 10 percent. To offset this decline, top management made the decision to place greater emphasis on research and development in the hope that the introduction of new and improved products would reverse the trend. Very little additional attention was paid to the other functional departments.

The new emphasis on research and development was initiated by the hiring of a brilliant young scientist who was known not only for scientific ability but also for a familiarity with the behavioral sciences. The new R & D director was soon surrounded with a competent team of researchers, most of whom were eager to apply their specialized talents on behalf of the corporation's R & D effort.

The director made several significant changes in the corporation's traditional approach to R & D. The staff was organized into research teams, with each team held responsible for an allotted number of projects. Under this arrangement, each team member was allowed to work on that portion of the project in which he or she was most interested and to which his or her abilities were best suited. The teams met regularly with the director to discuss the objectives, strategies, and problems of the various projects. The director remained constantly informed as to the progress being made on the major projects and, in the process, developed a personal acquaintance with most of the members of the staff. The director instituted a compensation plan that placed strong emphasis on individual merit; the staff members were recognized for their achievements in the form of merit raises and, in some cases, direct bonuses. Senior scientists were also eligible for optional forms of deferred compensation. In addition, the corporation financed professional society memberships, travel expenses to conventions and seminars, and released time for periodic educational "refueling."

The R & D effort has exceeded the expectations of the corporation's top management. A new line of products is being offered, and the quality of older products is again being recognized. The R & D director reports that morale is high among the members of the staff. The rate of turnover within the department has been reduced to an all-time low. The management of Blueridge Manufacturing is now beginning to think about the possibility of applying this same approach in other departments of the organization. They are very much aware of the fact that the successful implementation of the approach will be limited by greater size and diversity, cost considerations, and a lower level of sophistication on the part of the employees. Yet results tend to speak for themselves.

a. How do you account for the improved performance of the R & D group? What actions did the R & D director take to improve performance and how did the compensation system support these actions?

b. What do you think of the policy to send scientists to professional meetings? What are the advantages and disadvantages to having such a policy?

c. Discuss the role of economic and noneconomic rewards in achieving the director's objectives. How do you think each of these types of rewards impacted performance?

References

[1] M.C. Knowles, "Labour Turnover: Aspects of Its Significance," *Industrial Relations* (Australia) 18 (1976): pp. 67-75.

[2] See for example, Thomas A. DeCottis and Daniel J. Koys, "The Identification and Measurement of the Dimensions of Organizational Climate" in Richard C. Huseman, ed., *Proceedings of the Academy of Management*, Detroit, Michigan, August 1980, pp. 171–175.

[3] J. R. Hackman and Edward E. Lawler III, "Employee Reactions to Job Characteristics," *Journal of Applied Psychology* 55 (1971): pp. 267–283.

[4] *Ibid.*

[5] John P. Wanous, "Who Wants Job Enrichment?" *Advanced Management Journal* 41 (Summer 1976): p. 16.

[6] *Ibid.*

[7] David C. McClelland and David H. Burnham, "Power Is the Great Motivator," *Harvard Business Review* 54 (March-April 1976): pp. 100–110.

[8] David C. McClelland, "Business Drive and National Achievement," *Harvard Business Review* 40 (July-August 1962): pp. 104–105.

[9] Hackman and Lawler, "Employee Reactions to Job Characteristics."

[10] Frederick Herzberg, Bernard Mausner, and Barbara Snyderman, *The Motivation to Work*, 2d ed. (New York: Wiley, 1959).

[11] See for example, Fred E. Fiedler, *Personality and Situational Determinants of Leadership*, Department of Psychology, University of Washington, Technical Report 71-18, June 1971; and Jay W. Lorsch and John J. Morse, *Organizations and Their Membership: A Contingency Approach* (New York: Harper and Row, 1974).

[12] Howard Baumgartel, "Leadership Style as a Variable in Research Administration," *Administrative Science Quarterly* 2 (1957): pp. 344–360.

[13] J. R. Hackman, Edward Lawler, and Lyman Porter, *Perspectives in Behavior in Organizations* (New York: McGraw-Hill, 1977): p. 225.

[14] Hackman and Lawler, "Employee Reactions to Job Characteristics."

[15] See for example, Robert N. Ford, "Job Enrichment Lessons from ATO," *Harvard Business Review* 51 (January-February 1973): pp. 96–106.

[16] Antone F. Alber, "The Real Cost of Job Enrichment," *Business Horizons* 22 (February 1979): pp. 60–61.

[17] J. R. Hackman and Greg Oldham, *A Flexible Approach to Working Hours* (New York: AMACOM, 1978): p. 55.

[18] William F. Glueck, "Changing Hours of Work: A Review and Analysis of the Research," *Personnel Administrator* 24 (March 1979): p. 47.

[19] Jay S. Kim and Anthony F. Campagne, "Effects of Flextime on Employee Attendance and Performance: A Field Experiment," *Academy of Management Journal* 24 (December 1981): p. 739.

[20] For examples of research on flexitime, see Donald J. Petersen, "Flexitime in the United States: The Lessons of Experience," *Personnel* 57 (January-February 1980): pp. 21-31; and Stanley D. Nolan and Virginia H. Martin, *Alternative Work Schedules, Part I: Flexitime* (New York: AMACOM, 1978).

[21] Space does not permit a full discussion of the approaches to management development nor the benefits accruing from such programs. Interested readers may wish to refer to a basic chapter on management development in any standard personnel text. One good source is Wendell L. French, *The Personnel Management Process*, 5th ed. (Boston: Houghton-Mifflin, 1982), Chapter 17, pp. 378-399.

[22] Bureau of National Affairs, *Employee Promotion and Transfer Policies*, Personnel Policies Forum no. 120, January 1978, pp. 12-15.

[23] For a discussion on the importance of allowing employees to self-select into jobs see: John Wanous, "Effects of a Realistic Job Preview on Job Acceptance, Job Attitudes, and Job Survival," *Journal of Applied Psychology* 53, December. 1973, pp. 327-332.

[24] French, *The Personnel Management Process*, pp. 378-399.

[25] Thomas Delone, "What Do Middle Managers Really Want from First-Line Supervisors?" *Supervisory Management*, September 1977, pp. 8-12.

[26] Clyde W. Summers, "Protecting All Employees against Unjust Dismissal," *Harvard Business Review* 58 (January-February 1980): pp. 132-139.

[27] Julius G. Getman, "Good Cause Compromise," *The Wall Street Journal*, August 1980, p. 10.

[28] Ed Yager, "Examining the Quality Control Circle," *Personnel Journal* 58 (October 1979): pp. 682-684.

[29] Elaine Rendall, "Quality Circles—A Third Wave of Intervention," *Training and Development Journal* 35 (March 1981): p. 29.

[30] M. Scott Meyer, "Every Employee a Manager," *California Management Review* 10 (Spring 1968): pp. 9-20. Suzanne Secias, "Fringe Benefits: Yours vs. the Best," *Money*, July 6, 1977, p. 38.

[31] R. B. Dunham and F. J. Smith, *Organizational Surveys* (Glenview, Ill: Scott, Foresman, 1979).

[32] *Ibid.*

CHAPTER

16

Compensation

Administration

and Control

· **Learning Objectives**

· **Introduction**

· **Responsibility for Compensation Management**

Compensation Staff Personnel
Organization Line Managers
Line Managers and Compensation Staff Relationships
Top Management Decision Making

· **Maintenance of the Wage Level**

Wage Surveys
Cost of Living Allowances
Supply Shortages
The Wage Level Adjustment Decision

· **Maintenance of the Wage Structure**

Job Content Changes
Job Reanalysis

· **Pay for Performance Administration and Control**

Size of Merit Increases
The Unit Allocation Problem
Conducting Performance Appraisals

· **Administration of Pay Change Transactions**

· **Wage and Salary and Standard Hours Budgets**

Wage and Salary Budgets
Standard Hours Budgets

· **Legal Controls**

Federal Contract Holders
Overtime, Child Labor, and Minimum Wage Legislation
Equal Opportunity and Affirmative Action Regulations
Employee Retirement Income Security Act of 1974
Social Security
Labor Contracts
Wage and Price Guidelines

· **Communication of Compensation Information to Employees**

The Importance of Communication
Communication of Wage Levels and Structures
Communicating Pay Increase Information
Communicating Merit, Market, and COLA Increases
Benefits Communication

· **Exercises**

437

Learning Objectives

To learn about compensation administration and control in general.
To learn who is involved in various compensation decisions—the organization's management and the compensation staff.
To learn how organizations maintain a comprehensive wage and benefits system once the system has been designed and implemented.
To learn how to administer wage change transactions.
To learn how wage decisions are tied into organizational budgets.
To reexamine legal issues from an administration and control standpoint.
To learn how to communicate wage and benefit information to employees.

Introduction

The discussion in the text has focused upon the elements and design of a comprehensive compensation system. The first chapters established the goals and the theory behind compensation programs, while later chapters discussed how a compensation system is designed.

Throughout these chapters numerous policy issues were implied. The purpose of Chapter 16 is to discuss the administrative process of managing the compensation system once it is established. Also, policy issues that have not been discussed elsewhere are covered here. This chapter is meant to provide a clear knowledge of what goes into managing a compensation system.

Responsibility for Compensation Management

Numerous personnel within an organization have input into the compensation decision-making activity. Although the text refers to a "compensation decision maker," in reality many individuals contribute to the decision-making process. Some of the more important roles in the organization that are involved in compensation decision making are clarified here.

Compensation Staff Personnel

Many of the individuals involved in compensation management are compensation staff personnel.

Organizations of 250 or more employees (and sometimes smaller ones) usually employ a staff person whose job is to manage the compensation system. If the organization is relatively small this job may be the responsibility of the personnel manager or personnel director. In a relatively large firm the title is likely to be compensation manager or director. Very large organizations may employ a whole group of compensation professionals, including one or more compensation managers, benefits managers, pension plan managers, and job analysts. The titles for these positions suggest the responsibilities of each job.

Staff personnel in modern organizations have several different roles. Among the more important roles are to provide expert advice to other managers; to assist line managers by handling the administrative work involved in compensation decision making; and to actually make decisions on some issues. For example, suppose a staff person is asked by the organization to conduct a wage and salary survey in the labor market. The staff person may draw up a list of potential organizations to be included in the survey and recommend which firms will actually be surveyed. This would be the advisory role. In this case the staff specialist does not make a decision as to which firms to survey, but makes only a recommendation. The staff person may then conduct the survey by contacting the selected firms to gather information on wage rates for key jobs in the other organizations. This is an example of the role of carrying out the administrative details. Finally, the staff specialist may unilaterally decide how to summarize the data for use by higher management. In this last case the individual is acting as a decision maker. Staff specialists perform a combination of these three roles simultaneously. The various roles of the organization's management and compensation staff in compensation decision making are presented in Exhibit 16.1.

Organization Line Managers

The group of managers that has control over the operations of the company is known as line managers. Job titles of line managers might include first line supervisor, department manager, regional manager, area manager, and vice-president of production. Line managers as a general rule have final responsibility for operations within their part of the organization. This responsibility includes final decision-making power over any decisions that directly impact their area.

Line Managers and Compensation Staff Relationships

In effective organizations line and compensation managers work closely together to achieve organization objectives, including compensation management. Compensation staff professionals conduct job analysis to provide input into job evaluation. Job evaluation is a shared responsibility of both line management and compensation specialists. In the case of job evaluation, the compensation staff provides the expertise on the job evaluation process, and line managers may then define compensable factors, and slot the jobs into the job structure.

Some decisions are made only by line managers; for example, decisions about the performance levels of subordinates. In this decision the line managers are the most informed about the subordinates' performance. In other decisions lower line managers may only make recommendations. For example, few lower line managers make the final decision on the merit pay increase for their subordinates. This manager may recommend a pay increase, and the increase is approved when the manager's supervisor and the personnel or compensation specialist both concur. This example shows that many decisions are shared decisions to provide a system of checks and balances.

Exhibit 16.1 *Summary of Who Is Involved in Compensation Decision Making*

Distribution of Responses on Decisions over Wage and Salary Activities

Personnel Activities	Decision Response 1 (Personnel administrators in this firm make final decisions on their own for this activity.)	Decision Response 2 (Line managers make the final decision on their own for this activity.)	Decision Response 3 (Personnel administrators and line managers jointly decide on this activity.)	Decision Response 4 (Decisions on this activity are made by senior or executive management.)	Decision Response 5 (Consultants make final decisions on this activity.)	Decision Response 6 (Not applicable—this activity is not a part of this firm's personnel procedures.)	Multiple Response
Activity 1. Developing wage and salary budgets (including annual merit or improvement pay). (*n* = 319.)	12%	4%	21%	53%	0%	5%	2%
Activity 2. Job evaluation: Comparison of jobs by a systematic procedure such as ranking jobs, point-factor technique, etc. (*n* = 317.)	41	1	40	9	0	6	2
Activity 3. Developing a wage and salary structure of grades, classifications, or rates of pay. (*n* = 320.)	53	1	14	26	1	2	5

continued

Exhibit 16.1 *continued*

Distribution of Responses on Decisions over Wage and Salary Activities

Personnel Activities	Decision Response 1 (Personnel administrators in this firm make final decisions on their own for this activity.)	Decision Response 2 (Line managers make the final decision on their own for this activity.)	Decision Response 3 (Personnel administrators and line managers jointly decide on this activity.)	Decision Response 4 (Decisions on this activity are made by senior or executive management.)	Decision Response 5 (Consultants make final decisions on this activity.)	Decision Response 6 (Not applicable—this activity is not a part of this firm's personnel procedures.)	Multiple Response
Activity 4. Making changes in a wage and salary grade, classification or rate of pay. (n = 320.)	36	2	40	18	1	1	5
Activity 5. Choosing appropriate survey data for comparison of pay rates to those of your firm. (n = 321.)	80	0	9	4	0	3	3
Activity 6. Appraisal of individual employees for the purpose of salary adjustments (n = 321.)	4	54	31	5	1	4	3

Note: Percentage totals may not equal 100% due to rounding.

Source: (Used with permission of the *Journal of Management.* N. Fredric Crandall, "Wage and Salary Administrative Practices and Decision Process;" *Journal of Management,* 1979, Vol. 5, number 1, pp. 81–82. Copyright 1979, Southern Management Association.

Top Management Decision Making

Certain compensation decisions are made by top management such as presidents, chief executive officer, or the compensation committee. Compensation committees are comprised of a subset of the board of directors. Usually some of these board members are also senior level executives. These individuals provide collective top management judgment for any action to be taken.

Examples of decisions that are almost exclusively the purview of top management are any increase in the wage level; the decision to allocate more money to lower level jobs than higher level jobs; the decision to increase the benefit level; the decision to implement a profit-sharing or a pension plan. Each of these decisions involves the organization as a whole, and each will have a substantial impact upon labor costs. Not surprisingly, top management will make these decisions. The role of top management in compensation decision making is also presented in Exhibit 16.1.

Maintenance of the Wage Level

Once an organization has designed and implemented a comprehensive compensation system, one of the first decisions that must be made is when and how to adjust wage levels through time. For example, over time wages in other organizations in both the product and the labor market will probably increase. Inflationary forces in the economy can also make an organization's wage level obsolete. Shortages of labor in particular sublabor markets may push wages in those markets up at unusually rapid rates, as well. Each of these conditions suggests a need to periodically readjust the wage level for the organization as a whole or for particular job families.

Wage Surveys

Systematic maintenance of the organization's wage level suggests that the wage level be regularly reviewed, perhaps annually. The criteria for adjusting wage levels are product market wage survey data (focusing on the ability-to-pay constraint), labor market survey data (focusing on the need to motivate employees to join and stay), cost of living allowance increases, and labor shortages in specific submarkets. Product and labor market changes are probably the most critical, and Chapters 9 and 10 detail the process of obtaining and using these data. Cost of living allowances and labor shortage adjustments are discussed below.

Cost of Living Allowances

Some organizations in the economy use a cost of living allowance (COLA) to increase wage levels. These increases result from inflationary pressures in the economy. A typical COLA increases wages a certain percentage each time inflation drives the cost of living up by a given percentage. The COLA is typically measured with respect to changes in the Consumer Price Index. When the index increases by 3 percent, for example, the organization adjusts the overall wage level by 3 percent or less, according to company policy. Most COLA arrangements do not allow for wage increases equal to the rise in the index. Usually the wage increase is less, such as a 1 percent COLA increase for each 2 percent Consumer Price Index increase. The rationale behind COLA increases is to combat decreases in **real wages**, or the buying power of wages. If inflation, for example, moves at a rate of 6 percent over a year, then employees will need a six percent increase to offset the effects of inflation.

In spite of the popularity of COLA increases among some firms, they should be implemented with caution. These increases imply that the firm is in an industry in which it can readily pass along labor cost increases to the consumer or make up labor cost increases through greater productivity. Since most firms have rather fixed production functions in the short run and relatively fixed labor cost functions per unit of output, the first of these two constraints must be met in order for a COLA policy to be realistic.

Supply Shortages

Some organizations employ particular types of labor that are in short supply relative to demand (such as engineers, currently). These organizations may have problems keeping wage levels competitive with the external market while still maintaining internal equity. When wages based on internal equity relationships lag the market so much that the firm has difficulty attracting and retaining these employees, then the wage level for subsets of employees must be adjusted rather than for the entire organization. As noted in Chapter 10, job evaluation programs may be conducted within job families. Evaluations of job family wage structures are preferable administratively since these evaluations do not need to be concerned with the issue of inter-job family equity considerations.

The Wage Level Adjustment Decision

The decision process for adjusting wage levels involves several different decision steps that are summarized in Exhibit 16.2.

The first step in the process is to accumulate relevant data for decision making, including current wage levels in both the product market and the

---

Exhibit 16.2 *Summary of Steps in Adjusting the Wage Level*

1. Obtain current labor and product market wage data.
2. Organize data and make recommendations to the decision makers.
3. Make the decision.
4. Implement the decision.

---

labor market. This step may also include obtaining data on the change in the Consumer Price Index and analyzing particular job families that are experiencing labor shortages relative to demand. The employee who performs this step is usually a compensation staff person and may have the title of compensation analyst, compensation manager, personnel manager, or the like. In smaller companies a line manager may be assigned responsibility for gathering the data.

In the second step in the process recommendations are made to top management. The responsibility for preparing the recommendations usually rests with the compensation staff.

The third step in adjusting the wage level is to arrive at a decision as to the specific change that will be made. In small companies this decision may be made by the president or the chief executive officer; in larger companies it may be made by the compensation committee.

The fourth and final step in adjusting the wage level is to implement the decision. An adjustment in wage level usually implies that the entire wage structure (or only the wage structure for a specific job family) will be shifted upward equally. The base, midpoint, and maximum rate for each job grade will shift up by the percentage increment which is decided upon in step three.

Unequal Percentage Adjustments in the Wage Structure   Organizations may not increase wages by a constant percentage throughout the wage structure. Often wages at the bottom of the structure are increased at a faster rate than at the top of the structure. In spite of the fact that internal equity considerations suggest the need to maintain the distances in pay rates between grades, compelling reasons exist for giving lower level grades larger increases.

One argument for granting larger increases to jobs lower in the wage structure is that low-paid jobs are more susceptible to inflationary pressures. Inflation hits low-wage employees much harder than high-wage employees because a greater proportion of the low-wage income goes for necessary items (such as food, clothes, and shelter), and therefore, they should receive larger increases. Another argument is that low-level jobs are most susceptible to market pressures. Since low-level jobs are usually entry-level jobs, they are the first ones to feel labor market competition.[1] Thus, they should receive larger percentage increases. Another compelling reason is that the organization may simply have limited funds to increase wages. Different percentage increases may be given to different groups simply because of the limited financial resources of the organization.

Wage Compression and Expansion   Any decision to provide for differential increases to different jobs throughout the pay structure will result in wage compression or wage expansion.[2] Wage compression occurs when the midpoint wage between job grades shrinks.[3] In other words jobs at different wage levels are paid at closer wage rates. Conversely, wage expansion occurs when jobs with different midpoint wages become more different in their wages. Both of these forces are likely to upset internal equity in the wage structure, and should be allowed only when the firm has no other choice.[4] For example, when market pressures are extremely great for entry-level jobs, then larger increases may need to go to entry-level jobs. However, the organization should correct this compression at the first opportunity. Although no data are known to exist on this point, it is generally better to have the entire organization share in limited funds than to make one or more subgroups of jobholders suffer. This general rule cannot always be abided by in times of extreme inflation or market pressure on certain jobs.

The Special Impact of Labor Unions   Labor unions attempt to influence the wage level and wage structure of jobs held by their members. Unions also have an indirect influence on nonunion jobs in two ways. First, in order for the organization to provide for internal equity, nonunion production jobs may have to receive wage increases when the union negotiates higher rates for union jobs. In this case nonunion job pay rates are tied to union job pay rates.

Second, an increase in the wage level of union members' jobs can have an impact upon wages of supervisory jobs. For example, the organization will normally want to keep supervisors' pay equitable with top-level union production jobs, which may necessitate increasing supervisory rates. Pressures from union jobs can eventually create compression in the wage structures between operative and supervisory jobs, with a higher percentage increase given to low-level managers (supervisors) and a lower one to higher level managers. Chapter 4 contains a detailed discussion of the impact of labor unions on compensation decision making.

Maintenance of the Wage Structure

As the previous section shows, wage structure and wage level decision making are not totally independent of each other. Decisions to increase the wage level in the firm are tied to the wage structure decision. Increasing wage rates at differential rates throughout the wage structure is a wage structure decision.

Job Content Changes

Another consideration that an organization must face in maintaining the wage structure, besides keeping wages current, is changes in job content. As noted in Chapters 7 and 8, most wage structures are based on an assessment of the relative contributions or inputs of the jobs. In job evaluation, jobs are examined in terms of their relative worth on these inputs (such as skill, effort, and level of responsibility). Job evaluation assumes there is stability in job content—that the contributions change relatively little over time.

The reality of organizational life is that most jobs do eventually change over time, and may vary in their inputs or contributions required over time. If this change is substantial, some jobs should move up to higher pay grades, while other jobs should move down the pay grade structure. These changes are typically due to changes in technology or the redesign of jobs (the reallocation of tasks among jobs).

Job Reanalysis

Every organization needs to deal with job content changes. There must be an administrative mechanism to reevaluate jobs when they change in content. Many organizations that use formal job evaluation plans have a staff specialist, titled compensation analyst. The compensation analyst typically reanalyzes jobs. Reanalysis may occur at the request of the job incumbent or the immediate superior, or at the time major changes are made in the content of a job, or when technology has altered the duties of the job. Reanalysis of the job can result in three outcomes: no change in the job's grade assignment; an increase in the job's grade assignment; or a decrease in the job's grade assignment.

Job Analysis and Evaluation Committees   Compensation analysts should not be allowed to make the decision to move a job from one grade to another. Although the analyst may have gathered all of the information on the job and reevaluated the job using the job evaluation manual, a decision as to the final new grade should be made only by the compensation manager and the line managers in the unit where the job is located. Some job incumbents may attempt to bargain for higher wages by manipulating the job evaluation system. Also, there should be checks on the accuracy of the analyst's work. The line managers and the compensation manager can determine the accuracy of the evaluation.

Chapter 7 pointed out the dangers of having just one person evaluate jobs. One of the important roles of the job evaluation committee is to provide stability in judgments about the relative value of jobs. Job reevaluation also should be conducted by committees and not by individuals, although this is not traditional compensation practice. To the extent that single evaluators introduce bias into assignment of jobs to grades, then the value of the entire wage structure is biased. By inference, internal equity is also likely to be threatened.

A Mechanism for Job Reanalysis   The organization should provide a mechanism for line managers and job incumbents to request reevaluation of a job. A simple requisition form, such as that in Exhibit 16.3, should be provided.

The form in Exhibit 16.3 first identifies the job title and current grade for the job being reevaluated. Second, there is space for the person requesting the reevaluation to identify reasons why the job's grade should change. Third, also required are the name and title of the requisitioner and the date the requisition was filled out. Fourth, the analyst provides recommended action, the reasons for the proposed action, the analyst's name, the date of the action, and the name of the supervisor of that job. This form provides a record of requests for

---

Exhibit 16.3 *Sample of a Job Reanalysis Requisition Form*

Date: _____

Reanalysis/reevaluation requested by:

Title _____

Name _____

Dept. _____

Jobs to be reevaluated—specify all jobs:

Job title _____

Job title _____

Job title _____

Reason for request (check one or more):

        Reassignment of tasks among jobs   _____

        Technological change   _____

        Earlier misclassification   _____

Analyst:

    Name _____

    Date of reanalysis/reevaluation _____

    Current job grade _____

    Recommended new job grade _____

Action by Compensation Director and Line Manager

*Approve change   *No change   Signatures_____

---

reevaluation, and may be used to audit requests for reevaluation. For example, if the compensation department is constantly receiving requests for reevaluation by incumbents of a certain job, there may be real inequities in the assignment of this or other jobs to pay grades.

Pay for Performance Administration and Control

Pay increases that are based on seniority are relatively easy to administer. On the employee's anniversary date, an increase is processed. The amount of the increase is normally the next step in grade amount established with the pay range. Pay increases that are allocated on the basis of merit or performance are considerably more complex.[5]

Size of Merit Increases

First, a major policy decision must be made as to the magnitude of the merit pay increase. Usually a decision is made to grant a specified percentage increase. In theory the percentage increase would have been established at the time decisions were made about the width of pay grades. For example, the decision to have a 30 percent pay range around the midpoint suggests that the organization could give average increases of 6 percent over five years. However, in practice the amount of the increase is usually determined each year for numerous reasons.

One reason is that organizations often confuse general increases for COLA or labor market adjustments with merit increase budgets. Also, organizations often wait till the end of the year to determine merit increases because of the financial health of the organization. These reasons are poor since market adjustments and COLA adjustments relate to the wage level decision and not to merit increase decisions. The organization's financial health and ability to pay should have been considered when the pay ranges were first established—the ranges should have been based on the financial constraints of the organization. The midpoint of pay grades was originally anchored to the labor or product market survey data, which should not be affected by COLA increases or the organization's financial health.

The Unit Allocation Problem

Another problem in allocating merit pay increases is sometimes referred to as the unit allocation problem. Should all organization units get the same percentage increase for merit, or should different units get different percentage increases based on top management's perceptions about unit performance? This problem is caused partly by confusion over the purposes of merit pay. If merit pay is supposed to reward individual merit, then only under the assumption that individual performance is not normally distributed among units would granting different increases to different units be justifiable. In short, it may take a considerable leap in faith to make such an assertion since there is no apparent reason why average employee performance levels vary systematically by unit. At the same time this is frequently done.

Conducting Performance Appraisals

Role of the Immediate Supervisor   The immediate supervisor should evaluate an employee's performance. This is standard practice and also is consistent with legal principles discussed in the Stockham Valve case in Chapter 12. These performance reviews ought to then be reviewed by at least one higher level of management to assure that reviews are conducted properly. It is a good policy to have appraisals reviewed at the level above the supervisor also to assure that performance levels of employees are known to someone besides the immediate supervisor.

When Are Reviews Conducted? Another policy consideration in performance assessment is whether performance appraisals should be conducted annually for everyone at the same time or should be staggered according to employees' anniversary dates. Conducting all appraisals at fixed intervals has the advantage of forcing managers to concentrate on the appraisal process in some detail. Using fixed intervals also makes budgeting of the pay increases easier since the average increase is easier to divide among all of the employees. The disadvantage is that they consume a large amount of time at the fixed interval date.

Appraisals conducted on anniversary dates have the advantage of distributing the paperwork over time. However, anniversary date reviews may cause managers to do a less thorough job of appraising performance. Experience also suggests that some managers have a tendency to forget individual anniversary dates. Although purely judgmental, it may be easier, on balance, to conduct appraisals at fixed intervals of time rather than on anniversary dates.

Monitoring Performance Appraisal Information The level of management above the manager doing the performance ratings should monitor the appraisals to assure that they have been conducted, and that someone else is aware of the employee's performance level.

Performance appraisal information should also be monitored by the human resources department for several reasons. First, the department can be another check on whether or not managers are appraising their subordinates. Second, the department can assure that there are not problems with the appraisal that might result in a potential civil rights lawsuit. For example, average performance evaluation scores for women and men (or blacks and whites) should be monitored to assure that there are not average differences between the groups. Should the department find that there are average differences, this finding should be immediately investigated. The difference in performance scores may be justifiable and legitimate. However, the organization should not assume that this is the case, and it should substantiate any mean differences to its satisfaction.

Similarly, average pay increases should be monitored to determine if men and women, for example, receive equal increases, on average. Any discrepancies should be immediately investigated to determine if the mean differences are justifiable.

Translating Performance Appraisal Outcomes into Money Under a pay for performance policy, the performance appraisal outcomes for individuals determine the magnitude of the pay increases received.

Actual pay increase recommendations should rest with the immediate supervisor. The supervisor should have information about pay ranges and about the average percentage increase being made. The immediate supervisor makes recommendations on the increases for the department's employees based on the performance appraisals and the pay guidelines. Increases must not push the employee past the maximum of the range for the job, and the average increase cannot exceed the average of the budget for increases.[6]

As noted in Chapter 12, guidecharts are often developed to help managers recommend pay increases for employees. The key feature of the guidechart is that the percentage increase available to an employee is dependent upon the current position in the pay range and the current performance evaluation score. Guidecharts, while useful administratively, may work against the pay and performance relationship. Using the guidechart, poor performing employees at the bottom of the job pay range will receive larger percentage increases than higher performing employees near the top of the job pay range.

Comparatio   Another tool for compensation administration is the comparatio, or average wage expressed as a percentage of midpoint pay. The organization may want to plan in advance for pay increases to all employees within job grades. At the same time the costs associated with these pay increases need to be controlled. One way to do this is with the comparatio.

The comparatio formula is the total wage or salary of all of the employees within a grade or job, divided by the midpoint of the salary grade or job, multiplied by the number of employees in that grade or job, multiplied by 100. The resulting ratio expresses the average pay for the grade or job relative to the midpoint of the grade or job. Fox example, suppose that there are three employees in a given job within a department. These employees earn $17,000, $17,500, and $19,000 per year. The midpoint for this salary grade is $18,000. The current comparatio for this job grade in the department is: [$53,500 ÷ ($18,000 × 3)] × 100 = 99. In this case actual average pay is 99 percent of the midpoint for the range.

The comparatio has several uses. As a budget control mechanism it allows the organization to control wage costs across departments. For example, if the current comparatio for a job group is 100, the average wage is exactly at the midpoint of the pay range for that job. If a decision is made to increase average pay by 7 percent the comparatio after the pay increase will be 107. Managers will be allowed to exercise discretion in pay increases for subordinates so long as the overall comparatio does not exceed 107.

The comparatio also has other uses. Two of the more prominent ones are to monitor wage changes and to examine turnover as it impacts wage costs. For example, if the comparatio for a job group currently stands at 120, then wages are 20 percent above the median. If the employer has established a 35 percent pay range around the median, no wage increases should be allowed for the group as a whole since average wages are already above the range. Extremely high or low comparatios also imply extremely low or high turnover among incumbents on these jobs.

Administration of Pay Change Transactions

Numerous personnel transactions result in pay changes for employees. The more common reasons for a pay change are:

1. Promotion
2. Demotion
3. Lateral transfer with change in pay
4. Merit increase
5. Seniority increase
6. COLA adjustment
7. Job reclassification
8. Geographic COLA differential.

The organization must monitor pay changes and maintain pay records. In a small organization, a simple card in the employee's personnel file can be used to keep track of the amounts of these various changes, the date of the change, and the reason for the change. If payroll records are computerized, it is a small programming job to maintain pay change information in the electronic file. Pay change records are also useful for analysis of pay changes by race, ethnic, and sex groups for equal employment opportunity and affirmative action purposes.

Wage and Salary and Standard Hours Budgets

Budgets can be efficient planning and control devices when properly used. They force managers to plan for future expenditures. Once planned budgets are approved they can be effective and efficient control devices: managers can be held accountable for planned expenditures. Numerous kinds of budgets are used by organizations, including capital expenditure budgets, contingency budgets, and operating budgets.

Capital expenditure budgets allow for planning and control of capital outlays—the purchase of land, buildings, and equipment. Contingency budgets plan for different states of the future—for example, what will revenues and expenses be if sales volume is $10 million, or what will revenues and expenses be if sales are $12 million? Operating budgets plan and control expenditures for a definite period of time, such as a week, month, or year.

Two operating budgets for controlling the compensation program are unit payroll (wage and salary) budgets and standard hours budgets. Although these budgets may be integrated into one budget document, they are discussed separately here.

Wage and Salary Budgets

An example of a wage and salary budget is depicted in Exhibit 16.4.

The example in Exhibit 16.4 is a budget for one calendar year. Several features of this budget are notable. First, the planned salary and wage for each line-position is recorded for each month. Second, each line-position is designated so that there is not confusion about the number of authorized positions. This point is critical since a department manager may be tempted to convert one $40,000 position into two $20,000 positions. This action would be inconsis-

Exhibit 16.4 Wage and Salary Budget

Job Title/Incumbent	January	February	March	April	May	June	...	December	Total
Assistant Department Manager/Smith	$ 2,000	$ 2,000	$ 2,000	$2,140[a]	$ 2,140	$ 2,140	. . .	$ 2,140	$ 25,260
Department Secretary/Hoyt	1,200	1,200	1,200	1,200	1,200	1,280[a]	. . .	1,280	14,988
Clerk III/Jones	1,000	1,000	1,000	1,000	1,000	1,070[a]	. . .	1,070	12,070
Assembler B/Carter	1,400	1,400	1,400	1,400	1,400	1,400	. . .	1,498[a]	16,898
Machine Attendant/(Vacant)	[b]				1,100	1,100	. . .	1,100	8,500
. . .	.	.	.	.	.	.	. . .	.	.
Machine Attendant/Nelson	1,100	1,177[a]	1,177	1,177	1,177	1,177	. . .	1,177	13,970
Total planned	41,350	41,427	41,427	41,900	42,400	42,600	. . .	44,100	516,640
Total actual	40,050	41,000	41,600	42,500	41,400	44,400	. . .	44,400	518,380
Difference	$ 1,300	$ 427	$ (173)	$ (600)	$(1,000)	$ 200	. . .	$(300)	$(1,740)

[a] Annual anniversary date—planned 7 percent increase.
[b] Position authorized to be filled in May.

tent with control purposes. Presumably there is a justification for each position in the budget, and transforming a particular position into a different position suggests that the manager is not acting consistent with planned staffing levels for various types of labor. Further, conversion of one position into two positions will result in higher total labor costs to the organization because of the increased costs of providing employee benefits for two people as opposed to one person.

A third feature of the budget in Exhibit 16.4 is that planned pay increases are identified in the budget. The assistant department manager and the clerk III are to receive annual pay increases of 7 percent in April and June respectively (the employment anniversary dates). This percentage increase is based on the organization's policy decision as to the average increase for seniority or merit in the budget year. Any employee may receive more or less than the average, but for planning purposes the average is entered.

Fourth, the budget in Exhibit 16.4 allows for the addition of new line-positions throughout the year. The example budgets a machine attendant position to be filled in May of this budget year.

Fifth, by totaling the columns of data, the manager knows the monthly budget for the department. Similarly, by totaling the rows the manager knows the budgeted wage and salary for each person (or line-position) in the department.

Finally, the manager can compare total planned expenditures with total actual expenditures. Variances must then be accounted for. Normally in the course of the budget year some variances may be authorized. For example, if the assistant department manager receives a 10 percent merit increase in April, the dollar amount of this above-average increase is an authorized budget variance. Similar authorized variances might occur if the department needed to expand or contract because of business conditions.

Normally wage and salary budgets are planned once a year. Some organizations will use a rolling budget. A rolling budget is updated periodically, such as every three months. For example, if a department started with the budget in Exhibit 16.4 on January 1, the budget would be redeveloped April 1 for a 12-month period. With the advent of modern computers, updating budgets, even monthly, is relatively easy and allows for better control of variances. Wage and salary budgets can be developed by the day, week, month, or year depending upon a specific organization's requirements.

Standard Hours Budgets

When nearly all of the employees in a department are exempt (salaried) there is less concern with controlling hours of work. However, when most of the employees in a department are nonexempt and qualify for overtime, it is important to control actual hours worked. Overtime for nonexempt employees can increase the direct wage bill 50 percent faster than paying straight-time will, and these costs must be controlled. One method of control is with a standard hours budget. An example of a standard hours budget is depicted in Exhibit 16.5.

A standard hours budget identifies each job within a department and identifies the authorized number of full-time equivalent positions for each job. A policy decision that managers can staff up to the full-time equivalent but not pay overtime will effectively control labor costs. In the example in Exhibit 16.5, the manager can authorize up to a maximum of ten overtime hours for assembler A positions only.

Standard hours budgets, to be effective, must be developed to reflect anticipated business conditions. Budgets in highly stable work environments may need to be developed only every six months, or once a year. When business conditions fluctuate, budgets may need to be developed weekly or even daily.

Legal Controls

Every organization is faced with a myriad of laws and regulations that constrain compensation decision making.[7] Awareness of these laws and their ramifications for compensation is essential. Chapter 3 of the text reviewed the major legislation. In this section the important major components are reviewed from the administration and control viewpoint.

Federal Contract Holders

Organizations that hold federal contracts must comply with the provisions of the Davis-Bacon Act, the Walsh-Healy Act, and the McNamara-O'Hara Act. These three acts establish "going wage rate" requirements for firms with government contracts in excess of a specified dollar value. The secretary of labor determines the going wage rates for employees who work on these contracts.

Exhibit 16.5   *Standard Hours Budget*

	Number of Full-Time Equivalent Positions	Authorized Hours	Authorized Overtime Hours
Assistant Manager	1.0	40	0
Secretary	1.0	40	0
Clerk III	1.0	40	0
Clerk II	1.0	40	0
Clerk I	0.5	20	0
Assembler A	6.5	260	10
Assembler B	4.0	160	0
Assembler C	2.0	80	0
	20.0	680	10

The organization must know these rates in order to bid on the contract, as well as to assure that its pay practices conform to the law.

Overtime, Child Labor, and Minimum Wage Legislation

The principal piece of legislation regulating overtime and child labor is the Fair Labor Standards Act (FLSA) of 1938. There may also be state laws regulating these issues; however, normally the federal standards are more stringent than state standards.

Every employer must make sure that the jobs it considers exempt are truly exempt according to the FLSA. Employees in jobs considered exempt are exempt from the overtime provisions of the FLSA. All other jobs are nonexempt from the overtime provisions. The Wage and Hour Division of the Department of Labor can provide the organization with a test against which the organization's jobs can be compared. A job that meets the standards in the test is considered exempt for overtime purposes. An employer should not assume that any job is exempt under FLSA standards, regardless of the job's title, until it is tested to determine its legal status.

The FLSA also establishes provisions for child labor. With few exceptions (such as newspaper carriers), it is illegal to employ individuals under 16 years of age. Further, in addition to federal law there are usually state laws regulating child labor. In many states individuals between the ages of 16 and 18 must have state-issued work permits. Specific details of the state requirements can be obtained from a state's Department of Commerce or Industry, or the state's Labor Department.

Jobs under the purview of the FLSA must be paid at least the minimum wage (currently $3.35 per hour), as set by Congress. Organizations should be sure they meet this standard.

Equal Opportunity and Affirmative Action Regulations

As discussed in Chapter 3, most organizations are subject to the provisions of Title VII of the Civil Rights Act of 1964. Employers are also subject to the Equal Pay Act of 1963, and government contractors are subject to Executive Order 11246, which regulates affirmative action plans. Collectively, these three pieces of legislation represent the major constraints dealing with discrimination in pay (see Chapter 11 for a more detailed discussion of pay discrimination).

As a matter of policy every organization should monitor average pay rates for the protected race, ethnic, and sex groups within job groups or grades. Where average differences in wages between any two groups exist, the employer should examine the reasons for those differences. For example, if women earn only 80 percent of what men make for performing the same job, then it is imperative to examine why this differential exists.[8] In this example the differences may be justifiable (such as average differences in quantity or quality of production between the groups), or it may be an illegal differential (for example, managers are systematically giving women smaller raises for no good reason). Whenever differentials exist the organization should assume that they are illegal until it can justify them. The issue of examining pay differentials and justifying them was covered in detail in Chapter 11.

Just as there cannot be illegal pay differentials between various race, ethnic, or sex groups within the organization, there should not be differentials between the levels of employee benefits for protected groups.[9] For example, it is illegal to provide different levels of health insurance for men and women, or blacks and whites. It would also be illegal to provide more vacation or sick time to one protected group than another.

Performance appraisal systems that result in pay increases for employees must also be monitored. If average differences in performance scores exist between protected groups, then the reasons should be investigated to insure that the differences are valid and not discriminatory.[10]

The organization's job evaluation system should also be monitored to determine that the factors used in evaluation do not discriminate. The recent controversy over comparable worth pay discrimination is related directly to this issue, and is discussed in detail in Chapter 11. An employer may be subject to a pay discrimination charge if the factors used in job evaluation plans are biased or if the application of the factors is biased.[11]

Finally, under federal affirmative action guidelines, the organization should compile and analyze reports of average pay for all jobs in the organization. This data needs to be broken down by race, ethnic, and sex groups within job grades. Under affirmative action plans, as with equal pay and Title VII analysis, the focus is on whether protected groups receive different amounts of pay relative to each other.

Employee Retirement Income Security Act of 1974

The major provisions of the Employee Retirement Income Security Act (ERISA) were discussed in Chapter 5. Retirement plans that meet federal standards are insured by the federal government. Employers must meet these standards in order to qualify for tax deductions for contributions made to the plan. Employers can contact the U.S. Department of Labor and the Internal Revenue Service for the appropriate information on standards and reporting requirements.

Social Security

The organization will want to be sure that it keeps current in sending in both the organization's and employees' contributions to Social Security. Normally, these funds must be paid at least quarterly. The employer should contact the nearest federal Internal Revenue Service office to determine where these funds are to be paid.

Labor Contracts

Employers who have a labor union representing some or all of their work force must comply with the labor contract between the organization and the union. Most contracts specify the frequency of wage payments, the rate of pay, and often overtime and other additional forms of payment. The labor contract is a business contract between labor and management. The organization must respect the provisions of that contract so that it does not engage in an unfair management practice.

Wage and Price Guidelines

Wage and price guidelines have been issued by presidents of the United States from time to time. Such guidelines may be issued during periods of rapid inflation or during periods of restricted labor supply (such as in times of war).[12] Wage and price guidelines are intended to control inflationary pressures on wages and prices.[13] Such guidelines do not have the force of law; however, the president of the United States may attempt to penalize firms for not conforming to such guidelines. Penalties can range from public censure to threats to withhold government contracts. While it is highly doubtful that such guidelines do much good, especially in the long run, organizations should make an effort to conform to any guidelines in effect.

Communication of Compensation Information to Employees

One of the most important areas of compensation administration and control is the communication of compensation information to employees.[14] Communication between management and employees about compensation matters is usually poor. This section discusses the importance of compensation information and suggests how organizations might do an effective job of communicating with employees.[15]

The Importance of Communication

As Chapter 1 stated, one of the major goals of compensation is to motivate individuals to elicit the behaviors desired by the organization. This major goal has three subparts: (1) to motivate individuals to join the organization; (2) to motivate individuals to stay with the organization; and (3) to motivate individuals to high levels of performance. For employees to understand how they are treated in terms of compensation, the organization needs to communicate information about the compensation system. More specifically, since the organization wants to influence perceptions of equity on the part of employees, it needs to communicate information about pay levels and structures to employees. The organization will also want to communicate pay increase information to employees so that the instrumentality and expectancy model is operationalized. Finally, the organization will want to communicate information about benefits so that it receives credit in the eyes of the employees for these benefits. Each of these important components of communication is discussed next.

Communication of Wage Levels and Structures

Communicating pay information to employees is constrained by two important considerations. First, individual perceptions of reality may not conform to reality. One classic study found that employees systematically underestimate the pay level of their superiors and overestimate the pay level of their peers.[16] This study found that this was due in part to the fact that pay was kept secret in the organization. At least one subsequent study found that even where pay information was less secret, employees still made substantial perceptual errors about the pay of superiors and peers.[17] These data suggest that it is extremely difficult to communicate effectively about pay.[18]

The second major constraint on communications about pay is that employers must be concerned about the privacy of employees. While this is not a legal stipulation, there is a genuine ethical issue as to what rights an individual has with respect to privacy in personal life. Many consider wages and salary to be within the domain of personal privacy. To reveal one employee's pay to another employee could be considered a violation of the first employee's right to privacy in personal life, creating a dilemma for the organization. In order for the organization to be sure that employees perceive the pay system as fair, the employees must be informed of the pay system. The dilemma can be resolved by not communicating information about individuals but rather communicating information about the pay system itself.

Specifically, information about pay policy should be communicated to employees. Each employee should be told what the median wage rate is for his or her job along with the pay range. Communication of this information tells the employee the minimum, median, and maximum of the job. Further, it is recommended that the organization communicate information about how the wage level and structure were arrived at in the first place. The wage structure question can be dealt with by communicating the fact that a process of job evaluation was used to establish internal pay equity relationships. Employers with a valid job evaluation plan have little to fear by communicating with employees on how their jobs ended up at a particular place in the wage structure.

The communication of wage levels can also be straightforward. The organization should have used some type of market survey to arrive at equitable wage rates, and if the surveys are sound there is no reason why employees should not know how these rates were established. Should labor market or product market wage rates be communicated to employees? There is no definitive answer to the question. However, as a general rule the employer will probably want to communicate only the information which is most favorable to it. On the other hand, the organization may be naive in believing its employees accept the information.

If there is great disparity between labor and product market data and the firm uses the lower of the two rates, an explanation should be given to the employees. Where labor market rates are the lower of the two, the explanation is straightforward—the firm is paying the going rate in the labor market. Where product market rates are lower the explanation will need to be more detailed. Employees often do not readily understand the economic constraints faced by the employer. However, with open and candid communications the employer can help employees understand the economic constraints it faces. Thus, employers may want to communicate where their pay rates stand relative to one or both markets, perhaps by communicating that the firm is paying at the 60th percentile of the labor or product market, for example.

Communicating Pay Increase Information

It should go without saying that if an organization wants employees to see an association between pay and performance it must communicate information about pay increases. However, experience suggests that this is usually poorly done. For example, suppose that an employee is appraised as a superior performer and receives a 7 percent pay increase. The employee may be told that the 7 percent is based on superior efforts. However, without any information about the pay increases of others, the employee cannot arrive at a judgment about the performance and pay relationship. How can the organization communicate pay increase information without violating the privacy of other employees' pay increases?

The recommended solution is to communicate to employees the average percentage increase given in the appraisal cycle and to inform them of their individual percentage increases. The employee learns only his or her increase but can assess the increase relative to the average increase. To the extent that the individual percentage increase is consistent with the performance evaluation, the employee may arrive at an independent judgment that the increase is commensurate with performance. This should also strengthen the performance and pay relationship in future reward cycles.

Communicating Merit, Market, and COLA Increases

Organizations give pay increases for reasons other than performance or seniority. Periodically the organization may need to give pay increases to keep wage rates on a par with market wage rates. This type of increase should not be confused with merit or seniority increases. Organizations that confuse these adjustments to the wage structure (that is, all rates shift equally) will most likely damage the performance and pay relationship.

The same type of problem occurs when performance increases are confused with cost of living allowance increases. COLAs are usually given to employees in highly inflationary times to offset the loss of buying power of wages. Such increases should be thought of as adjustments to the entire wage structure, just as are market adjustments, and should not be confused with performance or seniority increases.

Both compensation decision makers and employees may confuse these various types of increases in wages. In order to keep the increases distinct, they can be given at different points in time. It is also recommended that each increase be communicated separately to employees so that there is no misunderstanding about which increase is rewarding performance or seniority and which is based on equity considerations.

Benefits Communication

Benefits communication is probably one area in which organizations have done an exceedingly poor job until recently. With the rise in the magnitude of benefits (as a proportion of the total compensation package), it is becoming more and more important that organizations successfully communicate the benefits package to employees.[19] There are two parts to communicating benefits effectively: to communicate the types of benefits offered to employees, and to communicate the value of those benefits to employees.

Communicating the types of benefits offered to employees should be done repeatedly. Communication of benefits for the first time should occur shortly after initial employment during orientation training. At this stage the employee may not remember or understand all of the benefits available, so subsequent communications should occur. Employees may be reminded once a year of the types of benefits available to them. Any time there is a change in the benefits package (such as a change in sick pay policy, change in retirement policy, or change in health insurance), there should be systematic communication to all employees affected.

In addition to the communication about the types of benefits that employees qualify for, there should also be communications about the value of those benefits. In recent years more and more organizations are communicating this value. One way to do this is with an annual benefits report such as the one depicted in Exhibit 16.6.

The benefits report form in Exhibit 16.6 shows several types of benefits the employee receives and the dollar value of these benefits.[20] It also shows the total value of these benefits as a proportion of base pay. This type of report is intended to communicate both types and amounts of benefits to keep employees informed about which benefits they have and the total value of the benefits.[21]

Many firms send benefits reports directly to the employee's home. This is done so that spouses also realize the benefits they are receiving from the employing organization.

Summary

This chapter discussed issues in compensation administration and control. The chapter began with a discussion of the roles of production and compensation staff in compensation decision making. Both types of managers are involved in compensation decision making.

Exhibit 16.6   *Employee Benefits Report Form*

Employee name: Sally Doe   S.S. #: *999-99-9999*

Based on salary of $20,000 per year, your benefit package is valued at $9,670, which represents 48.35 percent of your annual salary.

The benefits you have at XYZ Corporation are:

Benefit	Annual Dollar Cost	Percent of Annual Pay[a]
Health insurance	$2,000	10%
Retirement plan (includes Social Security)	3,470	17.35
Sick pay allowance (26 days per year)	2,000	10
Paid holidays	1,000	5
Life insurance	200	1
Other (includes workers' compensation, unemployment insurance, etc.)	1,000	5
Total[b]	$9,670	48.35

[a] XYZ's contributions only.
[b] This does not include other nonmonetary benefits, such as reduced ticket prices for the Midvale Art Center. Contact Employee Services for a listing of these benefits for which you qualify.

The discussion then turned to maintenance of the compensation system, including wage level and wage structure decisions. Administration of performance pay systems was covered next. The importance of budgets as planning and control devices was examined. The various legal requirements for compensation administration were also reviewed.

The chapter discussed the communication of compensation decisions to employees. Emphasis was placed on accuracy and honesty in these communications. Communications also involve the employer achieving recognition for the funds spent on employee benefits.

Discussion Questions

1. What is the comparatio?

2. What purposes does an annual payroll budget serve?

3. Who should be involved in monitoring the performance appraisal and merit pay system? Why?

4. (A library research project.) There are numerous pieces of legislation that apply to compensation management. Identify each piece of legislation, what it requires in the way of reporting, and the address of the agency where such reports are filed.

5. Why is it important to communicate information about compensation to employees?

6. How should wage rate data be communicated—which data should be communicated and why?

7. Discuss the communication of employee benefits. What problems might you foresee in communicating benefits information to employees?

Exercises

1. You are the supervisor of operations at the Utopian National Bank.

You are the immediate supervisor of 12 bank employees. Their names and demographic information appear on the computer summary sheet in Exhibit 1, which also contains your numeric performance evaluation for each employee. These represent accurate, unbiased performance scores.

The 12 employees work in one of two jobs, teller or bank services representative. The job descriptions for these two jobs appear in Exhibits 2 and 3. Wage information for these two jobs appears in Exhibit 4.

Utopian National Bank has a merit pay policy. Excerpts of the merit pay policy appear in Exhibit 5.

In your personnel log are several notes and memos from your employees and others, which are presented in Exhibit 6. Exhibit 7 presents a guidechart for granting merit pay increases to bank employees.

You must make pay increase decisions for the 12 employees. Your decisions should be made in accordance with Utopian National Bank pay policy, which is designed to achieve the bank's goals. The president of the bank has authorized a merit pay budget of 6 percent for the current annual pay increase decision.

Use Exhibits 1 through 7 to prepare the following documents:

a. A specific pay increase recommendation for each employee.

b. A one-half- to one-page written narrative that presents the rationale for your decision for each employee.

c. A summary budget report to your supervisor, including:
    i. Your recommended pay increase decision for each employee.
    ii. A report on the new and old comparatio.

d. A written report that identifies any problems with your decisions and suggests solutions to those problems or otherwise reveals that you are aware of the problems.

e. A written report of what you learned from the exercise (2-5 pages).

Exhibit 1   *Computer Summary Sheet*

	Sex	Race	Current Pay	Years in Job	Performance Evaluation Score
Tellers:					
Ray Flack	Male	Black	$13,500	3	5
Linda Hanson	Female	White	11,000	1	5
Melissa Hines	Female	White	12,600	4	3
Ed Motley	Male	Black	10,700	0	4
Judy Ames	Female	White	11,900	2	3
Karla West	Female	White	13,400	6	4
Nate Jones	Male	Black	10,400	0	4
Norma Burke	Female	White	12,600	3	3
Bank services representatives:					
Sam North	Male	White	14,800	4	3
Lena Scott	Female	Black	12,174	0	5
Tom Snell	Male	White	15,700	6	5
Edna Loy	Female	Black	13,500	3	4

5 = Superior; 4 = Above average; 3 = Average; 2 = Below average; 1 = Inferior.

Exhibit 2   *Teller Job Description*

Title: Bank Teller

Date prepared: 1985
FLSA: Nonexempt

General Summary

Receives and pays out money and keeps records of each transaction.

Principal Duties and Responsibilities

1. Receives cash and checks for deposit.
2. Verifies amount of deposit and notes endorsement on checks.
3. Cashes checks and disburses savings account withdrawals.
4. Receives mortgage, land contract, bank card, and public utility payments.
5. Sells and cashes government bonds, cashier's and certified checks.
6. Sells savings certificates.
7. Posts interest, automatic deposits, and service charges.
8. Processes business deposits and signs out night money bags to business customers.
9. Processes installment loan payments, late charges, and payoffs.
10. Disburses approved cash advances.
11. Keeps a running total of transactions and balances the day's accounts using teller machines and computer terminals.
12. Balances 24-hour teller machines.
13. Balances all branch bank windows on a rotating basis.

continued

Exhibit 2   *continued*

14. Pulls and files closed signature cards to verify signatures and endorsements.
15. Helps customers access safe deposit boxes.
16. Balances customers' savings and checking accounts.
17. Processes assigned night deposits.
18. Helps tellers who have not balanced to balance their accounts by checking money drawers and other auditing procedures.
19. Counts cash on hand and prepares cash for the vault.
20. Sorts checks and deposit slips.
21. Refers problems to appropriate personnel.
22. Performs clerical duties occasionally.
23. Shares break room clean-up duties.

Equipment and Materials Used

1. Computer terminals
2. Microfiche and viewers
3. Typewriters
4. Adding machines
5. Coin machines
6. Bank tickets and other forms
7. 24-hour teller machines

Knowledge, Skills, and Abilities

1. Tellers should have the following abilities: To read; to perform arithmetic operations quickly and accurately; to see details and recognize errors in numbers and spelling; to present information effectively; to work within precise limits of accuracy; to follow instructions; to accept responsibility for money handled; and to be tactful and patient with others. These abilities are normally acquired at the high school diploma or equivalent level.
2. Approximately six months to one year of on-the-job experience is required after the two-week teller training class is completed in order to develop teller skills and to learn bank policies and procedures.
3. The physical demands of the position are light. Working rapidly and standing for long periods are occasionally required.
4. The emotional demands of the position include frequent customer contact, meeting deadlines under pressure, and the threat of robbery.
5. Using machines, sitting, standing, and speaking with customers comprise the majority of daily physical activity.

Working Conditions

Physical surroundings and working conditions are good, with occasional noise, temperature variation, and ventilation problems. There are rarely any health or safety hazards.

Advancement

Tellers may become bank services representatives.

Exhibit 3 *Bank Services Representative Job Description*

Title: Bank Services Representative   Date prepared: 1985
                                                        FLSA: Nonexempt

General Summary

Provides services to bank customers, such as opening new accounts, stopping payments, extending loans, closing accounts, and setting up land contracts. In addition, performs other bank duties such as balancing the vault, traveler's check accounts, and safe deposit accounts; processing return items; and conducting monthly audits.

Principal Duties and Responsibilities

1. Opens various new accounts.
2. Answers customer questions concerning new and existing accounts in person and by telephone.
3. Processes Series E bonds into Series H bonds.
4. Sells money to tellers for their daily money needs.
5. Verifies all currency returned to the vault by tellers.
6. Deducts traveler's checks from bank reserves and sends commission to the holding bank.
7. Audits and balances traveler's check account.
8. Orders and keeps records of time certificates and bank and personal money orders.
9. Orders and compiles all new savings and checking account packages.
10. Counsels customers and determines the type of accounts best suited to customer needs.
11. Balances and audits safety deposit register and sends monthly billings to customers.
12. Conducts unannounced audits of tellers once a month and prepares audit report.
13. Conducts monthly branch transaction audits to determine the amount of activity (number of transactions rather than money) at the branch and compiles reports.
14. Processes returned items, such as bad checks and overdrawn savings accounts, by contacting the concerned party by telephone or written notice or both.
15. Processes stop payment and loan extension requests.
16. Arranges for direct deposits from customers.
17. Rents safe deposit boxes and closes accounts.
18. Sets up land contracts and issues time certificates.
19. Keeps records of disbursements for promotional materials.
20. Coaches other employees in the performance of their duties.
21. Prepares money shipments to, and receives shipments from, the main bank office.
22. Performs the duties of regular teller when necessary.
23. Refers problems to superiors.

Equipment and Materials Used

1. Computer terminals
2. Microfiche and viewers
3. Typewriters
4. Adding machines
5. Coin machines
6. Bank tickets and other forms
7. 24-hour teller machines
8. Currency counter
9. Protectograph
10. Telephones.

continued

Exhibit 3   continued

Knowledge, Skills, and Abilities

1. Bank service representatives should have the following abilities: To read; to perform arithmetic operations quickly and accurately; to see details and recognize errors in numbers and spelling; to present information effectively; to work within precise limits of accuracy; to follow instructions; to accept responsibility for money handled; to be tactful and patient with others; to gain familiarity with a variety of forms; to perform a variety of tasks that may change often; to gain familiarity with accounting procedures; and to make decisions based upon personal judgment and measurable standards. These abilities are normally acquired at the high school diploma or equivalent level.
2. Physical demands are light. Working rapidly, excessive listening and speaking, and standing for long periods are frequently required.
3. Emotional demands of the position are frequent contact with customers and the general public, occasional close supervision, meeting deadlines under pressure, irregularly scheduled activities, working alone, and the threat of robbery.
4. Speaking with customers comprises the majority of daily physical activity.

Working Conditions

Physical surroundings and working conditions are good, with occasional noise, temperature variation, and ventilation problems. There are rarely any health or safety hazards.

Advancement

Bank services representatives may advance to management trainee positions.

Exhibit 4   *Wage Information Guidechart for Two Bank Jobs*

	Bank Services Representative	Teller
Maximum	$15,826	$13,566
75th percentile	14,913	12,783
Midpoint	14,000	12,000
25th percentile	13,087	11,218
Minimum	12,174	10,435

Exhibit 5   *Utopian National Bank Pay Policy*

Utopian National Bank has a policy of paying our employees a fair and equitable wage while permitting us to be competitive within the banking industry. One of our goals is to attract and retain capable employees at Utopian National Bank. To this end, it is our policy to continually survey wages in the banking industry and to pay at the 80th percentile of the industry.

Another goal at Utopian National Bank is to reward employees on the basis of their performance. It is our philosophy that individuals will contribute their maximum when they realize that they will be rewarded accordingly. To that end, the bank encourages all employees to do their best. You will be rewarded accordingly.

Exhibit 6   *Notes and Memos*

TO: Supervisor of Operations
FROM: Jill Smith, EEO/AA Officer
RE: EEO/AA Goals

This memo is to bring to your attention the fact that your department has not yet achieved its goal of 50 percent minority representation in jobs within your department.

As you know, Utopian National Bank has a federally mandated EEO/AA program. It is important that each department achieve its race and ethnic goals if the overall corporation is to achieve its goals.

Please advise my office of when you will anticipate another opening. In other words, when do you foresee that you will be able to bring your department into line with its parity goal?

TO: Supervisor of Operations
FROM: Nate Jones
RE: New Employment Opportunity

As we discussed yesterday, I have an opportunity to go to work at Buchanon Machine Shop as a machine attendant. They are offering me a starting wage of $13,000 annually.

I know that you will be communicating to us our annual pay increase next week and I don't want to leave Utopian Bank until I know what kind of increase I'll get. I really love the bank and if you can match the Buchanon offer, I'll stay at the bank.

I hope you can match the offer since I really want to stay on.

P.S. I don't want to sound like I'm griping, but how come Ed Motley and I are paid so poorly relative to other tellers?

TO: Supervisor of Operations
FROM: Melissa Hines
RE: My Pay Increase

You asked me to put in writing why I deserve a big pay increase. Well, I'll tell you why.

First, I got four kids to support. Ever since my husband walked out on me last year, it's been tough.

Second, I'll lose my house unless I get more money. It costs so much to feed the kids and keep up my personal appearance (for my job) that I'm falling behind on the mortgage payments. (Just $100 a month more would get me over the worst of it.)

TO: Supervisor of Operations
FROM: Tom Snell
RE: My Promotion

I'm getting sick and tired of not getting the promotion you promised me.

You told me that I'd be getting the promotion this year and it hasn't happened yet. Here I've worked my fanny off for six years and then the bank doesn't follow through on its word.

Well, either I get a promotion this year, or I get a big pay raise, or I'm going to quit.

---

continued

Exhibit 6   continued

TO: Supervisor of Operations
FROM: Norma Burke
RE: The Old Days

This isn't really the time or place to write this, but I was just thinking about the great time we had in Williamsburg last fall.

Do you remember how we went to that great restaurant in Virginia Beach and you bought me that fantastic veal? And, of course, afterward . . . .

It would sure be fun if we could do that again this year.

TO: Supervisor of Operations
FROM: Lena Scott
RE: Pay Inequities

As you know, I'm heavily involved in the women's rights movement in town. Well, to be very blunt—how come Edna and I make so much less than Tom and Sam?

If we could discuss this problem and if you could adjust our wages next week when you make pay increases, then I think the problem will be solved.

TO: Supervisor of Operations
FROM: Lena Scott
RE: Pay Inequity

I have a basic question about why I don't receive higher pay.

Specifically, why do I only get a little over $1,000 per month? I have a Master's degree in secondary education and I'm certainly worth more than that.

To: Operations Supervisor
Utopian National Bank
Anytown, USA

Dear [Supervisor]:

Sam and I would like to invite you to a small informal dinner at our house next Saturday night.

The get-together is in honor of the mayor, who is celebrating 40 years on the job.

Sam and I would be honored if you and your spouse or guest would join the four of us.

Sincerely,

Mrs. Sam (Emily) North
Vice President, Kiln Enterprises

P.S. RSVP—regrets only—989-9919

Exhibit 7   *Guidechart for Merit Pay Increases*

Performance Level

Current Pay	Superior	Above Average	Average	Below Average	Inferior
Maximum	0–7%	0–5%	0–2%	0%	0%
75th percentile	7–10	5–7	2–5	0	0
50th percentile	8–12	6–8	4–6	0–1	0
25th percentile	10–14	7–10	5–7	0–2	0
Minimum					

---

2. The ABC Corporation has a COLA policy in effect. According to the policy, each time the cost of living increases by 2.5 percent in any six-month period (beginning January 1 of each year), the employees will receive a 1 percent COLA increase for each 2 percent increase in the cost of living, up to a maximum of 3 percent in any six-month period. The changes in the Consumer Price Index (on which the corporation bases the cost of living) for the past five years follow.

Period	Consumer Price Index[a]	Annual Wage Bill	Percent Change From Previous Period
January 1 to June 30, 1980	247	$12,000,000	?
July 1 to December 31, 1980	249	?	?
January 1 to June 30, 1981	254	?	?
July 1 to December 31, 1981	260		
January 1 to June 30, 1982	264		
July 1 to December 31, 1982	268		
January 1 to June 30, 1983	270		
July 1 to December 31, 1983	272		
January 1 to June 30, 1984	282		
July 1 to December 31, 1984	284		

[a] Based on 1967=100.

Using this information, calculate the impact this policy will have on the firm's total wage bill. What percentage is this?

References

[1] Thomas J. Bergmann, Frederick S. Hills, and Laurel Priefert, "Pay Compression, Causes, Results, and Possible Solutions," *Compensation Review* 15, number 2 (second quarter, 1983): pp. 17–26.

[2] F. S. Hills, "The Pay-for-Performance Dilemma," *Personnel* 56, number 5: pp. 23–31.

[3] Roger Lopata, "Salary Compensation: Are Workers Outearning Bosses?" *Iron Age* 223, number 39: pp. 49–51.

[4] Michael Seitzinger, "Planning Supervisor/Subordinate Pay Differentials," *Personnel Administrator* 28, number 2: pp. 74–77.

[5] C. R. Farmer, "Merit Pay: Viable?" *Personnel* 55, number 5: pp. 57–63.

[6] W. C. Hamner, "How to Ruin Motivation with Pay," *Compensation Review* 7, number 3: pp. 17–27.

[7] B. G. Costello, "A Primer on Regulations and Controls Affecting Employee Compensation," *Health Care Management Review* 7, number 4: pp. 59–69.

[8] Karen Greenberg and Mary Zippo, "How Can You Determine Whether Salary Discrimination Is Sex-Based?" *Personnel* 60, number 1: pp. 57–58.

[9] R. L. Haneberg, "Employee Benefit Plans—What Constitutes Sex Discrimination?" *Risk Management* 26, number 1: pp. 10–15.

[10] "Guidelines for Effective and Defensible Performance Appraisal Systems," *Personnel Journal* 61, number 10: pp. 776–782.

[11] J. T. Brinks, "The Comparable Worth Issue: A Salary Administration Bombshell," *Personnel Administration* 26, number 11: pp. 37–40. T. G. Cody, "Comparable Worth Rules: Another Weight to Balance," *Management Review* 68, number 5: p. 31.

[12] "Companies Can Live with 7 Percent," *Business Week,* November 1978, pp. 26–27.

[13] "A Break for Labor in Revised Guidelines," *Business Week,* December 1978, pp. 34–35.

[14] T. H. Patten, Jr., "Open Communication Systems and Effective Salary Administration," *Human Resource Management* 17, number 4: pp. 5–14.

[15] W. H. Wagel, "Bringing Salary Administration out of the Closet," *Personnel* 55, number 4: pp. 4–10.

[16] E. E. Lawler, III, "Managers' Perceptions of Their Subordinates' Pay and of Their Superiors' Pay," *Personnel Psychology* 18 (1965): pp. 413–423.

[17] E. E. Lawler, III, "Secrecy about Management Compensation: Are There Hidden Costs?" *Organizational Behavior and Human Performance* 2 (1967): pp. 182–189.

[18] See also George T. Milkovich and Philip H. Anderson, "Management Compensation and Secrecy Policies," *Personnel Psychology* 25 (1972): pp. 293–302.

[19] T. W. Hourihan, "Help Employees to Understand Their Benefits," *Personnel Administrator* 28, number 4: pp. 92–95, 98.

[20] D. Bartz, "Employees Can Be Motivated by 'Selling' Benefits via Clearly Written Booklets, Personal Statements," *Supermarketing* 33, number 10: pp. 18–20.

[21] B. R. Ellig, "What's Ahead in Compensation and Benefits," *Management Review* 72, number 8: pp. 56–61.

Name Index

Ackoff, R. L., 262
Adams, J. S., 41
Alber, A. F., 435
Alderfer, C. P., 26, 40
Alewine, T., 347
Anderson, P. H., 470
Andrews, J. R., 41
Arvey, R. D., 188
Atkinson, J. W., 41
Back, K., 295
Baker, R. P., 104
Barret, J. T., 104
Bartlett, F., 379
Bartz, D., 470
Bass, A. W., Jr., 220
Batten, J. D., 41
Baumgartel, H., 435
Bavelas, A., 381
Baytos, L., 380
Beatty, J. R., 103
Beatty, R. W., 103
Becker, J. W., 41
Belcher, D. W., 263, 379
Benge, E. J., 220
Bentley, L., 379, 380
Berger, C., 295
Bergmann, T. J., 21, 103, 134, 313, 469
Berkowitz, L., 41
Berlew, D., 41
Bernardin, H. J., 162, 348
Bexson, J. D., 188
Bildersee, R. A., 411
Blinder, A. S., 313
Bloch, H. R., 262
Blum, M. L., 348
Borman, W. C., 348
Boudreau, J., 295

Bridwell, L. G., 40
Brinks, J. T., 187, 470
Bronfenbrenner, M., 66
Brown, B. A., 134
Brown, D. G., 262
Burcke, J. M., 411
Burnham, D. H., 435
Burns, J. E., 134
Burns, K. G., 134
Burton, J. F., Jr., 66, 262
Bushardt, S. C., 40
Campagne, A. F., 435
Campbell, J. P., 40, 348
Carroll, S. J., 348
Chamberlain, N. W., 104
Charles, A. W., 221
Chesler, D. J., 220
Clark, K. L., 187
Cockrum, R. B., 411
Cody, T. G., 470
Cohen, S., 104, 134
Conley, J. R., 21
Costello, B. G., 469
Creed, B. B., 134
Crystal, G. S., 66, 263, 295, 380
Cummings, L. L., 348
Dalaba, O., 381
Dalton, D. R., 295
Daly, P., 380
DeCotiis, T. A., 348, 435
Delone, T., 436
Densmore, B., 411
Dertien, M. G., 187
Dobofsky, M., 103
Doeringer, P. B., 103
Dougherty, M. F., 104
Douty, H. M., 66
Dulles, F. R., 103

Dunham, R. B., 436
Dunlop, J. T., 65, 66, 103, 104, 188
Dunnette, M. D., 40, 42, 161, 162, 221, 348, 380
Einstein, A., 19
Elisburg, D., 134
Elkin, J. M., 411
Ellig, B. R., 295, 470
Farmer, C. R., 469
Ferguson, R. H., 104
Festinger, L. S., 295
Fiedler, F. E., 435
Fielder, B. L., 262
Flanagan, J. C., 162
Florkowski, G., 380
Fogel, W., 262
Ford, J., 103
Ford, R. N., 435
Fossum, J. A., 104, 187
Foster, K. E., 187
Foulkes, F. K., 411
Fowler, A. R., 40
Franklin, W. H., 40
Freeman, R. B., 104, 295
French, J. R. P., Jr., 347
French, W. L., 21, 436
Friedman, A., 41
Gantt, H. L., 359, 380
Gayle, J. B., 40
Geare, A., 380
Geisel, J., 411
George, C. S., Jr., 103
Getman, J. G., 436
Glueck, W. F., 435
Goldfarb, R. S., 134
Gomez-Mejia, L. R., 221, 294
Goodman, P., 41

Greenberg, K., 470
Grossman, P., 21, 313, 348
Gruenwald, A. E., 66
Guion, R. M., 348
Hackman, J. R., 41, 435
Hall, D. T., 41
Hallman, G. V., 104, 262
Halsey, F. A., 359, 380
Hamblin, R., 380
Hamner, W. C., 469
Haneberg, R. L., 470
Hartmann, H. I., 187, 313
Hay, E. N., 220, 221
Henderson, R. I., 187
Henemann, H. G., III, 41, 103,
    187, 295, 348
Heneman, H. G., Jr., 21, 134
Herzberg, F., 27, 40, 435
Hicks, J. R., 104
Hildebrand, G. H., 104
Hills, F. S., 21, 41, 103, 134, 262,
    295, 313, 348, 379, 411,
    469
Hirsch, B. T., 104
Hourihan, T. W., 470
Hughes, R. E., 103, 262, 411
Husband, T. M., 221
Huseman, R. C., 435
Janes, H. D., 187
Jaques, E., 187, 207, 221
Kahn, S. C., 134
Kay, E., 347
Kerr, C., 103
Kim, J. S., 435
Knowles, M. C., 435
Kochan, T. A., 104
Kotter, J., 41
Koys, D. J., 435
Krackhardt, D. M., 295
Krefting, L. A., 295
Krzystofiak, F., 156, 162
Kulberg, R., 221
Lacombe, J. J., III, 21
Lawler, E., 40, 41, 348, 379, 380,
    435, 470
Lee, J. A., 187, 220
Lester, R., 262
Levinson, H., 348
Lewis, G., 41
Livernash, E. R., 221, 294, 295,
    313
Lochner, A. H., 348
Lopata, R., 469
Lorsch, J. W., 435
Lubben, G., 348
Mace, C., 380
Maddi, S. R., 41
Madigan, R. M., 220
Mahoney, T. A., 65, 66, 187, 221,
    295, 381
Maldonado, K. F., 411
Manger, E. I., 134
March, J. G., 41
Martin, D., 104
Martin, J. L., 411
Martin, V. H., 436
Maslow, A. H., 24, 40
Matsui, T., 41
Mausner, B., 40, 435
McCaffery, R. M., 134, 262
McClelland, D. C., 28, 41, 435
McCleod, J. S., 188

McConkie, M. L., 348
McConnell, C. R., 65, 66
McCormick, E. J., 104, 154, 155,
    161, 162, 221
McCroskey, J., 411
Mecham, R. C., 220
Mendoza, J. L., 187, 220
Merrick, D. W., 357, 380
Meyer, H. H., 347
Meyer, M. S., 411, 436
Middlemist, D., 41
Milkovich, G. T., 313, 470
Miller, E., 41
Miller, L., 380
Mills, D. Q., 104
Mitchell, D. J. B., 104
Mitchell, T., 42
Moore, B., 380, 381
Morrall, J. F., III, 134
Morse, J. J., 435
Mossholder, K., 313
Mowday, R., 40
Murphy, K. R., 162
Murphy, M. J., 221, 295
Murray, H. A., 26, 40
Naylor, J. C., 348
Nemmers, E. E., 66
Newman, J., 156, 162
Nolan, S. D., 436
Oldham, G., 435
Oliver, P. M., 188
Olson, C., 295
Olson, R., 380
Opsahl, R. L., 42, 380
Otteman, R., 262
Palmer, L., 411
Parker, J. E., 66, 262
Paterson, T. T., 221
Patrick, P., 221
Patten, T. H., Jr., 162, 380, 470
Patton, J. A., 295
Paul, R. D., 411
Pennington, R. L., 262
Petersen, D. J., 436
Peterson, D., 294
Peterson, R., 41
Pierson, F. C., 188, 294
Piore, M. J., 103
Porter, L. W., 40, 41, 435
Priefert, L., 469
Pritchard, R. D., 41
Pugel, T. A., 262
Pursell, R. B., 188
Purves, D., 220, 221
Raube, S. A., 262
Reder, M. W., 65
Reinharth, L., 41
Remick, H., 103
Rendall, E., 436
Reynolds, L. G., 21, 66, 294
Roberts, H. V., 313
Rosen, B., 187, 221
Rosenbaum, W., 41
Rosenbloom, J. S., 104, 262
Rosow, J. M., 21
Ross, T., 380, 381
Rothe, H., 380, 381
Rowan, R. L., 359
Rowland, K. M., 103
Rucker, A. W., 372
Rynes, S., 187, 188, 221
Sanders, M. S., 41

Sandvar, M. G., 103
Sangerman, H., 134
Scanlon, J., 371
Schein, E. H., 104
Scheinder, B., 40
Schlei, B. L., 21, 313, 348
Schneir, C. E., 348
Schuster, J., 380
Schuster, M., 380
Schwab, D. P., 41, 162, 221, 294,
    348
Searle, F. R., 40
Secias, S., 436
Seitzinger, M., 469
Seligman, D., 104
Shaw, E. A., 221
Shimmin, S., 379, 380
Sibson, R. E., 262, 411
Simchak, M. M., 134
Simon, H. A., 41
Skinner, B. F., 42
Smith, A., 45, 66
Smith, E. C., 262
Smith, F. J., 436
Smith, P. C., 161, 162, 348
Smyth, R. C., 221, 295
Snyderman, B., 40, 435
Sovereign, M. G., 103
Starke, F., 41
Steer, R., 40
Steiner, G. A., 21
Steiner, J. F., 21
Stepp, J. R., 104
Stevens, C. M., 104
Stevens, S. N., 348
Stone, T. H., 161
Stouder, D., 41
Strauss, G., 381
Summers, C. W., 436
Suttle, J. L., 41
Szilagyi, A. D., 21
Taylor, F. W., 357, 380
Taylor, G. W., 188, 294
Teel, K. S., 348
Thomsen, D. J., 187, 220
Thomson, W. R., 380
Thorndike, E. L., 42
Todor, W. D., 295
Tornow, W., 221
Torrence, G. W., 221
Trieman, D. J., 187, 313
Turner, W. D., 220
Vroman, S., 104
Vroom, V. H., 34, 41, 347
Wagel, W. H., 470
Wahba, M. A., 40, 41
Wallace, M. J., Jr., 161
Walton, R. E., 21
Wanous, J. P., 435, 436
Wegener, E., 187
Weick, K. E., Jr., 40
White, W. L., 41
Whyte, W. F., 380, 381
Witte, E. E., 103
Wollenberger, J., 347
Wonderlic, E. F., 348
Wren, D. A., 162
Yager, E., 436
Yankelovich, D., 41
Yoder, D., 21, 134
Young, H. A., 104
Zalusky, J., 187
Zepke, B. E., 134
Zippo, M., 411, 470

Subject Index

Ability to Pay, 4, 12, 16, 17, 18, 44, 52, 56, 227, 233, 280
importance of, 59–63
Accident Insurance, 403
Achievement, 419
Advisory Arbitration, 89
Affirmative Action Plan, 76, 129
written plan, 129
AFSCME v. State of Washington, 311
Age Discrimination in Employment Act, 129, 209, 334
Alderfer's Need Theory, 26
American Federation of State, County, and Municipal Employees (AFSCME), 309
Antitrust Law, 233
Arbitration, 89
Behaviorally Anchored Rating Scales, 340–341
Binding Arbitration, 89, 99
Black Caucus, 9
Bonus Plans, 367–370
Brand Demand, 61
Briggs vs City of Madison, 310
Budgets, 451–454
pay increase, 343–344
standard hours, 453
wage and salary, 451
Cafeteria Benefit Plans, 409
Central Tendency, 328
Certification Election, 84
Child Labor Laws, 109, 455
Civil Rights Act of 1964 (CRA), 9, 17, 127–129, 298–299, 301, 303, 309, 331, 334, 455
and compensation decision making, 128
Collective Bargaining, 18, 85–89
bargaining committee, 85
bargaining in good faith, 84
bargaining issues, 85
mandatory, 85, 86
permissive, 85
prohibited, 85
bargaining process, 87–89
give back offers, 87
settlement ranges, 87
Commissions (Salesperson), 363–364
Commonwealth of Massachusetts v. Hunt, 80
Communications, 457–460
and COLA, 459
importance of, 457
of benefits, 460
of market rates, 459
of merit, 459
of pay increases, 459
of wage levels and structures, 458
Comparable Worth, 75, 269, 309–312
Comparatio, 450
Compensable Factors (defined, 143), 166, 170–173
commonly accepted, 170
criteria for choosing, 172
and job analysis, 143
who selects, 173
Compensation (defined, 10)
Compensation Goals, 12–18
Compensation Staff, 438–439
Consumer Credit Protection Act, 119

Conducting Performance Appraisals, 448–450
Contrast Bias, 329
Contract Work Hours Standard Act, 113
Contributory Benefits, 400, 408
Cost of Living Allowances (COLA), 92, 93, 442, 448
communication of, 459
Cottage System, 79
Criterion Contamination, 325
Criterion Deficiency, 325
Critical Incidence Method, 340
Critical Incident Technique, 150
Davis-Bacon Act, 17, 112, 114, 454
Defined Benefits Pension Plan, 395
Defined Contribution Pension Plan, 395
Demand Elasticity, 59–61
for the brand, 61
for the product, 59–60
Demand For Labor, 44, 46, 49
Dental Insurance, 403
Derived Demand (for labor), 46
Dictionary of Occupational Titles (DOT), 154
Difference Bias, 329
Direct Observation Job Analysis, 149
Discounts on Goods and Services, 404
Discrimination (forms of)
adverse impact, 127, 301, 331
adverse/unequal treatment, 127, 301
age, 129
analyzing discrimination, 304–308
class action suits, 304, 309
comparable worth discrimination, 309–312
components of, 299
direct pay discrimination, 129, 302–308
examples of, 299
fair, 298
illegal, 299
doctrines of, 300–302
indirect pay discrimination, 129, 308–309
legal, 299
and performance assessment, 331–334
present effect of past discrimination, 302
reasonable accommodation discrimination, 302
unfair, 298
Due Process, 98, 426
Earnings, 6
Economy of Scale, 48
Employee Attitude Surveys, 429–431
Employee Benefits (defined 11, 386). see Chapter 14; specific benefits
communication of, 460
growth in, 387–392
taxation of, 409
trends in, 408–410
Employee Retirement Income Security Act (ERISA), 17, 121–123, 393–395, 456

and compensation decision making, 123
and fiduciary standards, 121, 394
and funding, 121, 394
and pension benefit guaranty corporation, 395
and portability, 122
and vesting, 122, 394
Employee Stock Ownership Plans, 369
Employee Training and Development, 433
Employment Exchange Contract, 29, 31
Equal Employment Opportunity Commission (EEOC), 17, 124, 127, 129, 304, 306
Equal Pay Act (EPA), 7, 9, 17, 124–127, 302, 303, 305, 332, 334, 455
and compensation decision making, 126
Equity Theory, 31–33
Establishing Pay Grades, 269–273
Excessive Leniency, 328
Excessive Strictness, 328
Executive Bonuses, 367–370
long-term bonuses, 369
short-term bonuses, 368
Executive Order, 11246, 129, 455
Exempt Employees, 106
External Equity (defined, 13), 14, 33, 267, 278–280
External Labor Market, 18
Extrinsic Job Rewards, 419–420
Factor Comparison Method of Job Evaluation, 191–200
Factory System, 80
Failure to Discriminate, 330
Fair Labor Standards Act 1938 (FLSA), 9, 106–112, 455
and compensation, 111
enforcement, 111
and record keeping, 110
Federal Mediation and Conciliation Service, 84, 89
Fiduciary Standards, 17
Flat Rate Pay System, 285
Flexitime, 423, 432
401K Plans, 396
Freehand Line, 274
Fringe Benefits. see Employee Benefits; specific benefits
Functional Job Analysis, 153
Gain Sharing Plans, 372–373
Gantt Plan, 359
Garnishments, 119
Giveback Offer, 87
Goals of Compensation, 12–18
Going Wage Rate, 39
Grading Rules in Job Evaluation, 182
Graphic Rating Scales for Performance Assessment, 335–340
Green Circle Rate, 287
Grievance Procedure, 99, 426
Group Incentive Plans, 351–352
cost reduction plans, 371–372
gain sharing plans, 372–374
plant wide, 370
small group, 370
Guaranteed Annual Wage, 94
Guide Charts, 344, 450

Gunther v. County of Washington, 311
Halo Effect, 328
Halsey Plan, 359
Hawthorne Studies, 420, 426
Hay Method of Job Evaluation, 211
Health Insurance, 399–403
  and costs, 401
Health Maintenance Act, 120
Health Maintenance Organization, 120, 402
Herzberg's Need Theory, 27–28
High Wage Employer, 64
Holiday Pay, 397
Human Capital Variables, 305
Human Relations Training, 426
Incentive Plan Committees and Unions, 95
Incentive Plans, 350–352
  group, 351–352
  individual, 351–352
  piece rate, 352–358
  problems with, 359–362
Individual Incentive Plans, 351–352
  managerial, 367–369
  for salespersons, 362–366
Inducements/Contributions Contract, 29–30
Industry Wage Surveys. *see* Product Market Wage/ Benefit Survey
Inside Sales, 364
Instrumentality Expectancy Theory, 34–37, 318, 350–351
  implications for compensation, 38–39
Insurances, 399–404. *see* specific type
Interest Arbitration, 89
Internal Equity (defined, 14), 34, 164, 190, 226, 273–278
Internal Labor Markets, 12, 18, 69, 72, 73, 74
  and degree of openness, 74
  implications for compensation, 74
  and isolation effect, 74
  and port of entry, 73
Internal Revenue Service, 123
Interviewing for Job Analysis, 151–153
Intrinsic Job Rewards, 418–419
James v. Stockham Valve and Fittings Company, 331
Job (defined, 73, 140)
Job Analysis, 446–447, (see Chapter 6)
  custom designed, 156
  steps in conducting, 143–147
  techniques and methods, 147–158
  uses of data, 141–143
Job Analysis Questionaire (JAQ), 156
Job Autonomy, 418
Job Bidding, 424
Job Classification Method, 179–183
Job Description (defined, 158)
Job Design, 421–423, 432
  and unions, 98
Job Enlargement, 422
Job Enrichment, 423

Job Evaluation (defined, 143), 34, 79
  committees and unions, 95, 446
  direct market method, 211
  employee attribute techniques, 208
  evolution of, 168–170
  factor comparison method, 165, 191–200
    advantages and disadvantages of, 198–200
    steps in conducting, 191–198
  Hay method, 210
  and internal equity, 34
  and job analysis, 143
  job classification method, 165, 179–183
    advantages and disadvantages of, 182–183
    steps in conducting, 179–182
  and labor unions, 95
  maturity curves, 209
  non-quantitative methods (see Chapter 7)
  and pay grades, 269–273
  point method, 165, 200–207
    advantages and disadvantages of, 207
    steps in conducting, 200–207
  position analysis questionaire method, 211
  quantitative methods (see Chapter 8)
  ranking method, 165, 173–179
    advantages and disadvantages of, 176–178
    steps in conducting, 174–178
  single factor method, 207
  whole job method, 178
Job Evaluation Committee, 446
Job Grades (see Pay Grades)
Job Inventories, 156
Job Posting, 424
Job Pricing, 79
Job Service, 119
Job Specifications (defined, 159)
Joint Decision Making (labor and management), 94–99
Just Wage Doctrine, 9
Key Jobs, 64
Labor Costs, 7, 61, 280
  and labor unions, 91, 95
Labor/Management Contracts, 457
Labor Market Wage/Benefit Survey, 33, 227–230
  and benefits structure, 407
  conducting, 234–254
  consultant surveys, 235, 242
  custom designed surveys, 243–253
  and external equity, 33
  federal government surveys, 234–235
  geographic scope of, 228
  occupational level and, 230
  organizations included in, 227
  professional association surveys, 235, 240
  summarizing survey data, 254–257
Labor Supply, 51
Labor Supply Shortages, 443
Labor Unions, 69, 79
  as criminal conspiracies, 80
  impact on compensation, 89–99

income security, 94
labor's share of national income, 90
preventive labor policy, 91
union and non-union wage rates, 90
wage and benefit levels, 91
wage structure, 91, 92
and job design, 98
and job evaluation, 95
and the labor movement, 79–85
lockout, 88
membership, 80–84
and the right to organize, 80
strike, 88
union shop, 84
Law of Diminishing Marginal Proportions, 49
Leadership, 14
Leadership Styles, 420
Legal Constraints, 7, 17. *see* Chapter 5
Lemons v. City and County of Denver, 310
Letter of Right to Sue, 17
Life Insurance, 403
Line Managers, 439
Lockout, 88
Long Term Disability Insurance, 403
Low Wage Employer, 63
Management by Objectives, 341–343, 429
Managerial Incentive Plans, 367–369
Marginal Revenue Productivity Theory (MRP), 44, 46–56
  and ability to pay, 52
  and average productivity, 49
  and average revenue productivity, 49
  and demand schedule for labor, 50
  and marginal productivity, 49
  and marginal revenue productivity, 49
Maslow's Needs Hierarchy, 24–26, 415
Maturity Curve, 209
McClelland's Need Theory, 28
McNamara-O'Hara Act, 113, 454
Merit Increases, 448
Merit Pay. *see* Pay for Performance
  communication of, 459
Merit Rating. *see* Performance Assessment
Merrick Plan, 357
Minimum Wage, 455
  changes in, 10
  civil rights act, 455
  equal pay act, 455
  FLSA Provisions, 109
Minnesota Satisfaction Questionaire, 430
Motivation
  content theories, 24–29
  and equity theory, 31–34
  and extrinsic factors, 27
  and human needs, 24–29
  instrumentality and expectancy theory, 34–39
  and intrinsic factors, 27
  to join, 12, 33
  and money, 28, 38
  to perform, 12, 14, 34

Motivation
(Continued)
  process models, 31–39
  reinforcement theory, 37
  to stay, 12, 13, 33
Moving Expenses, 405
Multiple Evaluators, 324. *see*
    Performance Assessment
Multiple Wage Structures,
  268–269
Murray's Need Theory, 26
National Academy of Sciences,
  311
National Association for the
  Advancement of Colored
  People (NAACP), 9
National Labor Relations Act. *see*
  Wagner Act
National Labor Relations Board,
  84
National Organization of Women,
  9
Needs Hierarchy, 26
Noncontributory Benefits, 400,
  408
Noneconomic Rewards (see
  Chapter 15)
  costs of, 431–433
  and economic rewards, 414
  and human needs, 415
Nonexempt Employees, 106
Nonlinear Wage Lines, 281
Nonpecuniary Rewards (defined,
  11)
Nonquantitative Job Evaluation.
  see Chapter 7; specific
  method
Nonrecurring Financial Rewards
  (defined, 11)
Office of Federal Contract
  Compliance Programs
  (OFCCP), 132
Order Effect, 329
Organization Status, 420
Outside Sales, 364
Overtime, 108, 455
Pay for Performance, 447–450,
  457–459
  administration of, 447–450
  communication of, 457–459
Pay for Time Not Worked,
  397–399
  holiday benefits, 397
  indirect costs of, 399
  other, 397
  vacation benefits, 397
Pay Grades, 269–273
Pay Increase Budgets, 343, 344
Pay Ranges, 267, 282–288
Peer Evaluations, 323
Pension Benefits Guaranty
  Corporation, 395
Pension Plans, 392–397
  costs, 396
  fiduciary standards, 394
  funding, 394
  objectives of, 392
  types of, 395–397
  vesting, 394
Performance Appraisal. *see*
    Performance Assessment
Performance Appraisal Paradox,
  319
Performance Assessment. *see*
    Chapter 12
  bias and errors, 327–329

and compensation decision
  making, 343–345
  conducting, 448–450
  legal considerations, 331–334
  and money, 449
  monitoring appraisals, 449
  problems with, 325–331
  techniques, 334–343
  who conducts, 323–325, 449
Performance Evaluation. *see*
    Performance Assessment
Performance Ratings. *see*
    Performance Assessment
Performance Standards (defined,
  159)
Perquisites, 386
Piece Rate Plans, 352–358. *see*
  Individual Incentive Plans
Point Method of Job Evaluation,
  200–207
Portability, 17
Port of Entry, 73
Position (defined, 73, 140)
Position Analysis Questionaire
  (PAQ), 154, 211
Power and Influence, 419
Prevailing Wages, 112
Primacy Bias, 329
Product Demand, 59
Product Market Wage/Benefit
  Survey, 44, 58, 231–233
  and anti-trust law, 233
  and benefit level, 407
  conducting, 234–254
  consultant surveys, 235, 242
  custom-designed surveys,
  243–253
  federal government surveys,
  234–235
  geographic scope of, 231
  importance of, 58–63
  organizations included, 231
  professional association
  surveys, 235, 240
  purposes of, 233
  summarizing survey data,
  254–257
  and technology, 231
Professional Development, 424
Profit Sharing Plans (see Gain
  Sharing Plans)
Quality Circles, 426, 433
Quality of Labor, 63, 64
Quanitative Job Evaluation. *see*
  Chapter 8; specific method
Random Sampling, 230, 252
Ranking Methods of Job
  Evaluation, 173–178
Ranking Methods of Performance
  Assessment, 334
Rater Bias, 327–329
Rater Error, 327–329
Recency Tendency, 328
Red Circle Rate, 287–288
Regression Analysis, 275,
  305–308
Reinforcement Theory, 37
Retirement Plans, 409. *see*
  Pension Plans
Right-to-Work Clause, 84
Rights Arbitration, 89
Rowan Plan, 359
Rucker Plan, 372
Salary Reduction Pension Plans,
  395

Salesperson Compensation,
  362–366
  problems with, 366
Scanlon Plan, 371, 372
Seniority, 283–284, 285
Similiarity Bias, 329
Simplified Pension Plans, 396
Size of Merit Increases, 448
Social Interaction, 420
Social Security, 406, 456
Social Security Act, 9, 118, 406
Soldiering, 361
Standard Hours Budgets, 453
Standard Hours Plans, 358–359
State Legislation, 132–133
Stock Option Plans, 369
Stock Purchase Plans, 396
Stratified Random Sampling, 253
Strike, 88
Subordinate Evaluations, 323
Subsidized Meals, 405
Superordinate Goals, 330
Supervisory Recognition, 419
Supplementary Unemployment
  Benefits (SUB), 94
Taft-Hartley Act, 84
Tandom Wage Adjustments, 269
Task (defined, 140)
Task Completion, 419
Taylor Plan, 357
Theory of Relativity, 19
Thrift Plans, 396
Time and Motion Study, 352
Time Span of Discretion, 207
Top Management, 442
Turnover, 63, 64
Unemployment Compensation,
  406
Unemployment Insurance, 118
Union Shop (defined, 84)
Vacation Pay, 397
Vesting, 17, 394
Wage and Benefits Survey
  Committees and Unions, 95
Wage and Hour Division (USDL),
  111, 114, 119
Wage/Benefits Survey. *see*
  Chapter 9; Product Market
  Wage/Benefit Survey;
  Labor Market Wage/Benefit
  Survey
Wage Comparison, 6
Wage Compression, 444
Wage Differentials, 45
Wage Fairness, 7
Wage Level (defined, 13), 56, 64
  adjustments, 442–445
  communication of, 458
  maintenance of, 442–445
Wage/Pay Structure, 265–288.
  see Chapter 10
  communication of, 286
  and external equity, 278–280
  implementing, 286
  and internal equity, 273–278
  maintenance, 288
  and management training, 289
  multiple wage structures,
  268–269
  and product market constraint,
  280
  reasons for, 266–268
Wage/Price Guidelines, 457
Wage Range (see Pay Ranges)
Wage Rate (defined, 10, 64)
Wages (defined, 6)

Wage Structure (defined, 14), 56,
    266–268
  communication of, 286, 458
  maintenance of, 288–289,
    445–447
Wage Surveys, 442
Wagner Act (National Labor
    Relations Act), 9, 80, 84

Walsh-Healy Act, 113, 454
Weber v. Kaiser Aluminum, 76,
    77–78
Willingness to Pay, 18
Work Adjustment Theory,
    416–418
Workers Compensation, 406

Workers Compensation Laws, 9,
    114–117
  and compensation decision
    making, 117
Work Methods Job Analysis, 149
Work Rules, 321
Written Affirmative Action Plan,
    129